SURVEY
OF
SOCIAL
SCIENCE

SURVEY
OF
SOCIAL
SCIENCE

GOVERNMENT AND POLITICS SERIES

Volume 4
1355-1808

Organized Crime and Political Corruption—Self-Interest in Politics

Edited by
FRANK N. MAGILL

Consulting Editor
JOSEPH M. BESSETTE
CLAREMONT MCKENNA COLLEGE

SALEM PRESS

Pasadena, California   Englewood Cliffs, New Jersey

Library of Congress Cataloging-in-Publication Data
Survey of social science: government and politics series /
edited by Frank N. Magill; consulting editor Joseph M.
Bessette.
    p.   cm.
Includes bibliographical references and index.
    1. Political science—Encyclopedias. 2. United States—
Politics and government—Encyclopedias. I. Magill,
Frank Northen, 1907-   . II. Bessette, Joseph M.
JA61.S88   1995
320'.03—dc20
ISBN 0-89356-745-0 (set)   95-30408
ISBN 0-89356-749-3 (volume 4)   CIP

PRINTED IN THE UNITED STATES OF AMERICA

CONTENTS

GOVERNMENT AND POLITICS

SURVEY
OF
SOCIAL
SCIENCE

ORGANIZED CRIME AND POLITICAL CORRUPTION

Field of study: Politics

Organized crime includes groups that utilize violence or threats of violence, that involve illicit enterprises in illegal goods that are in public demand, and that assure immunity of operation through political corruption and enforcement. Such political corruption, which is indispensable for organized crime operations, has dominated cities, states, and even entire countries.

Principal terms

COMMISSION TRIALS: series of organized crime prosecutions by the federal government in the 1980's that crippled the mafia

COSA NOSTRA: "this thing of ours"; alleged name of the mafia in the United States

ETHNIC SUCCESSION: theory that organized crime has been a means of upward mobility for various ethnic groups

MAFIA: popular name given for Italian-American organized crime

ORGANIZED CRIME CONTROL ACT (1970): most sweeping and comprehensive legislation passed against organized crime in the United States

POLITICAL CORRUPTION: misuse of public office by public officials for their own personal gain, including accepting bribes, kickbacks, and other favors

RICO: Racketeering Influence in Corrupt Organizations statute of the Organized Crime Control Act (1970); forbids proceeds from illegal operations from being used to acquire legitimate businesses

Overview

Organized crime has been variously defined by the public, legislatures, scholars, and academics. In general, it comprises groups that use or threaten violence, that operate illicit enterprises that supply illegal services that are in public demand, or that provide for immunity of operation through political corruption and enforcement. Organized crime is not restricted to traditional mafia groups, but may include corrupt business executives, members of the professions, public officials, and members of other occupational groups.

Political corruption entails the misuse of official duty for personal benefit. This may include the acceptance of bribes, kickbacks, and other favors by officeholders in exchange for ignoring their public duty. Blackmail and bribery are essential elements of organized crime operations. Political corruption and the connivance of public officials is, in fact, the largest factor in the breakdown of law enforcement in dealing with organized crime. Financing political corruption is the largest operating cost of organized crime, similar to an underground tax. Organized crime has been successful at compromising entire cities, counties, states, and even countries. Political machines in larger cities, such as Tammany Hall in nineteenth century New York City, had elaborate relationships with local crime syndicates. In some countries, such as post-World War II Japan and Italy, organized crime groups were employed by their governments to defeat communist elements. Once their task was accomplished, however, these same governments had to confront newly entrenched groups that had infiltrated the power structure. In Latin America, the power and wealth of drug cartels in the late twentieth century so compromised and intimidated political leadership that organized crime groups controlled major parts of the government, particularly in pre-Castro Cuba, the Bahamas, Colombia, Mexico, and Panama.

Organized crime has a variety of expressions, which include traditional crime syndicates. The latter are highly organized and are characterized by hierarchy, restricted membership, secrecy, violence, provision of illicit goods, profit orientation, and immunity of operations through corruption. These crime syndicates include the Japanese Yakuza, Chinese Triads, U.S. mafia, Neapolitan Camorra, and Unione Corse in Corsica. Nontraditional organized crime groups include many African American, Latino, Jamaican, Vietnamese, and other ethnic-based gangs in the United States. The role of political corruption in organized crime can be illustrated by local politically controlled organized crime groups, which consist of those in which the local power structures are not simply corrupt allies, but actual partners in organized crime operations. National politically controlled organized crime involves national authorities who actively participate in the operations of organized crime. Crime cartels may include political figures, law enforcement officials, and drug traffickers.

The "mafia myth" is the erroneous assumption that organized crime did not begin in the United States until the large-scale immigration of Italians in the late nineteenth and early twentieth century. The widespread popular identification of immigrants with organized crime has given rise to the ethnic succession theory of crime. It claims that organized crime has acted as an alternative means of upward mobility for various ethnic minorities who, because of discrimination or lack of skills, have fewer legal opportunities. Prior to the Italian American ascendancy to domination of organized crime in the United States from 1930 to 1990, organized crime was dominated by Anglo-Saxon, Jewish, and Irish gangs. Since 1990, African American, Latino, and other gangs have moved into the turf abandoned by an aging mafia.

Some of the largest organized crime groups in the world are powerful drug trafficking cartels, such as the Medellín and Cali groups of Colombia. These groups often act in complicity with officials at the highest levels of their own and other countries. At times politicians act not merely as paid off allies, but as active partners in organized crime operations. The international narcotics industry probably could not prosper as it has without the cooperation of corrupt governments.

By far the most popular theory of organized crime relates to the so-called Cosa Nostra. The term "cosa nostra" (literally, "this thing of ours") was first revealed by mafia informant Joseph Valachi during the McClellan Commission Hearings on Organized Crime in 1963. The Cosa Nostra was believed to consist of some twenty-four families or groups in the United States with more than five thousand male members in the 1960's. Overseeing these families was a national commission made up of the heads of the more powerful families. Each family was headed by a don or boss, and had a chain of command consisting of various underbosses, *consiglieris* (advisers), *caporegimas* (lieutenants), and "soldiers." These members were charged with corrupting police and public officials, and with enforcing discipline over members and nonmember associates through assault, mayhem, and murder. Together with their nonmember associates, Cosa Nostra members have been able to make illegal gains through such activities as narcotics trafficking, labor racketeering, gambling and bookmaking, loansharking, and extortion. Profits made in these operations are then used to infiltrate legitimate businesses, such as meat distribution, waterfront activities, garbage disposal, vending machines, realty, bars and taverns, labor unions, restaurants, garment manufacturers, and the produce business.

An event that transformed small mobs into large powerful syndicates in the United States was Prohibition, which lasted from 1919 to 1933. The government had unwittingly created an illegal monopoly for organized criminal groups. The immense profits from illegal liquor sales were used, in part, to corrupt law enforcement and public officials. After the repeal of Prohibition, first gambling and later drugs became the major sources of organized crime profits. Success at illegal enterprises gave organized crime the money and power to move into legitimate businesses and activities. Four labor unions that were found to have substantial organized crime influence in the late twentieth century were the International Longshoremen's Association, the Laborers International Union of North America, the Hotel and Restaurant Employees' Union, and the International Brotherhood of Teamsters. Businesses such as vending machines and bars have been fertile grounds for "skimming," or hiding money earned so as to avoid taxes. Even big business, such as banking, construction, entertainment, insurance, real estate, and Wall Street, has not been immune to mob operations.

Organized criminal groups also have been implicated in high-level government operations and political corruption. In "Operation Mongoose," for example, Central Intelligence Agency operatives used mafia figures in an attempt to assassinate Cuban premier Fidel Castro during the 1960's. In 1979, the House Assassinations Committee concluded that there was very likely a conspiracy in the assassination of President John Kennedy and, in their opinion, organized crime was most likely involved. While not all authorities would agree with such a conclusion, the fact that a congressional committee would make this finding is a testament to the perceived power of organized crime.

Applications

Organized crime had its beginnings in the New World with colonial pirates in the employ of England in her war with Spain. They maintained a vast underworld market in forbidden goods. Organized crime was also a basic part of politics and political corruption in early U.S. cities, with "robber barons" looting the industrial landscape of early capitalism and politicians cooperating with criminal gangs in various rackets. Organized criminals, police, and politicians ran illicit enterprises to serve the public demand for vice. Until 1920, organized crime was confined to small local mobs. Prohibition, however, was a bonanza for organized crime. Large segments of the public craved the illegal alcohol supplied by organized criminals. In Chicago in the 1920's, Al Capone provided an almost stereotypical picture of the mob and its power. At the same time, in New York City, a power struggle resulted in the founding of Cosa Nostra. The eventual victor, Salvatore Maranzano, was assassinated by his own followers, Charles "Lucky" Luciano and Vito Genovese, two figures who succeeded each other in running the Cosa Nostra into the 1950's. The post-World War II period found the mob moving into the casino-building business in Las Vegas. They also were the subject of the Senate's televised Kefauver Commission Hearings, which focused attention on labor racketeering and other mob activities.

In 1957, a planned Cosa Nostra meeting in a small western New York hamlet was raided by police, destroying much of the anonymity previously enjoyed by the syndicate. It had become harder for figures such as Federal Bureau of Investigation Director J. Edgar Hoover to claim that there was no such thing as organized crime in the United States and to dispense with the problem by ignoring it. Allegations have been made that Hoover himself may have been compromised by organized criminals in return for free gambling arrangements and other favors. The Apalachin raid, the Kefauver hearings, and the later McClellan Commission Hearings confirmed the existence of a mafia or Cosa Nostra.

The biggest strike against the Italian American syndicate took place in the mid-1980's with the indictment of the bosses of sixteen of the twenty-four mafia families. The so-called Commission Trials convicted some of these bosses as being members of the commission established by Lucky Luciano in 1931 to settle disputes and authorize mob killings. The last survivor of the New York City mafia families was John Gotti, who had become known as the "Teflon don," because none of the charges against him seemed to stick. In 1992, after he was convicted, he was dubbed the "Velcro don," because the charges stuck. The American mafia in the 1990's was a dwindling empire, with some strongholds remaining in New York City and the Chicago suburbs. A variety of organized crime groups have succeeded the mafia, such as the Herrera organization from Mexico, outlaw motorcycle gangs, Colombian cocaine cartels, African American and Latino street gangs, and Russian and Asian gangs. In the late 1980's, twenty-two defendants went to trial in New York City on charges that they ran a $1.7 billion drug trafficking organization in the United States using pizza parlors as fronts. This group of Sicilians was revealed to U.S. authorities by Sicilian mobster and informant Tommaso Buscetta.

Context

A variety of investigative tools exists to attack organized crime and political corruption, including financial analysis, electronic surveillance, use of informants and undercover agents, computer assistance, and citizens' commissions. There are also specific laws that have particular importance in the fight against organized crime and political corruption. These include the Hobbs Act; the Organized Crime Control Act, especially its RICO statute; the Bank Secrecy Act; and assets forfeiture or seizure laws.

The Hobbs Act is an antiracketeering act passed in the mid-1940's that considers any interference with interstate commerce as a violation of law. In one case of political corruption, politicians in Newark, New Jersey, were convicted of accepting kickbacks from contractors who had obtained their supplies from out of state. "Sting operations" involve police undercover operatives pretending to be involved in criminal schemes in order to catch criminals. This same tool is also used to catch corrupt politicians. The FBI conducted a sting operation known as Abscam, in which a man impersonating a wealthy Arab offered bribes to members of Congress. Eight members of Congress were convicted before the investigation was revealed. In 1983, an FBI sting operation targeting the Cook County, Illinois, judiciary resulted in more than sixty persons being convicted of political corruption, including eleven judges, and police officers, lawyers, and court officials. The Organized Crime Control Act of 1970 has been the most effective piece of legislation passed in the United States to attack organized crime activity. A major feature of the act is the Racketeering Influence in Corrupt Organizations (RICO) statute. This prohibits the use of the profits derived from the proceeds of criminal activity from being used to infiltrate legitimate businesses that are involved in interstate commerce. A "pattern of racketeering" is broadly defined as any two specified crimes, for example, murder or extortion, within a ten-year period.

The Organized Crime Control Act contains other important features. It provides for the creation of special grand juries to investigate organized crime and general immunity for witnesses appearing before the grand jury. The privilege against self-incrimination is suspended in return for protection against the use of such compelled testimony in any future criminal proceeding. A recalcitrant witness provision enables the jailing of immunized witnesses who refuse to testify. The conviction of individuals based on irreconcilably inconsistent declarations under oath—that is, perjury—is authorized, as is a provision for safe houses and protected facilities for housing government witnesses and their families. The government is also given the power to preserve and introduce testimony by the use of depositions (written declarations) in a criminal proceeding, a right that previously had been granted only to the defense. The act also prohibits challenges to the admissibility of evidence based on the government's having unlawfully gathered such evidence, if such activity occurred five years before the event the government is seeking to prove. Illegal gambling businesses were also defined as a violation.

The Bank Secrecy Act (1970) is an attempt to control money laundering by requiring banks to report all transactions over ten thousand dollars and to report when such amounts leave or enter the country. It also requires that foreign bank accounts must be reported by individuals on their tax returns. Assets forfeiture or seizure laws have become a valuable means of attacking criminal enterprises, as well as persons receiving political bribes. Such seizure of assets curtails the financial capability of enterprises to continue their criminal businesses. These assets may include money, property, businesses, cars, boats, or any item that was derived from or involved in criminal operations.

Bibliography

Abadinsky, Howard. *Organized Crime*. 4th ed. Chicago: Nelson-Hall, 1994. The most comprehensive source on this subject.

Albanese, Jay. *Organized Crime in America*. 2d ed. Cincinnati, Ohio: Anderson, 1989. Useful accounts of the Commission Trial and investigations.

Albini, Joseph. *The American Mafia: Genesis of a Legend*. New York: Appleton-Century-Crofts, 1971. This scholarly work traces the history and origins of the mafia.

Blakey, G. Robert, and Richard Billing. *The Plot to Kill the President: Organized Crime Assassinated JFK*. New York: New York Times Books, 1981. Blakey was the chief counsel to the House Assassinations Committee (1978), which concluded that there was organized crime complicity in President Kennedy's murder.

Bresler, Fenton. *The Chinese Mafia*. New York: Stein & Day, 1980. Fascinating account of triads, tongs, and the rituals and numerology of Chinese organized crime.

Chin, Ko-Lin. *Chinese Subculture and Criminality*. Westport, Conn.: Greenwood, 1990. Author cautions against the perpetration of myths regarding Chinese organized crime and examines its structure and operations, particularly in the United States.

Cressey, Donald. *The Theft of the Nation: The Structure and Operations of Organized Crime in America*. New York: Harper & Row, 1969. Principal consultant and sociologist to the President's Crime Commission of 1967 describes the structure and functions of the Cosa Nostra.

Kaplan, David E., and Alec Dubro. *Yakuza: The Explosive Account of Japan's Criminal Underworld*. Reading, Mass.: Addison-Wesley, 1986. Japanese organized crime and its control over legitimate and illegal businesses are described.

Maas, Peter. *The Valachi Papers*. New York: Bantam Books, 1968. Biography of Joseph Valachi, the first member of the Cosa Nostra to reveal its inner operations.

Mills, James. *The Underground Empire: Where Crime and Governments Embrace*. New York: Doubleday, 1986. Describes an underground empire of nations of institutionalized state-supported crime and drug trafficking.

Pennsylvania Crime Commission. *Organized Crime in Pennsylvania: A Decade of Change, 1990 Report*. Conshohocken: Pennsylvania Crime Commission, 1991. This update of 1970 and 1980 reports describes the evolving nature of organized crime. This volume pays special attention to newer African American, Asian, and Latino groups.

Sterling, Claire. *The Octopus: The Long Reach of the International Sicilian Mafia*. New York: W. W. Norton, 1990. Account of the Sicilian mafia, which has assassinated judges and police chiefs, has been condemned by the pope and the Italian government, and was the subject of a massive crackdown by the Italian military.

Frank E. Hagan

Cross-References

Business and Government, p. 177; Law Enforcement, p. 1059; Political Crimes, p. 1448; Political Ethics, p. 1461; Political Machines and Bosses, p. 1468; Self-Interest in Politics, p. 1802.

PACIFIC ISLANDER GOVERNMENTS

Field of study: Comparative government

Pacific islander governments include many of the world's newest nations. Despite great differences, they share common challenges of attaining political autonomy from their former administrators, encouraging sustainable economic development, and preserving cultural integrity. These similarities provide the basis for establishing a broad regional identity.

Principal terms

COMMONWEALTH: political unit that has local autonomy but voluntarily unites with another nation

COMPACT OF FREE ASSOCIATION: agreement between two sovereign nations, whereby the more powerful nation receives preferential access to the lands and waters of the less powerful nation, in exchange for providing it with military protection and foreign aid

DECOLONIZE: process of achieving political independence from a foreign occupier or administrator

DEPENDENCY: people or nation that is beholden to another nation because of a lack of economic and military resources

OCEANIA: Pacific's lands and waters, including Melanesia, Micronesia, and Polynesia

SOVEREIGNTY: legal characteristic of a state by which it is free of external control and has full authority over its body politic

Overview

The Pacific islands lie in the world's largest geographic area, the Pacific Ocean. Over the vast expanse of 13.5 million square miles lie 10,000 islands with a combined land mass of 379,365 square miles. All told, 7.1 million people live on the Pacific islands (half on Papua New Guinea, alone) and are subject to the rule of twenty-five separate political entities. To facilitate comparisons and to better understand linguistic, cultural, and political differences among the islands, scholars divide the massive region into three relatively distinct island groups: Melanesia, including islands west of the international date line and below the equator; Micronesia, including islands west of the international date line and mostly north of the equator; and Polynesia, encompassing the area of a triangle from the Hawaiian Islands at the apex, southeastward to Easter Island just off the Chilean coast, and extending westward to New Zealand, although not including it.

In so vast a region, it is difficult to generalize about island cultures. Among the island groups, however, the small islands of Polynesia and Micronesia do exhibit similarities. In each, the land is scarce, which led to hierarchical social structures based on leaders' dominion over the land. In the more rugged and larger Melanesian islands, land is not as scarce a resource, and therefore was less significant in defining relative social standing. Accordingly, societies were more egalitarian. Languages in the Pacific have similar roots, reflecting the prehistoric migrations of people across the Pacific. Most are members of the Austronesian language family, except certain islands in Melanesia that have Papuan roots.

Beginning in the 1960's, the inhabited islands were transformed from powerful nations' colonial possessions to governments with varying degrees of political independence. At the end of the twentieth century, relationships between the islands and their former colonial trustees remained close. Many Pacific islander governments have modeled their institutions after those of their former trustees or overseers.

Because of their undeveloped economies, small populations, and strategic locations in the Pacific trade routes, the islands were vulnerable to colonization. While their distance from the major powers shielded the islands for centuries, by the fifteenth century, Europeans had developed oceangoing ships and were traveling the Pacific and beginning to occupy the islands. In 1494, through a treaty concession, Spain acquired titular control over the entire Pacific.

The fortunes of the major powers ebbed and flowed over the next 450 years. Great Britain, France, and the United States played dominant roles, but Spain, Germany, The Netherlands, Japan, and Britain's former colonies of Australia and New Zealand, all controlled interests in Oceania at some point. After World War II, as the major powers began what was, for them, the painful process of decolonization, especially in Africa and Southeast Asia, the Pacific islands were still under trusteeship and domain. It was not until the 1960's that the process of self-determination began in the Pacific. Most islands chose the path of self-governance. Some opted for association or commonwealth status, in which they exert control over internal affairs but leave varying degrees of diplomatic and security arrangements to their partners. Nations that associate with a power, such as the Cook Islands with New Zealand or Palau with the United States, retain their political independence but allow preferential access to their lands and waters; commonwealths, such as the Northern Mariana Islands, unite politically with another nation. Other islands, for example, Western Samoa, became fully sovereign with complete control over internal and external affairs. Almost all nations have retained security relationships with their former administrators, since self-defense against even minimal threats is impractical.

Melanesia, including Fiji, the Solomon Islands, and Vanuata, was under joint British-French administration. The French have continued to hold New Calendonia as an overseas possession. The Australians last administered New Guinea and Papua, which combined to form the single nation of Papua New Guinea in 1975. Aside from New Calendonia, these islands became independent during the 1970's. The larger islands of Melanesia contain more natural resources, leading to greater self-sufficiency and political independence compared to Micronesia or Polynesia. These latter regions tend to have islands that are smaller, contain fewer resources, and are more reliant on foreign aid.

Micronesia was mostly under U.S. control, with Nauru jointly managed by Australia, Great Britain and New Zealand, and the Gilberts (Kiribati) under British mandate.

The United States has continued its connection with the Federated States of Micronesia (including Yap, Truk, Ponape, and Kosrae), the Marshall Islands, and Palau as self-governing associated states. While these states control their internal affairs, the United States may intervene in their internal affairs if there are threats to the security of islanders. In exchange, the United States continues to provide a large amount of direct financial assistance. In each case, the security agreements may only be terminated with the consent of both; this leads some observers to conclude that these governments are not fully sovereign. Guam is a self-governing territory and the Northern Marianas (of which Saipan, Tinian, and Rota are the major islands) is a United States commonwealth.

Polynesia, the largest island group, had the greatest differentiation of trustees. The first territory to achieve independence was Western Samoa in 1962. It remains the only island formerly controlled by New Zealand that has since become independent. Niue and the Cook Islands remain associated states and Tokelau is a New Zealander dependency. The British granted independence to Tonga and Tuvalu (Ellice Island); only tiny Pitcairn remained a British colony. Wallis, Futuna, and French Polynesia remained overseas territories of France. Chile's close neighbor Rapanui (Easter Island) is a part of Chile proper. American Samoa remained an overseas territory of the United States; the Hawaiian Islands petitioned and became one of fifty states within the United States.

All the Pacific islands exert dominant control over their internal affairs. Most islands that have chosen not to be independent do so either because they are so small, such as Pitcairn with fewer than one hundred inhabitants, or they do not possess the expertise or inclination to fully handle external relations, such as the Cook Islands. With few exceptions, islander governments adopted the government structure of their former administrators. U.S. possessions, such as the Commonwealth of the Northern Mariana Islands (CNMI), adopted presidential systems to govern internal affairs. The CNMI has a chief executive, a governor, elected by all citizens; a nine-member Senate that allocates representation by territory rather than by people; a fourteen-member House of Representatives apportioned by population; and a commonwealth trial court that handles internal legal matters.

Former British colonies adopted Westminster-style parliamentary governments, in which the legislative body makes the laws without a separate chief executive wielding a veto over legislative acts. Kiribati's forty-one member House of Assembly, for example, has complete lawmaking authority. Western Samoa adopted a forty-seven member Legislative Assembly modeled after New Zealand's House of Representatives.

One clear point of distinction from their former administrators is that many islander governments have attempted to protect the role traditional chiefs or leaders play in decision making. In parts of Polynesia, the role is formal, with traditional leaders in Wallis and Futuna, for example, sharing power with a French administrator and the Territorial Assembly. In Tonga, a king retains the greatest amount of political influence; the nation does not have periodic elections. In other nations, such as Palau, traditional leaders play a less formal role, rarely seeking public office but retaining a large degree of informal influence. These roles reflect the fact that the vast majority of the islands are still rural and communal, with the extended family or clans playing a paramount role in society.

The greatest challenges facing Pacific islander governments are social and economic. Crime, alcohol and drug dependency, and population growth are vexing problems threatening local culture and traditional ways. Traditional societies are threatened too by the change from subsistence-based economies to the reality of becoming part of the international market economy. Phosphate-rich Nauru provides the region's best standard of living to its citizens; others, such as the Solomons, have substantial natural resources that are extractable. Islands such as Palau, Guam, or the Cook Islands hope that tourism may eventually improve standards of living. One promising sign of increasing economic independence is that the Pacific states in 1979 declared 200-mile economic zones around their islands, consistent with the United Nations Law of the Sea Treaty. This will serve to protect the natural resources upon which many of these islands rely for fishing, tourism, or seabed mining. Nevertheless, the unfortunate reality is that few have any hope of economic independence. In fact, many islands are reluctant to seek political independence as it might threaten the amount of aid that otherwise comes from their administrators or associated states.

Regional cooperation is perhaps the region's best hope of strengthening itself. In December, 1986, the nations of the South Pacific, assisted by New Zealand, ratified The Treaty of Rarotonga establishing the South Pacific Nuclear Free Zone. The effort represented years of cooperation among the islands and was a significant step in asserting independence vis-a-vis the major nuclear powers such as the United States, Great Britain, France, and China. The South Pacific Forum and the South Pacific Bureau for Economic Cooperation also represent efforts to better coordinate action on regional political issues and economic problems. The major challenge for regional organizations is to try to build a consensus among disparate islands, so as to better strengthen themselves in their relations with other international organizations and major nations.

Applications

On October 1, 1994, at 1:01 P.M. local time, Palau became the Pacific's newest independent nation when the Compact of Free Association with the United States took effect. Palau is located just east of the Philippines and north of Papua New Guinea. Palauans voted in November, 1993, to ratify the compact, following actions of the United States Congress in 1986 and 1989. Palauan independence marked the end of the United Nations Trust Territory of the Pacific Islands (TTPI), which the United States had administered since 1947. Palau, like the Marshall Islands and the Federated States of Micronesia, chose to retain sovereignty over its affairs, as opposed to the Northern Marianas, which opted for commonwealth status.

The compact continues the Palau-United States relationship indefinitely. For the first fifty years, the United States retains the right to use Palau for military bases and may prevent access to it by any nation the United States deems hostile. One sticking point that had prevented earlier ratification of the compact was a Palauan constitutional provision banning nuclear weapons from its lands and seas. The United States has been steadfast in its refusal to confirm or deny the presence of nuclear weapons on its navy fleet, and thus refused to abide by the constitutional provision. To change the Palauan constitution, however, required a three-fourths vote, making a procompact vote difficult to pass. Seven previous referenda were defeated; ratification only occurred after Palau amended its constitution in such a way that the antinuclear provision would not apply to the compact.

Under the agreement, Palauans have the right to live and work in the United States, and Palau will receive $517 million in U.S. aid over fifteen years. Most of the money will go toward infrastructure, communications, and road improvements, as Palau faces the challenge of developing its domestic economy. Like many of its island neighbors, Palau has an overcrowded capital, Koror, and isolated villages scattered among many of its two hundred islands, only eight of which have significant populations. Major projects will better connect many of the islands, clear paths for roadways, and augment local harbors. Its education and health care systems also are in dire need of enhancement.

With these improvements, Palau hopes to build on its economic resources. Its pristine environment—particularly its waters, which are among the best diving spots in the world—are a significant draw for tourism and annually offer a bountiful harvest of tuna. The nation's proximity to cheap labor and the compact's provision to allow Palauan goods to enter the United States duty-free also promise to attract significant foreign investment, especially by the nearby Asian nations. Foreigners continue to control much of Palau's industry, raising the question of whether these assets will benefit Palauans, allowing them to retain one of the Pacific's best standards of living, or merely be shipped overseas.

Palauan politics is another challenge. Since its constitution took effect in 1980, one president has been assassinated and, after a corruption scandal, another was found dead, an apparent suicide. The nation is perhaps the world's most governed society. In addition to a president and vice president, Palau has a bicameral legislature, the Ol Biil Era Kelulau, with a sixteen-member House of Delegates and a fourteen-member Senate. Palau is also a federal nation with sixteen states, each of which has its own constitution, governor, and legislature. Overlapping all of this is a separate clan structure, which exerts considerable influence in political affairs. Coordinating and integrating the work of all these centers of authority will be difficult.

Context

Many political observers predict the Pacific region will be the world's most significant in the twenty first century. Bountiful economic growth in nations such as Japan, China, Korea, and the smaller nation-states such as Malaysia are the factors usually cited. Nevertheless, Great Britain, France, New Zealand, and the United States believe the Pacific islands are important enough to continue their extension of financial assistance and military protection. At the same time, most of the direct economic investment comes from Asia, rather than from private firms in the West. These international interests and the crucial strategic positions of the islands undoubtedly will continue to make them important.

Even with the political violence in Palau, and similar episodes in New Calendonia and Fiji, the process of decolonization and greater independence in the Pacific has gone well, especially when compared with the violent experiences of decolonization in Africa and Southeast Asia. The region does, however, share the tests facing many of the world's newest nations. Oceania's long-term challenges, in fact, may be more complicated. All new nations face travails in their first years of sovereignty; the United States, the world's foremost military and economic power in the late twentieth century, had a destructive civil war and political instability for much of its first hundred years.

The region's challenges are compounded by a desire to protect indigenous cultures that, for many, define their very existence. How to do that in a world that is increasingly interdependent economically, environmentally, and strategically may be the most difficult question to answer. Creating sustainable economies capable of adequately providing for citizens is also a dilemma. The assets to provide decent standards of living—such as natural resources and strong education systems—are lacking. Alongside these problems are rapidly burgeoning populations that require greater economic growth simply for the nations to maintain their standards of living. It appears likely that the overwhelming majority of islands will continue their dependency on foreign nations.

While by themselves few islands have the wherewithal to acquire real political independence and self-sufficiency, regional cooperation among the islands may be the best hope. Much of Polynesia and Melanesia are nuclear-free zones, thanks to the determined actions of the islands. Forging common positions is a difficult process when the region's widespread diversity, geographic distances, cultures, and economies are considered, but the common issues of the region—development, a desire for greater political autonomy, and their precarious strategic positions—provide the bases for cooperation.

Bibliography

Bunge, Frederica M., and Melinda W. Cooke, eds. *Oceania: A Regional Study*. 2d ed. Washington, D.C.: U.S.G.P.O., 1984. Excellent overview of the Pacific islands, including their histories, cultures, economies, and challenges for the future.

Douglas, Norman. *Pacific Islands Yearbook*. 16th ed. North Ryde, New South Wales, Australia: Angus & Robertson, 1989. Basic introduction to the Pacific islands.

Elliott, Jennifer. *An Introduction to Sustainable Development*. London: Routledge, 1994. Useful for analyzing the challenges developing nations, such as the Pacific islands, face in balancing economic growth with environmental resources.

Kluge, P. F. *The Edge of Paradise: America in Micronesia*. New York: Random House, 1991. First-hand account of the effects of development on traditional societies. Highly readable. Written by a former Peace Corps volunteer.

Meller, Norman. "The Pacific Island Microstates." *Journal of International Affairs* 41 (Summer/Fall, 1987): 109-134. Description of the recent history and political situation facing the Pacific islands. Includes useful charts on island political histories and economic situations.

Pacific Studies. 1977-. Semiannual journal published by the Hawaii campus of the Brigham Young University. Provides scholarly articles on recent developments in the Pacific, its islands, and adjacent countries.

Stephen D. Van Beek

Cross-References

Asia: Politics and Governments, p. 108; Colonial Government, p. 344; Colonialism and Anticolonialism, p. 351; Commonwealths, p. 364; Comparative Government, p. 384; Developed and Developing Nations, p. 533; Environmental Protection, p. 617; Independence Movements and Transitions, p. 896; Nationalism, p. 1268; Regional Governments, p. 1672; Self-Determination, p. 1796; United Nations, p. 2045.

PAN-AFRICANISM

Field of study: Comparative government

Pan-Africanism encompasses a set of ideas, emotions, and ideologies that espouse unity and solidarity among all Africans—those living on the continent and those of the worldwide diaspora.

Principal terms

DIASPORA: dispersal of Africans and their descendants to places outside the continent

ETHIOPIANISM: movement for independent black churches and religious empowerment

IMPERIALISM: imposition of a nation's rule or domination over a foreign territory

NATIONALISM: belief in and maintenance of a self-governing nation-state

SELF-DETERMINATION: right of communities to determine for themselves how they are governed

Overview

Pan-Africanism is familiar to many people, especially blacks, but it defies easy definition. Pan-Africanism is a complex concept. For example, at a conference held in 1960 by the American Society of African Culture at the University of Pennsylvania, Philadelphia, to examine pan-Africanism, several conflicting views of what pan-Africanism is were expressed. Definitions ranged from African self-government to worldwide black economic, social, and cultural development. Others spoke of pan-Africanism as being synonymous with the terms "African personality" and "negritude." There is an element of acceptability in all these definitions because at the broadest interpretation, pan-Africanism is about the advancement of blacks everywhere; the ideas and methods for achieving this goal may sometimes diverge.

Pan-Africanism is an idea, a movement, and an ideology. W. E. B. Du Bois, one of the architects of pan-Africanism, saw it as an intellectual movement aimed at achieving understanding and cooperation among all peoples of African descent. He hoped such cooperation would bring about their industrial and spiritual emancipation. To Colin Legum, the British journalist and political commentator on Africa, however, pan-Africanism is "essentially a movement of ideas and emotions."

Expressed in its broadest terms, pan-Africanism is a set of ideas, emotions, and ideologies that espouse unity among Africans living on the continent and those of African descent in the diaspora. Underlying pan-Africanism is a sense of common bond and unity of black peoples everywhere. Pan-Africanism recognizes a common history of black struggle against oppression, colonialism, slavery, and white domination. As a historical movement, pan-Africanism has at one time or other incorporated goals for the political, social, cultural, economic, and spiritual advancement of blacks.

Its major elements may be identified as: recognition of Africa as the homeland of all persons of African origin, solidarity among people of African descent, belief in a distinct African personality, pride in African history and culture, empowerment of Africans in government, church, and economics, and hope for a glorious, united Africa.

It is not known exactly when or by whom the term "pan-African" was first used. What is known is that the term did not gain currency until after the Pan-African Congress in 1900. What is also known is that the ideas and emotions that came to be embodied in pan-Africanism were born out of centuries of humiliation and degradation suffered by African descendants in the Americas. The ideas and emotions of pan-Africanism were rooted in a determination to recover an identity and a heritage nearly destroyed by slavery and racism. The origins of pan-Africanism therefore lay outside the continent of Africa among diasporan blacks who were rendered homeless by being taken from Africa and subjugated to an alien culture.

Pan-Africanism's origins can be traced as far back as the eighteenth century. As early as 1787, Prince Hall, a Boston minister from Barbados and Grand Master of the African Lodge, petitioned the Legislative Assembly of Massachusetts over repatriation to Africa. The emigration movement was further advocated by Paul Cuffee (1759-1817), a Quaker merchant and shipbuilder, who made two visits to Sierra Leone in West Africa in the 1810's, founded a settlement there, and established an association to provide a link between Africans, and repatriated forty blacks at his own expense. Olaudah Equiano, an enslaved Nigerian who later secured his freedom during the late eighteenth century and moved from the United States to England, where he wrote his classic autobiographical experiences of slavery, similarly assisted in the repatriation of several blacks.

Other early pan-Africanists were Jamaican journalist John B. Russwurm (who went to Liberia in 1830 and established a newspaper there), George Charles (president of the African Emigration Association, who petitioned the U.S. Congress in 1886 about establishing a United States of Africa), John Duport (from St. Kitts, who went to settle in Guinea in 1855), Bishop Henry McNeil Turner (a leading proponent of the Back to Africa movement), and publisher Timothy Thomas Fortune (whose Afro-American League was a model United States of Africa).

At the same time that these early pan-Africanist activities were being initiated in the diaspora, the flame of African nationalism was being lighted in West Africa. Its torchbearers included James Africanus Horton, a Sierra Leonean who assumed the name "Africanus" as a demonstration of pride in his heritage. A medical officer and colonial administrator, Horton decried Africa's victimization at the hands of European imperialism and held out hope for an African future under the control of Africans. James "Holy" Johnson, a Nigerian minister of the Anglican Church Missionary Society, preached about a distinctive African character that he termed the "African personality." Perhaps the most influential pan-African advocate of his time in Africa was Edward Blyden. Born in St. Thomas in 1832, Blyden emigrated to Liberia, where he became a newspaper editor, minister, professor, and president of Liberia College. Blyden believed Africans must advance by their own methods and "show that we are able to go alone, to carve our own way."

It was out of these beginnings that pan-Africanism evolved from a movement of emotions and ideas into an organization of social protest and political action. The institutionalization of pan-Africanism as a movement may be credited to the 1893 Chicago Congress of Africa, where the term "pan-African" was used for the first time. The Congress criticized the threat of European imperial expansion in Africa. The African Association was founded in England in 1897 essentially as an anti-imperialist organization.

Applications

Between 1900 and 1945, five Pan-African Congresses were held in various cities in Europe and the United States. They served as the primary vehicles for the application and dissemination of pan-Africanist ideas. The first of these congresses was convened in London in 1900 by Trinidadian barrister Henry Sylvester Williams. It protested against the "scramble for Africa" and discussed ways of bringing about closer communication among blacks. It also called for the cessation of discrimination based on race and color, petitioned the great powers of the time to respect the autonomy of the black-ruled nations of Abyssinia (Ethiopia), Haiti, and Liberia, and sent a protest to Queen Victoria of Great Britain against the treatment blacks were receiving in southern Africa.

The second Pan-African Congress (1919) coincided with the Paris Peace Conference. It was the first of several to be held under the direction of W. E. B. Du Bois. It attempted to persuade the international community that Woodrow Wilson's principle of self-determination should apply to Africa. Though the resolutions were moderate in tone, calling for the right of Africans "to participate in the government as fast as their development permits," the fifty-six delegates spoke in the name of black people everywhere in proclaiming African rights.

The author of more than twenty books on black history and culture, Du Bois was one of the most prominent pan-Africanists for over half a century. A founder of the Niagara Movement and of the National Association for the Advancement of Colored People, Du Bois made his imprint indelibly on two important organizations committed to black rights.

Du Bois held views regarding the restoration of dignity for blacks that differed from those of another foremost pan-Africanist, Jamaican-born Marcus Garvey (1887-1940). Du Bois viewed the discrimination that blacks suffered in the diaspora and Africa as part of a global struggle. Since the struggle was everywhere, there was little point in going home. Garvey advocated separatism and African repatriation. He founded the Universal Negro Improvement Association (UNIA) with the slogans "Back to Africa" and "Africa for the Africans." In 1916, Garvey moved the UNIA from Kingston, Jamaica, to Harlem, New York, where he convened the first Black Parliament and developed a framework that was to influence pan-Africanism for a long time.

One of the guiding principles of Garveyism was the economic empowerment of the

African. Toward this end, he undertook a number of economic ventures, including creating an international shipping scheme, the Black Star Line, operating small enterprises in Harlem, and investing in Liberia. A second principle was religious empowerment in a form that subsequently came to be identified as Ethiopianism. A third principle of Garveyism was the fostering of a deep sense of pride in Africa. Garvey accomplished this third principle on a scale never before attained in the diaspora. His First International Convention of the Negro Peoples of the Globe at New York's Madison Square Garden, for instance, attracted 25,000 representatives. Fiercely proud of his "Africanness," Garvey used ceremony and symbols in seeking to regain for blacks a dignity that had been shattered by slavery and colonialism. He created an African national anthem and conferred titles of honor such as "Duke of the Nile," "Earl of the Congo," and "Baron of the Zambezi." Garvey's philosophy influenced generations of pan-Africanists in America, the Caribbean, Europe, and Africa. Although he never set foot on African soil, he instilled a real sense of solidarity among Africans and people of African descent for the first time. Garvey transformed pan-Africanism from a largely intellectual movement into a mass movement.

The next Pan-African Congress, held under the leadership of W. E. B. Du Bois, met in 1921 in London and Brussels. It was perhaps the most radical of the early congresses in the tone of its resolutions. Delegates openly condemned colonialism in Africa and racism in the United States and again demanded recognition of the integrity of Ethiopia, Haiti, and Liberia.

The 1923 (London and Lisbon) and 1927 (New York) congresses continued with condemnations of racism and demanded a voice for Africans in their own governments. The congresses also demanded that the development of Africa be for the benefit of Africans. The 1927 congress was the last to be held under Du Bois's direct leadership.

Meanwhile, in the United States, a cultural manifestation of pan-Africanism was flowering in the movement known as the Harlem Renaissance, which affirmed black pride. Langston Hughes, one of the literary giants of this movement, captured the emotions underlying the pan-Africanist movement:

> You from Africa
> We are related—you and I
> You from the West Indies,
> I from Kentucky
> We are related—you and I
> You from Africa
> I from these States
> We are brothers—you and I.

A subject that has not received adequate attention is the role of women in pan-Africanism. In addition to the active involvement of individual women, each chapter of Marcus Garvey's UNIA had a "lady president." Garvey's first wife, Amy Ashwood, cofounded the UNIA with her husband. An activist, Amy traveled and wrote extensively, and was prominent in the protests against the Italian invasion of Ethiopia in 1934. Garvey's second wife, Amy Jacques, ran the UNIA during the period of her husband's incarceration. Another leading woman pan-Africanist was Henrietta Vinton Davis, who worked as director of the Black Star Line. Other leading women pan-Africanists included Mme M. T. L. De Mena and Queen Mother Moore, who were both active in UNIA and the committee for the defense of Ethiopia. Prominent delegates at the 1921, 1923, and 1927 congresses also included Jessie Fauset (teacher), Helen Curtis (social worker and NAACP activist), and Addie W. Hunton (one of the organizers of the 1927 congress). In Africa, Adelaide Casely-Hayford helped in the dissemination of pan-Africanist ideas through her participation in the 1927 congress and her role as lady president of the Freetown branch of UNIA.

In 1934, when the Italian dictator Benito Mussolini made plans to attack Ethiopia, the threat signaled a rallying point for pan-Africanists everywhere, for whom Ethiopia symbolized African independence and greatness. Blacks living in London formed the International African Friends of Abyssinia to defend Ethiopia. Headed by the Trinidadian historian and writer C. L. R. James, the Guyanese physician Peter Milliard, and the future Kenyan nationalist leader Jomo Kenyatta, the association campaigned against Italian fascism and imperialism. It was later joined by the Trinidadian George Padmore when he moved to England in 1935. Subsequently, various organizations for the defense of Ethiopia were established throughout Africa, Europe, and the United States. Among them were the International African Service Bureau led by Guyanese T. Ras Makonnen and the West African Youth League founded by the Sierra Leonean I. T. A. Wallace-Johnson.

In many respects the Fifth Pan-African Congress (Manchester, United Kingdom, 1945) was the most significant of all the congresses. First, it made resolutions that went beyond the familiar condemnations of imperialism and racial discrimination of past congresses. The fifth congress called on European governments to implement the Atlantic Charter and grant immediate independence to African colonies. Second, Manchester marked a watershed in the pan-African movement. It was attended by many Africans who were soon to become leaders of nationalist movements in their own countries, including, notably, Obafemi Awolowo from Nigeria, Kwame Nkrumah from the Gold Coast (now Ghana), and Dr. Hastings K. Banda from Nyasaland (now Malawi). Third, the participation of eighteen trade unions in the congress marked the entry of labor organizations as a key element in the nationalist struggle in Africa. Finally, Manchester marked a transition in the battlefront of the nationalist element of pan-Africanism to African soil, where the ideas that had been formulated in the diaspora were put into action in the liberation of the continent. The next Pan-African Congress, as an example of this transition, was held in Africa, in Dar es Salaam, Tanzania, in 1974.

Context

When the Gold Coast became independent as Ghana in 1957 (the first African nation south of the Sahara to achieve this distinction), Kwame Nkrumah declared his pan-African vision for the future of Africa: "The independence of Ghana is meaning-less unless it is linked up with the total liberation of the continent." Following Ghana's lead, and, in some cases, with Nkrumah's vigorous support, nationalist leaders in various parts of Africa intensified their campaigns for self-government. By 1961, most former colonies were liberated from colonialism.

With the virtual elimination of imperialism in Africa questions have been raised concerning the contemporary relevance of pan-Africanism and its continuing role. Those with a limited notion of pan-Africanism like to suggest that insofar as the primary impetus of the movement was derived from a commitment to the liberation of blacks, pan-Africanism is a thing of the past. The majority of pan-Africanists, however, see a continued relevance for pan-Africanism as long as oppression, dis-crimination, and exploitation of blacks exist anywhere in the world. The ongoing struggle for the total elimination of oppression and discrimination has continued to inspire various pan-Africanist movements, ranging from the Organization of African Unity and negritude to Black Power.

The driving force behind the pan-African movement in Africa, Kwame Nkrumah convened two major conferences in Accra soon after Ghana's independence: the Conference of Independent African States and the All-African People's Conference. These conferences marked an important shift in pan-Africanism away from a concern with the grievances of black people worldwide toward a concern for the unity of the newly emerging African states. Toward this goal, Nkrumah established, along with Sékou Touré of Guinea and Modibo Keita of Mali, a union of their three countries which would be the nucleus of a union of West African states and eventually of all Africa. Nkrumah's strategy of continental union government was rejected, however, by the leaders of many African states that feared losing their individual sovereignties. Rival and competing blocs of states with divergent concepts of African unity emerged. When the Organization of African Unity (OAU) was created in Addis Ababa in 1963, the delegates rejected continental political unity and opted for functional cooperation. The OAU charter aimed at promoting the unity and solidarity of African states through commissions on economic and social development, mediation, defense, and health. In retrospect, the loosely structured OAU has had limited success. It was largely ineffec-tual in resolving major conflicts such as the Congo and Nigerian crises.

Other groups and movements have shared the pan-African spirit. Begun among francophone Caribbean and African students studying in Paris in the 1930's (notably Aimé Césaire and Leon Damas), negritude was a pan-African expression of African nationalism, an affirmation of black pride, and a critique of colonial injustices. Negritude emphasized the need for blacks to strip themselves of the French cultural cover so that they might rediscover their true Africanness. In its accommodation of French civilization, negritude was inherently self-contradictory.

During the 1960's, many African Americans, exasperated at the slow pace of the Civil Rights movement, began to form organizations with more radical strategies and ideologies. The vanguard groups included the Student Non-Violent Coordinating Committee, the older Congress of Racial Equality, and more militant organizations such as the Black Panthers and Black Muslims. Though espousing divergent philosophical approaches, all these civil rights organizations advanced, in varying degrees, pan-Africanist ideas (pride in blackness, rediscovery of African roots and history, and black empowerment) that came to be embodied in the concept of black power. Many of the leaders of the Civil Rights movement projected pan-Africanist orientations in their pronouncements. As Malcolm X declared to an OAU summit meeting in 1963, African American activists recognized that

> We find ourselves in a strange land that has rejected us, and, like the prodigal son, we are turning to our elder brothers [Africans] for help. . . . Your problems will never be fully solved until and unless ours are solved. You will never be fully respected unless we are also respected.

Pan-Africanism has also found expression in the worldwide campaign that culminated in the dismantling of apartheid (the official policy of racial discrimination and segregation of nonwhite peoples in South Africa) in the 1990's. Persistent public demonstrations, the movement for the divestment of businesses and investments from South Africa, and pressure on the U.S. Congress to pass sanctions against South Africa unified pan-Africanists everywhere. Inside South Africa, antiapartheid leaders such as Steven Biko were influenced by the black consciousness movement in the United States, which advocated militancy.

The Rastafari movement, born in Jamaica (named after Ras Tafari, who became Emperor Haile Selassie of Ethiopia), is another expression of pan-Africanism. Its message of resistance to white oppression is universal. Rastafarianism is exemplified by the popular lyrics of one of the songs of Bob Marley, the most influential Rasta:

> Get up, stand up, stand up for your rights;
> Get up, stand up, don't give up the fight.

At the close of the twentieth century, there was an increasing diffusion of pan-African thinking and practices among African Americans. The African identity of American blacks was widely accepted. African art, culture, and attire, and African-inspired practices such as Kwanza and rites of passage had also gained a foothold in African American culture.

Insofar as black oppression and underdevelopment exist, there is a continued relevance for pan-Africanist ideas. What is needed is a continual rededication to pan-Africanist thinking. Pan-Africanism has come a long way from Garvey's initial idea of repatriation to Africa, and should be recognized as a dynamic force in the struggle for individual, group, and community liberation.

Bibliography

Esedebe, P. O. *Pan-Africanism: The Idea and Movement, 1776-1963*. Washington, D.C.: Howard University Press, 1982. Comprehensive discussion of Pan-Africanism from its inception to the OAU.

Legum, Colin. *Pan-Africanism: A Short Political Guide.* New York: Praeger, 1965. Classic study by one of the best known political commentators on the subject.

Lemelle, Sidney. *Pan-Africanism for Beginners.* New York: Writers and Readers, 1992. Brief, highly readable account, creatively illustrated and written for the general reader.

Ras Makonnen. *Pan-Africanism from Within.* Edited by Kenneth King. New York: Oxford University Press, 1973. Provocative analysis that presents the author's views on a movement with which he was personally involved.

Walters, Ronald W. *Pan Africanism in the African Diaspora.* Detroit: Wayne State University Press, 1993. Comparative examination of the interactive involvement of blacks in the United States, Latin America, and the United Kingdom in pan-Africanism.

Joseph K. Adjaye

Cross-References

Africa: Politics and Governments, p. 21; African American Politics, p. 28; Colonial Government, p. 344; Colonialism and Anticolonialism, p. 351; Independence Movements and Transitions, p. 896; Indigenous Peoples' Governments, p. 903; Nationalism, p. 1268; Self-Determination, p. 1796; World Government Movements, p. 2174; World Political Organization, p. 2186.

PARLIAMENTARY GOVERNMENT

Field of study: Types of government

The most common form of democratic rule in the late twentieth century, parliamentary government joins the executive and lawmaking branches of government by making the executive responsible to a majority in the popularly elected house of the legislative body.

Principal terms

CENTRALIZED PARTY: political party whose parliamentary leaders control the vote of party members inside parliament

COLLECTIVE RESPONSIBILITY: system in which the entire cabinet, not only the prime minister, is responsible to a parliamentary majority and must resign in the event of a no-confidence vote

MINISTERIAL RESPONSIBILITY: the basic requirement of parliamentary government—that the head of government or the entire cabinet is dependent on and responsible to a majority in the legislature

NO-CONFIDENCE VOTE: upon the expression by a legislative majority of "no confidence" in the existing leadership, the executive must resign and a new government be formed; in some parliamentary systems this vote necessitates new elections

PARTY GOVERNMENT: control of the executive by the same party that controls a majority of votes in the parliamentary house to which the executive is responsible; also known as party rule

Overview

Great Britain proudly and correctly proclaims itself the birthplace of parliamentary democracy. The gestation period, however, was a long one. In a sense, both democracy and parliamentary government in Britain have been evolving for more than seven hundred years.

The Norman monarchy established in England after 1066 by William the Conqueror was a relatively undifferentiated one. King William was the state, and the business of the state was relatively simple and conducted in a highly personal manner by the monarch. As the realm expanded and the complexity of the state's business increased, a specialization and institutionalization of tasks gradually began to emerge; the king alone could no longer manage effectively all the affairs of state. To assist him, there emerged, at first informally, a council of agents and counselors. Over time, the individual counselors developed areas of expertise in place of tendering general advice on all matters, and in this emergent king-in-council arrangement can be found the embryo of the modern British state in general and its administrative-executive branch in particular.

The legislative branch of government in England can also trace its origin to the king's council, although in this instance the relevant council was not the king's inner circle of advisers at court but the crown's larger, outer council of agents throughout the realm. Initially composed of the king's knights, the members of this council performed a double task in feudal England. They enforced the king's law in their respective locales, and at irregular intervals they were summoned to court to meet together with the inner council as a council of the whole, to advise the king on matters of broad concern.

During the thirteenth century, the British Parliament evolved from this outer council. As the country's commercial centers grew in importance, the king added burghers, representatives of England's emerging business class, to the outer council. At approximately the same time, the council began to meet more regularly. By 1265, most of the sources of influence in the realm were represented—the great barons, the upper clergy, the knights, and the burghers—and the term "parliament" (from the French verb for "to speak") was being regularly used to characterize its sessions. In the model parliament of 1295, the large assembly divided into two groups. The upper nobility of the state and church began to meet together in what shortly became the British House of Lords; the knights and burghers began to meet regularly in what subsequently became the House of Commons.

By the fourteenth century, the institutional components of a parliamentary system already surrounded the king: an executive council at court serving as an increasingly specialized, differentiated part of the executive in charge of administering the affairs of the state; and a bicameral legislature participating at increasingly regular intervals in shaping the policy made by the king. Still, it required another five centuries for the changing relationships between these bodies to cast parliamentary government into its modern form.

It was not until the seventeenth century that an epic struggle for supremacy between the king and Parliament was finally resolved, in favor of Parliament. The monarch remained sovereign in theory, but when William and Mary signed the English Bill of Rights of 1689 upon succeeding to the throne, they were acknowledging a de facto supremacy of Parliament that has never subsequently been challenged.

During the eighteenth century, the cabinet emerged as the instrument to reconcile the gap between theory and practice in the British political system. Although theoretically the members of the cabinet were the king's men, in practice it became necessary for the king to appoint to it men drawn from and acceptable to Parliament. At approximately the same time, the development of parties inside Parliament provided a means of gaining, by partisan vote, the Parliament's official approval of the cabinet and its head, the prime minister. With the expansion of the suffrage and the development of grassroots party organizations during the nineteenth century, the system developed its democratic nature as the cabinet became responsible to a directly elected parliamentary majority in the House of Commons, the dominant house of Parliament in the late twentieth century.

Unlike the U.S. system of separation of powers, parliamentary government was not created by a constitution struck at a single moment of time, but emerged as the product of an organic development spanning centuries. The executive-administrative and legislative branches, both springing from the same historical source, have remained united in their modern form as well, with the executive in Great Britain accountable to a majority in the House of Commons.

Applications

Parliamentary government has become the most common form of democratic government in the world. Two principal reasons account for its appeal: It fits well in political systems based on the concept of popular sovereignty, and it is widely associated with the concept of energetic, majority-rule government. Outside of the land of its birth, however, parliamentary government has seldom provided countries with both popular and energetic government.

The U.S. system of government is based on the premise that the majority must be controlled, and to accomplish this, divides political power among three different branches by means of a written constitution difficult to amend. Parliamentary government, on the other hand, rests on the assumptions that government derives its power directly from the consent of the people, and that it exists to implement the will of the majority. In the twentieth century, the first assumption has typically led to arrangements making the government, either the chief executive of the entire cabinet, accountable to a majority in the popularly elected house of the legislature.

By wedding executive and legislative powers, parliamentary government offers a way for the government to govern with less likelihood of gridlock than in a separation-of-powers system, especially one in which the executive and lawmaking bodies are controlled by rival political parties. Where the executive branch commands the support of a majority in the popularly elected house, it can steer through the parliament the laws it has promised it will implement in running for office or that it determines are necessary to serve the general welfare while it is in office. Energy and accountability in government are thereby assured, in theory.

In practice, parliamentary government has required two other elements to function energetically, both of which have been historically present in the British political system, but rarely have been coupled elsewhere in the democratic world: a two-party system to assure a continuous, coherent majority in the popularly elected house of parliament; and a system of centralized parties in which the party leaders can control the votes of their members in parliament, so that campaign promises will be implemented. Where these elements have been lacking, the result has frequently been weak and indecisive government in parliamentary systems or the adoption of substantial deviations from the parliamentary model to make the system more effective in policy-making.

Principally as a result of the traditional homogeneity of the British political culture, there has rarely been enough substantial political disagreement in Britain to support a system of more than two parties. Although third parties have been present, in virtually every British election during the nineteenth and twentieth centuries only two parties had a chance of winning enough votes to govern without having to form a coalition cabinet. These same two parties rotated over time in office, and after each election a single party was able to govern without coalition partners. Only the faces changed over time. During the nineteenth century, British politics revolved around the issue of church-state relations, with the two principal parties being the Conservatives (pro-union) and Liberals (supporting disestablishment of church and state). In the twentieth century, class issues displaced religion as the pivotal issues in British politics. The Conservative Party, as the party of the traditional ruling class, continued to flourish, but the Liberal party was displaced permanently as Britain's second party by the Labour Party. Significantly, in all three parties, the parliamentary leadership has normally controlled party nominations, enabling the party's leaders in parliament to command the vote of their members in parliament. Those voting with the opposition, especially on key issues or no-confidence votes, could count on not being renominated. As a result, only once in the twentieth century (1979) was the opposition party able to bring down a government in Britain by successfully calling for a "no-confidence" vote.

In Western Europe, parliamentary government has had to function in quite a different environment. National political cultures there historically have been fragmented along class, religious, ideological, regional, and generational lines. Nationwide party organizations did not effectively develop in many countries until after World War II. The principle of popular sovereignty usually translated into parliaments composed of many small, diverse political parties, and fragile, multiparty coalition cabinets constructed to obtain the approval of a parliamentary majority, but prone to paralysis and collapse in the face of serious problems because of their differences. The Third French Republic, for example, had more than ninety cabinets between 1870 and 1940; the Fourth French Republic (1946-1958) had more than twenty. The more the parliaments have reflected the diversity of the people electing them, the less effective they have been as bodies for energetic government.

Given this history of stalemate in European parliamentary systems, including the Weimar system in Germany between World War I and World War II, the architects of constitutions written in Western Europe since World War II have tended to depart from the purer British model of parliamentary democracy in an effort to make the system more effective. There has been a decline in enthusiasm for proportional representation election systems, which guarantee parties a share of seats in parliament proportional to their share of the popular vote; where these arrangements have been selected, they usually have been subject to qualifying restraints. The most common device has been a variation of West Germany's 5 percent clause, a provision of the Federal Republic of Germany's 1949 constitution intended to inhibit the development in postwar Germany of the extreme multiparty system, multiparty parliament, and weak multiparty coalition cabinets that failed to govern Germany effectively during the 1920's. Under the 5 percent clause, only those parties that win at least 5 percent of the nationwide vote are entitled to seats in Germany's popularly elected house of parliament.

Modifications of the 5 percent requirement have been incorporated in many parliamentary systems throughout the Western world. Perhaps the most interesting of the efforts to achieve energetic government in a country traditionally earmarked by a fragmented political culture and propensity towards multiparty stalemate has been France's. At the height of that country's 1958 crisis over whether to fight to retain Algeria as an overseas part of France or allow it to have independence, Charles de Gaulle was summoned to govern France. De Gaulle demanded the right to draft a new constitution for France, one that could overcome the traditional centrifugal tendencies in French society and make France democratically governable. His solution, embodied in the constitution of the Fifth French Republic in 1958, was a hybrid system with two executives: a premier accountable to the Chamber of Deputies in the French assembly to give France a parliamentary system in normal times; and a powerful French president, directly elected by the people, possessing substantial authority to coax decisions out of the cabinet and assembly during normal times, and empowered to govern France for six months directly by executive decree in moments of crisis.

Context

With such modifications, the parliamentary system of popular sovereignty and fusion of legislative and executive functions continued to be extremely popular throughout the twentieth century. Spread by the European colonial powers into their colonies, or established in their imperial possessions on the eve of self-government, parliamentary forms of government developed on every continent: in Canada in North America, in former British and French territories in South America, in Australia, in Asia (including India), and in Africa.

Parliamentary government also quickly became the democratic model of choice in the former Soviet Union and Eastern and Central Europe following the collapse of the Union of Soviet Socialist Republics and its Eastern European empire in the early 1990's. The need for a strong central government to manage the political transition to democracy and the economic transition to a mixed market, combined with the popular desire for democracy, dictated the choice. The U.S. model of separated and rival branches of government appeared too disjointed, too inefficient, and too likely to lead to paralysis to fit their needs. Conversely, the British system of strong party government in a parliamentary system had great appeal, except for two things: Few countries in Eastern and Central Europe had the homogeneity of the political culture in Britain, and the British political process renders all government power, including judicial power, subject to the control of a majority in the House of Commons. Consequently, in Russia the system chosen leaned towards the French hybrid of presidential and parliamentary democracy. Elsewhere, the German model of parliamentary government, with a constitutionally strong prime minister, most often provided the model for constitutional government in part because the fragmented political terrain in Germany was more akin to that of Eastern Europe than to that of Britain. Furthermore, the form of democracy developed in the postwar Federal Republic of Germany was itself something of a hybrid: a traditional parliamentary form of government with the executive and legislative powers joined, but borrowing from the United States an independent judiciary empowered to protect the constitutionally guaranteed rights of the people against abuse by the parliament.

Parliamentary government thus continues to be tested, to spread, and often to flourish in the democratic world. It has been most successful where democratic political values and goals have been broadly diffused among the members of society, and where there are two centralized and disciplined parties whose members in parliament are constrained to vote as instructed by their leadership. It has also functioned well, however, in more fragmented landscapes even in the face of serious political problems, although usually in a modified form. Whatever the final tailored product, the pattern of parliamentary democracy generally set the style for democratic government in the twentieth century.

Bibliography

Budge, Ian, et al. *The Changing British Political System: Into the 1990's*. 2d ed. New York: Longman, 1988. A particularly interesting study of parliamentary government in Great Britain at the moment when European integration was making substantial inroads into the traditional sovereignty of parliament, and the traditional two-party system had broken down.

Dicey, A. V. *Introduction to the Study of the Law of the Constitution*. 7th ed. London: Macmillan, 1908. Excellent study of the development of parliamentary government in its unique birthplace, a country without a written constitution.

Friedrich, Carl J. *Constitutional Government and Democracy: Theory and Practice in Europe and America*. Boston: Ginn, 1946. Classic examination of all forms of democratic government, and the point-of-departure for anyone researching this topic.

Gooch, R. K. *The Government of England*. New York: D. Van Nostrand, 1937. One of the great studies of British government by an American political scientist. The section of the evolution of parliamentary government in Britain is still among the best, most succinct treatments available in U.S. libraries.

Greenberg, Douglas, et al. *Constitutionalism and Democracy: Transitions in the Contemporary World*. New York: Oxford University Press, 1993. Outstanding collection of essays on the quest for constitutional government, including in the new democracies of the Third World and Eastern Europe.

Kornberg, Allan, ed. *Legislatures in Comparative Perspective*. New York: David McKay, 1973. Older but still useful study of legislatures in a variety of parliamentary and nonparliamentary systems. Outstanding group of contributors.

Loewenberg, Gerhard, ed. *Modern Parliaments: Change or Decline?* Chicago: Aldine Atherton, 1971. Another older work of immense value. The essays focus on the twentieth century decline in the importance of legislatures in most democracies.

Rose, Richard. *Politics in England: Change and Persistence*. 5th ed. Glenview, Ill.: Scott, Foresman, 1989. Study of the model of parliamentary government and its link to the British party system, written by the ranking expert on British politics in the English-speaking world.

Joseph R. Rudolph, Jr.

Cross-References

The British Parliamentary System, p. 146; Cabinet Government, p. 184; The Canadian Parliamentary System, p. 190; Government Types, p. 785; Legislative Body Types, p. 1091; Modern Monarchy, p. 1209; Monarchy in Constitutional Governments, p. 1215; Montesquieu's Political Philosophy, p. 1228; Multiparty Systems, p. 1235; Policy Development and Implementation, p. 1414.

PATRIOTISM

Field of study: Politics

The acute sense that makes a good citizen in war and in peace, patriotism is a political virtue that encourages strong devotion and readiness to make sacrifices for the welfare of one's homeland and fellow citizens. Closely related to nationalism, patriotism underlies the basis of statehood, especially of nation-statehood and occasionally of subnational loyalty, in all cases promoting intragroup cohesion, but at times intergroup conflict.

Principal terms

ANTIPATRIOTISM: belief that citizens should not participate in wars against other states

CHAUVINISM: exaggerated, excessive, or blind patriotism

INSULARITY: inward-looking orientation and exclusiveness that dichotomizes the "we-group" and the "they-group," a feeling enhanced by patriotism and nationalism

JINGOISM: clamorous chauvinism or arrogant and uncritical nationalism

MESSIANISM: belief in a deliverer who will save a nation or a people who have a monopoly on truth

NATION: people connected by supposed or actual ties of blood; often evidenced by a common language, culture, history, religion, or other objective criteria, but also a group perception of commonality

NATIONALISM: devotion to, or advocacy of, national interest, national unity, or independence

PROPAGANDA: information or education provided by governments that is designed to enhance patriotism

XENOPHOBIA: suspicion, dislike, or fear of foreigners; often accompanies extreme forms of patriotism or nationalism

Overview

Usually defined as love of country, national pride, and readiness to make sacrifices, patriotism is a form of civic virtue. The focus of the solidarity involving patriotism tends to be territory—broadly defined—with which citizens identify memories of childhood, familiar environment, and common experiences. By contrast, nationalism tends to center on descent (ancestry), language, or culture. Accordingly, patriotism means giving highest preference to the interests of one's countrymen regardless of their race, ethnicity, religion, or other characteristics. Historically, this has been so since the sixteenth century when Niccolò Machiavelli, Italian statesman and political philosopher, declared that he preferred his country to the safety of his soul, and when most men stopped giving their highest allegiance to the Church.

For all that, patriotism has different emphases since the so-called public good toward which patriotism strives is rarely self-evident. In a general way, love of country is equated with pride in such values (at least in the United States) as freedom, fairness, opportunity for all, a democratic system of government, the country's natural beauty, and the need to sacrifice for its development and security—in short, the shared national heritage. But more narrowly, patriotism may focus on combat culture stressing the need for military service. Or, in its "quiet patriotism" variety, it may dwell on the seemingly intractable problems of peace rather than training for war. Indeed, quiet patriotism plays up civic virtues such as principle, honor, and service, not self-aggrandizement or private interest. It was expressed by the words of President John F. Kennedy at his 1961 inaugural address, when he declared, "Ask not what your country can do for you, but what you can do for your country." The focus may be even more abstract as when President Ronald Reagan's "new patriotism" in the 1980's emphasized national pride in the American spirit.

Ambivalence about the true nature of patriotism has led to many controversies in different societies. Just as there is not always agreement about what public good demands each citizen's highest allegiance, there is not always consensus about where lines should be drawn between political dissent and disloyalty, freedom of expression and government authority, and treason and patriotism. The Vietnam War, for example, evoked powerfully divergent responses among Americans, with both its supporters and its opponents laying claim to be true American patriots.

Despite such confusion, there is broad agreement that patriotism has three elements. These include love of one's country; desire for its welfare, as measured by the accretion of territory, population, wealth, prestige, glory, and other attributes; and willingness to serve it—even to the point of making the ultimate sacrifice for the country's survival and development.

At its best, then, patriotism binds the diverse segments of a society into an integrated whole, while at its worst, patriotism may degenerate into chauvinism or other forms of fanaticism. That is because cohesive civic culture can easily deteriorate into combat culture. For example, in 1846, many Americans wished to delineate the border of the Oregon Territory and Britain's Canadian territory more favorably and coined the slogan "Fifty-four forty or fight." In the Spanish-American War of 1898, the war cry was "Remember the Maine!"—referring to the U.S. battleship that mysteriously exploded in Havana harbor. Indeed, in a public opinion survey taken in 1991, the year of the Persian Gulf War, 88 percent of Americans who were polled perceived themselves as being "very patriotic," while 55 percent agreed with the statement that "we should all be willing to fight for our country whether it is right or wrong." On the downside, the feeling of patriotism is exclusive, often implying or even expressing superiority over other groups, for patriotism thrives largely on differences among nations, real or imagined.

But despite occasional vocal criticism by some of this "gross and harmful delusion" for causing violence and grief across the centuries, patriotism continues to be a powerful motivational force. It may well be asked why this is so and why patriotism has been so successful in its dominance over alternative appeals to ultimate loyalty by universal "brotherhoods" of various kinds, such as Christianity, international communism, pacifism, world trade unionism, and world federalism. By the same token, why does this ultimate loyalty generally coincide with the territorial definition of a country?

To answer such questions, one must examine the socialization, the conditioning aided and abetted by propaganda, even brainwashing, that promote loyalty to one's country. These processes use such emotional patriotic symbols as national flags, anthems, revered documents, folklore heroes, and other trappings motivating citizens to devotion, unity, and the willingness to make civic sacrifices. Such indoctrination occurs with children at an early age at home, in schools, and elsewhere. In 1991, for example, President George Bush referred to "American values" to justify United States involvement and leadership in the Persian Gulf War.

Perhaps more important, individuals are motivated by patriotism because they derive from it life-satisfactions—psychic and material benefits of various kinds—from sharing a community of feeling. As George Washington himself noted, patriotism without interests or other rewards in return is insufficient for the citizen to face adversity for long.

Because of the stress on the long-honored values of combat culture taught in schools, patriotism has found its highest expressions in the realm of conflict, not peace. Leaders often have aspired to joining the pantheons of their national military heroes who, in the minds of many, epitomize patriotism. In other words, there is a tendency to channelize patriotic sentiments into admiration for individuals who have become national idols. For that reason, the reputations of leaders such as France's Napoleon Bonaparte or Turkey's Mustafa Kemal Ataturk are more closely identified with the military exploits of these leaders than with the more significant and lasting civic contributions that they made to achieve "the moral equivalent of war," as American philosopher William James called it. Napoleon's greatest civic achievement was endowing his country with a public administration and judicial code second to none. Ataturk's achievement was modernizing and secularizing the core of the anemic Ottoman Empire into the Turkish Republic.

Applications

If bravery in wartime can be equated with patriotism, a collective example would be the tiny Mediterranean island of Malta. During World War II, when Malta was a British Crown Colony, it was subjected to three thousand German and Italian bombings that destroyed thirty thousand buildings. In April, 1942, Britain's King George VI conferred the George Cross on all of Malta's three hundred thousand residents for their heroism.

Also, Soviet leader Joseph Stalin waged his "Great Patriotic War" against the onslaught of Nazi Germany and its allies in 1941-1945. By appealing to duty and honor in fighting for "Mother Russia," the dictator hoped that Soviet citizens would prefer loyalty to the homeland and overlook the oppression and forced sacrifice to which they had been subjected. Religion is often pressed into the service of patriotism. In

Iran, Ayatollah Ruhollah Khomeini, the country's Shiite Muslim spiritual head, tried to stiffen the citizens' resistance to the Iraqi attack of 1980 by arousing their religious passions.

These appeals to patriotism work with most but not with all. Even in the United States, where World War II, like World War I, elicited more public expressions of support than any other conflict, there are examples. The likes of aviator-pioneer Charles Lindbergh, whose America First movement advocated the country's noninvolvement in the war, and poet Ezra Pound, who sided with Fascist Italy and publicly charged President Franklin Roosevelt with "licking British vomit up from every lamppost" through his Radio Rome broadcasts, helped to confuse the issue of what patriotism is or to reinforce the view that no person is wholly a patriot or wholly a traitor, but that everyone is a little of each.

On a broader scale, consider the case of Japanese Americans in the United States during World War II. Mass hysteria and public policy led to the relocation of more than 100,000 people of Japanese descent—mostly American citizens—on the West Coast after the Japanese attack on Pearl Harbor in December, 1941. Entire families were ordered to leave their homes and businesses, meaning great financial loss to many. The substandard conditions existing in temporary assembly centers with barbed-wire fences, roving searchlights, armed guards, mess-hall food, and the crowding of families into single rooms led to many grievances and even riots. The more permanent relocation camps far from the coast in the semi-arid inland regions of the West were little better. Occasionally the inmates—some with as little as one-sixteenth Japanese blood—were threatened with the loss of U.S. citizenship. In January, 1943, a new policy mandated inmates to declare their loyalty or disloyalty to the United States, as it was now the goal to empty the centers and even to accept volunteers for an all-Nisei U.S. Army unit. Some 31,000 Japanese Americans swore unqualified allegiance to their country while more than 6,000 refused to do so and 3,000 others qualified their answers or refused to register at all. (In fact, no Japanese American was ever convicted of espionage or sabotage.) The "loyal" ones were allowed to leave the centers while the "troublemakers" were moved to another camp.

In Hawaii, where no evacuation of Japanese Americans had taken place, one out of every three eligible males eighteen to thirty-eight years of age offered his services, but on the mainland only one out of fourteen volunteered, seemingly because of their resentment of the deprivation, discrimination, and isolation which they had endured. Indeed, specific circumstances in particular camps played a major role in how they responded. This episode in American history may evidence the truth in the aphorism of former Illinois governor and U.S. presidential candidate Adlai Stevenson when he remarked: "To strike freedom of the mind with the fist of patriotism is an old and ugly subtlety."

Some countries have managed to blend aspects of military and civic service. For instance, French military conscripts in peacetime are given the option to serve part of their duty performing civilian duties, such as teaching in France's former African colonies if they possess the appropriate skills. In the United States, conscientious objectors are exempted from compulsory military service during wartime in exchange for performing community service in hospitals, nursing homes, and the like.

Context

As a sense of duty, discipline, and obligation to one's country, patriotism reinforces the social and political glue that holds a society together and prompts it to work toward a common goal. Patriotism in a society will not necessarily always be aroused, even by the kinds of leaders mentioned earlier. This is because not all individuals identify with the same intensity with a given community whose citizens they may happen to be. Indeed, the loyalty of some such citizens may lie elsewhere. For example, in the mid-1990's, the nationalist feelings of the Chechens, based on history, ethnicity, and religion, promoted them to give their ultimate allegiance to the autonomous province of Chechnya rather than to the Russian Federation of which they where citizens. During the Civil War in the United States, Southerners fought and died for the Confederate States of America rather than for the United States into which they had been born.

Have political leaders taken advantage of patriotism to promote their own agendas? In 1982, for example, the military government of Argentina seized the British-ruled Falkland Islands (Malvinas), apparently to divert attention from Argentina's economic problems by fanning patriotic fervor in a popular cause. Some people have charged George Bush with starting the Persian Gulf War against Iraq in 1991 as a means to improve his re-election chances. By the same token, in the 1992 campaign, questions were raised about candidate Bill Clinton's military status during the Vietnam War and about his loyalty because of his antiwar protests abroad. The future American president argued that in his opinion, it was more patriotic to voice his opposition to what he considered a misguided engagement and unjust war than to do otherwise. It is apparent that patriotism, like beauty, is in the eyes of the beholder.

Bibliography

Cecil, Andrew R. *Three Sources of National Strength.* Dallas: University of Texas at Dallas, 1986. A distinguished scholar argues that freedom, patriotism, and economic stability—not military oppression—make nations great. Draws a sharp distinction between "unselfish, altruistic" patriotism and "self-interested" nationalism.

Curti, Merle E. *The Roots of American Loyalty.* New York: Columbia University Press, 1946. A noted American historian explains in this pioneering work and in simple language but from various perspectives the roots of Anglo-American and European patriotism.

Grodzins, Morton. *The Loyal and the Disloyal: Social Boundaries of Patriotism and Treason.* Chicago: University of Chicago Press, 1956. Argues that patriotism and treason are not opposites, since "every man is a little of each."

Kosok, Paul. *Modern Germany: A Study of Conflicting Loyalties.* Chicago: University of Chicago Press, 1933. Study of interwar German nationalism, explaining the success of Adolf Hitler's brand of fascism.

Mathews, Shailer. *Patriotism and Religion.* New York: Macmillan, 1918. Examination of the religious basis of patriotism and patriotic war in the closing months of World War I.

Murdock, Eugene C. *Patriotism Limited, 1862-1865: The Civil War Draft and the Bounty System.* Kent, Ohio: Kent State University Press, 1967. Using New York State to illustrate behavior in the North, Murdock argues that the first national military draft and the commutation fees that the wealthy paid to avoid military service color any assessment of patriotism in Union Army ranks.

Ravitch, Diane, ed. *The American Reader: Words That Moved a Nation.* New York: HarperCollins, 1990. Selection of patriotic songs, literature, and artwork illustrating the emotional underpinning of patriotism.

Simpson, Carolyn. *The Value of Patriotism.* New York: Rosen, 1993. Written for young adults, this book examines the various manifestations of patriotism.

Wingield-Stratford, Esmé. *The History of English Patriotism.* 2 vols. London: John Lane, 1913. Masterly work tracing the British variety from its Norman and Saxon origins to the close of the nineteenth century.

Peter B. Heller

Cross-References

Citizenship in World Governments, p. 254; Civic Education, p. 278; Civil Wars, p. 325; Demagoguery, p. 507; Fascism and Nazism, p. 656; Immigrants and Politics, p. 861; Independence Movements and Transitions, p. 896; Islam and Government, p. 994; Liberal Nationalism, p. 1111; The Nation-State, p. 1241; Nationalism, p. 1268; Propaganda, p. 1615; The State, p. 1878; World Political Organization, p. 2186.

PEACE

Field of study: International government and politics

Peacemaking and peacekeeping constitute two twentieth century approaches to mobilizing international resources to maintain international peace and security. Peacemaking has generally failed, while peacekeeping has achieved considerable success.

Principal terms
AGGRESSION: unlawful use of force by a state
LEAGUE OF NATIONS: international organization founded in 1920, terminated in 1946
PEACEKEEPING: interposition of international forces to contain a conflict
PEACEMAKING: collective military action to suppress aggression
SECURITY COUNCIL: principal organ of the United Nations to deal with aggression and threats to the peace
UNITED NATIONS: international organization founded in 1945
VETO POWER: authority of permanent members of the Security Council to prevent a decision from going into effect

Overview

Peacemaking and peacekeeping are two related, although different, strategies to maintain international peace and security. Both involve the use of military forces under international authority, but the nature and purpose of peacemaking and peacekeeping forces differ. Peacemaking is defined as the mobilization, under international authority, of military forces either to deter or suppress aggression. This concept is referred to popularly as "enforcement," and in the literature of international politics as "collective security." This definition focuses on the military aspect of peacemaking, although the use of economic sanctions by the international community may also be considered a form of peacemaking. Whether the instrument is military force or economic sanctions, peacemaking involves an element of coercion.

Peacekeeping is quite different. Former United Nations official Brian Urquhart described peacekeeping as the use of multinational military personnel and formations not in a fighting or enforcement role but as a means to end hostilities and to act as a buffer between hostile forces. The most significant differences from peacemaking forces are that peacekeeping forces do not fight, operate only with the consent of the host country, and are politically neutral. One of the architects of U.N. peacekeeping, Secretary-General Dag Hammarskjold, often used the term "preventive diplomacy" to describe peacekeeping.

The idea of peacemaking has a lengthy heritage, but it was only in the twentieth century that an effort was made to put it into practice. Peacemaking was one of the primary objectives of both the League of Nations and the United Nations. The League of Nations was created in the aftermath of World War I to curb states from engaging in aggressive war. Although the word "peacemaking" was not in the League Covenant, some of its articles, notably numbers 10 and 16, contain the essence of what is called the principle of collective security. Article 10 stated, "The Members of the league undertake to respect and preserve as against external aggression the territorial integrity and existing political independence of all Members of the League." Article 16 provided that a member that resorted to war without recourse to peaceful means of settling a dispute was to be considered at war with all members. These commitments to assist the victim of aggression were not accompanied by a workable mechanism to put them into practice. No organ of the league had the power to mobilize an international army that could have been used against an aggressor. In fact, the league remained helpless in the face of German and Japanese aggression during the period between the two world wars.

The one significant league effort to stop an aggressor was the application of economic sanctions against Italy in October, 1935, as a result of Benito Mussolini's invasion of Ethiopia. The sanctions voted were weak and ineffective: They did not embargo oil or close the Suez Canal to Italian troops. In the end, they failed to stop Italy's aggression. The outbreak of World War II in 1939 marked the demise of the league and the failure of humanity's first serious effort to apply peacemaking on a global scale.

In the aftermath of World War II, the great powers attempted again to institutionalize collective security or peacemaking with the creation of the United Nations. Under the assumption that the League of Nations had failed because it lacked universality (the United States never joined) and that it lacked enforcement powers, the United Nations system was constructed to overcome the league's deficiencies. To induce the great powers—the United States, France, Great Britain, the Soviet Union, and China—to join, they were given permanent membership on the Security Council with the right to veto. The idea was that the great powers would police the world, although they themselves would be immune from sanctions by virtue of the veto. The system of collective security is spelled out in Chapter 7 of the U.N. Charter, under the title "Action with Respect to Threats to the Peace, Breaches of the Peace, and Acts of Aggression."

Potentially, the United Nations has considerable peacemaking powers. The charter empowers the Security Council to determine when aggression has occurred and resist it through collective measures, which may include economic or military sanctions. A decision to take collective measures is binding on all members of the United Nations, according to Article 25. The Charter provides two methods by which the Security Council might undertake enforcement measures. One is directly, by the application of armed forces under its control. Such forces are to be organized through the contribution by individual members of military forces, including national air forces, to the Security Council (Articles 43 and 45). Command of these forces is to rest with a Military Staff Committee (Article 47). Articles 43 and 45 long remained dormant, as no state ever put any of its armed forces under the command of the Military Staff Committee. A second potential method for the application of collective measures would be for the

Security Council to call upon all or some of the United Nations membership to act on its behalf (Article 48).

Applications

The United Nations has never exercised its peacemaking powers according to the provisions of its Charter. The United Nations has intervened in a variety of ways in many of the conflicts and wars since World War II, but has not become the guarantor of international peace and security that its founding members hoped it would be. Only twice has the United Nations become a partner in a large-scale effort to stop aggression: in Korea from 1950 to 1952, and in the Persian Gulf in 1990 and 1991.

The attack by North Korean forces against South Korea on June 25, 1950, was a flagrant act of aggression, to which the Security Council responded swiftly. It was able to avoid a veto because the Soviet delegate had chosen to absent himself from the proceedings of the United Nations. The Security Council recommended that the members of the United Nations assist the Republic of Korea in repelling the armed attack, and it established a unified command under the United States. North Korean troops were eventually expelled from South Korea and a front approximately along the original boundary was established, although an armistice was not formally signed until July 27, 1953.

Although South Korean independence was preserved by collective means, this action was not a true example of United Nation's peacemaking for several reasons. First, the United States and South Korea provided the bulk of armed forces, and all armed forces were under United States command exclusively. In addition, the U.S. decision to intervene was made independent of Security Council action. Finally, the Security Council only recommended that military forces be contributed and only a few number countries actually did so.

Forty years after the Korean War, the United Nations again was involved in a military action to reverse an act of aggression. On August 2, 1990, Iraqi armed forces invaded and proceeded to annex Kuwait, its oil-rich neighbor. The United States again took the initiative to mobilize a coalition of forces to expel Iraq from Kuwait. On November 29, the U.N. Security Council authorized the United States-led coalition to use all means necessary to liberate Kuwait, giving Iraq a deadline of January 15, 1991. In January, Iraq was hit with a massive air strike; by the end of February, Iraq had capitulated. This action demonstrated the value of U.N. endorsement for a war against aggression, but again the action took place only because the United States took the initiative and provided the bulk of military forces. It was not peacemaking, although it had elements of peacemaking.

Peacemaking by the United Nations has proven to be no more successful than it was under the League of Nations. The standard explanation for the paralysis of the Security Council has been the veto. Not only does the veto protect the permanent members from U.N. action, but it protects the allies and clients of the great powers as well. Throughout the period of the Cold War (1945-1990) each superpower frequently used the veto against others. The fact that the Security Council has not functioned as an instrument of collective security in the post-Cold War period suggests that the difficulties of peacemaking are more fundamental. National sovereignty continues to stand as a barrier to collective action. States are unwilling to put large numbers of their armed forces under international command, and are disinclined to war on aggressors unless their own vital interests are affected by the aggression.

While collective security has been a failure, peacekeeping has developed into one of the United Nations's more successful activities in the security field. Peacekeeping emerged as a nonenforcement alternative to collective security. More modest in scope than peacemaking, peacekeeping has proven to be more practical. The earlier U.N. peacekeeping operations were created to oversee truces and to separate combatants who had agreed to stop fighting. A major expansion of United Nations peacekeeping came with the creation of the first United Nations Emergency Force in the Middle East in 1956. Organized by Secretary-General Dag Hammarskjold, UNEF became a model for United Nations efforts to keep the peace by interposing international forces between belligerents.

A few U.N. peacekeeping operations were compelled by circumstances to violate the nonfighting rule and, in so doing, compromised the neutrality of the U.N. operations. Such was the case with United Nations forces in the Congo in the 1960's and in Somalia in the 1990's. Over the years, United Nations peacekeeping forces have performed the following functions: investigation, monitoring cease fires, interpositions between hostile forces, restoring civil order, observing the withdrawal of occupying troops, supervising elections, conducting referenda, supervising the restructuring of governmental administration, and providing humanitarian supplies to refugees. Between 1945 and 1994, U.N. peacekeeping operations have been deployed in the Balkans, India and Pakistan, the Sinai, Lebanon, the Congo (now Zaïre), New Guinea, Yemen, Cyprus, the Golan Heights, Afghanistan, Iran, Iraq, Angola, Namibia, Central America, Kuwait, El Salvador, Western Sahara, Cambodia, Croatia, Bosnia and Herzegovina, Somalia, Mozambique, and Rwanda.

Context

In the 1990's, a decided shift in the scope of United Nations peacekeeping operations took place. The end of the Cold War opened up new possibilities for cooperation among the permanent members of the Security Council. They agreed to try to avoid using the veto, and to rely more on compromise and persuasion. The nonaligned members on the Security Council abandoned their traditional caucus, thus making easier the job of rounding up the necessary nine of fifteen votes to reach a decision. Along with the decline in Security Council divisions came a demand for international assistance on a new range of issues. The operation in Namibia in 1989 differed from previous operations: Peacekeepers were sent not to keep belligerents from fighting each other but to assist a new state in building its political infrastructure as it became independent from the Republic of South Africa. The success of the Namibian operation encouraged further United Nations oversight of voting in the Western Sahara, Central America, and Cambodia.

Traditional peacekeeping was stretched even further in the early 1990's with the use of United Nations forces in Somalia and Bosnia-Herzegovina for humanitarian purposes. On March 17, 1992, the Security Council voted unanimously to send a peacekeeping force to Somalia to complement the earlier United States intervention to relieve widespread starvation. United Nations forces found themselves under assault by forces loyal to Somali warlord General Mohammed Farah Aidid, and when they sought to apprehend Aidid, U.N. peacekeepers became enmeshed in the country's ethnic civil war. The escalation of purpose from humanitarian ends to political involvement alienated many Somalis and brought widespread criticism to the mission.

In Bosnia, United Nations forces in 1993 and 1994 found themselves trying to aid the refugees of a vicious civil war before the fighting had ceased, and ended up being criticized by Bosnian partisans for failing to take more vigorous action to protect the Muslims and by the Serbs for being partisan against them. Humanitarian intervention proved to be more complex than originally contemplated, because it operated in an active war zone.

The new activism in peacekeeping has raised new problems. One of the most serious is financial. In 1994, there were approximately seventy thousand United Nations peacekeepers deployed, at an approximate annual cost of $3 billion. This sum exceeded the normal United Nations regular budget. In 1992, the unpaid arrears for peacekeeping operations exceeded $800 million. On occasion, financial considerations limited the United Nations' response for peacekeepers, for example, in Rwanda and Yemen in 1994. Secretary-General Boutros Boutros-Ghali cited the need to acquire funding to meet the demands for peacekeeping as a major challenge to U.N. members.

Since participation in peacekeeping is strictly voluntary, each operation must be organized on an ad hoc basis among those states willing to make troops available. The United Nations does not know what forces it can count upon. In 1990, the secretary general surveyed the United Nations membership to determine what military personnel might be made available for peacekeeping operations. Few members replied. The secretary general stressed that logistic units posed a particular problem, as few states could afford to spare such units. The United Nations had to rely on the logistical support of the United States and a few other developed states. Because the need for peacekeeping often arises suddenly and an effective response might necessitate a quick United Nations reaction, the U.N. administrative structure was revised on March 1, 1992, to create a United Nations Department of Peacekeeping Operations headed by an undersecretary general. In recognition of their contribution toward global peace, United Nations peacekeepers were awarded the Nobel Peace Prize in 1988.

Bibliography

Burns, Arthur Lee, and Nina Heathcote. *Peace-keeping by U.N. Forces, from Suez to the Congo.* New York: Praeger, 1963. Systematic examination of the formative years in the evolution of peacekeeping.

Durch, William J., ed. *The Evolution of UN Peacekeeping: Case Studies and Com-*

parative Analysis. New York: St. Martin's Press, 1993. Twenty-four essays by five experts analyze U.N. peacekeeping operations through 1992. Thoroughly documented with an index and bibliography.

Martin, Andrew. *Collective Security*. Paris: UNESCO, 1952. Classic study of the origin of collective security in both the League of Nations and the United Nations.

United Nations. *The Blue Helmets: A Review of United Nations Peace-keeping*. 2d ed. New York: United Nations, Dept. of Public Information, 1990. The single best reference of U.N. peacekeeping through 1989. Detailed, complete, and authoritative. Three appendices contain statistics, tables of organization, and maps of each operation.

Walters, F. P. *A History of the League of Nations*. London: Oxford University Press, 1969. The definitive history of the League of Nations in one volume.

Joseph L. Nogee

Cross-References

Ambassadors and Embassies, p. 53; Conflict Resolution, p. 397; International Relations, p. 969; North Atlantic Treaty Organization, p. 1332; Sanctions, p. 1777; Superpowers and World Politics, p. 1916; Supranational Government Institutions, p. 1922; United Nations, p. 2045; War, p. 2129; World Political Organization, p. 2186.

PLATO'S POLITICAL PHILOSOPHY

Field of study: Political philosophy

Plato, perhaps the greatest of the ancient Greek philosophers, turned his creative mind to political theory more than once, creating a legacy of thought for all who followed.

Principal terms

DIALECTIC: conversational method of questions and answers that leads to knowledge

FORM OF THE GOOD: supreme Good and the source of absolute knowledge

OLIGARCHY: rule by the few

POLIS: city-state, community

RHETORIC: art of public communication using argument and persuasion

WORLD OF FORMS: unchanging world, above the ever-changing world of sense perception, containing the perfect Form of everything in the universe

Overview

Plato (c. 428 B.C.E.-348 or 347 B.C.E.) was born into one of the most noble families of ancient Athens and came to manhood in the closing years of the Peloponnesian War (431-404 B.C.E.). His stepfather was aligned with the moderate democratic faction that held political power during the war, and for a brief time Plato considered a political career. About the time he would have begun, the Athenian democracy capitulated to the Spartan monarchy. Plato blamed Athens' defeat upon its democratic institutions. He became an early supporter of the oligarchic regime that came to power in the political revolt following the war's end. But rule by the wealthy few proved no better than rule by the people. Indeed, the reign of terror that followed the ascendancy of the new government made the old democracy look good. In the unstable political climate following the war, it was not long before a counterrevolution restored the old democrats.

At first, the restored leaders behaved decently, leading Plato again to consider entering the political arena. Any political ambitions he may have harbored, however, were quickly shattered. The reinstated leaders unambiguously proved their unworthiness when they tried and executed his beloved teacher, Socrates, for what they called practicing impiety and corrupting the youth of Athens. Totally disillusioned by this politically motivated execution, Plato concluded that all politics was morally corrupt.

Socrates had devoted his life to what he considered his divinely ordered task, to question and provoke debate among the citizens of Athens, for the betterment of their souls. He believed that their betterment could only be achieved through knowledge of the highest Good—the Good to which all good things are united.

Under the influence of Socrates, Plato too had come to believe in the unity of all virtue. It was also from his teacher that he acquired the idea that virtue is knowledge and that it can be taught. If someone is taught the virtues, he or she will behave virtuously. Plato took Socrates' teachings to the level of political philosophy and concluded that only when those who held political power were armed with true knowledge of the Good would a just and well-ordered society be possible. The death of Socrates convinced Plato that bad states produce bad people.

It was, Plato believed, the teachers known as the Sophists, not Socrates, who were the true corruptors of Athenian youth. Proclaiming to teach the skills necessary to get ahead in life, the Sophists turned young men away from the pursuit of truth. The Sophists taught rhetoric, the art of public communication by means of argument and persuasion. This subject could not help but appeal to wealthy young men who harbored political ambitions. To use a modern analogy, the Sophists turned their students into lawyers, able to argue either side of an issue with great persuasive ability but with a perhaps cynical disregard for ultimate truth. Socrates, on the other hand, had turned his students into something like campus radicals, who went about questioning every-thing, including authority.

Athens was a direct democracy, and political careers were made and broken in its main legislative body, a sovereign assembly of all male Athenians, and in the law courts, where litigants were expected to represent themselves. Under such conditions, the ability to speak persuasively facilitated political success. Some Sophists were impressive thinkers and teachers, but most taught little more than debating skills for the sole purpose of manipulating the opinions of others. In Plato's mind, the spirit of Sophistic education had come to mean the substitution of theoretical skepticism in place of the quest for philosophical truth. The Sophists denied the possibility of absolute knowledge, which led to moral relativism and the rejection of universal standards of right and wrong behavior.

The Sophists also adhered to the notion, shared by most Greeks of the time, that virtue meant the ability to effectively attain a given end. They parted company with Socrates, Plato, and the rest of the Greeks, however, when they argued that human happiness could only be acquired through the attainment of wealth, honor, and status. Viewed from this perspective, political virtue was no more than the successful attainment of political power for its own sake.

Plato's political philosophy is a long polemic against the skepticism and moral relativism at the core of the sophist curriculum. He founded a school of philosophy to wage this battle. The Academy, as his school came to be known, became the center for the development of a new philosophical movement grounded upon the theory that truth is real and absolute moral standards do exist. Here Plato studied, taught, and wrote until his death at the approximate age of eighty.

Applications

Plato's philosophy is preserved in the more than two-dozen dramatic dialogues that can safely be attributed to his authorship. Usually, Socrates, the chief character and narrator, is shown engaged in a dialectical inquiry with his companions. The term "dialectic" is derived from the Greek word that means "to discourse," and this is very close to the meaning it had for the historical Socrates. In Plato's dialogues, however, this takes on a greater meaning. The figure of Socrates is used to portray Plato's belief that the dialectical method is the way to understanding that everything in the universe is explained by reference to the absolute Good. Plato wrote the dialogues during intervals in a fifty-year period. Each is part of a whole, which means that neither the parts nor the whole can be understood separately. Consequently, three dialogues—*The Republic*, the *Statesman*, and *The Laws*—that deal most directly with Plato's political ideas cannot be understood without reference to his much wider philosophical system.

The core of Plato's philosophy is the theory of Forms. He understood that to combat the problems posed by the moral relativism of the Sophists he needed to provide a secure foundation for morality. He found the solution in his theory of Forms. While granting that the world people experience through their senses is subject to change, he denied that this world was the entire universe. Above the ever-changing world of sense perception, he believed, there exists a permanent and unchanging world of Forms. These Forms were not mere abstract ideas; they had a real existence. Everything in the world (stones, trees, cats, humans), as well as its characteristics (hard, tall, black, healthy), has a perfect counterpart in the world of Forms to which it relates as a shadow relates to a physical object. Within the world of Forms there is a hierarchy. At the top, the highest and most noble of them all was the Form of the Good.

Plato's moral philosophy was derived from his theory of Forms. To avoid moral relativism and corruption, the goal of human existence must be to enter as fully as possible into the realm of Forms. The ethical Forms—temperance, courage, justice, etc.—provide permanent and universal moral standards for the constantly changing political world.

The Republic, Plato's first systematic treatment of political philosophy, describes the Form of an ideal polis. This Form serves as a measuring rod for the evaluation of existing city-states. The dialogue begins when a conversation between Socrates and his companions turns to talk about the nature of justice. After a survey of traditional definitions of justice reveals them to be unsatisfactory, Socrates leads the discussion toward a true description of the just city and the just individual.

He suggests the inquiry begin at the state level, since the polis is no more than its citizenry. In other words, the just state reflects the just souls of its citizens. No one is entirely self-sufficient; the city-state exists to provide the cooperative effort necessary to fulfill the needs of its citizens.

This cooperative fulfillment of human needs was also the rationale for the tripartite class structure of *The Republic*. Each of the classes—workers, guardians, and rulers—fulfills a specific need. The workers provide the material goods necessary for the existence of the state. Left to itself, however, this class is the potential source for the state's destruction: Economic activities need ordering principles; uncontrolled, they cause internal conflict and provoke attack by external enemies.

It is the guardian class that enforces the ordering principles that keep the economic system from self-destructing. Plato sometimes refers to this class as soldiers, but they are much more than this. The guardians' duty is selfless work for the common good. Such uncommon unselfishness is the result of a formal education in which members of this class are taught to regard the polis as their own family, and a communal form of living in which wives, children, and property are held in common. Devoid of private concerns, they are entrusted with official governmental power.

The guardians alone implement and enforce public policy, but they do not make it. For this they turn to the ruling class, Plato's famous philosopher kings. This class holds ultimate authority within the state, and it formulates the state's ordering principles. Selected from the wisest of the guardians, the source of their authority is knowledge. These philosopher kings know the supreme Good, and, therefore, the pattern to which all things ought to be ordered, including the just polis.

The embodiment of political justice, Plato tells us, is the proper functioning of this class system. In other words, when each class does its own work without meddling in the affairs of the others, justice exists in the state.

True to Socrates' assertion that the state mirrors the soul of its citizens, the tripartite class structure of *The Republic* matches the souls of its citizens. The part of the soul that desires material things is the counterpart to the working class; the spirited part of the soul that is the source of the passions corresponds to the guardian class; and reason is associated with the ruling class. When reason leads the passions and appetite, each person will find peace and harmony through active participation in the class that he or she is best suited for. People who behave this way are righteous or just. In the republic, justice exists at once in the whole and in all of the parts.

The just republic can only come to be under the direction of the truly wise, whose knowledge is not that of the ordinary politician. Such knowledge comes only to those who prove capable of surviving a long and arduous educational curriculum. For this purpose, Plato advocated a system of universal education, open to any child regardless of sex or social status. At the very start, students undergo rigorous academic, physical, and moral testing. Those who drop out early become workers; those who drop out before the age of thirty become guardians; finally, those who complete five more years studying the dialectic and fifteen years of practical experience become rulers.

No earthly city-state could achieve the eternal Form of the ideal polis. Therefore, *The Republic* ends with the admission that even if the closest possible approximation of this ideal were to be attained it could not last forever. Sooner or later, its fate would be the same as what awaits all worldly things—degeneration. Once again the world of politics would be devoid of justice.

Plato's political thought does not end with *The Republic*. In *Statesman*, Plato turns his attention to practical politics. Here philosopher kings do not exist. The question becomes, what kind of state is second best? Plato's answer is that state in which the laws conform as closely as possible to the true dictates of reason. There are three kinds of lawful states (monarchy, aristocracy, and democracy), and each has its unlawful counterpart (tyranny, oligarchy, lawless democracy). In the lawful state, those in power rule in the interest of the state; in the unlawful state, those in power unscrupulously serve their own self-interest at the expense of the good of the community.

In *Statesman*, Plato seems to soften his attitude toward democracy, to the extent that he is willing to distinguish between lawful and unlawful democracies. Moreover, in the first part of *The Laws*, written in the last ten years of his life, the bitterness he had about democracy in the past seems to have totally disappeared. In *The Laws*, he goes into elaborate detail describing the constitution and the specific institutions for a second-best state. Magnasia, as this imaginary polis is called, is a mixed regime in which political harmony is achieved through a lawful blending of the monarchial principle of wisdom with the democratic principle of freedom. The glue that holds this society together turns out to be, however, a dogmatic creed that the citizenry must accept if public order is to be maintained.

In *The Laws*, enforcement of this dogmatic creed is turned over to the Nocturnal Council, a body of men of extraordinary virtue, who are granted unlimited power for constitutional revision. Reminiscent of philosopher kings, members of the Council undergo training in a special curriculum at the end of which they appear to approach, but stop just short of, the knowledge of the Good. What is to prevent them from using their power of constitutional revision to dispense with the democratic principle of popular control? We are never told. What is apparent is that Plato never really rejected the elitist principles of *The Republic* and remained an aristocrat until the end.

Context

Alfred North Whitehead (1861-1947), the British mathematician and philosopher, once characterized Western philosophy as no more than a footnote to Plato. This is hardly an exaggeration; no other philosopher—ancient, medieval, or modern—had as great an influence upon subsequent ages. His only possible rival, Aristotle, was Plato's student, and all of Aristotle's work bears the stamp of his teacher.

From ancient times until the disintegration of the Roman Empire in the fifth century C.E., scholars continued to read *The Republic* and to imitate its style. Throughout the centuries, Plato's influence waxed and waned, but it never disappeared. From the first to the third century C.E., Platonism came into competition with mystery religions, Christianity, and Hebrew thought.

Its influence faded, until the third century C.E., when Plato's philosophy came to be transmitted through the movement known as neo-Platonism. Though the neo-Platonist paid scant attention to the political aspects of Platonic philosophy, it was through this movement that Saint Augustine of Hippo (354-430) came to know Plato's writings. Augustine's attempt to synthesize Platonism and Christianity, after purging the former of its pagan elements, did much to lay the foundations for the political outlook of the early medieval world. From roughly 500 to 1450, however, except for some fragments, the writings of Plato were lost to the West. Eventually, the texts were rediscovered, and there was a Platonic revival in the fifteenth century when utopian speculation flourished. The driving force behind this resuscitation of Platonism was *The Republic*.

Twenty-three centuries after his death, Plato's work still has not lost its impact. In 1945, his political theory became the focus of a controversy, when the Anglo-Austrian natural and social philosopher Karl Popper branded Plato as the father of totalitarianism. For Popper, the ideal state depicted in *The Republic* is totally closed and utterly hostile to the individual freedom and equality characteristic of democratic societies. In the spate of polemical works that followed, such prestigious philosophers as John Wild and John Halowell defended Plato. Foremost among modern neo-Platonists are the students of the eminent philosopher Leo Strauss, who taught at the University of Chicago until his retirement in 1964. The Straussians, as his followers are called, teach at colleges and universities throughout the United States. They are living testimony to the everlasting endurance of Plato's political philosophy.

Bibliography

Barker, Ernest. *Greek Political Theory: Plato and His Predecessors*. 3d ed. New York: Methuen, 1947. The time-honored commentary on Plato's political philosophy.

Klosko, George. *The Development of Plato's Political Theory*. New York: Methuen, 1986. Readable introduction to Plato's political philosophy; less encyclopedic than Ernest Barker's classic.

Plato. *The Laws*. Translated by Trevor J. Saunders. New York: Penguin Books, 1970. Translation and interpretive essay that discusses the vexing problem of Plato's totalitarianism.

_____. *The Republic*. Translated by Allan Bloom. New York: Basic Books, 1943. Excellent translation and interpretive essay.

_____. *Statesman*. Translated by J. B. Skemp. Edited by Martin Ostwald. New York: Liberal Arts Press, 1957. Ostwald's introduction places the *Statesman* within the context of Plato's political theory.

Zeitlin, Irving M. *Plato's Vision: The Classical Origins of Social and Political Thought*. Englewood Cliffs, N.J.: Prentice-Hall, 1993. Covers the social and political structure Plato wrote about, the intellectual tradition he inherited, and a balanced discussion of his political writings.

Thomas J. Mortillaro

Cross-References

Aristocracy, Oligarchy, and Plutocracy, p. 78; Aristotle's Political Philosophy, p. 83; Augustine's Political Philosophy, p. 121; Autocracy and Absolutism, p. 127; The City-State, p. 272; Dialecticism, p. 540; Elitism, p. 591; Epicurean Political Philosophy, p. 624; Idealism, p. 855; Ochlocracy, p. 1338; Oligarchy, p. 1344; Political Philosophy, p. 1505; Statesmanship, p. 1898; Stoic Political Philosophy, p. 1904; Thomas Aquinas' Political Philosophy, p. 1974.

PLURALISM

Field of study: Political philosophy

Pluralism refers to institutional arrangements for distributing and sharing governmental power. It is also an approach for understanding political behavior and a benchmark for comparing different countries' political institutions and values.

Principal terms

NON-EUCLIDEANISM: view that systems of thought built on logic rather than empirical knowledge, including democratic, moral, and higher law, and natural rights theories, are not absolute because, as non-Euclidean geometry reveals, any number of systems of thought are possible, depending on first assumptions

POSITIVISM: doctrine that holds that human knowledge is based on what is known through actual practice, sense perceptions, and reliance on scientific methods, not on moral values or ideals

RELATIVISM: theory that conceptions of moral values and truth are not absolute, but are relative to the institutions, people, and groups holding such values

SCIENTIFIC NATURALISM: view that the only real knowledge is what is collected and verified through the application of scientific methods

TOTALITARIANISM: form of government in which political leaders exercise centralized and absolute control over all aspects of life, political and cultural expression is suppressed, and individuals, groups, and institutions are not permitted to be autonomous

Overview

The pluralist approach to American politics makes six assumptions about American political institutions and politics. The first is that widespread opportunities exist for all who wish to influence the American government. The second is that an important source of such opportunities, which are central to sustaining democratic government, are private groups in the American political system. The third is that the high number and changing nature of diverse social, economic, religious, professional, and cultural groups who make demands on the government ensure the dispersal of political power. Fourth, public policies are moderate, incremental, innovative, and fair because they are compromises of the interests of groups that have crosscutting interests. Fifth, because leaders of interest groups fear loss of support and the formation of opposing groups, they are sensitive to the needs of group members. Similarly, because elected public officials fear replacement, they are sensitive to the needs of voters. Finally, leaders of private groups, elected officials, and elites generally, who are far more knowledgeable than the general citizenry, are the protectors of American democracy.

These six assumptions represent a summary of the interpretations of American politics by David Truman and Robert Dahl, the two leading proponents of the pluralist approach to American politics. Truman argues that interest group interactions with government, viewed as a complex system of multiple access points, are central to democracy. He also has argued that leaders of private groups protect the changing interests of the membership because they fear the loss of their leadership positions. Interest group leaders are attuned to democratic principles and are aware that people organize; leaders are, therefore, open to members' demands for change. These demands then filter their way into the political system. Finally, overlapping membership in various groups by members of each interest group, the large number of access points to government, and the widespread belief in the need for compromise in government decision making ensure moderation in public policy.

Robert Dahl argues that America's cultural consensus in support of democracy, the presence of large numbers of dispersed minorities, and numerous policy arenas result in government by different and changing minorities, rather than rule by a simple majority or a closed power elite. Some of these minorities are large in number, such as the poor or voters. Others are small in number and based on wealth, for example bankers. Still others are based on race and education. Government has shifting policy arenas that are open to the demands of these minorities. Democracy is not based on a faith in constitutional principles, in checks and balances, or in adherence to absolute principles. Democracy, according to Dahl, is based on political, social, and economic elites' faith in a democratic political culture, compromise, and adherence to the rules of the game.

For Dahl and Truman, observable, open politics, not a closed power elite or class interests, as Marxists would suggest, explain public policies. For Dahl and Truman the key values of the American regime are supported by adherence to norms that are most clearly articulated and supported by public officials, leaders of private groups, and other elites. These norms include fair elections, freedom of speech and dissent, and equal protection of the law. Truman emphasizes that change within organized groups that make demands on government is the major cause of political change. Dahl emphasizes that the democratic nature of the U.S. political system is caused by the ability of elected officials to shape public policy, to articulate the interests of the unorganized, and to protect democratic norms.

Pluralist interpretations of American politics are based on a relativist theory of democracy. This theory emphasizes that the study of American politics, democratic theory, and American government in general, does not rest on adherence to absolute conceptions of morality, which is the premise of traditional democratic and constitutional theories. The role of political science, in relativist theory, is to create a new democratic theory based on the study of the realities of the people, institutions, and groups as they actually operate.

Since America has been generally viewed as a well-functioning, democratic political system, especially when compared to, for example, Nazi Germany or Russia, America's pluralistic institutions were seen as central to its democracy. Scholars addressed the question of why American politics was democratic even though elites, rather than the general citizenry, were the most active participants in the political process. Their answers varied according to their interpretation of the interests and goodwill of the elites. Democratic theory lost its traditional function as a gadfly and glossed over the glaring discrepancies of wealth and power in American society. The pluralist view of politics is based on complacent attitudes and overoptimistic evaluations of American politics.

In raising questions about the validity of pluralist interpretations of American politics and democracy, Theodore Lowi chronicles how pluralism developed as an ideology that governs the way politics in America is viewed. Pluralism replaced capitalist ideology's strong faith in the autonomy of the market and of economic institutions from government. The nation lost its faith in undiluted capitalism and in capitalism as a governing ideology because of the problems caused by capitalist production, including urbanization, unemployment, and the poor health of the workers. The increased division of labor and specialization of production that was needed to secure greater efficiencies in production caused the establishment of public and private institutions to administer capitalist production, markets, and the formation of capital. There was an expansion of the services and institutions that capitalism needed to function efficiently, such as insurance, legal instruments and courts, and downtown areas to house these services and institutions. The growth of trade associations allowed firms to communicate with each other and with government. Other groups formed to deal with the negative effects of industrialization.

Pluralism was an excellent ideology. It made sense of the role of trade associations and other interest groups and their links to government. At the core of pluralism is a faith in bargaining among groups with political or economic market power. By bargaining, they may deal with the effects of competition, have control over the terms of their agreements, and can administer rather than merely respond to their environment. Bargaining, in a pluralistic society, becomes a workable alternative to violence and coercion. The pluralistic system is viewed as stable, peaceful, and self-regulating. Pluralism is viewed as working well and as the way government ought to work.

The faith that scholars, public officials, and citizens have placed in pluralism has brought damaging results. Government became a forum for private interests to bargain. Government officials and groups achieved a self-serving equilibrium and stability among themselves rather than reach equitable compromises through high-minded contention. Pluralism turned Federalist No. 10 on its head. Federalist No. 10 warns of factions (political organizations with private interests) and argues for government to define and protect the aggregate, public interests of the nation. Under pluralism, government is a forum for bargaining among private interests and not, as in Federalist No. 10, as a forum to protect minorities from factions and to protect the public from private interests. The legitimacy of government declines along with the ability of public officials to limit private power.

Applications

Pluralism has influenced the analysis of urban politics and the place of the Supreme Court in American politics. The classic pluralist account of urban politics is Robert

Dahl's 1961 study of New Haven, Connecticut, politics, *Who Governs?* In this book, Dahl emphasizes that political resources through which different groups of citizens secure political influence, such as votes, wealth, education, social stature, race, and organizational skills, tend to be equal. The open structure of political decision making and the ease with which any group can mobilize its different political resources also equalizes group power. The fluidity of group formation, the presence of many different and changing policy arenas, and the presence of a skilled mayor (whose major concern is to anticipate the needs of the wider voting public, including citizens not yet represented by organized groups), results, Dahl concludes, in a condition in which no one group, coalition of groups, or leader dominates New Haven politics. As in most pluralist accounts of American politics, *Who Governs?* portrays interest groups and political and social elites as safeguarding the stability of democracy. The groups respect democratic values. The likelihood is quite limited that mass politics, as found in totalitarian regimes, will occur in pluralist democracies.

Robert Dahl has also presented a pluralist interpretation of the Supreme Court. Dahl views the Supreme Court as part of a dominant national coalition. The Supreme Court supports the general policies of the majority coalition. Dahl does not mind that the Supreme Court follows election returns, because, he argues, the primary objective of a democratic political system is to ensure plural, majority rule, not to ensure that fundamental rights in the Constitution are protected. Dahl argues that the majority coalition is better at protecting minorities' rights than the Supreme Court. The primary role for the Supreme Court is to confer legitimacy on the majority coalition.

Dahl's faith in the pluralist political system manifests itself in the following way: The standard for evaluating the Supreme Court is not whether the Court upholds the Constitution. Dahl redefines the role assigned to the Supreme Court by the Founders, which is to counter majoritarian laws when they violate the principles of the Constitution, to one of supporting the governing coalition of the political system. Dahl belittles the primary role of the Supreme Court in the U.S. constitutional scheme, which is to limit the abuse of government power and to protect the rights of citizens, especially minorities. Moreover, no longer, in pluralistic theory, are law and politics, or courts and political institutions, to be viewed as separate or autonomous spheres. Most important, like other relativist scholars, Dahl assumes that the Supreme Court uses principles, precedents, and facts instrumentally when making constitutional law. That is, Dahl assumes that justices, like policymakers in political institutions, use constitutional principles to justify their policy choices. Ronald Kahn argues that pluralist scholars grossly understate the autonomy of the Supreme Court from politics, misunderstand Supreme Court decision making, and misperceive the effect of the Supreme Court on social and political change.

Context
Pluralism can be better understood if one considers developments in political thought and political science in the twentieth century. From 1900 to the 1930's the growth of respect for positivism and scientific naturalism undermined respect for

traditional democratic theory, moral philosophy, and ethical absolutes. Scholars attacked the view that moral principles, deductive and inductive logic, and higher law principles could provide the bases of knowledge, law, or politics because they could not be proved. Non-Euclidean geometry revealed that a priori reasoning and logic were not knowledge. Scientific naturalism assumed that knowledge was verifiable only if it could be tested scientifically. No method of human reasoning could be viewed as knowledge, because no such method could be proved empirically. "We hold these truths to be self-evident" was viewed as opinion and ethical assumption.

This view fostered a moral relativism that questioned the legitimacy of moral principles. Scholars in the 1930's and 1940's argued that truth and ethical propositions cannot be proven by induction or deduction. Therefore, moral ideals—such as a faith in democracy, the rationality of citizens, and individual rights—were left without a rational foundation. Empirical studies of American politics by scientific naturalists led to questioning of, and ultimately rejection of, the three cardinal principles of democratic government: the possibility of a government of laws rather than people, the rationality of human behavior, and the practical possibility of popular government.

The question of how to justify democratic values and theory in an age of moral relativism and totalitarian atrocities became an essential one for social, political, and legal scholars. They were faced with the question that if moral values are not provable, what way could there be to demonstrate the superiority of democracy? Pragmatist John Dewey framed this debate about democracy. Dewey argued that as long as all facts could be publicly and critically examined in light of their social consequences, people could freely make up their minds about the nature of truth. Moreover, unlike authoritarian regimes, in democracies there is no authoritative ruling group or set of beliefs. Democracy is experimentalist in outlook while totalitarian regimes are absolutist in thought and authoritarian in structure. If truth is relative and not absolute, the truth will not be found in a regime of absolutism.

After World War II the correlation between intellectual relativism and democracy was widely accepted. The culture that underlay democratic political forms denied absolute truths, remained intellectually flexible and critical, valued diversity, and drew strength from innumerable competing groups.

The relativist theory of democracy was the major research paradigm in political science from World War II through the middle 1960's. The dualism between plural American democracy and absolutist tyranny became the primary political assumption of American intellectuals of the time. The relativist theory of democracy is the foundation upon which pluralist interpretations of American politics are based.

Bibliography

Dahl, Robert. *A Preface to Democratic Theory*. Chicago: University of Chicago Press, 1956. A thorough statement on the pluralist approach to American politics, this work argues that central to the stability and fairness of American politics are pluralist principles, such as faith in compromise, rule by elites who fear not being reelected, and the ease of access to political institutions by all who organize.

_____. *Who Governs?* New Haven, Conn.: Yale University Press, 1961. A study of politics and decision making in New Haven, Connecticut, which seeks to demonstrate that the pluralist approach can explain local as well as national politics. This study helped set the tone for the later study of urban politics.

Greenstone, J. David. "Group Theories." In *Micropolitical Theory*, edited by Fred I. Greenstein and Nelson W. Polsby. Vol. 2 in *Handbook of Political Science*. Reading, Mass.: Addison-Wesley, 1975. A persuasive statement on how group theories of American politics, such as those by Arthur Bentley and David Truman and the scholarly reaction to them by Grant McConnell and Theodore Lowi, have formed the intellectual core of the study of American politics since the 1950's.

Kahn, Ronald. *The Supreme Court and Constitutional Theory, 1953-1993*. Lawrence: University Press of Kansas, 1994. Argues that Supreme Court decision making has been misunderstood since 1953 because pluralist scholars view its justices as similar to elected officials, that is, as following election returns, their own policy wants, or the policy objectives of the presidents who have appointed them. This book argues further that pluralist scholars have understated the place of foundational constitutional polity and rights principles, precedent, and the role of the Court as an institution to counter majority pressure in its decision making.

Lowi, Theodore J. *The End of Liberalism: The Second Republic of the United States*. 2d ed. New York: W. W. Norton, 1979. Powerful statement on the development of pluralist principles of government and how their acceptance by political elites, citizens, and scholars has undermined American faith in political institutions.

McConnell, Grant. *Private Power and American Democracy*. New York: Alfred A. Knopf, 1966. Statement about the role of groups in American politics that counters David Truman's pluralist approach.

Purcell, Edward A., Jr. *The Crisis of Democratic Theory: Scientific Naturalism and the Problem of Value*. Lexington: University Press of Kentucky, 1973. Cogent analysis of the intellectual history behind the decline of national faith in foundational principles of democracy, rule of law, and constitutionalism and of the growth of relativist interpretations of law and politics, which are at the core of pluralist interpretations of American politics and legal institutions.

Truman, David. *The Government Process: Political Interests and Public Opinion*. New York: Alfred A. Knopf, 1964. First published in 1951, this influential interpretation of American politics emphasizes the role of interest groups in political change.

Ronald C. Kahn

Cross-References

The Constitution of the United States, p. 425; Democracy, p. 513; Elitism, p. 591; Equality and Egalitarianism, p. 630; Interest Groups, p. 936; Invisible Government, p. 975; Liberalism, p. 1118; Ochlocracy, p. 1338; Political Participation, p. 1479; Political Representation in the United States, p. 1525; Power Divisions in Governments, p. 1578; The Supreme Court: Organization and Purpose, p. 1929.

POLICE STATES

Field of study: Types of government

Police states are a form of nondemocratic or authoritarian government characterized by the preeminence of police organizations over competing institutions in terms of political power, and marked by the purposeful and ongoing use of state terror as a basis for governance.

Principal terms

AUTHORITARIANISM: nondemocratic forms of government, including one-party rule, military rule, personal and corporatist dictatorships, and police states

GESTAPO: secret political police of the Nazi regime, created in 1933 and, under the leadership of Heinrich Himmler, attained a preeminent and feared position

NAZI REGIME: German government from 1933 to 1945 under the leadership of Adolf Hitler and the National Socialist Party

POLICE STATE: authoritarian regime in which police institutions are the primary basis for power, and operate independently of party, civil, or military control

SS AND THE WAFFEN SS: *Schutzstaffeln*, the elite guard of the Nazi regime, with the Waffen SS a premier paramilitary wing, under the direction of Heinrich Himmler

STATE TERRORISM: state use of violence to induce extreme fear, for the purpose of producing desired behavior among both victims and observers

TOTALITARIANISM: form of authoritarianism in which a regime not only clings to power, but also works to remake individuals and society according to ideological beliefs

Overview

The distinction between democratic and nondemocratic political systems can be stated with some clarity and consensus. Democratic regimes are marked by a respect for individual rights, free and active political opposition, independent media, and free and fair elections, while nondemocratic systems lack or severely limit these features. Police states fall into the latter camp, to be sure, but the application of the uncomplimentary label "police state" to a given state is often marked by more confusion than clarity. In describing nondemocratic regimes, after all, many terms are routinely employed: autocracy, tyranny, dictatorship, military rule, authoritarianism, totalitarianism, state terrorism, and, of course, police states. It is rarely clear, however—particularly in the popular media—whether these terms are intended to refer to the same or different types of nondemocratic political systems.

Many academic discussions do try to clarify and delineate these concepts from one another. While police states are related to and significantly overlap some of these other concepts, they represent a particular form of nondemocratic regime, with unique characteristics, organization, and rationale. While the term "dictatorship" correctly refers to any and all nondemocratic systems, "police state" only refers to a relatively small number of these systems. Police states can be identified from the others by the prominence, independence, and use of state police powers.

Amos Perlmutter, in *Modern Authoritarianism: A Comparative Institutional Analysis* (1981), has provided the most thorough effort to differentiate systematically among types of dictatorial or authoritarian governments. He argues that authoritarian governments vary according to the relative power of three features: a dominant political party, state institutions, such as the military and bureaucracy, and what he calls parallel-auxiliary structures: propaganda and police. Each of these structures can be the basis of political control in a nondemocratic system. Control can be exercised through the organization and personnel of a strong, ideological party. The clearest example of this is the dominant role played by the Communist Party in the Soviet Union until the demise of the regime, although there are lesser-known examples as well, such as the role of the Ba'ath Socialist party in Iraq. In these cases, the real locus of power and decision making resides in the single party, with the alternative institutions of the civil bureaucracy, the military, and the police subordinate to the party. Party cadres and officers are infiltrated into, or placed in control of, these alternative institutions.

Similarly, state institutions may be employed as the basis for nondemocratic rule, and, in fact, this is most common. Direct military rule, so common in many parts of the developing world, is authoritarianism of this form. Control may also be exercised through a dominant civil bureaucracy, or, more likely, a coalition of the bureaucracy and the military. In Latin America in the 1970's, for example, there was a great deal of interest in this form of so-called "bureaucratic authoritarianism," where bureaucratic and military elites ruled, not in the name of some party ideology, but in the cause of stability and rational economic growth and development.

Finally, nondemocratic rule may be exercised through what Perlmutter has called parallel-auxiliary structures, primarily the police. These are the regimes properly labeled police states. In these cases, with the clearest being post-1937 Nazi Germany, police organizations assume a dominant political position. In more typical authoritarian regimes, the police are directed by and answerable to other state agencies. In contrast, in a police state, police organizations are independent and autonomous of the bureaucracy and military, answerable only to the political elite. By 1938, for example, Heinrich Himmler's police organizations, including both the SS and the Gestapo, were answerable only to Adolf Hitler himself, not to the military, or interior ministry, or anyone else. Indeed, the state institutions were subordinate to Himmler's independent police organizations.

All governments have police organizations, including regimes of single-party rule, bureaucratic regimes, and military authoritarian regimes. These police organizations may be large, expansive, and brutal, as was certainly the case in the Soviet Union. Outside of the period of the great party purges, however, the police and KGB were clearly subordinate to the party. The police acted at the direction of party leaders, not independent of them. This contrasts markedly with the latter stages of Nazi rule, wherein the bureaucracy and often even the military acted at the direction of the police. While all regimes have police, they only assume an independent and dominant role in a police state.

The characteristics and activities of the police within a police state usually take several forms, often sequentially. During the drive to power, the police or quasi police are committed to overt, often public acts of violence and intimidation. The effort is to subdue, frighten, and overcome political opponents. In the history of Nazism, for instance, this is the period of street thugs and of the brownshirts. The police organization is not yet dominant, but exists to provide the muscle in the pursuit of political power.

Once a regime is in power, the police may move through several stages of development on the road to the establishment of an actual police state, as described in detail by Brian Chapman in *Police State* (1970). While the suppression of real or imagined political opponents continues, indeed, often expands, police may also strive for greater power within the regime, a strategy which usually takes several forms. First, there is often a concerted effort to centralize all police functions, both civil and political, into one supreme organization, and, ultimately, to strengthen the organization through the development of a paramilitary wing, such as the Waffen SS. These steps create a monolithic police apparatus with the ability to compete with the military's capacity for mass coercion. Second, there is an effort by this police apparatus to challenge other state institutions. The police maneuver to free themselves of bureaucratic rules and control, to become autonomous of and equal to the bureaucracy and military. Once this is achieved, a modern police state has been established.

Chapman also argues that if and when the police move beyond independence from party and state institutions to the actual infiltration and dominance of these institutions, then what is happening is the development of a totalitarian police state, a state within which the police are the supreme political institution. This was the case under the Nazis, as well as during the period of party purges in the Soviet Union, when the Communist Party itself became the object of police surveillance and coercion.

In a police state, the police take on several characteristics and strategies: repression or elimination of regime opponents, organizational development as a national, centralized, and often paramilitary institution, intragovernmental competition to achieve political independence, and, in its ultimate form, total domination through the suppression, surveillance, and intimidation of party and state institutions. This is a police state in its full development.

Applications

The course of Nazi rule was marked by a steady accumulation of power by police institutions. When the Nazis assumed power in 1933, the party, bureaucracy, and military were the preeminent institutions. At the time, there was no national police force. This changed quickly with the establishment of the *Geheimestaatspolizei*—the Gestapo—on April 26, 1933, and, once put in motion, the process led to the formation of history's most prime example of a police state and of a totalitarian police state.

This was not, however, an immediate development, but one that emerged over a period of years, as police institutions moved steadily in several directions, toward expansion and centralization, independence from civil control, and penetration of party and state institutions. The pattern is clear. The Gestapo was created as a secret political police force, but was originally subordinate to regional civil authorities. Later in 1933, Himmler was appointed "Political Police Commander of the State," a position from which he quickly nationalized the Gestapo and all other political police functions. In November, 1933, the Gestapo was removed from control of the Ministry of Interior and allowed to report directly to Hermann Göring, then minister-president of the regime. In February, 1936, many of the duties of the Ministry of Interior were then formally transferred to the Gestapo. In June, 1936, Himmler was made chief of all German police and head of the SS, a step that centralized all police, including regional and civil police, and tied them to the SS and Gestapo. In September, 1939, Himmler assumed control of the new *Reichssicherheitshauptamt* (RSHA), or Reich Security Headquarters, absorbing all of the Nazi Party's intelligence files and duties. There was a steady progression, in other words, of expanded, nationalized, centralized, and independent duties. By this stage, the police were clearly an independent political force; a police state was in place.

The process continued, however, with the police moving beyond independence from party, bureaucracy, and military, to a position of supremacy over these institutions. The Nazi state developed into a totalitarian police state. The police came to dominate the party through the creation of the RSHA; when they took over the party's intelligence functions, they assumed the responsibility for surveillance of the party itself. The military was the most difficult institution for the police to challenge, but they were able to do so successfully as a result of the development of the elite Waffen SS, the paramilitary shock troops of the regime, which were loyal to Hitler and Himmler, not the general staff of the military. The police came to dominate the bureaucracy by means of the personal loyalty to Hitler, and the power to ignore and supersede the bureaucracy for reasons of administrative necessity. The process was complete when, in August 1943, Himmler himself, in addition to his police duties, was appointed to head the Interior Ministry.

The circle was complete. In 1933, the Gestapo was created and answerable to civil authorities. In 1943, the head of the Gestapo, and of all other police functions, was in charge of the civil authorities. Politically, Himmler had surpassed all competitors, and was clearly the second power in the regime, second only to Hitler. In Chapman's words, "The police were in supreme control. They were better ideologues than the party, better soldiers than the army, better administrators than the civil service, and better executioners than the judges." This was the world's clearest and most thoroughly developed example of a totalitarian police state. By dint of terror and intimidation, loyalty and sycophancy, administrative efficiency and political acumen, the Nazi secret police reached a position of dominance from which they were all but synonymous with the regime itself.

Context

The distinction between democratic and nondemocratic regimes is that between respect for the individual and contempt, between free expression and compliance, between choice and imposition, and, at its most fundamental level, it is all too often between life and death. For all the concern over antigovernmental violence in the form of terrorism, riots, assassination, guerrilla war, and so on, the fact remains that most political violence is committed by governments against their own people. Most political violence—torture, terrorism, and killing—is government violence. Nearly all government violence is committed by nondemocratic regimes, including police states. The chief operational characteristic of police states is terror.

All police states seek compliance and submission, and totalitarian police states go further still, seeking unanimity of thought and positive demonstrations of support as well. State terror is the method employed to achieve these goals. Violence is employed not only to eliminate political, social, economic, and ideological enemies, but to induce fear in observers that they could be victims of future violence. Individuals and whole classes of people are victimized to serve as examples for the rest of the population. Police in a police state operate in secret and above legal and judicial restrictions. Spies infiltrate all manner of social organizations. Citizens are encouraged to inform on neighbors and even family members. Opponents simply disappear. Tortured and abused citizens are returned to communities as examples. Fear and terror are made pervasive as a means of control. State terror is not the exclusive province of police states, but it is a defining characteristic, and the human cost of such terror in the twentieth century was staggering.

No society, of course, can operate without some policing; police institutions are essential to governance, for the provision of necessary order and stability. Democratic regimes contrast with police states in their desire and ability to limit and control police institutions. Police states impose few if any limits on police, with police being unaccountable to broader civil authorities, and able to intercede in all institutions and aspects of society. Police states allow an independence of action for policing institutions that is inherently inconsistent with a respect for human rights and dignity, or for open political debate and competition.

It is important to put the concept of police states in perspective. In the long list of authoritarian regimes around the world in the twentieth century, fully developed police states are rather rare. Other forms of authoritarianism, particularly those that rely on military and state institutions for dominance, are far more common. Knowledge of, and prevention of, the rise of a police state remains important, however, because of the human toll such regimes have exacted. The Nazi police state and Soviet police state during Stalin's purges were so horrific that other states must remember not to follow them. Many regimes nevertheless take steps in the direction of a police state.

Bibliography

Arendt, Hannah. *Totalitarianism*. New York: Harcourt, Brace & World, 1968. Difficult but pioneering work on the issue, with particularly compelling discussions on the role of secret police.

Chapman, Brian. *Police State*. New York: Praeger, 1970. Outlines the distinctions between traditional, modern, and totalitarian police states, with contemporary examples.

Conquest, Robert. *The Great Terror: A Reassessment*. New York: Oxford University Press, 1990. Discussion of the secret police and terror in Stalin's Soviet Union, including the rise and dominance of the police over the Communist Party and the military.

Friedrich, Carl J., and Zbigniew K. Brzezinski. *Totalitarian Dictatorship and Autocracy*. 2d ed. New York: Praeger, 1965. Compelling discussion of the unique nature and development of totalitarianism, and the roles of the secret police and terror.

Hohne, Heinz. *The Order of the Death's Head: The Story of Hitler's SS*. Translated by Richard Barry. New York: Coward, McCann & Geoghegan, 1970. Readable history of the SS, including its formation, Himmler's rise to power, the Gestapo, competition with party and state institutions, and the Waffen SS.

Perlmutter, Amos. *Modern Authoritarianism: A Comparative Institutional Analysis*. New Haven, Conn.: Yale University Press, 1981. Influential discussion of authoritarian governance, outlining the similarities and differences in the political systems of the various forms of authoritarianism including police states.

Shirer, William L. *The Nightmare Years, 1930-1940*. Vol. 2 in *Twentieth Century Journey: A Memoir of a Life and the Times*. Boston: Little, Brown, 1984. Readable autobiographical and eyewitness account of the creation and workings of the Nazi regime, from one of the century's leading journalists.

Stohl, Michael, and George A. Lopez, eds. *Government Violence and Repression: An Agenda for Research*. Westport, Conn.: Greenwood Press, 1986. One of the few treatments of state terrorism, a series of essays defining state terror, the political basis for employing such terror, and the links between state terror and genocide, drawing heavily from the Nazi experience.

Vassiltchikov, Marie. *Berlin Diaries, 1940-1945*. New York: Vintage Books, 1987. Diaries of a Russian princess living through the height of Nazi terror, who knew many conspirators involved in the 1944 plot to kill Hitler. Captures the intense fear and intimidation the regime generated.

David Carleton

Cross-References

POLICY DEVELOPMENT AND IMPLEMENTATION

Field of study: Functions of government

Policy development in government is the process of identifying important public issues, bringing them to the attention of decision makers, and the formation of laws or regulations intended to resolve the issues. Policy implementation is the administration of public policy.

Principal terms

AGENDA: issues and problems to be considered by a policy-making body

BUREAUCRACY: organizational structure intended to enhance efficiency through hierarchical control, task routinization and specialization, and rule making

ELITISM: public policy development as an effort of small, powerful groups to maintain their control of social systems

EXTERNALITIES: unplanned effects of policy decisions

INCREMENTALISM: policy development through small changes, often called "fine tuning" of existing public programs or processes

OVERSIGHT: congressional or executive function of reviewing and evaluating the implementation of public policy

PLURALISM: policy development in which power is distributed among numerous groups who individually or in coalitions exert influence on public policymakers

PUBLIC INTEREST: common good, of benefit to the entire community

RATIONAL-COMPREHENSIVE: logical process of decision making in which problems are identified, all alternatives considered, and solutions arrived at by selecting the best alternative

Overview

Making public policy is what governments do. They implement programs to solve public needs, and they finance these activities through taxation. Policy development involves identification of a problem, having the problem placed on the agenda of political decision makers, developing proposed solutions, gathering support for a solution, and formalizing the solution into policy through law. Policy implementation occurs when public officials provide for the realization of public policies through budgeted funds, assignment of administrative responsibility, and appropriate legislative or executive oversight.

Policy-making processes are extremely complex; they can involve hundreds or thousands of people. Often, the most important individuals in the policy process are public decision makers in the legislative, executive, and frequently the judicial branches of government. Some public policies cross levels of government, originating at the local levels before being accepted as important issues at the federal level of government. Often the reverse is true as well, as federal policies, often referred to as federal mandates, are passed down to the state and local levels of government. Other actors in the policy process include government agencies, pressure groups, the media, and the general public.

Adding to the complexity of public policy-making is the complicated nature of most public issues. Issues such as education, health, energy, welfare, the environment, the economy, and defense involve complicated systems often extending beyond the capacity of most policymakers to be fully informed. In addition to the intrinsic difficulty of these subjects, decision makers must also deal with the externalities of their policy decisions. Decisions regarding energy, for example, will often affect the environment. Tax policy decisions significantly affect national income and the economy.

The policy-making process has been studied to see if there is a consistent pattern. Most people envision policy-making as an orderly process in which decision makers identify a problem, consider all the applicable alternatives, select the one that is most efficient and effective in solving the problem, and implement that solution by assigning the responsibility to an appropriate government agency and allocating the necessary budget. When one thinks of the time and intellectual resources that must be committed every time a policy is made, however, it is not surprising that this rational-comprehensive model is more the exception than the rule in making public policy.

More often public policy is made by making modest changes to existing policies. Scientists call this the incremental theory of public policy. Instead of identifying and studying a problem and searching for every possible solution, decision makers engage in "satisfying," in which, because of time and information constraints, they settle on the first available solution that satisfies most persons or groups interested in the problem. For example, economic policy is not reinvented annually; instead, government agencies make minor adjustments in the amount of federal spending or in setting interest rates. A new direction in education policy usually means the government is introducing a program that makes a small variation in the overall education policy. It would simply take too much effort and time to come up with completely new policies every time a problem was identified.

There is much discussion about who really has the greatest influence in the policy process. Some scholars have shown that policies are often generated within government structures like Congress, the office of the president, or in bureaucratic agencies. In this case, policy-making follows an institutional model. Other researchers have demonstrated that American public policy is understood best in a framework of pluralism. Under this pattern most policies are developed through the involvement of interest groups seeking to fulfill their own purposes. Others argue that the public policy process does not follow these methods, but instead, policy is made to satisfy the interests of an elite group that currently holds considerable power and influences the making of public policy and so works to retain that power.

Public officials make policy by passing laws, establishing programs, and creating incentives for public participation. At the federal level, for example, the president may propose an agenda for domestic and foreign policies in a state of the union address and in proposed legislation for Congress to consider. Members of Congress may then take up some of these policy proposals by writing and debating bills in congressional committees and on the floors of Congress. Eventually a bill is passed assigning an executive agency the responsibility of implementing the policy. Public policy may also be created through less formal means. Executive agency officials in the Internal Revenue Service, for example, adopt policy when they set rules for the collection of taxes. The State Department, in the way it approaches an international crisis, makes policy.

Applications

During the Great Depression of the 1930's, poverty in the United States reached its highest levels in modern times. More than one third of Americans were out of work, and many lost their life savings, family farms, and their homes. During this difficult time, state governments were overwhelmed by the large number of people in need. The president and most members of Congress saw an urgent need for national policies to help the poor. Several programs were enacted to put people back to work, help those in retirement, and assist families who needed financial aid. One of these programs, the Social Security Act, helped the elderly to secure an adequate retirement. Part of the Act also provided assistance to widows with children; it became known as "welfare," or more formally, Aid to Families with Dependent Children (AFDC). Over the ensuing years, AFDC was slowly modified from assistance to widows to include any woman with children who has little or no income and without someone else living in the home who can earn an income. This last provision created a policy externality by encouraging the breaking apart of poor families. The father, who might be unemployed but still capable of work, would make his wife and children ineligible for financial assistance if he remained in the home.

Even after decades of positive economic growth many Americans were still suffering in poverty while the rest of the nation prospered. By the early 1960's a number of federal agencies and private philanthropies were operating additional programs to assist the poor without the detrimental effects on the family.

In 1963, President John F. Kennedy involved his Council of Economic Advisors in developing proposals for a comprehensive plan to attack poverty. Following Kennedy's death, President Lyndon B. Johnson identified poverty in America as "the great unfinished work of our society." He then declared, "To finish that work I have called for a national war on poverty." Johnson acted quickly to bring poverty to the national policy agenda. Federal bureaucracies and important members of Congress were brought together to develop a program for helping lift the poor out of poverty. Sargent Shriver, an influential leader, formerly of the Peace Corps, was appointed to coordinate the development of Johnson's poverty program. After only a few months, a plan was introduced to Congress. Debate was brief; the congressional sponsors pushed the Economic Opportunity Act of 1964 through both houses without significant amendment.

In the case of the Economic Opportunity Act of 1964, two presidents saw the need for a change in policy toward the poor. Following the assassination of President Kennedy, the country, including Congress, was sympathetic to the policies proposed by the late president. Legislation was developed through the efforts of many actors including state and local officials, academics, federal agency officials, and public interest groups. Absent from these discussions, however, were the poor themselves. In the political world of special interest groups, those who do not have the resources to organize to protect their own interests are seldom represented.

A second example of public policy development and implementation illustrates how a federal agency can adopt a policy that affects state and local governments and the public without necessarily going through Congress to enact legislation. Part of Ronald Reagan's presidential campaign was based on reforming America's education system. Reagan's strong belief in a new federalism, returning many responsibilities back to state and local governments, prompted him to propose the elimination of the federal Department of Education. After he entered office in 1980, President Reagan appointed Terrel Bell as secretary of education with the mission of abolishing the department.

The Reagan Administration soon realized, however, that the state of education in the United States required more help, not less. Secretary Bell launched a major study of the American education system and identified several serious problems demanding public policy attention. President Reagan's second secretary of education, William Bennett, proposed a major restructuring of the education system by returning to fundamental knowledge and skills. Bennett aggressively campaigned across the country to emphasize the urgency and importance of the problems in education.

The next administration, under President George Bush, adopted the theme of education reform into its platform. Bush's second secretary of education developed a plan proposing several changes in the education status quo. Education secretary Lamar Alexander proposed uniform testing of education outcomes by school so parents and communities could judge how their schools were performing. He proposed that the federal government establish model schools in every legislative district, and that teacher quality should be improved through pay incentives and new ways of demonstrating teaching competency in academic subjects. An important part of Alexander's plan was to let parents choose the schools that their children could attend. Through an open-market concept, competition between schools could produce greater educational opportunities overall.

The proposals for education reform of presidents Reagan and Bush used few dollars and required little action by Congress. These administrations did increase the public discussion about the need for educational reform and developed several alternatives for public discussion. Change generally has occurred incrementally in the American education system, and it is the state and local governments that make many of the important policy decisions, including how to pay for the changes in local schools. In many states, education accounts for more than half of all state government expenditures.

Context

The purpose of government is to develop and implement public policy. When governments were first created, their primary mission was to protect citizens from dangers and to provide public services. The decision to organize and take action as a community was essentially public policy development. The formation of a police force or an army for protection and the construction of streets, sewers, and public buildings were examples of policy implementation. Governments continue to provide the same fundamental services that they did thousands of years ago, but policy development and implementation have changed considerably since that time.

Traditionally, governments have provided protection and some limited public services. Today, governments are involved in virtually every aspect of their citizens' lives, from the day one is born to the day one dies. Governments regulate hospitals and health care, child care, and public education. They tax wage earners for hundreds of public services, and they provide benefits to retirees. Governments control where and how one can be buried and have a say in what happens to the deceased's estate.

Another important change in modern government is the way policy is developed and implemented. In ancient times a ruler could establish policy through his or her own word, possibly with the advice of a few close advisers. Today, policy decisions have become much more complicated. In a pluralist society, many interest groups have an opportunity to express their opinions and exert what influence they can in an effort to persuade government officials to accept their point of view. Many policy decisions are made by a select elite composed of government officials, key industrial leaders, and important members of Congress. This can and does change, however, in cases of increased media exposure of decision making. Also, a virtual explosion of special interest groups, with considerable power to influence, has helped broaden the power base.

Bibliography

Anderson, James E. *Public Policymaking: An Introduction*. 2d ed. Boston: Houghton Mifflin, 1994. Solid introduction to policy-making in the United States.

Downs, Anthony. *Inside Bureaucracy*. Boston: Little, Brown, 1967. Provides a critical look at the dynamics of bureaucracies.

Dye, Thomas R. *Understanding Public Policy*. 7th ed. Englewood Cliffs, N.J.: Prentice-Hall, 1992. Classic text describing the models of political decision making as they relate to public policy.

Easton, David. *A Systems Analysis of Political Life*. Chicago: University of Chicago Press, 1979. Easton is well known for his work in systems theory as it relates to public policy. This work describes policy-making as a result of political inputs and the workings of governmental institutions.

Kingdon, John W. *Agendas, Alternatives, and Public Policies*. Boston: Little, Brown, 1984. Describes agenda setting and decision making in the policy-making process. Kingdon uses interesting metaphors such as policy streams, garbage cans and primeval soup to describe the processes of public policy-making.

Kruschke, Earl R., and Byron M. Jackson. *The Public Policy Dictionary.* Santa Barbara, Calif.: ABC-Clio, 1987. Useful supplement to other readings in public policy that defines the most important terms used in public policy-making.

Lindblom, Charles E. *The Policy-making Process.* 3d ed. Englewood Cliffs, N.J.: Prentice-Hall, 1993. Considers policy-making from several approaches, including an institutional model, group theory, and elite theory.

Mills, C. Wright. *The Power Elite.* New York: Oxford University Press, 1959. Examination of public policy using the elite theory of policy-making.

Schattschneider, E. E. *The Semisovereign People.* New York: Holt, Rinehart and Winston, 1960. Classic examination of group theory and social conflict as models of policy analysis.

W. David Patton

Cross-References

Budgets of National Governments, p. 158; Civil Rights and Liberties, p. 298; Commerce Regulation, p. 357; Constitutional Law in the United States, p. 439; Executive Functions in U.S. Government, p. 636; Federal Mandates, p. 662; Filibuster, p. 694; Funding of Government, p. 724; Government Agencies, p. 765; Judicial Review, p. 1012; Labor Relations, p. 1038; Legislative Functions of Government, p. 1098; Public Policy, p. 1633; State and Local Government, p. 1885; Taxation and Appropriation, p. 1941.

POLITICAL ACTION COMMITTEES

Field of study: Politics

Political action committees (often called PACs) are conduits for campaign contributions. As organizations that collect funds from supporters of interest groups or political causes, they distribute funds in political campaigns in the name of their contributors.

Principal terms

> ACCESS CONTRIBUTION: money intended to ensure a contributor communication access to the recipient
>
> CHALLENGER: candidate who runs against an incumbent
>
> CONNECTED PAC: committee sponsored by an organization such as a corporation, labor union, or association
>
> FAT CAT: slang term for rich campaign contributor who has undue influence on government policy
>
> INCUMBENT: candidate seeking re-election to an office already held
>
> INDEPENDENT EXPENDITURE: money that PACs spend in their own campaigns, rather than contributed to candidates
>
> NONCONNECTED PAC: committee without a sponsor that is responsible for its own financing and administrative costs
>
> OPEN-SEAT CANDIDATE: person running for an office for which no incumbent is running
>
> OVERHEAD: purely administrative costs of running an organization— such as office space, supplies, staff, mailing, and telephones

Overview

The first political action committee (PAC) was created by the Congress of Industrial Organizations labor union in the 1940's. The PAC collected funds from the union's members and contributed them in the union's name to candidates for political office. A few other corporations, unions, and associations formed PACs in the 1950's and 1960's, but PACs did not become an important part of the U.S. political system until the 1970's, when concern over large contributions from wealthy contributors, commonly known as "fat cats," and illegal donations from corporate treasuries led to the passage of campaign finance reform legislation. Reformers hoped that a legal conduit (such as a political action committee) through which corporate, union, and association supporters could contribute limited funds would end the role of fat cats and reduce the appeal of illegal contributions.

Legislation passed by the U.S. Congress and decisions issued by the Federal Election Commission and U.S. Supreme Court established guidelines for PAC behavior. Political action committees may both make contributions to candidates and expend funds directly in their own campaigns. They may make total contributions of no more than $5,000 to any one candidate in a single election. This limits them to $10,000 per candidate in each election cycle, $5,000 for the primary election to obtain the party nomination, and $5,000 for the general election to be elected to office. By contrast, independent expenditures which directly fund PAC campaigns for or against a candidate or cause are subject to no limit. Contributions account for 90 to 95 percent and independent expenditures 5 to 10 percent of PACs' total campaign spending.

A sizable majority of political action committees, those referred to as connected PACs, are sponsored by established organizations such as corporations, labor unions, or associations. A smaller proportion, those known as nonconnected PACs, have no sponsoring organizations. Nonconnected PACs are often much more visible to the public because most solicit funds through mass mailings and telephone solicitations. However, nonconnected PACs face a more precarious financial situation than connected PACs, because soliciting the general public yields relatively small returns, and nonconnected PACs must pay their own overhead costs, which consume most of their revenues, leaving only a small proportion for campaign spending. Connected PACs have the advantage that their likely contributors are more easily identified: Corporate PACs solicit their sponsors' stockholders and employees (most successfully management-level employees) and union and association PACs solicit their sponsors' members. In addition, connected PACs' sponsors can legally pay overhead costs necessary to solicit funds so that connected PACs can use all donations they receive as contributions and independent expenditures.

More than 4,000 PACs are registered with the federal government at any moment. In 1992 this figure included approximately 2,000 corporate, less than 400 labor union, about 800 association, and 1,300 nonconnected PACs. PACs account for between $150 and $200 million in contributions during each two-year election cycle. Corporate PACs usually account for a bit over 35 percent, labor union PACs a little under 25 percent, association PACs about 30 percent, and nonconnected PACs the remaining 10 percent of that total. PACs vary greatly in their financial resources. About one-third of all registered PACs make no contributions, and another quarter contribute less than $5,000 each within a given election cycle. The richest 450 PACs account for more than three-quarters of all PAC campaign funds. Some of the largest PACs are corporate PACs: the American Telephone and Telegraph and United Parcel Service (each averaging about $1.5 million) and RJ Reynolds Tobacco/Nabisco Inc. ($850,000); labor union PACs: the Teamsters ($2.5 million), National Education Association ($2.3 million), and United Auto Workers ($2.2 million); association PACs: Realtors ($3 million), American Medical Association ($2.9 million), and Trial Lawyers ($2.2 million); and nonconnected PACs: National PAC, which supports U.S. assistance for Israel ($700,000), the National Abortion Rights Action League ($400,000), and EMILY'S List, which was formed to help women win elective office ($350,000).

Two major contribution tactics have been identified: access and electoral. Access contributions are intended to provide access to officeholders, assuring the PAC or its sponsor an opportunity to lobby and persuade the official of the wisdom of its policy preferences. As a consequence, these contributions are generally directed to candidates who are expected to win, with little regard to the candidates' ideological and policy positions. Incumbent House candidates' overwhelming reelection rates (more than 90 percent of those who run are reelected) lead PACs to concentrate their access contributions on House incumbents. Access contributions are also directed to Senate candidates, but incumbent senators' lower reelection rates (commonly around 70 to 80 percent) lead to a lower concentration of access contributions on Senate incumbents.

Electoral tactics are intended to influence voters and are generally directed to candidates with whom the contributor agrees on ideological or policy grounds. These contributions are concentrated in more competitive races because the expenditure of campaign funds in such races promises the greatest probability of influencing who will win. Some challengers and incumbents receive electoral contributions, but a larger share of these funds is directed to candidates in open seat races because contests without incumbents are generally more competitive. Few access or electoral dollars are directed to challengers because of their poor electoral prospects.

During the late twentieth century political action committees in each category tended to rely more on one contribution tactic or the other. Corporate PACs were noted for their commitment to access contributions. In the House of Representatives, incumbent Democrats received a substantial proportion of corporate PACs' contributions, despite their reputation as being less probusiness than Republicans, because the Democrats were usually in the majority. Labor union PACs directed a larger proportion of their funds with the intention of influencing elections. Labor PACs contributed heavily to Democratic incumbents and candidates for open seats but rarely to Republicans. The contribution tactics of PACs within the association category were more diverse than PACs within the corporate or labor category. A majority of association PACs relied on electoral tactics though many employed access tactics. The net result was that Republicans benefited slightly more than Democrats from association PACs' contributions. Finally, nonconnected PACS were the most committed to electoral contributions. Although a substantial share of nonconnected PACs were conservative, Democratic candidates received slightly more funds from nonconnected PACs than did Republicans. In addition, nonconnected PACs accounted for the overwhelming majority of independent expenditures. Such spending allowed these PACs to increase the chance of influencing election outcomes by concentrating funds on campaigns for or against particular candidates. This in turn made it easier for these PACs to take credit for electing allies and defeating opponents, helping in their efforts to persuade potential donors to contribute to each PAC.

The net result of PACs' contribution tactics can be seen in the receipts of different categories of candidates in the 1992 elections. While about 43 percent of House candidates' campaign funds came from PACs, proportions varied among different types of candidates—from a high of about 50 percent of total receipts for Democratic incumbents down to less than 10 percent for Republican challengers. PACs accounted for about 21 percent of Senate candidates' campaign receipts, and—as with the House—Democratic incumbents received the highest proportion, approximately 35 percent, and Republican challengers the lowest, under 10 percent.

Two other classes of PACs, actually subcategories of nonconnected PACs, should be noted. Those in the first group are called "leadership" PACs and are used with increasing frequency by U.S. House and Senate leaders and candidates for leadership positions. Though small in number of financial assets relative to other categories, these PACs play an important role. Congressional party and committee leaders use their personal PACs to help other members' campaign efforts. In so doing they gain the gratitude and indebtedness of other members. These PACs can help congressional leaders build congressional majorities for policies that the leaders support. They can also help line up support for a legislator's presidential candidacy.

PACs in the second group, referred to as "candidate" PACs, are used by presidential candidates to jump start their campaigns and supplement their official campaign spending. Presidential candidates must accept limits on their campaign spending as a condition of receiving federal campaign funds. They establish PACs as a means around those limits. Candidate PACs carry out such tasks as identifying potential contributors, setting up the framework and identifying personnel for campaign operations, and providing financial support for potential allies. All this spending is immune to limits placed on presidential candidates' campaign spending.

Applications

The impact of PAC campaign spending on elections and government policy is widely debated. Specific cases of PAC-sponsored campaigns to influence election results and PAC contributions directed to candidates to facilitate access to officeholders illuminates the issues involved.

Money for "independent expenditures" has received a good deal of notoriety and is widely perceived as a powerful campaign weapon. The most highly publicized use of independent expenditures is the 1980 campaign of the National Conservative Political Action Committee (NCPAC) against six liberal Democratic senators. When four of the six senators targeted by NCPAC were defeated in their campaigns for reelection, the media widely reported NCPAC's claim that its independent expenditures were the cause of the senators' defeat. While NCPAC and many media commentators concluded from this experience that independent expenditures were an extremely powerful weapon which could be used to alter election outcomes, however, much of the available evidence leads one to question that conclusion.

Political action committees' independent expenditures probably have less impact than is widely perceived. The power of PAC campaigns is contingent on other factors involved in an election. For example, NCPAC's spending was only one of the elements which contributed to the defeat of the four senate incumbents. The 1980 elections were marked by widespread voter skepticism about liberal and Democratic candidates, and the ideological leanings of the senators targeted by NCPAC were particularly out of step with the more conservative states they represented. In addition, a majority of these six senators were noted for having "lost touch" with their constituents. In sum, independent expenditures may contribute to a change in election outcomes when they are part of a broader campaign or trend, but in isolation their influence is likely to be limited.

Growth in the public's perception of highly funded PAC campaigns as an unwarranted intrusion into local elections has further eroded the potential impact of PACs' independent spending. Andy Jacobs, a member of the House of Representatives, claims that the 1986 American Medical Association (AMA) campaign against his reelection actually increased his share of the vote. Jacobs reported that the AMA's campaign was widely perceived by district residents as outside interference in their local election, leading a number of his constituents who had traditionally voted for his opponents to vote for him.

The influence of access contributions is also in question. Access-oriented contributors hope to insure for themselves an opportunity to convince decision makers to write policy in a manner the contributors favor. Ironically, the public is generally less informed about more influential access contributions. This is because media attention toward the influence of such contributions is limited.

PAC access contributions have their greatest influence over policy on which few of the PACs' potential adversaries are active. When a policy question stirs little notice, PAC money tends to have more influence. In such circumstances, officials who respond to PAC contributors' preferences need have little fear of incurring retribution from the interest's opponents. As a wider range of the population becomes aware of a policy, the probability increases that opposition to the PAC contributor's preferences will increase. As opposition rises, officials who side with a PAC contributor bear an increasing risk of controversy. This risk may lead officeholders to hesitate in their support for contributors' preferences.

Health care policy provides a good example. President Bill Clinton's 1992 campaign promise to reform health care policy inspired the media to focus attention on the contributions of health care industry PACs. It also motivated opponents of the health care industry among consumer groups, labor unions, and the public at large to lobby their legislators. While the dollar value of health care and insurance industry contributions was impressive in the early 1990's—reaching over $41 million in the 1991-1992 election cycle—so was the attention of health care industry opponents. The industry's influence on policy was probably greater during the preceding decade during which time health care PACs contributed smaller sums. The lower level of interest in health care issues during the 1980's meant that health care industry interests faced fewer active opponents, and as a result, the industry had greater influence. Indeed, health care industry contributions may have helped keep reform (generally opposed by members of the industry) off the legislative agenda. Once the issue became visible to a larger share of its opponents, however, the industry's influence declined even as its contributions increased.

Context

Political action committees are playing an increasingly important role in U.S. electoral politics. Since the 1960's election campaigns have become less labor intensive and more capital intensive. Until the 1960's much of the work of campaigning was centered in political parties, which depended heavily on volunteers to do door-to-door canvassing and other personal campaigning. The decline of voter loyalty to the parties and the rise in public attention to the media made candidates increase their reliance on campaign technology (such as television, direct mail, and opinion polls) and campaign professionals (like pollsters and campaign consultants). The need to buy media space and time and to hire professionals greatly increased campaign costs. For example, between 1974 and 1992 the average cost of campaigning for the Senate increased more than sixfold (to $2.89 million) and for the House of Representatives more than sevenfold (to about $410 thousand).

During that same period PACs accounted for a steadily increasing share of candidates' campaign funds. They accounted for more than one-fifth of U.S. Senate and more than one-third of House candidates' 1992 campaign receipts. PACs are also important sources of funds for national and state party organizations and for leadership and candidate PACs. In addition, PACs are spending increasing sums on contributions to candidates for state office. Critics charge that PACs have become the new fat cats, trading large sums of money for influence on government policy.

Critics also note that because incumbents are generally at an electoral advantage, PACs' concentration of funds on incumbents further undermines the competitiveness of elections. This, in turn, makes it costly for legislators to reform campaign finance laws, because reform would be likely to cost them more campaign receipts than it would their future opponents.

PAC leaders defend PACs as a vehicle that offers average citizens an easily accessible means of political action, increasing citizen participation in the political system. They also defend access contributions as insurance which assures the interests they represent an opportunity to "make their case" to elected officials, and they defend electoral contributions as a legitimate means for citizens to influence elections. Still, the role of PACs remains controversial.

Bibliography

Barone, Michael. *The Almanac of American Politics*. Washington, D.C.: National Journal, biennial. Provides information regarding the level of PAC contributions to specific candidates for the U.S. Congress.

Congressional Quarterly Weekly Report. Washington, D.C.: Congressional Quarterly Press. Provides up-to-date information about PACs and congressional elections.

Fritz, Sara, and Morris Dwight. *Gold-Plated Politics*. Washington, D.C.: Congressional Quarterly Press, 1992. Describes the sources of campaign funds and reasons for increasing costs of running for the U.S. Congress in the 1990's.

Jackson, Brooks. *Honest Graft*. Rev. ed. Washington, D.C.: Farragut, 1990. Examines the efforts of Tony Coelho as chair of Democratic Congressional Campaign Committee to attract PAC contributions to Democratic candidates for the House of Representatives.

Sabato, Larry. *PAC Power: Inside the World of Political Action Committees*. New York:

W. W. Norton, 1985. Deals with PACs' relationship to interest groups and political parties and the implications for PACs of proposed election finance reforms.

Sorauf, Frank. *Money in American Elections*. Glenview, Ill.: Scott, Foresman, Little, Brown College Division, 1988. Overview of the sources and expenditure of campaign funds. An entire chapter is devoted to the role of political action committees.

Stanley, Harold. *Vital Statistics on American Politics*. 4th ed. Washington, D.C.: Congressional Quarterly Press, 1994. Identifies the richest PACs by name and presents summary statistics about general PAC contribution patterns.

Frank L. Davis

Cross-References

POLITICAL CAMPAIGNING, PLANNING, AND FINANCING

Field of study: Politics

Political campaigns consist of the activities undertaken by candidates and their supporters in order to win elections. The most important campaign activities include raising money, promoting the candidate, and motivating supporters to vote.

Principal terms

DEMOCRATIC CONGRESSIONAL CAMPAIGN COMMITTEE: committee made up of a small number of Democratic members of the U.S. House of Representatives that raises and contributes campaign money to Democratic candidates

DIRECT MAIL: mailings sent out to targeted groups of people in an attempt to raise campaign contributions and promote a candidate

GRASSROOTS ORGANIZATION: local volunteers and professional staff who work to identify potential supporters, register voters, and promote candidates

FEDERAL ELECTION CAMPAIGN ACT OF 1971: bill specifying how federal candidates can raise and spend money for their campaigns; amended in 1974, 1976, and 1979

INDEPENDENT EXPENDITURES: campaign spending by persons or groups that is not made directly in cooperation with a candidate and is, therefore, not subject to the limitations of the Federal Election Campaign Act

POLITICAL ACTION COMMITTEE: legally constituted committee that can raise and donate money to federal candidates' political campaigns, subject to the restrictions of federal law

SOFT MONEY: campaign contributions given to state party organizations for registration drives and other grassroots activities, circumventing the restrictions of the Federal Election Campaign Act

Overview

The purpose of a political campaign is to convey information that will motivate people to vote for a particular candidate. The success of a campaign in meeting this goal is often dependent on the amount of money that can be raised. It is not uncommon for candidates seeking a high-level office, such as a seat in the United States Senate, to raise millions of dollars. Because candidates running for a city council seat or other low-level offices need to appeal to relatively few voters, they require much less money to run effective campaigns. Virtually every candidate must raise some money, if only to pay for the costs of printing campaign literature or placing advertisements in newspapers.

Candidates for high-level offices often hire a direct mail company to help them raise money. These companies identify potential campaign contributors and contact them requesting campaign contributions. Some candidates also receive money from local, state, or national campaign organizations. For example, Democratic candidates seeking seats in the House of Representatives may receive funds from the Democratic Congressional Campaign Committee, a group comprising a select number of Democratic members of Congress. This committee solicits money from individuals and political action committees, and then makes contributions to Democratic congressional candidates.

Laws regulating campaign finance vary depending on the type of office being sought and the state in which a candidate is seeking it. States differ in how they regulate the financing of campaigns for statewide and local offices. Some states limit the amount of money individuals and interest groups can give to candidates running for particular offices. Several states ban direct contributions to candidates from corporations; a few states prohibit contributions from labor unions. Other states have less stringent laws. While all states have some sort of disclosure requirement, several states have no limits on the amount of money individuals or groups can give to state or local candidates.

Candidates running for the presidential nomination of a major party are subject to the provisions of the Federal Election Campaign Act and its amendments. This law limits the total amount of money candidates can spend during the presidential nomination process (approximately $33 million in 1992). There are also restrictions on how much money candidates can spend in each state. A person is allowed to give no more than $1,000, and political action committees no more than $5,000, to a presidential candidate. Candidates may contribute up to $50,000 of their own money to their campaign.

Corporations and unions may not give money directly to presidential candidates, although they may use corporate or union funds to establish a political action committee. All contributions of $200 or more must be reported to the Federal Election Commission, a government agency. A candidate who raises $5,000 in each of twenty states, thus demonstrating his or her viability, becomes eligible for public financing. The federal government will contribute a dollar to a candidate's campaign for each dollar that the candidate raises from individuals, although only the first $250 of each person's donation is matched. The money the government gives to candidates is derived from a voluntary checkoff on the federal income tax, whereby individuals indicate that a dollar of their tax payment should be used for this purpose.

Laws regulating campaign spending in the general election for president differ from the laws pertaining to the presidential nomination process. The federal government offers each candidate a lump sum (approximately $55 million in 1992) to pay the costs of his or her campaign. If a candidate accepts this payment, and all major party candidates had accepted it as of 1992, then the candidate is precluded from raising money from other sources except for the purpose of complying with the reporting requirements. National party organizations, however, are allowed to spend several million additional dollars promoting their presidential candidates. Candidates who choose not to accept public funding, such as H. Ross Perot in the 1992 election, may raise and spend as much money as they wish.

There are loopholes in the campaign finance laws. First, the law allows state party organizations to spend an unlimited amount of so-called soft money on such activities as registration drives, polling, and advertisements for nonfederal candidates. Since such activities inevitably benefit federal as well as nonfederal candidates—a newly registered voter is as likely to vote for a presidential candidate as a nonfederal office seeker—presidential candidates encourage campaign contributors to give money to state party organizations.

Second, the law allows for independent expenditures. Individuals and organizations can spend unlimited amounts of money in support of a candidate, providing they do not consult with the candidate or the candidate's campaign staff regarding how the money will be spent.

The financing laws that pertain to congressional candidates differ in some respects from the laws regulating presidential contests. While individual contributors and political action committees are subject to the same contribution limitations that pertain to presidential elections, there is no public financing, and candidates are free to raise and spend an unlimited amount of money. There are no limits on the amount of money congressional candidates can contribute to their own campaigns. When John D. Rockefeller IV ran for the Senate in 1984, he spent $11 million of his own money. National party organizations, congressional campaign committees, and state party committees are also allowed to contribute to congressional candidates.

One way campaign organizations promote a candidate is by setting up a grassroots organization. Typically, volunteers are recruited to go door-to-door to register voters, talk to people about a candidate, and drop off campaign literature. In the days immediately preceding an election, volunteers telephone people and remind them to vote or offer them rides to the polls. Sometimes candidates will coordinate their grassroots activity with local party organizations thus benefiting from the assistance of party leaders who are interested in electing candidates for a variety of offices.

The second method of candidate promotion is to use the media. Advertisements are placed in newspapers and promotional spots are run on the radio and television. In order to increase their name recognition, most office seekers still distribute such traditional campaign materials as posters, bumper stickers, yard signs, and buttons. In addition, attempts are made to influence how the press covers the candidate. Many campaign organizations have a press secretary who is responsible for informing the news media of the candidate's public appearances and for writing press releases that convey the candidate's qualifications and positions on the issues.

Office seekers with substantial resources often hire campaign consultants to help them devise and implement an effective campaign strategy. Based on their interpretation of poll results, consultants often advise candidates to adopt particular campaign themes and suggest snappy one-liners that the candidates can use to attract the attention of the press. Consultants also produce radio and television advertisements, and suggest when they should be aired.

Ever since the televised debates between John F. Kennedy and Richard Nixon during the election of 1960, such confrontations have become a regular feature of presidential contests. Televised debates between congressional and gubernatorial candidates became more common in the 1980's and 1990's.

Applications

In 1988, Michael Dukakis won the Democratic Party's presidential nomination but was defeated in the general election by George Bush. How these candidates campaigned illustrates the effects of campaign finance law and some important features of campaigns in the late twentieth century.

In seeking the Democratic presidential nomination, Dukakis was required to conform to the provisions of the Federal Election Campaign Act. He qualified for federal matching funds by raising $5,000 in each of twenty states. From that point, the first $250 of every contribution he received from individual contributors was matched by the federal government. By the end of his campaign, he had raised more than $19 million and received $9 million in matching funds. Unlike most other presidential hopefuls, Dukakis refused to accept money from political action committees. Dukakis' contributions came from 114,000 contributors who gave an average donation of $171. The Dukakis campaign solicited contributions through direct mail, fund-raising events, and direct requests from the candidate and his supporters.

George Bush also qualified for matching funds and spent all the money allowed under federal law. He raised his money from both individual contributions and political action committees, but most of his donations came from individuals.

In order to finance his general election campaign, Dukakis elected to accept a grant of $46,100,000 from the public treasury. By accepting this grant, his campaign organization was precluded from accepting private contributions, except monies that were raised to defray legal and accounting expenses. The law did not prevent Dukakis' supporters from raising soft money for the state parties. In fact, the major fund-raiser for the Dukakis campaign, Robert Farmer, raised more than $20 million in soft money that was used for various grassroots activities such as get-out-the-vote drives.

About two-thirds of the funds Dukakis received from the public treasury was spent on broadcast media. Most of the money spent on television was devoted to brief advertisements, which initially emphasized the central theme of his campaign: that he was a stronger and more competent leader than his opponent. When this campaign theme failed to be effective, Dukakis changed to a more policy-oriented message that emphasized his empathy with the electorate's concerns about the trade deficit, housing, and health care. Funds were also used to pay for polls, direct mail, travel, staff salaries, printing, and telephone charges.

The Bush campaign also used soft money to its advantage. Twenty-two million dollars in soft money was spent by the Republicans in 1988 on grassroots activities. Like Dukakis, Bush spent most of his $46,100,000 federal grant on media. Unlike Dukakis, Bush opted for a negative campaign theme. He attacked his Democratic opponent by claiming he was weak, naïve, and too liberal. Bush's television advertisements attacked Dukakis' positions on the death penalty, prison furloughs, and his veto of a bill that would have required teachers in Massachusetts to recite the Pledge of Allegiance.

Dukakis and Bush engaged in two televised debates. The vice presidential candidates also debated each other. After hearing his Republican opponent, Dan Quayle, compare himself to John F. Kennedy, the Democratic vice presidential nominee, Lloyd Bentsen, noted that he had been a friend of the former president and then unleashed one of the many one-liners that have become characteristic of modern-day, media-centered campaigns: "Senator, you're no Jack Kennedy."

Context

Both the characteristics of campaign organizations and the manner in which campaigns are financed has changed over time. The decline of the patronage system, changes in state laws that now allow many candidates to be elected in primaries rather than chosen in party conventions, and the decline in party loyalty within the electorate, have weakened party organizations. Thus, candidates in the late twentieth century have relied less on party organizations than in the past. While most candidates still coordinate their campaign with a state party organization, candidates for federal or statewide office often raise most of their own money. Control over funding enables candidates to hire their own staff and make independent decisions about how to promote their candidacy.

The technologies used in campaigns also have changed. Although candidates still rely on volunteers to pass out campaign buttons and distribute literature, well-financed office seekers also take polls, customize mailings to select groups of voters, and flood the airways with hundreds of thirty-second commercials. Advertisements that attack an opponent have been found to be particularly effective and, therefore, have been used increasingly. Candidates' speeches, which in an earlier era were often lengthy discussions of public policy, have become more likely to consist of a few pithy remarks that the candidate hopes will be considered interesting enough to be included in a televised evening news program.

Modern-day campaigns for high-level offices are likely to include televised debates. In most presidential debates, candidates have been required to answer questions posed by journalists and deliver a closing statement. In the 1992 presidential contest, however, one debate was structured so that the candidates answered questions from people in a studio audience. In 1992, presidential candidates also attempted to communicate with voters by appearing on television talk shows, a format that had been shunned by most candidates in previous elections.

The laws regulating how candidates for federal offices raise money have changed over time. In the nineteenth century, people and businesses could give unlimited amounts of money directly to political candidates. In the election of 1896, Mark Hanna, a Republican Party leader, asked banks to contribute a proportion of their capital to William McKinley's election campaign. In 1907, the Tillman Act was passed, which limited corporate contributions to federal candidates. Eventually unions and utilities were also prohibited from making political contributions. These laws were not strictly enforced and contained many loopholes. In 1971, Congress passed the Federal Election Campaign Act. While this legislation has some loopholes that allow wealthy individuals, corporations, and unions to spend millions of dollars in support of political candidates, it has forced federal candidates to solicit money from a multitude of people and political action committees in relatively small amounts. No longer can a candidate seeking a party's presidential nomination solicit unlimited contributions from wealthy individuals.

Bibliography

Alexander, Herbert E. *Financing Politics: Money, Elections, and Political Reform.* 4th ed. Washington, D.C.: Congressional Quarterly Press, 1992. Recounts the history of campaign finance law; excellent discussion of independent expenditures and soft money. Although most of the book focuses on federal laws, one chapter is devoted to state and local campaign financing.

Drew, Elizabeth. *Politics and Money: The New Road to Corruption.* New York: Macmillan, 1983. Although somewhat dated, this is still the best book on campaign finance. It is filled with quotes from political insiders that reveal the role political action committees play in raising money for political candidates.

Germond, Jack W., and Jules Witcover. *Whose Broad Stripes and Bright Stars: The Trivial Pursuit of the Presidency 1988.* New York: Warner Books, 1989. Highly readable account of the presidential nomination and general election campaigns of Michael Dukakis and George Bush in 1988. The inclusion of numerous quotes from those most closely involved in the campaigns captures the sense of drama and excitement surrounding presidential campaigns.

McCubbins, Mathew D., ed. *Under the Watchful Eye: Managing Presidential Campaigns in the Television Era.* San Diego, Calif.: Congressional Quarterly Press, 1992. Includes five articles about presidential campaigns. The role of political parties, paid advertising, and the press in campaigns is discussed.

Salmore, Stephen A., and Barbara G. Salmore. *Candidates, Parties, and Campaigns: Electoral Politics in America.* 2d rev. ed. Washington, D.C.: Congressional Quarterly Press, 1989. Describes how campaigns have changed over time as political party organizations' role in elections has declined. Good discussion of how campaign strategies are influenced by the type of office being sought and whether or not the candidate is an incumbent or a challenger.

Sorauf, Frank J. *Inside Campaign Finance.* New Haven, Conn.: Yale University Press, 1992. Good discussion of the sources of campaign contributions and various proposals for reform.

Wayne, Steven J. *The Road to the White House 1992: The Politics of Presidential Elections.* 4th ed. New York: St. Martin's Press, 1992. Excellent discussion of the presidential nomination process and candidates' campaign organizations, strategies, and tactics.

Paul Bradford Raymond

Cross-References

The Democratic Party, p. 520; Elections, p. 578; Grassroots Politics, p. 797; The Media and Elections, p. 1161; Nomination Processes, p. 1312; Political Action Committees, p. 1420; Political Campaigns in U.S. History, p. 1434; Political Party Conventions, p. 1492; Presidential Elections in the United States, p. 1596; Primary Elections, p. 1603; The Republican Party, p. 1699; Voting Behavior in the United States, p. 2109.

POLITICAL CAMPAIGNS IN U.S. HISTORY

Field of study: Politics

Under a democratic system, political campaigns are designed to convince a majority of the voters to cast their ballots in favor of a particular candidate, or to approve certain policies or programs. In Western democracies, especially in the United States, political parties have traditionally played key roles in election campaigns.

Principal terms

CAUCUS: meeting of key political party leaders, usually to decide party policy or select a candidate

CONVENTION: gathering of delegates representing members of a political party, who adopt a party platform and nominate candidates for office

DIRTY TRICKS: unethical or illegal activities designed to embarrass, discredit, and defeat political opponents

GENERAL ELECTION: election during which all registered voters have the opportunity to cast ballots for candidates

NEGATIVE CAMPAIGNING: attacks on real or imagined flaws in an opponent, often using slurs and innuendo

PARLIAMENTARY SYSTEM: political system in which voters select members of a legislative body; the majority party in that body then chooses the executive branch of government, usually known as the cabinet

PRIMARY ELECTION: election during which the members of a political party cast their ballot for the candidates they wish to represent the party in the general election

STUMP SPEECH: direct address by a candidate to voters, often repeated with minor variations throughout a campaign

Overview

In the United States, as in most Western democracies, elections can be either direct or indirect. During a direct election, the voters themselves vote for the candidates of their choice and the one with a majority of votes (in some cases a plurality) is elected to office. When the election is indirect, representatives of the voters, such as the electoral college, cast the votes to fill a public position. While political campaigning is more overtly associated with direct elections, it exists in indirect elections as well.

American political campaigns began well before the United States was established. Colonial governments generally had a royal governor, appointed by the British monarch, and assemblies whose members were elected by the eligible voters, white males who owned a sufficient amount of property. Through the American Revolution, and during the early years of the republic, these campaigns were, by modern standards, low-key affairs. The number of voters was relatively low, often a homogenous group, and often well acquainted, as was the case in Massachusetts and Virginia. The exceptions were in states with a significant division between the coastal areas and the upcountry, such as in South Carolina. In either case, the prevailing fear of factions, as political parties were known, helped restrain the public vigor with which campaigns were waged.

This changed following the presidency of George Washington, as Federalists, those associated with men such as Alexander Hamilton and John Adams, vied with the Republicans (later called Democrats), those associated with leaders such as Thomas Jefferson and James Madison. In 1800, the nation saw its first contested presidential election, and this national division was replicated at the state and local levels.

Although a residue of restraint remained, and candidates were discouraged from taking too active a public role, the growth of political parties and the westward expansion of the nation inevitably changed the way in which campaigns were conceived, organized, and run. By the time of Andrew Jackson, popular democracy had created a situation where active campaigning was required. This was clearly demonstrated in the 1840 election, when the Whigs, successors of the Federalists, defeated the incumbent Martin Van Buren through a well-organized and active campaign.

The Whig campaign included many now-familiar trappings of U.S. elections, including rallies, parades, symbols—such as the log cabin where Whig candidate William Henry Harrison had supposedly been born—theme songs, political cartoons, campaign literature, and stump speeches. Lapel badges and ribbons, which later evolved into campaign buttons, and posters and other visible signs of support were also in place. Although modified by technological progress and adapted to particular elections, these techniques remained basically unchanged until the advent of the electronic media.

During this period, the three methods of choosing party candidates in the United States were developed: the caucus, the convention, and primaries. In a caucus, a relatively small but influential group of party leaders determines which of the available candidates best represents the party's platform and has the greatest chance of winning, though not necessarily in that order of importance. The caucus was the dominant form of nominating candidates during the early period of U.S. political campaigns; in the 1830's and 1840's, it was replaced by the convention.

Delegates at a party convention, whether local, state or national, were free, in theory, to nominate any person they desired. In practice, however, delegates were soon pledged to a particular candidate, sometimes indefinitely and sometimes only for a specific number of ballots. At national conventions, governors or senators who wished to play the role of power broker could have themselves nominated as a "favorite son" of their state, in order to hold their delegates as a bloc vote that could serve as a bargaining point during the convention. From time to time, however, conventions would be swayed by emotion or a charismatic figure, as happened with the Democratic convention in 1892, when William Jennings Bryan made his famous "Cross of Gold" speech in support of free silver. Bryan was converted instantly from an almost unknown Nebraska congressman to presidential nominee.

After the progressive reform movement of the early 1900's, popular primaries became key factors in political campaigns. In these preliminary elections, members of a political party can express directly their choice for the party's nominee. Because the primary is such an important step in the electoral process, it has become a full-fledged part of the campaign, and candidates devote much of their time, energy, and funds to the efforts. This is especially true in presidential primaries, which have become much more powerful than the actual convention in selecting a party's nominee.

Caucus, convention, and primary all rely on the existence of an organized political party, and the chief characteristic of political campaigns in the United States until the 1890's was the dominant role played by the party. Candidates were clearly secondary to the party machinery, whose discipline and loyalty assured massive turnout of the votes on election day. In 1840, for example, more than 80 percent of the eligible voters cast a ballot in the presidential contests. In state races, the numbers could be even higher, such as the 88 percent who voted in Mississippi that year, or the 92 percent who went to the polls in New York. Most of this was attributable to the well-organized and well-directed party efforts.

A second and enduring characteristic that emerged during this time was the relative roles played by the major parties. The Democratic Party was distributed nationally but found its greatest strength in the South, in urban areas, among the middle and lower classes, and, especially after the 1830's, among immigrants. Consequently, Democratic campaigns on all levels were often geared towards populist economic issues that were of key concern to the party's constituency. By contrast, first the Whigs and later the Republicans were strongest in the Northeast and Midwest and among big business and the wealthy. Whig and Republican candidates and their platforms naturally advocated policies that favored these supporters. After the Civil War, the Republicans incorporated a strong appeal to patriotism in their party's campaigns and often tried to smear their Democratic rivals with the taint of treason.

Although many methods of campaigning were employed, debates and stump speeches were the most used. In debates, rival candidates discussed the issues of the election before crowds or audiences of voters, sometimes speaking for hours as they exchanged thrusts and responses. The Lincoln-Douglas debates of 1858, which propelled Lincoln into national prominence, were an example of this. Stump speeches, in which the candidate or his surrogate addressed the crowd, were also a key means of reaching voters, especially in state and local contests. During a time when politics seemed woven into the very fabric of everyday life, this close, almost intimate contact between electorate and candidate was an integral fact of political campaigns.

This relationship weakened following the Civil War. The tremendous growth of the nation, along with developments in technology, made it more difficult to approach voters individually, while making it easier to communicate with them en masse. At the same time, the two major parties were undergoing a gradual but telling weakening of their power, caused by several factors, including public disgust over the endemic corruption of the post-Civil War Republican administrations; a growing distrust in the traditional party machinery; and an increase in education and sophistication among the voters. These trends culminated during the 1892 presidential race between Grover Cleveland and Benjamin Harrison when, for the first time in decades, the nominees overshadowed their parties and became the prime focus of voters.

The election of 1892 has been cited by historians as the first modern political campaign, during which professionally produced literature, public relations, and advertising, and intense use of transportation, especially railroads, were in wide use. These techniques, which remained dominant until the advent of the electronic media, were employed on state and local levels as well. While they did not fully replace the traditional stump speech, they made it possible for candidates to reach more voters in a more effective and efficient fashion. At the same time, however, they further weakened the role of the political parties, since they reinforced the role of the candidate as an individual, rather than merely the representative of the party.

Another major shift occurred in 1932, when Franklin Delano Roosevelt, the Democratic nominee, began to put together what is known as the "New Deal coalition," an alliance of interest groups such as organized labor, farmers, the urban middle and lower classes, and, later, African Americans. This coalition forced Democratic campaigns to be more inclusive, appealing to a variety of constituencies. Roosevelt, one of the nation's most masterful politicians, helped bind this coalition together through the power of his personality and, using the mass media, especially radio, sought to arouse support for his programs and policies among the general public.

It was left to the electronic media to complete the transformation of American political campaigns. By the 1960 election, there were enough television sets in the United States that seventy million viewers were able to watch the famous Kennedy-Nixon debates. Conventional political wisdom holds that John F. Kennedy's performance in these events, especially his poise and coolness when compared to Vice President Richard Nixon, was a pivotal factor in the extremely close election. Since then there have been debates between presidential contenders, and on the state level, but political campaigns have mainly used the electronic media in a different fashion—by producing their own messages and purchasing time for them.

By the 1964 election, thirty- and sixty-second television commercials were a familiar staple of elections. By the 1980's, candidates on every level recognized the need to present their message on television. Expensive to produce and place, these commercials forced up the costs of running a campaign, and soon it was common for even statewide races to cost hundreds of thousands of dollars.

In the 1990's, political campaigns in the United States retained all the essential elements that were present in the beginning: a two-party system that stressed discipline and organization; candidates who were obliged to present their message in a clear, compelling fashion to the electorate; and the voters, whose decisions were made amid a background of competing voices and messages.

Applications

Whether on the local, state, or national level, American political campaigns share many features, and differences are mainly of degree, rather than kind. For example, the techniques and methods now commonplace in national presidential elections came to the state level in Texas as early as 1948 in the intense primary battle for the Democratic nomination to the Senate between Representative Lyndon Johnson and well-respected former governor Coke Stevenson. Running an uphill campaign, Johnson used modern transportation such as a helicopter; dramatically increased his radio advertisements and print material; and, at the same time, utilized the old-fashioned politics of stump speeches and personal appearances. Under what some observers called questionable circumstances (including, possibly, outright fraud at the polls), Johnson won the Democratic primary by fewer than a hundred votes, earning him the nickname "Landslide Lyndon." He easily won the general election and went on to become a powerful Senator and eventually President.

An unfortunate role is played in American political campaigns by "dirty tricks," unethical and sometimes illegal activities that are aimed at derailing an opponent's strategy. The 1972 burglary of Democratic National Headquarters in the Watergate Hotel by operatives of the Committee to Re-Elect the President (known as CREEP), was one of the most infamous dirty tricks of modern politics. It eventually led to the resignation of President Richard Nixon.

An even more unfortunate and increasingly prevalent technique is that of "negative campaigning," which uses distortions, innuendoes, and sometimes lies against an opponent. A notable example of this tactic came in the 1988 presidential race, when Republican strategists attacked Democratic contender Michael Dukakis on several fronts. First, the Republicans noted that Dukakis had opposed making the Pledge of Allegiance mandatory for students; this, Republicans implied, was tantamount to being un-American. Candidate George Bush even staged visits to flag factories to underscore his patriotism. Next, nominee Bush described Dukakis as "a card-carrying member of the ACLU [American Civil Liberties Union]," raising memories of the Red scares of the 1950's, when persons were branded as being card-carrying members of the Communist Party. Again, the connection of Dukakis with unpatriotic activities was clear, if unspoken.

Finally, the Republican campaign portrayed Dukakis as soft on crime, and played upon lingering tinges of racism. Willie Horton, an inmate who had fled a state-sponsored prison furlough program in Massachusetts, later committed murder and rape in Maryland. Television ads suggested Dukakis was personally responsible for the furlough, and a photograph of Horton, heavily bearded and obviously African American, was central to the ads. Although many commentators denounced the ads, they were a key part of the strategy that resulted in George Bush's election as president in 1988.

Context

American political campaigns are often viewed as contests between individual candidates, with a clear winner and loser. This is especially true in statewide or national elections, and it has become common for a defeated presidential candidate to face the end of a political career. This is not necessarily the case in many other democratic societies, especially those with parliamentary government.

An example is Great Britain, where the actual head of government, the prime minister, is not selected directly by the voters, but by the majority party in the British Parliament. The leader of the majority party is asked by the monarch to form a government, which is composed of members of Parliament, who continue to take part in the ongoing debates and votes of that body. By contrast, members of the president's cabinet in the United States cannot be members of Congress.

Elections occur at regular intervals in the United States, and hopeful candidates begin preparation and even campaigning months or years before election day. By contrast, while the British Parliament can be in session for no longer than five years, elections can be held sooner if there is a vote of no confidence in the government or if the prime minister calls for an election—often when the government in power enjoys substantial public popularity. Because of this, British political campaigns are much briefer than those in the United States, lasting a matter of weeks rather than months. Furthermore, since a party rather than personal victory is essential for control of the government, British parties such as Labour, the Conservatives, or the Social Democrats traditionally have maintained tighter discipline than their counterparts in the United States.

In other parliamentary democracies, such as France or Italy, the multiplicity of parties makes stability difficult and elections frequent. In such cases, where parties tend to become doctrinaire and rigid, unlike the more pragmatic and flexible Republicans and Democrats in the United States, political campaigns often fail to resolve issues more than momentarily.

By contrast with other nations, political campaigns in the United States, while they may appear to be confused, chaotic, and even destructive, have proven to be a way of bringing stability and direction to the process of government from the local to the national level.

Bibliography

Archer, Jules. *Winners and Losers: How Elections Work in America*. San Diego, Calif.: Harcourt Brace Jovanovich, 1984. Introductory primer to the U.S. political process that provides concise, easily understood information on such topics as how the system works and what it takes to be a candidate.

Kelly, Kate. *Election Day: an American Holiday, an American History*. New York: Facts on File, 1991. Popular history of how Americans have voted and reported the results since colonial times. Excellent source for charting the changes in the electoral system over the centuries and how those changes have impacted political campaigns.

Kleppner, Paul, et al. *The Evolution of American Electoral Systems*. Westport, Conn.: Greenwood Press, 1981. This collection of essays, part of the *Contributions in*

American History series, is especially useful for its study of political parties and their roles in campaigns.

Mitchell, Jack. *How to Get Elected*. New York: St. Martin's Press, 1992. Informally subtitled "An anecdotal history of mudslinging, red-baiting, vote-stealing, and dirty tricks in American politics," this slim but fact-filled volume offers an often amusing, sometimes appalling, view of the less seemly side of political campaigns.

O'Neill, Tip, with Gary Hymel. *All Politics Is Local*. New York: Times Books, 1994. In this brief but engaging book, Tip O'Neill, a congressman from 1952 to 1986, and Speaker of the House for ten years, gives the practical rules of political campaigns, from approaching the average voter to raising campaign funds. Indispensable book for those who want to learn how U.S. political campaigns really work.

Silbey, Joel, et al, eds. *The History of American Electoral Behavior*. Princeton, N.J.: Princeton University Press, 1978. Essays that explores the interrelated phenomenon of candidates, parties, voters, and the campaign process. Contains several good studies of urban political machines and their impact on election campaigns.

Michael Witkoski

Cross-References

Elections, p. 578; The Media and Elections, p. 1161; The New Right, p. 1293; Nomination Processes, p. 1312; Political Action Committees, p. 1420; Political Campaigning, Planning, and Financing, p. 1427; Political Participation, p. 1479; Political Parties, p. 1485; Political Party Conventions, p. 1492; Political Platforms, p. 1512; Presidential Elections in the United States, p. 1596; Primary Elections, p. 1603; Two-Party Systems, p. 2033.

POLITICAL CORRECTNESS

Field of study: Civil rights and liberties

An ideologically charged concept, political correctness involves issues of civility, free speech, and censorship. Although attempts to apply the concept can highlight certain limitations of political and social discourse, particularly in academic settings, the concept is often used in ways that are misleading and manipulative.

Principal terms

CENSORSHIP: suppression of the publication or public expression of ideas regarded as objectionable

CIVIL RIGHTS ACTIVIST: advocate of aggressive policies designed to advance racial and sexual equality in the United States

CONSERVATIVE: in the most general sense, one who accepts the status quo; conservatives are among the strongest critics of political correctness concepts

FEMINIST: advocate of recognition of women's rights and related issues

FREE SPEECH: unrestricted expression—a First Amendment right in the United States that many observers believe is threatened by political correctness advocates

LIBERAL: in the context of political correctness, one who advocates correcting stereotyping or biases directed against disadvantaged groups

MULTICULTURALISM: movement that promotes teaching subjects in their broadest cultural and global perspectives in order to enhance students' appreciation of human diversity

RIGHT-WINGER: extreme conservative

Overview

The term "politically correct," or "PC," came into vogue in the United States during the late 1980's. In its most basic form, it refers to certain attitudes and manners of speech or expression thought to be polite, acceptable, and correct—according to certain liberal, or left-of-center, orthodoxies. The reverse meaning of the concept is applied to attitudes and forms of expression that these same orthodoxies consider to be unacceptable or "incorrect." Incorrect attitudes are subject to various kinds of administrative, social, and other group pressures, including censorship. The concept of political correctness serves as the nucleus of a body of criticism aimed at liberal or left-wing causes, groups, and strategies. Such criticism often takes the form of satire or sarcasm, but it has a serious theme, the threat to the First Amendment right of free speech. Criticism of political correctness also sometimes comes from within the ranks of liberalism itself. In such cases, political correctness might be understood as a form of political self-criticism.

The objects of political correctness criticism have become numerous. At the outset, however, there were two main targets: feminists and civil rights activists. These remain the primary targets of political correctness criticism.

Critics of political correctness allege that it has become unreasonably difficult candidly to express honest opinions or to question values and policies concerning racial and sexual equality in the United States. Hardline advocates of political correctness reject outright the validity of open debate about certain racial questions, such as the justness of affirmative action policies, the extent to which African Americans themselves are responsible for continuing racial inequalities, possible connections between race and intelligence, and the merits of prominent African Americans such as Jesse Jackson. Extreme political correctness tenets deny any hint of racial inferiority and raise accusations of bias when members of minority groups are criticized. Associated with these issues is hostility expressed toward noncon-forming black conservatives by many mainstream African American intellectuals and commentators.

Critics of political correctness charge that feminists are guilty of severely limiting permissible expression within academia. Examples include feminist advocacy of constricting the parameters of discussion about abortion, family values, and sexual liberation. At an extreme, feminists have been accused of being humorless, tyrannical "femi-nazis," a term popularized by radio and television personality Rush Limbaugh. Such intentionally provocative language exemplifies how the case against political correctness can be subjected to exaggeration and rhetorical flourishes that are meant to score points with impressionable audiences. This seems to be particularly true when the targets are feminists.

Both racial justice advocates and feminists are among groups accused of censoring free speech on college campuses by fostering overly narrow (or vague) campus guidelines restricting expression deemed to be hateful or even insensitive toward women and members of various minorities. Gay and lesbian groups are also often cited in this last regard by critics of political correctness. Political correctness is likely to brand as "homophobic" anyone who questions the amount of civil rights protection that should be afforded homosexuals, the appropriateness of teaching tolerance of homosexuality in schools, and other related issues.

The concept of political correctness has been expanded to cover many disadvan-taged groups, including handicapped persons, Jews, Latinos, and Native Americans, as well as issues such as environmentalism, animal rights, welfare, homelessness, and multiculturalism. This last issue in particular has become a central target for critics of political correctness. Such critics believe that the emphasis on diversity constitutes a dogmatic and inappropriate devaluation of American (and Western) culture that fosters fragmentation within American society over consensus and cohesion.

What most political correctness concerns have in common is that they represent a liberal or left-wing desire either to bring relief to oppressed groups within American society or to expand American consciousness beyond narrow nationalist or chauvinist parameters. They are associated with a negative view of traditional American eco-nomic, social, and political institutions. Occasionally, this negative view extends even to American ideals and basic values. Critics of political correctness usually argue that these negative assessments lack validity, and they sometimes assign blame for the shortcomings of American society to liberals or even to advocacy of political correctness itself. They argue that political correctness's negative portrayal of traditional American culture, society, and politics has been promoted to such a degree that political correctness is itself one of society's primary oppressors. More specifically, political correctness is said to comprise a new orthodoxy severely limiting fruitful discourse and threatening basic freedom of expression.

The debate over political correctness is politically charged and often polemical in nature. Critics of political correctness are typically concerned not only with the excesses but also with the basic causes of political correctness advocates. They wish to use criticism of political correctness to discredit liberalism and various causes under that umbrella category and to weaken the identification of liberalism with greater regard for maximizing freedom and alleviating oppression. They seek to show liberals and related groups as the real oppressors and the real threats to free thinking and free speech.

There are at least two other categories of political correctness critics: those who sympathize with liberal causes but believe that fostering orthodoxy is not the right way to proceed, and those who regard political correctness primarily as an object of humor, expanding the concept to absurdity in order to exploit its entertainment value. Some critics of political correctness are sympathetic to liberal causes but believe that transforming liberal beliefs into a rigidly enforced orthodoxy will ultimately be counterproductive. Unlike their counterparts on the Right, these critics admit that political correctness is appealing in a world in which prejudice, inequality, and various forms of domination by powerful classes and groups remain largely unalleviated. They also emphasize the fact that political repression has been used at least as often by conservatives and right-wingers as by the liberal Left. Their point is that liberals lose credibility when they appear to be as repressive as their political opponents and that, in the long run, only unhampered free expression will contribute to the emergence of truth and justice. These critics also make it clear that they do not see political correctness as the primary problem facing American society. Rather, they see it as an undesirable product of the struggle for genuine liberation and enhanced social justice.

The interests of some critics of political correctness lie more in the field of entertainment than in politics. These observers have produced an abundance of satire on the issue, the effect of which has been to associate the concept of political correctness to trivial issues. Supposedly politically correct terms have, for example, been created for baldness ("follicle impairment") and shortness ("vertically challenged"). Although this sort of satire seems irrelevant (and quickly grows tedious), it has roots in some of the rhetorical gymnastics of political correctness in its quest to formulate nonoffensive and nondiscriminatory terms for conditions that are often objects of disdain and bias in American society.

There is no agreement on the extent to which political correctness thinking permeates American society or on its consequences. Although many critics chide academia for giving in to political correctness, there is also no evidence that colleges and universities actively exclude views regarded as politically incorrect any more than they exclude various left-wing or other unconventional views that have little to do with political correctness. In reality, the academic world presents a variety of prejudices depending on the educational institutions, individual departments, or even geographic locations. The mass media appear to have some prejudices linked to political correctness (for example, one against fundamentalism and perhaps even religion in general), but politically incorrect commentary and humor abounds on television and radio as well as in various print media. Broadcast news programs often convey negative images of minorities and radical feminists, among others.

There is no clear agreement that political correctness is a problem in or benefit to society. Some advocates of political correctness argue that some censorship measures are necessary to ensure civility and equal opportunity. They argue that the alternatives are not between censorship and freedom but rather between a benign and relatively open-minded left-wing political correctness vision or a right-wing orthodoxy that would be far more repressive, if perhaps more subtle, in matters relating to free speech and even freedom of religion.

Some analysts, whether or not they are critical of political correctness, believe that a perfectly free market of ideas never exists. They believe that real freedom of thought is won in opposition to various dogmatically held ideological barriers. For these observers, political correctness is simply standard operating procedure for human discourse even at its best.

Applications

The concept of political correctness has numerous applications but is probably most vitally connected to the institutions that see themselves as bastions of free discourse—educational institutions and mass media.

In education, political correctness allegedly has affected the public school curriculum, branding certain controversial topics as taboo and promoting certain slants on information about topics such as American history and culture. Grade school textbooks especially have been adapted for political correctness. In higher education, political correctness has been accused of limiting the academic freedom of faculty members, affecting hiring practices in ways that discriminate against scholars with politically incorrect views, and adversely inhibiting the spirit of free inquiry (and funding) necessary in honest scholarly research. On both levels, students are said to be hampered by undue restraints on classroom discussions and on free expression in extracurricular activities.

The mass media, particularly at the national level, are often accused of being biased in favor of political correctness. This is an extension of an older claim that the mass media have a liberal bias leading to prejudice against religion, big business, and conservative right-wingers. On the other hand, people who work in mass media tend to see themselves as objective. Some have disapprovingly noted demands made upon them in the name of political correctness. People in the entertainment industry who see themselves as advocates of free expression have also been accused of supporting political correctness. One example involving both news media and entertainment is that of political cartoonists. They have been especially interested in raising the issue of how political correctness affects their art because they see theirs as a form of expression that is by its special nature offensive.

In Canada, research on crime allegedly has been hampered by the prohibition placed on noting the race of lawbreakers. Business has seen the emergence of a new specialty: diversity management, which aims to foster "correct" racial, ethnic, and gender mixes in the workplace. In the field of environmentalism, political correctness is seen by some as fostering an imbalance of priorities in which legitimate economic development needs are slighted in favor of advocacy for the environment.

Some critics of political correctness see it as creating an overall atmosphere of self-censorship that threatens not only academia and mass media but also the entire American society, including the workplace. According to these observers, political correctness threatens the extinction of spontaneity, candor, free expression, and even free thought.

Context

The debate over political correctness is part of a larger debate between the Left and Right in American politics. Some of the issues of contention can be traced back to the 1930's, when Franklin D. Roosevelt's New Deal programs were implemented in response to the Great Depression. Debates concerned such issues as whether the unemployed should receive aid and whether they or impersonal big business were to blame for their plight. The great bulk of political correctness debate and the often harsh passions that accompany it come directly from the political tumult of the mid- to late 1960's. At this point, American institutions were subjected to radical criticism aimed primarily, but not entirely, at the war in Vietnam (and the international U.S. role), poverty, and other forms of inequality, especially those linked to race and gender discrimination. These challenges to the national self-image were met almost immediately by a vigorous backlash from traditionalists and reactionaries who saw critics from the Left as unpatriotic and even un-American.

Although the majority of Americans remained centrist (or moderate) through the late twentieth century and were suspicious of extremists, the Right and the Left continued to be driving forces in American politics, with the Right finding a home of sorts in the Republican Party and the Left doing the same in the Democratic Party. The Right attempted to roll back many liberal programs and policies from the 1960's and early 1970's while the Left attempted to defend its gains. In addition, each group battled to sell its overall vision of what American society and government should be to mainstream Americans. The political correctness debate became part of this ongoing rhetorical struggle.

The future for this war of words seemed grim. On the bright side, some politicians and intellectuals attempted to synthesize what is valuable in both liberalism and conservatism into a strategy for solving difficult public policy questions as well as healing the wounds of the 1960's. On the other hand, the accusatory rhetoric of the political correctness debate, with charges such as racism, sexism, and a lack of patriotism being hurled, continued to flourish. The potential consequences of the political correctness debate remained open to question. Although it could be seen as a legitimate and perhaps even fruitful form of conflict, it also inflamed passions that may become politically unmanageable, leading to further fragmentation and perhaps even to civil disorder.

Bibliography

Beard, Henry, and Christopher Cerf. *The Official Politically Correct Dictionary and Handbook.* New York: Villard Books, 1992. Although a work of humor, this book illustrates the broad range of issues to which the concept of political correctness can apply. It also illustrates one of the central issues for critics of political correctness: the substitution of fuzzy, equivocating language for that which is clear and to the point.

Henry, William. *In Defense of Elitism.* New York: Doubleday, 1994. Henry, a culture critic for *Time* magazine before his death in 1994, takes on egalitarianism, multiculturalism, affirmative action, and radical feminists in this elegantly written diatribe against political correctness. Although Henry recognizes the legitimate concerns underlying political correctness, he often opts for bombastic rhetoric, sacrificing precision for impact and quoting opponents out of context.

Hentoff, Nat. *Free Speech for Me—But Not for Thee: How the American Left and Right Relentlessly Censor Each Other.* New York: HarperCollins, 1992. Hentoff's book is especially valuable because it can be seen as self-criticism from the Left by a civil libertarian with impeccable counterculture credentials. Hentoff clearly sympathizes with the concerns of African Americans, Jews, feminists, homosexuals, and other historically oppressed groups tempted to employ censorship in the name of social justice or civility, but thinks that freedom of speech is too important to be subordinated to even the most worthy causes.

Kimball, Roger. "From Farce to Tragedy." *Partisan Review* 60 (Fall, 1993): 564-569. Part of a series of articles on political correctness (related articles appear in the same issue). Kimball argues that the rapid expansion of political correctness throughout American society has transformed the political correctness problem from farce to tragedy.

Platt, Steve, Walt McDougall, Graeame Keyes, and Signe Wilkinson. "The Right to Be Offensive." *New Statesman and Society*, March 18, 1994, 25-40. Concerns the special challenge of political correctness to editorial cartoonists, who often see their willingness to offend readers as a measure of their professional integrity and effectiveness.

Rawson, Claude. "PC, the Rancid Right, and Universities." *Sewanee Review* 102 (Spring, 1994): 270-285. Discusses the dangers of political correctness in academia, warning that scholars and teachers may be judged by their opinions rather than their abilities.

Wrong, Dennis. "PR on PC." *Dissent* 41 (Spring, 1994): 275-277. In a reply to the *Partisan Review* articles noted above, Wrong concludes that the articles overestimate the problem of political correctness and serve no significant constructive purpose.

Ira Smolensky

Cross-References

Activist Politics, p. 7; Civil Rights and Liberties, p. 298; Conservatism, p. 419; Feminist Politics, p. 682; Gay and Lesbian Politics, p. 732; Gender Politics, p. 738; Interest Groups, p. 936; The Left and the Right, p. 1079; Liberalism, p. 1118; Neo-Conservatism, p. 1281; The New Right, p. 1293; Postmodernism, p. 1570; Protest Movements, p. 1621; Race and Ethnicity, p. 1654; Radicalism, p. 1661.

POLITICAL CRIMES

Field of study: Civil rights and liberties

Political crime is any criminal activity that is committed for ideological purposes. Political criminals believe they are following a higher law that transcends present society and its laws. Political offenses include crimes by government as well as crimes against government.

Principal terms

CRIMES AGAINST GOVERNMENT: violations of law, ranging from protest and civil disobedience to terrorism, performed in response to an ideological commitment

CRIMES BY GOVERNMENT: violations of human rights, civil liberties, and constitutional privileges; also, illegal behavior that occurs in the process of enforcing the law or maintaining the status quo

ESPIONAGE: stealing of secrets

IDEOLOGY: distinctive belief system or strongly held, abstract ideals

RAISON D'ETAT (REASON OF STATE): belief that some violations of the law by state officials are necessary for the public good; attributed to political philosopher Niccolò Machiavelli

TERRORISM: unlawful use of force or violence against persons or property to intimidate or coerce a government or its people in furtherance of political or social objectives

Overview

Political crime is defined as illegal or immoral actions that are committed for ideological purposes. There are two forms of political crime: crime by government and crime against government. Political crime by government has a specific meaning that excludes ordinary political corruption and bribery, which are generally motivated by greed rather than by conviction to a cause. Crimes by government include violations by secret police, abuses of human rights and constitutional privileges, and genocide, as well as crimes committed by government officials in the act of enforcing the law. Crimes against government range from protests, illegal demonstrations, and strikes, to espionage, political whistle-blowing, political assassination, and terrorism.

All governments have laws forbidding activities that threaten the state. The Anglo-American legal tradition does not give special recognition to political crime as such, but deals with such activities under more traditional, nonpolitical laws. The Nuremberg principle was established by the victorious Allies at the end of World War II in condemning Nazi war criminals. It set the precedent that individuals faced with the dilemma of either obeying orders that involved war crimes or crimes against humanity, or following their moral consciences, should disobey unjust dictates. The defense of "following orders" was deemed unacceptable. Similar documents in the Western political tradition, as well as the United Nations's Universal Declaration of Human Rights (1948), provide customs and standards for international conduct. This includes respecting the integrity of basic human needs and civil liberties. Despite the intentions of these documents, international law has been handicapped by the lack of a consensual world community and by inadequate powers of enforcement.

Since states seldom choose to label or prosecute their actions as criminal, crime by government is more a sociological than a legal entity. Secret police are units of the state's internal security police that have as their mission the suppression of serious or threatening political opposition and the control of political activity. The activities of secret police may include illegal surveillance, searches, detention, and violations of human rights. Political prisoners include those who have seriously threatened the existing government, and also prisoners of conscience who are sent into exile, tortured, or murdered. Amnesty International, an organization that locates and defends political prisoners, finds totalitarian regimes to be the worst offenders. Genocide, the mass destruction or annihilation of human populations, is the ultimate violent crime by government. In 1948, the U.N. Convention on Genocide defined it as a crime, but the United Nations has been less than vigilant in condemning such activity. Political crime by the police includes violation of due process, freedom of speech, invasion of privacy, and other offenses against the constitutional rights of the individual. These activities are often committed in the name of preserving law and order and attempting to protect the existing political system.

Additional abuses by government agents include illegal surveillance and undermining and disrupting legitimate democratic processes. This may entail character assassination (damaging a person's reputation by spreading vicious lies) as well as secret experiments on unsuspecting subjects. During the Cold War, United States government agencies covertly exposed civilians and their own military personnel to harmful nuclear, chemical, and biological experiments, and conducted drug and mind-control experiments without the informed consent of the subjects.

Crimes against government involve activities such as protest and dissent in opposition to the status quo, as well as reactionary resistance to recent changes that may have taken place in the existing order. Dissident activities in opposition to the existing system is represented by the civil rights, antiwar, and labor movements of the past, while reactionary forces can be found in right-wing "death squads," the Ku Klux Klan, and the American Nazi Party. Social movements advocate change in the current system and often conflict with responding authorities. Martin Luther King, Jr., and the Civil Rights movement utilized civil disobedience, a strategy of violating unjust laws through passive nonviolent resistance. Other such movements include the pro-life, pro-choice, antinuclear, and animal rights groups.

Political espionage involves stealing state secrets and is a common international practice of intelligence agencies. While spies in the late twentieth century have often been motivated by financial gain, many spies have been ideologically oriented, such as communists Julius and Ethel Rosenberg, who altered post-World War II history by giving United States atomic secrets to the Soviets. The betrayal of one's country out of commitment to either a political ideology or a foreign state constitutes the crime of treason, which is the only crime specifically mentioned in the United States Constitution. Political whistle-blowers are those who violate state secrecy laws to expose situations or activities that they believe the public has a right to know about.

Terrorism is the use of violence and cruelty as a means to spread fear within a civilian population in order to gain political power or support for a cause. While much terrorism involves offenses against the state, official or state terrorism involves offenses by state officials and agents as a means of obtaining power. A new form of terrorism was begun in Algeria in the late 1950's by the National Liberation Front, which popularized the random attack on civilians. Indiscriminate terror became more widespread with the invention of more effective explosives and modern mass media coverage. Terrorist groups are often small in membership and rely on mass media coverage of their "propaganda by deed" in order to attract attention to their cause. Incidents of international terrorism, particularly with U.S. citizens as targets, decreased with the end of the Cold War, and terrorism inside the United States remained at a relatively low level. The 1993 bomb attack on the World Trade Center in New York City by Islamic fundamentalists, while dramatic, was atypical.

Applications

Persons who commit political crimes in service of their government generally are motivated less by self-interest than by a conviction that they are defending the status quo or the existing system. Secret police are often involved in illegal surveillance, searches, detention, or arrest; as a matter of practice, they may violate human rights. Some governments encourage their agents to commit crime. Infamous secret police such as Adolf Hitler's Gestapo, Stalin's Unified State Political Administration (UGPU), and Haiti's Tonton Macoutes used midnight raids, torture, and disappearances as a general method of operation.

International violation of human rights is illustrated by the thousands of political prisoners—persons who have committed no crimes other than their espousal of controversial ideas—who are tortured, murdered, or "disappeared" throughout the world. Amnesty International has reported that authoritarian and totalitarian regimes of the Left and the Right are the least tolerant of dissent and are the major violators. Slavery and child prostitution are still practiced in many countries, despite their prohibition in the U.N. Declaration of Human Rights. Diplomatic and economic relations between countries often take precedence over the suffering of political prisoners and human rights violations.

Genocidal conflicts have a long history, from Roman persecutions of Christians and medieval pogroms against the Jews, to Adolf Hitler's Holocaust and Serbian ethnic cleansing in Bosnia. The latter involves killing, starving, raping, and sending to containment camps members of a target ethnic group in order to resettle the area with members of the offender's group. Despite the 1948 U.N. Convention on Genocide, the United Nations has been inconsistent in condemning such activities.

In democratic societies, governments are expected not only to enforce the law, but also to obey the law and respect the constitutional rights of their citizens in doing so. Prior to the success of the Civil Rights movement, police officials in the southern United States routinely violated federal law, committing murders, lynchings, and beatings in preserving a racist caste system. Other abuses by government officials may include illegal surveillance of citizens, disruption of conventional democratic process, and secret experiments with the public as unknowing subjects. The U.S. Select Committee to Study Government Operations (1979) revealed that the Central Intelligence Agency and Federal Bureau of Investigation had secretly harassed Martin Luther King, Jr., by sending anonymous letters, tapping his telephone, and disrupting his speaking engagements with false fire alarms in an effort to discredit him. Agents provocateurs also were used to infiltrate dissenting groups, radicalizing and discrediting them.

U.S. intelligence agencies and the military in the 1950's and 1960's conducted mind control and interrogation experiments involving extrasensory perception, drugs, polygraphs, hypnosis, shock therapy, surgery, and radiation, often without the permission of unsuspecting subjects.

Crimes against government can be illustrated by various illegal protests, demonstrations, and strikes associated with social movements that advocate change in the existing society. Martin Luther King, Jr., and the Southern Christian Leadership Conference encouraged nonviolent resistance, civil disobedience similar to that employed by Mohandas Gandhi in overcoming British rule in India. By disobeying unjust laws, but willingly accepting the punishment, such protesters hoped to appeal to public conscience and make the public confront the hypocrisy of such laws in democratic societies.

Espionage, the secretive theft of information, has been a practice since early recorded history. While the name Benedict Arnold, who betrayed the American revolutionaries to the British, lives in infamy, the name of Nathan Hale, an American spy executed by the British, is held in high honor in the United States. Ideologically motivated spies are seen as political criminals condemned as traitors in one country, while heralded as heroes in the nation that benefited by their activities. Julius and Ethel Rosenberg were the first and only native-born U.S. citizens to be executed for treason, in March, 1951, for having given U.S. atomic secrets to the Soviet Union. The Rosenbergs were devoted communists, as were the British spies Guy Burgess, Donald Maclean, Kim Philby, and Anthony Blunt. These "establishment spies" were recruited as Cambridge University students in the 1930's and rose to the highest levels as "moles" (deep-cover agents) in British intelligence. After the end of the Cold War, the ideological motivation of spies was replaced for the most part by mercenary motivations.

Political whistle-blowing is illustrated by the case of Daniel Ellsberg, an employee of the Rand Corporation, a private think tank and research organization. He violated his oath of secrecy and revealed a classified study, *The Pentagon Papers*, to the U.S. press. Ellsberg felt that the public's right to be aware that the government had deceived it regarding U.S. involvement in the Vietnam War exceeded his duty to keep government secrets.

Terrorism may be distinguished from tragic incidents of war by the willful and calculated targeting of innocents. Most modern terrorism has been directed against democratic states, with little aimed at more totalitarian countries. Some well-known international terrorist groups of the second half of the twentieth century included Abu Nidal's group, the Basque ETA, Islamic Jihad, the Palestine Liberation Organization, the Provisional Irish Republican Army, and Sikh separatists. Domestic terrorist groups in the United States have included Puerto Rican independence groups, right-wing Ku Klux Klan and neo-Nazi hate groups, and extensions of international groups.

Context

Political criminals view crime as a means of achieving a higher moral goal. They conceive of their behavior as important either in the preservation of society—crime by government—or in bringing about change in society—crime against government. Political criminals operate within subcultures that view their behavior as appropriate. Whether their issue is racial supremacy, preservation of the status quo, terrorist attacks, genocide, or nonviolent civil disobedience, political offenders have the support of their peers and are often convinced of the rightness of their actions.

Political crime's sociological nature can be illustrated by its relativity with respect to time and place. While the Rosenbergs were condemned as traitors in the United States, they were heralded as heroes in the Soviet Union. The slaughter of eleven members of the Israeli Olympic team during the 1972 Munich Olympics was applauded in some areas of the Arab world. Such disagreements in international ideologies explains in part the inability of world bodies such as the United Nations to act in unison in condemning atrocities and terrorism. On the other hand, some former political prisoners live to see victory for their cause. In May, 1994, Nelson Mandela, who had been a political prisoner for nearly three decades, was sworn in as the first African president of South Africa.

Since they threaten the status quo of society, crimes against the government generally receive a strong, negative societal reaction. Reactions to crimes by government usually are milder. This is a result of the belief that since the government makes and enforces the law, it cannot violate the law. In the United States, public opinion in this regard has changed since the events of Watergate. This involved agents in the employ of President Richard Nixon burglarizing the Democratic National Committee Headquarters in the Watergate complex in Washington, D.C. Nixon's coverup and deceit led to his resignation.

The more complex, populous, and interrelated the world community becomes, the more possible it becomes for a small, dedicated minority to threaten the well-being of society using noncombatants as targets. The rapidly changing world order can continue to be expected to generate new demands for change; depending on the response to these demands, new political criminals may emerge, either in the form of overly eager guardians of the society or as agents of change.

Bibliography

Kelman, Herbert C., and V. Lee Hamilton. *Crimes of Obedience: Toward a Social Psychology of Authority and Responsibility.* New Haven, Conn.: Yale University Press, 1989. Beginning with an account of the My Lai Massacre during the Vietnam War, this book describes what takes place when authority gives orders exceeding the bounds of morality or law. Explores issues such as responsibility in authority situations, denial of responsibility, and breaking the habit of unquestioned obedience.

Kittrie, Nicholas N., and Eldon D. Wedlock, Jr., eds. *The Tree of Liberty: A Documentary History of Rebellion and Political Crime in America.* Baltimore: The Johns Hopkins Press, 1986. Excellent collection of more than four hundred primary documents tells the story of dissent, disobedience, violence, and rebellion in the United States. Documents range from King Edward III's Treason Law of 1352 to a 1985 *New York Times* article on the sanctuary movement for Central American refugees.

Laqueur, Walter. *The Age of Terrorism.* Boston: Little, Brown, 1987. First American edition of the definitive historical and contemporary work on terrorism. Discusses myths regarding terrorism, including the false beliefs that terrorism is a new phenomenon, that it is a politically loaded term, that it is always left-wing, and that it takes place when conditions are at their worst.

Proal, Louis. *Political Crime.* Montclair, N.J.: Patterson Smith, 1973. Reprint of the classic 1898 edition. Proal gives groundbreaking accounts of political crime issues including discussions of Machiavellianism, political assassination and tyrannicide, anarchism, political hatreds, and political hypocrisy.

Roebuck, Julian, and Stanley G. Weeber. *Political Crime in the United States: Analyzing Crime by and Against Government.* New York: Praeger, 1978. Informative descriptions and analysis of crimes by government, such as human rights violations, and secret police activities, as well as crimes against the government, such as illegal protests, dissent, and terrorism.

Schafer, Stephen. *The Political Criminal: The Problem of Morality and Crime.* New York: Free Press, 1974. Readable account of criminals who are convinced of the rightness of their actions. The moral relativity of political crime takes place where social changes for the benefit of the people may be forced through violation of the law.

Turk, Austin. *Political Criminality: The Defiance and Defense of Authority.* Beverly Hills, Calif.: Sage Publications, 1982. Interesting discussion of political policing, internal security police who preserve the existing state. This may include assassination, torture of political offenders, human rights violations and agents provocateurs (spies who manipulate groups).

Frank E. Hagan

Cross-References

Autocracy and Absolutism, p. 127; Civil Disobedience, p. 285; Civil Rights and Liberties, p. 298; Civil Unrest and Rioting, p. 317; Despotism and Tyranny, p. 527; Genocide, p. 752; Human Rights and International Politics, p. 848; National Security, p. 1261; Organized Crime and Political Corruption, p. 1355; Police States, p. 1408; Political Ethics, p. 1461; Political Violence, p. 1539; Populism, p. 1551; Protest Movements, p. 1621; Revolutions, p. 1738; Terrorism, p. 1962; Totalitarianism, p. 1987.

POLITICAL ECONOMY

Field of study: Political philosophy

Political economy is the study of the relationship between politics and economics. This interdisciplinary field examines the role of government in the production and distribution of goods.

Principal terms

ECONOMIC RATIONALITY: rational appraisal of alternative courses of action, leading to the choice of the action that promises the greatest net gain

ECONOMICS: social science concerned with the production, distribution, and consumption of goods and services, or the material welfare of humans

NORMATIVE ECONOMICS: analysis involving value judgments about economic events; for example, recommending what should be done to control inflation

PARETO OPTIMALITY: economic system in which resources are distributed in such a way that it is impossible to make anyone in the system better off without making someone else worse off

POLITICAL: of or pertaining to the state or its government

POSITIVE ECONOMICS: analysis of economic events without making value judgments; for example, reporting the facts and causes of inflation

UTILITY: satisfaction one receives from consuming commodities

Overview

Political economy is the study of the relationship between the world of public power and decision making (politics) and the world of production and distribution (economics). Holders of public power include federal, state, and local governments, and big business. Prior to the eighteenth century, the academic disciplines of political science and economics existed as two separate functions. Even in this early period, however, it was clear that politics and economics were not self-sufficient in any real sense. It has always been apparent that institutions of power such as governments and big business affect the production and distribution of goods and services. Similarly, economic conditions affect which people or organizations seize and maintain power. For example, it is commonly thought that the economic conditions in Russia in the early twentieth century led to the Russian Revolution and Lenin's rise to power.

Nevertheless, politics and economics have often been studied as separate disciplines. Traditional economists viewed society as being composed of free, self-interested people interacting as equals in the marketplace. These economists did not explicitly include forces of power such as governments or big business in explaining or predicting economic behavior. They thought that a society of free, self-interested individuals each trying to maximize his or her own self-interest would lead to Pareto optimality for society. Government was not seen as playing a central role, but was merely an agency through which individuals accomplished their ends. Furthermore, traditional economists saw economics as primarily a positive discipline, that is, similar to a physical science in which phenomena are studied without making value judgments.

The intellectual basis for this view was economist Adam Smith's *An Inquiry into the Nature and Causes of the Wealth of Nations* (1776). The key insight of *Wealth of Nations* is simple: If an exchange between two parties is voluntary, it will not take place unless both parties believe that they will benefit from it. Smith recognized that prices emerged from the voluntary transactions between buyers and sellers and these prices could coordinate the activity of millions of people, each seeking his own interest so that Pareto optimality would result. This is referred to as the price mechanism, which functions without the interference or assistance of government. When governments interfere with the price system, shortages and oversupplies can occur. For example, when a government agency puts a ceiling on the price of corn, there will be a corn shortage. Similarly, when the government imposes a price floor, there will be an oversupply of corn, at least temporarily. Adam Smith argued that governments should not interfere with the natural workings of the price system.

A second group of economists is referred to as "welfare economists." Welfare economists have tried to develop a general welfare function, that is, a way of achieving the greatest happiness for the greatest number of people. In direct contradiction to the assumptions of traditional economists, welfare economists argued that it was the job of the government to maximize the utility of its citizens. By itself, they argued, the price mechanism could not assure the greatest utility for the greatest number of people. Welfare economists also supported the idea of a normative economics and therefore wished to suggest ways to achieve societal goals, such as the elimination of poverty. Many held that the general welfare function would only be achieved after the collapse of capitalism.

The welfare economists recognized some limitations in traditional economics. One was that the assumptions of economics cannot easily accommodate the phenomenon of coercive power, since economics rests on freely choosing, utility-maximizing persons. Similarly, political science cannot accept the economist's notion of the economic person who acts with unconstrained rationality in a world of conflict, misunderstanding, and coercion. This group believed the best interests of people would be served by large institutions and governments.

The intellectual basis for this view, and arguably the most significant twentieth century development in political economy, was John Maynard Keynes's *General Theory of Employment, Interest, and Money* (1937). Keynes's book justified the intervention of governments in the economies of industrialized countries. Keynes argued that government regulation was needed to optimize the well-being of society.

Acceptance of his ideas enabled politicians consciously to manipulate the economy to generate changes in investment and employment. Once Keynesian theory gave politicians a justified role in economics, economic theory could no longer be closed to political variables. After Keynes, in describing how economies functioned, economists had to explicitly show the effects of political variables such as income taxes, property taxes, and other government policies.

The tension between traditional economists and welfare economists has resulted in what is generally referred to as the "new political economy." The approaches of the new political economy are referred to as rational choice and public choice. Its adherents claim that the new political economy offers a new and better understanding of politics and other forms of social behavior than is provided by other disciplines, such as political science. Proponents of the new political economy suggest that the notion of the rational, utility-maximizing individual may be useful in understanding certain social and political processes.

Most economists view human behavior as involving conscious choices on the part of persons or organizations confronted with certain decisions. Economic actors are assumed to have a capacity for making rational decisions and the ability to choose the most efficient resolution of their choice dilemmas. These assumptions were useful to the traditional economist who was investigating free-market situations, such as those described in *Wealth of Nations*. This basic conception has been extended to include nonmarket processes or situations, especially those involving government. The political economist studying a democratic political situation views the situation as allowing exchanges between citizens, political parties, and governments. Voters are thought of as buyers of public goods and services, while governments and political parties are suppliers of these goods and services, including education, roads, national defense, police protection, and so on. The voters obtain utility when they consume the public goods or services, and they pay for this utility with taxes and with the votes they cast on election day.

One can differentiate between economics and the new political economy by comparing some of the basic questions that are addressed by economists with those addressed by political economists. Where economists ask, "What goods are produced in the free market place, and in what quantities?" the political economist asks, "What public goods are produced, and in what quantities?" Where an economist might ask, "How are goods distributed?" the political economist would ask "Who gets how much of the benefits produced and distributed by the government?"

Applications

Political economists address a wide variety of problems. One domestic problem in the United States is the declining quality of public elementary education. Parents complain that their children are not learning as well as children did in past generations. Not only is there a declining level of learning quality in general, but also there is a wide discrepancy in the quality of education provided by school districts in different areas. Children attending poor, inner-city schools generally receive an inferior education compared with children attending school in more affluent districts. Schools are frequently not a place of learning, but rather a place where children are concerned with their own safety because of the presence of gangs and guns. The new political economy offers insights into how to address these problems.

First, using a new political economy framework, one can think of the parent and the child as the consumers or purchasers of public education, and the teacher and the school administrators as the producers or sellers of the education. Because the teachers and administrators are government employees, the taxpayers are purchasing public education from the government. Political economists see a basic problem in the fact that the purchasers of public elementary education, especially the poor, are severely limited in their choice of sellers of public education, because the student typically must attend school in the school district in which he or she lives. A proposed remedy for this problem is to allow the parent and the child to purchase the education anywhere they like, from any of a number of different sellers of education. The seller of elementary education could be a public or a private school. This is consistent with what is referred to as a voucher system, a concept that was developed by economist Milton Friedman. Friedman's argument is as follows. The parents of each elementary school child would be given a voucher each year, which is redeemable only for public elementary education. The voucher indicates the amount it costs to educate an elementary school student in a public elementary school for a year, say $3,500. The parent may spend the voucher at the school where she believes the child would receive the best education. Suppliers of education, both public and private schools, would, in effect, be charging tuition that would be paid in vouchers. Consistent with Adam Smith's theories, students and parents would elect the schools where the best education could be obtained. In such a free marketplace, schools providing an inferior product would go out of business.

Political economists also have addressed issues related to the licensing of certain professions. In most states in the United States, one must have a license to practice a wide variety of occupations, including law, medicine, dentistry, plumbing, and home building. Welfare economists argue that licensing is a legitimate function of government because licensing requirements safeguard the public. This safeguarding results because those seeking to enter the occupation must first demonstrate proficiency at that occupation. After licensing, the practitioner is often required to complete continuing professional education in order to remain proficient. Those who are licensed also usually must agree to comply with a code of ethics. Thus, licensing requirements protect the public from incompetent or unethical practitioners. According to the new political economy, citizens purchase licensing services from the government because they are incapable of judging who is competent and ethical and who is not.

Other economists argue that while licensing requirements may advance the best interests of the public to a limited degree, the principal beneficiaries of licensing requirements are those who are licensed. Licensing is a way of limiting entrance to certain professions and maintaining a high wage for those who are currently licensed, similar to limiting the supply of a certain commodity in an effort to keep the price of that commodity high. As an illustration, these economists point to the high wages often earned by attorneys in the United States, and suggest that licensing requirements have been a major factor in keeping these wages high. Licensing boards in the United States effectively limit the number of suppliers of legal services. Licensing is only available to those who have completed certain coursework, passed the bar exam, and so forth. The requirement to be licensed as an attorney effectively prevents competent people, such as paralegals, from performing certain routine services, such as the preparation of a simple will, typically provided by attorneys. If a paralegal assists someone in writing a will, the authorities can charge the paralegal with practicing law without a license. So one consequence of licensing is that the cost of routine legal assistance is higher than it would otherwise be, because licensed attorneys can charge more than paralegals. Citizens purchasing licensing services from the government should be aware of the total costs of licensing. The price of licensing services is paid in votes, tax dollars, and higher prices for certain services.

Context

The new political economy can also be applied to international issues, that is, the relationship between economics and politics on a worldwide basis. Decisions made by politicians in one region may profoundly affect the economy and the well-being of citizens in another country. These issues are likely to receive more discussion as the number of financial transactions occurring among nations increases.

To illustrate, consider the effects of tariffs and other restrictions on international trade between the United States, Canada, and Mexico. In 1993, the Clinton Administration supported the passage of the North American Free Trade Agreement (NAFTA). One effect of NAFTA would be to reduce or eliminate the tariffs that had been levied on the sale of manufactured goods among the United States, Canada, and Mexico. NAFTA also would make it easier for U.S. manufacturers to relocate their manufacturing facilities outside of the United States. This led to concern in the United States that manufacturing jobs would be lost to Mexico if NAFTA were ratified. This issue was hotly debated in 1993, when supporters and opponents of NAFTA assessed the potential economic impacts of unrestricted free trade with Mexico and Canada. The Clinton Administration argued that citizens of all three nations would be better off if NAFTA were passed, and this argument was supported by several well-known economists. The result was that the U.S. Congress passed NAFTA.

Although policymakers may look to political economists to support their policy decisions, political economists often differ in their explanations of economic and political events. The predictions of different political economists are often contradictory. There is rarely an indisputable solution to complex domestic or international problems. There is no single theory of political economy; there are multiple theories that attempt to describe the relationships between political and economic processes. Since a variety of assumptions and values underlie each theory of political economy, each theory is open to criticism. Thus, political economy is an ongoing intellectual enterprise and all reasonable viewpoints should be heard.

Bibliography

Friedman, Milton, and Rose Friedman. *Free to Choose*. New York: Harcourt Brace Jovanovich, 1980. Clearly written, easy-to-read book that presents the virtues of free markets. First outlines Adam Smith's price theory, then discusses a variety of current issues related to economics, including monetary inflation, labor unions, welfare payments, wage and price controls, and public education.

Heilbroner, Robert L. *The Worldly Philosophers: The Lives, Times and Ideas of the Great Economic Thinkers*. 4th rev. ed. New York: Simon and Schuster, 1972. Readable, nonmathematical book outlining the personal lives and economic ideas of Adam Smith, Karl Marx, and John Maynard Keynes, among others. In writing about these and other economists, Heilbroner provides a chronological outline of how economic ideas have developed over time.

Keynes, John Maynard. *The General Theory of Employment, Interest, and Money*. New York: Harcourt, Brace & World, 1965. While portions of the book are clearly written, the general reader will have difficulty understanding Keynes's classic. Extensive mathematical notation, with regular digressions.

McCloskey, Donald N. *If You're So Smart*. Chicago: University of Chicago Press, 1990. In this entertaining, nonmathematical book, McCloskey argues that economists use fact, logic, metaphor, and story to explain and predict economic events.

Mitchell, William. "The New Political Economy." *Social Research* 35 (Spring, 1968): 76-110. Although somewhat dated, this article provides an interesting, easy-to-read summary of the new political economy. Mitchell provides a chart that clearly shows the questions addressed by traditional economists and the new political economists.

Smith, Adam. *An Inquiry into the Nature and Causes of the Wealth of Nations*. Edited by Edwin Cannan. New York: The Modern Library, 1937. A masterpiece of economic thought, but probably not for the general reader. Much mathematical notation and frequent digressions from the main points under discussion.

Staniland, Martin. *What is Political Economy?* New Haven, Conn.: Yale University Press, 1985. Generally easy-to-understand summary of the basic issues underlying political economy. Clear discussion illustrating why it has been so difficult for political science and economics to merge. Discussion of Marxism and international political economy.

Jack M. Ruhl

Cross-References

POLITICAL ETHICS

Field of study: Political philosophy

Political ethics are the standards of conduct that should guide the behavior of governmental officials, such as the expectation that they be honest, responsible, and accountable in the performance of their public duties. Officials typically disagree with one another and with the public about the meaning of these ethical standards.

Principal terms

ACCOUNTABILITY: requires that government activity be conducted in the open, so that citizens can evaluate the actions of public officials

ADMINISTRATION: managing the tasks of government with economy and efficiency

BUREAUCRACY: organization of specialists in which positions are filled on the basis of merit and decisions are based on rules and impersonal relationships

POLITICS: arena of public action in which politicians determine allocations in government budgets and make laws

RESPONSIBILITY: expectation that politicians and bureaucrats serve the public interest in a democratic manner and adhere to a set of moral values consistent with this end

RESULTS-BASED ETHICS: consequences of decisions determine their rightness or wrongness

RULE-BASED ETHICS: universal moral principles such as honesty, liberty, and equality that serve as ethical standards

Overview

Western and American political philosophy and ethics are based in the Judeo-Christian religious legacy; the Greek ethical tradition, including the Socratic dialogues, Plato's *Republic*, and Aristotle's Nicomachean ethics and politics; the Roman ethical tradition; and the European Enlightenment. The Judeo-Christian legacy promoted a political ethics standard associated with religion and its moral influence in promoting the right behavior of individuals. In the Greek ethics tradition, Socrates (c. 470-399 B.C.E.), the founder of Western political philosophy and political ethics, examined the reasons behind why governments exist. Plato (427-347 B.C.E.), a student of Socrates, explored "what was the best political order, the best order of the city compatible with the nature of man." In the Roman ethical tradition, Marcus Tullius Cicero (106-43 B.C.E.), the foremost Roman political ethicist, examined what is the best political order. The classical political philosophy and ethics tradition suggested that the virtuous community was tied to the common good, wherein people could strive for moral perfection.

In the pre-European Enlightenment era, Niccolò Machiavelli radically departed from classical political philosophy and ethics and explored questions of actual rather than moral behavior. His view was that people could not achieve moral perfection because they lived only to satisfy the lower passions of political life. In the European Enlightenment era, Francis Bacon, a disciple of Machiavelli, addressed the nature of the best state or model of a commonwealth. Bacon argued that the origins of states and commonwealths lie in human desires. Thomas Hobbes, a student of both Machiavelli and Bacon, posited that natural law was the best means to understand the passions of the political man in a brutish world, where the sovereign (the state) had absolute power. Other modern political philosophers were equally important in the early American ethical debate on the nature of citizens and the state, including René Descartes, Benedict Spinoza, John Locke, Montesquieu, and Jean-Jacques Rousseau.

The Founders of the United States were profoundly influenced by both classical and modern political philosophy and ethics. Because governments and bureaucracies are run by people, the Founders sought to reconcile the classical tradition of the human search for moral perfection with the modern tradition of pursuit of self-interest. The ideal was to build a nation based on democratic ideals and the principles of open government, which would take both traditions into account.

The Founders began this nation-building task by developing a small and efficient bureaucracy run by public servants who were the cream of the new American aristocracy. They required that legislators serve good government and act only in the public interest. James Madison, a principal designer of the U.S. Constitution, in Federalist No. 51, spoke directly to the need of ethics in government: "The aim of every political constitution is, or ought to be, first to obtain for rulers men who possess the most wisdom to discern, and the most virtue to pursue, the common good of the society; and in the next place, to take the most effectual precautions for keeping them virtuous whilst they continue to hold their public trust."

The Founders, keenly aware of the tension between ethics and politics and of the tendency of human beings to maximize their self-interests to the detriment of the public good, sought to develop a representative government that would be responsive to the needs of citizens in a pluralistic society. They developed a national consensus on the ethical standards and moral values that citizens and the society as a whole would respect.

The national consensus on ethics nourished by the Founders, however, began to unravel by the mid-eighteenth century because of the tremendous growth of the American government and the tendency of legislators, appointed officials, and bureaucrats in government to satisfy their personal and partisan interests at the expense of the American people. As a result, no universal definition of American political ethics is accepted by elected officials in the legislative and executive branches of government, by appointed or unappointed officials in the federal bureaucracy, or by appointed judges in the federal judiciary. Instead, three standards of political ethics became an integral part of the federal government; they are at odds with the ethical standard of the Founders and of the American people. First, legislative ethics encompass standards of conduct applied to elected members of Congress. Second, bureaucratic ethics apply to all appointed and nonappointed public servants working in the U.S. Congress and in the executive branch of government. Third, judicial ethics pertains to the behavior of judges in the federal judiciary. Specifically, the American people view the universal standard of political ethics as the requirement that all public officials exhibit judgment, professional courage, discretion, openness, accountability, responsibility, forthrightness, and integrity. The significance of political ethics lies in the expectation that public servants will act responsibly, as required by law and by accepted, unwritten public standards of good moral behavior. At the most basic level of ethics, bribes, lapses of character, personal venality, conflicts of interests, corruption, and lying are not condoned by the American people. This definition of political ethics by the American people has stood the tests of history and of politics.

The different ethical standards of the three branches of American government and those held by the American people are clearly illustrated in the grey area of campaign contributions. Elected officials can accept money in the form of campaign contributions; appointed officials cannot. Because elected officials can accept campaign contributions, the line of what constitutes ethical behavior is much more difficult to know for these officials than it is for appointed officials. Ethical behavior of elected officials should not cross the boundary of impropriety or even have the appearance of illegality. Virtually any money given to a federal judge or a civil servant is a bribe and hence not only unethical but also often illegal. In contrast, the line between a legitimate campaign contribution and a bribe is much harder to distinguish for members of Congress. For example, the American people, adhering to rule-based ethics, expect members of Congress to accept campaign contributions within the limits of national law and to refrain from casting their votes on federal legislation based on the money they are given by lobbyists, political action committees, or wealthy individuals.

Members of Congress tend to use results-based ethical standards. In this context, accepting campaign contributions is not viewed as inappropriate by politicians because it helps them, as they see it, to improve public decisions. The problem is that rule-based ethics supported by the American people can clash with results-based ethics adhered to by politicians, especially when politicians accept large sums of money from contributors and vote to satisfy their personal and partisan interests instead of the public interest.

Applications

Members of the U.S. Congress often have an ethical standard different from that held by the American people. Legislative ethics has generally meant not acting in an illegal manner and is less stringent than the public's expectation of good ethical behavior. For the public, even the appearance of impropriety is unacceptable. In the area of campaign contributions, for example, the public is likely to blur the distinction between a bribe (which is illegal) and a campaign contribution when a politician aids a campaign contributor. In contrast, members of Congress have argued that there is nothing ethically wrong with helping individuals who contribute to their campaign chests. An illustrative case of this ethical grey area is the savings and loan scandal of the 1980's.

On November 15, 1990, U.S. senators Alan Cranston of California, Dennis DeConcini of Arizona, John Glenn of Ohio, Donald W. Riegle, Jr., of Michigan, and John McCain of Arizona faced charges before the Senate Ethics Committee of assisting the California-based Lincoln Savings and Loan Association's head, Charles H. Keating, Jr. A federal investigation suggested that Keating had defrauded his public investors through illegal financial transactions. The committee was charged with determining if the senators had used their political influence to assist Keating in return for campaign contributions.

The Keating Five, as the senators were called, denied that they had used their influence to convince government regulators to ignore Keating's activities, or that they even knew of Keating's financial fraud. Special Counsel Robert S. Bennett, who questioned the Keating Five on their alleged influence peddling with Keating, argued to the contrary. He claimed that the five senators' behavior was both illegal and improper. On January 16, 1991, the Senate Ethics Committee rebuked four senators for their poor ethical judgment but allowed DeConcini, Glenn, Riegle, and McCain to retain their Senate seats. The committee accused Cranston of using his influence to protect Keating in exchange for money. Cranston retired from the Senate having been censured for unethical behavior but not prosecuted for committing a crime. Keating was convicted of financial fraud and sent to prison. The fact that Cranston proclaimed his innocence to the end indicates the different standards held by politicians and by the public about which standard of political ethics should have supremacy, legislative ethics or public ethics.

Historically, the conflict between the adherents of rule-based and results-based ethics is illustrated in the American democratic experiment. The Founders designed the U.S. Constitution to foster in public servants the ethics of accountability and responsibility, along with the democratic ideal that they were trustees and not overseers of the public trust. The Founders created an open and representative democracy with an executive and a legislative branch made accountable to the American people through periodic elections, and a judicial branch to interpret and solve constitutional disputes between the executive and legislative branches. The Founders believed that the system of checks and balances would discourage politicians in the federal government from exclusively pursuing their self-interests and would promote the development of dedication to the public interest. In this context, they developed a legislative ethical standard to make members of Congress accountable and responsive to the American people. It included sanctions for improper behavior and disbarment from office for criminal acts. In the new American bureaucracy, they emphasized administration and the values of efficiency and economy over partisan politics. In the federal judiciary, the Founders developed ethical standards for sitting federal judges, whose charge was to protect the U.S. Constitution and the rule of law. Sanctions were included to censure, impeach, and disbar judges who committed crimes while in office.

The universal ethic of public service developed by the Founders had its first practical expression in George Washington's administration. Washington appointed men to the American bureaucracy noted for their competence, character, trustworthiness, and loyalty. He set the high moral tone for what was to follow by his pioneering dedication to ethics in government. In the administrations of John Adams, Thomas Jefferson, and others who followed, merit and character were reinforced as the basis for entry into public service. In the first decades of the American democratic experiment, the Congress, the executive branch, and the federal bureaucracy performed well in carrying out the ethical ideals of the Founders.

Andrew Jackson became president in 1829 and initiated a major historical and political reversal from the ethical precepts of the Founders toward the "democratization" of the federal government. Jackson, an advocate of the "common people," strongly believed that the aristocrats who had controlled government in the early decades of the United States had done so at the expense of the American people. This reversal meant that appointed positions in the federal government would be staffed by nonaristocrats, and appointments would be based more on applicants' allegiance to politicians than on their ability to do their jobs. This meant that bureaucrats and politicians could pursue power and wealth while in the public service, and it signaled the decline of the Founders' ideal of dedication to the ideals of moral perfection and right conduct in the public service. It also signaled the rise of politicians who directly controlled bureaucrats in the executive and legislative branches.

Jackson became the standard-bearer of the new American spoils system. In his administration, four arguments were presented to justify the supremacy of rule-based ethics over results-based ethics. First, it was argued that aristocrats in the early American public service had been corrupt in their support of rule-based ethics because they served the interests of the wealthy. Second, results-based ethics was a superior form of political ethics, as it took into account the needs of all Americans in a competitive market system. Third, the consequences of public decisions determined the rightness or wrongness of a public decision and did not depend on who in the federal government might benefit from public decisions. Finally, it was argued that there was no moral tension between ethics and good government, and that individuals in the public service could maximize their personal interests as long as the needs of the American public were met. In summary, the Jacksonian adherents of rule-based ethics believed that they should rightly profit from their service in the federal government, as they were representatives of all the people.

Context

The long-standing political conflict between rule-based ethics and results-based ethics has had the effect of preventing a national U.S. consensus on a standard of political ethics applicable to all public officials. Basically discounted is the rule-based ethical standard of the American people and of the Founders, which calls for both responsive and efficient policy action to solve national problems. Members of both political parties, concerned primarily with the benefits of results-based ethical standards, have tended to look at and solve national problems in response to their own self-interests and partisan political agendas, not the desires of the American people.

Ethics has always played a role in politics. Politics concerns allocations of goods, whether directly through government budgeting or indirectly through laws establishing rights and privileges. Politicians therefore must always have in mind some concept of the "good" to be served in the allocation process; this implies some ethical views on the world. Politicians also face personal ethical questions of behavior in terms of influences on their actions such as campaign contributions and bribes. They must employ some ethical standard in deciding whose influences to follow, particularly when the interests of campaign contributors conflict with those of constituents as a whole. The ethics of politicians, unfortunately, do not always match the ethics of the citizenry.

Bibliography

Beard, Edmund, and Stephen Horn. *Congressional Ethics: The View from the House*. Washington, D.C.: Brookings Institution, 1975. Good introduction on ethics in the U.S. House of Representatives. Index. Bibliography is dated.

Cooper, Terry L. *The Responsible Administrator: An Approach to Ethics for the Administrative Role*. San Francisco: Jossey-Bass, 1990. Excellent discussion on the need for responsibility and accountability by the American public administrator. Index and bibliography.

Denhardt, Kathryn. *The Ethics of Public Service: Resolving Moral Dilemmas in Public Organizations*. New York: Greenwood Press, 1988. Well-balanced treatment of the universal and the relative morals and values conflicts in political ethics. Index and bibliography.

Donahue, Anne Marie, ed. *Ethics in Politics and Government*. New York: H. W. Wilson, 1989. Good survey on the theory of public ethics in American politics and in the federal government. Index and bibliography.

Garment, Suzanne. *Scandal: The Culture of Mistrust in American Politics*. New York: Anchor Books, 1992. Fine analysis of the historical impact of scandals in American politics and their negative consequences for ethics in government. Index and bibliography.

Rohr, John A. *To Run a Constitution: The Legitimacy of the Administrative State*. Lawrence: University Press of Kansas, 1986. Fine exposition on the values of equality, freedom, and property in the U.S. Constitution, as the standard for the practice of good political ethics. Index and bibliography.

Stern, Philip M. *The Best Congress Money Can Buy*. New York: Pantheon, 1988. Strong critique of the impact of money on the voting behavior of members of both houses of the U.S. Congress. Index and bibliography.

Timmins, William M. *A Casebook of Public Ethics and Issues*. Pacific Grove, Calif.: Brooks/Cole, 1990. Good introduction for high school and college students. Case studies look at major public policy issues facing the United States. Index and bibliography.

Michael J. Siler

Cross-References

Accountability in U.S. Government, p. 1; Bureaucracy, p. 164; Democracy, p. 513; Elected Versus Appointed Offices in the United States, p. 572; Machiavelli's Political Philosophy, p. 1148; Organized Crime and Political Corruption, p. 1355; Political Crimes, p. 1448; Political Machines and Bosses, p. 1468; Political Participation, p. 1479; Political Representation in the United States, p. 1525; The Presidency in the United States, p. 1590; Self-Interest in Politics, p. 1802; Separation of Powers: Political Philosophy, p. 1809; Social Darwinism, p. 1833.

POLITICAL MACHINES AND BOSSES

Field of study: Local and regional government

Political machines and the "boss politicians" that led them dominated the politics of many cities in the United States from the mid-1800's to the mid-1900's. Studying them yields insight into urban history, the workings of local government, and the roles of different ethnic groups and social classes in local politics.

Principal terms

BOSS: leader and most powerful member of a political machine

ETHNIC GROUPS: various religious, cultural, racial, or nationality groups that are identifiable within a larger society

PATRONAGE: resources, rewards, and favors controlled by government, especially jobs, contracts, or the like

POLITICAL MACHINE: powerful political organization that operates through a local political party, and dominates the politics of a city

PROGRESSIVE REFORM MOVEMENT: persons and groups who sought to oust the political machines from power

SOCIAL CLASS: group in society distinguished by its economic, educational, and cultural factors

Overview

One enduring influence on the politics of city government in the United States has been the existence of political machines and the bosses that controlled them. Political machines were informal political organizations, that is, not created in law or through constitutions, that controlled local government and politics in many major U.S. cities from the mid-1800's through the mid-1900's. They primarily worked through the less formal local political party mechanisms and served as a link among various local political and economic interests, especially recently arrived immigrant groups, city workers, and the rapidly growing urban business sector. By working to bring these interests together, machine politicians were able to build strong political bases. In many cities, they directly controlled and manipulated local elections, and thus the formal offices of local government, that is, the Mayor's office and city council. Having attained such power, machines could control the spending of local government revenues, award government jobs, do favors for loyal supporters, and grant contracts to supportive businesses. Through trading such favors and rewards for political support machines further strengthened their control over most of a city's affairs to the point that little could happen in the governmental or business sectors without the machine having a hand in it.

To understand the emergence of machine politics in many cities, one must examine the massive transformations cities experienced during this period. In the mid-1800's, as industrialization changed the economic structure of society and forced more people to seek jobs in the growing urban, manufacturing centers, immigrants were increasingly settling in the cities, rather than in the vast U.S. territories. Whereas most of the immigrants of the late 1700's and early 1800's were Protestants from places such as England, Germany, and Scandinavia, the immigrants of the late 1800's and early 1900's tended to be Roman Catholic and come from countries such as Ireland, Italy, and Poland. Significant numbers of Eastern Europeans and Jews came toward the end of that period.

Mostly poor, facing anti-immigrant and religious discrimination, and in immediate need of housing, food, and jobs, the new ethnic populations created a large, extraordinarily diverse, urban working class in towns that previously had been much smaller, populated by people of the same ethnic and socioeconomic background, and not yet affected by industrialization. This phenomenon of intensive immigration into the cities, in conjunction with the dramatic economic changes prompted by industrialization, placed enormous demands on the existing local governments and their abilities to serve the needs of the rapidly growing population. Even major cities, such as New York, Boston, Chicago, and Philadelphia, were overwhelmed by these changes.

Such transformations injected new conflicts into local political affairs. Economic background, religion, language, nationality, and other cultural differences divided the once homogeneous local populations into factions with diverse political and economic interests. As growing numbers of immigrants became citizens, the native residents often mounted determined efforts to oppose the growing political power of ethnic voters, giving rise to severe ethnic conflict and frequent riots. Ethnic political leadership in many of the country's largest cities began to win seats on city councils, and as these populations grew, working-class ethnic voters gradually became the dominant force in local electoral politics.

Since existing local governmental institutions were overwhelmed by these emergent needs and conflicts, the cities' new political leadership, supported by the growing ethnic working class, began to use the more informal mechanisms of the local political parties to consolidate their political power and centralize decision making. The party organizations provided a strict hierarchical, top-down chain of command that was essential to the workings of the machine organizations.

The leader or boss of the machine frequently was the chairman of one of the city's political parties and might also hold elected or appointed office, such as the mayor's seat or a position on the city council. Although machines could use any political party to serve their purposes, local Democratic parties were especially associated with machine politics, because that was usually the party to which most of the working-class ethnic voters belonged. Beneath the boss, the machine's chain of command encompassed other elected officials supportive of the machine, government employees, and party leaders or captains at the district, neighborhood, precinct, and block levels.

The fuel that sustained the machine and gave it power was an elaborate system of patronage, through which government jobs, favors, contracts, and other benefits were awarded in return for service and loyalty to the machine organization. Public officials and city employees who relied on a machine for their jobs could ignore orders from those higher in the organization only at their own risk. To win support from voters, machines not only were able to draw on the power of ethnic solidarity, but also could offer jobs and personal assistance in times of trouble. It was the duty of the machine's block captains, for example, to determine the needs of voters residing on a given block in the city, report those needs up through the ranks of the organization, and then bring about a response that was intended to win the political support of the individuals in question. A city job, a timely word to a landlord who was demanding late rent payments, a turkey at Thanksgiving, or a bucket of coal in the winter, were some of the things the machine might provide. Of course, what the machine gave, it also could take away, and the average voter understood that the machine could punish as well as reward its constituents. The payoff was on election day, when the block captain would make sure that all those who supported or had received favors from the machine went out to vote for its candidates.

Business was another important player in machine organizations. Not only was business booming in the late 1800's and early 1900's because of industrialization, but also the needs of rapidly growing cities for the construction of public roads, schools, government buildings, and parks made winning local government contracts a particularly lucrative enterprise. In exchange for contracts financed by local taxpayers, businesses often provided payoffs and kickbacks to machine leaders, or promised to hire machine supporters to fill the jobs created through government contracts and franchises. In some cities, machines even were accused of striking deals with organized crime, especially during the Prohibition era of the 1920's and 1930's when the manufacture and sale of alcoholic beverages was illegal. For allowing crime leaders to operate without interference, machine politicians received additional monies that either went back into the machine organization or went into the pockets of bosses.

While many stories about machine corruption are true, in politics, things are rarely viewed as being entirely good or entirely bad, and the political machines are no different in this regard. At a time when cities experienced unprecedented change, and existing local governments could not effectively deal with the demands for services, jobs, housing, schools, roads, and other necessities of life, machines fulfilled numerous critical needs. They served as employment agency, granter of contracts, welfare agency, vehicle for upward mobility, and symbol of the political power of working-class ethnic groups. Nevertheless, the often blatant graft, corruption, and favoritism that seemed an inevitable part of machine politics proved to be a primary factor in their decline.

Because machines were not created as formal political institutions, but were identified and characterized by their general approach to local governance, it is not always possible to state precisely which political organizations were truly political machines. Generally, however, a political machine can be described as a political organization that possessed most, if not all, of the following characteristics: It was organized in line with the structure and functioning of the local political party organizations. It had a hierarchical structure and a strict chain of command, with a boss at the top, and subsequent layers of public officials and party leaders below. It was concerned primarily with patronage matters involving jobs, contracts, and the distribution of the rewards that could be controlled by government. Finally, it supplied these things in exchange for political and financial support from constituents and businesses who supported the machine leaders, kept its candidates in office, and enabled it to accumulate more power and support over time.

Applications

Over a period of approximately one hundred years, numerous political machines existed in many American cities. Not all operated the same way, and not all were equally powerful. Some existed only as long as a particular boss was in power, while others operated for decades through numerous changes in leadership. Despite this variability, there are some classic examples that are repeatedly referred to in the literature on machine politics. The Tammany Hall machine of New York City, especially when it was run by boss William Marcy Tweed, from the late 1850's to the early 1870's, still stands as one of the best examples of the powerful, sometimes ruthless, often corrupt machine organization. The Chicago machine from the mid-1950's through the mid-1970's, under the leadership of Mayor Richard J. Daley, is one of the best examples of a more contemporary machine organization. Indeed, some consider Daley's Chicago organization the last of the classic political machines.

Tammany Hall was the name of the mostly Irish faction of the New York City Democratic Party. Although the local party had been fragmented among competing ethnic groups, under Boss Tweed's control, the various factions came together. Tweed was a tireless politician who often held several important elected and appointed positions at the same time. He had worked his way up in the machine organization from the lowest block captain position, eventually being elected to serve as a city councilman, state senator, county supervisor, and U.S. congressman. Throughout his tenure as boss, however, Tweed's most powerful position was his chairmanship of the Tammany Hall Democratic Party organization. From that position, he was able to have his supporters elected or appointed to almost any position in the city government, including mayor, and he held tight control over the granting of contracts for huge public works and construction projects. Tweed used kickbacks from contracts, and contributions and bribes from wealthy supporters, both to enrich himself and to consolidate his power. In the process, he made numerous enemies, and after an 1871 investigation that revealed the breadth and depth of his wrongdoing, he was convicted on various public corruption charges and died in prison in 1878. Tweed left a much stronger Tammany Hall machine, however, and over the next fifty years under various bosses, Tammany controlled the local Democratic Party and much of what went on in New York City.

Richard J. Daley of Chicago was both mayor of Chicago and chair of the Cook County Democratic Party organization from 1955 until the time of his death in 1976. Like Tweed, Daley worked his way up through the ranks of the local Democratic Party, until he sat at the top of the machine's elaborate system of patronage. Under Daley, it was estimated that the Chicago machine controlled more than thirty thousand jobs, from part-time elevator operators to well-paid city government department heads.

Daley's strength was evident in his ability to work with and win support from a broader coalition than had supported most machines. He had strong ties to the federal government and several presidents, especially John F. Kennedy and Lyndon Johnson, and established particularly good relations with the business community. Despite recurrent charges of political corruption, Daley viewed himself as a professional manager and gained a reputation for his ability to get things done.

By the 1970's, however, even Daley's machine began to go the way of its predecessors. The voters who traditionally supported the machines became more successful and independent, needing the machine for fewer things. Public disapproval of corruption and the old style of politics also cut into machine support. The federal government took over many of the social welfare functions the machines had provided, and overall, the machines had come to outlive their usefulness. Political machines came into existence to fulfill various social, political, and economic needs, and began to die out when those needs were no longer as evident.

Context

Political machines cannot be fully understood by focusing on them independent of their broader political and governmental contexts. In virtually every city where machine politics was evident, opposing political forces organized and sought to oust the machine from power. These opposition forces were generally known as progressive reformers, and they attempted, and at times succeeded, to beat the machines at their own political game.

Usually headed by affluent and middle-class social and political activists, reformers forged alliances with like-minded citizens, journalists, educators, state legislators, and businessmen. Most were sincerely interested in bringing an end to machine corruption, although the reform movement also frequently exhibited anti-immigrant and anti-Catholic sentiments. One prominent reformer of the late 1800's wrote that under machine rule, local governments had come to be controlled by "a crowd of illiterate peasants, freshly raked in from Irish bogs, or Bohemian mines, or Italian robber nests." The fundamental struggle between machine and reform politics, however, was a struggle for power between ethnic and class-based interests.

Local reformers were particularly interested in undercutting the machines by changing the rules and institutions of local government. They generally sought to weaken the power of the mayor's office, make local elections nonpartisan, and fill government jobs through a professional civil service. All such reforms were aimed at undermining the machines and their control over patronage and the local political parties. Between the efforts of the reformers and the overall changes in the social, political, and economic conditions of U.S. cities, machines gradually disappeared.

Bibliography

Glazer, Nathan, and Daniel Patrick Moynihan. *Beyond the Melting Pot: The Negroes, Puerto Ricans, Jews, Italians, and Irish of New York City*. Cambridge, Mass.: MIT

Press, 1963. A groundbreaking work that drew attention to and shaped thinking on the broader issue of ethnic politics in U.S. cities.

Judd, Dennis, and Paul Kantor, eds. *Enduring Tensions in Urban Politics*. New York: Macmillan, 1992. Best selection of academic, popular, historical, and contemporary articles on a variety of topics related to urban politics. Ten articles on machine and reform politics provide competing perspectives on the subject.

Rakove, Milton. *Don't Make No Waves ... Don't Back No Losers: An Insider's Analysis of the Daley Machine*. Bloomington: Indiana University Press, 1975. Colorful and generally sympathetic analysis of the workings of the Daley machine. A good contrast to the book by Royko.

Riordan, William L. *Plunkitt of Tammany Hall*. Edited by Terrence J. McDonald. Boston: Bedford Books of St. Martin's Press, 1993. A fine introductory essay leads to a reprint of a short book, originally published in the early 1900's, based on conversations with George Washington Plunkitt, a Tammany district leader in the late 1800's. Best source available on the general views of machine politicians themselves.

Royko, Mike. *Boss: Richard J. Daley of Chicago*. New York: Dutton, 1971. Written by a popular Chicago journalist, this volume is probably the most widely read book on machine politics. It offers a critical view of the Daley machine, but provides sharp, objective insights into its internal workings.

Christopher L. Warren

Cross-References

City Government in the United States, p. 266; Clientelism, p. 337; Cult of Personality, p. 477; The Democratic Party, p. 520; Immigrants and Politics, p. 861; Industrialization, p. 916; Local Governments, p. 1136; Organized Crime and Political Corruption, p. 1355; Political Crimes, p. 1448; Populism, p. 1551; Race and Ethnicity, p. 1654; The Republican Party, p. 1699; State and Local Government, p. 1885; Urbanization, p. 2071.

POLITICAL MYTHS AND THE PHILOSOPHIES OF MOSCA AND PARETO

Field of study: Political philosophy

Gaetano Mosca and Vilfredo Pareto were the first political theorists to draw sharp distinctions between the masses and the elite minorities who govern them. According to Mosca, all governments—regardless of their forms—are ruled by elites. Pareto adds that all governing elites constantly compete with rising new elites as their own grasp of power inevitably weakens.

Principal terms
    CIRCULATION OF ELITES: Pareto's theory that ruling elites constantly replace each other
    DEMOCRATIC MYTH: belief that the masses truly govern themselves
    ELITE: minority power group within a government
    LOGICAL ACTION: action that a person links to an end based on a scientific judgment that can be confirmed by an independent observer
    MYTH: belief or story of unknown origin that explains a cultural value or system, such as a type of government
    NONLOGICAL ACTION: action based on impulse and desire
    POLITICAL FORMULA: myth or belief system that a governing elite invents to preserve its own authority

Overview

Born in Sicily, the Italian jurist and political scientist Gaetano Mosca (1858-1941) took a law degree at Palermo (1881), where he lectured in constitutional law until moving to the Italian mainland in 1888. While holding professorships at Turin and Rome, he was elected a deputy to the national assembly (1909-1919), and he served in the cabinet of Prime Minister Antonio Salandra during World War I. In 1919 he became a life senator. His lasting significance, however, is as a political theorist, and he is particularly remembered for The Ruling Class (1896 and 1923), which was first published in English in 1939.

Because of his particular philosophical interests, Mosca is often compared to another Italian pioneer of social science, Vilfredo Pareto (1848-1923). The son of a Genoese exile living in France, Pareto was born in Paris, but his family returned to Italy when he was a child. After taking a degree in civil engineering at Turin's Polytechnic, he practiced that profession from 1870 to 1892 and also served as a director of a major railroad company. Around 1891 he chanced to meet the economist Maffeo Pantaleoni, whose work got him interested in economics and led him to study the writings of French economist Leo Walras. When Walras retired from Switzerland's University of Lausanne in 1893, he recommended that Pareto succeed him there.

Pareto's subsequent assumption of the position marks the beginning of his career in the social sciences. In 1916, he published his masterwork, *Tráttáto di sòciología generále* (*The Mind and Society: A Treatise on General Sociology*). Meanwhile, his receipt of a large inheritance in 1898 allowed him to retire to a Lake Geneva village. He refrained from participating in government until the year before he died. In 1922 Benito Mussolini made him a senator, and he also worked on the Fascist journal *Gerárchia* (Hierarchy).

As thinkers Mosca and Pareto were alike in many ways, but they also diverged in other ways. For example, they both pioneered in proposing a realistic theory of elites, but Mosca—unlike Pareto—did not construct a system of general sociology. Also, they expressed themselves quite differently. Mosca's language is often warm with feeling and impressive in its fearless honesty. Pareto's words tend to be cool and calculating, impressive in their precise analysis and objectivity, although sometimes fiery with contempt. Both men had contempt for democracy; however, Mosca eventually relented and acknowledged some virtues to representative government. Mosca so disapproved of Mussolini's resort to violence that he delivered an anti-Fascist speech and retired to private life.

Mosca's main contributions to political science include his pioneering use of purely descriptive data drawn from history to reach inductive conclusions about human behavior. He also contributed the original view that minority elites rule regardless of the form of government and that they base their power on a myth to which the governed subscribe. He also posited a law explaining the oscillation of elites as attributable to their inevitable dissolution from aging. Finally, he offered original explanations of the relation of Christianity to socialism, as well as to materialistic atheism. It is significant to note that although Mosca concluded that parliaments were invariably corrupt, because they serve private interests, he believed that democracy is a workable form of government.

Mosca saw his theory of the ruling class as a "scientific truth," in contrast to a "metaphysical abstraction" like the "political formula" that justifies any elite group's rule. To possess authority in the minds of the masses, the ruling class needs a myth or belief system to guarantee a government by law, whether it be the Feudal Myth, the Papal Myth, the Monarchial Myth, the Fascist Myth, the Communist Myth, or the Democratic Myth. Such myths may involve narratives or they may contain only sets of principles.

In comparing Christianity to socialism, Mosca notes that they share a "hunger for justice and the ideal" that is natural to human beings and that both must exist in a world filled with iniquities. Otherwise, Christianity and socialism are direct opposites. Like any religion, Christianity is based on feeling, not reason; whereas socialism emerged from the rationalism, materialism, and atheism of the French Enlightenment. According to Mosca, socialism teaches that "happiness lies in satisfying earthly instincts and passions" and does not address spiritual needs. While Christianity teaches people to love God and one's neighbor, socialism teaches class hatred—hatred of the bourgeois and the capitalist, who are regarded as the oppressors of the working class.

Unlike Mosca, Pareto was predominantly a mathematical economist and general sociologist. He analyzed some important ideas relevant to political science, however, and he systematized and developed some political ideas that Mosca had been the first to propose. For example, he treated Mosca's theory of the ruling class in terms of "the elite," whereas Mosca generally used the term "the political class." Pareto spoke of Mosca's idea of the cyclical recurrence of elites as "the circulation of elites." Mosca unmasks democracy and popular sovereignty as metaphysical pretensions based upon mythical appeal. In *Mind and Society*, Pareto states that one purpose of this work is to "strip realities of such veilings of sentiment." Pareto's analysis of human acts as "logical" and "nonlogical" and as consisting also of "residues" (biogenetic drives) and "derivations" (rationalizations) are both relevant to political science.

Pareto tried to develop a concept of "theories that surpass experience," which he relates to "residues" rather than to cognitive psychological factors. In doing so, he emphasizes two main classes of residues: "the instinct of combinations" (the ability of a group to adapt easily to situational exigencies) and the "persistence of aggregates" (the tendency of a group to keep commitments once they have been institutionalized). Having developed the theory of a "circulation of elites," Pareto holds that oscillation occurs between two kinds of social groups: a group whose members are "more actuated by the 'combinations' residues, or the 'foxes,'" and a group whose members are "more actuated by the 'persistence' residues, or the 'lions.'" He shows that in a political context the lions tend to resort to force, whereas the foxes tend to lack sufficient concern about social instability.

To Pareto, a "logical" action is one in which the actor sees his action as a means to an end that is scientifically verifiable by both him and an independent observer. A "nonlogical" (not to be confused with "illogical") action is one not in the category of "logical." This analysis is important in a political context.

Applications

Mosca maintained that the ability of an elite class to govern depends on how deeply its political myth is accepted by the people whom the elite govern. Indeed, the quality of its "juridical defense" (government of law) also depends on this factor. Further, the successful operation of the government also depends on the "collective moral sense" displayed by the ruling class and even on whether the governed possess requisite moral, cultural, and aesthetic sensibility. Pareto developed Mosca's ideas of elite minority rule further in regard to the importance of political myth and the inevitability of the ruling class's decline and replacement by another elite minority group. He concluded that subjectivity and feeling hold more sway over human behavior than objectivity and reason and he thought that this was the main source of error in the world. For social science to be scientific to an important degree, it must recognize the reality of this state of affairs. Pareto sharply distinguishes between the truth of reality and the desirability of the ideal. To him it is right to act on the knowledge that the majority never truly rule in a democracy or any other form of government. Further, the scientific approach to social phenomena must disregard political propaganda. After

Mussolini secured a mandate from the king and accepted the office of prime minister, he showed himself to be the "Machiavellian Prince," thereby proving Pareto's political theory.

Context

Mosca and Pareto were the first thinkers to assert the reality of minority elitist rule in all forms of government. Taking their cue from Giambattista Vico, they emphasized the importance and power of political myth, whether religious or secular. A case in point is Pareto's comparison and contrast between Christian and communist myths. In their researches, Mosca and Pareto developed ideas and suggestions they encountered in their reading of Plato, Machiavelli, Newton, Vico, Comte, Rousseau, Macauley, Taine, Spencer, and Poincaré. Both emphasized theories about elites and myths that support government through practical illusions. In his exposition of the differences between Christianity and socialism, Pareto was especially influenced by Georges Sorel's *Reflections on Violence* (1908). A French social philosopher, Sorel invented the "syndicalist myth" after dreaming that the working class had taken over the government under the pressure of a massive general strike, with the result that a worker's paradise had come into being. Mosca and Pareto have their own followers in the French political economist Francis Delaisi, the American sociologist Talcot Parsons, and others.

Bibliography

Albertoni, Ettore. *Mosca and the Theory of Elitism*. Translated by Paul Goodrick. New York: Basil Blackwell, 1987. Sympathetic but critical assessment of Mosca's theory of the elite and views on democracy.

Delaisi, Francis. *Political Myths and Economic Realities*. New York: Viking Press, 1927. Clear, highly interesting account of the various political myths that have historically supported different forms of government.

Meisel, James Hans. *The Myth of the Ruling Class: Gaetano Mosca and the "Elite."* Ann Arbor: University of Michigan Press, 1962. Antielitist critique of Mosca's theory of elitism.

——————, ed. *Pareto and Mosca*. Englewood Cliffs, N.J.: Prentice-Hall, 1965. Collection of essays, including eight on Pareto and five on Mosca.

Powers, Charles H. *Vilfredo Pareto*. Newberry Park, Calif.: Sage Publications, 1987. Basic introduction to the principles that Pareto sees as underlying social function.

Tudor, Henry. *Political Myth*. New York: Praeger, 1972. Helpful discussion of the general aspects of political mythology.

Richard P. Benton

Cross-References

Aristocracy, Oligarchy, and Plutocracy, p. 78; Elitism, p. 591; Equality and Egalitarianism, p. 630; Fascism and Nazism, p. 656; Force, p. 712; Irrationalism in Politics,

POLITICAL PARTICIPATION

Field of study: Politics

Political participation concerns the manner in which citizens interact with government. Through active participation in government, citizens attempt to convey their needs to public officials in the hope of having these needs met.

Principal terms

CITIZEN-INITIATED CONTACT: contacting of government officials by members of the public through phone calls, letters, or other means

CIVIL DISOBEDIENCE: open and intentional breaking of a law in an attempt to be arrested and draw attention to a particular issue

INITIATIVE: procedure through which citizens can force a decision on an issue by collecting a certain number of signatures on a petition, after which the issue will be voted on either by the legislature or by a public vote

PUBLIC HEARING: public meeting where government officials invite members of the public to share their comments regarding a particular matter

RECALL ELECTION: election in which the public decides whether to retain or dismiss an elected official prior to the expiration of the official's term

REFERENDUM: a public vote on a specific issue

Overview

Legislators, chief executives, and judges are all key participants in the policy process. Political participation, however, is not limited to those elected and appointed officials. Most people participate in government and politics to some extent.

When discussing political participation, political scientists are likely to distinguish between conventional and unconventional modes of participation. Conventional means of participation are those that are more common and accepted. Unconventional ones are less ordinary and are sometimes viewed as less acceptable.

One conventional manner of participation is for citizens to initiate contact with government officials. This type of participation can take many forms. Citizens may phone, write, fax, sign a petition, or send a telegram to their elected representatives or other government officials. This contact could be regarding a pending piece of legislation affecting many people or a problem specific to the individual making the contact. Because government officials, especially elected ones, like to keep their constituents happy, this sort of participation can be very effective.

Sometimes government does not wait for citizens to approach it with their concerns. Instead, government will invite comments from the public on a variety of matters. Such is the case with public hearings. A public hearing will frequently be held prior to a legislative body's taking action on an issue. The passage of a local government's budget, the rezoning of a piece of property, and a decision regarding a public utility's rate hike request are examples of situations often subject to public hearings. At these proceedings, citizens may give the decision-making body their views concerning the pending action. In addition to formal public hearings, many local governments set aside time during their meetings for public comments.

Comments are not sought only by legislative bodies. Executive agencies charged with implementing legislation frequently seek public input regarding proposed rules and regulations. On the federal level, the process by which agencies solicit such feedback is governed by the Federal Administrative Procedures Act of 1946 (FAPA). This act requires that agencies publish proposed rules in the *Federal Register*, a document produced every business day, and invite written comments from members of the public. Only after a public comment period can an agency produce its final rules. Many states have comparable laws requiring agencies to include the public in the rule-making process.

Some governments go beyond simply inviting public comments by establishing citizen advisory boards. Sometimes these bodies monitor a particular governmental function or department. Other citizen advisory boards are given a more general charge, such as to help assemble a budget or site a landfill.

The most common form of political participation is the act of voting. Within broad parameters provided by the federal constitution, voting in the United States is regulated by the states. States have extensive control, for example, over registration requirements. Some states require registration well in advance of an election; others permit registration on the day of an election. States also set the hours during which polls will be open and establish rules for absentee balloting.

A more active form of participation than simply voting is working on a political campaign. There are a number of important tasks that need to be performed in almost every campaign. Candidates for public office need volunteers to stuff envelopes, knock on doors, and make phone calls. Campaigns, however, are not limited to those for a particular office. Many people volunteer their efforts in behalf of an issue. This can involve campaigning for or against specific ballot measures, especially in locations that make extensive use of initiative, referendum, and recall.

The initiative is a device that gives citizens greater control over what sorts of things are on the governmental agenda. If a state constitution or municipal charter allows for this technique, citizens can force a decision on an issue by collecting a specified number of signatures in a petition drive. Once sufficient signatures are obtained, the constitution or charter requires that either the appropriate legislative body decide the issue or the question be put directly to the voters in a public vote known as a referendum.

Although many referenda are held as a result of successful initiative petition drives, there are other circumstances under which they are utilized. Many state constitutions and municipal charters, even those that do not contain provisions for the initiative process, mandate that certain sorts of decisions be approved by public referendum. Financial decisions, particularly those involving large amounts of public debt, as well as amendments to constitutions and charters, often fall into this category.

Recall is the firing of a public official by the voters prior to the expiration of the person's term. The usual procedure involves obtaining a certain number of signatures on a petition calling for the official's removal. Once the requisite signatures are obtained, a special recall election will be held. The voters then decide whether to retain the office holder. Not all states or municipalities have recall provisions in their constitutions or charters.

Political participation can also take the form of active participation in an organized interest group. In addition to lobbying government officials, many interest groups become involved in elections, supporting candidates in the hope that candidates will support their cause if they are elected. Nonpartisan groups, such as the League of Women Voters, also provide an opportunity for citizens to become active in politics.

The ultimate form of conventional political participation is running for public office. There are thousands of offices up for election in the United States, ranging from president of the United States to members of a local school board. Most of these positions have no eligibility requirements other than that candidates be registered voters within the jurisdiction of the particular office. Major exceptions include president or vice president of the United States, for which candidates must be thirty-five years of age or older and be born citizens of the United States; United States Senate, where candidates must be twenty-five years of age or older; and many state and local judicial posts, where candidates must be attorneys. Depending on the position being sought, running for office can be an expensive affair, in terms of both time and money. It can also be a rewarding experience.

Not all forms of participation are classified as conventional. Unconventional forms of participation include such activities as protests, civil disobedience, and political violence. Civil disobedience involves intentional efforts to be arrested in order to draw attention to a cause. Civil disobedience, therefore, is a more extreme form of participation than a simple protest. The most radical form of political participation, however, is politically motivated violence. Bombings, assassinations, and riots can all be examples of this.

Most citizens do not opt to participate in political violence. Neither do they all choose to write letters to elected officials, speak at public meetings, or even vote. Political scientists, therefore, are interested in factors associated with political participation. Studies have demonstrated that voter turnout in the United States is relatively low compared to many other democracies. Other studies have shown that factors such as age, income, and education are positively related to political participation.

Applications

In many respects, Spence Barch of Harrison Township, Pennsylvania, led a typical life. Upon graduation from high school in 1974, he attended college, eventually receiving a masters in business in 1983. He worked as an accountant and was active in church and community organizations. What set Barch apart from most citizens in the United States was the extent to which he participated in politics. Not only did he vote in every election since he turned eighteen, but he also was a candidate in many of them. At the age of nineteen, he was elected to a two-year term as Republican committeeperson, the youngest in the state. This nonpaid position gave him a unique vantage point from which to view the workings of Harrison Township government. He regularly attended township commissioners' meetings and occasionally spoke at them. Barch did not like everything he saw at these meetings. His biggest concern was that the same group of people seemed to be running the township, as Republicans seldom ran for commissioner. Because he believed that people needed a choice, in 1979, at the age of twenty-two, Barch ran for township commissioner. He won the Republican primary, but lost the general election by a narrow margin in a township where the majority of the voters were registered Democrats.

Three years later, Barch ran for a seat on the Highlands school board. Again Barch won the Republican primary but lost the general election, this time by an even narrower margin. Despite two losses in three years, Barch entered the electoral arena for a third time at the age of twenty-six, when he again sought a seat on the school board. This time he was successful, winning a four-year term by a wide margin. Barch won reelection to the school board four years later, but lost his bid for a third term. His tenure on the school board convinced Barch that for education to improve, there would need to be changes at the state level. Hence, Barch decided to run for a seat on the state legislature in 1992 in the hope of serving on that body's education committee. This time Barch was defeated in the Republican primary.

Despite several defeats at the polls, Barch accomplished several goals during his time in public office, including helping to defeat two tax increases and to pass a policy prohibiting corporal punishment in his school district. Through his continuing involvement in electoral politics, Barch demonstrated that one person who makes the choice to participate can have an impact on the policy process.

While the case of Spence Barch illustrates conventional political participation, the residents of the Love Canal neighborhood of Niagara Falls, New York, used both conventional and unconventional means to persuade federal and state officials to fund the relocation of hundreds of families. Residents sought the relocation effort after studies conducted in the late 1970's found that the area was contaminated by toxic chemicals that had been buried years earlier. These chemicals, it was believed, were to blame for a series of health problems that afflicted inhabitants of the area. The residents initially employed conventional techniques to convey their sentiments to government leaders. Homeowners called, petitioned, and wrote letters to federal, state, and local officials. They also voiced their concerns at a number of public meetings. It was an unconventional technique, however, that attracted the most attention to their cause.

In May, 1980, the preliminary results of a new federal study began to leak out. The study suggested that several residents of Love Canal had suffered chromosomal damage as a result of their exposure to chemicals seeping up to the surface. This, coupled with the perception that the Carter Administration was dragging its feet on relocation efforts, caused residents to abandon conventional methods of participation in favor of more drastic ones.

On the evening of May 19, 1980, area residents held two federal officials in the office of the Love Canal Homeowners Association. Although they were not physically restrained, the two Environmental Protection Agency (EPA) administrators were in a building surrounded by several hundred angry Love Canal residents. The association's leader, Lois Gibbs, labeled the officials "hostages" in an attempt to appease the crowd. During the course of the confrontation, there was considerable shouting and at least one of the office's windows was shattered. After several tense hours and an ultimatum from the FBI, the residents allowed federal and local police to escort the EPA officials out of the building. Although there were no arrests, the incident did serve to further impress upon federal and state officials the seriousness of the situation. Two days after the incident, the federal government announced that the president had approved funding for a temporary relocation plan. For the residents, this announcement was the culmination of several years of political participation, both conventional and unconventional.

Context

Political participation is a critical aspect of any system of government, especially democratic ones. Without such involvement it would be extremely difficult for government to discern, let alone address, the needs of the public. In the absence of feedback from its citizenry, government would be forced to either rely on its own perceptions of the people's desires or spend a large amount of time and money conducting frequent surveys on countless issues.

One problem with relying on people to communicate their needs to decision makers, however, is that some people do not do so. Often the needs of groups that neither vote nor contact their elected representatives receive low priority. Politicians are much more likely to cater to the desires of the types of people who participate, the types who can make or break an official seeking reelection. This raises the fundamental question of fairness. Regardless of how one answers this question, political participation is vital to government.

Political participation serves another purpose: aiding in the legitimation of policy. Public policy is much easier to implement if citizens accept choices made by their leaders, even if they don't necessarily agree with those decisions. The chances of this happening are dramatically increased when the public feels that it has been consulted in the making of the decision. Thus, providing persons with an opportunity to speak at public meetings and forming citizen advisory committees not only provides government with information that might make for a better decision from a technical standpoint, but also can increase the acceptance of unpopular decisions. If people are still unhappy with policy choices, the most basic form of conventional political participation—voting—is again an option. The knowledge that in subsequent elections they can vote against the officials who made the decision with which they disagree keeps most citizens from turning to more radical, unconventional means of political participation.

Bibliography

Conway, M. Margaret. *Political Participation in the United States.* 2d ed. Washington, D.C.: Congressional Quarterly Press, 1991. Excellent review of the literature on political participation. The chapter on characteristics associated with participation is particularly useful.

DeSario, Jack, and Stuart Langton, eds. *Citizen Participation in Public Decision Making.* New York: Greenwood Press, 1987. Ten articles, each of which places the topic of political participation in an applied context. All deal with government efforts to solicit public participation.

Gibbs, Lois M. *Love Canal: My Story.* Albany: State University of New York Press, 1982. Story of how the residents of Love Canal convinced the government to buy their chemically contaminated homes, as told by the housewife who became the head of the Love Canal Homeowners Association. Her account of the events surrounding the crisis demonstrates how ordinary citizens can influence government actions.

Langton, Stuart, ed. *Citizen Participation in America: Essays on the State of the Art.* Lexington, Mass.: Lexington Books, 1978. Essays on various aspects of citizen participation. Topics range from the nature of political participation to ways in which government can use public participation to its advantage. Essay on matching method to purpose contains an exhaustive list of participation techniques.

Milbrath, Lester W. *Political Participation: How and Why Do People Get Involved in Politics?* Chicago: Rand McNally, 1965. Classic work on political participation. Its discussion of variables related to participation is both well-organized and reader-friendly.

Verba, Sidney, Norman H. Nie, and Jae-on Kim. *Participation and Political Equality: A Seven-Nation Comparison.* New York: Cambridge University Press, 1978. Compares political participation in the United States and six other nations. Although knowledge of advanced statistical techniques is helpful in interpreting some of the data, most of the findings are presented as percentages. The general reader should thus be able to comprehend most of the material.

Kevin R. Hardwick

Cross-References

POLITICAL PARTIES

Field of study: Politics

Parties play significant roles in all political systems, but especially in democratic systems, whose health often depends on the success of parties in linking the people to the political process and recruiting qualified people to run for office and serve when elected.

Principal terms

CATCH-ALL PARTY (UMBRELLA PARTY): party that appeals to diverse interests, usually by adopting a general or vague platform

CENTRALIZED PARTY: party whose leadership controls all nominations and the votes of party members who hold legislative seats

DECENTRALIZED PARTY: loosely structured party whose central headquarters has little control over the party's organizational wings or governmental members

MULTIPARTY SYSTEM: political process in which numerous parties compete; frequently produces coalition governments in parliamentary systems

THIRD PARTY: minor political party that tries to challenge the major parties in a two-party system

TWO-PARTY SYSTEM: system in which only two parties have a realistic chance of winning control of the government

Overview

Political parties are organizations that seek to influence governments by capturing their elective offices. Although parties are found in authoritarian and pluralist systems, they are an essential political ingredient only in democracies. Indeed, it has been often said that democracy is not found within parties but among parties—in the choices that competing parties offer by running candidates for office and in the role that they play as organizations that can be held accountable for the actions of government. Nor are these the only roles fulfilled by parties in democracies. In addition to linking citizens organizationally and psychologically to their governments, parties recruit new groups into the electorate, they find qualified personnel for appointed offices, and they present candidates to run for offices in elections. They also consolidate and articulate the demands of the diverse groups and interests found in contemporary, pluralist democracies. Finally, they often train future leaders for the tasks of governance, even as they provide the mechanisms for turning campaign promises into governmental policies in democratic systems.

The success of parties in discharging these roles varies, but normally their effectiveness follows their forms. The more structured a party is, and the greater a national party leadership's control is over its grassroots organization, party nominations, and (consequently) the votes of its members in legislatures, the more successful the party is likely to be in discharging its linkage, aggregation, recruitment, electoral, and decision-making roles. Although no system's parties perform all these roles well all the time, the centralized, highly structured parties of parliamentary democracies normally perform most of these roles well most of the time—a state of affairs that reflects both national political cultures and national election systems. Throughout Western Europe, for example, national political cultures generally emphasize the need for aggressive, majority-rule democracy. Parties are expected actually to implement their platforms when they take power. Moreover, in many of these countries, elections might occur at any time, at the request of a prime minister or as the result of a no-confidence vote being passed against the government within a legislative body. This contrasts with the American system of elections as calendar events that can occur only at regular intervals. As a consequence, political parties in parliamentary systems—unlike American parties—do not usually have the luxury of hibernating after elections. They must be prepared to contest an election at any moment, providing round-the-year linkages between the people and government and continuously discharging the roles of parties in democratic systems. Most—but by no means all—of the world's major parties are to be found in Western Europe.

Applications

Two of the world's major parties are in the United States: the Democratic Party and Republican Party. Other parties may be older, but few have enjoyed the durability of the two major parties. For most of the twentieth century, the two dominant American parties have exercised hegemony over political power at all levels in the United States. Third parties have come and gone, sometimes influencing the behavior of the major parties; however, not since the Civil War has any third party seriously threatened to displace either of them in the country's party system.

Significant differences separate the two major American parties, especially on policy issues. The Republican Party has a more conservative membership (80 percent of which describes itself as "conservative," against only a third of the Democratic Party membership), and it has therefore consistently adopted a more conservative platform than its rival—projecting itself as the party of capitalism, smaller government, anticommunism, and traditional family values. Meanwhile, the Democratic Party has tended to be composed of approximately equal numbers of members who call themselves liberals, moderates, and conservatives. As the creator of the social welfare state during the 1930's and as the architect of strong civil rights legislation in the 1960's, the Democratic Party continues to draft platforms slightly left of center in terms of the government's role in protecting minority rights, problem solving, and quality-of-life issues.

Policy emphasis notwithstanding, both parties are doctrinally loose, middle-of-the-road umbrella parties that try to appeal to as many voters as possible. Both are also highly decentralized organizations largely unable to control even the choices of party candidates (who are now generally selected in primary elections conducted by state governments) or control the voting of their elected officials. The parties' organizational weakness often undercuts their capacity to perform the functions of parties in democracies. On the other hand, their character mirrors the individualistic nature of the national political culture, which would look unkindly on national party leaders telling local representatives how to vote. The umbrella nature of the major parties has been an asset to the extent that it has left third parties with little opportunity to acquire their own followings in the United States.

By contrast, the principal parties in Great Britain's two-party system, though not without their internal divisions, have tended to be highly centralized and less catch-all in nature than American parties. The Labour Party still reflects its nineteenth century trade union origins and its commitment to pragmatic socialism. The Conservative Party—the world's oldest continuously functioning party (with roots predating Britain's Glorious Revolution of 1689)—likewise remains true to its commitments. It favors a unitary Great Britain, free-market capitalism, and its own image as the party of Britain's traditional ruling class, even though many of its late twentieth century leaders (Edward Heath, Margaret Thatcher, and John Major) have come from working-class backgrounds. At the same time, the party's pragmatic approach to conservatism (including a willingness to embrace most of the welfare state created by the Labour Party after World War II) has kept it politically competitive, allowing it to attract a large bloc of working-class votes, as well as a large share of the expanding middle class.

Only during the 1980's did these parties veer far from the British political center, and with ill-effects to both. Following its defeat in the 1979 general elections, Labour lurched sharply to the left on several major issues. For example, it advocated more nationalization of industry and proposed weakening Britain's ties to NATO and the United States. In taking these stands, the party distanced itself from a large share of the middle-of-the-road vote and alienated the moderate element in its own parliamentary wing. During the 1983 general election, a celebrated segment of its members in Parliament broke away to found the Social Democratic Party, which subsequently spawned a breakaway segment now allied with the British Liberal Party (in the Social Liberal Alliance). The net effect was to leave the Conservatives with such fragmented opposition that it was relatively easy for Prime Minister Margaret Thatcher to win reelection in both 1983 and 1987 with enlarged parliamentary majorities, even though the Conservative Party had a net loss in total votes in both elections, compared to 1979 returns.

The opposition's split also enabled Thatcher to move the Conservatives doctrinally more to the right on economic policy than might have otherwise occurred because there was little electoral risk in doing so. At the same time, the voters' inability to hold the Conservatives electorally accountable for this policy drift contributed to a sharp drop in deference to political authority in Britain. What appeared to emerge was a "one-and-a-half-party system," in which only the Conservatives could contest elections with any chance of governing without a coalition partner. All other parties (including Labour) could only hope to govern in a coalition format.

Contrary to the traditional, two-party model of Anglo-American politics, parties on the European continent have usually functioned within moderate (three to five parties) to intense (more than five) multiparty frameworks, with French parties in particular being numerous and historically weak. Only since the Fifth French Republic began in 1958 have France's parties become modern, nationwide, catch-more political organizations capable of anchoring stable ruling coalitions within the French Assembly. Their development in part reflects the post-World War II setting of French politics, which has been generally favorable to the formation of a moderate multiparty system of true national parties. As citizens have become more willing to participate in politics, ideologies have declined in importance. Urbanization and industrialization have leveled regional differences and undercut parochial issues. Still, skillful party builders, such as François Mitterrand, also played a major role in transforming the postwar nature of French party politics.

Mitterrand is the father of the modern French Socialist Party (PSF), which he built during the 1960's into a centralized, nationwide organization out of the small, quarrelsome local socialist organizations, which previously represented a small part of the country's political spectrum. In defining the PSF's commitment to working-class interests pragmatically rather than rigidly, Mitterrand also widened the party's appeal beyond the working class to the many citizens entering middle-class jobs in the French bureaucracy during the 1980's. The PSF consequently became France's largest vote getter during that decade, with Mitterrand himself winning the powerful French presidency in 1981 (retaining it until 1988) and the PSF capturing control of France's parliament on two occasions. Moreover, even when it declined during the early 1990's, the PSF continued to represent the largest bloc of votes in France as the party of the Left, while the electorate on the Right continued to divide its votes among several parties with sizeable followings.

Meanwhile across the Rhine River, for most of its post-World War II history, democratic Germany has been governed by the Christian Democratic Union and its Bavarian wing, the Christian Social Union (CDU/CSU)—the party which championed reunification when the Federal German Republic became self-governing in 1949, and which presided over reunification when the communist regime in East Germany collapsed in 1990. Founded in postwar Germany under the guiding hand of the allied occupiers, the CDU/CSU became the party of Konrad Adenauer, religious values, West Germany's economic "miracle," and militant anticommunism. In the 1950's it also became—along with other major German parties—a catch-all, centrist organization as postwar affluence produced a middle-class society in the Federal German Republic (FDR). Profiting from this strategy and its economic and political accomplishments, the party controlled the FDR's chancellorship during all but thirteen of the forty years of the Federal Republic's pre-reunification history. Only during the 1970's did it become the opposition, when a new generation of Germans raised in the postwar period of economic prosperity embraced a series of quality-of-life issues that were mainly identified with the Social Democrats (SDP). After the global economic downturn of the 1980's again made economic issues the primary concern of the

German electorate, voters returned the CDU/CSU to office. Indeed, even during its period in the opposition, the CDU/CSU never received less than 44.5 percent of the vote and often received more than the SPD, which was able to govern only with the support of the small Free Democrat Party.

Japan's Liberal Democratic Party (LDP) provides the last example from the developed democratic world. Formed in 1955 by the merger of the Liberal and Democratic parties at the insistence of Japan's business community, the LDP was designed to provide the country with a single, essentially probusiness party capable of continuing to control the government despite the recent reunification of Japan's Socialist party. The result was a party that dominated every Japanese election until 1993, and which held an absolute majority in Japan's house of representatives after every election except two between 1955 and 1993.

The LDP's success can be widely explained by two factors: its pragmatic adaptation to postwar Japan's changing political scene and its ability to hold together the personal political machines that it encompassed until the 1990's. Like the German CDU/CSU, the LDP began as pro-American in its foreign policy and self-consciously procapitalist at home. Over time, however, by creating Japan's postwar welfare system and other postwar redistributional policies, the LDP transformed itself into a catch-all party that appealed to all segments of the Japanese electorate. Meanwhile, though often ruthlessly pragmatic in sacrificing the leaders of its internal factions when tales of scandal or corruption made it politically expedient to do so, the party also did well in sustaining the essentially male-dominated, Tokyo University educated coalition of leaders of its internal factions upon which its ability to dominate Japanese politics depended. Not until the late 1980's, when a series of scandals combined with an unpopular sales tax to undermine the party's following, did the party become vulnerable—and then only because some of its internal factions at last began breaking away. Nevertheless, the LDP remained the largest party in Japan's essentially moderate, multiparty system.

Finally, there is a lone representative from the Third World, the Indian National Congress party. India's largest party, its history is inseparably linked to that of its country. Founded in 1885 to mobilize India's religious and linguistic communities behind a drive for self-rule, the Indian National Congress eventually won independence for India in 1947. Under the leadership of Jawaharlal Nehru, it subsequently became the system-wide governing party of independent India. Under Nehru's successors—including his daughter Indira Gandhi and her son Rajiv Gandhi—the party successfully steered India through a turbulent half century of democracy—a feat that some observers say may be unique among Third World states.

To be sure, neither the Congress Party nor India was spared the growing pangs of democracy. After 1947, the party basically became a political machine under the personalized and often domineering control of its leaders, functioning not so much as a catch-all party, but as a syndicate of leaders willing to champion whatever necessary to stay in power in a country whose voters remain perhaps 50 percent illiterate. Power has also been personally costly to the party. Spiritual leader Mahatma Gandhi, Prime Minister Indira Gandhi, and Prime Minister Rajiv Gandhi all died at the hands of assassins—the last while campaigning for reelection in 1991. Rajiv's death also affected the party's organization, leaving behind a leadership vacuum in the party which had continued to govern India even after the party's split into contesting wings in 1969. When the elections resumed after Rajiv's death in 1991, the party received its lowest vote since independence. Its decline, however, had begun almost a quarter century earlier, with the party's vote slipping from 44 percent in 1971 to under 40 percent in all subsequent national elections except that of 1984. As a consequence, the political hegemony which the party enjoyed as late as 1970 steadily eroded. Still, like the other parties surveyed, the party remained an influential actor in Indian politics. Indeed, it remains the centerpiece of India's multiparty system, as well as the single largest vote getter in the democratic world, given the enormous size of India's electorate.

Context

The picture of democratic party politics which emerges from these studies is a consistent if not altogether positive one. Although some parties have had a strongly ideological component at birth, the major parties in the electorally competitive democratic world have flourished and maintained their support by adopting platforms of a more or less pragmatic and catch-all nature. Doing so has not always been cost free. Pragmatism can antagonize the true believers within parties even as forces in society may distance the parties from their traditional electorates. Most of the Western parties, for example, have been built on class issues to some degree; however, the shift from industrialized to postindustrial societies in the developed world has undercut class as a cohesive force. Worse, it has generated a host of new issues, often commandeered by opposition parties, outside the realm of class-based politics (such as privacy, environmental, and other quality of life issues). As a result, most of these parties have faced strains within their relationships with their traditional supporters.

Governing for long periods has also been a mixed blessing. Staying in power continuously confers abundant resources with which to reward supporters; however, it also means being held responsible for bad times (such as those resulting from the global economic decline of the 1980's) and having constantly to wrestle with issues that cannot be resolved without straining the internal components of a catch-all political organization. Organizational strains and electoral setbacks thus become inevitable, but the most successful parties in the world's largest and most powerful democracies have continued to influence their political systems. Furthermore, by their example they have often influenced those peoples opting for democracy in the former Soviet Union and those pursuing the difficult road to it in the developing world.

Bibliography

Duverger, Maurice. *Modern Democracies: Economic Power Versus Political Power.* Translated by Charles L. Markmann. Hinsdale, Ill.: Dryden Press, 1974. Classic study of western systems by one of France's leading political scientists.
Hauss, Charles. *Comparative Politics: Domestic Responses to Global Challenges.*

Minneapolis, Minn.: West, 1994. Ideal starting point for research on the principal countries of today's world and their leading political parties, including those of the communist world.

Lawson, Kay. *The Comparative Study of Political Parties*. New York: St. Martin's Press, 1976. Excellent guide to the topic, using as case studies the principal parties in the United States and France, as well as Africa's Guinea.

Rose, Richard. *Do Parties Make a Difference?* Chatham, N.J.: Chatham House, 1980. Detailed study of British political parties and their impact on national policy-making.

Wattenberg, Martin P. *The Decline of American Political Parties: 1952-1988*. Cambridge, Mass.: Harvard University Press, 1990. Examination of electoral drift, dealignment and party decentralization and decay in the postwar political process in the United States.

Joseph R. Rudolph, Jr.

Cross-References

Accountability in U.S. Government, p. 1; Class Conflict, p. 331; Communist Parties, p. 377; The Democratic Party, p. 520; Mexico: Politics and Government, p. 1179; Multiparty Systems, p. 1235; Nonpartisan Political Organizations, p. 1326; One-Party Systems, p. 1350; Political Machines and Bosses, p. 1468; Political Party Conventions, p. 1492; Political Party Roles, p. 1499; Political Platforms, p. 1512; The Republican Party, p. 1699; Social Democratic Parties, p. 1846; Two-Party Systems, p. 2033.

POLITICAL PARTY CONVENTIONS

Field of study: Politics

At an American political party convention, delegates choose candidates for president and vice president of the United States, and the party creates a party platform, or statement on issues. These functions are superficial, however; other less obvious functions are very important.

Principal terms

DELEGATE: party member who, based on party loyalty, service, and support for a particular presidential candidate, is chosen to represent local party units at the national party convention

NOMINATION: the selection, by delegates' vote, of the official party candidates for president and vice president

PLANKS: single issue statements within the platform, the exact ideological orientation of which is often used as a bargaining chip in seeking party unity

PLATFORM: statement of the official party position on a variety of issues a work of compromise that is usually vague, disjointed, and ignored

PRIMARY: statewide electoral contest within parties, designed to choose, by popular vote, party nominees and to choose delegates (based on the popularity of the presidential candidate they support) for the national party conventions

Overview

The political party convention is the governing body of a political party in the United States. Both the Democrats and Republicans hold their national conventions once every four years. The political party convention is a gathering of party supporters who have been sent by their state party organizations to represent their locality in the party's deliberations.

Initiated by the Anti-Masonic Party in 1831, and now used by all major American parties, the convention has been the body responsible for selecting the party's presidential and vice presidential nominees. The other major function of the convention is the creation of the party platform, which is a statement of the party's official position on important issues of the day.

Conventions do more than these primary functions, but providing an overview of American political party conventions is difficult for two reasons. First, political party conventions are dynamic, with their composition, organization, and rules of function constantly changing. Any specific description of convention structure could be quickly outdated. Second, those elements of the conventions that are consistent are not of real consequence. For example, the choice of a party presidential nominee, once the main purpose of a convention, is decided by primary elections long before the convention is held, making the continuing practice of voting in the convention usually a mere formality. Another example is the party platform, a proclamation of the ideology of the delegates that happen to control the convention that year. Ultimately it is read by almost no voters, and its planks, which address specific issues, are often disregarded by even the candidates.

The most visible parts of the convention are in fact just window dressing, but this does not mean that these giant party gatherings are without effect. Conventions serve several essential functions in furthering party goals, such as serving as a deliberative body. The convention delegates have been selected by other party members to deliberate as a body on candidates and issues. With some exceptions, most delegates have not been legally or formally bound to vote for a certain issue position. The delegates' commitment to the presidential candidate holds only through the first ballot. The primary voters do not and, for practical reasons, cannot bind delegates to vote in certain ways on platform or procedural matters.

Another function is that of national campaign rally. Party faithful gather from all parts of the country to mingle with one another, meet old friends, share new ideas, meet the candidates and party leaders, listen to motivational speeches, and have fun. The delegates are supposed to become whipped into a frenzy by the time they leave, so that they will carry their enthusiasm to the faithful back home and convince them to support actively the party's nominees.

Third, the national party convention serves as a reward system for party faithfulness and activity. Devoted party workers are rewarded for their service to the party by selection as a delegate to the national convention. It is intended that the goal of national convention participation will be a spur for committed service to the party.

A fourth function is one of legitimizing, consensus building, and hatchet burying. Before the convention the party may have experienced a bruising struggle. Though one candidate may have the nomination, the wound of party division needs healing. The final nominating vote and the calls for unity from former opponents establish the victor's role as the nominee of the party. A convention provides legitimacy for a nominee.

Although these traditional functions continue to be served, television has altered the role of the convention. Often, this alteration has hampered the convention's ability to perform its functions. During the convention itself, the presence of television cameras makes the process of deliberation difficult. Serious bargaining and cajoling cannot be accomplished on the floor of the convention for fear that television cameras and reporters will be attracted and eavesdrop. Serious negotiation on party business must be done off the floor, in private chambers, away from the camera's eye.

Television also hampers compromise in another way. When a political leader is interviewed on camera and states a particular position, he or she is committed in front of not only those at the convention, but also to a few million others in their homes. A tentative initial stance soon becomes a hardened public position. Later change or compromise involves losing face and therefore is more difficult to undertake. Leaders and delegates involved in bargaining must hedge on public statements (a practice that incurs the wrath of the press), or not compromise at all.

Television also has affected the campaign rally function. The presence of television has led to a reduction in rallies. Since the advent of television coverage in 1952, the convention sessions have been shortened, most spontaneous demonstrations have been prohibited, favorite son nominations (used to recognize state or regional party figures) have been reduced or eliminated, and the numerous lengthy seconding speeches have been substantially reduced. Television has demanded a convention that fits its needs for fast-paced action and strict time constraints. The presence of television has added a benefit, however, to the campaign rally function. Now, not only can several thousand delegates feel the effects of the rally, but millions of voters can join in as viewers, thus reinforcing their party identification.

Television is capable of distorting the image of the convention and diluting the campaign rally function for viewers. For example, while delegates are on the floor hearing rally speeches from the podium, viewers may be treated to commentary from a television anchorperson, a question-and-answer session with a delegation leader on some wild rumor, a human-interest story on an unusual delegate, or a commercial. The rally function for viewers becomes diluted because television does not have an obligation to help the convention fulfill that function. In fact, television has an obligation to remain impartial.

The reward system function also has been affected by television, though more indirectly. By commenting on the erratic or indifferent behavior of delegates—at times demonstrating, at other times sleeping, and sometimes not even present—and especially in the 1968 and 1972 conventions, on the unrepresentative composition of the delegation, television has encouraged a negative image of delegates as political hacks. This has provoked calls for delegate selection reforms. These reforms resulted in the exclusion of traditional party leaders and loyalists. Through the primary system of delegate selection, allegiance to a particular candidate has become the criterion for selection rather than faithful service to the party.

Finally television has played a major role in damaging the conventions' function of legitimizing and consensus building. Television's effect on this function perhaps is the most serious because the party may well fragment after the convention rather than coalesce if this function is not carried out.

Compromise is an essential aspect of the legitimizing and consensus-building function. Defeated candidates and their supporters must be allowed to return to the fold and have their opposition forgotten in order to create a consensus for the fall campaign. Television, with an interest in highlighting conflict, will emphasize the conflicts within a party in order to provide engrossing viewing.

The camera also provides a forum for ideologues seeking national exposure. Television gives these people a level of importance beyond their number of supporters or actual influence at the convention. Those who do not or cannot win at the convention may use the media to achieve some measure of victory, leading to fragmentation and resistance to compromise.

For many voters the convention coverage is their first attention to the campaign and their first real exposure to the nominees. Party leaders realize that in the media age, the campaign really begins with the convention. Aware of this significance, the party has structured the convention to meet television's needs. The objective is to make convention viewing convenient and attractive to the voter. For example, sessions are held in the evening when more viewers can watch, key speeches are scheduled in prime time, and entertainment by Hollywood figures is included. The presence of television has provided greater opportunity for fulfillment of some convention functions, such as getting voter attention for a nominee. Conversely, there has been a greater strain on the ability of the convention to fulfill other functions, such as deliberating and building consensus.

The presence of television cameras in conventions has not had merely a narrow effect in terms of convention timing and spontaneity of demonstrations, but very likely has had a broad effect in weakening the convention's ability to carry out important functions.

Applications

In the modern, primary-dominated presidential selection process, the traditional functions of a convention (choosing nominees and creating a platform) are of limited importance. Despite this fact, the conventions still can influence who wins the race to the White House. With the vast exposure provided by media coverage of the conventions, a good convention performance, well received by the press, can give a significant boost to a candidate. Conversely, poor press coverage of a convention can severely damage a candidacy.

The 1992 national party conventions provided a dramatic contrast in media perceptions of the parties' and candidates' convention performances. The coverage of the conventions appears to have directly influenced the popularity of the candidates in the early stages of the general election campaign.

The Democrats held their convention first. They portrayed themselves, through the platform and the tone of the speakers, as more centrist than in recent memory. The speech of the party's presidential nominee focused on a new image for the Democrats as defenders of the middle ground. Though their party is often divided and fractious, the Democrats in 1992 were united behind their new image. The delegates were enthusiastic and confident, and the positives of the convention bubbled over into the media coverage. Bill Clinton, who just a few weeks before had been in third place in some polls (behind the Republican candidate George Bush and independent H. Ross Perot), by the convention's end held a twenty-point lead over the incumbent president.

The Republicans had a much different experience. Behind in the polls, they knew they had to stage a perfect event, but they failed. With major challenges coming to President George Bush from the conservative wing of his party, the platform and the speeches were often far to the right of the candidate and a majority of the voters. Many in the party also chose to attack the elites of entertainment and media over the issue of family values. President Bush's speech was drafted at the last moment and was not well received.

The media coverage of the Republican convention emphasized the controversy of the event, between elements within the party and between the party and the nation's culture. Viewers saw convention delegates calling for the removal of Vice President Dan Quayle from the ticket; they saw defeated presidential candidate Pat Buchanan not boosting the party's nominee, but instead using his speech to attack homosexuals and feminists; and they saw a controversial televangelist speak as a prominent member of the party. These were not the acts of a party intent on building a consensus. The press commentary accompanying the convention events was usually downbeat, negative, and critical—perhaps justifiably so, considering that the Republicans were often attacking one another.

The Republican convention failed to accomplish its purposes as a positive campaign rally, as a legitimizing forum for the nominees, and as a consensus-building show of party unity. The convention rather served as a podium for the ideologues of the party, thus alienating more voters than were gained. The convention gave Bush a boost of only a few points in the polls, which evaporated in only a few days.

The convention season of 1992 produced a drastic shift in the electoral future of the major party candidates. The media depicted the Republicans as divided and out of touch with mainstream America, while it portrayed the Democrats as united and sensitive to American values. The Democrats gained an advantage over the Republicans that did not wane before the general election in November. America watched one party fail to fulfill the real convention purposes of compromising, consensus building, and rallying, and watched the other party succeed.

Context

The Republicans had an unsuccessful convention in 1992, but the Democrats had a debacle in 1968. After the Democratic convention in 1968, the party leadership, especially those from the party's left wing, began to evaluate the effectiveness of the convention as a representative institution. An advisory commission, established to recommend rules changes, suggested major revisions in the delegate selection processes. Changes included quotas for minorities, elimination of seats reserved for public or party officials, and an end to the practices of unit rule (a whole delegation voting in a bloc), proxy voting, and appointment rather than election of delegates. After the 1972 Democratic convention, and the general election results, doubts arose about the wisdom of the reforms. The party supposedly with the most representative convention had suffered one of the worst defeats in its history. Many Democratic leaders and party members had abandoned the party. It was argued that the reforms had caused the damage.

Several subsequent reform efforts followed through the 1970's and 1980's. The tide of reform ultimately turned back toward greater roles for elected officials and party leaders as convention delegates. By the 1992 Democratic convention, approximately 14 percent of delegate seats were reserved for "super delegates," or those delegates not elected through primaries and caucuses. The greater importance given to primaries initiated by earlier reforms, however, continued unabated. In 1992, thirty-nine states held presidential primaries.

Selection of delegates through state primaries and caucuses continued to undermine the role of the convention as the deciding voice in the presidential nomination process. In most campaigns since 1972, one candidate has secured a majority of the delegates, through arduous campaigning in the primaries, long before the convention opens. The candidate is usually so assured of victory that often the selection of a vice presidential running mate is made before the presidential candidate is even nominated. In 1984 and 1992, the Democratic nominees chose running mates even before the conventions began.

The dominance of the eventual nominee's delegates at the convention guarantees that the vice presidential candidate choice will be easily ratified. This was remarkably illustrated in 1988, when Republican convention delegates unanimously selected Indiana senator Dan Quayle as their vice presidential nominee. They did so despite the fact that Quayle was in the midst of a scandal about whether he used political connections to join the National Guard to evade more onerous military service during the Vietnam War.

The conventions have been termed "dinosaurs" in the modern age of primaries, but they have demonstrated a remarkable adaptability in shifting from deliberative bodies for presidential nominations to televised campaign rallies and showcases for the parties and their nominees. Mark Twain once said that reports of his death were greatly exaggerated; the same could be said about the conventions.

Bibliography

David, Paul T., Ralph M. Goldman, and Richard C. Bain. *The Politics of National Party Conventions*. Washington, D.C.: Brookings Institution, 1960. Comprehensive examination of the presidential electoral process, with a close look at the conventions.

Davis, James W. *National Conventions in an Age of Party Reform*. Westport, Conn.: Greenwood Press, 1983. Nuts-and-bolts account of the history, organization, procedures, and functions of national party conventions.

Polsby, Nelson W. *Consequences of Party Reform*. New York: Oxford University Press, 1983. Survey of the consequences of party reforms since 1968.

Shafer, Byron E. *Bifurcated Politics: Evolution and Reform in the National Party Convention*. Cambridge, Mass.: Harvard University Press, 1988. Describes the changing functions of conventions since the reforms of the 1970's and 1980's and discusses where convention evolution may lead.

Smith, Larry David, and Dan Nimmo. *Cordial Occurrence: Orchestrating National Party Conventions in the Telepolitical Age*. New York: Praeger, 1991. A look at how conventions are being molded to fit the media age, turning them into spectacles, and in the process giving them new purpose and vitality.

Richard Davis
Vincent James Strickler

Cross-References

Delegates, p. 501; The Democratic Party, p. 520; Elections, p. 578; The Media and Elections, p. 1161; Political Machines and Bosses, p. 1468; Political Parties, p. 1485; Political Party Roles, p. 1499; Political Platforms, p. 1512; Populism, p. 1551; Presidential Elections in the United States, p. 1596; Primary Elections, p. 1603; The Republican Party, p. 1699.

POLITICAL PARTY ROLES

Field of study: Political philosophy

Political parties are organizing units for political groups. Parties generally fall outside of the formal governmental structure. They are a political tool used by government officials to mobilize voters and interest groups to support or oppose political policies.

Principal terms

CENTRALIZED PARTY: political party that gives elected officials considerable control over party nominations and policy formation

CONVENTIONS: gathering of party members to plan party strategy and, in some cases, to make nominations for public office

DECENTRALIZED PARTY: political party that grants considerable control over party nominations to the electorate

ELECTORAL CAUCUS: group of party loyalists who meet to determine who will be the party's nominees to public office

PRIMARY ELECTION: election that permits voters to determine who the party's nominee will be for the general election

Overview

Political parties are usually one of two types: They are either legislative parties that help organize governmental activities or they are electoral parties that try to influence who will hold governmental office. Political parties in one form or another have existed for centuries, but formal parties that develop political platforms and have clearly established membership are largely the result of developments that occurred during the nineteenth and twentieth centuries. There is a parallel between the development of democratic governments and the development of political parties.

Political parties began as collections of like-minded people hoping to consolidate their influence in a way that would enhance their ability to control governmental decisions and actions. Most political parties began as some other type of organization. Clubs, trade associations, and churches have all had organized political groups that have demonstrated the potential to become political parties. Organizations that attempt to influence government to achieve economic, social, or religious objectives occasionally become so caught up in political activity that they begin to function more like a political party than an interest group. The transition occurs when the groups want members to occupy political offices instead of merely influencing them.

Legislative parties (sometimes referred to as parliamentary or congressional parties) originated when legislative chambers began to possess significant political authority. As legislative chambers became policymakers instead of advisers to policymakers, party divisions became more common within the organizations. The most important distinction to make among legislative parties is based on the percentage of the legislators who are members of a particular party. Within a two-party system, there is a majority party and a minority party. In a multiparty system there can be a majority party as well but the minority parties have a decidedly different role when they are numerous and fragmented.

Majority parties, regardless of the type of party system, have the responsibility of organizing the legislative chamber and trying to determine the legislative agenda. In many political systems this party is referred to as the party in government or as the governmental party. The minority party or parties are frequently referred to as the opposition party or parties. Just as it is the majority parties' job to determine the direction of governmental policies, it is the responsibility of the opposition party to critique the majority party and propose alternative policies to those being presented by the majority.

Electoral parties, like legislative parties, have become more common as democracies have become more common. Electoral parties attempt to influence governmental policies by getting candidates they support elected to public offices. Electoral parties will usually take an active part in trying to recruit candidates for political office and in trying to mobilize voters for those candidates on election day. The usual goal of electoral parties is to get enough of their candidates elected so they can be the majority party in the government.

While there is no one sure way for parties to develop, it is most common for legislative parties to develop within the legislature and then for that party to begin to organize electoral party units. The most sophisticated party units build their electoral campaigns around the successes or failures of the legislative parties. Although many electoral parties begin as local organizations, a sign of their ultimate success is determined by their ability to unite and work with one of the legislative parties.

The most important decision that any party system must make is how it will go about selecting or nominating its candidates for public office. The two main models historically have been the centralized British system and the decentralized American system. A centralized party system is one that gives the legislative party considerable control over the nominating process; a decentralized party system is one that leaves the nominating process to other constituent groups. In the United States, for example, nominations usually take place in local conventions, caucuses, or primary elections. In all of these nominating systems, members of the legislative party may take an active part, but they do not control the process. They become part of a larger group of party activists or voters who make the party's nominations.

The simplest and most unified parties are those associated with a parliamentary system of government. In parliamentary democracies the only elected representatives are the members of parliament. Once the parliamentary elections are over, all other political positions are determined by votes within parliament. The voters' task is limited to determining whom they would like to have as their parliamentary representative and which party they would like to see organize parliament. The relative simplicity of this system makes meshing the interests of the legislative party and electoral party fairly easy.

In a presidential system, such as that found in the United States of America, party systems are fragmented. For example, voters may vote for one party in a legislative election and another in the presidential election. In fact, there are a number of party scholars who contend that America's major parties can be divided into a presidential organization and a congressional organization. The main point to this is simply that presidential systems generally produce greater obstacles to party unification than do parliamentary systems.

Political parties were developed to permit large groups of individuals to work together to advance a common political agenda or set of principles. This is as true of legislative parties as it is of electoral parties. In most cases, the larger the group being organized, the more important the party's role is in the process. Mass democracies are unmanageable without the organization of political parties. Political parties establish competing political agendas, policy programs, and political principles from which voters may choose.

Party systems may be defined in a variety of ways, but the most common methods focus on either the types of parties utilized within the party system or the number of parties that can sustain a significant influence over governmental policies. Systems defined by the types of parties may be so general that they consider little more than whether the parties are centralized or decentralized. They may also identify parties by attempting to determine the nature of party cohesion. Under such a system parties would be described according to type of interests that bond the members together: ideological, economic, single-issue, personality, factional, and so on.

The easiest way to define a party system is according to the number of parties it regularly accommodates. Part of the attractiveness of this method is that it permits only three options: multiparty system, two-party system, and single-party system.

It is not uncommon for party systems to accommodate a wide range of types of parties either permanently or periodically. Clearly the most important determinants for shaping party systems are the electoral systems within the government. Electoral systems that utilize single-member districts with winner-takes-all elections usually favor two-party systems. Governments that provide for proportional representation encourage multiparty systems.

Applications

The purpose of political parties is to help large groups of citizens come together and work for common political ends. In legislatures this is accomplished by organizing caucuses and providing leadership to coordinate and educate party members. Legislative parties set political agendas and sponsor legislation to support those political agendas. How party leaders set their political agenda and how they advance that agenda varies considerably from system to system. What is constant in all political systems is the need to forge a coalition that is capable of governing.

In multiparty systems building and maintaining a coalition is an ongoing process. The party's efforts to mobilize voters during elections is distinct from two-party systems in that they must attempt to counter a wider range of alternatives. What remains constant in all democracies is that periodic elections generally provide a mechanism for assessing voters' satisfaction (or lack thereof) with the policies of the party or coalition that currently controls the government. The party or coalition that controls the government must defend its policies and record while the opposition party or parties must critique the current policies and offer alternatives.

Multiparty systems provide the electorate with a wider range of policy alternatives during elections. The negative to this wider range of political options is that it increases the likelihood of no one party receiving a majority of the votes. It is the absence of a clear majority party in government that leads to coalition governments. The electorate cannot know in advance what kind of compromises the party leaders will make in order to forge a majority coalition.

In fact, the electorate cannot even be sure that the party receiving the highest percentage of votes will be part of the ruling coalition. The more homogeneous the coalition, the clearer the policies advanced by the coalition will be, but all coalitions are patchworks to some extent. The trick is trying to adjust and compromise policy positions without sacrificing the basic principles of the parties involved. This is not always possible.

The advantage of a two-party system is that one of the two parties will emerge from the election with a majority of the votes. The extent of voter approval of the principles and policies of the victorious party is generally determined by the size of the majority vote. Parties that win elections with significant percentage of the popular vote are said to have a clear mandate from the electorate.

Mandates permit the victorious party to start working on their campaign agenda immediately. When the next election comes up the majority party will have to defend its record. This defense will usually focus on the party's ability to implement the policies advocated during the election and the success of those policies once they were implemented. In this sense, two-party systems make it easier to turn elections into a political referendum on the ruling party.

Single-party systems confront a different set of challenges, but their task is still very similar to the one confronting other types of party systems. Single-party systems generally exist in a political system with a high degree of homogeneity. Single-party systems are often associated with totalitarian regimes, but these are not the only models that exist in party history. The United States of America had a strong single-party system in the southern states for over a century following its Civil War.

Single-party systems must organize governmental operations and educate the citizens as in any other type of party system. Within totalitarian systems the single party protects the government from rebellion and revolution. To accomplish this task, the party cannot ignore the needs and wants of the general citizenry. It must also convince citizens that the government is serving their interests.

Regardless of the type of party system, political parties must ensure that government operations are conducted on a daily basis and provide communication between the government and the general citizenry. The role parties play in providing channels of communication is central to every other task they perform.

Context

It is difficult to think of any kind of popular government without a party system. Historically parties were utilized to give a political voice to groups of citizens who believed that the governmental machinery had ignored or abandoned them. The role parties performed in monarchical and aristocratic regimes was one of educating the ruler about the needs and desires of the masses. Many political writers thought that parties were unnecessary when the masses were given a political voice through elected representatives. During the nineteenth century parties developed a new role within governmental systems. Democratic governments discovered that parties could be as helpful in communicating and defending the actions of government to the masses as they had been in communicating the needs of the masses to government in earlier centuries.

The channels of communication provided by party connections proved as valuable within the government as they did between the government and the general citizenry. Parliamentary systems found parties ideally suited for their organizational needs. They not only provide a system for identifying friends and foes, but also furnish a mechanism for building an executive cabinet. The concept of a party government reveals just how much parliamentary systems have become dependent on political parties.

A majority party within a parliamentary system not only controls the legislature but selects its key leaders for the executive cabinet as well. In the simplest terms, party government means the party that gains a majority of seats in parliament controls every branch of the government; stated differently, the majority party becomes the government.

Presidential systems use political parties as a communication bridge between and among the different branches of government. A defining characteristic of presidential systems is separation of powers. A major role of political parties within these systems is to provide the separate branches of government with a common set of political objectives.

Party platforms are statements designed to give party members and the general public a sense of what the party believes. The ability of party leaders to formulate a strong and attractive platform is important if they expect candidates for public office to accept the party's principles and policies as their own.

The ability of political parties to unify a variety of different groups under a common political banner is what distinguishes political parties from other types of political factions. It is the job of political parties to find common political ground that can unify a broad cross section of religious, economic, and social groups. Building such a coalition requires enormous political skills, because each group will be forced to compromise and moderate aspects of its own particular narrow interests. This is how majority coalitions are forged in mass democratic societies.

Many political parties began as interest groups, local political clubs, or as groups backing a particular political figure. It is only as these groups grew and matured politically that they developed the potential to be considered true political parties. At their best, political parties are founded on political principles that should strengthen the political system of which they are a part. Conflicting visions over what is the best course of action for the political system to pursue should be the defining characteristic of competing parties in any political system.

Bibliography

Duverger, Maurice. *Political Parties, Their Organization and Activity in the Modern State*. New York: John Wiley & Sons, 1954. Comprehensive work on the general topic of political parties. Sound comparison of the different types of party systems.

Mansfield, Harvey. *Statesmanship and Party Government: A Study of Burke and Bolingbroke*. Chicago: The University of Chicago Press, 1965. Clear statement on the origin and development of the British party system.

Ostrogorski, M. I. *Democracy and the Organization of Political Parties*. 2 vols. New York: Macmillan Company, 1902. One of the first systematic studies of political parties. While some of the information is dated, it is still a classic study of political parties.

Schattschneider, E. E. *Party Government*. New York: Holt, Reinhart and Winston, 1942. Discusses how the U.S. party system could be transformed into a more centralized system.

Wilson, James Q. *Political Organizations*. New York: Basic Books, 1973. A theoretical work that develops the relationship between interest groups and political parties.

Donald V. Weatherman

Cross-References

POLITICAL PHILOSOPHY

Field of study: Political philosophy

Political philosophy is the inquiry into the fundamental concepts concerning political life, such as the nature of the state, justice, law, liberty, authority, community, citizenship, and political obligation.

Principal terms

LIBERAL DEMOCRACY: form of government of the United States and Western Europe; characterized by protection of fundamental individual rights and limited government (classical liberalism) and free elections with widespread popular participation (representative democracy)

NORMATIVE THEORY: theory of how things ought to be, as opposed to positive theory, which concerns how things are

PHILOSOPHY: exploration of the fundamental principles of a subject, using rigorous intellectual methods such as logic, language analysis, dialectics, and others

POLITICS: process in which a group (whose views, opinions, and interests may differ) reaches decisions that are binding on all members of the group

THE STATE: association of people encompassing all lesser associations that claims the right to make binding rules, backed by sanctions, on its members and others who live within the territorial borders over which it claims sovereignty

Overview

Western political philosophy has its origin in the culture of ancient Greece. Sometimes conceived as a branch of moral philosophy, political philosophy addresses basic concepts related to political life. Political philosophy is sometimes distinguished from political theory, though not often well. The words "philosophy" and "theory" are derived from Greek. "Philosophy" is composed of two Greek words, philos, meaning love, and *sophia*, meaning wisdom. "Philosophy" literally means "love of wisdom." In the original Greek sense, the love of wisdom took on the aura of an almost erotic quest.

"Theory" is derived from the Greek words for God (*theos*) and for seeing or watching (*theorin*). Originally a "theorist" was sent by one city-state to another to report on the other's religious festivals. *Theoria* came to mean a journey undertaken to observe the different values and institutions of other lands.

Philosophers are sometimes thought of as those who undertake a painstaking examination of linguistic propositions regarding abstract intellectual problems, while theorists are thought of as being less concerned with linguistic or logical precision and more concerned with more concrete "visions" of societies and their morally and politically relevant characteristics. Despite such distinctions between theory and philosophy, the differences are often ignored. Accordingly, both should be considered together.

One concept that political philosophers discuss is nature of the state. Political philosophy began in ancient Greece in the fifth and fourth centuries B.C.E. Greece was divided into city-states, which were composed of a city and surrounding territory. The first great political philosophers, Plato and Aristotle, were concerned with the character of the state. For each, the state has an ethical end or purpose, namely the pursuit of the good life. This good life could not be achieved without a just social order.

For Plato, the state is like the human body. This simile is known as the "organic analogy." The body politic is like the body physical because it may be divided into classes of people who perform functions that are like bodily functions. Thus, the ruling part of the state is like the head, which is dominated by reason. The protective parts ("guardians" or soldiers) are ruled by the spirited element (the emotions stirred when people are attacked). The farmers and artisans making up the remainder are ruled by desires and are accordingly called the "appetitive" element. In his *Republic*, Plato lays out an imaginary state composed of each class of person. The whole is ruled by philosopher-kings, who have attained knowledge of the good through rigorous study. Since reason rules the whole, the state is well ordered, as reflected in its complete harmony. The imaginary state has no "politics" in the usual sense. Plato calls this harmony justice. Plato's work is the foundation of normative political philosophy.

For Aristotle, the state should be seen as a part of nature. Human nature is fully developed only in the state because only within a state can a person achieve full development. People are naturally citizens, members of the state, because, in Aristotle's famous words, "man is a political animal." Citizens are those who rule and are ruled in turn. States differ in how they are ruled but rightly ordered states are always ruled for the good of the whole. For Aristotle as well as Plato, ethics and politics are intertwined. If a king or social class rules for its own interest only, the state is morally disordered and illegitimate.

In Aristotle's view, people form the state merely to survive, but they maintain it for a higher purpose, attainment of the ethically good life. Each state's way of life incorporates an idea of the good life. The ways of life of states and people differ, but there is only one good life, and it is one that fulfills a person's nature. This is the contemplative life, which exercises the faculty exclusive to humanity, the rational faculty. Aristotle's *Politics* classifies governments and explains that rationale for their existence. Aristotle's work is the foundation of positive political philosophy.

Modern political philosophers have expressed views on the nature of the state that differ with those of the ancient masters. For Jean-Jacques Rousseau, for example, the state is not a natural growth but a human artifact. This view is consistent with Rousseau's notion that the best state should be conceived as originating in a contract. Rousseau admired what he considered the moral simplicity of ancient republics. Most states corrupt their members by encouraging personal dependence on the state and, in some cases, by luxury. Personal dependence makes people anxious and fawning, placing them in a state of psychological bondage. The properly constituted state, however, accomplishes the moral regeneration of its citizens. It is ruled by constitutional law made collectively by its members. Personal dependence on individuals is replaced by impersonal dependence on law. Bondage is replaced by freedom.

After Rousseau, other philosophers of modern liberalism emphasized the liberty of people to live in accordance with their own version of the good life. Rather than insisting that the state is organized around a common conception of the good life, modern liberal political philosophy defends fundamental individual liberties of conscience, expression, and association. The liberal state also protects a private sphere, unknown to the ancients, which is none of the state's business. For the ancients, there was no distinction between "society" and the "state." The liberal state recognizes the right of individuals to form, within legal limits, autonomous, self-governing associations. This autonomous realm is called "civil society."

Democracy has accompanied the liberal state and has been a means of achieving individual liberty. The English liberal philosopher Jeremy Bentham and American constitutional theorist and statesman James Madison (both most active in the late eighteenth century) saw the state as the arena of the struggle of interested groups that would use state power for their selfish purposes whenever possible. Bentham's solution was to inform democratic public opinion by means of a free press and open government and to allow elections to act as sanctions against wrongdoing. Madison's solution was the extended republic, which would encompass so many selfish interests that none could dominate.

The French theorist Alexis de Tocqueville, author of *Democracy in America* (1835), added a further caveat to maintain liberty when social conditions are relatively equal and public opinion is a potent force. He argued that personal liberty is best maintained in modern democracies through membership in a variety of organizations. Such groups could shield the individual from the domination of any one group. "Multiply your associations and be free," he wrote.

Karl Marx, however, denied that the modern democratic state safeguards liberty. Marx argued that employees, especially industrial workers, are exploited by the wealthy owners of the means of production. The liberal state was a sham. Stripped of its intellectual disguises and exposed for what it is, the state is merely the "ruling committee" of the owners of the means of production. Only a revolution, he argued, by oppressed workers can ensure a free society. With the demise of communism, the liberal-democratic view of the state appears to have triumphed. Some critics, however, believe that liberal democracy is in the process of being replaced by a different system, cultural democracy. Under the latter system, the liberty of the individual is submerged in membership in a society's various cultures.

Another central concept of political philosophy is liberty versus authority. A perennial problem for political philosophers is the conflict between the interests of the individual and the interests of society. Authority, embodied in the state, represents the interests of society as a whole. Society is a necessity for the individual, who needs human solidarity and protection, but individuals also need liberty. Simply the idea of "the individual" implies human separateness and the need for space and autonomy. Human beings are members of groups and are separate; each aspect of being human raises its own problems. The needs of the individual and society can clash. Liberty and authority are potentially in conflict because order is necessary for society to exist. To maintain order, individual desires, such as sexual and aggressive urges, must be curbed. Too much suppression of individual desire, however, leads to neurosis and unhappiness.

One of the champions of authority is the seventeenth century English philosopher Thomas Hobbes. Hobbes feared the "masterless man" who lacked the restraining influence of authority. Basing his thought in part on the legal traditions of his time, in *Leviathan* (1651) Hobbes conceived the solution to the conflict between individual and authority as a contract. People are driven to make this contract because without the state they live a miserable, brief existence. Without the state, people do battle with one another in a "war of all against all." Hobbes believed that people must give up their natural rights to freedom, except their right to protect their individual lives. That is, they must consent to total obedience to common authority. The individual's interest in freedom is sacrificed to authority; protection is gained as compensation.

John Locke, by contrast, offered a libertarian version of contract theory in his *Second Treatise of Civil Government* (1690), which became the basis for the Declaration of Independence. Locke's version of the contract emphasized the rights retained by the individual in consenting to authority. Locke even justified violent revolution against authority that abused its power.

A third approach to the contract between liberty and authority was offered by Rousseau. In *The Social Contract* (1762), Rousseau postulated the individual in two roles, first as a citizen, who, in consenting to join the state and agreeing to its constitution, is a legislator. The citizen's second role is a subject of the law, obliged to obey. Consent reconciles these two roles. In joining the social order, people give up their entire selves, including their natural rights, to the whole community. They receive back civil rights and as much freedom as is compatible with the welfare of the whole. In submitting to everyone, citizens submit to no one. Citizens disobeying the law may be compelled to obey it. According to Rousseau's famous "paradox of freedom," in being compelled to obey, the citizen is "forced to be free." In obeying the law one has made, one only follows his own will. The conflict between liberty and authority is thus fully reconciled.

Whether or not one agrees with a philosopher's treatment of conflict between liberty and authority, reading the great philosophers provokes one to consider the problem. In so doing one may become reconciled to a rule of law that often requires one to restrain one's appetites for the good of the whole.

Applications

At various times in history, people have attempted to put the ideas of political philosophers into practice. One such idea is that of equality. At the dawn of the American republic, Thomas Jefferson wrote that "all men are created equal." He was echoing a millennia-old concern of political philosophers stretching back to Aristotle, who examined the meaning of equality as applied to politics and justice. Presently, many are concerned with how the idea of equality is applied to citizens in a democracy. A problem regarding equality discussed by philosophers is the conflict between liberty and equality. This conflict was examined at length by de Tocqueville in 1835. Discussions of the application of equality lead to whether these applications are destructive of liberty.

One kind of equality is "equality of condition." Karl Marx and Friedrich Engels proposed a version of this kind of equality in *The Communist Manifesto* (1848), in which they suggest that under communism wealth would be distributed according to the formula "from each according to his abilities, to each according to his needs." Perhaps not absolute equality of condition, but something like it, would be instituted in such a society.

A host of communal experiments in living, beginning with early Christian communities of centuries ago up to the present, have tried to approximate the ideal of equality of condition. In Israel, communalist kibbutzim (collective farms) were established after 1947, and in the United States and Canada hundreds of such experiments were begun since the early nineteenth century.

Equality of condition can be achieved two ways. First, people can voluntarily share their wealth. Second, the state can practice involuntary social leveling on people. It has been found, however, that attempts to create complete equality of condition require an authoritarian or totalitarian state. A few nations, such as Sweden, have submitted to exceptionally high levels of taxation to pay for a comprehensive welfare state; but complete equality of condition has not been sought. In Israel, about 3 percent of the population volunteer to live on kibbutzim. Thus, 97 percent reject equality of condition. It is noteworthy that the first proposal for complete equality of condition in Western philosophy is found in Plato's *Republic*, which proposes a tightly controlled, repressive, Sparta-like society among the guardian, or warrior, class. All but a handful of the world's people submit to rigorous equality of condition.

A second form of equality is equality of opportunity, in which no one is to be excluded from consideration in the distribution of society's benefits on account of irrelevant criteria. For example, a rule that no one with blond hair shall be admitted to the state university uses an irrelevant criterion, since hair color has no bearing on academic performance.

Controversy has arisen over how to achieve equal opportunity. Some argue that policies that prefer one group over another in the distribution of certain social goods are justified if there is a pattern of inequality that needs to be reversed. If preferential policies favor some groups over others, are those unfavored wrongly discriminated against? If all citizens are to have equal opportunity, are those not favored treated unfairly? One may argue that equality does not last for long; wealth and success attract more of the same, the poor lose their chances. One may argue that, therefore, equality of opportunity can only be maintained by giving greater (that is, unequal) opportunity to the disadvantaged.

Some philosophers argue that the good of society as a whole or compensation for past injustice requires the temporary sacrifice of equal opportunity of some for others less well off. Others argue that the metaphorical level playing field does not exist in the presence of preferential policies. These people argue that preferential policies amount to the punishment of the innocent and are destructive of liberty because they undermine the equal protection of the laws, a fundamental principle of liberal democracy. Questions of what various forms of equality mean and how they should be applied to society are perennial problems of political philosophy.

Context

Political philosophy—the study of normative or moral questions—may be contrasted with the empirical study of politics, which deals mainly with the description and analysis of political phenomena and theories that explain them. Political philosophers have concerned themselves with the idea of civic virtue, according to which the good citizen of a republic places the public good before private interest. Political philosophers also have discussed civic virtues, those characteristics of the citizen (such as compassion, civility, and concern for public affairs) that are conducive to the effective and healthy functioning of the body politic.

Students of empirical politics study, among other topics, political and social behavior and the practical difficulties that may arise from certain behavior. For example, students of empirical politics may study the effects and social dislocation that result from high crime rates or the meaning and consequences of a decline in political participation. By definition, however, empirical political science does not attempt to answer moral questions or moral problems.

Empirical political science does answer questions regarding the ends of political life, such as what a good society or a good life are, or, to use the classical frame of reference, what the best regime or the good life might be. Empirical political science does not explain if and why people should feel obligated to obey authority. Instead, empirical studies describe what people think about these matters and may describe the consequences of the breakdown of authority or of the sense of political obligation.

Bibliography

Arendt, Hannah. *The Human Condition*. Chicago: University of Chicago Press, 1958. Acclaimed work of political thought that makes full use of classical and modern philosophy to describe what it means to be human.

Dahl, Robert A. *Democracy and Its Critics*. New Haven, Conn.: Yale University Press, 1989. Masterwork of a master political scientist. Some argue that it presents a more able defense of democracy than do the works of renowned philosophers such as John Stuart Mill.

Fonte, John. "Ill Liberalism." *The National Review*, February 6, 1995, 48-54. Fascinating and astute essay about what the author believes is the decline of American liberalism and the rise of a new dominant political philosophy, cultural democracy.

Sabine, George H. *A History of Political Theory*. 3d ed. New York: Holt, Rinehart, and Winston, 1961. The most comprehensive work in English on the history of Western political thought.

Strauss, Leo. *Natural Right and History*. Chicago: University of Chicago Press, 1953. Argues that the ancient Greek view of man and nature and their proper relation in a well-governed state is superior to modern ideas, because modern philosophers wrongly abandon nature as the moral standard by which human society should be governed.

Tinder, Glenn. *Political Thinking: The Perennial Questions*. 5th ed. New York: HarperCollins, 1991. Readable philosophical questions and answers about the means and ends of power, equality and inequality, and other topics.

Wilson, James Q. *The Moral Sense*. New York: Free Press, 1993. A respected social scientist writes philosophy, arguing that human beings have an innate moral sense that is blotted out or ignored at the peril of grave social disorder.

Charles F. Bahmueller

Cross-References

Anarchism, p. 66; Capitalism, p. 197; Conservatism, p. 419; Equality and Egalitarianism, p. 630; Existentialism, p. 642; Idealism, p. 855; Irrationalism in Politics, p. 987; Liberalism, p. 1118; Marxism-Leninism, p. 1155; Neo-Conservatism, p. 1281; Neo-Idealism, p. 1287; Political Pragmatism, p. 1519; Political Science, p. 1532; Postmodernism, p. 1570; Republicanism, p. 1706; Scientific Humanism, p. 1784; Social Darwinism, p. 1833; Socialism, p. 1865; Utilitarianism, p. 2077; Utopianism, p. 2084.

POLITICAL PLATFORMS

Field of study: Politics

A political platform is a statement of principles, goals, and programs developed and supported by a political party and its candidates. Platforms are drafted by committees and approved and modified by delegates attending national, state, or county party conventions.

Principal terms

COALITION BUILDING: process of expanding interparty political support in order to win elections

CONVENTION DELEGATE: person selected to attend a convention

MINORITY REPORT: attempt to modify a platform by convincing a majority of the delegates to vote for change

NATIONAL CONVENTION: assembly of delegates who select the party's presidential nominees and approve the platform

NATIONAL PARTY CHAIR: person selected to speak for the party—also is responsible for raising money, selecting candidates, and assisting in campaigns

PLATFORM COMMITTEE: responsible for drafting the party platform prior to the national convention and then submitting the platform to the convention for approval

Overview

In American politics, the business of national party conventions is to select presidential and vice presidential candidates, rally the party faithful, kick off the national campaigns, and draft the political platforms. The customary view is that political platforms are meaningless documents filled with lofty rhetoric designed to win voter support. This view is reflected in the cliché, "A platform is to run on, not to stand on."

If platforms are meaningless, then why do they evoke so much attention from interest groups, the media, political activists, and candidates? Major platform disputes have occurred at both the Democratic and the Republican national conventions. Platform disputes are often cited as primary reasons why a political party loses an election. Some platform disputes are so intense that they cause major disruptions at the conventions and in the presidential elections. At the 1948 Democratic convention, for example, many Southern delegates were so upset at a minority report on civil rights, which was approved by the delegates, that they walked out of the convention. Several weeks later they held their own convention and formed a new party, the States' Rights, or "Dixiecrat Party." Governor Strom Thurmond of South Carolina was selected as the Dixiecrats' presidential candidate, and the party captured the electoral votes of four southern states and 23 percent of the Southern presidential vote.

There are two dominant views on how American political parties formulate their political positions on issues—the responsible parties model and the economic rationality model. The first approach maintains that each party should develop its public policy positions on the basis of ideology. For example, Republicans would offer a conservative position on issues and Democrats would provide the liberal alternative. The divergent views of the parties would offer a clear and distinct choice of alternatives to the voters. Critics of the responsible parties model argue that American political parties are pragmatic and not ideological. In fact, critics contend that when Republicans have moved too far to the right and Democrats have moved too far to the left, the American voters have rejected the party and its candidates.

The economic rationality approach argues that parties are pressured by public opinion in formulating their policy positions. Each party seeks to maximize its votes by measuring public opinion in order to adopt positions that will reflect the dominant views. According to this model, in the American two-party system the parties will seek positions close to the political center. In other words, Republicans and Democrats take similar positions on many issues.

The above two views are the major approaches to explaining how political parties develop their policy stands. There is another approach: The "cleavage" theory maintains that although political parties are influenced by public opinion in their quest for votes, other factors also influence policy stands. For example, parties must take into consideration the views of party activists, interest groups, and party leaders before determining their policy positions. Numerous studies have demonstrated that Democratic Party activists are far more liberal than rank-and-file Democrats, just as Republican Party activists tend to be far more conservative than rank-and-file Republicans. Activists, exert greater influence over the parties' policy stands than will the nominal party member.

The Republican and Democratic parties each appoint a platform committee, also known as a committee on resolutions, to prepare a platform draft before the convention begins. For example, in 1992, the Republican platform committee consisted of 107 people and the Democratic platform committee had a membership of 2 chairs, 10 vice chairs, and 186 members. Much of the work of the platform committee may be split among various subcommittees that focus on such issues as the economy or national defense. The Democrats selected 16 members of the platform committee to prepare the initial draft of the 1988 platform, which was then submitted to the other members of the committee for modification. Prior to writing the platform, both parties usually hold regional meetings in various parts of the country. The purpose of such meetings is to allow individuals and organizations who are a key part of the parties' constituency to provide input on issues of concern.

One of the constant debates in drafting political platforms is whether they should be brief documents enunciating the general principles of the party, or expansive documents that discuss the party's programs and positions. The first Democratic Party platform, in 1840, contained fewer than 1,000 words. In contrast, the 1984 Democratic platform was longer than one hundred pages and contained more than 45,000 words. In order to avoid a repetition of the 1984 Democratic platform, which was criticized as offering something to everyone, Democratic National Committee Chairman Paul G. Kirk, Jr., urged the platform committee to avoid listing a string of words and positions designed to woo various interest groups but lacking in a simple, cohesive message that large numbers of people could identify with. Democratic leader Jim Wright reminded the platform committee that the Ten Commandments were short and to the point. In 1992, the Democratic platform was a mere 16 pages, while the Republicans needed 133 pages to present their platform.

Another factor affects the drafting of political platforms: whether the party's presidential nominee currently occupies the White House. The president has a great influence over the membership of the platform committee and the composition of the platform. Presidents will exert their influence to remove anything in the platform that might be critical of the administration. For example, at the 1992 Republican convention, President George Bush forced a change in the platform that referred to Bush's 1990 reversal of his 1988 campaign pledge, "Read my lips: no new taxes," as a "mistake."

Once the platform committee has finished writing the platform, it is submitted to convention delegates for their approval. Approval is not always automatic, and spirited battles may develop on the convention floor. In 1968, a three-hour floor debate occurred at the Democratic convention in Chicago concerning what the platform would say about U.S. policy in Vietnam. Four years later, the Democratic platform positions on abortion and gay rights triggered the longest platform debate in American convention history.

Minority reports may be submitted to the convention floor by delegates who believe the platform position on a particular issue is in error. Frequently minority reports are offered by candidates who failed to secure the party's nomination but who want to influence the party's position on certain issues. In 1980, Senator Edward Kennedy of Massachusetts challenged the incumbent president of his own party, Democrat Jimmy Carter. Kennedy and his supporters offered twenty-three minority reports. The convention delegates approved fourteen, defeated seven, and withdrew two. The final platform was filled with so many concessions to the Kennedy forces that President Carter gave the platform only a halfhearted endorsement. Democratic presidential nominee Bill Clinton and his supporters were able to defeat all twenty-two amendments to the platform offered by rival candidate Jerry Brown at the 1992 convention.

Applications

Although the public is cynical about political platforms and believe that the parties use vague and flowery language only to attract supporters, it is clear that the platforms of the two major American parties contain substantial differences. Republican platforms have generally placed more emphasis on national defense and foreign affairs, while Democratic platforms have stressed issues such as the economy, welfare, and health care. This distinction has developed because the Republicans have been regarded as the party better able to handle issues of war and peace while the Democrats, in contrast, have been viewed as being more capable of handling domestic policy. In other words, both parties emphasize their own areas of strength.

As might be expected, the parties tend to see things in a different light. In their 1992 platform, Republicans looked at twelve years of Republican control of the White House, and concluded that Republicans had "launched an era of growth and prosperity such as the world had never seen." Through Democratic eyes, the economy and America were "on the wrong track. The American people are hurting. The American dream of expanding opportunity has faded."

The most glaring difference between the parties has been on the issue of abortion. The 1992 Democratic platform supported "the right of every woman to choose," whereas the Republican document argued that abortion should be made illegal in all circumstances, even after rape and incest. The Republican position on abortion went beyond what President George Bush supported. A vocal minority opposed the platform's rigid position. First Lady Barbara Bush argued that abortion should not be in the platform, pro or con. Governor William Weld of Massachusetts pleaded that the Republicans could be "losing touch with mainstream America and forfeiting our role as a bulwark against government intrusion."

On other social issues, Democrats tend to favor civil rights laws protecting homosexuals, while Republicans attack Democrats for including "sexual preference as a protected minority receiving preferential status under civil rights statutes." With respect to public support for the arts, Republicans "condemn the use of public funds to subsidize obscenity and blasphemy masquerading as art." Democrats urge public support for the arts "free from political manipulation and firmly rooted in the First Amendment's freedom of expression guarantee."

Major differences have separated the two political parties with respect to education, health care, and foreign affairs. Democrats said that they "deplore the Bush Administration's efforts to bankrupt the public school system," and they also deplored "the savage inequalities among public schools across the land." The Republican platform, meanwhile, praised President Bush for pushing for school vouchers. People could use these vouchers to send their children to the school of their choice—public, private, or religious.

Both parties have agreed that health care needs to be reformed, but they have offered substantially different alternatives. Republicans have wanted to keep the federal government out of the health care system. "We believe health care choices should remain in the hands of the people, not government bureaucrats." The Democrats, by contrast, have supported a major role for government in reforming the health care system. In 1992 the Democratic platform pledged that "all Americans should have universal access to quality, affordable health care—not as a privilege but as a right."

Finally, in the area of foreign affairs, Republican platforms praised the accomplishments of the Reagan-Bush years. The collapse of the Soviet empire, the liberation of Eastern Europe, the reunification of Germany, and the success of the 1991 Gulf War are cited as examples of Republican leadership. Democrats have attacked the Republican foreign policy as "rooted in the past, divorced from our values, fearful of change and unable to meet its challenges." International crises, under the Bush Administration, "have been managed rather than prevented."

Many of the divisions between the parties can be traced to the differing philosophies concerning the role of the federal government. For Democrats, federal government is the answer to many of the nation's problems. For Republicans, the federal government is the cause of many of the nation's problems. The 1992 Democratic platform called for "an activist government, but it must work in a different, more responsive way." The 1992 Republican platform quoted Abraham Lincoln, the party's first president: "In all that people can individually do well for themselves, Government ought not to interfere."

Although political platforms indicate consistent differences between the Democrats and Republicans, the parties are not always consistent in their positions. This inconsistency is nowhere better illustrated than in the 1992 Democratic platform. While the platform rejected Republican conservatism, it also rejected traditional Democratic liberalism in favor of what is called a "third way." This "third way" was to steer a course between the laissez-faire capitalism of the Republicans and the welfare-state economics normally associated with the Democrats. The 1992 Democratic platform, for example, called for such unconventional Democratic planks as emphasizing economic expansion, upholding law and order, and using military force when necessary. In addition, the platform called welfare "a second chance, not a way of life," and asked for a cutoff of benefits after two years. In a final departure, the platform supported the right of states to enact death penalty statutes.

Context

Political platforms have existed as long as political parties. Although the length and content of the platforms have changed over time, the intent of political platforms remains the same. Platforms are devices by which the parties highlight their accomplishments and criticize the opposition. Platforms also contain specific pledges about policy goals the party hopes to achieve in the future. The objective of the platform is to assist the party in expanding its political support so that it can put together a winning coalition on election day.

Gerald Pomper, a political scientist, evaluates political platforms over a twenty-year period in his book Elections in America (1980). Pomper points out that approximately 20 percent of political platforms consists of rhetoric and fact, 40 percent consists of evaluating the record and past performances of the parties, and 40 percent consists of statements of future policies and pledges. In evaluating the party records, the party in control of the White House dwells on its achievements. The other party focuses on blunders committed by the president's party. One of the most surprising things to emerge from Pomper's study is that slightly more than half of platform pledges were fulfilled, and only 10 percent were completely ignored. The parties take seriously the pledges they make to the American electorate.

Platforms are not read by most delegates at the national conventions, who must approve these documents, let alone by the average voter. The party with the congressional majority also frequently ignores the platform, and even presidential candidates have disassociated themselves from their party platforms. Yet this does not mean that political platforms are not worth the paper on which they are printed.

Political platforms do offer the public some important pieces of information. Platforms assist voters in summarizing and crystallizing their views about a political party and the candidates who are running under the party's banner. Platforms indicate when the parties are continuing along their traditional paths and when they are breaking new ground. Finally, platforms reflect the commitment of the parties to future public policy objectives. Platforms do indicate the future direction of the parties and, as such, become a device by which voters can hold the parties accountable. The failure to carry out political promises as reflected in the platforms may become an important determinant in whether the electorate decides to return the dominant party to office.

Bibliography

Congressional Quarterly's Guide to U.S. Elections. 3d ed. Washington, D.C.: Congressional Quarterly Press, 1993. Contains useful summaries of all party platforms to 1992.

Congressional Quarterly Weekly Report. Washington, D.C.: Congressional Quarterly Press, 1992. The July 18 and August 22, 1992, issues contain the Democratic and the Republican platforms for that year. Articles discuss the drafting process as well as platform controversies.

Downs, Anthony. *An Economic Theory of Democracy.* New York: Harper & Row, 1957. Argues that, in order to maximize voters, parties utilize an economic rationality approach.

Johnson, Donald B. *National Party Platforms.* Champaign: University of Illinois Press, 1978. Compilation of party platforms from their origins in 1840 to 1976.

Kirkpatrick, Evron M. "Toward a More Responsible Two-Party System: Political Science, Policy Science, or Pseudo-Science?" *American Political Science Review* 65 (December, 1971): 965-990. Argues that the parties should formulate policy based on ideology, thereby offering a clear and distinct choice to the voters.

Monroe, Alan D. "American Party Platforms and Public Opinion." *American Journal of Political Science* 27 (February, 1983): 27-42. Analysis of Republican and Democratic platforms from 1960 to 1980.

Ostrogorski, Mosei. *Democracy and the Organization of Political Parties.* 2 vols. Edited by Seymour M. Lipset. Garden City, N.J.: Anchor Books, 1964. Classic condemnation of platforms as meaningless documents.

Pomper, Gerald. *Elections in America.* 2d ed. New York: Longmans Green, 1980. Perhaps the best analysis of platform content and the ability of parties to fulfill their promises.

Darryl Paulson

Cross-References

POLITICAL PRAGMATISM

Field of study: Political philosophy

Abandoning traditional philosophies' search for absolute values, political pragmatism asserted that truth is relative, and springs from a person's reasoned analysis of his or her actions and experiences; thus it should be directed toward reforming society and extending democracy beyond politics to all walks of life.

Principal terms

GROWTH: in John Dewey's version of political pragmatism, signifies the full release of an individual's abilities

INDIRECT-CONSEQUENCES TEST: guideline for determining if government intervention is necessary when actions by one group unexpectedly affect larger groups

INSTRUMENTALISM: doctrine that ideas are instruments of action, and their usefulness determines their truth

METHOD OF INTELLIGENCE: Dewey's shorthand for the scientific method, which he believed would solve humanity's age-old problems when widely applied

PLURALISM: condition of society in which diverse cultural, ethnic, racial, religious, and minority groups, and a diversity of private interests, are tolerated

POSITIVISM: theory that knowledge derives from scientifically verified facts about natural phenomena and their properties, not from sentiments, emotions, intuitions, tradition, or values

PRAGMATISM: philosophy holding that truth is not absolute but is relative to different times, places, and cultures, and is discovered through people's reasoned actions and experiences

PUBLICS: word used by political pragmatists to indicate the plurality of cultural and special interests within a society

RADICAL EMPIRICISM: pragmatic theory that all human knowledge derives from experience

Overview

The appearance of political pragmatism coincided with the unfolding of the Progressive Era in the United States and with its counterparts in Great Britain and Western European countries. The Progressive Era in the United States began in the 1890's and withered away after 1917 upon the entrance of the United States into World War I. For a quarter of a century, however, Progressivism touched nearly all major areas of life in the United States—political, economic, social, and intellectual—often in contradictory and controversial ways. Some of the more important objectives embodied in the Progressive movement were directed toward bringing greater measures of genuine democracy into operation at all levels of the country's political institutions and political processes. Progressives often noted that there was nothing wrong with democracy except that too little of it really had been tried in the United States.

Seeking to extend political democracy, therefore, Progressives battled on many fronts to reformulate the nation's political morality and to renovate its political machinery. Accordingly, they assailed the power of both rural and urban political bosses. They fought to ensure the direct election of U.S. senators. They struggled to align federal political and legal authority against corporate trusts and monopolies. They supported direct primary elections for the selection of party candidates and won their campaigns calling for the introduction of the secret ballot. They successfully championed laws on behalf of popular legislative initiatives, legislative referenda, and the recall of elected officials. For a time, their demands dominated the country's political agenda.

As part of the Progressive movement, political pragmatists generally acknowledged the need for reforms that promised more democracy in the nation's political life. For them, however, perceptions of what democracy meant ranged far beyond reforms that might be achieved within the relatively narrow realm of politics. Political pragmatists were intent upon making a democratic ethos, and the democratic practices that hopefully flowed from it, integral parts of the entire fabric of life.

Nearly all political pragmatists were intellectuals: reform-minded academics, such as philosophers, historians, political economists, scientists, and educators, along with a few lawyers, judges, authors, ministers, and social workers. Among political pragmatists in the United States, none ultimately was more distinguished than John Dewey (1859-1952), whose reputation as a social philosopher became international. There were other twentieth century Americans whose pragmatism carried political implications: Oliver Wendell Holmes, Jr., Jerome Frank, Lewis Mumford, Chauncey Wright, Carl Becker, Charles and Mary Beard, Karl Llewellyn, and Charles I. Lewis, for example. Their European brethren, who were likewise predominantly intellectuals, included Sir Isaiah Berlin, Karl Popper, Bertrand Russell, Henri Poincaré, and Pierre Duhem.

British and European progressivism evinced stronger class biases than American Progressivism did, and was often closely identified with left wing, or at least differently nuanced, ideas about what constituted social and political democracy. Nevertheless, United States and European political pragmatists shared the general conviction that ideas were not fixed but evolved with their cultures, and that they were instruments of action whose truth was determined by their usefulness.

Political pragmatists drew important parts of their ideas from a deep pool of thinkers. Many of the intellectual issues they explored had been addressed by philosophers in every era since ancient Greece. Immediate influences upon their ideas, however, derived from a handful of late nineteenth and early twentieth century thinkers who identified themselves as "Pragmatists"—without the word "political." Chief among these pragmatists were Charles Sanders Peirce, Nicholas St. John Green, William James, and George Herbert Mead. Charles Darwin's theory of evolution, which posited that all life represented continuous adaptations to its environments, supported the pragmatists' view that humankind, too, was a product of evolutionary adaptations. For pragmatists the law of life was change, and humankind's rational capacities placed the ability to effect such change in its hands.

Despite their intellectual diversity, pragmatists and political pragmatists held certain philosophical principles in common. Unlike many earlier philosophers, they believed that investigations of major scientific and social questions could not be resolved by following a single philosophical formula or by imposing absolute values inherited from the past. They asserted that knowledge, ideas, and claims to truth evolved from humankind's ongoing interpretations of human actions and experiences. To them, such knowledge, ideas, and truths were relative, that is, subject to changing interpretations and validity depending upon the individuals, the times, and the cultures involved.

Many pragmatists, even those whose views included observations on politics, confined themselves to philosophical writings on truth, reality, the nature of history and law, religion, and mathematical logic. To the confusion of people hoping to understand pragmatism, pragmatists often were reluctant to define their credo precisely: They considered doing so to be antipragmatic. Consequently, their theories were explored and criticized almost exclusively within the ambit of relatively small intellectual communities. They rarely claimed the interest or the attention of wider publics, either through discussions or their actions.

Applications

While drawing upon and sharing the philosophical interests of many other pragmatists, John Dewey, both by his writings and actions, affected the lives of the vast majority of Americans directly and indirectly—if nowhere else, through their public schools. Before his death in 1952, Dewey was regarded in intellectual circles, both in the United States and abroad, as the foremost social philosopher of the United States, a veritable philosopher of democracy.

Dewey's intellectual efforts began with his own reconstruction of philosophy. For him, the goal of philosophy was to further social progress in the present, real world rather than to search for eternal verities. His objectives were twofold. First, he sought to create a comprehensive political concept of democracy that was more universal than any conceived by previous thinkers. The political philosophers of his predecessors, in his view, had preoccupied themselves too narrowly with the state and other formal political institutions. Although he also concerned himself with these institutions, he sought to formulate a democratic political vision that took into account ever-changing historical conditions, and included the applied philosophy of education, epistemology, esthetics, ethics, logic, the philosophy of science, social problems, and social reform.

Dewey's second objective was defined by his own vigorous criticisms of the exploitation of the community by one class that sought to ensure its future at the expense of others: exploitation, that is, by a ruling class or, in his day, by a capitalist class. Dewey was not a Marxist, despite his agreement with many of the fundamentals in Karl Marx's critique of capitalist societies. Dewey strongly dissented from Marx's call for violent class struggle as the way to usher in a new age. He found merit, however, in Marx's materialistic concept of history and in his economic determinism. Dewey frankly asserted that some form of socialism was inevitable, principally because capitalism prevented the development of sound human relationships, but believed that his approach to socialism was unmistakably different from Marx's advocacy of class civil war.

Dewey's approach to solving social problems was through the application of what he called his "method of intelligence." This employed Dewey's version of the familiar scientific method, an investigatory technique that called for observation; experimentation; reflective reasoning, or the observation of facts; establishing hypotheses; and testing the results. Conceptually, the method of intelligence was not new. Dewey's concern was that it had never been applied to politics. Politicians and political institutions, he insisted, suffered from cultural lag: a failure to comprehend the vast changes wrought by technology and the subjugation of nature.

Dewey hoped that applying the method of intelligence to political activity, as well as to all other walks of life, would open up society and maximize every individual's capacity for growth. To Dewey, growth meant the realization of everyone's full potential within the bounds of a tolerant, multicultural community composed of diverse publics. That people could always achieve growth alone seemed unlikely to Dewey. He thus proposed a criterion for determining when government intervention into people's lives was required. He called his test the "indirect-consequences test," and said it should be used when the actions of one group unintentionally affected the lives of other groups. For example, if a trade union in a parts plant in one city strikes to improve its working conditions, the strike halts delivery of parts to plants elsewhere, stops their production, and idles thousands of workers in other parts of the country. This causes economic losses in several communities, consumers everywhere are hurt either by lessened choices or higher prices, and there are unpleasant psychological consequences for everyone involved. Such situations, in Dewey's view, signaled the occasion for government intervention.

As powerfully as he argued for the creation of political and social conditions that maximized individual growth, Dewey conceived of this growth taking place within the associations or social groups that were essential to human development. In his judgment, there were two kinds of these associations. The first, and in many ways the most important, were local, face-to-face relationships such as the family, school, and church, where the roots of character and personal values were formed. Such groups typically lay outside the realm of politics. But associations that transcended local ones, he felt, frequently worked at cross purposes, struggled with one another, and incited civil strife, all at the expense of efforts that might better have been spent on growth. It was the function of the state, a secondary association, to regulate and ameliorate such struggles, and to ensure social harmony.

As conceived by Dewey, the state would be much more than an umpire for society's conflicts. Utilizing the method of intelligence and the indirect-consequences test, the state would be a positive force. In certain circumstances, Dewey invested the state with a vision that lay beyond the capacity of individuals. While wary of totalitarianism, Dewey believed that the state's positive and legitimate role was to evaluate the purposes of other associations, ascertain their intentions, assess the consequences of their actions, and act accordingly.

Dewey was politically active in promulgating his comprehensive democratic philosophy in university communities, in public educational forums, in newspaper and magazine articles, in lectures, in trade unions and social settlements.

Context

Political pragmatism developed in large measure from divisions within modern liberalism. Liberals agreed on the objective of creating societies that afforded the utmost possible liberty for individuals, but a substantial and successful group of liberals emphasized individualism in economic affairs—laissez-faire capitalism—to the exclusion of much else. Increasingly, other liberals decried the conditions in which the mass of human beings lived largely because of the decisions of laissez-faire capitalists. For them liberalism, particularly in the United States early in the twentieth century, had made only feeble attempts to alter the fundamental workings of the political economy to ameliorate poverty or expand the horizons of ordinary working people. For them, supposedly liberal or democratic societies actually functioned chiefly to satisfy the interests of the few.

Political pragmatists were liberals of this latter stamp. As a consequence, its U.S. adherents in the early twentieth century joined, in spirit at least, with the Progressive movement. But for those who had reflective and philosophical minds, such as John Dewey, political Progressivism seemed committed to little more than mechanical tinkering with the country's political machinery. Commendable as those efforts may have been, they fell short of setting both broader and deeper goals. This was the difficulty that led independent thinkers such as Lewis Mumford, for example, to flirt briefly with Marxism and anarchism and eventually to write brilliant, comprehensive analyses of technology's impacts, and human's maladjustments to them, upon urban societies. A similar political pragmatism brought Dewey's colleagues at the University of Chicago, including George Herbert Mead, Addison W. Moore, and James Tufts, to stress the social dimensions of human actions: dimensions that, for them, implied that human behavior was not primarily the result of biological or physiological adaptations to the environment. They viewed the social and political dimensions of human life as new products of evolution. They likewise integrated change in the shape of social reform into their understanding of evolution.

British and European intellectuals produced their own versions of political pragmatism. Among them were England's Bertrand Russell, the son of a liberal nineteenth century reformer. Russell was one of the world's most distinguished philosophers and mathematicians, and eventually won a Nobel Prize in Literature. He premised his lifelong, but selective, pacifist campaigns and his practical social reformism on an empirically based logical atomism that underscored the reliance of knowledge on original human experiences. Experience, particularly as viewed by people of genius, was the fount of knowledge, but knowledge was relative and continuously changing. Russell was deeply involved in educational reform such as at the Beacon Hill School. He was a passionate enemy of extremism, promoted the idea of relativism in human affairs, and profoundly believed in the power of rationality.

After the mid-twentieth century, most of the first generation of political pragmatists were dead and interest in pragmatism, and reform, generally had faded. Their passing coincided with liberalism's decline throughout the Western world, a decline linked to the apathy, cynicism, and confusion attending decades of world wars and the Cold War, and the abandonment of social reform to large, highly bureaucratized governments. In addition, there had always been a division between U.S. pragmatists and those with somewhat analogous views in Great Britain and in Europe. Russell, for example, was contemptuous of James's and Dewey's work, and German philosopher Martin Heidegger, in the same vein, wrote that the "American interpretation of Americanism by means of pragmatism" remains outside of the metaphysical realm. There was, however, a revived interest in pragmatism and its political connotations between the 1970's and 1990's in the writings of Willard Van Ormond Quine, Donald Davidson, and Richard Rorty.

Bibliography

Dewey, John. *Reconstruction in Philosophy.* New York: New American Library, 1950. Originally published in 1920, this remains an excellent introduction to Dewey's philosophical position and his political objectives.

Murphy, John P. *Pragmatism.* Boulder, Colo.: Westview Press, 1990. Clearly written for non-specialists, this covers pragmatist thinkers from C. S. Peirce to Donald Davidson showing the evolution of pragmatic thought. Informative introduction by Richard Rorty. Excellent.

Scheffler, Israel. *Four Pragmatists.* London: Routledge & Kegan Paul, 1974. Excellent critical introduction to Peirce, James, Mead, and Dewey.

West, Cornel. *The American Evasion of Philosophy.* Madison: University of Wisconsin Press, 1989. Well-written genealogy of pragmatism from Ralph Waldo Emerson to Quine, Rorty, Roberto Unger, and Michel Foucault. Indispensable work for those interested in political pragmatism during the generation after the mid-twentieth century.

Clifton K. Yearley

Cross-References

Democracy, p. 513; Idealism, p. 855; Liberalism, p. 1118; Political Philosophy, p. 1505; Social Democracies, p. 1839; Socialism, p. 1865; The State, p. 1878.

POLITICAL REPRESENTATION IN THE UNITED STATES

Field of study: Politics

Political representation in American politics is based on the idea that elected officials engage in making decisions on governmental policy that represent the interests of those who elected them.

Principal terms

CLASSICAL LIBERALISM: school of political thought guided by the belief that individuals are rational beings who have the right and responsibility to make political decisions

CONSTITUTIONALISM: belief in limited government guaranteed through a written or understood contract

CONTRACT THEORY: idea that governments should be created through a social contract between people and government

DEMOCRACY: government in which the people are directly or indirectly involved in policy decisions

NATURAL RIGHTS: rights belonging to all human beings, received from nature, rather than a human institution

PLURALISM: belief that individuals participate in government by joining competing groups that influence government

POLITICAL REPRESENTATION: responsibility of governmental officials to serve as political voice of the people

POPULAR SOVEREIGNTY: belief that ultimate authority for government belongs to the people

REPUBLIC: indirect democracy in which voters elect representatives to make governmental decisions

STATE OF NATURE: imagined condition of life before government

Overview

The basis for political representation in the United States was set forth in 1776 when Thomas Jefferson wrote in the Declaration of Independence that governments derive their power from the consent of the governed. Such a system is a democracy, which may be either direct or indirect. In a direct democracy, the people govern themselves, and each person has an equal voice. An indirect democracy, on the other hand, requires that individuals choose others to represent them in a decision-making body. Another word for an indirect democracy is a republic. The United States was created as a republic. In 1787, when the Constitution was written, the Founders believed that few people were wise enough or educated enough to know how to run a government. A republic allowed the people to vote for representatives who would serve as their voice in the newly created government.

When the Founders met in Philadelphia in 1787 and began writing a Constitution, they did not have to start from scratch. They were able to build on the English system of government. Starting with Magna Carta in 1215, the English began to believe that the people had a right to a voice in government and even to rebel against their government, as they did in 1642.

The concept of political representation was realized to its fullest extent with the birth of classical liberalism in the writings of the seventeenth century English philosopher Thomas Hobbes. Hobbes argued that without government, people were in a state of nature. He saw this state as hostile because, even though individuals in such a state are equal and able to make their own decisions, they are never safe from the actions of others. Hobbes maintained that individuals are willing to trade their perfect equality and freedom for the security of government. Thus, the people come together, negotiate a contract for government, and choose a sovereign. The sovereign then represents the people according to his or her own interests. This contract, in Hobbes's view, could never be broken.

The classical liberal belief that individuals possess the ability to reason and therefore engage in political decisions was further refined by John Locke, another seventeenth century English philosopher. Like Hobbes, Locke wrote of a state of nature, but he believed this state was basically cooperative. Locke agreed with Hobbes that individuals are eager to leave the state of nature for the security of government; however, he argued that the negotiated contract between the people and the government could be broken if the government ceased to honor the terms of the contract. Although individuals exchanged their perfect equality and freedom for the security of government, Locke maintained that certain rights could never be taken away by government as part of the contract. These natural rights were given to individuals by God, not a government; no government could take them away. These rights he identified as the right to life, liberty, and property. Of all classical liberals, Locke has been the strongest influence on the American political system. His words were interpreted by Thomas Jefferson in the Declaration of Independence as the right to "life, liberty, and the pursuit of happiness." Locke is said to be an unofficial Founder of the American Constitution.

Jean-Jacques Rousseau, an eighteenth century French philosopher, also believed in government by social contract. Rousseau contended, however, that governments, once created, enslaved individuals. He argued against representative government because he believed that representatives expressed only their own voices and that assigning the right to make policy decisions to others deprived individuals of a voice in government.

The first political philosopher to insist that women should also have a voice in government was Mary Wollstonecraft. Although she was English, she spent much of her life in France and engaged in heated debate with Rousseau over the nature of women and their ability to exercise rational judgment.

The nineteenth century English philosopher John Stuart Mill agreed with Wollstonecraft. Mill suggested, as had classical Greek philosopher Plato, that no society could afford to ignore the gifts of half its population. With Mill, the classical liberal belief that the guarantee of individuality (granting individual rights and encouraging individuals to pursue their own goals) found its strongest advocate. Mill believed that representative government was the most practical form of government, but he maintained that only one man in a hundred was capable of making wise decisions. Representatives should be wise enough to make political decisions for those who could not make them. Significantly, protection of minority voices in decision making was, in Mill's view, inherent in maintaining liberty.

When the North American colonies declared their independence from Great Britain in 1776, it was chiefly because they had no political representation in the English Parliament, which was levying heavy taxes to pay for their own military. "No taxation without representation" became the rallying cry of the dissatisfied colonists. At that time, each colony had its own legislature made up of elected representatives; however, most of these legislatures could be dismissed by the royal governors appointed by the British king.

In order to work together to fight the revolution, the new states negotiated their first contract, the Articles of Confederation. This contract allowed each state to retain its independence. A legislature made up of representatives from all thirteen states, with equal voting representation, was the entire national government. There was neither an executive nor a judiciary. Additionally, the economic scene was grim because the legislature had no power to tax, so there was little money to run the national government.

A number of educated people who had studied Hobbes, Locke, and other philosophers argued that a convention should be called to create a government that would be strong enough to solve the existing problems and still allow for some autonomy for each state. This convention began in Philadelphia in May of 1787 and lasted until a new constitution was signed on September 17, 1787. Twelve states (excluding Rhode Island) chose to send representatives to the Philadelphia Convention to represent the voice of the people and the interests of the states. These representatives were all white male property owners. They tended to be affluent, well educated, and former members of the military or legislatures.

It was a foregone conclusion that the Framers of the Constitution would create a system based on popular sovereignty or control of government by the people. This republic evolved from classical liberal beliefs and combined dependence on rational individuals choosing political leaders through elections with rational leaders who were capable of running a government. The Framers believed that all individuals—including those that ran the government—were self-interested and unlikely to work for the public without specific limits on their power. As constitutionalists, the Framers designed a contract that would limit the powers of the government so that it could allow individuals to control their own lives. The Framers were not concerned with equality in the way that it came to be defined in the twentieth century. To them, equality meant individuals having the opportunity to pursue and achieve their own goals.

Even though the system created in Philadelphia resulted in indirect political representation, it was argued that the people would have an active voice in government beyond voting for those who made policy decisions. James Madison, who is one of the intellectual authors of the Constitution and who became the fourth president of the United States, explained to doubters that the new system was based on pluralism. Madison believed that self-interested individuals would join groups that promoted their common interests to political leaders. As each group worked to promote its own interests, Madison contended, they would serve as the voice of the people and would check any one group from having too much power. The people and the government would, therefore, be safe from tyranny by either the majority or the minority.

The pluralist system allowed minority groups to demand political participation. The move toward full participation for African Americans began with the Antislavery movement. After the Civil War, three Reconstruction amendments to the Constitution were designed to grant political rights to former slaves. The Thirteenth Amendment (1865) abolished slavery, the Fourteenth Amendment (1868) guaranteed rights of citizenship to former slaves, and the Fifteenth Amendment (1870) guaranteed black males the right to vote. It was not until the 1960's, however, that the Civil Rights movement was successful in using the Fourteenth and Fifteenth Amendments to bring about true political representation for African Americans. Civil rights advocates were able to achieve passage of the Civil Rights Act of 1964 and the Voting Rights Act of 1965. These two acts guaranteed black suffrage and provided means of challenging discrimination in all aspects of American society. The Supreme Court played a significant role by handing down decisions such as *Brown v. Board of Education* (1954), which ended the separate but equal doctrine.

The movement toward full political representation for women officially began with the Seneca Falls convention (1848). Achieving suffrage was the early focus of the women's movement, and most of its leaders also worked in the Antislavery movement. Women were granted suffrage with the passage of the Nineteenth Amendment (1920). They began to push for full political representation only with the revival of the women's movement in the 1960's.

After such reforms were instituted, all minority groups were able to vote for representation; however, minorities continued to make up a small number of representatives in all areas of government.

Applications

At the national level, American citizens are represented by members of Congress, by the president, and by the vice president. Congress is divided into two groups: the House of Representatives and the Senate. In the House, representation is based on population, so that states such as California and New York, with large populations, have more representatives than the smallest state, Rhode Island, or a large state with a small population, such as Alaska. In a state with only one representative, the representative represents the entire state. In most cases, the state is divided into districts, with one representative for each district. For example, Georgia has eleven congressional districts and has eleven members of the House. There are 435 members of the House of Representatives. The Senate was designed to represent the states rather than the people. In the Senate, each state has two senators to represent it, for a total of one hundred senators.

The president and vice president are the only elected officials who represent the entire country. They are chosen indirectly by the people. Each state has electors equal to its number of representatives in Congress. These electors (along with three for Washington, D.C.) make up the electoral college, which votes directly for the president and vice president.

Two other groups are involved in significant policy-making activities at the national level, but neither of these groups is elected by the people. Both groups are made up of people who are appointed by the president and confirmed by the Senate. The first is the federal judiciary, which includes the U.S. Supreme Court, appellate courts (which hear appeals from lower courts), and district courts (which conduct federal trials). The second is made up of executives, such as the secretary of state and the secretary of defense, and bureaucrats, including the heads of agencies such as the Internal Revenue Service and the Social Security Administration.

Despite political reforms designed to grant universal political representation, minorities continue to make up small percentages of both houses of Congress, the federal courts, the Cabinet, and governmental agencies. For example, after the 1992 election, in Congress there were fifty-five women, forty African Americans, nineteen Hispanics, and one Native American. There has never been a president or vice president who is recognized as a member of a minority group. It might be argued, therefore, that American representation is representing the same class that went to Philadelphia in 1787.

Context

It is necessary to examine what political representation means in practice rather than in theory. It is necessary to question whether representation simply means suffrage, or if it includes the right to be a representative who makes policy decisions. It is necessary to question whether representatives who are not of an underrepresented group can identify and promote that group's interests. Also of interest is the fact that voter turnout in the United States tends to remain within a few points of 50 percent, indicating that roughly half the population has no active voice in who represents them. Finally, political representation must deal with the ratio of representatives to those represented.

Hanna Pitkin, a noted scholar on issues of representation, identifies three methods of representation. One is the descriptive method, which requires that representatives mirror the characteristics of those represented. For example, under this method, women, who make up 51 percent of the population, would comprise 51 of the 100 senators. A second is the symbolic method, which dictates that any person in a particular group serves as a symbol of that group and causes other representatives to consider their interests. It might be said, then, that Carol Moseley Braun, as the only African American woman in the Senate in the 103d Congress, served as a symbol of both women and African Americans. A third method, one Pitkin prefers, is the "acting for" method of representation, which requires representatives to stand in as voices of all those whom they represent.

The right to vote on representatives is inherent to a democracy, but it does not guarantee an equal voice in decision making. Only representatives who act for the minority as well as the majority can do that. This is not to say that a representative must be a woman in order to understand women's interests, or that only an African American or a Native American can speak for members of those groups. Many white members of congress have joined the battle for civil rights. Presidents have signed legislation and appointed minorities to prestigious positions, and white males in the courts have refused to allow restrictions on minority rights.

The courts have played a significant role in protecting the concept of "one person, one vote" in the United States. Before a series of court cases in the 1960's, each state could determine the apportionment of each legislative district at both the state and national levels. It was common to have an urban representative representing three to four times as many people as did a rural representative. The Court reformed this practice in state house districts in *Baker v. Carr* (1962), in state senate districts in *Reynolds v. Sims* (1964), and in U.S. House districts in *Wesberry v. Sanders* (1964). A census is taken every ten years, and reapportionment of all legislative seats except the U.S. Senate takes place according to formulas established by courts.

Native-born Americans tend to take the right to vote for granted. Most believe that it is a right that can never be taken away; therefore, there is no need to protect it. American politics is very complex, and making a decision on which candidate to vote for often seems an impossible task. Since the election of Ronald Reagan in 1980, partisan politics has become more common. For those who seek an easy solution, voting a party ticket is likely. Americans are bombarded with campaign ads that are highly sophisticated and extremely contradictory and with media analysis that allows someone else to do the thinking. Many citizens claim they do not know whom or what to believe.

Americans are represented, whether or not they choose to exercise their right to vote, by those people elected and appointed to policy-making positions. Those people respond to demands made by others in their field, voters, interest groups, political action committees, and political parties. Pluralism, therefore, allows each American to be part of that demand for representation. Each person must decide whether his or her voice will be heard.

Bibliography

Abzug, Bella. *Gender Gap: Bella Abzug's Guide to Political Power for American Women.* Boston: Houghton Mifflin, 1984. Written by a former congresswoman, this is a highly readable account of the lack of political representation for women, with profiles of female representatives.

Barker, Lucius J., and Mack H. Jones. *African Americans and the American Political System.* 3d ed. Englewood Cliffs, N.J.: Prentice Hall, 1994. Excellent account of how African Americans fit into the overall system of political representation, using both historical and contemporary examples.

Becker, Carl L. *The Declaration of Independence: A Study in the History of Political Ideas*. New York: Vintage Books, 1958. Detailed account of why and how the American system was derived from classical liberalism.

Boxer, Barbara. *Strangers in the Senate: Politics and the New Revolution of Women in America*. Washington, D.C.: National Press Books, 1994. California's Senator Boxer examines the history of women in the U.S. Senate and identifies the events that led to the unprecedented inclusion of seven women in the Senate after the 1992 election.

Hobbes, Thomas. *Leviathan*. Edited by C. B. Macpherson. New York: Penguin Books, 1968. Classic work, originally published in 1650, that refutes the theory of divine right and argues for a social contract.

Kammen, Michael, ed. *The Origins of the American Constitution: A Documentary History*. New York: Penguin Books, 1986. Important historical documents explain the reasons for the design of the American system of representative democracy. Includes the Federalist Papers, the Anti-Federalist Papers, and private correspondence of the Founders.

Mill, John Stuart. *Three Essays*. New York: Oxford University Press, 1975. Includes three essays, with noteworthy explanation of classical liberalism and major concepts of democratic politics.

Pitkin, Hanna Fenichel. *The Concept of Representation*. Berkeley: University of California Press, 1967. Examines all aspects of representation and argues for improved methods.

Rousseau, Jean-Jacques. *The Social Contract*. New York: Hafner Press, 1947. Presents classical liberal argument against political representation and arguments for social contracts.

Elizabeth Rholetter Purdy

Cross-References

POLITICAL SCIENCE

Field of study: Politics

Political science is an academic discipline akin to anthropology, economics, history, psychology, and sociology that studies political institutions, political processes, and political behavior.

Principal terms
BEHAVIORALISM: movement within political science that sought to make the discipline more scientific by focusing on quantitative research techniques
ELITISM: theory of politics that argues that all political systems, including modern democracy, are controlled by small elites
EMPIRICAL THEORY: political theory concerned with what is, instead of what may be or should be
NORMATIVE THEORY: theory emphasizing norms—rules and standards—of political behavior
PLURALISM: theory and practice regarding multiple social, economic, and political groups
POSTBEHAVIORALISM: intellectual movement that responds to the nonjudgmental and scientific assertions of behavioralism, emphasizing the importance of public policy and addressing contemporary political problems and issues

Overview

The youngest of all social science disciplines, political science is about one hundred years old. Although the history of the study of politics can be traced back to classics on ethics and moral philosophy, starting with the Greek thinkers such as Plato and Aristotle, through medieval, Renaissance, and modern political thinkers, the development of the discipline as a systematic and scientific study of politics began in the late nineteenth century. In the United States, the discipline began assuming an independent status with the founding of the School of Political Science at Columbia University in 1880. Thereafter, political science was organized as a distinct discipline in many universities. In 1903 its professional body, the American Political Science Association, was established for the purpose of advancing the "scientific study of politics."

The development of political science as a discipline and the advancements in theoretical and empirical knowledge within its various subfields are mainly associated with the contribution of scholars teaching in American universities. These scholars have dominated, especially since World War II, the debate within the discipline, making the field virtually an American science. In 1988, there were 121 institutions in the United States that granted doctoral degrees in political science. These institutions have produced approximately 70 percent of the world's trained political scientists.

Political science lacks a central paradigm and there is no universally accepted subject area or definition of the discipline. Contending definitions have been advanced by political scientists of various methodological, epistemological, and theoretical persuasions. During the last century the focus of the discipline changed and expanded. Various approaches to the definition of the discipline can be identified. In the late nineteenth century and the first two decades of the twentieth, political science was defined in institutional terms. Political scientists such as Woodrow Wilson, W. Willoughy, and James Bryce rejected the philosophical and normative approach to the study of politics for being unscientific. They sought to devise a value-free and scientific definition of politics by focusing on the study of empirically observable phenomena. The state was identified as the defining and organizing concept and the discipline was equated with the scientific study of the state.

The state—an entity having four attributes: population, territory, government, and sovereignty—became the object of political inquiry. Scholarly attention was focused on the study of constitutions, law, and formal structures of government, and how to improve them. There was an outpouring of descriptive literature during this period. The institutional approach was found to be too narrow, legal, and restrictive, however; other political scientists, who defined politics as a power relationship between and among individuals and groups of individuals, began to study the dynamic rather than the static elements of politics. Scholars such as Harold Lasswell, Hans Morgenthau, Gaetano Mosca, and G. Catlin broadened the scope of political science by defining politics as the struggle for power. With the power approach, the focus of study shifted from the state to the individual or group. The central question of political inquiry, as defined by Lasswell, is: Who gets what, when, and how.

Pluralist theorists such as Robert Dahl, Seymour Martin Lipset, Charles Lindblom, Arthur Bentley, Arnold Rose, and David Truman advanced the third conception of politics by defining politics as a process of interest accommodation. Pluralism emphasizes groups as the basis of politics and believes that modern societies consist of a variety of interest groups. Political decisions, in this view, involve processes of bargaining, negotiating, conciliation, and compromise among groups. Power is viewed to be widely dispersed among organized interest groups, associations, governmental officials, and private individuals. Refuting the elitist view that the elites make all major decisions and govern the masses, pluralists posit that in modern democracies the government acts essentially as a broker to facilitate compromise among competing interest groups.

Behavioralism, which became the dominant approach in political science for two to three decades following World War II, advanced a fourth approach through its scientific idioms of structural functionalism and general systems theory. David Easton provided an empirically oriented and enduring definition of politics centered on the concept of a political system, which, according to Easton, involves those actions related to the "authoritative allocation of values" for the social system as a whole. Building on the systems framework, structural-functionalism identified functions performed by all political systems. There are, according to this approach, four process functions: interest articulation, interest aggregation, policy-making, and policy implementation. There are also three system functions: socialization, recruitment, and communication. This approach was considered superior since it could be used to study developed and democratic systems as well as developing and nondemocratic ones.

The synthetic definition of the discipline provided by political scientists in the postbehavioral era after 1969 combines the scientific thrust of behavioralism with the normative concerns of traditional political theorists. It is now commonly agreed that the discipline of political science includes the study of political institutions, political processes, and political behavior in the public realm.

Applications

Since political science covers a wide area of inquiry, the discipline has over the years become compartmentalized into various subfields, such as American politics and political behavior, comparative politics, international relations, political sociology, political theory, public administration, public law, public policy, and state and local government—with their specific subject matters, concepts, and approaches. Courses in these areas are offered at both the graduate and undergraduate level. Advancements in three particular subfields, however, have been central to the development of the discipline. Those subfields are political theory, comparative politics, and international relations.

Political theory, which had its origins in general political philosophy, was traditionally defined as the study of the history of political ideas, which were to be found in the classical texts of politics. In the wake of the behavioral revolution of the 1950's and 1960's, however, a positivist distinction was made between historical and scientific political theory. Rejecting the history of political theory as the basic meaning of theory in political science, David Easton, in *The Political System* (1953), distinguished between value theory and causal theory. Value theory, according to Easton, is primarily concerned with the normative question of what ought to happen in politics—rules and standards of political behavior—based on political insights achieved by philosophers from Plato to Marx. Causal theory, on the other hand, is an empirical theory of politics, modeled after the methodology of the natural sciences. It represents a body of generalizations (or laws) based on a concern with what is—empirically observable phenomena—using scientific techniques and scientific rigor.

Marginalized in the discipline, traditional political theory in the 1970's moved toward an autonomous endeavor. In the 1970's and 1980's, political theory began assessing, under the influence of John Rawls's *A Theory of Justice* (1971), the outcome of public policy. Also, theory became more empirically aware. As the discipline recognized that its approaches and theories are in fact value laden, the distinction between normative and empirical theory was no longer considered important.

In the 1980's, some theorists moved in the direction of formal model building. Political scientists of this persuasion—Anthony Downs, David Held, Jon Elster, Ian McLean, Adam Przeworski, Russel Hardin, and Brian Barry, to name a few—were inspired by theoretical economics, game theory, and rational choice theory. They believed that formal models are aids to clarify thinking about the major concerns of traditional political theory, such as the nature and conditions of good forms of government. Since formal political theory has remained highly technical, it has had limited adherents within the profession and almost no audience outside the profession. There is growing recognition of a symbiotic relationship between normative and empirical political theory, but now the trend is toward development within separate theoretical arenas, not toward a synthesis of various theories for developing a systematic theory of politics.

Comparative politics, which emerged as a separate subfield only after World War I, deals with similarities and differences in political processes, structures, and behaviors. In the beginning it studied comparative government and focused on formal legal and constitutional aspects of government. The field changed after the rise of the behavioral movement and the decolonization of Asia and Africa in the 1950's and 1960's. Behavioralism provided new concepts, research tools, techniques, and methodologies used to study Western as well as newly independent states. The developing nations, in particular, became the laboratory for empirical research and theory building for a large number of scholars—Lloyd and Susanne Rudolph, Leonard Binder, David Apter, Aristide Zolberg, Myron Weiner, and Lucian Pye, to name a few—who played an important role in the development of the field.

Comparative politics scholars are heavily indebted to other social science disciplines, particularly sociology and anthropology. Significant theoretical advancements in the subfield took place during the 1960's and 1980's. Structural functionalism was the first systematic effort toward making comparative politics truly global. In *The Civic Culture* (1963), Gabriel Almond and Sidney Verba advanced the model of an ideal democratic culture based on a comparative study of five democracies (Britain, the United States, Italy, Mexico, and Germany) using survey research methodology. With the shift in focus from the developed to the developing nations, modernization and developmentalism emerged as the dominant framework of comparative research in the 1960's, which argued that there is a unilinear and evolutionary path of development, and suggested that the developing nations emulate the historical pattern of development of the West. This approach was severely criticized by dependency theory in the late 1960's and 1970's for ignoring the developing nations' colonial past, which had contributed to their underdevelopment.

In the 1970's and 1980's, alternative approaches to modernization and development were advanced: authoritarianism, corporatism, and state-society relations, for example. With the end of authoritarian regimes in Latin America and other parts of the world, and the collapse of communism in Europe in the 1980's, the subfield began focusing on the issues of democratic transition and democratic consolidation in newly democratic states. In the 1990's, comparativists turned to an examination of the phenomenon of ultranationalism based on ethnic, tribal, and religious differences, in countries such as the former Yugoslavia, Somalia, Rwanda, and many parts of the former Soviet Union.

The field of international relations concerns itself mainly with questions about war and peace, and power and security. With changes in the international system, the scope of the field has expanded. Since the 1970's, economic and social relations among states have assumed the same importance as the study of security issues. The major subjects of study in international relations include the study of forces such as multinational corporations, international governmental organizations (the United Nations, European Union, World Bank, International Monetary Fund), regional organizations, international regimes, terrorist organizations, liberation movements, political parties, social classes, and pressure groups, in addition to the traditional study of states as international forces.

Four theoretical perspectives on international relations can be identified in the literature: idealism, realism, behavioralism, and neoliberal institutionalism. Scholars of international relations during the 1920's and 1930's adopted a legalistic-moralistic approach to the study of war and peace. They believed that the elimination of war depended on the development of international institutions such as the League of Nations. The rise of Adolf Hitler to power in Germany, followed by World War II, led to the emergence of realism, which became the dominant school of thought in the 1950's. It remains the most influential perspective. Realist thinkers defined international politics as a struggle for power. In their foreign policies states promote their national self-interest, which is the acquisition of power.

The behavioralists launched an attack on the realists (and idealists) in the 1960's. The behaviorists wanted to build a genuine science of international relations by concentrating on understanding recurring patterns and causal relations of international behavior. In doing so they borrowed concepts from other disciplines, including mathematics, making international relations the most interdisciplinary field in political science. Behavioralists tried to make international relations a separate discipline but were unsuccessful.

The emphasis of neoliberal instrumentalism is on interstate cooperation. Through the use of theories of complex interdependence, international regimes, and hegemonic stability, neoliberals analyze complex global economic, social, and ecological problems in the contemporary world.

Context

The development of political science as an academic discipline in the United States began in the late nineteenth century. It was influenced by America's democratic tradition. Political science came to be viewed by many in the profession as a science of democracy, but the discipline has continuously changed in response to the changing domestic and international environment. There are three distinct phases—traditional, behavioral, and postbehavioral—in the development of the discipline.

Traditional political scientists were influenced by the normative and philosophical ideas of thinkers from Plato to Marx. The rise of dictatorships in Germany, Italy, and the Soviet Union, and the horrors of World War II, however, led many young political scientists to ask why the prevailing institutional approach could not explain these phenomena. These political scientists, believing in the value principles of liberal pluralism, brought about a shift in emphasis from institutions to actual political behavior. Since behavioralism emphasized quantification, measurement, theory construction, and value-free research, survey research emerged as the most scientific method. Political science essentially became sociology. By the late 1960's, however, behavioralism was criticized for its academic detachment, its preoccupation with methodological questions, and its neglect of the ethical, moral, and policy dimensions of contemporary political problems, such as the Vietnam War and poverty in urban America.

The postbehavioral era has been marked by a diversity of approaches, a development of middle-range and area-specific theory, and eclecticism. The failure of behavioralism to explain contemporary national and international problems led some political scientists to seek explanations using Marxism, especially in its structural, neo-Marxist form. The revival of the Marxist tradition and its analyses of the capitalist state has contributed to efforts by state-centric scholars to "bring the state back" into political analysis after more than two decades of academic neglect. Scholarly attention also has gone to the political economy approach because of the increasing importance of economic factors in domestic and international politics.

Historic changes in the 1980's and early 1990's provided new contexts in which political scientists developed concepts relevant for examining and explaining contemporary political reality. The study of democracy, especially the phenomena of democratic transition and democratic consolidation in newly democratic states, emerged as a major subject in the 1990's. New concepts and approaches were developed for studying the rise of the ultranationalism that has resulted in ethnic and tribal violence in many countries. As the discipline matured in the postbehavioral era, political scientists increasingly became eclectic in their approaches.

Bibliography

Ball, Terence, ed. *Idioms of Inquiry: Critique and Renewal in Political Science.* Albany: State University of New York Press, 1987. The ten contributors to this volume on political theory argue for a pluralism of approaches and explore alternative idioms of political inquiry.

Easton, David. "Political Science in the United States: Past and Present." In *The Development of Political Science: A Comparative Study.* Edited by David Easton, John Gunnell, and Luigi Graziano. New York: Routledge, Chapman & Hall, 1991. In this short, perceptive essay, Easton analyzes major developments in the discipline.

Finifter, Ada W., ed. *Political Science: The State of the Discipline.* Washington, D.C.: American Political Science Association, 1983. Survey of the discipline in nineteen essays, each dealing with a subfield.

Leftwich, Adrian, ed. *New Developments in Political Science: An International Review of Achievements and Prospects.* Hants, England: Edward Elgar, 1990. A dozen essays deal with developments in different subfields of the discipline.

Ricci, David. *The Tragedy of Political Science: Politics, Scholarship, and Democracy.*

New Haven, Conn.: Yale University Press, 1984. Deals with the discipline's scientific claims and its attachment to American liberal democratic culture.

Seidelman, Raymond, and Edward J. Harpham. *Disenchanted Realists: Political Science and the American Crisis, 1884-1984*. Albany: State University of New York Press, 1985. Argues that the development of political science in the United States has been associated with disenchantment with government and mass politics.

Somit, Albert, and Joseph Tanenhaus. *The Development of American Political Science: From Burgess to Behavioralism*. Enlarged ed. New York: Irvington, 1982. Provides a detailed study of the rise of political science from the beginning of the twentieth century to behavioralism.

Sunil K. Sahu

Cross-References

Democracy, p. 513; Elitism, p. 591; Liberalism, p. 1118; Pluralism, p. 1402; Political Philosophy, p. 1505; Power in Politics, p. 1584; Public Opinion Polling, p. 1627; The State, p. 1878; Voting Behavior in the United States, p. 2109.

POLITICAL VIOLENCE

Field of study: Politics

Political violence is the use of intentionally coercive actions committed to achieve political ends, as well as the unintentional violence resulting from political action.

Principal terms

ASSASSINATION: killing of a public figure, often for political purposes

CIVIL WAR: war within a country rather than between countries

COUP D'ÉTAT: violent removal of state leadership, often including assassination of the leader

GENOCIDE: systematic killing of members of an ethnic or religious group with the intent of eliminating the group entirely

GUERRILLA WARFARE: low-intensity conflict characterized by scattered armed attacks

HUMAN RIGHTS VIOLATION: use or threat of violence or other illegal or repressive acts by a government or its agents against a person

MASS UPRISINGS: large-scale demonstrations in opposition to government policies

POLITICAL TERRORISM: use or threat of extraordinary violence for political purposes

REVOLUTION: overthrow of a government, resulting in a fundamental change in the political elite

Overview

A common manifestation of political conflict, violence can be used to influence elections, to discourage or eliminate political opposition, or to gain control over scarce resources. It can also be an unintended consequence of political action when unpopular political events provoke violent responses.

Maintenance of civic order is generally considered a fundamental responsibility of government. The fear of civil disorder is often used as a justification for increased government power at the expense of individual civil liberties.

Political violence can be used by governments against their own citizens or against citizens of other nations. To some extent, all governments are coercive in that they regulate the behavior of citizens, redistribute resources to the advantage of some groups over others, and punish citizens who violate laws. Indeed, a common definition of government is an agency with a monopoly over the legitimate, or legal, use of violence.

When government coercion takes the form of extraordinary violence, contrary to that government's own law or the accepted tenets of human rights, it is terroristic. State terrorism is the use or threat of violence by government authorities or their agents to intimidate citizens. Most commonly, state terrorism is used to discourage political opposition and to maintain a regime in power. Governments frequently deny sponsorship of their own terrorist agents and some terrorists may operate without direct government sponsorship, but with the government's approval. Examples include state police agencies in the Soviet Union that enjoyed full government support, death squads sponsored directly or indirectly by government officials in Central America, and Ku Klux Klan groups in the United States that were at least tacitly supported by local officials. The range of violent tactics includes beatings, torture, rape, murder, mutilation, burning, and other forms of intimidation and coercion.

Political violence, too, may be used by incompetent regimes to maintain their authority when they are unable to deliver needed services. Such official political violence is more common when resources are scarce and officials are either unable to provide minimal services or cannot effectively reallocate resources to meet needs. Intimidation of constituents serves to reduce the pressure to perform well.

Violence by citizens against governments takes many forms. The spontaneous violence of riots was familiar in the United States and Western Europe during the 1960's and early 1970's. Such angry violence generally lacks focus, although individual targets (such as people, public buildings, and stores) may be identified. The Los Angeles riots of 1992, following the verdict in the Rodney King beating case, for example, seemed to lack focus, although there were a few attacks on city offices. Most of the violence was directed against private businesses and a few individuals. Studies of the urban riots in the United States during the 1960's and 1970's produced several explanations for the violence, most suggesting that the violence was related to increasing economic frustration rather than the absolute poverty levels. Two of the more prominent explanations were theories of relative deprivation, arguing that people were frustrated because they were poor compared to most in their cities and had little hope of catching up economically, and theories of rising expectations, meaning that people were frustrated because promised economic and political equality was not being realized.

As violence against government authorities escalates, political purposes and targets generally become clearer. Assassinations, coups d'état, and other direct attacks are seldom misunderstood. There is often a presumption that violent opponents desire to overthrow the government, but their political goals may be much more limited. Violent tactics serve to get public and official attention when nonviolent tactics do not.

Following World War II, studies of low-intensity conflict described a continuum of violence. The wars that led to the collapse of colonial empires in Asia and Africa tended to follow common patterns. The first stage was low-scale terrorist attacks against colonial authorities, often very deliberately avoiding attacks on police and military authorities in favor of attacks on more vulnerable civilian targets and symbolic facilities. As popular support increased, and as authorities proved unable to stop the attacks, national liberation forces increased the level of their attacks. The second stage was guerrilla warfare, meaning more frequent and directed attacks on government personnel and facilities. Successful guerrilla raids elevated the violence to the third and final stage, civil war. The belief that revolutionary violence tends to escalate affects perceptions of antigovernment violence today. The United States government's "no negotiation, no compromise" policy toward terrorists is based on the belief that the level of violence will increase if the terrorists are successful in achieving their political goals through the use of violence. Some experts argue that giving in to reasonable or legitimate terrorist demands helps remove the motivation to use violence.

In international affairs, the political violence of national governments includes state-sponsored terrorist groups and insurgency movements, as well as international war. Here, too, there is some expectation of an escalation from terrorism to guerrilla warfare to full-scale war. The use of military force is as old as the institution of government. The history of warfare has been characterized by an escalation of the scope and level of violence. Expanding alliances broadened the scope of international conflict and technological advances increased the destructive power. Thermonuclear weapons pushed the level of violence to the point of its being irrational for both sides.

Whether political violence is justifiable is both an interesting philosophical question and a critically important practical question. Analysts of terrorist violence frequently refer to the cliché that "one man's terrorist is another man's freedom fighter." Political violence has its uses. The violence of war is frequently justified in terms of threats to national interest and the inhumanity of the enemy. When the public has been unwilling to accept the official justification, it has been difficult to continue wars. For example, the United States was forced to withdraw from Vietnam in the 1970's and France was forced to withdraw from Vietnam in the 1950's and Algeria in the 1960's. There are also strong arguments for "just wars." When basic human values are threatened, or when war becomes a matter of self-preservation, people may be driven to war. Philosophical discussions of "just wars" may, too, suggest that there is an obligation to go to war if a government has violated its responsibility to the people or to the world community. That obligation was mentioned in the debates about whether the United Nations should get involved in Bosnia and Rwanda in order to stop the killing of thousands of civilians, in the early 1990's. The practical problem, however, of how to end the conflicts was more often the point of controversy than the philosophical argument.

Some governments and political cultures encourage or, at least, condone political violence. The level of violence in American politics, for example, is high compared with most other nations in the world. American officials, too, have argued that stopping international terrorist violence has been difficult because some nations, such as France and Mexico, have revolutionary traditions that accept violence as being justifiable and have tended to provide sanctuary to terrorist organizations. A less supportive international culture, it is argued, would reduce the attractiveness of terrorism as a tactic and would eliminate some of the safe havens for terrorists.

There have been several trends in political violence since World War II. The nuclear balance of terror, it is argued, kept the superpowers from using their nuclear weapons, although the use of tactical nuclear weapons was discussed periodically. Conventional warfare also became an increasingly expensive option. The strategic balance limited the gains that a superpower might make through conventional force. Limited wars, such as the Korean and Vietnam wars, became frustrating experiences because complete victory was not possible, nor even sought. Unconventional forces proved more flexible and more appropriate for the scope of warfare. Wars of national liberation were largely over by the early 1970's. Communist insurrections gave way to other nationalistic movements, some democratic, some socialistic, and some mixed. Low-intensity political violence became less ideological and more ethnic and separatist. In the United States and Western Europe, the violence of left-wing groups was largely replaced by the violence of right-wing groups. In the United States, violence became more characteristic of antitax groups, antiabortionists, drug dealers, and radical environmentalists. At the same time, analysts noted increasing racial violence and hate crime.

Applications

The conflict in Bosnia-Herzegovina following its declared independence from Yugoslavia in 1991 created an international crisis. From its founding after World War II, Yugoslavia experienced considerable political conflict among its numerous ethnic groups. It was frequently joked that the only Yugoslav was President Tito. Everyone else in the country, the assumption behind the joke was, was a Serb, a Croat, or some other member of an ethnic group—not a member of a nation. When Tito died, a collective presidency (with the office of president rotating among the leaders of the separate republics and autonomous regions) held the state together only briefly.

The Yugoslav military, organized to discourage a Soviet invasion, had its equipment decentralized and its local units generally capable of operating independently. The national army was dominated by the Serbs. When the conflict began, the large number of armed local militia very quickly escalated the level of violence. These local militia were trained military units. They were not necessarily well trained or well equipped, but they were there, with the Serbian forces generally stronger.

The population of Bosnia and Herzegovina tended to be intermixed ethnically, particularly in the larger cities such as Sarajevo. To gain political advantage, the Serbs took control of as much territory as possible. Attacks were designed to terrorize the Muslims and to force them to flee, so that Serbian units could take Muslim villages and lands. Artillery shelling and sniper fire created uncertainty and fear. Rape and torture of Muslim civilians served to terrorize the populations of other Muslim villages. Such terroristic tactics helped accomplish the task that more conventional tactics might not have, that is, forcing the Muslim population to flee.

The international dilemma became how to separate the antagonists who were so intermixed geographically, and how to find a solution before the Serb advantage became so great that they would be unwilling to compromise.

In some respects, the political violence in Bosnia is not a new phenomenon. Axis and Allied forces during World War II used terrorism to demoralize enemy forces. The Allied firebombing of Dresden and saturation bombings of other German cities were conducted for their psychological impact. The use of German buzz bombs against

London was designed to lessen the British will to fight. The United States hoped that dropping atomic bombs on Hiroshima and Nagasaki would end the war in the Pacific before Allied troops had to invade the Japanese mainland. Civilian populations became military targets. Rumors, as well as documented reports, of atrocities motivated civilian populations to support the war efforts on both sides. Such events have been common throughout the history of war.

Context

Political violence is often viewed as representing a failure to find peaceful means of resolving conflicts. Some would argue that there is absolutely no justification for using violence. Others argue that political violence is necessary as a means of breaking free of the past. Frantz Fanon, for example, in The Wretched of the Earth (1963), argues that violence is a necessary means to break the mental bonds created by colonialism. Marxist theory is unclear on the need for violence to realize utopia, although communist interpreters of Marx are often very clear about the utility of violence. When viewed as a political instrument, violence may be secondary to the political goals being sought. If one finds justification for the political goals, one also has justification for the violent means. The idea that the end justifies the means is part of the philosophy of war; by that philosophy, violence becomes legitimate.

Many believe that there are always peaceful solutions to political problems. Moral force, Mohandas Gandhi suggested, can ultimately overcome physical force, as well as the most unjust and violent opponents. There are political conflicts, however, for which there are no acceptable compromise solutions for the parties involved. Some such political conflicts have lasted for centuries. Artificial political boundaries, often set by colonial governments, have made it difficult to separate hostile cultures.

Aside from the philosophical arguments for and against the use of violence, there have been fundamental changes in how violence is perceived around the world. It was common in the years immediately following World War II for national liberation forces to use bombs without shrapnel, that is, bombs that were designed to make loud noises, without killing people. The purpose was to show that many people could be killed if changes were not made. Relatively few people were killed during the initial period of terrorist violence in the 1950's and 1960's. By the late 1960's, however, violence had escalated tremendously. There were often dozens or even hundreds of civilian casualties when bombs exploded. Acts of terrorism, to get desired media attention, needed casualties.

Political violence, from racist attacks to tribal warfare, is increasing as people and nations show less tolerance of others and economic limitations create more competition for scarce resources.

Bibliography

Eckstein, Harry. *Internal War: Problems and Approaches.* New York: Free Press, 1964. Historical and modern interpretations of political violence and revolution. A classic.
Fanon, Frantz. *The Wretched of the Earth.* Foreword by Jean-Paul Sartre. Translated

by Constance Farrington. New York: Grove Press, 1963. Argument for the necessity of violence in overthrowing colonial regimes.

Frey, R. G., and Christopher W. Morris, eds. *Violence, Terrorism, and Justice*. Cambridge, England: Cambridge University Press, 1991. Considers the purposes and tactics of terrorists from philosophical perspectives.

Gurr, Ted Robert, ed. *Protest, Rebellion, Reform*. Vol. 2 in *Violence in America*. Newbury Park, Calif.: Sage Publications, 1989. A sequel to the classic *Violence in America*, published in 1969.

Laqueur, Walter, ed. *The Guerrilla Reader: A Historical Anthology*. New York: New American Library, 1977. Philosophers, analysts, and guerrillas describe and offer justification for political violence.

Nieburg, H. L. *Political Violence: The Behavioral Process*. New York: St. Martin's Press, 1969. Nieburg examines the political violence of the 1960's, particularly the assassination of President Kennedy, and its place in the politics of the time.

Thackrah, John Richard. *Encyclopedia of Terrorism and Political Violence*. London: Routledge & Kegan Paul, 1987. Definitions of hundreds of terms and names relating to contemporary terrorist and antiterrorist organizations, acts of violence, and related phenomena.

Walter, Eugene V. *Terror and Resistance*. New York: Oxford University Press, 1969. Classic study of political violence in African societies, providing understanding of how social structures and government authority interacted to create violence.

Wilkinson, Paul. *Terrorism and the Liberal State*. New York: John Wiley & Sons, 1977. Discussion of the dilemma that political violence poses for democratic government, that is, how to stop violence without sacrificing civil liberties.

William L. Waugh, Jr.

Cross-References

POLITY

Field of study: Types of government

Polity is the general name for a political organization, or, more specifically, it is the name for inclusive constitutional government.

Principal terms

CONSTITUTIONALISM: doctrine that political arrangements, institutions, and processes should be governed by basic, well-publicized, usually written law

FEDERAL REPUBLIC: generally large political organization with power constitutionally divided between one inclusive and a number of less extensive governments

PLURALISM: view that democracy and fairness are preserved when a political organization comprises multiple and distinct groups and interests

POLITICS: activity of forming and carrying out public choices

POLYARCHY: government by more than three people, or a contemporary, large-scale, usually industrialized polity

Overview

One basic distinction between governments is qualitative: good and bad. Good governments exercise rule in the interests of all members of the society, while bad governments use political power for the advantage of only a few. Closely related to this distinction is that between governments under the rule of law and those that rule by arbitrary command. In just, constitutional government, political power is defined and limited by a fundamental, usually written constitutional law. In unjust, despotic government, political power is not limited and is thus liable to invade all areas of life.

In theory, there is no reason why just constitutional government may not rest safely in the hands of a relatively few persons, or even of a monarch chosen for life. In practice, however, there are three difficulties with any such arrangement. First, any small group of rulers is liable to be familiar with only a narrow range of opinions and interests. Assuming the group's good intentions, it nevertheless is going to govern with incomplete information. Second, long and uninterrupted tenure in public office tends to result in either neglect or corruption. Finally, the valuable experience of exercising public authority is restricted to a few in any elitist system.

The most desirable constitutional government, then, is one in which there is widespread participation by a variety of people. This form of government is polity. As the ancient Greek political philosopher Aristotle (384-322 B.C.E.) has noted, polity, the general name for a political association, is, more specifically, the name for inclusive constitutional government.

Aristotle's reasoning is as follows. Every political community is complex and made up of parts. It is a plurality, not a unity. Different groups, classes, and kinds of people perform different functions and contribute in different ways to the community. What makes a community most genuinely political, then, is that all or almost all of its members enter, in one way or another, into political life and the process of governing. As a result, polity is not of the whole, but by only a part; it is of the whole, by all the parts that make up the whole. To paraphrase the American statesman Abraham Lincoln, polity is government of, by, and for the people.

Polity is a practical and not an ideal form of government. Its advocates recognize that people differ from one another in a number of ways. The most politically relevant differences are economic in two senses. First, in any complex and reasonably prosperous community, there is a significant division of labor in the processes of production and distribution. This results in a variety of occupational groups and classes, each of which possesses interests of its own. Second, members of these occupational groups receive differing monetary and status rewards, both within a given group and between different groups. In short, functional economic differences lead to inequalities in material wealth and economic power.

The fundamental task faced by any given polity is to prevent these economic differences and inequalities from reaching a point where they destroy political life. If the economically advantaged and powerful rule, this is government by a part (almost certainly a minority) over the whole. In this situation, there can be no meaningful political life for most people. Polity must also guard, however, against allowing politics to become so pervasive that it destroys the stability and prosperity of the economic system. In polity, political life and involvement is the end, but economic prosperity is an indispensable means.

Prosperity is not, however, the only precondition for polity. Polity is highly unlikely unless a large proportion of its citizens reach a relatively high level of not only economic but also moral and educational development. It is impossible to create a polity where most are poor, immoral, and ignorant. Accordingly, public affairs in a polity are concerned generally with the private economic, moral, and educational issues that concern the continued existence of the polity.

Despite this general concern, a line is drawn between public and private matters as they relate to the individual. For the most part, a polity leaves private concerns to private institutions. It largely leaves the economy to various businesses, corporations, and labor organizations. It leaves education to churches and schools. It leaves the rearing of children to families. It allows a wide variety of informal and voluntary organizations. Within the context of a broad supervision aimed at ensuring well-balanced economic, moral, and educational development, public policy in a polity is intended to encourage private attention to these matters. This is in keeping with the fundamental principle of polity that the community is a plurality, each part of which is well suited to perform its particular function.

Balance, moderation, and watchful but unobtrusive supervision are, then, the basic political principles of a polity. It follows that individuals possessing these characteristics are the most appropriate officeholders. The middle class in a polity is that group midway between wealth and poverty, between highly public and highly private life, between rigid conservatism and revolutionary radicalism, and between complete inequality and complete equality. The middle class is possessed of a sufficiency both material and psychological, enabling them to hold office for a time and to relinquish it so that others may take part in public life.

No polity may persist without a fair number of such middle-class people. It is unrealistic to expect, however, that this sort of middle class will be a majority in all societies. Those with both more and less than an average amount of property and other resources must be included in public life, if polity is to achieve its goal of widespread participation. It is likely that those above and below the middle form distinct political parties. Membership and activity in these parties, at local, regional, and national levels, provides involvement in politics for those who do not hold public office.

Typically, the party of the relatively rich will favor less public involvement in government (an oligarchy), while that of the relatively poor will favor more (a democracy). The constitution of a polity channels these fundamental political positions and the resulting debate between them, into regular, free, competitive elections. The very broad purposes of electoral politics in a polity are as follows. First, electoral politics ensure that public debate occurs regularly and is heard widely. Second, it provides frequent opportunities for citizens to compete freely for political offices, including those within parties. Third, it permits adjustment and readjustment of the balance between a more and a less active government, as required by domestic and international political conditions. Last, it reminds every member of the polity that citizenship means participating actively and repeatedly in helping to make and execute public choices. These purposes are served when offices are numerous, elections are frequent, rotation in office is mandated or strongly encouraged, and electoral participation is viewed as a requirement of citizenship.

Polity succeeds to the extent to which the balance between public and private life is maintained. In practice, this requires that competition between political parties is preserved and moderated. Moderation necessitates the expansion of the size and political influence of the middle class. Middle-class citizens embody the norm of a polity. It violates, however, basic principles of polity—plurality and diversity—if the middle class grows so large and influential that it dominates all others. This would exclude from political life all non-middle-class people and thus destroy the polity.

Applications

For practical purposes, any constitutional government having free elections, competitive political parties, and widespread electoral participation may be considered a polity. American political scientist Robert A. Dahl, in Polyarchy (1971), calculated that there were between two dozen and three dozen such countries in the world at that time. This is roughly one-fifth of the world's nations. Most polities (or polyarchies, in Dahl's term) are Western European or Anglo American, but India, Japan, and Costa Rica are also included in his list.

It is undeniable that formal democratic institutions are necessary if a polity is to exist. A country in which the citizens are unable to choose freely between rival political programs and leaders cannot be considered a polity. It is possible to imagine a polity, however, in which voting is the sole act of political participation for most citizens. Further, it is possible to call a nation in which the major issue between two leading rival parties is how best to provide for economic prosperity, full employment, and relative income equality a polity. In this situation, the major public concern is economic well-being, for the country as a whole and for the people within it. The major purpose of public activity may be to serve private interests; almost all the citizens of a polity may remain private.

The tendency of a polity to combine the public and the private into what the twentieth century political philosopher Hannah Arendt (1906-1975) calls the social is one of two directions it may take. One direction is a high combination of the public and the private. An example of this direction may be found in the Scandinavian social democracies, particularly Sweden. These countries have settled, consensus-oriented constitutional politics, in part resulting from their international political neutrality and in part because relatively equalitarian economic well-being and extensive social welfare programs are firmly established. A consensus exists to use public institutions and resources to serve private purposes; these countries are therefore more social and less political.

The other direction is exemplified by the Anglo American countries, particularly the United States. In American politics, active debate continues on two fundamental constitutional questions. First, there is the question of what is and is not a public, governmental function. In the early and mid-1990's, for example, the issue of whether individual health insurance is an essentially public or essentially private responsibility dominated American domestic political debate. From the perspective of Scandinavian and Western European welfare states, the United States is considered backward in this area. From the American perspective, however, the health insurance debate was not yet settled.

The second question is equally fundamental. Assuming that a given issue is determined to be public, in the American federal system the question inevitably arises of which level of government should address it. If, after discussion and debate, the matter is held to be a state or local concern, then national uniformity in this area is precluded. Instead, dozens, hundreds, or thousands of different programs come into being. The result is a mind-boggling diversity and complexity, rendering simple, efficient legal and public administrative systems impossible, and rendering corruption in the face of public ignorance, inattention, or confusion, quite possible. The question then arises to whether this is a problem to be solved by substituting uniformity for diversity.

Context

The examples given indicate some of the basic practical issues of polity as a form of government. The American case shows that a complex constitutional structure has the potential for a rich and diverse public life. In the United States, there is political activity at national, state, county, municipal, and neighborhood levels, thus involving a very large number of citizens in the governing process. Such widespread activity is essential to a polity: Practically speaking, it is the meaning of the term.

The American case also shows how a complex polity needs a constitution. Unless clear and decisive distinctions are drawn and observed between public and private concerns, and among national, state, and local functions, the result is a multiplication of public programs and a confusion of responsibilities. In such a situation, a healthy pluralism becomes virtual anarchy, with multiple groups and interest at every governmental level competing to exercise control over every area of human life. The likely outcome is this paradox: Government effectivenss breaks down precisely because government is everywhere.

The difficulty suggested by the American case, then, is a pluralism exaggerated to the point of anarchy. A nearly opposite problem is possible with the Scandinavian and Western European social democracies. In them, the potential exists for a unity of opinion, and thus of policy, that diminishes pluralism to the vanishing point. A near-universal consensus on the role of the state means the effective end of politics. All fundamental political issues, especially regarding the question of what is public and what is private, would then be considered resolved. The only question remaining would be the technical one of how best to deliver governmental services. Whether these services were to be provided bureaucratically or capitalistically, almost all citizens would be functionaries, recipients, or both. They could not be citizens actively deciding fundamental public questions.

The deep problem facing current polities, then, is the possibility of either too much or too little politics. Both possibilities exist. In a complex constitutional situation, a tilt toward too much politics results in too much pluralism and competition; in a simple one, it results in too little. Polity, however, cannot operate successfully if there is either too much disagreement or too little. Too much disagreement tears a community apart; too little puts it to sleep. Either way, it ceases to exist actively.

This problem has no easy solution and, in any case, it is the business of each polity to decide what its problems and solutions are. The political science of polity, however, has a contribution to make. Modern political theory tends to understand the private as the individual. This is not a sound philosophical foundation for polity. The individual is utterly disproportionate, in strength, to the state, which is how the public is now understood. Given these terms, it is inevitable that public will overwhelm private. The ancient Greek political theorists, the philosophical founders of polity, understood the private to be the household, a term roughly encompassing a family and its property. Their thesis is that strong households underlie and support strong polities. Their thesis deserves renewed consideration.

Bibliography

Arendt, Hannah. *The Human Condition*. Chicago: University of Chicago Press, 1958.
    Discusses the changing understanding of the political. Part 2 is of special interest.
Aristotle. *The Politics*. Translated by Ernest Barker. New York: Oxford University

Press, 1958. The classic, indispensable source on polity, by its greatest theorist.

Dahl, Robert A. *Polyarchy*. New Haven, Conn.: Yale University Press, 1971. A contemporary interpretation of polity as pluralistic democracy.

Hamilton, Alexander, James Madison, and John Jay. *The Federalist Papers*. Edited by Clinton Rossiter. New York: New American Library, 1961. The classic American treatment of the extended republic in which political activity is multiplied, checked, and balanced.

Ladd, Everett Carll. *The American Polity*. 3d ed. New York: W. W. Norton, 1989. Ladd sees the American Constitution as the modern realization of Aristotelian polity.

Lowi, Theodore J. *The End of Liberalism*. 2d ed. New York: W. W. Norton, 1979. An indictment of contemporary interest group politics.

John F. Wilson

Cross-References

Aristotle's Political Philosophy, p. 83; Citizenship Rights and Responsibilities, p. 260; The Constitution of the United States, p. 425; Constitutional Governments, p. 432; Democracy, p. 513; Government Types, p. 785; Interest Groups, p. 936; Ochlocracy, p. 1338; Oligarchy, p. 1344; Pluralism, p. 1402; Political Participation, p. 1479; Political Party Roles, p. 1499; Republicanism, p. 1706; Separation of Powers: Political Philosophy, p. 1809; Social Democracies, p. 1839; Two-Party Systems, p. 2033.

POPULISM

Field of study: Political philosophy

Populism is the appeal, often tinged with cynicism, of a charismatic leader or a political movement to the common people.

Principal terms
AUTOCRATIC: government in which one individual has complete power

BIMETALISM: monetary policy of use of two metals, such as silver and gold, as a standard

CHARISMATIC LEADER: one who gains a large following, often through emotional speeches

DEMAGOGUE: political figure who makes wild promises to the masses but whose goal is personal power

GRASSROOTS: of widespread, popular origin

OLIGARCHY: rule by a small elite group

PLATFORM: statement of the goals of a political party

RADICALS: group that seeks great changes in society

Overview

Populist movements, which usually seek reform, arose in North America and in Russia in the late nineteenth century, and in twentieth century Latin America. While each of these movements grew out of specific circumstances at the time, they all share certain characteristics: lower- and middle-class groups who believe that they have been betrayed by those who rule, a desire for political power to effect reforms, and charismatic leaders who rally disparate groups.

Populist movements reflect the grievances of groups in transition. When social and economic changes threaten their livelihood, for example, they seek protection from the government and demand reform. Populism was perhaps the first political movement in the United States to claim that the federal government has some responsibility to the common people. While populist coalitions have occurred in many countries, in the United States it is most closely associated with the post-Civil War agrarian movement and the People's Party of the 1890's.

Midwestern and Southern farmers faced a number of problems, both economic and social, after a period of prosperity in the mid-nineteenth century. Expansion into regions west of the Mississippi River had been subsidized by railroad companies and the federal government. This encouraged many farmers to migrate westward. Abundant rainfall in the immediate postwar years weakened the reputation of the prairies as deserts, bringing a net population increase of more than one and one-half million to Kansas, Nebraska, and the Dakotas. The boom mentality attracted investments from the East Coast, as rising land values and increasing production made farms good collateral for loans. Circumstances began to change in 1886 when the average rainfall fell below normal. Crops began to fail, and thousands of farmers began to leave the region. Covered wagons traveled eastward with signs saying, "In God we trusted, in Kansas we busted." Mortgages were foreclosed, and no new money was forthcoming. As the boom turned to bust, farmers began to suspect that Eastern financiers were the only ones who had profited from their hard work.

The circumstances were different for the farmers in the Southern states, but the outcome was similar frustration. The Civil War had destroyed the plantation economy, and agriculture was increasingly dominated by sharecropping. Sharecroppers needed credit and often found it in advances made by local merchants. The advances, along with rent for the land, were to be paid when the crops were harvested. The dilemma for these sharecroppers was that the more they produced, the lower the value of their crops, with the result that they were unable to repay their debts. Circumstances were similar for both black and white farmers, and they both sank deeper into poverty. They became angry that others were benefiting from their increasing misery.

Farmers were told that overproduction was responsible for their economic woes. They thought, however, that high transportation costs were to blame, and began to accuse the railroad companies of monopolistic control over routes and unfair prices. All railroad companies became the target for the farmers' anger, along with their supposed allies, the grain elevator operators. The small farmers of both the South and the Midwest had a common enemy, and reformers who spoke out against the railroads found much support in these areas. These reformers sought an end to the monopolies of railroads and grain elevator companies. Publicity about monopoly trusts brought out other groups who claimed that government tariffs only encouraged a concentration of capital and harmed the common folk, who had to pay higher prices.

Farmers began to organize to address these problems. The National Farmers' Alliance in the North was formed in the 1870's, and a National Farmers' Alliance and Industrial Union in the South was joined by a Colored Farmers' Alliance. J. B. Rayner, a black populist leader from Texas, was a tireless reformer who influenced the movement. Although there were regional and local splits among the organizations, there was basic agreement on three issues: land, transportation, and finance.

It was an affiliation between the Farmers' Alliance and the Democratic Party that brought the farmers' demands into the political arena. First in South Carolina, under the leadership of Benjamin Tillman, there was a tacit merger of the two groups in 1888 when farmer candidates were elected as Democrats. Farmers' groups in North Carolina and in several Midwestern states gained political influence, making the idea of a third political party more acceptable. With the onset of a severe economic depression, the People's Party was established in Kansas in 1890 and nominated a candidate for governor. Similar movements followed in the surrounding states. Campaigns were colorful events, with musical parodies and fiery speeches by speakers such as Mary Elizabeth Lease of Kansas, who reportedly told farmers to raise less corn and more hell. Farmers blamed railroads, Wall Street, and lack of credit for their ills. Candidates blamed the problems of the common people on the rich and the powerful, and wanted to be elected to make reforms. The People's Party platform of 1892 stated that the powers of government, equated by them with that of the people, should be expanded. Beginning with this campaign, silver coinage became an issue that brought Western miner owners, Midwestern and Southern farmers, and Eastern labor into a coalition.

In 1873, Congress had discontinued silver coins as a monetary standard. The gold-only standard led to an overvalued dollar and a decline in prices. This fiscal policy favored investors, who were repaid with appreciating dollars, over borrowers, who had to sell more to earn the same amount in dollars. This issue united farmers with silver mining states that favored bimetalism—a gold and silver standard.

The union of Free Silver supporters, farmers, and the Democratic Party was accomplished in 1896 in the nomination of William Jennings Bryan as the presidential candidate on a platform of free silver. He was endorsed by the People's Party, which had contested elections in 1892 and 1894. The fusion of these two parties became complete and represented the end of a separate populist political party. Bryan was a brilliant speaker who electrified the convention. He lost the election. The silver issue receded as economic prosperity returned. Populism ceased to reflect the goals of farmers alone and became a force representing popular reforms, eventually influencing the Progressive Movement of the early twentieth century.

Applications

Populism has also arisen in several other regions of the world. In the latter half of the nineteenth century, Russia experienced significant social and economic change. In the 1860's the serfs were freed, and by the 1880's the Industrial Revolution had reached Russia. Foreign investments rose, railway lines were expanded, and industrial output rose. The growth of a middle class and an industrial working class made Russia more fertile ground for socialist and reformist political doctrines from the West.

Despite increasing industrialization, Russia remained an overwhelmingly rural country, and the majority of its population were peasants. Rural society revolved around the village community. The community controlled allocation of land, and individual peasants were not free to leave without village permission. Twin pressures of increasing population and the need for exports to pay for the foreign loans used to industrialize led to a land hunger among the peasants. Much land was controlled by the aristocrats or by wealthy individual farmers; peasants remained unsatisfied with government policy.

Historically, Russian peasants were more revolutionary than their Western counterparts. The great Pugachev Rebellion of the late 1700's had been a serious challenge to the government of Catherine the Great. By the end of the 1800's peasants were ripe for revolt, but lacked the leadership. This leadership came from reformist intellectuals, many of whom saw the true nature of Russia not in the autocratic rule of a czar, but in the communal cooperation of the village community. Some became members of the People's Will, and assassinated Czar Alexander II in 1881. Others traveled into the countryside to teach peasants to read. This group of intellectuals held a mystical reverence for the power of Russian peasant society. Peasant desire for land led to a revolutionary doctrine that would stand in contrast to Marxism and its focus on the industrial worker. Russian populists wanted to ameliorate the problems faced by farmers, spoke out against great landowners, and preached of a revolution that would avoid the evils of capitalist development for agrarian cooperation based on village life.

Russian populists were to have great influence on the course of revolution in Russia. Some, exiled to Western Europe, helped form the organization that would eventually become the Marxist Social Democratic Party. Others, rejecting Marxism, formed in 1901 the Social Revolutionary Party, which embodied many of the goals of earlier populists.

In the twentieth century populism emerged in Latin America as an urban rather than rural movement, with a focus on the grievances of the labor movement rather than farmers. It has exhibited some of the same goals and characteristics as other forms of populism: coalitions of groups seeking to take power away from elites, and charismatic leadership. Perhaps the best example in modern Latin America comes from Argentina, with the emergence of Juan Perón as a populist leader.

After 1880, Argentina changed dramatically from a poorly unified country with minimal economic ties to Europe to a unified state whose capital, Buenos Aires, grew to a large urban center. First, through export of agricultural products and then, when increasing demand for labor brought millions of immigrants, to a commercial and industrial center, Buenos Aires came to hold nearly one-third of all the people of the country. This rapid urban growth created the conditions of poverty and unemployment that reformers used to criticize the government's reliance on capitalist market forces to resolve urban ills. Housing was in short supply and expensive. Limited public transportation provided few opportunities for workers to live in the less expensive outlying districts. Disease brought death during frequent epidemics: Overcrowded housing and unhealthy conditions were often to blame for high death rates among tenement dwellers.

Populism emerged in Argentina first as a reform movement among elites who criticized a limited democracy that allowed an oligarchy of wealthy landowners to control the government. The Radical Party eventually obtained the presidency in 1916 with the election of Hipólito Irigoyen as president. Irigoyen instituted reforms aimed at improving the lives of the urban working class. Unions were accorded more rights to press their demands for better working conditions and increased wages. Housing projects were built. Radical Party functionaries sought grassroots support and assisted constituents with food baskets at holiday times or helped them secure housing. This alliance between middle-class reformers and workers reduced the power of the landowning elite. That elite reasserted itself through a military coup in September, 1930, when Irigoyen was overthrown.

During the 1930's the military dominated Argentina's government, but a reformist group of army officers took power in 1943 in another coup. Juan Perón emerged as one of the leaders of this reform group, and eventually became a powerful force in the government, controlling the labor department. Perón's alliance of reformist army officers and organized labor brought him growing power and, in 1946, he was elected president. Perón's policies reflected a desire to protect the working class through social legislation. Paid holidays and vacations were granted, vacation resorts provided low-cost workers' villages, social security legislation was passed, and housing projects helped to solve some of the problems of urban growth.

Perón began to lose support from more conservative elements of his coalition as a result of his economic policies and the power of his popular wife, Evita. After he was overthrown by a military coup in 1955, no political group could retain power without the support of his followers, and many of his social policies continued under subsequent regimes. Perón's popularity continued even while he remained in exile, and in 1973 he was allowed to return to Argentina. Perón was elected president, but died in office a year later. His legacy continued, however, and the Peronist Party captured the presidency in 1989.

Context

Populism in American history has been the subject of much debate. John D. Hicks's book The Populist Revolt (1931) saw populism as an agrarian protest movement and, along with the work of C. Vann Woodward, linked populism to early twentieth century reform movements, including the Progressive Movement and the New Deal. Richard Hofstadter, in *The Age of Reform* (1955), emphasized the nativist, anti-immigrant aspects of populism and its links to Father Coughlin, a Catholic priest of the 1930's whose radio programs criticized the New Deal and liberal reforms in virulent, anti-Semitic and xenophobic terms, and to Senator Joseph McCarthy's anticommunist crusade. Since the 1960's however, populism has been used to describe several grassroots movements that have challenged traditional political parties. The first of these was the surprising support for Alabaman George Wallace in 1968 and 1972, when he won the Democratic primary in Michigan with his platform against busing and his criticism of elite intellectuals who he said ran the Democratic Party. His unsuccessful candidacy brought together voters who were discontented with their party and its leadership. In 1972 the candidacy of George McGovern on an antiwar platform brought him control of the Democratic Party, but not the election victory. In 1992 H. Ross Perot, a Texas billionaire, ran unsuccessfully for the presidency on a platform that united many different groups of anti-incumbent sentiment, the need to focus on the national debt, and disappointment with the two main candidates. Each of these events marks modern examples of populism in the United States, and follows the criteria of movements that seek to restore power to the common people, unite disparate groups, and follow a charismatic leader.

Worldwide, populism continues to express the desires of common people who feel betrayed by those in power. Russians in the 1990's have sought limits on political and economic changes that have led to chaos. In 1994 Italians voted out most incumbents and turned to a millionaire businessman who promised to return the government to the people. These movements appeal to people who are disillusioned with their current leaders, face uncomfortable changes, and are stirred by a charismatic leader. Populism as a political movement continues to be a powerful force.

Bibliography

Conniff, Michael L., ed. *Latin American Populism in Comparative Perspective.* Albuquerque: University of New Mexico Press, 1982. Focuses on Latin American populist movements of the twentieth century, with articles on Russian and American populism.

Cunningham, Raymond J., ed. *The Populists in Historical Perspective.* Lexington, Mass.: D. C. Heath, 1968. Selections from American historians highlight Frederick Jackson Turner and his theory of the West and revisionists such as Hofstadter.

Hicks, John D. *The Populist Revolt: A History of the Farmers' Alliance and the People's Party.* Lincoln: University of Nebraska Press, 1961. Originally published in 1931, a classic work sympathetic to the Populist movement.

Hofstadter, Richard. *The Age of Reform from Bryan to F. D. R.* New York: Alfred A. Knopf, 1960. Revisionist view of populism as an undercurrent of popular resentments and nativist sentiments.

McKenna, George, ed. *American Populism.* New York: G. P. Putnam's Sons, 1974. Traces populist roots from Jefferson to George Wallace and George McGovern, arguing that populism is an entrenched American political style.

Riasanovsky, Nicholas V. *A History of Russia.* 4th ed. New York: Oxford University Press, 1984. For populism, see the chapter on Czar Alexander II and the radicals.

Woodward, C. Vann. *Origins of the New South, 1877-1913.* Baton Rouge: Louisiana State University Press, 1951. Presents additional information about the South's importance in the Populist movement, especially the relationship between the Farmers' Alliance and the Democratic Party.

James A. Baer

Cross-References

POSITIVISM

Field of study: Political philosophy

A philosophy of history elaborated by Auguste Comte in the first half of the nineteenth century, positivism stressed the importance of applying scientific methods to social issues and contributed to the acceptance of sociology as a tool for promoting order and progress.

Principal terms

HIERARCHY OF THE SCIENCES: positivist principle that all scientific knowledge grows from the simple to the complex, building on its predecessors

LAW OF THE THREE STAGES: principle that intellectual development begins with a theological stage, evolves to a metaphysical stage, and culminates in a positive stage

ORDER AND PROGRESS: positivist creed; understanding the laws that govern society brings progress which in turn assures order, itself the culmination of progress

POSITIVE: scientific, real, verifiable; contrasted to the myths and abstractions of orthodox religion and philosophy

RELIGION OF HUMANITY: positivist alternative to Christianity; serves humanity rather than a deity

SOCIOLOGY: discipline that applies to society the criteria used in scientific investigations

Overview

Positivism expresses some of the tensions present in nineteenth century European society. It can be understood as an attempt to extend principles elaborated during the eighteenth century Enlightenment to a nineteenth century world transformed by the French Revolution. It insists on the need for a scientific explanation of progress, positing that an understanding of the natural laws that govern society will allow the replacement of the political system destroyed by the French Revolution with one appropriate for the new industrial age, linking order and progress.

A French mathematician, Auguste Comte (1798-1857), formalized the philosophy of history and government defined as positivism. Comte was much influenced by Enlightenment thinkers, particularly the Baron de Montesquieu and the Marquis de Condorcet, who contended that society should be subjected to a careful scrutiny based on observable phenomena in order to understand the laws of progress of civilization. It was, nevertheless, to a contemporary that Comte owed his greatest debt: Henri Saint-Simon, the socialist utopian, whom the young Comte served as secretary and collaborator. Saint-Simon influenced Comte particularly in shaping Comte's emphasis on the essential connection between scientific and historical method, and in reinforcing his sense of the need to create a secular religion to replace Christianity.

Trained in mathematics at the École Politechnique in Paris, Comte readily accepted the importance of scientific classification and natural law. Positivism grew from his elaboration of the law of the three stages of intellectual development. Comte believed that human experience passed through three distinct phases. Beginning with the theological stage, in which religious explanations were preeminent, it evolved to the metaphysical stage, which was under the rule of philosophy, finally culminating in the positive stage, which acknowledged the supreme importance of science. An important counterpart to the law of the three stages was Comte's elaboration of a hierarchy of the sciences. He claimed that as scientific knowledge progressed consistently from the simple to the complex, new fields of scientific inquiry emerged. In this system, astronomy was the simplest of the sciences, and from its development grew knowledge in physics, then chemistry, biology, and finally sociology. The next step in this hierarchy, according to Comte, would be the elaboration of a science of morals.

Comte also affirmed that sociology should divide its attention between statics and dynamics. Social statics examined cultures as organic wholes at a particular level of development. Social dynamics focused on the transformation of societies from one stage to the next. The most recent period of social dynamics, from Comte's point of view, had been the French Revolution, which, by destroying an outdated political system, had created the appropriate environment for elaborating a positive alternative. He saw his role as that of formally describing this alternative.

In the aftermath of the French Revolution during the nineteenth century, industry appeared to be the foremost generator of social change. Comte maintained that industrial activity should naturally be the focus of human endeavors, replacing outdated enterprises such as warfare. The close connection between science and industry caused Comte to see industry as the vehicle to progress. Industrial workers, then, would be most responsible for ushering in a positive era of progress. Comte's philosophy placed a strong emphasis on work, despising idleness as antisocial. Realizing the importance of workers in bringing about change, Comte also believed that they should play a more active role in government. Positivism favored the destruction of all class privileges prevalent before the French Revolution, proposing republicanism as the better form of government. It favored what Comte called a "sociocracy," in which government would work for the good of society as a whole, extending beyond even the interests of all classes in the present to include the good of future generations. Clearly, then, political direction must come from those who looked beyond their immediate class interests.

In order to include participation by the many in a government that would work for the good of the whole, positivists insisted on the need for universal education. Citizens must be taught in a uniform way, based on scientific precepts, to discount the theological and metaphysical in favor of the positive. Since disagreements about power and forms of government had brought political conflicts in the past, an educational system that instilled a common understanding of the scientific bases for social change would usher in an era of order.

Comte and his disciples maintained that orthodox religion, and particularly Protestant Christianity, had accentuated divisiveness and disorder in the past. The individualism it fostered, they argued, worked against the common good. Positivists, therefore, abandoned Christianity in favor of a religion of humanity that adopted some of the trappings of the church, including temples and high priests, but proposed that one should "live for humanity," recognizing that the good of humankind as a whole best availed individuals by allowing society's benefits to be shared alike by all.

Comte's most lasting contribution, however, would not be in the political or religious spheres. It was the principle of organizing social phenomena in an orderly, scientific fashion (a tenet inherited from the Enlightenment and shared by many of his contemporaries) that made positivism's founder so important to future generations. Comte coined the word "sociology" (replacing the term "social physics"), and while he was certainly not the originator of the concept of a social science, he did contribute much to its propagation, influencing future sociologists such as Émile Durkheim and Max Weber.

Applications

Positivism originated in France and had a profound effect on British thinkers such as John Stuart Mill and Herbert Spencer. Yet it was not in Europe but Latin America that it secured lasting political influence. Latin America was emerging from its colonial status at roughly the same time that Comte began writing. The wars for South American independence ended around 1825, while Comte's major works span the period from 1826 to the early 1850's. Most of the nations that emerged from the old Spanish Empire quickly traded monarchy for republicanism. Leaders of these new republics became convinced of the need to promote education and industry.

In Mexico, Gabino Barreda, a lawyer and physician whom Benito Juárez made his minister of education, used positivist principles to explain his nation's history. He argued that during the colonial period Mexico had experienced the theological stage, which had given way to the metaphysical stage during the wars for independence. In the aftermath of those wars, Mexico was now on the verge of entering the positive stage. Social order, Barreda believed, could be restored through a positivist system of education that would eradicate some of the more enduring vestiges of colonialism evident in the continued influence of the army and the clergy. Furthermore, he contended, Mexico must move from a military era into an industrial age in order to survive in a world where industry increasingly defined national strength. Mexican positivists promulgated an intellectual revolution, seeing in education the instrument to transform the mentality of their fellow nationals and create the preconditions for economic development.

The appeal of order and progress extended broadly through the Mexican bourgeoisie. Many who belonged to this group, however, championed order and industrial progress as a means of amassing individual wealth. They rejected Comte's "sociocracy" and religion of humanity in favor of John Stuart Mill's emphasis on individual freedom. Mexican positivists were quick to agree that political freedom must be subjugated to economic freedom. While they accepted the need to examine Mexico's social situation in a scientific manner, they also maintained that a strong state was essential to establish the order that would bring progress and wealth. They therefore supported the authoritarian, and sometimes despotic, government of President Porfirio Díaz (1876-1880, 1884-1911), which adopted positivism as its political creed. In fact, Díaz's closest advisers and collaborators were called *científicos*, a particularly optimistic term for positivist civil servants. Díaz's administration, however, placed into sharper focus not only the promise but also the problems harbored within positivism. His long administration illustrated the perceived need for political order to implement the economic progress: Republicanism in practice became dictatorship. The vision that the *científicos* held of a modern Mexico did not always coincide with the fundamental aspirations of the Mexican people, many of whom struggled daily simply to survive. Instead of adapting to the needs of the population, the Mexican political elite decried the ignorance of the people and embraced the concept of superior and inferior human beings. This concept justified their decision to grant privilege to a small group of Mexicans over the vast majority of their fellow citizens. The rule of Díaz saw Mexico emerge from a period of political and financial instability, but the oppression suffered by the majority of Mexicans during Diaz's administration worked against continued order. Although many—particularly foreigners—admired the apparent economic progress brought about during Díaz's tenure, the order preserved by a careful policing of the countryside and the suppression of all political opposition collapsed after 1910, when Mexico plunged into revolutionary violence that would last more than a decade.

Positivism also played a significant role in the political transformation of Brazil. Following independence from Portugal in 1822, Brazilians experienced sixty-seven years of parliamentary monarchy accompanied by economic vitality. This vitality was based on the export of sugar and coffee produced by slave labor. During the time of the monarchy, an educated urban middle class, attuned to developments in Europe, grew in importance. An increased emphasis on mathematics and science in secondary schools served for the propagation of positivist ideas among professors and students.

Brazilian positivists at mid-century accepted the importance of industry and wage labor, but also acknowledged that their own nation's economic strength continued to rely on the labor of slaves. While they overwhelmingly opposed African slavery, many Brazilian positivists supported a process of gradual, rather than immediate, emancipation. This position was reflected in the 1871 Free Birth law, which granted free status to all children born to slave women. Ultimately, however, the strength of the abolitionist movement grew, and a law ending slavery passed in 1888.

Positivism had a profound effect on a rapidly modernizing Brazilian military that hoped to see order and progress triumph in its homeland, especially after the end of the war with Paraguay in 1870. This combination of military science and positivist ideology contributed to the downfall of the emperor in 1889. The monarchy was replaced with a republican government. The role of positivism in the young Brazilian republic was reflected in the motto "order and progress" inscribed in the new flag. Positivist influence after the collapse of the empire was not, however, long lasting.

Instead, the economic interests of coffee producers came quickly to the fore; they dominated the presidency at least until 1930. Yet it was in Brazil that the religion of humanity took strongest hold, with the founding of several positivist temples and the emergence of an enduring local apostolate.

Context

Positivism has been important in the transition from aristocratic regimes to republican democracies in an industrializing world. Faith in science and industry and in the perfectibility of human society provided the conditions needed for positivism's emergence and growth. Positivism appealed to those in France who saw in the political void created by the French Revolution the opportunity to chart a constructive social and political alternative. It also attracted the support of people concerned with the transformation of society brought about by the Industrial Revolution. In this respect, Comte shared with Karl Marx the conviction that new means of accumulating capital and subordination of the laboring classes demanded a system that would assure social justice. Positivism's emphasis on universal education and on the participation of workers and women in the political process foreshadowed future trends. In the twentieth century, however, especially after World War II, positivism came to be defined as a rather narrow doctrine that stressed the supreme value of empirical evidence and professed a belief in the inevitable perfectibility of society. Nevertheless, Comte's insistence on the application of scientific principles to social issues broadened the avenues of inquiry, transforming the way people made sense of their world both in his own lifetime and in the generations that followed.

Bibliography

Comte, Auguste. *Auguste Comte and Positivism: The Essential Writings*. New York: Harper & Row, 1975. Selection of writings illustrating the major themes in Comte's work, with an introduction to positivism.

Costa, Cruz. *A History of Ideas in Brazil*. Translated by Suzette Macedo. Berkeley: University of California Press, 1964. Best analysis in English of the importance of positivism in nineteenth century Brazil.

Harrison, Frederic. *On Society*. New York: Macmillan, 1918. Essays written by one of Comte's British disciples. Particularly interesting for its discussion of the positivist religion of humanity.

Hawkins, Richmond Laurin. *Auguste Comte and the United States (1816-1853)*. Cambridge, Mass.: Harvard University Press, 1936. Documents the relative failure of positivism in Protestant America. Pays much attention to George Frederick Holmes's opposition to Comte's philosophy and includes some of the correspondence between the two men.

Kent, Christopher. *Brains and Numbers: Elitism, Comtism, and Democracy in Mid-Victorian England*. Toronto: University of Toronto Press, 1977. Analysis of the appeal of positivism to British intellectuals in the 1850's and 1860's, especially as it related to the role of the working class in industrial nations.

Mill, John Stuart. *Auguste Comte and Positivism*. Ann Arbor: University of Michigan Press, 1961. Reprint of John Stuart Mill's 1865 exposition of Comte's positivist philosophy.

Simon, Walter Michael. *European Positivism in the Nineteenth Century*. Ithaca, N.Y.: Cornell University Press, 1963. Examines the diffusion of positivism in France, England, and Germany during the nineteenth century.

Thompson, Kenneth. *Auguste Comte: The Foundation of Sociology*. New York: Wiley-Interscience, 1975. Excerpts from Comte's writings, with a good introduction to their fundamental tenets.

Zea, Leopoldo. *The Latin-American Mind*. Translated by James Abbott and Lowell Dunham. Norman: University of Oklahoma Press, 1963. Essential for understanding positivism in Spanish America.

Joan E. Meznar

Cross-References

Industrialization, p. 916; Mill's Political Philosophy, p. 1204; Montesquieu's Political Philosophy, p. 1228; Political Myths and the Philosophies of Mosca and Pareto, p. 1474; Rousseau's Political Philosophy, p. 1756; Social Darwinism, p. 1833; Utilitarianism, p. 2077; Utopianism, p. 2084.

POSTAL SERVICE

Field of study: Functions of government

Collecting, sorting, and distributing mail has been viewed as an appropriate function of government in most countries for thousands of years. Postal service enables the universal communications that underlie political control, human understanding, business dealings, and technological, cultural, and artistic growth—in short, civilization.

Principal terms

ANCILLARY POSTAL SERVICES: functions that have no direct relationship with the traditional postal activities, such as a savings bank

POSTAL CODES: alphanumeric codes indicating successively smaller postal centers or stations to ease mail delivery; in the United States, the five- or nine-digit Postal Improvement Plan (ZIP) code

POSTAL INSPECTION SERVICE: law enforcement, internal audit, and security arm of the United States Postal Service

POSTAL SERVICE: system under which written and printed matter, packages, and electronic messages are transmitted, generally for prepaid fees

UNITED STATES POSTAL SERVICE: semiautonomous federal government corporation initiated on July 1, 1971, in an attempt to make mail-handling businesslike and self-supporting

UNIVERSAL POSTAL UNION: agency of the United Nations that established uniform rules guiding the exchange of international mail

Overview

From antiquity, postal service has paralleled the growth of civilization. The ancient Egyptians, Persians, Greeks, Romans, and Chinese all had it. The latter operated a postal network of approximately three hundred thousand horses with relay stations every twenty-five to thirty miles along the most traveled routes. In medieval Europe, postal service was at first provided by the private sector—merchants, monasteries, and universities—to serve its needs. As nationalism and unity grew, the rulers of rising nation- or city-states established their own communications systems alongside the private networks. By the fifteenth century, government service was fairly well established in France and Britain. It followed in the Italian and German states. By the eighteenth century, governments monopolized mail service and opened it to an increasingly literate public.

The British government established the royal postal service in its American colonies. In 1753, England appointed Benjamin Franklin as assistant postmaster general in Philadelphia. Franklin increased the speed and frequency of service, established new routes, and improved transatlantic mail to New York and Charleston, South

Carolina, via packet lines. Franklin was dismissed by the British government in 1774 for his revolutionary activities, only to be reinstated, this time as postmaster general, by the Continental Congress in 1775.

Under the authority of the new U.S. Constitution, which went into force in 1789, Congress had the exclusive power to establish post offices and post roads. At that time, the United States had seventy-five post offices and two thousand miles of post roads. Samuel Osgood was appointed as the first postmaster general by President George Washington.

One of the most important milestones in postal development was the publication of British educator Rowland Hill's *Post Office Reform: Its Importance and Practicability* in 1838. To replace the complicated, time-consuming system then in effect, Hill recommended a uniform rate of postage regardless of distance, and that postage be prepaid by means of adhesive stamps sold at post offices, rather than collecting a fee on delivery. These measures were adopted in England by 1840. Hill's "penny post" was less expensive than the previous system, thus making the service available to the masses, who were poor. It also simplified postal organization, making possible the speedy, inexpensive, modern system. Soon, different classes of mail were established, for example, reduced rates were charged for newspapers and, in short order, other printed matter, such as advertising. Postcards, first introduced in 1869, soon became popular.

The use of railroads to carry most of the mail, and the introduction of postal railroad cars to facilitate sorting while in transit, began in England in 1838 and speeded the mail delivery even more. Now mail could be delivered in cities as far as four hundred miles from the sender by the following day.

The exchange of mail across borders was also growing, although more slowly than internal mail volume. International mail service was hampered by myriad diverse bilateral postal treaties that necessitated the maintenance of detailed accounts between the countries concerned. This was no small task, considering the large number of currencies and units of weights and measurements in use in the mid-1860's.

The Paris Postal Conference of 1863, convened at the suggestion of the U.S. postmaster general, was the first attempt to untangle the chaotic conditions that translated into high international postage rates. At the conference, important general principles for simplifying procedures were adopted as a model. The International Postal Congress, held in Bern, Switzerland, in 1874, and attended by twenty-two states, led to the establishment of the General Postal Union in 1875, which was restyled the Universal Postal Union (UPU) in 1878. The UPU, which became a specialized agency of the United Nations in 1948, provides a uniform framework of rules and procedures for the exchange of international mail. As new services were added by the various national postal administrations—money orders (1878), parcel post (1885), postal checks (1920), aerograms (1940), cash on delivery (1947), and postal savings banks (1957)—the UPU covered the resultant international transactions.

Technological progress in postal transport, the automation of mail handling, and frequent innovations are the most striking features of the postal service. After the railroad, the most notable innovation was the use of airmail. While balloons had been used earlier in extraordinary circumstances (for example, during the siege of Paris by the Prussians in 1870), it was not until fixed-winged aircraft came into service that airmail became dependable. England experimented with airmail in 1911, and France in 1913, but it was not until after World War I that regular airmail started in the United States between Washington and New York (1918). The first international service between London and Paris was initiated in 1919. Regular transatlantic airmail started in 1939. The speed and reliability of airmail have made its use very extensive, even in domestic service, at times without any surcharge.

At the close of the twentieth century, computer and data transmission technologies provided alternatives to traditional mail service in the form of electronic messages such as e-mail. In large post offices, technological advances have facilitated the preparation of mail for delivery. Letters are processed by large machines, in which they are faced, canceled, and then channeled into ZIP code bins by mechanical sorters. It is predicted that the postal system will one day be nearly completely automated, which could reduce costs and provide better service.

While most mail is generated and delivered in developed countries, the establishment of efficient postal systems may be as important in the many developing countries. A good postal network enables a government to maintain contact with its citizens for such purposes as education and public information. By being a major user of transport services, promoting capital expenditures in buildings, equipment, and vehicles, and providing employment, postal services can be an important vector of national unity and development. Some of the post offices' ancillary activities, such as postal savings banks, may be especially valuable in countries where infrastructures are underdeveloped. For that reason, technical assistance through the transfer of hardware and software, especially training of various types, has been promoted by the Universal Postal Union and other international and domestic agencies. Such programs cover postal planning, management, financing, and public information. The syllabus may be as broad as postal service in general or as narrow as stamp collecting.

Applications

In the early 1990's, the United States Postal Service (USPS) was moving more than 170 billion pieces of mail a year, approximately half of the world's total. This volume was handled by approximately 29,000 post offices, using more than 150,000 vehicles of all kinds, and employing approximately 700,000 employees. The USPS's 125,000 city routes and 36,000 rural routes are serviced by letter carriers who cover more than a million miles a day. With some exceptions, the USPS monopolizes first-class mail (letters) by law. It is the largest telecommunications and transportation system in the world.

Since the establishment of the first U.S. postal service, there has been a debate about whether handling the mail is a proper function of government and if so, where in the organizational chart it should be located. The first General Post Office Act of September 22, 1789, which created the service on a temporary basis, was silent on where the postal function should be positioned. Even the name change from General Post Office to Post Office Department was made informally around 1825. Also at that time, Congress accepted this separate identity for the department as Postmaster General John McLean began reporting directly to the president instead of the secretary of the treasury. President Andrew Jackson made the postmastership general a cabinet position in 1829.

Uncertainty over whether the function should be a private or a public one continued, especially as new services were introduced. When Samuel F. B. Morse asked Congress for funds to set up wires to test his new electromagnetic device in 1838, Congress was reluctant to provide them. In 1847, Congress and the executive changed their minds, allowing the telegraph to be developed by the dozens of companies that quickly sprung up. After several of the early companies failed, the Western Union Telegraph Company emerged as a near-monopoly by the 1870's. A similar reversal happened with the telephone several decades later. In 1918, the postmaster general took control of the country's telephone companies, but by the 1920's these were restored to their private owners. Since the Postal Reorganization Act of 1970 created the semiautonomous government corporation, the USPS, there have been similar controversies regarding overnight mail, parcel post, electronic forms of transmission, and even first-class mail.

Part of the argument revolves around whether the public or the private sector is more competitive, that is, which can provide universal service, equitable access, privacy, and quality at the lowest cost. There is also an ideological side to the debate. U.S. society has tended to prefer private to public ownership of businesses, even those vested with a public interest such as railroads, airlines, and other public or semipublic utilities, in contrast to most other Western countries. This is explained by the widespread American faith that competition, free enterprise, the pricing mechanism, and the profit motive will produce the best outcomes. There has also been a tendency in the United States to view government as inefficient, bureaucratic and tied up in red tape, wasteful, occasionally corrupt, even socialistic. In the case of the old Post Office Department, it was also considered, with reason, to be highly politicized and a provider of political plums. Therefore, it was not difficult for business interests to make a case for private ownership, and Congress responded to the pressure on several occasions. Even in Great Britain, where the Royal Mail has been viewed as part of the fabric of British life and culture, privatization was openly being considered as a viable alternative in the 1990's, provided quality of service and low rates were maintained.

The United States Postal Service was supposed to be a compromise between public and private ownership, using businesslike methods, operating with a balanced budget, and still providing reasonable service. The USPS, however, did not satisfy everyone. In the 1990's, for example, a complete overhaul of the fee-classification system was being recommended, with rates tied more closely to cost and market factors. Visions for the future included computer bar codes for all letters before the twenty-first century; performance-based incentives, not just for managers but for all postal workers; and integration into the electronic information highway.

In 1994, the USPS continued to be managed by an eleven-person board of governors, nine of whom were appointed to overlapping nine-year terms by the president with the advice and consent of the Senate. The nine members select a postmaster general, who picks the eleventh member as deputy postmaster general. An independent, president-appointed Postal Rate Commission recommends rate schedules for the governors' approval. The 1970 act also established a postal career service to remove the political influence in the hiring and promotion of personnel that had been widespread under the earlier Post Office Department. Collective bargaining rights were assured. Strikes were prohibited, but compulsory arbitration was mandatory.

Context

From the beginning, private enterprise has competed with government, often beneficially, for at least some segment of the service. For example, in April, 1860, the Pony Express, owned by the Central Overland Express Company, provided a speedy adjunct to government mail service between St. Joseph, Missouri, and Sacramento, California, using horses running in relays. The first run over these two thousand miles took ten days, but President Abraham Lincoln's inaugural address reached the West Coast in a little more than seven days. The first transcontinental telegraph service to the West Coast, which opened on October 22, 1861, ended the spectacular record of the Pony Express.

In the late twentieth century, Congress still agonized over the proper mix of private and public enterprise in delivering postal service. Although one of the reasons for making the USPS a semiautonomous government corporation was to achieve a balanced budget, in most years it has had a shortfall of between $1 billion and $2 billion a year, ultimately made up by the U.S. Treasury. Nevertheless, postal rates continued to rise and alternative services provided by the private sector frequently have been more competitive. Complaints that the postal service was neither swift nor reliable, or that it was mismanaged, were still heard. To counter the charges, the USPS has pointed to the exploding growth in volume, completely disproportionate to population increase or the number of postal employees.

Whatever the merits of the debate, there is no question that the development of postal service has paralleled the evolution of United States history. Since the establishment of the first post office in Boston in 1639, postage stamps (1847), registered mail (1855), rail-carried mail (1862), free city delivery (1863), money orders (1864), penny postcards (1873), special delivery (1885), free rural delivery (1896), the postal savings system (1911), parcel post (1913), airmail (1918), certified mail (1955), ZIP codes (1963), and express mail (1977) have been introduced. By the early 1990's, electronic data transmission technologies were providing services that were likely to become even more common. Simultaneously, the growth of mechanization and automation, such as letter sorting machines (LSMs), is expected to revolutionize the system further.

Whatever the future may hold, the postal service in all of its forms has touched more people, more often, in more ways, than any other public agency in the United States.

Bibliography

Adie, Douglas K. *Monopoly Mail: Privatizing the United States Postal Service*. New Brunswick, N.J.: Transaction, 1989. Evaluates the problems of the United States Postal Service since 1971 and the recommendations to privatize and restructure it to make it more competitive and user-friendly.

Codding, George A., Jr. *The Universal Postal Union: Coordinator of International Mails*. New York: New York University Press, 1964. Scholarly, nearly encyclopedic, heavily annotated history of the Universal Postal Union. Excellent bibliography of primary and secondary sources and interesting annexes.

Conkey, Kathleen. *The Postal Precipice: Can the U.S. Postal Service Be Saved?* Washington, D.C.: Center for Study of Responsive Law, 1983. Laundry list of the many shortcomings of the service and its possible outlook in the twenty-first century, prefaced by consumer advocate Ralph Nader.

Cullinan, Gerald. *The Post Office Department*. New York: Praeger, 1968. History of the service from colonial times to the mid-1960's. The author, a former manager of the Post Office Department, provides insight into the frequent politicization and occasional corruption and mismanagement before the department's conversion to the USPS.

Fowler, Dorothy Ganfield. *Unmailable: Congress and the Post Office*. Athens: University of Georgia Press, 1977. Discusses the struggle among Congress, the courts, and the postal service to define "unmailable" categories of traffic in light of constitutional provisions on freedom of speech and the press, and freedom from unreasonable searches and seizures.

Fuller, Wayne E. *The American Mail: Enlarger of the Common Life*. Chicago: University of Chicago Press, 1972. Retraces the evolution of the mail from the early years to the creation of the USPS in 1971, seeing the postal system within the broadest possible perspective as a part of the national experience.

Hill, Rowland. *Post Office Reform: Its Importance and Practicability*. 4th ed. London: C. Knight, 1838. A classic by the British reformer whose recommendation of the prepaid penny postage stamp revolutionized postal development worldwide.

Jackson, Donald Dale, et al. *Flying the Mail*. Alexandria, Va.: Time-Life Books, 1982. Easy-to-read, enticing account of early airmail in the 1920's and 1930's, and the growing role of planes in postal operations around the world. Lavishly illustrated.

Kahn, Ely J., Jr. *Fraud*. New York: Harper & Row, 1973. Short history of the little-known U.S. Postal Inspection Service "and some of the fools and knaves it has known." Out of thousands of unlawful acts of various descriptions perpetrated through use of the mails, the cases presented were selected with a view to interest and diversity.

Robinson, Howard. *The British Post Office: A History*. Princeton, N.J.: Princeton University Press, 1948. Scholarly study evidencing how many pioneering British postal services, following Britain's earlier administration of the thirteen American colonies, helped to mold the United States system.

Scheele, Carl H. *A Short History of the Mail Service*. Washington, D.C.: Smithsonian

Institution Press, 1970. Objective historical account, daintily illustrated, of the U.S. Post Office Department by the Smithsonian's associate curator in charge of philately and postal history.

Peter B. Heller

Cross-References

Business and Government, p. 177; The Civil Service in the United States, p. 310; Communications Management, p. 370; Consumer Politics, p. 445; Funding of Government, p. 724; Government Agencies, p. 765; Government Roles, p. 778; Political Economy, p. 1455; Public Policy, p. 1633; Public Utilities, p. 1640; Technology and Citizen-Government Relations, p. 1949.

POSTMODERNISM

Field of study: Political philosophy

A movement within the fields of philosophy, political theory, literary criticism, architecture, art, and other areas, postmodernism challenges all modern orthodoxies concerning styles, beliefs, and sensibilities. In their place, it offers eclectic and unorthodox ideas and styles that question or subvert the received ideas of Western civilization as a whole.

Principal terms
DECONSTRUCTION: method of critical analysis (particularly textual analysis) that denies the idea of a single "correct" reading, including that of a text's author, providing instead multiple readings from multiple perspectives leading to radical skepticism
ENLIGHTENMENT: Western philosophical movement emphasizing reason that arose in the late eighteenth century, when its proponents rejected many traditional political, social, and religious ideas
METANARRATIVE (GRAND NARRATIVE): account of matters relating to the nature and destiny of humanity, from religious or secular perspectives (such as Marxism) that give meaning to the life beyond the individual
MODERNISM: broadly applied term for currents of artistic, literary, and political thought and sensibility attached to modernity; encompasses such political currents as liberalism, human rights, socialist utopianism, Marxism, history as progress, and belief in reason and science
MODERNITY: era beginning in the late seventeenth century characterized by increasing dynamism, individuation, economic development, and wealth; its proponents champion reason, science, and, occasionally, the idea of progress, leading—according to some—to a global civilization
POSTMATERIALISM: attitude of those who place little value upon material possessions and physical economic security, seeking instead a sense of belonging, self-expression, and nonmaterial qualities of life

Overview

The term "postmodernism" describes certain twentieth century movements in architecture, art, literary criticism, political theory, and other areas. Although there is no single accepted meaning of the term, consideration of the relationship between postmodernism and modernism helps to elucidate the concept. The Modern Age was founded upon such values of Western civilization as the ancient Greek idea that the world makes sense. It also rests on secularized versions of Christianity and its notions of human unity and equality and its denial of state control of conscience. More immediately, the Modern Age takes many ideas from the eighteenth century Enlightenment, which stressed belief in the value and power of reason, faith in science, and the idea of applying reason and science to subdue nature in order to make of the earth a Utopia, a place of peace and plenty.

The Enlightenment idea of history reflected this view. History is the story of progress over "irrational" custom, "superstitions," religions, and oppressive politics of the past. History is like a stream, muddy at its source, but becoming clearer and purer as the passage of time deposits the dross of error on its banks. This view of history as a unified story with a bright conclusion—an essentially comic vision—was a secularized version of the Christian account, which sees the human drama as a coherent story with a beginning, a middle, and an end.

After the American and French revolutions, another key component of modernity entered history: the claim to universally applicable human rights. The "self-evident truths" of human rights found in the Declaration of Independence were repeated and elaborated in the French Declaration of the Rights of Man and the Citizen (1789), and became a stock-in-trade of liberal democracy in the West. By the nineteenth century the idea of progress as the application of reason and science to economic and social life was a defining characteristic of the age. With the speed of new inventions and industries a new dynamism began to shape the social order.

At the same time, industrialization gave rise to new political parties championing the interests of the new and downtrodden industrial workers. Socialism was introduced into the common stock of European ideas in both "utopian" and "scientific" variants. Karl Marx, claiming the mantle of science for his ideas, based them on the thought of the German philosopher G. F. W. Hegel and presented a grand unified view of human history that foretold its end and fulfillment with the inauguration of freedom and plenty after a workers' revolution. This account of human history was another version of secularized Christianity. Although nineteenth century writers quarreled over the nature of history, modernity never doubted that history makes sense, that it has an intelligible character.

Modernity was also reflected in other aspects of culture. In the twentieth century, modern architecture showed clean, smooth lines reflecting purity and simplicity of style. Gone were the signs of class distinctions, Gothic revivals, and other reminders of the past. The new, triumphant egalitarian ethos demanded the sameness of the modern office building. In addition to architecture, modernity was mirrored in art, popular culture, industrial design, and much else. Modernity has also been mirrored in politics. The same social and economic processes that fed the dynamism of capitalism influenced the creation of political ideas and political parties that serviced the newly emerging social classes. On the European Left, class solidarity, preached by working-class (especially Marxist) parties, was the order of the day. On the Right, gaining currency was the idea imported from the Middle Ages of a "corporate" society, a social organism analogous to the human body, living in harmony, once the toxic elements are controlled or eliminated. In both cases, advocacy of societal or class unity predominated. Only liberalism looked to the accommodation of social pluralism, to the acceptance of differing social parts within a framework of personal and political liberty. Liberalism, the heir to the Enlightenment, tended toward a vision of history in which light dawns on a dark world so that with human effort the future will grow brighter.

Postmodernism can be seen as a denial of the central characteristics of the Modern Age. In architecture, postmodernism rejects simplicity of style, attempting to "rehumanize" architecture by eliminating purism in order to embrace complexity and historical references. Sometimes postmodern styles embrace playful elements, such as those found in the garish commercial architecture and billboards of the casino-canyons and boulevards of Las Vegas.

Postmodernism in philosophy, political and social theory, and literary criticism challenges or denies outright the principal truths of Western civilization, especially those of the Enlightenment. These "truths," insofar as they present a coherent view of the human condition or of history, are known as "metanarratives" that render meaning to individual lives as part of larger wholes. Thus, the biblical account of humanity as expelled from Paradise and destined to find redemption in faith is a metanarrative.

The postmodernist project rejects wholesale all attempts to make sense of the human condition from a single (or "totalizing") point of view—such as a religion. It also rejects all universal values (such as "reason" and "human rights") and all metahistorical accounts that claim to explain history as a whole (such as Marxism). Thus, major religions and forms of theism are denied. Humanism, in the sense of a claim to the unity of humanity through a shared human nature and shared values, is also repudiated. All "totalizing" views, those claiming to summarize or speak for a whole (the whole of a text, of a group, or any sort of whole), are disavowed, and fragments or fragmentary views are embraced instead. To postmodernism, the horrors of the twentieth century prove that history as progress is bunk; and the steady triumph of reason and reason's value are exposed as illusions. Reason in the twentieth century led to the Jewish Holocaust in Germany, the Gulag Archipelago in the Soviet Union, and the nuclear nightmare throughout the world. The Enlightenment itself and all of its machinations, its utopian projects, are frauds. By the 1989 bicentennial of the French Revolution, French postmodern intellectuals had turned decisively against the Revolution and its claims to champion universal human rights.

No single "scientific," ideological, or religious perspective of politics, of philosophy, or indeed of postmodernism itself, can be "privileged." Totalizing ideas of universal "rights" fail to take into account the differences among people, fail to account for the "Other." "Difference" and "Other" are major categories in the postmodernist lexicon. Moreover, postmodernism in some hands, especially those of writers such as the Frenchman Jean-François Lyotard, amounts to the denial of any restriction on thought or interpretation. For such writers, in a world without values or ideals grounded in traditional "metanarratives," each moment may be lived within an attitude of playful ironic creativity. For the critics of the movement such as historian Gertrude

Himmelfarb, postmodernism inhabits a nihilistic world shorn of all basis for moral restraint. Modernists see the world as the ancient Greeks saw it—as intrinsically intelligible. Postmodernists, by contrast, often paint the world as disordered and unknowable, like the "chaos theory" fashionable in physics.

Many postmodernists have a sense of "coming after." They come after the great belief systems have lost their moorings. They come after Friedrich Nietzsche declared the "death of God," and they come after the death of communist socialism, the flagship of Marxism, after 1989—when threat of Soviet invasion was lifted and whole peoples rose up to rid themselves of its oppression. It is worth noting that postmodernists insist that it is a state of mind, not a cultural or political period. Thus, people can choose whether to dwell in postmodernism or not. Some find this state of mind liberating. Critics fear that postmodernism liberates people from the foundations of all decency—moral, political, and social.

A powerful vehicle in the process of dismantling received truth is the critical technique of deconstruction championed by the French theorist Jacques Derrida. In deconstruction, Derrida fashioned one of the most potent weapons in the war against modernity. Derrida put forward the notion that there is a gulf between those who intend to impart meaning (the signifier) and what is meant or meaning (the signified). Once detached from its author, who loses previously ascribed authority (a situation called "death of the author"), the signified (that which is meant) can take on many meanings—none of which is necessarily incorrect. No longer is the author of a text its definitive interpreter; no one is. Since any statement can be taken to be a "text," all religious, historical, political, philosophical, and other claims can be subjected to the radical skepticism that deconstruction represents. Many interpretations of texts are possible; none is definitive.

This radically skeptical view leads to a thorough-going moral relativism. One consequence of this relativism is the denial by postmodernists of all claims to universal values, such as those put forward with such urgent faith by the Enlightenment. Such claims can be reduced to "texts" and deconstructed. This universal deconstruction has led critics to suggest that deconstructionists turn their techniques on their own texts; and that these techniques be applied not only to their political opponents on the Right, but also to their political allies on the Left.

The postmodernist mood influences many avenues of social theory. Although the late French philosopher Michel Foucault is not considered entirely postmodern, he is included in most discussions of postmodernist political thought. Interested in the roots and history of power and its relationship to knowledge, Foucault liked to speak of the "archaeology" of knowledge. Power leads to "hegemony," a key term in the postmodern vocabulary that refers to the domination of a point of view and the group espousing it. Always negative, hegemony is rejected by postmodernists, though no basis for this rejection is ever offered, since postmodernism eliminates all foundations for moral objection. In *Discipline and Punish* (1979), *History of Sexuality* (1980), and other works, Foucault sought to uncover the history of the social institutions and attitudes that dominate modernity, intimating that this exposure undermines modernity's claims to authority and signals the intellectual's withdrawal of confidence in and allegiance to a social order in which "privileged" middle-class values exercise "hegemony."

Another line of attack on modernity is offered by certain feminists. To radical postmodernist feminism, the values of Western civilization, those of reason, science, liberal democracy, and history as a coherent, intelligible whole are essentially male ("his-story"). The "privileged" position of these "phallocentric" values is to be replaced by a new matriarchal feminism that eliminates patriarchal "hegemonic" male evils such as spousal abuse, war, and political oppression.

Applications

A postmodernist understanding of politics can be applied to much of the politics of Western Europe and the United States, though less so to Eastern Europe, where politics is still more of the modernist cast. (The existence of such environmentally oriented parties as the 1990's Polish "Beer-Drinkers Party" might, however, usefully be described as postmodernist.)

Postmodernist politics may be described as the politics of social fragments, of "difference." As postmodernism rejects unified social theory, so unifying political ideologies and parties are discarded. In their place are fragments of parties, often single-issue groups, corresponding with fragments of the population. Thus, postmodernists reject Marxism and Marxist parties as historical relics and embrace in their sphere of influence new fragmentary political ideologies, sects, and parties that provide evidence of the transformation of modernism.

These new political ideas and political formations include those of environmentalists, feminists, pro- and antiabortionists, gays and lesbians, and the like. In the 1992 American elections, the H. Ross Perot phenomenon, in which 19 percent of the American voters opted for an untried, acerbic Texas billionaire, might also be described as postmodern in its rebelliousness and rejection of traditional parties for a maverick—a fragmented singularity.

Also in the United States, the central fragmenting features of postmodernism might also be seen in what has been termed "the new American politician." This new man or woman is no longer beholden to traditional hierarchical leadership. Instead, with an autonomy gained through independently raising money once provided by party headquarters, the new politician can assert a new autonomy from party leadership, fragmenting power in Washington and state legislatures.

A similar phenomenon occurred in Britain in the 1970's and 1980's. Because of the character of modern British society, the traditional working class, whose sense of solidarity was proverbial, began disintegrating. This complex phenomenon could be seen in the breakup of trade union cooperation in strike policy, with single unions going their own way. This was especially visible among miners in the early 1980's, when radical and moderate wings of the miners union split on strike policy, with a sizeable fraction opting to continue working. The result was the failure of the miners strike and a major victory for the government of Prime Minister Margaret Thatcher. A principal reason for the split within the union was that some miners had become homeowners and would face foreclosure without their wages. The economic forces of modern society thus undermined traditional social formations to reveal what can be considered a "postmodern" condition. Even France discovered the politics of myriad interest groups known across the Atlantic for decades.

Context

Postmodernism can trace some of its roots to the nineteenth century rebels against the certainties of Christian Europe, of whom Friedrich Nietzsche was—and still is—the leading exponent. Cultural and intellectual rebels have been a feature of Europe for more than a century and a half. Earlier, Jean-Jacques Rousseau, enfant terrible of European letters, became the first modern alienated intellectual. By the twentieth century a host of alienated intellectuals, along with bohemian artists and others protesting the regimentation and rationalization of industrial capitalism, became a standard feature of the European and later the American scene.

The aftermath of World War I, which wiped out a generation of young European men, brought forth cultural melancholia, "a politics of cultural despair," among some artists and intellectuals in the 1920's. After World War II, postmodernism was born in keen remembrance of the horrors of fascism and Nazism, especially the Holocaust and the desolation of Europe. By the 1960's, the failure of major utopian projects was becoming visible, especially after the Soviet invasion of Czechoslovakia in 1968 and the failure of the French student uprising. The waning of faith in Marxism, combined with the continuing estrangement of the intellectual from bourgeois society in general and capitalism in particular (despite the life of ease, even opulence, supplied to large numbers of Western intellectuals by capitalism), provided fertile ground from which adherence to postmodernism would grow. Critics of the movement argued that many postmodernists appeared to be disillusioned utopians. Once schemes for social perfection became bankrupt, the disenchanted turned against belief itself, inclining instead to the radical skepticism of deconstruction and similar movements of the new mood that distanced itself from the Modern Age and its secure optimism and intellectual certitude.

In society at large, changes in taste, judgment, and belief were creating what has been called a "postmaterialist" society. Postmaterialists fed the ranks of postmodernist politics. The priorities of postmaterialists run to self-expression and belonging, to the nonmaterial values of life, as opposed to the economic substance of middle-class security. In the United States, such values were heralded in the 1950's by the "beatniks" and in 1960's social criticism. By the late 1960's a middle-class counterculture was in full swing across America and Western Europe. From the 1970's to the 1990's, intergenerational value change was charted in social, economic, and political life, manifesting itself in altered lifestyles; toleration of minorities; altered consumer patterns, gender roles, and fertility rates; and other markers of social transformation.

The postmaterialist generation tended to adhere to postmodernist politics. Rather than loyalty to traditional political parties with their rejection of single-issue politics, members of this generation tended to support fragmentary causes represented by the politics of gender, environment, race, ethnicity, abortion, and sexual preference. It remained unknown how a fragmented postmodernist politics could cope with the realities of political life, which demands coalition building and therefore limits introverted concentration on one's own group or cause.

Bibliography

Best, Steven, and Douglas Keller. *Postmodern Theory: Critical Interrogations*. New York: Guilford Press, 1991. Fascinating and sympathetic—but not uncritical—examination of the leading exponents of postmodernist thought, such as Michel Foucault, Jean Baudrillard, Jean-François Lyotard, Gilles Deleuze, Fredric Jameson, and others. Written in a relatively clear style, but its postmodernist jargon requires some effort to understand.

Heller, Agnes, and Ferenc Fehér. *The Postmodern Political Condition*. Cambridge, England: Polity Press, 1988. Exploration of the character of postmodern political thought and its consequences, including moral consequences. Discussion of neo-Aristotelian responses to postmodernism concludes that a consensus on moral ideas is impossible. The authors are especially concerned about the consequences of the "postmodern condition" for the future of Europe.

Himmelfarb, Gertrude. *On Looking into the Abyss*. New York: Alfred A. Knopf, 1994. A distinguished historian, Himmelfarb surveys postmodern views of history and finds herself in a moral abyss. Brilliantly written and engaging, the work challenges facile acceptance of postmodern views.

Pangle, Thomas L. *The Ennobling of Democracy: The Challenge of the Postmodern Era*. Baltimore: The Johns Hopkins University Press, 1992. Brilliant and lucid critique of postmodernist philosophy and its application to politics by an adherent of the ideas of the late Leo Strauss. In exploring the nihilistic and disintegrating potential of postmodernism, Pangle offers his own philosophical antidote, which includes advocacy of civic education as the heart of American public schooling.

Rose, Margaret A. *The Postmodern and the Post Industrial*. Cambridge, England: Cambridge University Press, 1991. Historical and critical guide to postmodernism and postindustrialism and their relationship. Discusses postmodern theorists such as Lyotard and Baudrillard but goes beyond philosophical thought to include extensive discussion of postmodern architecture and the work of architectural critic Charles Jenks.

Wakefield, Neville. *Postmodernism: Twilight of the Real*. Winchester, Mass.: Pluto Press, 1990. Lively discussion of the meaning of postmodernism. Includes chapters on semiology and aesthetics and postmodernist psychology. The author dissects certain aspects of contemporary culture such as films and certain popular entertainment.

Charles F. Bahmueller

Cross-References

POWER DIVISIONS IN GOVERNMENTS

Field of study: Political philosophy

The distribution of power within governments has been a topic of intense discussion within political science. Understanding how power is concentrated within government is critical because its distribution determines who has political authority.

Principal terms

CHECKS AND BALANCES: limitations and requirements for cooperation imposed on each branch of government in a system of separation of powers

CORPORATISM: theory that power in government is for the most part answerable only to a few large interest groups

DICTATORSHIP: complete control of government power by a single ruler

DIRECT DEMOCRACY: rule of the citizenry in day-to-day government

DIVIDED GOVERNMENT: control of the executive and legislature being split between parties

ELITISM: theory of government run by a select few

FEDERALISM: system in which power is shared by a national government and a number of regional or state governments

PARLIAMENTARY SYSTEM: system in which executive and legislative powers are combined with one institution and are controlled by one political party

PLURALISM: theory that power in government reflects competition in society between many small interest groups

SEPARATION OF POWERS: system in which executive, legislative, and judicial powers are placed in different institutions and are exercised by different people

Overview

Power can be distributed within governments in many ways. At one extreme is the concentration of all political authority in the hands of one person who rules by command, while all other members of the society must obey his or her will. The absolutist monarchs of Europe before the late 1700's ruled in this manner. Louis XIV of France, who assumed the powers of kingship in 1661, coined the famous phrase, "l'état, c'est moi," meaning "I am the state." More recently, dictators such as Adolf Hitler in Germany (1933-1945) and Joseph Stalin in the Soviet Union (1924-1953) have provided examples of highly concentrated political authority.

At the other extreme is a government by the people, in which all individuals in a society directly influence the decisions made by that society. All members of the society gather in a single place to discuss and then vote on policy. Each person has a single vote and therefore equal power. This idea comes from the work of eighteenth century French philosopher Jean-Jacques Rousseau, who argued that the people were sovereign, that they should govern directly, and that there ought to be no constraints on the popular will of the people. In the American vernacular, this type of government has been called direct democracy and is reflected in the town governments of New England and in the referendums that many states have on issues ranging from seat-belt use in cars to taxes. Versions of it have been advocated recurrently by politicians such as Thomas Jefferson and presidential candidate H. Ross Perot.

Nearly all societies have governments that fall somewhere between the extremes of dictatorship and direct democracy. Dictatorships violate notions of justice and democracy, while direct democracy is extremely laborious and impractical, as well as threatening to the rule of law. Dictatorships and direct democracy, however, do provide a useful measuring stick with which one may compare the distribution of power in governments throughout the world.

Power in the governments of most modern countries is quite decentralized. Democracy—majority rule through citizen participation in politics—is a norm. Yet the United States, for example, is not a direct but a representative democracy in which the people select others to represent them in government. As a result, power is not decentralized to the extent that all of society's members get an equal and direct say in government affairs. The representation of all demographic, geographic, and economic interests in government, however, means that a variety of groups will be able to influence government decisions and public policy.

Not all representative democracies are the same. Power in the parliamentary systems of countries such as the United Kingdom, Canada, Australia, and Germany, for example, is relatively concentrated. This is because two major functions of government, the executive and legislative, are exercised by the same political party. In parliamentary elections, the party that wins the most seats in the country's parliament or legislature is entitled to choose the executive. In parliamentary systems, positions within the executive branch are of the most prestige and power. They are occupied by party leaders, whose control over appointments maintain party loyalty. Parties in parliamentary systems tend to vote in blocks. This means that the leader of the party, who occupies the executive position, can also control the legislature. The result is that parliamentary systems in effect hand both the executive and legislative functions of government to one group of individuals or political party. Nevertheless, the behavior of the party in power is checked by popular elections and is dependent upon continued parliamentary majorities and upon cohesiveness within the party. The party in power is often able to transform its platform into public policy quite easily.

In contrast, the American government is structured to avoid the concentration of power. Borrowing from the ideas of seventeenth century English philosopher John Locke and eighteenth century French philosopher Montesquieu, Framers such as James Madison built a system of separation of powers. Locke and Montesquieu warned that allowing all government functions to congregate in a single pair of hands could lead to political power being used against, instead of for, the people. Unlike the parliamentary system, the American system of separation of powers therefore allows for separate elections for the executive and for Congress. The system also prevents an individual from occupying a position in any two branches of government simultaneously. Moreover, because Madison and his colleagues believed that human beings are greedy and power was of an encroaching nature, they created a system of checks and balances. The executive, legislative, and judicial branches of government were given the ability to protect themselves and their prerogatives from one another. Congress can, for example, impeach presidents and judges. Policy-making is, by design, a labyrinthine process in which the branches are forced to interact and cooperate. Congress can, for example, only make law if it acquires the signature of the president or can get two-thirds of its members to override a presidential veto.

The extent to which power is concentrated within the American government is usually contingent upon party control. When a party controls both the presidency and Congress, power can be quite concentrated. In the 1930's, Franklin Roosevelt showed that a president can turn many of his interests into public policy if Congress shares his party affiliation. President Lyndon B. Johnson was able to do this in the 1960's as well. When there is a divided government, however, and the Democratic and Republican parties split the presidency and Congress between them, both the executive and legislature will exercise their prerogatives and protect their interests to the fullest extent. Often, the result is that power is decentralized to the point that it becomes very difficult for the government to make any significant policy. Congress and the president hold each other's proposals hostage. This situation has been called "gridlock."

There are three theoretical traditions that view the distribution of power in modern representative democracies differently. One of these, elitism, believes that power in the governments of democracies is concentrated in the hands of a few, who in turn represent a single interest. The United States may have a system of separation of powers, for example, but presidents and members of Congress, whatever their party affiliation, are all members of a certain class and so work together as a unit to realize their common interest. Many theorists of elitism suggest that all members of the federal government are wealthy and have an interest in maintaining the profits of the country's rich and powerful.

Pluralism and corporatism, on the other hand, argue that power is quite decentralized. Looking at the United States, pluralists suggest that decisions made by government are the result of competition between an array of groups in society that all attempt to influence policy. In this way, the president and Congress are servants of the millions of citizens who join interest groups such as the American Association of Retired Persons, the National Rifle Association, and the National Abortion Rights Action League. In the pluralist view, power is greatly decentralized. Corporatists are like pluralists but suggest that society is not divided into myriad groups. Instead, only large interests, such as business and labor, are able to make government sensitive to their needs. Corporatism, therefore, sees power as more concentrated than does pluralism.

Power can also be distributed between governments within a country. This sharing of power is known as federalism. In some countries, such as the United States and Germany, the national government shares political power with state governments.

Residents of California, for example, are governed by laws made in Sacramento, in Washington, and in the city in which they live. In other countries, such as the United Kingdom and France, the national government holds nearly all the political power. Local and regional governments do exist, but they are servants rather than partners of the national government. Such systems are known as unitary systems. Power is likely to be less concentrated in federal systems.

Applications

The degree to which power is concentrated within government is reflected in the balance of the opposing virtues of inclusive government and coherent policy. In the United States, divided governments in the late 1980's and early 1990's were receptive to many interests within American society. As a result, many different policies were debated and considered. Republican presidents Ronald Reagan and George Bush called for tax cuts, reduced government spending on domestic programs, a stronger defense, a decrease in government regulation of the economy, and social policies that included school prayer and opposition to abortion. The Democratic Congresses of the same time called for better social welfare programs, cuts in military spending, and generally liberal social policies.

The result was often stalemate, in which the president would use the veto to block congressional initiatives and Congress would regularly defeat presidential initiatives in committee or votes on the floor. At times the government seemed paralyzed. When the government did pass policy, the policy was not what anybody really wanted. Budgets, for example, were compromises in which Republican presidents traded away their desire to reduce domestic spending in return for the acceptance of tax cuts by Democratic Congresses. Likewise, these Democratic Congresses only accepted tax cuts if the Republican presidents agreed to augment domestic spending. Not surprisingly, this led to budget deficits—in excess of three hundred billion dollars. Moreover, the disagreeable legislative process and result of this gridlock alienated voters of both parties.

Unified governments would have likely been able to pass more coherent policy more quickly. Social security, Medicare and Medicaid, and major civil rights legislation, for example, were all created during times of unified government. This is not to say that concentrated power is necessarily preferable, as the history of the Thatcher government may indicate.

Power was more concentrated in the government of the United Kingdom in the 1980's than it ever would be within the U.S. system of separation of powers. With large parliamentary majorities, Prime Minister Margaret Thatcher and her Conservative Party took control of both the executive and legislative functions of government. Legislation slashing taxes, eliminating welfare programs, attacking labor unions, privatizing government-owned industry, reorganizing local government, and deeply affecting education was passed. The government made quick and resolute decisions.

Strong government came with a price. The prime minister and her colleagues became so powerful that they were able to temper dissent. Television programs that criticized the government were banned. The Greater London Council, controlled by the opposition Labour Party, was shut down. Even the right to assembly was diminished. The system ignored the interests of many people, and many people became alienated from politics. People resorted to violent demonstrations to have their voices heard. Union members who had lost rights and students who had lost financial aid took to the streets in demonstrations that sometimes led to battles with the police. Many Britons began to think that their country's parliamentary system was an "elective dictatorship," in which all power was concentrated in the hands of the prime minister. By the late 1980's many were calling for changes to the country's constitution.

Context

Until the nineteenth century, power was extremely concentrated in most of the governments of the world. Most countries were ruled by monarchs or small groups of powerful aristocrats. Revolutions, democratic movements, and independence movements around the world changed all this.

Political power has continued to disperse since then. Governments in countries such as Russia and South Africa are becoming more democratic and responsive to all interests within their societies. What is more, there are decentralizing pressures even within traditionally democratic governments. During most of the 1980's, Germany lived with a coalition government in which two parties shared executive power because no single party was able to gain a parliamentary majority. In the United Kingdom a constitutional reform movement has called for a system of separation of powers. France lived with split-party control of the presidency and parliament for much of the 1980's and early 1990's. The United States experienced divided government for twenty-six years between 1955 and 1994.

That power should continue to divide and disperse within governments, however, is not inevitable. There have been many parties and movements throughout the world that believe that the concentration of power is critical for a society's well-being. The Italian Forza Italia Party led by Silvio Berlusconi, for example, wished to emphasize policy output over governmental process. Fascist parties in France and Germany emphasize strong leadership and wish to exclude racial and ethnic minorities from government.

Economic, political, and social crises of the 1990's worked in some cases to concentrate, and in other cases to divide, power. In eastern Europe power decentralized. Dictatorships were replaced by representative democracies that were in many cases based upon the U.S. system of separation of powers. Yet in some democratic countries, there existed a belief that too much democracy led to gridlock and it was time for centralization.

The values of a country's people are also likely to play a role. The American democratic tradition, and a powerful yet fragmented Congress, make it unlikely that any one group might concentrate power too greatly within the U.S. government. Indeed, as Jimmy Carter discovered in the late 1970's and Bill Clinton briefly discovered in the 1990's, even unified governments find it difficult to enact a large and coherent program of policies. The German, Japanese, and Russian cultures, which emphasize order, however, may make these countries particularly susceptible to future concentrations of power within government. Similarly, the British and French people will have to remain vigilant because their political systems have a propensity for allowing power to concentrate within government.

Bibliography

Bagehot, Walter. *The English Constitution*. Introduction by R. H. S. Crossman. Ithaca, N.Y.: Cornell University Press, 1966. An important work for students of the parliamentary system.

Fiorina, Morris. *Divided Government*. New York: Macmillan, 1992. Short, detailed, and engrossing introduction to the American phenomenon of divided government.

Hamilton, Alexander, James Madison, and John Jay. *The Federalist Papers*. Edited by Clinton Rossiter. New York: New American Library, 1961. Must-read. Of particular interest are essays 10 and 47 through 51.

Lijphart, Arend. *Democracies*. New Haven, Conn.: Yale University Press, 1984. Authoritative guide to the way power is distributed within democratic governments.

Mayhew, David R. *Divided We Govern: Party Control, Lawmaking, and Investigations, 1946-1990*. New Haven, Conn.: Yale University Press, 1991. Changed the way political scientists view divided government by suggesting that, as far as policy is concerned, it is no different from unified government.

Montesquieu. *Selected Political Writings*. Translated and edited by Melvin Richter. Indianapolis: Hackett, 1990. Introduction and selections from *The Spirit of the Laws* are particularly recommended.

Sundquist, James L. *Constitutional Reform and Effective Government*. Washington, D.C.: Brookings Institution, 1992. The authoritative critique of the American system of separation of powers. Challenges the myth that American government is perfect and offers a detailed catalog of reform.

Andrew J. Taylor

Cross-References

POWER IN POLITICS

Field of study: Politics

In politics, power is the ability to produce intended effects. Those who lack power are subject to the control of others, while those who have power are able to control others. There are various forms of power.

Principal terms

AUTHORITY: legitimate power or right to control

COERCION: threat of using force or punishment to control behavior

ELITISM: view that political and social power is centralized

FORCE: use of physical constraints to control behavior

INFLUENCE: use of friendship, rewards, or inducements to control behavior

MANIPULATION: withholding information in order to control behavior

PERSUASION: use of information and reasoning to control behavior

PLURALISM: view that political and social power is decentralized

Overview

"Power" has two distinct meanings. Power, as defined above, is the ability to produce effects. To paraphrase one of the experts, people have power to the extent that they have the ability to get others to do what they would not otherwise do. In this sense power is the ability to produce a result. Power may also be defined in terms of actual results: Those who prevail over others are defined as more powerful than those who lose. The difference between these two definitions can be illustrated by considering the relationship between the United States and Vietnam.

On the one hand, it seems obvious that the United States is more powerful than Vietnam. The United States has five times the population of Vietnam, is many times larger in land area, has more natural resources, including iron and oil, has much greater industrial and agricultural production, has more weapons, has more technologically advanced weapons, and so on. All these advantages produce effects greater than those that Vietnam might produce. On the other hand, the United States did not win the Vietnam War; hence, the results of that war show that at least in that context the United States was not more powerful than Vietnam. One meaning of power identifies the United States as more powerful, yet another meaning of power identifies Vietnam as more powerful.

One definition is more general and focuses on the situation before the exercise of power, the other is more specific and focuses on the outcome after power is exercised. This distinction can be illustrated by returning to the relationship between the United States and Vietnam.

Throughout the war, the United States had a much greater military capacity than Vietnam. For example, the huge stockpile of nuclear weapons possessed by the United

States gave the United States an enormous edge in military power over Vietnam. The United States never exercised its nuclear power or other powers that may have escalated the war to the point of direct confrontation with another country with nuclear power. This restricted the nature of the war, thereby contributing to Vietnam's success on the battlefield. Vietnam prevailed on the battlefield in the 1970's, but Vietnam was not generally considered more powerful than the United States. Most experts recognized that in other situations, the United States, as a larger, more industrialized society, still had a much greater capacity than Vietnam to produce intended effects in future conflicts.

Power, however it is defined, requires resources, and different types of power require different types of resources. For example, persuasion is a form of power which requires information resources. If the president is going to persuade members of Congress to change their views, the president will have to give them good reasons for making that change. The Central Intelligence Agency, Federal Bureau of Investigation, and other intelligence agencies report to the president, so one may argue, however speciously, that the president frequently has more information than Congress about events in the world. It is precisely because of this that the president is frequently able to persuade Congress to accept direction.

Other types of power require other resources. Coercion typically requires access to force. For example, governments use coercion to get people to obey the law: If people exceed the speed limit they are subject to a fine. Manipulation requires access to channels of communication and the flow of information. Influencing people to act in a particular way often requires access to resources. Since money is highly valued, influence is frequently associated with wealth. Wealth can be used to bribe people, to hire people, to contribute to campaigns, and to pay for advertisements.

Using power involves costs and these costs vary with different types of power. For example, those who use force to achieve their goals frequently are faced with resistance. Resistance increases the costs of using power, and resistance is not the only cost associated with the use of force. Force inevitably involves the depletion of resources. For example, when governments use military force to achieve their goals, the costs for the government include dead and injured military personnel, the expenditure of ammunition and supplies, the loss of equipment, and dislocations in the economy. Force is costly, so leaders usually prefer to achieve their goals by using other forms of power.

Authority is an efficient form of power because it costs very little to use authority. People who have authority expect to be obeyed automatically. For example, military officers are usually assumed to have the right to order their troops to attack an enemy. As long as their troops believe that the officers have this authority over them, the officers do not have to waste resources trying to bribe, threaten, or persuade their troops. If they have the authority, they have the right to give orders and the troops have the duty to obey.

Even though force is an expensive form of power to use, political leaders still find it necessary to use force from time to time in order to make their use of coercion more effective. The effectiveness of coercion depends on the credibility of the threat to hurt or punish anyone who does not act in the manner that is demanded. In order for a government's threat to send in troops to be credible, it must occasionally actually do so and take the risk that some of the troops may be killed or that those the troops are sent to dominate instead dominate the troops.

Outcomes are determined not only by which kind of power is used, but also by how much power different people possess. Those with greater power usually prevail over those with less. Although it is not always easy to determine which actor has more power, power usually can be measured.

For example, the president of the United States is much more powerful than a lieutenant because the president has the power to command many more people than the lieutenant. The president is the commander in chief of all the armed services as well as the chief executive of the civilian bureaucracy. In contrast to the thousands of people subject to the president's command, the lieutenant can only command the small number of people in his or her platoon. Power can also be measured in terms of the range of activities that can be controlled. For example, the government has control over more of the activities of military personnel than it has over the activities of people in the postal service. Finally, another way to measure power is to observe how many different forms of power people have at their disposal. People who can bribe, hire, threaten, and persuade others to get them to do something they would not otherwise do may be more powerful than those who are limited to persuasion, for example.

Each of the different types of power—coercion, persuasion, influence, and so on—can be combined into an overall strategy or plan of action. Most strategies involve the use of more than one type of power. Centuries ago, Niccolò Machiavelli, an Italian political theorist, asked whether it was better for a ruler to be loved or feared. This is another way of asking what the best strategy for using power is. Machiavelli said it would be wonderful for the ruler to be both loved and feared, but he recognized that it is difficult to love someone one fears or to fear someone one really loves. Therefore, a ruler has to choose. Machiavelli argued it is better to be feared than loved because love does not always inspire obedience as reliably as fear does. Apparently most government officials agree with Machiavelli's strategy because virtually all of them maintain armed forces and police to back the laws they make.

Applications

In August, 1990, Iraq invaded Kuwait. Both countries are oil-producing nations in the Middle East from which the United States and its allies purchase oil. The government of the United States wanted Iraq to withdraw from Kuwait and ultimately went to war to achieve this goal. The Persian Gulf crisis illustrates the way that various types of power are used to achieve goals.

The United States government gave conflicting signals to Iraq before the invasion of Kuwait occurred, so there is some question whether Saddam Hussein, the president of Iraq, believed that he was simply doing what the Americans wanted. This might have been a classic case of anticipated reactions—actions taken by less powerful people in anticipation of pleasing more powerful people—if after Iraq's invasion President George Bush had not made it clear that he wanted Iraq to withdraw its troops. In order to implement this goal, the Bush Administration devised a multifaceted strategy that included economic, military, and diplomatic moves aimed at getting Iraq out of Kuwait.

On the diplomatic front, the United States sought international support, including resolutions from the United Nations Security Council condemning the invasion and demanding Iraqi withdrawal. The United States was able to obtain this support, but only by using the power of persuasion and inducement. President Bush portrayed the Iraqi invasion of Kuwait as a ruthless assault on international order rather than simply an action which adversely affected the interests of the United States. All countries have an interest in maintaining international order, so President Bush was able to persuade some leaders in other countries to support the Security Council resolution. He gave them a good reason for condemning the Iraqi invasion. Persuasion was not always enough, however; sometimes President Bush had to couple persuasion with inducements. For example, to obtain the cooperation of the Soviet Union, the U.S. government made various promises of economic help.

On the economic front the United States was able to secure an embargo of Iraq which limited the flow of goods into and out of the country. Although the embargo did create problems for Iraq, neither it, diplomacy, nor the threat of military action were sufficient to get Iraq to withdraw from Kuwait. The failure of these forms of power caused the Bush Administration to decide that only the use of force would get Iraq out of Kuwait.

The president, as the commander in chief of the United States military forces, has the right to command American troops to take action, although it is Congress that has the right to declare war. President Bush was reluctant to use only U.S. military force because an American offensive into Kuwait might cause all the other Arab and Islamic nations in the region to view the United States as anti-Arab. Therefore it was very important that the military forces be seen as a United Nations' force and not simply as an American force. That meant that the Bush Administration had to persuade the leaders of other countries to provide troops and equipment. Although other countries did cooperate by sending troops and equipment, most notably Great Britain, France, Saudi Arabia, Egypt, and Syria, several others, including Germany and Japan, did not. This meant that the Bush Administration had to persuade Germany and Japan to support the military effort financially, which they ultimately did.

President Bush also had to deal with opposition to the use of American troops by the American public and the U.S. Congress. To gain support at home, he used what may be called manipulation or persuasion to drum up support. That support came, although there were indications that the people would not tolerate a long, costly war reminiscent of Vietnam. What President Bush needed was a quick war with few American casualties.

Saddam Hussein knew that most Americans would oppose a long and bloody war with Iraq, so it was to his advantage to release news stories about chemical and biological warfare. The more the American media talked about this possibility, the more likely it was that a war involving American troops would never occur.

To counter this move by Iraq, the Bush Administration told Congress it had a battle plan that could minimize American casualties and force Iraq to withdraw. Congress gave its approval, and Iraq was forced out of Kuwait in early 1991 with relatively few American casualties. For a brief period afterward, President Bush enjoyed great popular support among the American public. Like many forms of power, however, his popular support proved to be ephemeral; in November, 1992, Bush was defeated in his attempt to win a second term of office.

Context

Harold Lasswell, a major American political scientist, defined politics as the process that determines who gets what, when, how. Power enters into this definition in two ways. In the first place, people and groups use power to get what they want. In the second place, power is the very thing they are pursuing. Power is both an end and a means.

As a means, power has two primary uses. One is that power is used to dominate people. Power used to dominate an enemy may be seen as something good. In this sense power is associated with feelings of security, and it is for this reason that many people are willing to support a strong national military force. Power created for one purpose, however, can be used for other purposes with which one does not necessarily agree. In many countries of the world, the national military forces are used to dominate the citizens they are supposed to protect.

Power is also used to transform. In this sense power is used to empower people and make them better. For example, parents are expected to use their power over their children to help transform them into autonomous adults. Similarly, governments are often expected to use their power to transform the poor into productive citizens, to transform criminals into law-abiding citizens, and to transform victims of sexual, racial, and religious discrimination from second-class citizens into full-fledged citizens. Not everybody agrees that government should be used for all these purposes, and that is why so many groups and individuals come together to use their power to influence what activities their government pursues.

Since groups and individuals do organize to influence the policies and direction of government, the study of politics frequently focuses on the question of who has power. Two views of who has power in the United States fall under the labels of "pluralism" and "elitism." Pluralists see power as decentralized: No one group dominates all the important decisions in the country. The government has power, but so do many other groups, including business, labor, farm, and religious groups. Elitists see power as centralized: One group dominates all the important decisions in the country. Business leaders control the corporate world and the mass media, and through these resources they also control public opinion and the government.

In general, pluralists believe that the existing distribution of power in America is about right, while elitists believe that there should be more popular control of the governmental and economic institutions in American society. Conflict on these issues in turn affects preferences on defining power, with pluralists being less enthusiastic than elitists in defining power in terms of ability. Since these are disagreements on basic values, there will always be some disagreement on how to define and describe power, even among the experts.

Bibliography

Dahl, Robert A. *Modern Political Analysis*. 5th ed. Englewood Cliffs, N.J.: Prentice-Hall, 1991. Discussion of power from the pluralist perspective by one of the leading power experts.

Isaac, Jeffrey C. *Power and Marxist Theory: A Realist View*. Ithaca, N.Y.: Cornell University Press, 1987. Discussion of the structural view of power for the analysis of politics.

Lukes, Steven. *Power: A Radical View*. New York: Macmillan, 1974. Pluralist and elitist views of power in less than sixty pages.

Machiavelli, Niccolò. *The Prince*. New York: New American Library, 1980. Classic work on how to use power in the world of politics.

Neustadt, Richard E. *Presidential Power and the Modern Presidents: The Politics of Leadership from Roosevelt to Reagan*. New York: Free Press, 1990. Detailed case studies from nine presidencies.

Wartenberg, Thomas E. *The Forms of Power*. Philadelphia: Temple University Press, 1990. Includes an analysis of how feminists conceive of power.

Edward S. Malecki

Cross-References

Elitism, p. 591; Force, p. 712; Geopolitics, p. 759; Hegemony, p. 817; Interest Groups, p. 936; Intergovernmental Relations, p. 942; Invisible Government, p. 975; Machiavelli's Political Philosophy, p. 1148; Mercantilism, p. 1173; Pluralism, p. 1402; Power Divisions in Governments, p. 1578; Realpolitik, p. 1668; Superpowers and World Politics, p. 1916; Totalitarianism, p. 1987.

THE PRESIDENCY IN THE UNITED STATES

Field of study: Functions of government

The United States president is the chief executive of the national government. According to Article 2 of the Constitution, the president's powers include execution of national laws, command of the armed forces, conduct of foreign relations, and vetoing of legislation.

Principal terms

CABINET: collective body of department secretaries who advise and assist the president

COMMANDER IN CHIEF: the U.S. president, who exercises executive, civilian control of the armed forces

ELECTORAL COLLEGE: voting body that chooses the U.S. president and vice president

EXECUTIVE AGREEMENT: international agreement made by the president without the consent of the Senate, which is not binding

EXECUTIVE ORDER: rule or regulation issued by the president or by an official or agency under the president's authority

EXECUTIVE PRIVILEGE: implicit authority to withhold information

HEAD OF STATE: the U.S. president's symbolic role as representative of the United States of America

IMPOUNDMENT: president's power to refuse to spend funds

VETO POWER: president's constitutional power to reject bills passed by Congress, thus not making them laws

Overview

The U.S. president is the chief executive of the United States government. Article 2 of the Constitution vests all the authority of the executive branch in the president. The president is chosen for a four-year term by the electoral college. The electoral college consists of electors in all the states and the District of Columbia, who are selected by voters from the states and the district. The number of electors for each state is determined by the total number of U.S. representatives and senators from the state. According to the Twenty-third Amendment of the U.S. Constitution, the number of electors for the District of Columbia will not exceed that of the least populous state.

In order to win a presidential election, a candidate must win a majority of electoral votes. If no candidate receives a majority of electoral votes, then the U.S. House of Representatives chooses a president from among the presidential candidates who received the most electoral votes. The Twenty-second Amendment of the U.S. Constitution, adopted in 1951, prohibits any person from being elected president more than twice.

The president serves a variety of roles in American national government: chief administrator (managing the cabinet and the rest of the federal bureaucracy and assuring the execution of national laws), chief diplomat (negotiating treaties, recognizing new foreign governments, and making executive agreements), commander in chief of the armed forces, and head of state (symbolizing the United States of America in ceremonial functions). The president is also a political leader who initiates legislative proposals, vetoes or signs bills, and rallies popular support for various policies.

The Constitution is open to interpretation about the president's powers. For example, Article 2 states that the president is commander in chief of the armed forces, but Article 1 states that Congress has the power to declare war. Therefore the question arises as to whether the president may order the armed forces to wage war without first obtaining a declaration of war from Congress. Another example is that the president carries out the laws that Congress passes; not unexpectedly, Congress and the president may disagree on whether the president is truly carrying out the law as Congress understands it.

Different presidents have made different interpretations of their powers. A president's exercise of his or her constitutional powers varies according to whether he or she chooses a passive or active approach to the presidency. For example, President George Washington chose to limit himself to two terms and he rarely vetoed bills, even if he personally disagreed with their content. By contrast, President Franklin D. Roosevelt was elected to four terms of office, actively developed and promoted much of the New Deal legislation, vetoed 635 bills, and used executive agreements to provide military aid to Great Britain before the United States entered World War II.

In addition to a president's preference for activity or passivity, other factors influence the scope of presidential power. Major crises have often temporarily or permanently expanded presidential power. Shortly after the Civil War began, President Abraham Lincoln raised armies, began a naval blockade of Confederate States, and pledged the credit of the national government without first receiving Congress' authorization. As a result of widespread bank failures caused by the Great Depression, President Franklin D. Roosevelt ordered that all banks be closed for ten days in 1933. During the Korean War, President Harry S Truman ordered the government seizure of steel mills with defense contracts because of a threatened strike. In 1964, Congress passed the Gulf of Tonkin Resolution, which gave President Lyndon B. Johnson broad discretion to wage the Vietnam War.

The modern presidency is a more powerful office, especially in foreign and economic affairs, than it was when the federal government began in 1789. The Supreme Court and Congress have had some successes in limiting the growth of presidential powers. Through its power of judicial review, the Supreme Court ruled President Lincoln's suspension of the writ of habeas corpus, a civil liberty in criminal cases, to be unconstitutional in the *Milligan, Ex Parte* decision of 1866. In the *Schechter Poultry Corp. v. United States* case of 1935, the Supreme Court ruled the National Industrial Recovery Act to be unconstitutional partially because it delegated legislative powers to the president. In *United States v. Nixon*, in 1974, the Supreme Court ruled that while the president did have a limited, implicit power of executive privilege to protect the privacy of his communications, this power was not absolute.

The Supreme Court, therefore, required that President Richard M. Nixon provide tape recordings of his conversations in the White House to a special prosecutor.

By the 1970's, Congress increasingly believed that it must limit presidential power and reassert its authority, especially in foreign policy and in the spending of funds it appropriated. The War Powers Resolution of 1973 limited the president's power to commit U.S. armed forces abroad. The resolution specified time limits by which the president was to inform Congress of military actions and seek its approval. The Budget and Impoundment Act of 1974 required the president to seek and receive congressional approval to impound funds within forty-five days.

Finally, the extent of a president's power and effectiveness in achieving policy goals depends on his or her political skills. These skills include an ability to communicate persuasively policy goals to Congress, the media, his or her political party, and the public, to compromise with political opponents, to build alliances with foreign governments in international relations, and to manage the vast federal bureaucracy.

Applications

In 1933, during the first hundred days of the presidency of Franklin D. Roosevelt, more major domestic legislation was introduced to Congress and signed into law than during the first hundred days of any previous presidency. The domestic policies that were proposed and enacted between 1933 and 1939 are known as the New Deal. How President Roosevelt was able to propose, develop, persuade Congress to pass, and implement so much of the New Deal during his first hundred days in office reveals key features of the president's roles as chief legislator and party leader. Roosevelt's example also reveals a president's use of personal skills during a severe, prolonged domestic crisis to achieve his policy goals.

Unlike most previous presidents, President Roosevelt developed, wrote, and submitted many bills to Congress with the help of White House aides and cabinet members known as the Brain Trust. By lobbying Congress and appealing to the public through radio speeches, Roosevelt secured the passage and enactment of the National Industrial Recovery Act, the Emergency Relief Appropriation Act, and other economic policies. In general, the early New Deal sought to combat the Great Depression by providing public works jobs to the unemployed, establishing regulations to reform banks, and fostering policies to raise and stabilize agricultural prices and industrial wages.

Even though the Supreme Court later ruled some of the early New Deal laws to be unconstitutional, Roosevelt and leading Democrats in Congress later expanded the New Deal to include government-provided electricity in rural areas, stricter regulation of the stock market, soil and forest conservation, legal rights for labor unions, and unemployment insurance and old-age pensions through the Social Security Act of 1935. The development and enactment of New Deal legislation made Congress accustomed to presidential leadership in the legislative process.

President Roosevelt's legislative success during his first hundred days in office provides broad lessons about the factors that influence a president's success as chief legislator. In addition to Roosevelt's initiative regarding the legislative process, his personal communication and lobbying skills, and the crisis atmosphere of the Great Depression, this president's rapid, massive legislative success was also helped by his "honeymoon" with Congress and his mandate from the 1932 election. During the honeymoon, presidents usually experience their most cooperative, supportive relationship with Congress, the public, and the media. This honeymoon typically lasts for about the first hundred days that the president is in office.

Presidents are also more likely to achieve their legislative goals during their first hundred days if they and their party receive a clear mandate from the voters. In order to receive a mandate, presidential and congressional nominees of the same party will develop and promote a platform of policy positions during their campaigns. If they are elected, they, as well as their supporters and opponents, may interpret their electoral victories as public support for their policy ideas.

In 1932, Franklin D. Roosevelt received 57 percent of the popular vote and his fellow Democrats won large majorities in both houses of Congress. President Roosevelt claimed that most voters wanted the majority policy changes that the New Deal promised. By contrast, in the 1968 elections, Republican presidential nominee Richard M. Nixon won 43 percent of the popular vote while Democrats continued to control both houses of Congress. This situation made it difficult for President Nixon to achieve major domestic policy goals during his first hundred days.

The degree of legislative success that President Roosevelt achieved during his first hundred days in office shows how flexible and fluid presidential power is. Presidential power in the legislative process can expand or contract according to reactions by the other two branches of government, the personal skills and perception of the presidency held by a particular president, an atmosphere of crisis or harmony in a policy area, and the extent to which his or her party controls Congress.

Context

The presidency is described second in the Constitution and is given fewer and less specific powers than Congress in Article 1. Opponents of a strong, active presidency have often claimed that a careful interpretation of the Constitution shows that Congress should be the dominant branch in policy-making and that the president should have a limited role. Supporters of a strong, active presidency, in which a president provides the initiative and decisive leadership in foreign and domestic policies, point out that in the Federalist Papers, a series of articles explaining and advocating the Constitution, Alexander Hamilton, one of the three authors, asserts that a president needs to use his or her powers flexibly in order to provide the independent, energetic, decisive, and accountable leadership that the nation needs, especially during crises. Supporters of an active presidency also argue that the political and economic changes and demands of the modern world require the president to use powers that extend beyond a strict interpretation of Article 2, especially regarding economic management and national security.

From 1933 until the early 1970's, presidential power seemed to be growing constantly, inevitably, and, to many Americans, dangerously. Presidential power during this period grew in proportion to the growth of the federal bureaucracy, American international responsibilities and interests, the role of the federal government in the economy, and expectations of presidential performance. The successive crises of the Great Depression and World War II accustomed the American people, Congress, and the media to Franklin D. Roosevelt's active approach toward presidential power. His presidency marked the beginning of the modern presidency, characterized by a large administrative staff in the White House and, later, such agencies as the Central Intelligence Agency (CIA) and Council of Economic Advisers, which were devoted to assisting the president with information, advice, and direct implementation of presidential decisions.

Historian Arthur M. Schlesinger warned of the dangers of an "imperial presidency" that could lead to disastrous policies and abuses of executive power. The conduct of the Vietnam War by several presidents and the Watergate scandal of the Nixon presidency made these dangers more apparent. In the 1970's, several Supreme Court decisions and acts of Congress checked and limited presidential power. When President Jimmy Carter was confronted by the Iranian hostage crisis, the Soviet invasion of Afghanistan, and an energy crisis, some scholars worried that an "imperiled presidency" could no longer effectively satisfy the overwhelming demands made upon it. The ability of President Ronald Reagan, Carter's successor, in achieving his policy goals of higher defense spending, lower income tax rates, and budget cuts in some domestic programs during his first term reduced concern that the American presidency was becoming a weaker, less effective "imperiled" office.

Bibliography

Barber, James David. *The Presidential Character: Predicting Performance in the White House*. 3d ed. Englewood Cliffs, N.J.: Prentice-Hall, 1985. Develops a psychological theory about the various forces that influence individual presidents' behavior.

Cronin, Thomas E. "An Imperiled Presidency?" In *The Post-Imperial Presidency*. Edited by Vincent Davis. New Brunswick, N.J.: Transaction Books, 1980. A view of the presidency as a weaker, less effective office by the late 1970's.

Hamilton, Alexander, James Madison, and John Jay. *The Federalist Papers*. Edited by Clinton Rossiter. New York: New American Library, 1961. Essays 67 through 77 written by Hamilton, describe and justify the method of selection, term of office, and powers of the U.S. president.

Neustadt, Richard E. *Presidential Power and the Modern Presidents*. New York: Free Press, 1990. Useful and comprehensive survey of presidential leadership from Franklin D. Roosevelt to Ronald Reagan.

Reedy, George. *The Twilight of the Presidency*. New York: New American Library, 1970. Asserts that the modern president tends to become isolated from political forces outside the White House. Focuses on the presidency of Lyndon B. Johnson.

Savage, Sean J. *Roosevelt: The Party Leader, 1932-1945*. Lexington: University Press of Kentucky, 1991. Analysis of President Franklin D. Roosevelt's influence on the Democratic Party, especially through his development and pursuit of the New Deal.

Schlesinger, Arthur M. *The Imperial Presidency*. Boston: Houghton Mifflin, 1973. An insightful analysis of the danger of the growth of presidential power in the realm of foreign policy.

Thach, Charles C., Jr. *The Creation of the Presidency, 1775-1789*. Baltimore: Johns Hopkins University Press, 1969. Classic study of the conflicting ideas concerning executive power that influenced the creation of the American presidency, with a helpful contrast of federalist and antifederalist views.

Watson, Richard A., and Norman C. Thomas. *The Politics of the Presidency*. Washington, D.C.: Congressional Quarterly Press, 1988. Thorough survey of the U.S. president's powers, roles, and political relationships. Has an interesting theory that presidential power is protean, able to change its size and form according to political conditions.

Wayne, Stephen J. *The Road to the White House: The Politics of Presidential Elections*. 3d ed. New York: St. Martin's Press, 1988. Examines the presidential selection process, campaign methods, media relations, and changing party nomination rules.

Sean J. Savage

Cross-References

The Constitution of the United States, p. 425; Cult of Personality, p. 477; Democracy, p. 513; The Electoral College, p. 584; Executive Functions in U.S. Government, p. 636; Foreign Relations, p. 718; Heads of State, p. 804; Impeachment, p. 882; Leadership, p. 1066; National Security, p. 1261; Policy Development and Implementation, p. 1414; Presidential Elections in the United States, p. 1596; Separation of Powers: Presidential Government, p. 1815; Succession, p. 1909.

PRESIDENTIAL ELECTIONS IN THE UNITED STATES

Field of study: Politics

The office of president, chief officer of the executive branch of the United States federal government, is open for election every four years. Because the president is the most important figure in federal government, and because the office carries inherent power, the contest has become one of fierce contention between major political parties.

Principal terms

ELECTORAL COLLEGE: body of electors chosen by the voters of each U.S. state to select the president and vice president

MEDIA: agencies of mass communication, divided into the print media, such as newspapers and magazines, and the electronic media, such as radio and television

NOMINATING CONVENTION: meeting of a political party at which delegates draft the party platform and select nominees for president and vice president

PARTY PLATFORM: statement of principles and programs that a party's presidential candidate is pledged to support if elected

POLITICAL PARTY: group of individuals and special interest groups with common purposes or opinions, organized for the purpose of gaining control of government

PRIMARY ELECTION: preliminary election in which voters select, or indicate a preference for, a candidate for the general election

STUMPING: speaking to and meeting with voters one-on-one during an electoral campaign, as opposed to reaching them through the media

TICKET: the combination of candidates for president and vice president nominated by a political party

Overview

The president is the chief executive officer of the federal government, commander in chief of the armed forces of the United States, and, by general consensus, the leader of his or her political party. The presidential term runs four years, beginning on Inauguration Day, which was changed from March 4 to January 20 in 1936. In accordance with the Twenty-second Amendment to the Constitution, no one may serve more than two consecutive terms.

Technically, presidential elections are a two-part process. The popular vote takes place during the general election, in which voters cast their ballots for the nominees for president and vice president (the "ticket"). Actually, voters are selecting presidential electors, who cast their votes in the electoral college in accordance with the wishes of the voters in each state, as determined in the general election. Each state is allotted a number of electors equal to its congressional representation; only by securing a majority of these votes can a candidate achieve the office of the presidency. While the vote of the electoral college is the official and deciding vote for the office, presidential elections are traditionally determined in the general election. Any study of presidential elections in the United States must therefore concentrate on the popular vote and how it has been sought by parties and candidates.

Historically, American presidential politics have gone through five phases. The first period, that of passive candidates, was an outgrowth of the debates that occurred during the drafting of the Constitution. A fear of the divisive nature of party politics, "factions," as James Madison termed them, and the unanimous selection of George Washington as first president, established a tradition that with the presidency "the office seeks the man, not the man the office." In actual practice, party politics quickly developed, and before the end of Washington's second term, Federalists, favoring a strong central government that supported trade and industrial interests, opposed Republicans (now Democrats) whose base was found among farmers and small businesspeople, and in rural areas.

While the partisan battles were intense, presidential candidates professed disinterest. In the election of 1800, for example, Thomas Jefferson, the Republican nominee, removed himself to his Virginia farm instead of campaigning. Actually, Jefferson actively planned and carefully directed the efforts of his party through lieutenants. So successful were Jefferson's Republican-Democrats (as the party was then known) that the Federalists soon effectively ceased to exist, and presidential campaigns were for all practical purposes decided by meetings of party leaders who selected the nominees. This period reached its limit in 1820, when James Monroe was elected president with only a single electoral vote cast against him—and that only because of the sentiment that no one should match Washington's unanimous record.

Such a system was possible only while the United States remained a fairly small nation centered on the eastern seaboard. As the country expanded westward and its population grew, an irresistible urge to democratize presidential elections found its focus in Andrew Jackson. Jackson initiated the period of popular democracy and party control during the election of 1824, when he broke from the tradition of the passive candidate and promised to make known his views on issues—in other words, to campaign actively.

Active campaigning had increased dramatically by 1840, which marked the first truly popular presidential campaign in U.S. history. Both Democrats and Whigs, the successors of the Federalists, used songs, slogans, badges, rallies, and handouts to trumpet the virtues of their own candidate and the failures of their opponent. Political newspapers, outspoken and often scandalous in their views and vehemence, assumed massive importance as literacy increased and distribution improved. Party discipline and control increased until the candidate often was merely the symbol of the party, rather than an independent factor. This period saw a succession of one-term presidents with only one, Democrat James Knox Polk (president from 1845 to 1849), showing true executive leadership and strength through his capable handling of the Mexican War and United States expansion into the Southwest and California. It should be noted that Polk himself was a one-term president, although that was largely by choice.

The only counterbalance to this development was the 1854 formation of the Republican Party, which coalesced around the issue of antislavery. Its first presidential nominee, John Charles Fremont in the 1856 election, was a hero of the "liberation" of California during the war with Mexico and a dramatic and appealing campaign figure. Still, the fledgling Republicans lacked the strength and discipline to beat the veteran Democrats, whose well-practiced ranks easily elected a relative nonentity, James Buchanan.

The Democratic Party began splintering along the same fault lines as the nation, as northern and southern Democrats divided over the issues of slavery and states' rights. In 1860, their disunity allowed the Republican nominee, Abraham Lincoln, to win the White House with less than a majority of the popular vote.

After the Civil War, the Democrats, tainted by accusations of treason and deprived of their traditional base of strength in the South, were shut out of the White House by a string of corrupt or mediocre Republican administrations. It was not until the still-disputed election of 1876 that the two parties achieved some measure of parity and more balance was restored to presidential election contests, just as advances in communications and transportation moved the political world toward more modern campaign techniques.

These techniques arrived in the fourth phase, first fully seen in the 1896 contest between Republican nominee William McKinley and Democratic contender William Jennings Bryan. Bryan, made famous overnight with his riveting "Cross of Gold" speech at the party convention, initiated the technique of "stumping" the nation. During the election he visited twenty-seven states, traveling more than eighteen thousand miles, and making more than six hundred speeches, during which he addressed approximately five million voters. Bryan was the first presidential candidate to make effective use of the railroads to reach voters in towns and hamlets throughout the nation. By contrast, McKinley and the Republicans adopted a "front porch campaign," in which their candidate remained at home in Ohio while the vast Republican war chest (the largest spent by any party until 1920) carried the burden of the campaign.

Despite McKinley's victory, the efforts by Bryan and the Democrats had fundamentally altered the presidential campaign process. The 1912 campaign, in which Democrat Woodrow Wilson won the White House, was significant because it was the first time presidential primary elections played a major role. That year twelve states allowed voters to choose delegates to the national party conventions that nominated presidential candidates. Primaries and increased visibility of the candidates also made the personality of the candidates more central to the election. One Democratic leader asserted that Woodrow Wilson's personality was the winning factor in the election.

This period of presidential elections reached its apex during the campaigns of another Democratic nominee, Franklin Delano Roosevelt. First elected in 1932 while the nation struggled through the Great Depression, Roosevelt won the presidency a total of four times, and transformed the presidential office and presidential politics through his mastery of traditional stumping techniques and modern mass media. A consummate radio performer, Roosevelt used fireside chats to develop a sense of intimacy with the American people, while he cultivated the media through his virtuoso performances at press conferences—337 during his first term alone.

Roosevelt completed the process, which had begun as early as 1840, that made the candidate, rather than the party or its platform, the central figure of a presidential election. With the increasing potency of the mass media, especially the electronic media, this tendency accelerated. By 1956, Leonard Hall, chairman of the Republican Party, could openly admit that politics is "show business," and just four years later the Kennedy-Nixon debates firmly established the ascendancy of the electronic news media.

Presidential elections shifted inexorably to their next phase, one dominated by the electronic media and their shorter, more intense attention span. During the 1964 election battle between Lyndon Johnson and Barry Goldwater, thirty- and sixty-second television advertisements became standard. The techniques that were used to achieve Richard Nixon's 1968 presidential victory were exposed in the book *The Selling of the President*, which revealed how effectively Madison Avenue advertising techniques and Republican Party politics had merged. The book was thought shocking at the time, but the methods it detailed soon became standard in both major political parties.

There has been a clear progression in U.S. presidential elections: National growth and the improvements in transportation and communication have made it easier for candidates to present themselves to the electorate. At the same time, these changes have focused attention on the candidate and his or her image, rather than the message. This is nothing new: Henry Clay's character was an issue in the presidential election of 1844. The intensity of interest in the candidate as an individual seems to be an expression of a fundamental American desire to make all politics, even presidential elections, intimate and personal.

Applications

The presidential elections of 1852, 1904, and 1992 are representative examples respectively of the three major periods of electing the nation's chief executive: the era of popular democracy and party control; that of the "modern" campaign; and the time of the mass media, especially the electronic media, dominating the process.

In 1852, the Whig Party nominated Lieutenant General Winfield Scott, a hero of the Mexican War. Although the Whig strategy called for Scott to remain quiet, the old soldier could not obey, and during the summer he wrote numerous public letters to supporters. In September, he began a tour under the guise of inspecting military posts. Unfortunately for his cause, Scott made numerous gaffes in both his letters and stump remarks, providing the opposing Democrats with ammunition for attacks on him personally and on the Whig Party.

By contrast, the Democratic nominee, Franklin Pierce, maintained an almost complete silence, with surrogate speakers and the party organization addressing the voters. Pierce, who had served as a congressman and senator from New Hampshire, was a "dough face," that is a Northerner who was acceptable to the South; he therefore brought a superficial unity to the Democratic Party, which allowed its highly effective and well-organized machinery to work its customary political miracles. Pierce was easily elected, thanks largely to his own silence and his party's outstanding discipline.

In 1904, Theodore Roosevelt, who had succeeded to the presidency after the assassination of William McKinley, sought his own election to the office. In this typical "modern" campaign, Roosevelt combined the great power of the office with the influence of mass media to impose his personality on the election.

Roosevelt began his drive in 1903, making an extensive national tour and attracting large and enthusiastic crowds. He also used his power as titular head of the Republican Party to ensure his nomination. As 1904 arrived, however, Roosevelt and his advisers believed it would be more dignified if he restrained his campaign activities. Still, Roosevelt orchestrated the newspaper coverage that focused on his energetic personality. Without leaving the White House, he dominated the campaign.

The Democratic nominee, Alton B. Parker, was the antithesis of Roosevelt. Chief judge of the New York Court of Appeals, Parker lacked the charisma of his opponent. It was only close to the election that the Parker camp learned a potentially devastating bit of intelligence: Roosevelt, fearing that he would lose, had solicited and accepted huge donations from Wall Street firms and the "trusts" he had spoken and acted against during his first term as president.

Parker launched a sharp attack on Roosevelt's actions, but he was unable to provide incontestable proof of the contributions, allowing the Republicans the opportunity to shrug off the charges as groundless, and granting Roosevelt a landslide victory. Personality had triumphed over substance, thanks in large part to knowing manipulation of the mass media by the party in power.

The election of 1992 illustrates the pervasive influence of the mass media and the need for successful candidates to utilize that media to present their message, which is in large measure their personality, to the American voters. To a large respect, all presidential elections are referenda on the candidates; the election of 1992 made an almost one-to-one mapping of the candidates to the issues of the day.

As sitting president, George Bush should have entered the campaign in an unassailable position. He had succeeded the enormously popular Ronald Reagan in 1988, after a tough campaign that devastated his Democratic opponent through a combination of appeals to patriotism and racism—the first overt, the second, covert. As president, he had managed the successful coalition effort against Iraq's invasion of Kuwait; at one point, his approval rating was more than 90 percent. Still, Bush was vulnerable, primarily because he had alienated elements of the Republican Party and because he was perceived as having ignored, and perhaps not even recognized, the widespread economic recession that gripped the nation. Instead of addressing these issues, Bush seemed to ask voters to retain him as president simply because he deserved to hold the office.

By contrast, Bush's Democratic rival, Arkansas governor Bill Clinton, made change the keynote of his campaign. Using the media in a virtuoso fashion reminiscent of

Franklin D. Roosevelt, Clinton appeared on talk shows, phone-in radio broadcasts, and other nontraditional venues to present his case to the voters. When faced with potentially disastrous allegations about his personal life raised in tabloid newspapers, Clinton shrewdly responded through an innovative media strategy that defused the rumors. During the fall election campaign, Clinton dominated the three presidential debates by appealing to average voters by demonstrating that he understood, and shared, their concerns. Without the close, even intimate, connection forged by the electronic media, Clinton might not have been able to establish the rapport that was essential to his victory.

Context

The original Framers of the Constitution envisioned a system in which the voters had only an indirect voice in the election of their president and vice president. To some extent, in the presence of the electoral college, that system remains. For practical purposes, the development of the U.S. political system has replaced indirect and disinterested selection, untainted by party divisiveness, with direct and self-interested elections, directed by party strategies and concerns. This transformation initially took place during the generation in which the Constitution was written. American presidential elections since then have been modifications and enlargements of that shift.

To some observers, these changes have been negative, focusing attention on the personality of candidates over the substance of issues and making popularity, rather than ability, the quality needed for success at the polls. The impact of the mass media, in particular the electronic media, can be viewed as a prime culprit in this shift, as voters are bemused by irrelevant personal details rather than concentrating on substantive matters of policy.

Others believe the changes have broadened and opened up the political process, making it possible for more voters to have a closer and more personal involvement in the selection of their president. The increased scrutiny that presidential candidates face, while sometimes irrelevant to their actual goal of serving as chief executive, has given the electorate an unparalleled opportunity to test and judge the character and views of those who presume to follow in the steps of Washington, Jefferson, Lincoln, and Franklin Delano Roosevelt.

Bibliography

Boller, Paul F. *Presidential Campaigns*. New York: Oxford University Press, 1984. Witty, incisive look at the ways in which candidates and parties have vied for the White House during U.S. history. Boller has a keen eye for the telling anecdote and the revealing comment.

Reische, Diana. *Electing a U.S. President*. New York: Franklin Watts, 1992. Brief but comprehensive overview of the nuts and bolts of presidential elections, including an excellent discussion of fund-raising and financing.

Roseboom, Eugene, and Alfred E. Eckes, Jr. *A History of Presidential Elections, from George Washington to Jimmy Carter*. 4th ed. New York: Macmillan, 1979. Well-

1602 Government and Politics

written, accessible survey of contests for the White House that places the development of the various styles of campaigning into context.

Scott, Thomas G. *The Pursuit of the White House: A Handbook of Presidential Election Statistics and History.* Westport, Conn.: Greewood Press, 1987. Valuable statistical and historical study that provides hard data on voters, voting patterns, and shifts in political allegiance. An important tool in understanding the basic framework of presidential elections.

Shields-West, Eileen. *The World Almanac of Presidential Campaigns.* New York: World Almanac, 1992. Often amusing overview of the presidential political process with a penchant for the eccentric yet telling details.

Troy, Gil. *See How They Ran: The Changing Role of the Presidential Candidate.* New York: Free Press, 1991. Comprehensive review of presidential elections in the United States, with the candidate and his activities as the focus of the study. Especially good for charting the shift in popular attitudes toward elections.

Michael Witkoski

Cross-References

Delegates, p. 501; The Democratic Party, p. 520; Elections, p. 578; The Electoral College, p. 584; The Media and Elections, p. 1161; Nomination Processes, p. 1312; Political Campaigning, Planning, and Financing, p. 1427; Political Campaigns in U.S. History, p. 1434; Political Parties, p. 1485; Political Party Conventions, p. 1492; Political Platforms, p. 1512; The Presidency in the United States, p. 1590; Primary Elections, p. 1603; The Republican Party, p. 1699; Two-Party Systems, p. 2033.

PRIMARY ELECTIONS

Field of study: Politics

Primary elections are the major means by which political parties nominate candidates to run in general elections against candidates from other political parties. Primaries provide ordinary citizens an opportunity to involve themselves directly in selecting their party's candidates for public office.

Principal terms

BLANKET PRIMARY: election in which citizens vote for one candidate per office from any party

CAUCUS: meeting of registered party members to select representatives who will attend conventions at which delegates will select the party's presidential candidate

CLOSED PRIMARY: election in which only citizens who registered as party members before the election are permitted to vote

CONVENTION: meetings, at county, state, or national level, of delegates elected by party members to select the party's nominees for office and establish the party platform

CROSS-FILING: rule allowing candidates to be on more than one party's primary ballot; permitted in only a few states

DELEGATE: person authorized to cast a ballot for designated candidates at party conventions

DIRECT PRIMARY: election in which voters choose their party's nominee for office

NONPARTISAN PRIMARY: election in which candidates are not permitted to list their party affiliation on the ballot

OPEN PRIMARY: form of direct primary in which any qualified voter may participate, regardless of party affiliation

RUNOFF PRIMARY: a second primary election between the two highest vote-getters if no candidate receives a clear majority; required in nine states

Overview

Many electoral systems allow citizens to participate in the nomination of their parties' candidates in general elections by holding direct primary elections. A primary election necessarily precedes the general election in which candidates from all parties vie for office. Although a relatively recent development in electoral history by the late twentieth century, primary elections were the principal means by which candidates in democratic political systems were selected to stand in general elections. Direct primaries for nominating candidates to at least some offices occur in every state in the United States; in more than forty states, nominees for all offices are determined in primaries.

In the United States, primary elections generally are internal party processes. Nine states, however, permit citizens registered as members of one political party to vote for candidates in another party's primary election. Such systems are called open primaries. The majority of states have closed primaries, permitting only registered party members to vote. A dozen states require only that voters publicly acknowledge support for a party in order to vote in that party's primary. Voters who have declared themselves as independent voters are barred from voting in most closed primaries. Two states, Massachusetts and New Hampshire, permit independent voters to switch registration on primary election day to vote in an established political party's primary. A few states hold blanket primaries, in which voters can vote for a candidate from any party, but for only one candidate for each contested office. In Louisiana, and many county and local elections, primaries are nonpartisan. Candidates in nonpartisan primaries are not allowed to list their party affiliation on the ballot.

Nine states require candidates to win a clear majority (fifty percent plus one of all votes cast) in order to be nominated. If no candidate wins a clear majority, a runoff primary must be held between the two candidates with the most votes. A few states allow candidates to cross-file to become the nominee for more than one party. For example, in Connecticut, New York, and Vermont, a candidate can seek simultaneously to become the nominee of more than one party, as when Alfonse D'Amato became the Republican and the Conservative parties' nominee for the U.S. Senate in 1980.

Each state regulates the procedures required to place a name on the primary ballot. Consequently, there is a wide variety of qualifying rules. In most cases, prospective candidates must gather a certain number of signatures from supporters in order to qualify. The number of required signatures can vary from a few dozen to tens of thousands. Several states also require the approval of party conventions before a candidate is placed on the ballot. In these cases, there may be a threshold a potential candidate must pass in order to gain access to the ballot. For example, in Colorado, anyone receiving at least 20 percent of the ballots at the state convention is presented to the voters as a candidate for office. In several states, local party committees are guaranteed that any candidate endorsed by the official local organization will be placed on the ballot.

Connecticut and New York have instituted challenge primaries as an alternative route to the ballot. Normally, primaries precede conventions, but challenge primaries are held after the convention. For example, Connecticut guarantees that the convention nominee for office will appear on the general election ballot, unless the nominee is challenged in a primary after the convention and loses. A challenge can take place if a losing convention candidate, who received a certain minimum percentage of the delegates' votes, chooses to mount a challenge.

In the United States, voters in presidential primaries do not select candidates directly. Instead, voters choose delegates, who are pledged to support a particular candidate at the national party convention. Additional convention delegates are chosen in party caucuses and conventions in some states. A third group of delegates are persons who are automatically selected by virtue of the party post or elected position they hold. The majority of delegates, however, are determined by primary elections. Delegates selected in primaries usually are bound by law to vote for their declared candidate during the convention's first ballot, but if no candidate wins a clear majority, delegates are free to vote for whomever they please on subsequent ballots. The last time prior to the mid-1990's that more than one ballot was necessary to nominate a presidential candidate was at the 1952 Democratic convention; there three ballots were required before Adlai Stevenson won a majority of votes.

Primary elections are viewed as more democratic than either the caucus system or the old machine system in which top party officials selected the party's nominee. Caucus systems require citizens to invest more time in selecting candidates by actually meeting together, or "caucusing." This system attracts far fewer participants than primary systems. Even fewer people participate when the selection process is in the hands of party officials. Even so, turnout for primary elections is generally far below turnout for general elections. The only exceptions are in states in which one party is dominant; there the candidate who wins the primary election is virtually certain to win the general election, so more attention is paid to the primary election. Voters in primary elections are generally unrepresentative of both the general public and registered party members as a whole. Primary voters tend to be better informed, better educated, more ideological, and have higher socioeconomic status than the average voter or party member.

Because of low voter turnout and the costs of conducting primaries, it took some time before the primary system took hold in the United States. After initial enthusiasm for primaries in the first two decades of the twentieth century, primaries fell into relative disuse. By 1916, twenty states had presidential primaries, selecting half the delegates to the national conventions. By World War II, however, the number of presidential primaries had fallen to thirteen, in which only a third of the convention delegates were elected. Strong candidates avoided primaries, since entering a primary was thought to be a sign of weakness. Only candidates who needed to demonstrate their electability tended to run. For example, Dwight D. Eisenhower in 1952, John F. Kennedy in 1960, and Richard M. Nixon in 1968 ran in primaries to demonstrate that being a general, a Roman Catholic, or a once-defeated presidential candidate would not undermine their chances of winning the general election.

After the 1968 Democratic convention, in which Hubert Humphrey won the party's nomination for president without entering a single primary, reforms were instituted that made it essential for presidential candidates to run in primary elections. As a result, the number of presidential primaries increased from seventeen Democratic and sixteen Republican primaries in 1968, to thirty-four Democratic and thirty-five Republican primaries in 1988. In 1968, roughly a third of the delegates to the national conventions were elected through the primary process, but by 1988, between two-thirds and three-quarters of convention delegates were selected in primaries.

The post-1968 reforms resulted in the selection of delegates who were much more representative of the population as a whole. Comparing the 1968 and the 1972

Democratic Party conventions reveals a dramatic change in only one election cycle. In 1972, the number of women delegates increased from 13 percent to 40 percent; the number of African Americans tripled from 5 to 15 percent; and the median age declined from forty-nine to forty-two years of age, with eight times as many people under the age of thirty as there had been in 1968. On virtually every other measurable characteristic, the convention delegates more closely mirrored the characteristics of the United States population. The number of people participating in primary elections also exploded. In 1968, only twelve million people participated in either primaries or caucuses. By 1988, forty-six million voters were directly involved in choosing their party's nominee for the presidency.

Applications

Ever since the Progressives began agitating to institute primary elections during the first two decades of the twentieth century, debate has raged over the effects such a reform would have on political parties. Progressive politicians argued that primaries would increase party strength by giving the party's nominee greater legitimacy. A party nominee who won the nomination through an electoral victory, rather than by cutting a deal with party bosses in the proverbial smoke-filled room, would be more likely to gain the allegiance of the electorate. Activists who worked for losing candidates, it was argued, would not become alienated because the party's standard bearer would be seen as the person who, in the majority of the party's view, best represented the principles of the party. Other politicians, usually opponents of the Progressive movement, argued that opening up the nominating process would result in divisive primaries that would inflict deep wounds within the party, reveal weaknesses of candidates to the opposing party, waste financial resources better spent in the general election campaign, exhaust the candidate, use up speech material, and make it less likely that party members would rally around the winning candidate in the general election. In short, many party activists and observers feared that when deep animosities are aroused within the party, only the opposing party benefits in the general election. Party leaders also feared that giving up their monopoly on the nomination process would cause them to lose control over the party.

It took decades before the conventional wisdom that divisive primaries would hurt the party was put to an empirical test. The testing threatened to create deep divisions among political scientists, but, by the end of the twentieth century, a clearer picture of the effect of divisive primaries was coming into view. The first wave of studies concluded that the conventional wisdom was wrong. In 1965, Andrew Hacker concluded that a divisive gubernatorial or senatorial primary bore little relation to general election success. Later studies of local activists in Iowa, however, found that a significant proportion of activists who had worked for losing primary candidates cast votes for the opposition party's candidate in the general election. Furthermore, few supporters of losing primary candidates were remobilized to work for the party in the general election campaign. The disaffected activists, however, tended to be those with the least campaign experience. Party professionals tended to remain loyal to the party and work for whoever won the nomination. Overall, divisive primaries hurt the party's prospects in the general election largely by demobilizing recently mobilized activists.

Even though divisive primaries might affect the behavior of volunteers, the effect on general election results might be negligible because of the professionals' activities. In the mid-1970's, researchers began to look more systematically at divisive primaries at all electoral levels. One early study found that nonincumbents seemed to benefit from a divisive primary because of the added media attention paid to close races, but that overall the effect of divisive primaries at the gubernatorial level was negligible. Other case studies of activists in particular states seemed to confirm the earlier studies' findings that professionals remained active and were not affected by divisive primaries. By the late 1970's, the conventional wisdom that divisive primaries hurt was faring poorly.

Then, as the issue began to seem settled, one of Hacker's students, Richard Bernstein, proved that his teacher had misread the data. Bernstein concluded that the data consistently supported the conventional wisdom: A divisive primary reduced a candidate's prospects in the general election. The tide turned further in the direction of the conventional wisdom after a study of presidential primaries from 1932 to 1976 found that divisive primaries reduced the likelihood of winning the state's electoral vote. Other studies, however, raised enough doubts to warrant continued investigation. By the early 1980's, opinion remained divided. A small study of U.S. Senate races concluded divisive primaries had no effect, and a study of House elections found that challengers were helped by divisive primaries, but incumbents were unaffected.

As debate continued in the 1980's, the methods applied to the question became much more sophisticated. Armed with new models to estimate the effect of divisive primaries, a series of studies conducted by Patrick Kenney and Tom Rice overcame the defects in previous studies and presented a fairly clear picture. Kenney and Rice found that in gubernatorial elections, divisive primaries seemed to hurt the Democratic Party, but not the Republican Party. In U.S. Senate elections, however, both parties suffered in the general election after experiencing a divisive primary. At the presidential level, Kenney and Rice found that the candidate of the party with the more divisive presidential primary was at a greater disadvantage in the November election. For every percentage of the primary vote that a Democratic primary winner achieved, the candidate increased general election support by 0.07 percent. While the effect is small, it is enough to impact close races. For example, applying the Kenney and Rice model to the 1976 race, if Gerald Ford had not experienced the Ronald Reagan primary challenge, it is estimated Ford would have won the 1976 presidential election.

In sum, primary elections have had a significant impact on party strength. Once the nomination function was taken out of the hands of the party bosses, party control of the electoral environment diminished. When parties were no longer able to stifle rivalries with backroom deals, conflicts were settled in public, sometimes eroding the party's chances of electoral success. Given the increased legitimacy of candidates and the increased level of voter participation, however, the costs of potential divisiveness seem relatively low.

Context

Dissatisfied with an electoral system dominated by corrupt machine politicians, a reform movement advocating a wide variety of electoral changes emerged in the first two decades of the twentieth century. Among other reforms, the Progressive movement championed the commission system for local government, the initiative, recall, and referendum elections at the state level, direct election of U.S. senators, and primary elections in all electoral contests where political parties sponsored candidates. By the late twentieth century, primary elections had become the principal means by which political parties nominated candidates for office. The institution of primary elections democratized the electoral system and weakened the influence of party leaders. While sometimes criticized as a costly system that does not necessarily result in the most electable candidates being selected to run in general elections, direct primaries have become the most important twentieth century institutional innovation in the electoral system.

Bibliography

Grassmuck, George, ed. *Before Nomination; Our Primary Problems: A Conference.* Washington, D.C.: American Enterprise Institute for Public Policy Research, 1985. Scholarly articles covering a wide variety of issues surrounding primary elections. The discussions of possible reforms and of the effect of media coverage on the primary process are particularly useful.

Jewell, Malcolm E. *Parties and Primaries: Nominating State Governors.* New York: Praeger, 1984. Comprehensive study of primaries at the gubernatorial level.

Kenney, Patrick J. "Sorting Out the Effects of Primary Divisiveness in Congressional and Senatorial Elections." *Western Political Quarterly* 41 (December, 1988): 765-777. Excellent scholarly overview of recent research on divisive primaries.

Maisel, Sandy L. *Parties and Elections in America: The Electoral Process.* 2d ed. New York: McGraw Hill, 1993. Highly readable text covering political parties in general and the nominating process in particular, written by a scholar who ran for office himself.

Wayne, Stephen J. *The Road to the White House, 1992: The Politics of Presidential Elections.* 3d ed. New York: St. Martin's Press, 1992. This continually updated book is the best overall introduction to how U.S. presidents are elected. Well-written, comprehensive, fully documented, the book is essential reading for students of the electoral system.

Dana Ward

Cross-References

PROGRESSIVISM

Field of study: Political philosophy

Progressivism emerged in the United States during the early decades of the twentieth century, manifesting itself less as a political philosophy than as a broad political reform movement. It encompassed both major political parties and was most notably characterized by the personalities and careers of the two progressive presidents, Theodore Roosevelt, a Republican, and Woodrow Wilson, a Democrat.

Principal terms

LIBERALISM: progressive reform

NEW DEAL: Franklin D. Roosevelt's liberal reform movement of the 1930's in response to the ravages of the Great Depression

NEW FREEDOM: 1912 campaign slogan of Woodrow Wilson that implied antitrust actions as a key reform

NEW NATIONALISM: Theodore Roosevelt's Progressive Party campaign slogan in 1912, advocating a strong regulatory state

TRUST: combination of businesses or corporations that threaten to create a monopoly in some area of the economy

Overview

Progressivism was the name given to a broad reform movement that captured the interest of the American people during the first two decades of the twentieth century. Its most obvious manifestation was a political and social response from many levels of society to the massive changes that had occurred in the United States in the decades after the Civil War. During the late nineteenth and early twentieth centuries many Americans moved from the country to the city, leaving farms for factories and substituting machines for muscle power, both animal and human. In addition, new immigrants from eastern and southern Europe and from Asia began to affect the previous social, religious, and cultural homogeneity of the country, or so it was claimed. There were many advances, particularly in material production, but there were also fearful challenges in that new world of urbanization, industrialization, and immigration.

The term "progressivism" has had many interpretations over the years and the notion of a single, unified political philosophy or movement has been replaced by a more complex perception, suggesting a number of forces—political, economic, social, intellectual, and cultural—working at times separately and at other times in concert throughout society. An analysis of these sometimes contradictory definitions reveals the movement's disparate nature, one that has often been revised to accommodate the shifting perspectives of historians and commentators from later eras. Early students of the period emphasized what they saw as its democratic character. The first writers about progressivism, contemporary with the movement, developed what was for a long time the commonly accepted thesis of progressivism, that it was a political movement whose aim was to speak and act for the people against the growing power of the private corporations. Such corporations included United States Steel and John D. Rockefeller's Standard Oil, which threatened America's egalitarian traditions as well as the belief that the United States was the land of individual opportunity. Progressivism was thus a democratic movement reacting to the corrupting power of economic special interests. Progressives generally agreed that the central government must play a significant role in the battle against the interests. Nineteenth century liberalism, committed to laissez-faire, had become largely irrelevant. The people's government should take the lead in protecting and advancing the people's welfare. These are the ideas that the progressives believed. Later thinkers would make new claims about what progressivism was and who represented it.

The questions most often asked about progressivism are what were its origins and who were the progressives? One of the earliest claims was that progressivism evolved from the populist movement of the 1890's and the farmers' battle against the trusts and railroads. This interpretation stressed the rural roots of progressivism. After World War II the interpretative emphasis shifted to a middle-class small-town perspective with lawyers and newspaper editors and ordinary businessmen taking up the people's cause. Others agreed to the small-town nature of the movement but interpreted progressivism more negatively, as a reactionary social and political response by members of the nativist middle class to preserve their world not only from the new millionaires of monopoly but also from labor unions and the new immigrant groups. Still other commentators have attributed the motives and assumptions and actions of progressives to the religious and moral attitudes of the time.

The turbulent decade of the 1960's ushered in new interpretations of progressivism. Reflecting the civil rights movements of their era, some historians criticized the racist and sexist assumptions of many progressives, a contradiction to the progressives' stated democratic ideology. The small-town and the rural interpretations were countered by those who argued that progressivism was mainly urban, with Chicago and New York City the key centers. Social workers and labor leaders thus replaced middle-class lawyers and editors as the seminal figures of the movement. From the perspective of the New Left it was claimed that progressivism was a conservative movement designed to forestall the threat of socialism and other even more radical assaults upon private property.

With exceptions, much of the scholarship about progressivism of the 1970's and 1980's returned to an examination and restating of earlier interpretations of progressivism. One of the exceptions was the theory that progressivism in the United States had been strongly influenced by events in Europe, particularly in Germany and Great Britain as well as by examples in Australia and New Zealand. Certainly the most startling argument was that there was no progressive movement at all. Noting that there was neither philosophical nor programmatic nor class nor geographical commonality, one historian has stated that at best progressivism was a confused multiplicity of individuals and organizations, actions and responses, and whatever forms progressivism took, the history of the period was the product of forces much more significant than the efforts of the reformers. Progressivism was a cloak of many colors, and a cloak whose colors keep shifting from wearer to wearer and from observer to observer. The most enduring characteristic of what was perhaps the major reform movement in American history was that progressivism often became whatever a progressive wanted it to be.

Applications

One of the most notable accomplishments of the early progressive era was President Theodore Roosevelt's decision to use the Sherman Antitrust Act of 1890 against the Northern Securities Company. The latter was a holding company created by J. Pierpont Morgan, John D. Rockefeller, James J. Hill, and Edward H. Harriman, all famous but controversial businessmen, consolidating the Chicago, Burlington, Quincy, Northern Pacific, and the Great Northern railroads and creating a rail transportation monopoly. The supposed evils of transportation and industrial monopoly were hardly news— populists and others had frequently complained during the nineteenth century—but the Sherman Act had proved to be toothless. Roosevelt, who had succeeded to the presidency upon the assassination of William McKinley in 1901, decided to prosecute the mammoth monopoly, and in February, 1902 it was announced that the government was filing a suit against the Northern Securities Company under the Sherman Act. Many Americans were elated although the financial center of the country, Wall Street, was dismayed. Whatever the legal merits of the resulting Northern Securities case— the eminent jurist Oliver Wendell Holmes sided with the company when the case reached the Supreme Court—Roosevelt had astutely chosen obvious targets in Morgan and Rockefeller in the people's battle against the trusts and other special interests. In 1903 the Supreme Court ordered the Northern Securities Company dissolved.

The country applauded. Reformers were generally pleased. Roosevelt became known as the "trust-buster." Roosevelt never believed that breaking up big business was either necessary or a solution to the country's economic, social, or political problems, and ironically his conservative successor, William Howard Taft, prosecuted more trusts. Roosevelt argued that more could be accomplished through government regulation than by merely breaking up big business, that size in itself was not the issue. What he established in the Northern Securities case was the supremacy of the activist federal government, one that supported the people's welfare in the battle with private business interests.

What Roosevelt also succeeded in doing was to focus the heart and mind of the country upon the presidency. Leaving office after almost eight years in 1909, he was followed by his handpicked successor, William Howard Taft. The latter was by common agreement much less progressive than Roosevelt, although his antitrust policy perhaps satisfied more progressives than had Roosevelt's. For reasons political and philosophical but also personal, Roosevelt challenged Taft for the Republican presidential nomination in 1912, but Taft used the political power inherent in his position to fight off Roosevelt and gain renomination. The fight had been bitter and

Roosevelt and his supporters refused to accept the decision, which they claimed had been unfair and unjust. In reaction they founded the Progressive Party and nominated Roosevelt as their candidate. Many contemporaries described the near-religious passions that swept the convention—the delegates sang "Onward Christian Soldiers" and Roosevelt's acceptance address was titled "Confession of Faith."

In the United States the two-party system had been the norm: Third parties had rarely been successful. The hopes of the Progressive Party—nicknamed the Bull Moose Party—rested primarily upon Roosevelt, one of the most popular figures in all of American history. For the party and Roosevelt to win, it was necessary that their opponents be portrayed as obvious reactionaries. Taft's image could be made to fit the conservative paradigm, but the Democratic nominee, Woodrow Wilson, who had compiled a notable progressive record as governor of New Jersey, did not. After Wilson's nomination Roosevelt sensed defeat.

Nevertheless, the Progressive/Bull Moose campaign of 1912 is generally considered one of the high points of the progressive movement. Roosevelt headed one of the most progressive—most liberal—party platforms and subsequent campaigns in the history of presidential politics. The party demanded a federal trade commission to regulate business and industry and a tariff commission to set rates on imports; it also advocated direct democracy with the initiative, the referendum, and the recall being adopted for federal elections, and urged a national presidential primary in which all the voters could choose the candidates, not just convention delegates. What is more, in the area of social welfare, the progressives and Roosevelt staked out new territory during the campaign: Workman's compensation, prohibition of child labor, minimum wages for women, a federal law for labor disputes, additional conservation laws, and a federal health program were some of the controversial topics, many of which were later enacted into law. In part inspired by Herbert Croly's *Promise of American Life* (1909) and campaigning under the rubric of new nationalism, Roosevelt envisioned a strong national government, as advocated by Alexander Hamilton, being used to achieve Thomas Jefferson's democratic goals—life, liberty, and the pursuit of happiness.

Wilson, also a progressive, was less committed to increasing the powers of the national government. Wilson's "New Freedom" placed greater emphasis upon eliminating special privileges and barriers in order to allow the individual freedom to compete and thrive in the marketplace or elsewhere. Paradoxically, Wilson attacked Roosevelt for not being sufficiently in favor of antitrust actions, the issue by which Roosevelt had first made his fame as a progressive. Roosevelt desired to regulate monopolies and trusts through a more powerful federal government; Wilson wished to break them up.

The Democrats won in 1912: Wilson and the Democrats received 6,200,000 votes, Roosevelt's Progressives 4,100,000, the Republicans and Taft 3,400,000, and the Socialist Party of Eugene Debs 900,000. Personalities undoubtedly played an enormous part in the decision of 1912 but there seems little doubt that the voters were voting for more than mere personality: The country was in a progressive mood.

Context

Progressivism was unique to a particular time, but it also reflected the periodic reform impulses found throughout American history. The era of Andrew Jackson in the first half of the nineteenth century combined democratic aspirations, early industrial challenges, a feeling of optimism, and larger-than-life political leadership. Mention has already been made about the possible connections between the concerns of the populists of the 1890's and the progressives of the next generation. Many scholars have compared the progressive era with the New Deal of the 1930's. Both had their Roosevelts, both were committed to strong government action, and many old progressives were to be found in various New Deal agencies. There were, however, differences. In contrast to the New Deal, progressivism occurred largely during a period of economic prosperity. New Deal reformers may also have lacked some of the religious and moral fervor that often motivated the progressives. The liberalism of the 1930's was similar to, but also different from, earlier progressivism.

In asking the question about what happened to progressivism, historians have often looked to World War I and the administrations of Warren G. Harding and Calvin Coolidge. Wilson's war to make the world safe for democracy also ushered in an era of suspicion, persecution, censorship, and the Red Scare, and the pre-war reform coalition was one of the war's casualties. It also led to women's suffrage and to Prohibition. The Nineteenth Amendment seems easily to fit into progressivism, but what about Prohibition? Was that a progressive reform? Many agreed that it was, but differed as to whether the movement to abolish the consumption of alcohol proved the worth of progressivism or proved its fallacies. In addition to Prohibition, other new issues such as immigration restriction and religious fundamentalism divided individuals and groups who had been allies before the war. There was also a leadership vacuum during the postwar years: There was no new Woodrow Wilson or Theodore Roosevelt. Many of the progressive goals had been achieved, however: direct election of senators and women's suffrage, limitations and controls on business monopolies, a more powerful and regulatory central government (for example in the Pure Food and Drug Law and the Federal Reserve System), and significant conservation of the nation's resources. Finally, surviving progressives often had little empathy for many new elements of the century's third decade: Flappers, literary modernism, and Sigmund Freud were unwelcome strangers to the familiar landscape. Many if not all the progressives were representatives of the respectable middle class and their intellectual and social roots were in the nineteenth century. Still, many progressives in the 1920's still claimed to be forward-looking, not reactionary or conservative, and claimed that they represented the people, not the selfish few.

The continuing debate about the nature of progressivism may never be completely resolved. Progressivism was possibly only a collection of many distinct and diverse occurrences—the beliefs and actions of numerous individuals and groups. The progressive movement, however, perhaps because of its diffuse and diverse nature, is responsible for America's greatest era of reform.

Bibliography

Cooper, John Milton, Jr. *Pivotal Decades*. New York: W. W. Norton, 1990. Excellent survey of the years 1900 to 1920. Cooper has also written a superb dual biography of Theodore Roosevelt and Woodrow Wilson, *The Warrior and the Priest* (1985).

De Witt, Benjamin Parke. *The Progressive Movement*. Seattle: University of Washington Press, 1968. First published in 1915, this is one of the earliest accounts of progressivism. Presents the movement as the people against the trusts and their political allies.

Hofstadter, Richard. *The Age of Reform*. New York: Alfred A. Knopf, 1955. One of America's premier historians argues that progressivism was mainly a reaction to the loss of status experienced by older political elites.

Kolko, Gabriel. *The Triumph of Conservatism*. New York: Free Press of Glencoe, 1963. This controversial interpretation turns progressivism on its head: Instead of a liberal movement acting for the people against big business, it was a conservative movement to protect special interests from the people.

Link, Arthur S. *Woodrow Wilson and the Progressive Era, 1910-1917*. New York: Harper & Row, 1954. Readable volume in the New American Nation Series chronicles progressivism from 1910 to the onset of World War I.

Link, Arthur S., and Richard L. McCormick. *Progressivism*. Arlington Heights, Ill.: Harlan Davidson, 1983. Discusses the complexities, contradictions, and diversities of progressivism, and stresses the progressives' anger at the consequences of industrialization.

Mowry, George E. *The Era of Theodore Roosevelt, 1900-1912*. New York: Harper & Row, 1958. Argues that progressivism was primarily fueled by the small-town elites.

Eugene Larson

Cross-References

PROPAGANDA

Field of study: Functions of government

Propaganda is the use of communications media to influence numbers of people. It is a controversial term associated with malicious deceptions and with routine efforts of persuasion.

Principal terms

AUDIENCE: people who read, hear, or see a message

BROADCASTING: use of electronic signals (radio and television) to send the same message or program to large numbers of people

MASS MEDIA: methods of communication such as newspapers, film, radio, and television that send their messages to large audiences

PUBLIC OPINION SURVEYS: questions asked to a selected sample of people to estimate the general public attitude on given issues

SYMBOL: person or object that represents an abstraction, such as a flag's representing a nation

Overview

Propaganda is the use of the media to influence public attitudes and to alter public behavior. Slanted or biased messages, and even deceptions, are often part of propaganda. In the twentieth century the term "propaganda" acquired sinister connotations because of its use by the Nazis to implant their fascist ideas, by the Soviet Union to spread its communist doctrine, and by several democratic governments to arouse public support for war efforts. Many governments and political parties have used less inflammatory, more honest propaganda to gain recognition or support. As the mass media expanded in the twentieth century, most large organizations, including governments, began to use propaganda to establish favorable public images. Propaganda became a routine part of their operations. At the same time, the public became increasingly aware of propaganda and its purposes.

It is more accurate to think of propaganda simply as a tool for influencing the public. Propaganda is more than blatantly manipulative Nazi newsreels or American political campaign television advertisements. One must consider the purposes, the content, the methods of dissemination, and the effects of the propaganda in order to evaluate it.

Propaganda is often the effort of a government to build support for policies and programs. The purposes of government propaganda can range from the understandable need to mobilize mass support to deception and manipulation to cover up mistakes, malfeasance, and incompetence. Governments use the media to explain the importance of personal sacrifice during wartime. Appeals to patriotism and civic virtue are quite common. Wartime may also create situations in which the state controls reports from the fronts in order to present a favorable impression of the war effort.

Governments also use propaganda to influence citizens of other countries. In wartime, this process is called psychological warfare. Psychological warfare is intended to demoralize or to confuse the enemy with information (true, false, or in between) about a disaster at home or on the battlefield. Psychological warfare may also be directed against the civilian population of the enemy nation to create fear and discouragement in order to weaken citizen participation in the war effort. In peacetime, international propaganda is often more subtle. A government may distribute misleading information to influence the outcome of another government's election, or, to cite an extreme example, to attempt to incite opposition to an existing regime. In less hostile situations, the representatives of one nation may distribute information in another that tells about favorable economic and political conditions in their homeland, in order to encourage tourism, investments, and trade.

The content of propaganda is usually direct and simple although the implications of the message may be subtle and complex. One of the most common devices is the use of powerful symbols already known to and accepted by the intended audience. These symbols can be of a patriotic character such as a national flag, a national anthem, or a picture of a uniformed soldier. Such symbols arouse memories of shared national experiences in wars or other national emergencies. The use of a symbol tends to focus the memories and emotions of the general public on a single broadly accepted message that, if presented effectively, can bring large numbers of people of differing backgrounds into a unified movement. The party or government that gains this support may have little or no connection with the actual historical origins of the symbols used in the propaganda, but this fact is usually lost in the emotion-laden excitement surrounding the use of the symbol.

Among the most controversial aspects of propaganda is the use of distortions and lies. When such untruths involve ethnic or religious prejudice, propaganda exploits the emotions of the public.

Propaganda is found in all types of mass media. In fact, it may be argued that bias is inherent in all forms of personal communication. The oldest form of public communication is the speech delivered to a large audience in an auditorium or an open field. Another traditional form is the use of posters. The written word is also important and appears on the pages of pamphlets, newspapers, magazines, and books. Radio reaches listeners in a large variety of places—at home, at play, on the job, and in motor vehicles. Film has an especially strong appeal because of its ability to present visual images that are structured and artificial while bearing a close resemblance to reality. Television can broadcast films and present instantaneous coverage of staged events. Film and the broadcast media share with traditional speech making and posters a strong influence among people who are unaffected by the printed word.

Although the effects of propaganda are often difficult to measure, the expansion of the mass media and the increasing dependence of the general public on information and opinions distributed through mass media make the subject of the effects of propaganda one of obvious importance. Critics and commentators generally agree that the most harmful results occur when propaganda arouses the emotions of the audience and leads it to engage in irrational actions, perhaps to the point of engaging in violence against innocent individuals. Appeals to prejudice can divide communities into contending ethnic or religious factions or into antagonistic political groups. Propaganda has been a contributing factor in the coming of many of the major wars of the modern era.

Propaganda can also influence public attitudes on political and social issues. Public opinion surveys indicate that propaganda has a strong effect when it reinforces existing attitudes. Carefully designed mass media campaigns for elective office can determine voting choices of a large percent of the electorate and thereby often decide the outcome of the elections. Organizations such as churches, labor unions, and private corporations use propaganda to influence public opinion and, in that way, place pressure on legislatures and government agencies to enact policies. Government media campaigns in favor of good health practices and against the use of tobacco, cocaine, and other harmful substances apparently tend to reduce their consumption.

Applications

Adolf Hitler provided the twentieth century's most dramatic and drastic use of propaganda. Hitler and Joseph Goebbels—his minister of propaganda—grasped the value of propaganda in post-World War I Germany, where millions of people carried the burdens of military defeat, material destruction, and economic collapse. Hitler and Goebbels' main purposes were to capture the allegiance of the German people for the Nazi Party and, after 1933, for the Nazi government in Berlin. The content of their propaganda was a series of brief, simply worded messages that connected Hitler with the heroic elements of the German past and with the potential for the nation's return to greatness. The Nazis used virulent anti-Semitism to blame Germany's Jewish minority for the nation's problems. Hitler used several forms of propaganda, including political rallies that were public spectacles. Goebbels distributed colorful posters designed to reinforce the Nazi message. Aware of the value of radio, Goebbels provided the public with inexpensive receivers to extend the reach of Nazi broadcast propaganda. The Nazi state also took control of the press, including newspapers, magazines, and books, by a combination of force and intimidation. Both Goebbels and Hitler were fascinated with film and ordered the production of newsreels, feature films, and documentaries. Director Leni Riefenstahl's 1936 film *Triumph of the Will*, for example, remains as a classic example of the persuasive power of propaganda.

The image of the Nazi regime that survives in newsreel incarnations of Hitler's strident speeches and goose-stepping soldiers leads many to assume, with reason, that this propaganda was immensely successful. In fact, from 1928 to 1932 the Nazi Party vote rose from eight hundred thousand to fourteen million. After the German defeat in World War II, however, research indicated that Goebbels and Hitler were aware of significant failures in their propaganda effort. For example, lengthy political speeches tended to bore the audience so that by the late 1930's government radio broadcasts were mainly light music interspersed with brief speeches and bulletins. In 1938, after five years of intense propaganda, Hitler, in a secret speech to newspaper editors, admitted that the Nazi message had not won the support of key professionals and technicians. Nazi propaganda, while spectacular, also revealed the uncertainties involved in the assessment of the impact of propaganda.

While fighting Hitler's war machine in Europe, the United States also faced the challenge of war on a second front against the Japanese in the Pacific. With most able-bodied young men in military service, the United States had a labor shortage. The government and private industry decided to recruit women workers for factories, but this policy contradicted accepted gender roles. In order to recruit married women with young children, government and industry used a focused propaganda campaign that combined patriotism with reassurances about day-care centers and schools. The fictional character Rosie the Riveter symbolized the acceptance of women in heavy industry. Government and industry used newspaper advertisements and magazine articles in a propaganda campaign that eventually gained wide exposure in popular music and Hollywood films. In general, Rosie the Riveter was a successful propaganda device. Both men and women accepted the presence of women in heavy industrial jobs. Ironically, government and private industry advocates of this campaign rejected the idea of women as industrial workers after the war. Another propaganda campaign began after the war, this time to convince women to resume working at home.

The Cold War involved an extended propaganda struggle between two powerful nations—the United States and the Soviet Union. The United States created specialized government agencies to reach people in the Soviet Union, satellite countries under Soviet control, and Third World nations. The U.S. government used Radio Free Europe to broadcast directly into Communist countries in their national languages. The Voice of America extended radio propaganda to Africa, the Middle East, Asia, and Latin America. The communist presence in Cuba led to the creation of Radio Martí (named for a nineteenth century Cuban nationalist) in 1985 and Televisión Martí in 1990. These broadcasts usually had a strong anticommunist, prodemocracy slant mixed with news and entertainment programs. The impact of these broadcasts is difficult to assess, but expensive efforts to jam them by the governments of the target audiences indicates that these messages reached a significant number of people.

The U.S. Information Agency (USIA) employed methods that, in contrast to the direct approaches described above, were more subtle. With a billion-dollar budget and offices in more than one hundred countries, the USIA's main goal was to cultivate many channels of communication and influence in nations important to the foreign policy of the United States. The USIA sponsored libraries, lecture series, English-language fluency classes, magazines, books, and films. These activities gave wide audiences a friendly, positive exposure to U.S. culture and politics. These channels gave the USIA opportunities to present explanations of U.S. foreign policy.

Context

Propaganda has a long history that can be traced back to ancient times, but its modern forms date from the religious struggles between Catholics and Protestants in Europe in the 1500's and 1600's. To compete with the expansion of Protestantism, the Catholic church established the Sacra Congregatio de Propaganda Fide (Congregation for the Propagation of the Faith) in 1627. This marked the beginning of the deliberate use of propaganda as it later became known. Other major historical movements such as the American Revolution of 1776 and the French Revolution that began in 1789 saw extensive use of posters, popular art, and pamphlets.

Advances in technology in the nineteenth and twentieth centuries, however, gave propaganda a much more extensive role in the everyday lives of ordinary citizens. Innovations such as the high-speed printing press, telegraphy, photography, and railroads made possible the rapid distribution of information and opinion. In the early twentieth century, film emerged as a popular medium. These innovations came together in World War I to give the propagandist access to a much larger audience and to create the impression that propaganda was immensely powerful. The British placed selective and slanted information in the print media of the United States to turn American public opinion against Germany and against President Woodrow Wilson's neutrality policy. After the United States entered the war in 1917, the Wilson Administration's Committee on Public Information used propaganda in print and film to arouse public support for the war. Political commentators such as Walter Lippmann and John Dewey expressed a new pessimism about the place of democracy in an era in which the public fell under the sway of propaganda.

The British and American experiences in World War I and the rise of Hitler in Germany in the 1930's seemed to confirm the assumption that propaganda was an ominous weapon that could dominate great numbers of educated people, but more detailed research, including the use of public opinion surveys beginning in the 1930's, revealed the complexities in the process of mass persuasion. This research indicated that by the middle decades of the twentieth century people often could make discriminating judgments about the flow of information in the mass media, including the recognition of propaganda and interpretation of its relevance and validity. The newness of mass media such as film and radio began to wear off; audiences began to learn to make judgments about the content and purpose of mass propaganda. The evolution of commercial advertising in these years also made the work of the propagandist more difficult, because viewers, readers, and listeners became aware of various methods of persuasion. While the heavy-handed approaches of the early twentieth century are outmoded, newer, more subtle forms of propaganda—especially through television— have become widespread in politics, government bureaucracies, and corporate advertising. Propaganda operations such as the U.S. Information Agency have learned the necessity of staying ahead of audience awareness of the techniques of mass persuasion.

Bibliography

Altheide, David L., and John M. Johnson. *Bureaucratic Propaganda*. Newton, Mass.: Allyn & Bacon, 1980. Studies the routine use of propaganda by large organizations, from welfare agencies to the military to evangelical crusades.

Balfour, Michael. *Propaganda in War, 1939-1945: Organisations, Policies, and Publics, in Britain and Germany*. London: Routledge & Kegan Paul, 1979. Well-documented study of the propaganda war between Germany and Britain. Concentrates on the failures of many propaganda efforts, but does find important long-term effects of British propaganda after the war.

Ellul, Jacques. *Propaganda: The Formation of Men's Attitudes*. Translated by Konrad Kellen and Jean Lerner. New York: Alfred A. Knopf, 1965. Sees propaganda as powerful, inescapable, and essentially harmful because of its threat to individualism and democracy.

Fortner, Robert. *International Communication: History, Conflict, and Control of the Global Metropolis*. Belmont, Calif.: Wadsworth, 1993. Explores international communications in unprecedented depth with considerable coverage of propaganda in the Cold War period.

Honey, Maureen. *Creating Rosie the Riveter: Class, Gender, and Propaganda During World War II*. Amherst: University of Massachusetts Press, 1984. Excellent examination of a propaganda campaign based on research in government documents and mass media material. Focuses on a propaganda effort connected with media, gender, and class issues that remain contemporary.

Jowett, Garth, and Victoria O'Donnell. *Propaganda and Persuasion*. 2d ed. Newbury Park, Calif.: Sage Publications, 1992. Solid introduction to the subject based on recent research. Emphasis on the institutionalization of propaganda and its expanding role in modern society.

Knightley, Phillip. *The First Casualty: From the Crimea to Vietnam—The War Correspondent as Hero, Propagandist, and Myth Maker*. London: Pan Books, 1989. Emphasizes the struggles of journalists to report on modern wars while under pressure to write propaganda instead of news.

Reuth, Ralf Georg. *Goebbels*. Translated by Krishna Winston. New York: Harcourt Brace, 1993. Traces Goebbels' life from his tormented youth through the Nazi years to his death in 1945. Offers valuable insights on the strengths and weaknesses in Goebbels' propaganda work.

John A. Britton

Cross-References

Charismatic Leadership, p. 209; Civic Education, p. 278; Cult of Personality, p. 477; Demagoguery, p. 507; Education Management, p. 565; Fascism and Nazism, p. 656; Invisible Government, p. 975; The Media and Elections, p. 1161; The Media and the Conduct of Government, p. 1167; Patriotism, p. 1384; Public Opinion Polling, p. 1627; Revolutionary Governments, p. 1725; Voting Behavior in the United States, p. 2109.

PROTEST MOVEMENTS

Field of study: Politics

Political participation is crucial for a democracy to prosper. Protest is one form of political participation. Although protest is considered a fundamental right in democracies, there is considerable controversy over how it is actually conducted.

Principal terms

ALIENATION: feeling that social norms and institutions do not represent one's values or needs

CYNICISM: feeling that institutions are acting from base motives

EFFICACY: one's political activities actually influencing what government does

LEGITIMACY: widely shared acceptance that those who govern society have gotten their power by right; the feeling that the political process deserves public respect

MOBILIZATION: process by which candidates, political parties, activists, and groups induce other people to participate

UNCONVENTIONAL POLITICS: refers to forms of political participation that others regard as deviant, challenging to authority, or generally outside the normal ways of doing things in governmental and electoral processes

Overview

A democratic political process is designed to allow the preferences of citizens to be expressed through nonviolent political means and established political channels on a regular basis. Democratic practices, however, are not perfect. The demands for change may be blocked, and in such situations people are likely to resort to protest in an attempt to produce change. Protest can be used by forces of any political or social persuasion. Protest can be violent or nonviolent and can be employed to prevent change as well as to make change possible. Further, it can be used by the powerful as well as by the powerless. Government itself sometimes resorts to protest in dealing with politically sensitive and explosive situations. The point to be made, however, is that protest is a type of political participation that is vital for democracy. Political participation is necessary for a healthy and thriving democracy, and protest is one way of expressing views to governmental bodies and officials. The Framers of the U.S. Constitution established, primarily in the First Amendment, that citizens had a right to protest the actions of government and to join protest movements.

There are a variety of ways in which individuals can participate in politics. Writing letters to elected officials, voting, running for office, and protest are some forms of participation. Different forms of participation can be compared to how much effort and commitment are required. The easiest form of participation is simply talking about politics. More effort and commitment are required to write letters or make telephone calls. Voting is still more demanding because it requires registering, making a decision, and going out to cast a ballot. A still more demanding form of participation is protest. Commitments to join social movements and engage in protest activities carry high costs. This type of participation is often viewed as illegitimate or as an unconventional type of politics, so individuals involved in protest may be fired from a job, physically constrained by police, and jailed.

Many of the historic moments and great changes in U.S. politics have resulted from people acting against government and established authority. Women won the right to vote by protesting and eventually pressuring legislatures to ratify a voting rights amendment to the U.S. Constitution. The struggle for civil rights involved unconventional politics, including marches, sit-ins, boycotts, hunger strikes, and riots. Those protests were meant to get government and society to respond to the demands of African Americans and other disenfranchised groups.

The emergence of a protest movement entails a change of consciousness and of behavior. The change in consciousness has at least three distinct phases. First, in the minds of those who are to protest, the system loses legitimacy. Large numbers of people who ordinarily accept the authority of their rulers and the legitimacy of institutional arrangements come to believe that these rulers and these arrangements are unjust and wrong. Second, people who believe that existing arrangements are inevitable begin to consider and assert demands for change. Third, there is a new sense of efficacy; people who ordinarily consider themselves helpless come to believe that they have some capacity to alter their social and economic positions. This last change of consciousness is perhaps the most difficult to achieve because of the alienation and cynicism that an individual brings into the political process.

Change in behavior is equally important, and usually more easily recognized, at least when it takes the form of unconventional politics. Such behavior involves two distinguishing patterns. First, large numbers of people become defiant; they violate the traditions, rules, and laws to which they ordinarily acquiesce, and they criticize the authorities to whom they ordinarily defer. Second, their defiance is acted out collectively, as members of a group, and not as isolated individuals. Strikes and riots are forms of collective action, but even some forms of defiance which appear to be individual acts, such as crime or school truancy, may have a collective dimension, if those who engage in these acts may consider themselves to be part of a larger movement. Such individual acts can be considered movement events when those involved in the acts view themselves to be acting as members of a group, and when they share a common set of protest beliefs.

Protests develop in democratic societies for various reasons. Protesters may view governments as unresponsive to moral issues or involved in immoral actions. Protesters may simply want to make a moral statement and arouse the conscience of other individuals. Protest activities may be directed against the private sector rather than the public sector. For example, in the 1990's, antiabortion demonstrators gathered outside private medical clinics.

The most common reason for protest and rebellion is that protesters view themselves in a position of relative deprivation, or the feeling that one's group is being deprived of opportunities enjoyed by other groups in the society. This might entail, for example, one group fearing that it is losing power or influence, thus moving that group toward unconventional politics. Especially threatened groups often resort to violent means of protest.

Applications

There are many examples in U.S. history of protest movements' mobilizing individuals into collective action groups to challenge arrangements that served to disadvantage these groups. Organized labor struggled with little success until the decade of the 1930's, when prounion forces pressured the U.S. Congress to pass the National Labor Relations Act. This legislation created opportunities for collective bargaining between labor and management. Through difficult unionizing drives in the 1930's, organized labor succeeded in unionizing much of U.S. industry and improving the wages and working conditions of unionized workers. A common type of political activity was the labor strike.

African Americans and other racial groups were largely shut out of the mainstream U.S. society by a rigid system of segregation and widespread discrimination. Through the Civil Rights movement of the 1950's and 1960's, African Americans got most segregation legislation removed from the law books. The movement culminated in the 1964 Civil Rights Act, which outlawed discrimination in virtually all areas of public accommodations, and in the 1965 Voting Rights Act, which for the first time since the 1890's made it possible for large numbers of African Americans in the South to vote. The most dramatic illustration of the success of this legislation can be seen in the number of African American elected officials in the United States, which increased fivefold from 1,479 in 1970 to 7,335 in 1990. As in the labor movement, unconventional politics played a major role, with demonstrations and marches leading the way.

Women were for the most part denied the vote until 1919, and even after achieving the vote they remained on the sidelines of U.S. politics and institutional life for the next half-century. The woman suffrage movement of the early twentieth century was critical to women's achieving the right to vote. The women's movement of the 1970's and 1980's, in turn, was critical to effecting affirmative action programs for women, appointing more women to high political office, and passing laws sought by women's groups. It was not unusual for women to be confronted with strict police enforcement. In other words, women used protest to overcome rules and laws that kept them from voting, often taking the risk of being physically constrained and jailed.

These three examples of protest movements are ongoing. Leaders of protest movements must constantly call attention for the injustice, suffering, or deprivation they face so that outside groups or individuals will be moved to join the protest movement. How effective these appeals are depend on several factors: the actual degree of suffering, the extent to which outside groups regard this suffering as unjust, and the degree of legitimacy given to the protest movement by the general public. Finally, at the practical level, government must have resources to meet the demands of the protesters. If demands have not been fully met, even if leaders of protest movements have become engaged in conventional or mainstream forms of politics, they must occasionally resort to protest in order to keep attention on their movement. Leaders of protest movements must continuously be involved in the transformation of both consciousness and behavior. Consciousness raising and mobilization of others are constant tasks in maintaining an effective protest movement. This suggests, in turn, that effective leadership is a very significant factor in determining the success of a protest movement.

Context

Protest is more effective and protesters have a better chance of success when other, more powerful groups in society accept the objectives of the protest movement. It is helpful to a protest movement when influential politicians or public officials embrace the objectives of the movement, as when President John F. Kennedy lent some support to Martin Luther King, Jr., and the Civil Rights movement. Threats of disruption—making it difficult for society to carry on with its everyday activities—can sometimes be an effective means for protest movements. King combined appeals to influential politicians and threats of disruption in his nonviolent campaign. He knew that when the streets are blocked by demonstrators, the jails filled to overflowing capacity with protesters, and the court dockets congested with cases, everyday business comes to a halt. At these times, governments are more willing to listen to the grievances of the protest movement. Whatever strategy is used, protest movements are most successful when they gain legitimacy.

Many protest movements never reach the stage of legitimacy required to bring about change. Protest movements often run the risk of alienating potentially sympathetic groups and arousing opposing groups to action. Most often, protest movements confront intense opposition from official governmental bodies and officials that restrict the effectiveness of protest strategies. This official action is meant to destroy and stop the protest movement.

Official action against protesters is of five types: suppression, in which police powers are used against protesters in a physical and coercive way; discrediting, in which attempts are made to damage a group's credibility or legitimacy in the public arena; delay, in which the government appoints a commission or relegates a problem to study with the intent of never acting on recommendations from that study; tokenism, in which the government concedes a tiny fraction of what is desired while giving the impression that a significant concession has been made; and coopting, which the government establishes a very close relationship with protesters with the intent of persuading them to adopt the institution's norms and values.

These actions are taken step by step; if the first step does not work, the next step is taken, and so on. The intent is to make it costly on the protester to continue with the protest movement. Suppression, or outright brutal coercion, usually stops an individual from participating. The attempt to stop the protest movement may begin at the very beginning of the movement.

People who join protest movements must decide how much effort and commitment to the movements they are willing to give. They likely will be concerned about going to meetings that will be watched by police officers or even terrorist groups. People may worry that by attending public meetings or demonstrations they may be labeled as deviants, causing trouble with their friends, neighbors, workers, and even family members. People may balk at the thought of having to spend long hours on picket lines, doing mailings, gathering signatures on petitions, or trying to get elected officials to listen. In the end, although protest is one of the few political resources available to relatively powerless groups, its potential for success is often limited.

Even in a democracy, some needs are ignored and others are deliberately neglected. As society changes, some groups and individuals find their values and beliefs threatened, their expectations blocked. Such situations can lead to alienation and cynicism. The end result is that individuals choose not to participate in political and governmental processes. This nonparticipation is dangerous for a democracy.

There are many forms of participation available to people. Joining a protest movement is one way of participating. Deciding whether protest is justified is not easy, however, especially if protest is violent. Those that study democracy would say that when protest is used as a way for the weak to express themselves, when protest is carried out in a spirit of moral consciousness, and when goals are compatible with democratic values, then protest movements contribute to and improve human dignity and life.

Bibliography

Barbrook, Alec, and Christine Bolt. *Power and Protest in American Life*. New York: St. Martin's Press, 1980. Discussion on what issues prompt protest and how group power is exercised.

Blumberg, Rhoda Lois. *Civil Rights: The 1960's Freedom Struggle*. Boston: Twayne, 1991. Chronicles the Civil Rights movement, ending with reasons for the decline of that movement.

Epstein, Barbara. *Political Protest and Cultural Revolution: Nonviolent Direct Action in the 1970's and 1980's*. Berkeley: University of California Press, 1991. Case studies, with special attention given to use of nonviolent means of protest and their effectiveness.

Evans, Sarah H. *Born for Liberty: A History of Women in America*. New York: Free Press, 1988. Historical survey of the women's movement.

Feldman, Allen. *Formations of Violence: The Narrative of the Body and Political Terror in Northern Ireland*. Chicago: University of Chicago Press, 1991. Protest movements in comparative studies.

Gamson, William. *The Strategy of Social Protest*. 2d ed. Belmont, Calif.: Wadsworth, 1990. Introduction to unconventional politics, with special attention given to the use of violence.

Hero, Rodney E. *Latinos and the U.S. Political System: Two-Tiered Pluralism*. Philadelphia: Temple University Press, 1992. Mexican American, Cuban American, and

Puerto Rican politics. Historical section on reasons leading to protest among some members of these ethnic groups.

Wasserstrom, Jeffrey N., and Elizabeth J. Perry, eds. *Popular Protest and Political Culture in Modern China: Learning from 1989*. Boulder, Colo.: Westview Press, 1992. Protest movements in comparative studies.

Wei, William. *The Asian American Movement*. Philadelphia: Temple University Press, 1993. An account of Asian American political issues and concerns, strategies employed, and how Asian Americans generally have been led toward cooptation.

David E. Camacho

Cross-References

Activist Politics, p. 7; African American Politics, p. 28; Civil Disobedience, p. 285; Civil Unrest and Rioting, p. 317; Consumer Politics, p. 445; Gay and Lesbian Politics, p. 732; Grassroots Politics, p. 797; Latino Politics, p. 1052; The Left and the Right, p. 1079; Legitimacy, p. 1105; Political Correctness, p. 1441; Political Participation, p. 1479; Political Violence, p. 1539; Woman Suffrage, p. 2141; Women in Politics, p. 2147.

PUBLIC OPINION POLLING

Field of study: Politics

Public opinion polling is the process of surveying a sample group to represent a larger group of people on a variety of topics or issues. Polls are relied on by politicians, businesses, the media, and the public to assess the general will.

Principal terms

ATTITUDE: feeling of like or dislike, agreement or disagreement

BIAS: error in estimations of public opinion most often resulting from faulty sampling procedures or predisposing questions

NONPROBABILITY SAMPLE: sample in which not everyone in the relevant population has a possibility of being included

POPULATION: entire group whose opinions a poll seeks to gauge, whether it is a local community or neighborhood or all the nation's or world's inhabitants

PUBLIC: any group of people sharing common interests either of a general nature or on a specific topic

PUBLIC OPINION: collective expression of attitudes on topics of community interest

RANDOM SAMPLE: type of sample in which everyone in the population has an equal chance of selection

Overview

Public opinion polls are surveys conducted in order to learn the attitudes, beliefs, and opinions of people on various topics. They generally involve listing a sample group to represent a population, interviewing members of the group on topics of interest, and then analyzing and reporting the results. A variety of media now regularly feature polls. Newspapers carry columns written by professional pollsters, such as George Gallup, Jr., Elmo Burns Roper, Jr., or Lou Harris, who describe results of their polls, which may be paid for by the newspapers carrying their columns. In addition, media conduct their own polls, often in a print/broadcast combination. Chief among these combinations are CBS and *The New York Times*, NBC and *The Wall Street Journal*, ABC and *The Washington Post*, and CNN and *USA Today*.

Public opinion polls, or surveys, can be divided into two types: those based on nonprobability samples such as the straw vote polls prevalent from 1824 to 1936 and those based on probability samples in which selection is determined mathematically.

Nonprobability samples are made up of readily accessible respondents. In other words, pollsters ask questions of whoever might be available to answer them. This includes sampling a group of people gathered in one place, such as people shopping in a mall. Volunteer samples consist of people who select themselves because of particular interests or feelings, often negative, about a topic. This includes people who write letters to the editor or who call in to phone polls.

The type of nonprobability sample that was used extensively in election polls from 1936 to 1948 was a purposive or quota sample where respondents are selected on the basis of predetermined percentages.

Initially, public opinion polls were based on volunteer samples, beginning with the straw poll of the presidential election of 1824 published by the *Harrisburg Pennsylvanian*. This represents the first time that public opinion was measured and quantified in some way, although the importance of public opinion and its relation to public policy was discussed by the ancient Greeks. The newspaper correctly predicted that Andrew Jackson would receive the most electoral votes, although John Quincy Adams eventually won the election in the House of Representatives.

Straw polls were widely used to forecast election results until *Literary Digest* wrongly predicted that Alf Landon, the Republican candidate for president in 1936, would defeat Franklin D. Roosevelt. Straw polls were often conducted by partisan newspapers to downgrade the chances and denigrate the qualifications of opposing candidates and to exaggerate the chances of favored candidates. An early method to conduct such polls was simply to estimate attendance at rallies. The greater the attendance, the greater the support. Another method was to print sample ballots in the newspaper. Unfortunately, papers or other interested parties could stuff the collection boxes. Another method was to mail sample ballots to people on various lists. This prevented ballot stuffing but presented difficulties regarding accurate polling because of the potential bias in the lists and the volunteer aspect of returning the ballot. A third method, and one often found to be accurate when sufficient numbers were included, was to have interviewers solicit statements about voting preferences from members of the community. This was the precursor of the man-in-the-street interviews later used to represent public opinion.

The most famous, and infamous, straw poll was that conducted by *Literary Digest*. The *Digest* was a popular weekly news magazine that began conducting straw polls in 1916 as part of a strategy to increase circulation. In 1920, the magazine mailed more than eleven million ballots on which readers might indicate preferences for potential presidential candidates. In 1932, twenty million ballots were mailed, and although state returns were found to have systematically overestimated the Republican vote in earlier elections, the *Digest* nevertheless predicted the Roosevelt victory to within half a percentage point.

Professional pollsters such as George Gallup began using quota samples during the 1936 election. People were defined in terms of categories believed to be relevant to the topic of interest, such as political party, likelihood to vote, and demographic characteristics such as income, gender, educational level, occupation, and age. Interviewers then selected respondents who met the predetermined categories until the quota for that category was met.

Quota samples were widely used thereafter until the fateful election of 1948. In that election, all the major pollsters incorrectly predicted that Thomas Dewey would defeat Harry S Truman for president. The major pollsters then switched to probability sampling. All probability sampling is characterized by every member of the relevant population having an equal chance of being selected and by determining mathematically who is selected for questioning.

Pollsters often use a systematic sample. The first person polled is selected randomly, and then every second, or third, or fourth person is selected according to a system. Multistage sampling is a type of cluster sampling that involves selecting individual households or people within the household, rather than selecting groups as in quota sampling. In a four-stage sequence common to national polls, a specific geographic area, such as a county, is selected, then a smaller area is selected such as a group of blocks, then an individual block is selected and finally the household or individual is selected. Polls conducted in this way have been found to be extremely accurate.

Once the sample is selected, individuals have to be interviewed. Questionnaires can be administered by mail, by phone, or through personal interviews. Generally, costs increase moving from mail to personal interviews. On the other hand, the number of people who take the survey decreases in the opposite order. Although mail surveys can have an adequate response rate under special circumstances, they are generally not considered a reliable technique for representing a diverse population and hence are considered suspect as a representation of a larger population. Telephone surveys are often the method of choice because they can be completed quickly and are relatively inexpensive. Person-to-person interviews have the advantages of allowing additional, more complicated questions, and helping ensure the correct person is responding. They are, however, far more expensive to perform.

The poll's questions can be open-ended, in which case respondents provide answers in their own words, or close-ended, in which case respondents select an answer from one or more provided choices. The key in all questionnaire construction is to ensure that the questions (and answers, if they are provided) are not biased so that respondents are led to favor one answer over another. Bias can be the result of question wording or placement of the question. Asking questions that put one candidate in a negative light and then asking voters whom they favor in the election is an example. It might work like this: "Do you think Jones is guilty of the criminal charges he is facing?" "Are you voting for Jones?" Reputable pollsters pretest their questions and the questions' placement to guard against unforeseen bias.

Polls are quantified almost as quickly as the data are entered into a computer. Most polls simply report the frequencies of respondents' answering questions a particular way: how many favor a particular candidate or how strongly they favor a particular issue. These results can be analyzed according to demographic variables such as age, education, ethnic group, gender, and income, or they may be reported as part of a trend so that changes over time can be observed.

Applications

Most polls are conducted for private clients who are outside the political arena. Elmo Burns Roper got his start as a clock salesman who began surveying potential customers to get a better idea of which lines would sell. George Gallup began his work by measuring newspaper readership. While pollsters do most of their work with marketing surveys, polls done for candidates and on elections have attracted the most scrutiny. Election polls afford the opportunity of testing the validity of results.

In 1936, George Gallup, a marketing and newspaper researcher who had formed the American Institute of Public Opinion (the Gallup Poll) a year earlier, brashly predicted that his poll results would be more accurate than the famed *Literary Digest* poll. He was aware of the bias in the *Digest* poll resulting from sampling from lists of subscribers, telephone owners, and recent automobile purchasers—all people then more likely to be Republican. Gallup received national recognition after the success of his predictions, and public opinion polling began the process of becoming scientific. *Literary Digest* went out of business the following year.

In 1959, John F. Kennedy hired Lou Harris and Associates to conduct large-scale surveys in order to enhance the effectiveness of his candidacy for president. Harris proceeded to interview more people across the United States than had ever been done by a political analyst. For the Wisconsin primary alone, Harris interviewed some 23,000 people in various polls. Although Kennedy won the primary, it came out that his support was dominant in Roman Catholic districts while his opponent, Hubert Humphrey, won the predominantly Protestant districts. When Kennedy's support in West Virginia started to decline as voters became aware of his Catholicism, Harris strongly urged the campaign to face the issue directly. Kennedy did so and won the West Virginia primary. Many analysts, including Lou Harris, believed that the advice Kennedy got from the Harris polls was instrumental in winning the election. All major candidates for the presidency since then have hired polling firms to provide advice during the campaign.

Presidential elections since 1952 have generally been forecast correctly within two or three percentage points by major pollsters. The elections of 1968 and 1976 were declared too close to call and in 1980 pollsters correctly predicted the winner but by a much closer margin than the actual result. Polls taken five or more days before the election tend to be much less accurate in forecasting the actual vote. To ensure the relevant (that is, the voting) population is represented in election polls, up to a dozen questions are asked each person polled to gauge accurately whether the person will actually vote.

The likelihood of a particular person being selected for a probability sample is the number of people in the sample divided by the number of people in the population. For a typical national Gallup poll, which first selects households and then people within the household, this would be 1,500 (the number of people in the sample) divided by 93 million (the number of households in the country) or one out of 167,000. Selecting such a small percentage of people randomly is extremely expensive, so polls that are not probability dependent remain common, even if they are lacking in accuracy.

One such poll which attracted considerable attention was conducted by Sharon Hite in 1976 and published as a book, *The Hite Report*. Among other controversial findings, Hite said that 70 percent of women married more than five years were having an extramarital affair, 84 percent were not satisfied emotionally with their relationship, and 78 percent said they were treated as equals only sporadically. She had distributed 100,000 questionnaires, of which some 3,000 were returned, a low response rate of 3 percent.

Although such a sample can provide useful insights, it cannot be said with any confidence to represent the population at large. This was ultimately shown by an ABC/*Washington Post* survey based on a national probability sample of women, which found that only 6 percent said they were having an affair, 93 percent were satisfied with their relationship, and 81 percent were treated as equals in their relationship most of the time.

Evaluation of the validity of a poll depends on several factors. These factors should be reported by the media along with poll results. The factors are: who sponsored the poll, the exact wording of the questions, the sampling procedure (random, systematic, quota, call-ins), the sample size, completion rate, and associated sampling error (plus or minus amounts by which responses can validly vary), the data-gathering method used (personal, telephone), and the date of the survey. People can then have a basis for determining how seriously to take the poll.

Context

Private polling firms, universities, and government agencies conduct polls on topics ranging from candidate preferences to opinions on current issues to inclinations to buy a particular product to preferences about a particular television program. Politicians now routinely commission polls to track campaigns. Politicians also make campaign decisions based on poll results. Government agencies conduct polls to monitor the effectiveness of their programs. Universities use polls to research the effects of various topics on the setting of agendas and on voting decisions.

The media subsidize polls conducted by private firms to keep their audiences informed and to keep informed of their audiences. Network political polling began in earnest after the 1972 presidential election. *The New York Times* began conducting its own poll in 1975. Single major sources of information, such as *The New York Times*, base hundreds of stories on poll results during the course of a year. Polls are not only used routinely to add factual depth to a story, but also sometimes become the story.

Some concern for public opinion is evident in most political regimes. Concern is especially evident in democracies, in which government is dependent on the will of the public. Jean-Jacques Rousseau, an eighteenth century French philosopher, argued that all laws are based on public opinion. Alexis de Tocqueville, a nineteenth century Frenchman who traveled extensively in the United States, warned of the tyranny of the majority if government policy were to result solely from public opinion. Polling techniques have become extremely sophisticated, but it is still not clear what the proper role of polls should be. All the major media regularly report poll results. Polls are used both to assess and, less reassuringly, to mold public opinion. Polls may determine the quality of leadership in the country by influencing elections. Reporting polls may take precedence over analyzing issues. Polls, for better and for worse, have established themselves as an integral part of the public opinion process.

Bibliography

Asher, Herbert. *Polling and the Public: What Every Citizen Should Know.* 2d ed. Washington, D.C.: Congressional Quarterly Press, 1992. Discusses problems in conducting polls, including difficulties in measuring people's attitudes. Excellent cartoons on polls.

Bradburn, Norman M., and Seymour Sudman. *Polls and Surveys.* San Francisco: Jossey-Bass, 1988. History and explanation of how polls are conducted, with a particularly fine chapter on organizations that conduct polls.

Cantril, Albert H., ed. *Polling on the Issues.* Cabin John, Md.: Seven Locks Press, 1980. Major pollsters, including George Gallup, Elmo Burns Roper, Jr., Warren Mitofsky, Peter Hart, and Patrick Caddell discuss the impact of polls on voting in a panel discussion format.

Crespi, Irving. *Public Opinion, Polls, and Democracy.* Boulder, Colo.: Westview Press, 1989. Relying on twenty years' experience with the Gallup organization, Crespi provides insights on conducting polls properly, with especially useful analysis of question wording and the contribution of polling to the public debate.

Herbst, Susan. *Numbered Voices.* Chicago: University of Chicago Press, 1993. Readable history of polling with an emphasis on Max Weber's view that quantification is a means of representing rationality.

Lavrakas, Paul J., and Jack K. Holley. *Polling and Presidential Election Coverage.* Newbury Park, Calif.: Sage Publications, 1991. Prominent pollsters describe the 1988 Bush-Dukakis election campaign and how the national media used poll results.

Mann, Thomas E., and Gary R. Orren, eds. *Media Polls in American Politics.* Washington, D.C.: Brookings Institution, 1992. The editors include chapters on the proliferation of polls, the influence of technology on the polling process, and the impact of polls on the public, politicians, and the democratic process.

Moore, David W. *The Superpollsters: How They Measure and Manipulate Public Opinion in America.* New York: Four Walls Eight Windows, 1992. Biographical history of the people who developed the industry.

Nieburg, H. L. *Public Opinion: Tracking and Targeting.* New York: Praeger, 1984. Covers the essentials of polling techniques but is at its best discussing the implications of polling in a democratic society.

Roger D. Haney

Cross-References

PUBLIC POLICY

Field of study: Functions of government

Public policy is an abstract concept that describes the formal expression of intention by a governmental unit through whose written documents and actions it is communicated. Public policy indicates what beliefs and values are currently accepted and important to each governmental unit.

Principal terms

AGENDA SETTING: first phase of policy process, determines what issues are important

FORMULATION: production of the written documents that identify intentions and plans for governmental action

IMPLEMENTATION: government execution of formal policy

INTEREST GROUP: people with shared beliefs in a particular policy issue

ISSUE NETWORK: people and organizations who share interest in a particular policy issue

POLICY ENTREPRENEUR: person who applies resources to the development of a particular policy

PUBLIC POLICYMAKER: any elected or appointed government official with authority to create policy

Overview

Policy, an expression of intentions and goals, can be classified according to both initiators and fields. For example, if the initiator is a corporation, the policy is a corporate policy. If the initiator is a legitimate authorized governmental unit, the policy is a public policy. To the extent that the intentions and goals of policymakers match those of the people governed, public policy will reflect the views of the populace. If there are differences, public policy may reflect only the views of either the policymaker or the populace. Public policy is classified under such general headings as economy, environment, education, technology, and social policies.

Supranational organizations such as the United Nations, the North Atlantic Treaty Organization, the European Economic Community, the Organization of American States, and the Organization of Petroleum Exporting Countries articulate public policies pertaining to their organizational purposes. If these organizations can exert sufficient economic, military, social, or other power, both member and nonmember nations will support their policies. The public policies of supranational organizations are influenced by the prevailing distribution of power within the world, as well as by the factors related to each organization's primary purposes.

The public policies of individual nations depend on each nation's system of government and current philosophy. Nations typically have either unitary or federal systems of government. Within a unitary system, all local and regional governments are subordinate to a central government. In a federal system, local and regional governments are not fully subordinate to a central government. Public policy does not officially vary among the levels of government in unitary systems as it might in federal systems. A nation's current philosophy of government, or the accepted belief concerning who has a right to participate in government, affects all phases of a nation's policy-making process.

In the United States, policy-making processes fall into four general phases: agenda setting, formulation, implementation, and evaluation. Agenda setting determines what issues are important. Issues become important to governmental units through the efforts of lobbyists, special interest groups, the media, individuals, policy entrepreneurs, issue networks, and current economic, political, social, and natural events.

The formulation phase determines when one or more of the government units with legitimate authority for an issue will create or change formal written documents that deal with it. The written document can take many forms depending on the level of government, branch of government, and perceived importance of the issue.

The Congress, federal court system, and executive branch (president, councils, commissions, boards, agencies, and departments) are the three policy-making bodies at the federal level. Policy-making instruments consist of congressional legislation and appropriations, the decisions of the courts, and such executive branch actions as orders, regulations, rules, procedures, organizations, positions, and direct actions. State legislative bodies, state court systems, and the state executive branches (governors and state organizations) use similar policy-making instruments to create public policy at the state level. Public policy at the local level is also established by the legislative, judicial, and executive branches of local and regional governments and by the government units for special districts, such as schools and water.

Once public policy articulating intentions and goals exists in a formal written document, the implementation phase begins. From the international to the local levels, individual officers put policies into practice, thereby determining which goals are actually achieved. For implementation to be uniform and successful, the practical aspects of implementation must be considered in the formulation phase.

Public policy processes enter the evaluation phase when sufficient time elapses after implementation to enable assessment of a policy. There are several reasons why the espoused goals of a public policy may not be realized. For example, the assumptions about human behavior or the issues on which a policy is founded may be erroneous. Alternatively, lack of training or mistakes made by officials responsible for implementing a policy may obstruct proper implementation.

The goals of a policy may be stated clearly or may conflict with the goals of other policies that are more popular or easier to achieve. Funds sufficient to implement the policy successfully may not be available or may not be allocated by the appropriate legislative body. Public or private organizations, interest groups, or individuals oppose a policy and block its implementation. Finally, the factors influencing the issue may change, making the policy undesirable.

Official evaluation of public policies is often conducted by the implementing organizations at the request of the legislative bodies with oversight responsibilities. In addition, academicians in political science, public administration, and the discipline most concerned with each policy (such as water resources for water policies) study, evaluate, and publish research evaluating both public policy in general and specific policies.

Applications

Efforts to conserve wildlife predate the modern era. In the United States, the public policy of wildlife conservation was evident in the laws that were passed in the colonies as early as the 1600's. Although the early laws were largely ignored, the public effort became more successful in the 1800's through the passage and enforcement of state game laws and the federal creation of national parks, forests, and wildlife refuges.

Since 1945, international wildlife conservation has been promoted through organizations within the United Nations. Four organizations have participated in establishing wildlife conservation programs: the Food and Agriculture Organization, the U.N. Educational, Scientific, and Cultural Organization (UNESCO), the International Union for the Conservation of Nature and Natural Resources, and the World Wildlife Fund. National parks, wildlife reserves, and protected areas have been established around the world and species that were once nearing extinction have been identified, monitored, and enabled to survive.

In the United States, the Endangered Species Act was passed by Congress in 1973. Originally, the act limited the hunting, collection, and threatening of rare species. It prevented federal construction in the habitat of rare species. The law was later amended to exclude the construction of specified federal projects.

Under this law, the American bald eagle was listed as endangered in 1978. Adult nesting pairs in the forty-eight contiguous states numbered about 791 at that time. The protection afforded by the endangered listing and the 1972 banning of the pesticide dichloro-diphenyl-trichloroethane (DDT), which was harmful to the reproduction of many species, are credited with the eagle's comeback. After the number of adult bald eagle nesting pairs exceeded four thousand in 1993, the bald eagle was reclassified as a "threatened" species. The eagle's resurgence is an example of a successful wildlife conservation policy.

Although a public policy may be successful, the mechanisms responsible for its success may be difficult to maintain. For example, the restrictions in the Endangered Species Act on the use of private property by owners have been successfully challenged in federal courts. In addition, attempts have been made to reduce the funds available to the Department of the Interior to enforce this law.

By contrast, public policy concerning poverty provides an example of an unsuccessful social policy. Poverty is the condition of living below the standard considered adequate by a community. Since ancient times, conventional wisdom had been that there is personal responsibility for poverty. Because of this belief, government was not considered to be the part of society that should take a leading or even active role in dealing with poverty.

The prevailing view had been that charity was the sole responsibility of friends, relatives, and religious and private organizations. A few exceptions to this view occurred. For example, Great Britain created a system to provide some funds for the poor through local government units called parishes in 1601, and the United States provided some assistance for disabled veterans and surviving dependents of soldiers killed in action during the Civil War.

The worldwide economic slump in the 1930's, known as the Great Depression, changed conventional wisdom concerning poverty. After causes for poverty other than personal responsibility were widely acknowledged, dramatic changes in public policy ensued. Nations around the world passed laws to create public assistance programs funded by their governments. In the United States, the Social Security Act was passed in 1935 that became the foundation for later public assistance programs.

In the United States, when a household in providing its basic needs spends more than one third of its total income for food, that total income level is defined by the federal government as poverty. This income level is adjusted depending on marital status, number of children, age, and the current cost of living. Those who have incomes at or below this government calculated amount are offered assistance of six types: job opportunities, education and training, services, housing, access to food, and money.

In the enabling legislation in the 1930's, public assistance for able-bodied individuals was intended to be a temporary measure. The belief was that the social stigma of receiving money from the government would be sufficient to prevent individuals from becoming permanently dependent on government funds. Contrary to expectations, it became common in the 1990's for three and four successive generations within one family to receive public assistance.

As early as 1965, a rise in illegitimacy indicated that public welfare policy was profoundly affecting the family structure of inner-city minorities. By 1990, only 37 percent of inner-city African American children under the age of six were living within married-couple families. In 1964, 75 percent of black inner-city children lived in married-couple families. In 1992, one in seven American children were receiving welfare, with approximately two thousand more being added each day. Although these trends indicated a failure in public social policies designed to alleviate poverty, it was politically unpopular to initiate change when the trends were identified.

To finance modern warfare, the U.S. government spent considerably more money than it collected in taxes and revenues. The national debt rose sharply as a result, requiring that a large portion of federal revenue be used to pay the interest to service the debt. As a result of this financial pressure in the late 1970's, 1980's, and 1990's, the federal government was forced to reevaluate the money it was spending on all other activities. This closer scrutiny focused attention on public assistance programs and their effectiveness. The need to reduce all government spending made it more politically popular to acknowledge the ineffectiveness of existing public assistance programs in eliminating poverty. The scrutiny did not, however, result in a new consensus about what the public policy of government should be or will be concerning poverty.

Context

Public administration, a relatively young academic discipline, asserts that the 1887 publication of the essay "A Study in Administration" by future president Woodrow Wilson marked its beginning. Within universities in the United States, public administration appeared as a subfield of political science in the early 1900's. Opposition within political science to the development of public administration within political science surfaced as early as 1930 and gained strength during the 1950's and 1960's.

Concurrently with the emergence of public administration as a field of study on par with political science and the advent of separate academic departments of public administration, the 1960's marked the appearance of public policy as a subfield of study within political science. Public policy applies the theoretical studies of government to public affairs. While nomenclature does not necessarily preclude scholarship of any particular type within a discipline, the distinction here is similar to the distinction between theoretical physics and engineering physics. The former focuses on theory and the latter on application. Similarly, political science focuses on theory and public policy on application. The subfield of public policy thus filled a void created by the departure of the applied discipline of public administration from political science.

The study of public policy enables understanding and interpretation of the actions of governments. Effective participation in the formulation and implementation of public policy is also facilitated by this study. Several approaches to the study of public policy exist. One approach concerns identification of the principal participants in policy formulation. How policy is developed, in this approach, is seen as a direct result of who participates. Six models of policy-making (elite/mass, group, systems, institutionalist, neoinstitutionalist, and organized anarchy) are examples of this approach. For example, the elite/mass model asserts that public administrators are an elite group who—because of apathy and lack of information by the populace—create policy with the intent of preserving the status quo and pass it downward to a passive mass of people.

Another approach to the study of public policy focuses on how to formulate an effective public policy. Three models (incrementalist, rationalist, and strategic planning) attempt to aid the policymaker. The incrementalist perspective suggests that the safest course to follow is to limit policy choices to those that make the slightest changes to existing policies. The rationalist perspective describes an ideal process including an exhaustive search and evaluation of alternatives and selection and implementation of an optimal policy. The strategic planning perspective advocates development, prioritization, and communication of organizational objectives to make the basis for policy and decision making uniform.

An additional approach to public policy categorizes the intentions of public policy. Regulatory, distributive, redistributive, and constituent are the four types of commonly recognized intentions. Regulatory policy places limits on activities to protect the public. Distributive policy broadly distributes the pooled resources of the nation. Redistributive policy assigns the revenues collected from one group to the use of another group. Constituent policy is for the general benefit of the people or the government.

A final approach to public policy is concerned with changes in particular policies over time. If policies do not change, they are considered static in this approach. Cyclical policies alternate between two policy options. Policies displaying linear progress change incrementally over time. Discontinuous policies are those characterized by abrupt shifts, involving new objectives and programs.

Bibliography

Cartledge, Bryan, ed. *Energy and the Environment*. New York: Oxford University Press, 1993. Thorough review of international issues involved in conflicts among energy policy, economic policy, and environmental policy.

Dye, Thomas, and Virginia Gray, eds. *The Determinants of Public Policy*. Lexington, Mass.: Lexington Books, 1980. Overview of approaches to the study of public policy discusses examples of public policy at the federal, state, and local levels of government.

Gillroy, John Martin, and Maurice Wade, eds. *The Moral Dimensions of Public Policy Choice: Beyond the Market Paradigm*. Pittsburgh, Pa.: University of Pittsburgh Press, 1992. Compilation of essays examining the philosophical bases for public policy. Demonstrates the breadth of public policy literature.

Gordon, George J. *Public Administration in America*. 4th ed. New York: St. Martin's Press, 1992. A chapter on public policy describes the policy-making process, emphasizing governmental intentions and the complexity of policy-making mechanisms.

Henry, Nicholas. *Public Administration and Public Affairs*. 6th ed. Englewood Cliffs, N.J.: Prentice Hall, 1995. Chapter on public policy describes the variety of approaches to the study and improvement of public policy. Extensive citations of historical public policy literature.

Irwin, Steven. *Technology Policy and America's Future*. New York: St. Martin's Press, 1993. Excellent coverage of the rationale for government involvement in a new area of policy-making, technology policy.

Jones, Charles. *An Introduction to the Study of Public Policy*. 3d ed. Monterey, Calif.: Brooks/Cole, 1984. Primer on the complex variety and changeable nature of public policy. Examines government policymakers, the influence of organizations, and individuals outside of government who influence the policy process.

Lowry, William. *The Capacity for Wonder*. Washington, D.C.: Brookings Institution, 1994. Focusing on the preservation of America's national parks, this book provides insight into how the interplay of politics, bureaucracy, and existing policies make effective policy-making a challenge.

Rabin, Robert, ed. *Smoking Policy*. New York: Oxford University Press, 1993. Addresses the interaction between public attitudes and governmental action in regard to the politics of regulatory enactment and enforcement of tobacco advertising, cigarette litigation, and strategies of insurers and employers.

Rose, Richard, ed. *The Dynamics of Public Policy: A Comparative Analysis.* Beverly Hills, Calif.: Sage Publications, 1976. Contains succinct discussion of models of public policy and numerous comparisons of the public policies of developed nations.

Santa Falcone

Cross-References

Administrative Procedures in U.S. Government, p. 14; Alliances, p. 47; The Arts and Government, p. 101; Bureaucracy, p. 164; Elected Versus Appointed Offices in the United States, p. 572; Executive Functions in U.S. Government, p. 636; The Family and Politics in the United States, p. 649; Federal Mandates, p. 662; Government Roles, p. 778; Intergovernmental Relations, p. 942; Iron Triangles, p. 981; Legislative Functions of Government, p. 1098; Policy Development and Implementation, p. 1414; Political Science, p. 1532; Public Opinion Polling, p. 1627; United Nations, p. 2045.

PUBLIC UTILITIES

Field of study: Functions of government

Public utilities are services considered so basic and important that they belong to the public trust; therefore, they are subject to considerable government regulation if privately owned. Some public utilities are publicly owned. Public utilities include electric, natural gas, telephone, water, and sewer services.

Principal terms
    CERTIFICATE OF PUBLIC CONVENIENCE AND NECESSITY: construction permit certifying the need for new facilities
    MONOPOLY: provision of goods or services in the absence of competition by one or a small number of producers
    PUBLIC UTILITIES COMMISSION: state government body with regulatory powers over public utilities

Overview

A public utility is a service of fundamental importance to the community or locality served, usually provided within a specified territory through a single governmental or business organization, without direct competition. Government is concerned with the provision of such public utilities as electricity, natural gas, telecommunications, transportation, water, and sewer services because they are essential to practically all industry, business, and community life.

In most countries, public utility services are considered to be so essential to community life that they are provided directly and exclusively by government. In the United States, a mixed pattern of some government and some private ownership has developed over time. Where private ownership is allowed, it is generally accompanied by government regulation.

Public utilities are regulated by state commissions in all fifty states and the District of Columbia. Typically, state legislation provides authority for a state commission of three or more persons to set rates charged consumers, supervise standards of service, regulate the issuance of securities, and permit entry or expansion of facilities in markets within the state.

State commission jurisdiction generally applies to all privately owned firms. In many states, regulation is also applied to utilities owned by consumers (for example, rural electric cooperatives), and in a few states it may be asserted over activities of public municipal utility departments or over subdivisions of the state operating outside municipal boundaries. The federal government also regulates some rates, operations, and financial activities of public utilities that engage in interstate commerce.

The rationale for public utility regulation is based on the notion that a public service may be provided by either governmental or nongovernmental means, provided that communities and consumers are protected from excessive rates, poor service, or other abuses resulting from monopoly. Economist John Bauer has observed that utilities are distinguished from other businesses by the fact that their facilities are located extensively in the streets, highways, and other public places. As a practical matter, it would inconvenience the community if two or more distribution networks for the same service were located in the same area.

Furthermore, there are often financial advantages in serving an entire municipality, or larger service territory, with a single operating system. The large financial investment required for plant and distribution equipment makes it desirable to serve densely populated areas in their entirety. Duplication of facilities increases costs and divides available business, reducing the profits and financial stability of the producers.

According to economist James C. Bonbright, there was for a long period a general consensus among economists that the primary feature of public utility enterprise is to be found in a technology of production and transmission, which almost inevitably leads to a monopoly of the market for service. Public utility regulation, if chosen in preference to outright public ownership, is therefore a substitute for competition.

The familiar statement that a public utility is a "natural monopoly" means this type of business cannot be operated economically unless it enjoys a monopoly of its market. The disadvantages of direct competition in these circumstances are so substantial it is believed likely to lead to bankruptcy of the competitors. Even if competition is long-lived, it is wasteful of resources because it entails unnecessary duplication of equipment, such as power lines, substations, and underground pipes.

Thus, preventing unnecessary duplication of both physical facilities and financial investments is generally held to be fundamental in the regulation of public utilities and in the limiting of competition between them. William K. Jones, in an article in Columbia Law Review, suggests this view was not universally held, because California and a few other states took the position before 1920 that a threat of new competition could be used as a means to stimulate existing utilities to achieve efficiencies and charge reasonable rates.

To prevent unnecessary duplication, it is necessary to control the entry of new firms and the expansion of existing ones in available markets. Thus, construction of new facilities by public utilities generally may not be undertaken without a permit, often called a "certificate of public convenience and necessity," from a government commission. The certificate of public convenience and necessity is a regulatory device by which a government may exclude otherwise qualified applicants from a market if, in the judgment of the regulatory commission, the addition of more service providers would have no beneficial effect, or might ultimately have a detrimental effect, on rates charged to consumers. The certificate thus was conceived as an instrument to ensure reasonable rates to consumers for public utility services. It also serves to protect stockholders from the risks of bankruptcy that might result from competition.

Certification of construction of new facilities is an activity that is central to government regulation of investor-owned public utilities. Each of a number of alternative sites has a unique mix of financial, technical engineering, social, economic, and environmental consequences. The selection of one implies a preference for one set of costs and benefits over others.

Public utilities subject to state government regulation in the United States included approximately 1,640 electric utilities, 1,060 natural gas utilities, 560 combined natural gas, electric, and petroleum pipeline utilities, 8,300 water and sewer utilities, 20,860 telecommunications firms (telephone, cellular phone, mobile radio, paging, cable television, telegraph, and others), and about 37,400 motor carriers in 1990.

Among public utilities, electric utilities are the most extensive in geographic coverage, and the largest in both number of customers and annual revenues. Provision of electric service is the most capital-intensive industry in the country, borrowing funds in capital markets in amounts second only to the United States government. Each year, coal and oil-fired electric generating stations put more air pollutants into the atmosphere than any other industry.

Construction of electric power plants is big business, often creating hundreds or thousands of jobs for each multiyear project, increasing state income tax and local property tax bases, and stimulating considerable secondary or indirect business activity in the vicinity of construction. Capital expenditures by the electric utility industry in the 1980's were often in excess of $40 billion per year nationwide for generation, transmission, distribution, and associated facilities.

Electric utility generation and distribution facilities are physically connected by transmission lines in three large networks that blanket most of the North American continent. One network covers the eleven adjacent western states and parts of Nebraska, South Dakota, Texas, and two Canadian provinces, serving slightly more than half the area of the United States. A second network serves most of Texas, with no interstate connections. A third regional network covers the remainder of the eastern United States and four Canadian provinces. Several connections allow limited exchange of electric power between the large eastern and western networks. Total installed summer generating capability in the United States was 685,091 megawatts in 1990, the largest of any country.

Few factors in the development of electric power are limited to the boundaries of one state. The basic energy resources—coal, oil, gas, uranium—often originate, must be processed, or are converted to electric power in states other than those in which the electricity is consumed. Water for hydroelectric power generation and steam plant cooling almost invariably involves interstate, and often international, interests.

Electric utilities often find it necessary to secure financing and engineering design services in states other than those in which new facilities are to be constructed. They frequently must contract with construction firms and equipment suppliers, and draw on labor pools located in surrounding states. Air and water pollution, as well as electricity, often travel across state lines. Many large generating projects serve consumers in several states. For example, the coal-fired Missouri Basin Power Project Laramie River Station near Wheatland, Wyoming, serves consumers in Montana, Wyoming, Colorado, North Dakota, South Dakota, and Nebraska. The regional dimensions of electric utility operations often exceed the geographic jurisdiction of state commissions.

Ownership of generation, transmission, and distribution facilities in these networks is divided between investor-owned firms (73 percent), municipalities and state governments or their subdivisions (10 percent); national government agencies (8 percent); rural electric cooperatives (3 percent); and nonutility generators, for example, chemical, paper, mining, petroleum refining and other industrial sources (about 6 percent).

Development of connections between previously separate electric power systems was fostered by both private initiative and public policy to realize the benefits that come from coordinated system planning and operations. Coordination over a wide geographic area may minimize operating costs and capital expenditures for plant construction, enhance system stability and recovery capabilities during emergency operating conditions, and provide opportunities to minimize total construction. This coordination enables construction of facilities with minimum adverse environmental impact. The extent to which these benefits are realized, however, depends upon the degree of actual coordination between utilities, which has often been low.

Applications

The Colorado Public Utilities Commission is typical of state commissions regulating electric utilities. It has broad responsibilities for setting rates charged to consumers, supervising standards of service, specifying utility accounting systems, allowing or disallowing the issuance of securities, and issuing certificates of public convenience and necessity. The Colorado commission consists of three members appointed by the governor, with consent of the state senate, for staggered terms of six years.

In 1990, the number of utilities regulated by the Colorado commission was 219, of which forty-six provided electric service. These included two investor-owned firms, twenty-eight rural electric cooperatives, sixteen municipal electric organizations, and one combined gas and electric utility. The commission also had jurisdiction over eleven natural gas, thirty telecommunications, six water and sewer utilities, and 125 motor carriers.

The Colorado commission has exclusive regulatory jurisdiction over activities of all investor-owned electric utilities and all rural electric cooperatives within the state. State constitutional and statutory provisions exempt municipally owned utilities doing business within their territorial boundaries from the commission's regulatory authority. Municipally owned utilities furnishing service to customers beyond municipal boundaries, however, are subject to Colorado commission jurisdiction, but only over that portion of service provided outside the boundaries.

Construction of new electric power facilities prior to the Colorado commission's issuance of a certificate of public convenience and necessity is expressly prohibited by statute. In determining whether a certificate shall be granted, the Colorado commission must consider and avoid duplication of service. The applicant must therefore make an affirmative showing that existing sources of electric power will be inadequate to serve anticipated demand.

In addition to state commissions, several other offices of local, state, and national government have regulatory jurisdiction over different aspects of electric utility operations, depending on their scope, location of facilities, and technologies utilized.

These include the Federal Energy Regulatory Commission (construction of hydroelectric generators on navigable streams and wholesale sales of electricity in interstate commerce), the Nuclear Regulatory Commission (design, safety, and construction of nuclear reactors), and the Securities and Exchange Commission (financial transactions of firms doing interstate business).

More than half of the states have special procedures, often administered by agencies separate from state commissions, regulating the location and land use features of new electric facilities, which may also be regulated by local zoning and building code requirements. State and national public land management agencies have authority to grant or deny permits for facilities located on lands within their jurisdiction. Considerable overlap and duplication of jurisdiction is therefore a fact of life in government regulation of electric utilities.

Context

Requirements for a certificate of public convenience and necessity were first applied in regulation of railroads in 1869, later to gas and electric distribution and telecommunications. Central station electric power generation became commercially feasible in 1882. Early regulation of electric utilities was accomplished by municipal grants of franchises for specific territories when competition arose among local firms. It was not until the early 1900's that perceived problems appeared to require statewide solutions, such as creation of state commissions.

Increases in electric generation and transmission capacity gradually moved electric supply beyond the neighborhood level where it began making possible the operation of multistate networks of large-scale electric power facilities. The largest generating unit in 1900 was 1.5 megawatts as compared to 1,300 megawatts in the 1990's. Maximum transmission capacity was 60 kilovolts in 1901, increasing to 1,000 kilovolts in the 1990's.

Legislation requiring government approval of new construction has usually been expressed in ambiguous language, often providing little more guidance to regulators than that proposed facilities "serve the public convenience and necessity." This has been interpreted to involve balancing competing interests of producers and investors, several classes of residential and commercial consumers (some located in distant states), environmentalists, antinuclear activists, Native Americans, and any other citizens who can meet the legal requirements to participate in commission proceedings.

Although state commission legislation reveals a general bias towards economic growth and development, it typically does not establish clear priority between the multiple objectives to be served by regulation. Thus, considerable discretion, and little guidance concerning its exercise, are provided to state commissions in setting rates and certifying construction of new generating capacity. Consequently, regulatory proceedings concerning rates and new construction have often been politically contentious.

In the 1980's, slower growth in demand for electricity than in earlier periods and availability of excess generating capacity above immediate needs slowed the rate of construction of new plants. More than half the state regulatory commissions adopted least-cost planning methods during rate setting and review of new construction plans. Least-cost planning requires utilities to consider renewable resources technologies such as wind and solar power, nonutility generation such as conservation, along with conventional power plants powered by coal, natural gas, oil, and nuclear fuels.

To the extent this assisted utilities in identifying and implementing energy conservation measures and other new technologies, it also required less new construction of conventional power plants. The result was a shift in patterns of ownership within the industry, with increased entry by nonutility generators. In 1986, utilities constructed 80 percent of net additions to total generating capacity, but by 1990, nonutilities were building more than half of net capacity additions.

This shift was fostered by enactment of two national policies which deviated from the historical concept of public utilities as regulated monopolies.

The Public Utilities Regulatory Policy Act of 1978 requires utilities to purchase all electricity offered for sale by nonutility generators, providing them with guaranteed markets for production. The Energy Policy Act of 1992 increased authority of the Federal Energy Regulatory Commission to require utilities to provide access to their transmission facilities to nonutilities. This means that, in many circumstances, nonutilities cannot be prevented from selling electricity to consumers across a competing utility's own transmission lines. Many nonutility generators are also exempt from rate regulation by state commissions because they have no distribution facilities of their own and sell electric power only in wholesale markets, not directly to retail consumers.

Similar trends toward greater reliance on competition and less reliance on economic regulation of public utilities were evident in deregulation of the airlines industry and of wellhead prices of natural gas in the 1970's. Nevertheless, trends toward greater regulation of some public utilities and other industries were evident in the same period in areas concerning environmental protection (air and water pollution, hazardous chemicals, and radioactive waste) and consumer safety.

Consequently, it would be difficult to support the assertion that government functions concerning public utilities have moved significantly away from regulation toward increased reliance on competition. It may be more accurate to say government regulation of public utilities has been used more selectively to encourage, rather than as a substitute for, competition.

Bibliography

Bauer, John. *Transforming Public Utility Regulation*. New York: Harper & Row, 1950. Influential examination of public utility regulation by state commissions, with suggestions for reform, some of which have been implemented.

Bernstein, Marver H. *Regulating Business by Independent Commission*. Princeton, N.J.: Princeton University Press, 1955. Offers a life-cycle theory of regulatory behavior in which commissions begin with advocacy of consumer protection but eventually reach a debilitative state in which they either seek to protect the status quo or are "captured" by the regulated industry. This classic statement of capture theory suggests that business interests control a disproportionate share of political resources.

Bonbright, James C. *Principles of Public Utility Rates*. New York: Columbia University Press, 1961. Explains the origins of regulation of public utilities, and the role of rate setting in protecting consumers. Written in plain language.

Jones, William K. "Origins of the Certificate of Public Convenience and Necessity: Developments in the States, 1870-1920." *Columbia Law Review* 79 (1978): 426-516. Authoritative treatment of the use of permits by state commissions regulating public utilities.

Michael S. Hamilton

Cross-References

Business and Government, p. 177; Capitalism, p. 197; Clientelism, p. 337; Commerce Regulation, p. 357; Consumer Politics, p. 445; Energy Management, p. 604; Environmental Protection, p. 617; Government Agencies, p. 765; Government Powers, p. 772; Government Roles, p. 778; Industrialization, p. 916; Postal Service, p. 1563; Public Works, p. 1647; Regulatory Agencies in the United States, p. 1678; State and Local Government, p. 1885.

PUBLIC WORKS

Field of study: Functions of government

Public works are the physical components of government serving needs that can best be met by the entire community acting through its chosen governors. Public works projects include the infrastructure of the economic and social systems.

Principal terms

INFRASTRUCTURE: physical structures of a society that facilitate social functioning, including networks of communication, transportation, and sanitation

PERFORMANCE BOND: financial guarantee by a private contractor that work will be performed according to schedule and other specifications

PRIVATIZATION: assumption of public functions and services by private business enterprise

Overview

Publicly owned engineered structures comprise a vast array of facilities. They include water and sewer systems; streets, roads, and highways; energy producers and distributors; recreational sites; and telecommunications facilities, all of which also may be privately owned. As population density has increased, especially in urban areas, so has the need for public structures and facilities. Problems of contracting between parties for provision of infrastructure became nearly insurmountable as more parties became involved; governments therefore stepped in to provide infrastructure for the public good.

The first need of organized society was for defense, so some of the earliest public works were fortifications. Most of these have not survived or have done so only as archaeological remnants, but one of the most remarkable still exists. The Great Wall of China was begun in the third century B.C.E. by the Emperor Ch'in to protect his conquests. It was worked on intermittently until the fifteenth century C.E. It extends directly for more than eleven hundred miles, and loops and enclosures add nearly another thousand miles. One of the more famous modern fortifications is the Maginot Line, constructed by the French following World War I to protect the border with Germany. The success of the Germans in flanking the line in World War II, combined with the development of many forms of aerial assault, has lessened the worth of fortifications as public works. Societies now spend their money on mobile "fortifications" such as tanks, airplanes, and missiles.

As humans moved from primitive living conditions into social groups, which then expanded into cities, their most pressing need beyond defense was an adequate supply of water for agriculture. Some of the earliest civilizations developed in areas of dry climate, necessitating irrigation systems. Many archaeological remains of extensive irrigations systems exist in the Tigris-Euphrates Valley and in Egypt. The Indians of the American Southwest built irrigation systems for their fields, and their example was copied by the Mormons, who built an extensive irrigation system to water farms in Utah. The U.S. Bureau of Reclamation runs an extensive system of irrigation in the Southwest, notably in California, where a large portion of the U.S. agricultural output is produced from irrigated fields.

Although irrigation has been the principal object of public works to manage water, some public works are designed to keep water out. This is particularly true of the system of dikes developed by the Dutch to reclaim land along the North Sea coast, first from a freshwater lake, and then from the sea. The city of Venice, Italy, is built on land reclaimed from marshes bordering the Adriatic Sea. Its famous canals form an artificial system to manage water and channel it away from land used for buildings. Levees along major rivers in many countries are intended to keep water out of alluvial bottomlands used for farming.

In the late twentieth century, some large public structures have been built to accommodate sporting events. Notable among these is the Houston Astrodome, opened in 1965 and copied in a number of other American cities. The notion of public sporting arenas goes back to Roman times and the Colosseum.

Streets, roads, and highways are probably the most historically significant public works. Most early roads were intended for use by rulers. The road system of the Persian Empire (sixth century B.C.E.) is a classic example, as are the Roman roads. Begun to make it easy for the Roman legions to move from Rome to the frontier, by the time of Augustus in the first century B.C.E., the roads had become a network linking the entire Roman Empire. The empire had also a primitive postal system, utilizing the roads, for government use. At their largest extent, the Roman roads ran for some fifty thousand miles. For more than one thousand years, the Roman road system was effectively the only road system in Europe. It was not until the seventeenth century, in France, that new, centralized efforts were made to improve the road system. The French designed the crowned road, with an underlayment of one or two courses of tightly packed stone, topped by up to three feet of gravel packed solid by traffic.

Two English engineers, Thomas Telford and John McAdam, devised modern road-building techniques in the early nineteenth century. Both recommended that the road base be layers of small, preferably crushed, stones. The invention of the stone crusher in 1858 and of the steam road roller in 1859 vastly facilitated the construction of such all-weather roads. The invention of the bicycle in the late nineteenth century led to a demand for smooth surfaces on roads, which resulted in the blacktopped road of twentieth century road systems. The rapid expansion of the automobile following Henry Ford's development of the Model T in 1908 increased demand for hard-surfaced roads.

Although there had been a "national road" in the early days of the United States, a serious national road system was a product of the twentieth century. The first federal highway act was passed in 1921, imposing a tax on gasoline to pay for highways. Various states soon followed with their own taxes on gasoline to finance state highway systems. The federal highway system was vastly extended after World War II, with the construction of the interstate highway system, modeled on some European highways, particularly the famous Autobahn of Germany.

Until the development of modern forms of land transport, the most effective way of moving goods was by water. Rivers have at times served as the primary means by which goods were moved from one place to another, and they remain a prime means of circulation. A major role for government is keeping open the lanes of traffic on the waterways, often blocked by silting.

Over time, many natural waterways were supplemented by artificial ones. In the seventh century, the Chinese began to connect the Yellow and Yangtze rivers with the Grand Canal, and for many centuries that canal proved a major artery of commerce. At one time in ancient Egypt, a canal connected the Nile with the Red Sea. The major canals of the world are of modern construction. One of the most important in the United States was the Erie Canal, built by New York State between the Hudson River and the Great Lakes. Finished in 1825, it facilitated the settlement and economic development of the Midwest.

For global transport, the two most important canals are the Suez Canal, connecting the Red Sea and the Mediterranean, and the Panama Canal. The Suez Canal, constructed by a private consortium, has been government owned throughout most of its existence. It was begun in 1859 and finished in 1869. Since then, a second canal has been dug over part of the distance to make two-way traffic possible. The Panama Canal was begun by the same French interests that created the Suez Canal, but the United States took over construction in 1903 and completed the project in 1914. The canal continues to be heavily used by freighters. Modern port facilities have improved freight traffic, as have innovations such as containerization of cargoes.

Valuable cargo often travels by air, and the construction and operation of airports became a major governmental responsibility by the late twentieth century. Most airport and port facilities are owned and managed by public corporations.

One of the problems faced by a road system is that eventually it will need to cross a body of water, most often a river. Many cities are established on the banks of rivers, making easy crossing of rivers desirable. The principal builders of bridges in the ancient world were the Romans, who developed a hydraulic cement for use on piers for bridges. This cement enabled the mortar in foundations to harden under water. The largest Roman bridge crossed the Danube near the Iron Gate. Romans and, later, medieval builders relied on arch bridges, which necessitated piers placed close together, sharply restricting river traffic.

The nineteenth century and development of the iron and steel industry saw major new technology in the construction of bridges. The first innovation used the truss, based on the stability of the triangle. Most early railroad bridges were truss bridges. The truss made possible the first bridge across the Mississippi River, the Eads Bridge, finished in 1874. Its wide span made it possible for transportation on the river to continue. Even longer spans could be built after the development of the suspension bridge. The first great suspension bridge in the United States was the Brooklyn Bridge, finished in 1881. The two most notable U.S. suspension bridges are the George

Washington Bridge across the Hudson in New York City and the Golden Gate Bridge across the harbor in San Francisco.

The other way to cross a river was through a tunnel underneath. The first significant tunnel underneath a river was built under the Thames River in England in the 1830's. Tunneling under the Hudson River was begun in 1874 but not completed until 1904, when it became possible for rail lines to connect New Jersey with New York City.

With the rapid spread of the automobile, an auto tunnel became desirable. The Holland Tunnel was completed in 1934. An even more massive project, a tunnel underneath the English Channel, was completed in 1994. Tunnels have also been built to contain mass transit systems in large urban centers. The first segment of the Boston subway was opened in 1897. The London subway began operating in 1900, and construction began on the New York subway in 1900. Subway systems were major parts of many twentieth century urban mass transit systems.

Another method of transportation widely used in modern times is the pipeline. Pipelines transport both oil and gas from producing areas, and sometimes from ports, either to consumption centers or to ports at which the fuel can be loaded into tankers.

The transport of information is an important public service. Although the ancient world had rudimentary postal systems, they were for the use of officials. Transporting information for the benefit of all citizens is a modern development. National postal systems were created in the nineteenth century, supplemented by telegraph systems and later by telephone systems, and finally by wireless communication. Governments around the world have taken large roles in constructing the physical facilities for communications systems and in regulating their use.

Urban systems for dealing with water and sewerage constitute one of the most important forms of public works. Nearly all ancient efforts dealt with the supply of water; handling of sewage was not an important concern until development of the flush toilet in the late eighteenth century. The two are, however, closely linked, as was discovered in London in 1849 when the spread of cholera was found to be caused by waste pathogens seeping into the water supply. Following that discovery, cities rushed to build sewer systems that removed human waste from water supply sources. Most cities provide for thorough biological degradation of human waste through primary and secondary treatment systems.

A major problem for every water and sewer system is what to do with ground runoff during heavy rains. Most sewer systems are built to handle two or three times the average daily input, but an extremely heavy downpour can overwhelm a system. Chicago solved this problem by building extensive underground reservoirs to hold extra runoff until dry weather returns, but the enormous expense has deterred most other cities.

As urban populations grow, many cities have extended their reach for water. Rome's famous aqueducts extended many miles, especially into the mountains. The first modern works to use steam-driven pumps were designed by Benjamin Latrobe for Philadelphia in 1815. New York City began the development of its massive Croton Reservoir in the 1830's; today it draws water from as far away as the upper reaches of the Delaware River. Much of Los Angeles' water comes from more than two hundred miles away, by way of the Colorado River Aqueduct. Supplying potable water is one of the major responsibilities of public works managers.

The need for places for recreation has been recognized since the late eighteenth century, when Benjamin Thompson, Count Rumbord, laid out the "English Garden" in central Munich, Germany. The advent of the automobile gave city residents the ability to travel readily for recreation. State and national parks developed in response. The first and most famous national park is Yellowstone National Park, created by Congress in 1872. Since then a multitude of scenic wonders and historic sites have been added to the National Park System. Public works projects also include public monuments, such as the Eiffel Tower in Paris and the Lincoln and Jefferson memorials in Washington, D.C.

Applications

Modern public works are administered in a wide variety of ways, depending on the nature of the works in question. Most highways are built (generally under contract with private construction firms) by public authorities, although toll roads are often run by separate, public or semipublic corporations. Local streets are invariably the responsibility of local government and are generally maintained by a local public works department.

The typical municipal public works department is organized in two main branches. One branch is concerned with day-to-day maintenance such as patching holes, cleaning storm sewers, marking traffic lanes, maintaining traffic signals, and removing dead animals and other obstructions to traffic. One of the most important day-to-day responsibilities in northern cities is snow removal during the winter.

A second branch of municipal public works is concerned with planning changes in the road system and in traffic regulations. This branch draws up specifications for any new roads as well as for major reconstruction of any existing roads. Minor repairs tend to be handled by public works employees, but major renovations are generally contracted out.

A public works department, or at a minimum a road commissioner for a very small town, is almost a necessity for the lowest levels of government. Where the population is too sparse to support organization into a town, responsibilities for local roads are handled by counties, which also have their own public works departments. Most rural roads are county roads, and maintenance is a county responsibility. More heavily traveled roads are under the authority of the state highway department. Most state highway departments have become part of a state department of transportation.

Although most states have their own maintenance operations, a more visible part of state public works departments is concerned with new construction or reconstruction. State highway construction and maintenance is financed by special taxes on gasoline. Many states have segregated highway funds and provisions that the receipts from gas and other taxes (such as for heavy trucks) may be used only for highway purposes.

As interstate transportation has become more important, the role of the federal government has increased. The U.S. Bureau of Public Roads evolved out of an embryonic Office of Road Enquiry, established in 1893. The U.S. Public Roads Administration was established in 1923; it subsequently became the Federal Highway Administration and finally was absorbed into the Department of Transportation. The federal gasoline tax, introduced in 1921 to fund federal highway construction, is an important source of revenue for the federal government. The system of interstate highways, begun during the Dwight D. Eisenhower Administration, proved to be a major means of interstate transport by the end of the twentieth century.

Although both state and federal government have dedicated revenues to maintain roads and highways, many specialists maintain that expenditures on maintenance and improvement have not kept up with needs. The late twentieth century witnessed widespread agitation for greater spending on infrastructure, notably the road system. These concerns have led to demands for innovative financing. An expansion of toll roads has been widely recommended, though whether the necessary capital can be raised from purely private sources (without the guarantee of state or federal bonds) has been questioned. The movement for privatization, which has been especially pronounced in areas where traffic problems are acute, such as in California, has also spread to other kinds of public works.

The proliferation of environmental regulations dealing with waste of all kinds has resulted in substantial privatization of waste disposal. What used to be the "town dump" has become the "sanitary landfill," and more often than not it is operated by a private enterprise. Municipal trash haulers have been replaced by private firms, and most businesses take an active part in handling their own waste, in part through recycling.

Even when public entities maintain ownership of public works, the construction is almost invariably handled by private construction firms. Most states prescribe in detail the specifications for any public structure or facility, as well as the system for bidding on contracts and the terms of the contracts. Bonding is universal: Successful bidders must post performance bonds to ensure that the public will not lose if the contractor fails to perform adequately.

Context

As population density increases, the need for publicly financed facilities to make urban living successful also increases. Moreover, expectations of urban amenities have increased. The combination of this rising level of expectations and shortages of public funds have led to significant political conflicts in the late twentieth century in virtually all developed nations. In particular, there are differing opinions as to whether more resources should be put into physical capital in the form of public works or into human capital in the form of education, training, and health programs.

Public works are among the earliest of government-sponsored efforts. As modern politicians have emphasized, they are the material "capital" of a civilization, those installations without which social groups cannot function at their best. Governments, the managers of social groups, are the custodians of public works. Public works are in many respects the hallmarks of a civilization and account for a substantial portion of the investments each society makes. From the public works that any society chooses to create, one can form an excellent picture of the priorities of that society, or at least of the government that dominates it.

Bibliography

Ausubel, Jesse H., and Robert Herman, eds. *Cities and Their Vital Systems: Infrastructure Past, Present, and Future*. Washington, D.C.: National Academy Press, 1988. Each chapter is by a different author. Describes most of the modern public works in historical perspective. Bibliography.

Cristofano, Sam M., and William S. Foster, eds. *Management of Local Public Works*. Washington, D.C.: International City Management Association, 1986. Provides a detailed description of the organization and operation of a typical city public works department.

Kirby, Richard Shelton, et al. *Engineering in History*. New York: McGraw-Hill, 1956. Although lacking information on some modern technologies, this work contains very readable descriptions of most of the major engineering works of history.

Organization for Economic Co-operation and Development. *Urban Infrastructure: Finance and Management*. Paris: OECD, 1991. This little book gives an international perspective on urban infrastructure management.

Stein, Jay M., ed. *Public Infrastructure Planning and Management*. Newbury Park, Calif.: Sage Publications, 1988. Collection of articles by experts on questions of planning of future public works.

Nancy M. Gordon

Cross-References

City Government in the United States, p. 266; Communications Management, p. 370; Government Roles, p. 778; Land Management in the United States, p. 1045; Public Utilities, p. 1640; Resource Management, p. 1718; Transportation Management in the United States, p. 2006.

RACE AND ETHNICITY

Field of study: Civil rights and liberties

Race and ethnicity, as political factors, are complex and varied. The politics of race and ethnicity are influenced by economic, political, cultural, and social forces that vary historically as well as geographically.

Principal terms

AFFIRMATIVE ACTION: government policies that promote and require preferential treatment of minorities

ASSIMILATION: process by which a group adopts the values and beliefs of the larger society

CLASS: social stratification (ranking) based on achievement rather than ascribed traits such as family name

CULTURAL PLURALISM: maintaining one's cultural distinctiveness while assimilating economically and politically

DISCRIMINATION: act of drawing lines of distinction in such a way that widely accepted values and procedures are violated

ETHNICITY: cultural characteristics that set a group apart from other groups

MELTING POT: common metaphor for assimilation, involving the idea that different ethnic groups melt and blend together to form a uniform American culture

RACE: a subset of the human race that is identifiable by physical characteristics

RACISM: belief that one's own racial group is superior to other groups

Overview

The pattern of racial and ethnic politics in the United States is one of conflict and accommodation. Recent racial theory has been dominated by three approaches: ethnicity-based theory, class-based theory, and nation-based theory. These three approaches have been used to explain the patterns of conflict and accommodation experienced by racial and ethnic groups in the United States.

The main themes of ethnicity-based theories are assimilation, cultural pluralism, and how minority populations are incorporated into society. Ethnicity-based theories tend to blame the victim for the victim's lack of success and assimilation. Class-based theories incorporate economic themes to explain some of the realities of race and politics. Class-based theories examine the economic structures that produce unequal exchanges. Nation-based theories analyze the realities of racial separation and examine the role of minority-based political movements, such as pan-Africanism. Nation-based theories explore the dynamics of colonialism to explain racial relationships. Racial and ethnic minorities are viewed as groups who have been colonized, dominated, and exploited economically, socially, and politically.

Ethnicity theory was popular up through the mid-1960's as the major framework for explaining racial realities. Race was viewed as a component or characteristic of ethnicity, rather than the other way around. Ethnicity theory became popular again in the 1980's, and its resurgence was spearheaded by neoconservatives and the election of Ronald Reagan to the presidency of the United States in 1980 and of George Bush to the same office in 1988. This resurgence was nurtured by growing concern over affirmative (reverse) discrimination.

The United States is not a color-blind society, and race has always been a determinant or strongly influencing factor in one's political rights, position in the economy, and identity. One cannot understand the politics and history of the United States without examining questions of race and ethnicity. In order to understand the politics of race and ethnicity, one must study the history of racial politics.

An introduction to the history of racial politics can be found in the book *From Different Shores: Perspectives on Race and Ethnicity in America* (1994), edited by historian Ronald Takaki. Two articles in particular, one written by Takaki and the other written by sociologist Nathan Glazer, present opposing viewpoints concerning the history of racial politics in the United States. Glazer's article, "The Emergence of an American Ethnic Pattern," is reprinted from his controversial book *Affirmative Discrimination: Ethnic Inequality and Public Policy* (1975).

Glazer sees American history as having a tradition of inclusiveness. Except for a brief time from the 1890's to the 1930's, when the United States was exclusive, people of a variety of races and ethnicities were welcomed to the United States. Glazer argues that three decisions have guided the development of an American ethnic pattern. One is that anyone could enter the United States and that no group would be subordinate to another group. Another is that racial and ethnic groups could not establish their own nation or states. The third is that no group would be required to surrender their ethnic heritage and distinctiveness as a requirement for citizenship in the United States. Glazer believes that neither cultural pluralism nor total assimilation (the melting pot) has dominated the American ethnic pattern.

Takaki strongly questions Glazer's belief that American society is inclusive; his article provides page after page of evidence challenging Glazer's position. For example, the Naturalization Law of 1790 stated that only free white men were eligible for citizenship. Native Americans were not made individual citizens until 1924, although as early as 1887 Indians, by following the required steps of the Indian Allotment Act, could become citizens. The terms of the act specified that Native Americans seeking U.S. citizenship agree to assimilate and adopt a nonmigratory lifestyle. Takaki argues that American history is riddled with racism and exclusivity and that what emerges from U.S. history is a racial pattern of domination, exclusion, and exploitation. He also argues that race is a more powerful predictor of one's life outcomes than ethnicity. Takaki believes that as a result of the tradition of exclusivity, contemporary racial inequality and occupational stratification are often more powerful in restricting mobility than more direct forms of prejudice and discrimination are.

Glazer is supportive of equality of opportunity and believes the government should only ban racial discrimination. Members of racial and ethnic groups should be treated as individuals, not as members of special groups with certain benefits allotted only to them. Takaki is supportive of equality of condition, rather than equality of opportunity. He believes equality of opportunity is not possible in a society composed of unequal groups. Takaki supports special benefits and programs (affirmative action) to enhance the chances of upward mobility for disadvantaged groups, while Glazer believes these are not necessary and those who are disadvantaged should emulate the values and example of the white European immigrants of the 1800's and early 1900's.

Glazer is not the only critic of affirmative action. Others argue that immigrant groups such as the Japanese and West Indian blacks have suffered from discrimination as much as other minority groups but have overcome the obstacles of racism and discrimination and are economically successful. Others also argue that racial representation is not the same thing as racial development, and that after more than twenty years of affirmative action, the income gap between whites and blacks is greater than it was in the 1970's.

Applications

The vision of American policymakers throughout the history of the United States, according to Takaki, has been one of racial domination and exclusion. He finds Glazer's claim that U.S. history reflects an ethnic pattern of inclusion ridiculous and argues that Glazer's theory does not explain the history of racial groups in the United States. The history of racial groups in the United States can be told, in part, by listing the policies and legislation that excluded or restricted their full participation in society.

In response to increased Chinese immigration, white resentment, and an economic depression, policymakers enacted the Chinese Exclusion Act of 1882. The act limited Chinese immigration to a fraction of what it once was. The act was not repealed until 1943.

Native Americans have been controlled by the federal government since its beginning. President James Monroe proposed in 1825 that Indians were separate and not a part of the political society. This belief was formalized in the Indian Removal Act of 1830. President Andrew Jackson implemented the policies outlined in the Indian Removal Act of 1830 and began to relocate tribes west of the Mississippi River. The Cherokee, Creek, Chickasaw, Choctaw, and Seminole were relocated from the southeastern part of the United States to what is now the eastern part of Oklahoma. Policymakers were hoping to create an Indian territory.

Indian policy has evolved through five stages, beginning with the idea of separation, followed by coercive assimilation, tribal restoration, termination, and tribal restoration. The General Allotment Act of 1887, also known as the Dawes Act, was intended to force Indians to assimilate. Each head of a household was given 160 acres of farmland. Any excess land left on the reservations was sold to non-Indians. By 1934, according to Takaki, 60 percent of Indian land was owned by non-Indians.

Immigration by Italians, Greeks, and other central, southern, and eastern Europeans was nearly eliminated by the National Origins Quota Act of 1924. Policymakers, influenced by faulty and erroneous data provided by the Dillingham Commission, restricted immigration of those groups, thought to be prone to crime. People from those regions of Europe were believed to be genetically inferior and incapable of becoming Americanized. Immigration from those areas was restricted until 1965.

In response to the Japanese bombing of Pearl Harbor, President Franklin Roosevelt, on February 19, 1942, issued an executive order that led to the transfer of nearly 120,000 American citizens of Japanese descent from West Coast areas to detention centers. In December, 1944, the order was repealed and those held in the centers were allowed to return home. Italian Americans and German Americans had not been forced to relocate.

In 1896, the Supreme Court ruled in the *Plessy v. Ferguson* case that separate but equal facilities for African American was acceptable. The Supreme Court considered racism natural and impossible to eliminate. This decision had a monumental influence on race relations, especially in the South. Eligible black voters, during this time, were often barred from voting because of discriminatory literacy laws, poll tax laws, and grandfather clauses limiting voting rights to those who had voted prior to 1861 and their descendants.

From the 1920's to the 1950's, some colleges and universities, including Yale, Harvard, and Columbia, implemented restrictive quotas for Jewish students. Some medical and law schools limited the number of positions available for Jewish students, while many fraternities and sororities banned Jews from membership.

The Immigration and Nationality Act of 1965 limited legal immigration from Mexico to 20,000 persons per year while increasing the quotas for southern and eastern Europeans. The 1986 Immigration Reform and Control Act again limited immigration for Mexican and other non-European immigrants. Employers who hired undocumented workers became subject to stiff fines and penalties. While the 1990, 1965, and 1986 immigration acts have no exclusionary racial quotas, they do restrict the number of immigrants from any one country. The 1990 Immigration Act favors highly skilled workers, professionals, and wealthy individuals willing to create jobs in the United States.

Context

Political scientist Andrew Hacker, in his book *Two Nations: Black and White, Separate, Hostile, Unequal* (1992), concludes that a huge racial chasm exists in the United States and that he sees few indications that the gap will eventually close. Takaki argues that how people perceive the problem of racial inequality will determine how they work to resolve the problem of racial inequality. The resurgence of the political right wing during the 1980's and early 1990's to some extent stymied the progress of programs and policies to enhance equality of condition. The administrations of Ronald Reagan and George Bush were not as supportive of affirmative action legislation as previous administrations had been.

Political mobilization from the 1950's to the 1970's helped to bring about civil rights legislation, which contributed to the restructuring of the racial order in the United States. Racial and ethnic politics changed during that time from a war of maneuver, which involves primarily an inward struggle within a group or movement, to a war of position, which involves an outward confrontation with the powers that be and the state. With the changing racial order of the 1960's and 1970's, racial movements lost their momentum and political unity. Some sociologists claim that the racial movements were satisfied with moderate reforms created by government, although the more radical elements of the racial movements wanted more. In the end this radical element was contained and a new era of racial and ethnic politics emerged. Some sociologists believe that the public policies and legislation of the 1960's through the 1980's did not create a color-blind society and racial equality has not been achieved. These sociologists believe the immediate future will not likely see the breadth of racial political mobilization that existed from the 1950's to the 1970's.

Since 1965 and the liberalization of immigration policies, Asian and Latino populations have increased rapidly. The census bureau estimates that by the year 2010, Latinos will surpass African Americans as the largest minority group in the United States. The Asian population is expected to increase to 5 percent of the total U.S. population by 2010 and 10 percent of the total U.S. population by 2050. With this growth among Latinos and Asians has come more ethnic and class diversity. This diversity includes diversity within ethnic groups. Such diversity may hinder political mobilization among Latinos, who are, in fact, Mexicans, Puerto Ricans, Cubans, and Central and South Americans. There is also great diversity among Japanese, Chinese, Korean, Vietnamese, Laotian, Filipino, and other Asian nationality groups. Such diversity makes it difficult to talk of a shared experience when the life experiences of group members are varied and diverse, with wide differences of income, occupation, education, and culture.

Sociologist Felix Padilla in his book *Latino Ethnic Consciousness: The Case of Mexican Americans and Puerto Ricans in Chicago* (1985) is somewhat optimistic in his appraisal of racial movements. According to Padilla, the Latinos, though diverse, are a political ethnic group that can pursue collective political, economic, and social interests within the larger U.S. society. The key to Latino success in affecting public policy is the ability of distinct ethnic groups to adopt a new and different collective identity, one that shares cultural, linguistic, and structural similarities. A shared history of inequality aids in bridging the ethnic differences that might separate these Spanish-speaking groups. The experience of poverty and discrimination have brought about the development of a broader Latino ethnic consciousness.

No matter what one's viewpoint might be about the future of the politics of race and ethnicity, one can be assured that the issues of race and ethnicity will continue to be at the center of American life.

Bibliography

Glazer, Nathan. *Affirmative Discrimination: Ethnic Inequality and Public Policy.* New York: Basic Books, 1975. Addresses the question of why the United States shifted from an emphasis on individual rights to an emphasis on group rights to create policies to overcome and correct racial and ethnic group discrimination.

_____. *Ethnic Dilemmas, 1964-1982.* Cambridge, Mass.: Harvard University Press, 1983. Sixteen articles written from 1964 to 1982, analyzing issues of racial and ethnic conflict.

Glazer, Nathan, and Daniel Patrick Moynihan. *Beyond the Melting Pot: The Negroes, Puerto Ricans, Jews, Italians, and Irish of New York City.* 2d ed. Cambridge, Mass.: MIT Press, 1970. First published in 1963, this is one of the most important books on race, ethnicity, and politics in the early 1960's. The second edition includes a new introduction in which the authors update their positions. The central thesis is that the melting pot has never existed in the United States.

Hacker, Andrew. *Two Nations: Black and White, Separate, Hostile, Unequal.* New York: Charles Scribner's Sons, 1992. Hacker believes racial tensions serve too many purposes in U.S. society and therefore are unlikely to be done away with in the near future, and that there is little evidence to suggest that the majority of white Americans are willing to support redistributive programs to enhance equality.

Omi, Michael, and Howard Winant. *Racial Formation in the United States: From the 1960's to the 1980's.* New York: Routledge & Kegan Paul, 1986. Describes the process by which race has shaped U.S. politics.

Padilla, Felix. *Latino Ethnic Consciousness: The Case of Mexican Americans and Puerto Ricans in Chicago.* Notre Dame, Ind.: University of Notre Dame Press, 1985. Argues that the main purpose of Latino ethnic consciousness is to advance the collective political, economic, and social interests of the diverse Spanish-speaking population.

Sowell, Thomas. *The Economics and Politics of Race: An International Perspective.* New York: William Morrow, 1983. Investigates intergroup differences and the economic and political consequences of these differences.

_____. *Preferential Policies: An International Perspective.* New York: William Morrow, 1990. Offers the argument that elites benefit from preferential programs while nonelites suffer. Also examines the patterns of preferential policies in the United States, India, Malaysia, South Africa, Nigeria, and Sri Lanka.

Takaki, Ronald, ed. *From Different Shores: Perspectives on Race and Ethnicity in America.* 2d ed. New York: Oxford University Press, 1994. One of the best collections available on race and ethnicity.

Wilson, William Julius. *The Declining Significance of Race: Blacks and Changing American Institutions.* Chicago: University of Chicago Press, 1978. Argues that for most African Americans their life chances have more to do with economic class position than with racial identification. He does not discount the role of race but emphasizes class plays a more fundamental role than in the past.

William L. Smith

Cross-References

African American Politics, p. 28; Asian American Politics, p. 115; Civil Rights Protection, p. 304; Civil Unrest and Rioting, p. 317; Entitlements, p. 610; The Family and Politics in the United States, p. 649; Immigrants and Politics, p. 861; Immigration and Emigration, p. 868; Immigration Regulation, p. 875; Latino Politics, p. 1052; Pan-Africanism, p. 1369; Political Correctness, p. 1441; Slavery and U.S. Political History, p. 1821; Social Darwinism, p. 1833.

RADICALISM

Field of study: Political philosophy

Radicalism in the context of social and political philosophy and practice means going to the root of a problem through intellectual analysis or practical policy. Radicalism also sometimes refers to the degree of departure from previous or familiar practice.

Principal terms

ANARCHISM: doctrine holding that because society is natural and humans are naturally good, the state as source of oppressive authority can be abolished and alternative governance instituted

MARXISM: doctrine holding that class struggle is the heart of the historical process and that ownership of the means of production and distribution determines the nature of the social order; collective ownership will follow a class revolution

PHILOSOPHICAL RADICALISM: a political philosophy demanding that all social, political, and legal institutions conform to reason

UTILITARIANISM: concept that people strive to maximize utility, which consists of pleasure as positive utility and pain as negative utility

UTOPIANISM: advocacy of some version of a perfect, or nearly perfect, society

Overview

The ideas of political radicalism are outgrowths of Western culture that have spread throughout the world. In one use of the term, the characteristic common to all philosophies and ideas called "radical" is that they seek the root of human problems.

In this sense, Plato (427-347 B.C.E.) was the first radical philosopher. Plato saw the principal root of evil and turbulence in the political world as human ignorance combined with the inherent corruption of physical things. There is no permanent cure for the corruption of physical things, but there is a remedy for ignorance. The remedy, knowledge, is not available to everyone; the highest philosophical knowledge, knowledge of the good, can be achieved only by the talented few after years of hard study.

The next step in Plato's radical message was a political one. Only those who have obtained philosophical knowledge can govern a just, well-ordered state. Once a state is established in accordance with true philosophical ideas, it must reject cosmopolitanism, keep to itself, and never change. None of the states of his time met these criteria, nor would they begin to approximate them until, as he stated, "philosophers become kings or kings philosophers." Paradoxically, Plato's radical message was at once revolutionary, because it attacked all actual states, and profoundly conservative, because it looked forward to a regime that would remain unchanged as long as possible.

In the world of ancient and medieval Europe, the ideals of Christianity as applied to society were themselves a form of radicalism, seeking to find the root of human misery and evil in humanity's innate sinfulness and estrangement from God. Although Christianity never proposed that humanity could overcome sin and achieve perfection in this world, it did hold up the promise of perfection in another world into which believers would be received after death.

If Christian doctrine did not foresee the end of human misery and evil, Christian ideals, either undisguised or in a secular form, provided the source for the long series of utopias that have been proposed by the radical imagination. Radicalism in the form of utopianism is not always a call to action. A writer's purpose in describing a radically new social order may be to hold up a mirror to society to show it the full panoply of its blemishes.

The original utopia, in Sir Thomas More's Utopia (1516), had this aim. The book was not a plan for action. The utopian social order that More depicted was based upon reason alone. Private property had no place in it. It was not a "perfect" society, because it was not based on Christianity. More seemed to be urging his contemporaries to recognize the deep imperfections of their society by looking at one that was much better, even though it did not practice the true faith.

Whether or not it is utopian, radicalism has most often included a plan of action for social change as well as a critique of society. The Enlightenment in eighteenth century Europe and America spawned radical ideas that inspired generations to action. The ideas of the Enlightenment were radical sometimes because they sought the root of social ills or of society itself and sometimes because of the degree of social change they proposed. The radicalism of the Enlightenment usually stemmed from its attempt to apply reason to the social order or to create a political philosophy based upon reason alone.

Some writers saw private property as a root cause of human misery; others found the source of social oppression in organized religion and its championing of obscurantism and superstition. On the continent of Europe, especially in France, the Roman Catholic church was singled out for censure.

Ironically, one of the most influential writers of the eighteenth century was perceived to have proposed radical social change when he had no such intention. At the opening of his *A Treatise on the Social Contract* (1762), Jean-Jacques Rousseau wrote, "Man is born free but everywhere he is in chains." Generations of readers, including untold numbers of radicals, took this statement as a clarion call for oppressed humanity to throw off its chains, but that was not what Rousseau meant. Almost immediately after declaring man to be "in chains," he wrote, "What can render it legitimate? I believe that I can settle this question." "Chains" for Rousseau meant social obligations; he could scarcely envisage a society with no obligations, which would be a total anarchy. Instead, his treatise explained how the principles of a just society legitimate the obligations (chains) it imposes upon its members.

When radicalism moved from thought to action in the eighteenth century, it took the form of revolution, first in America, then in France. The American Revolution that officially began in 1776 has often been described as less than truly revolutionary and therefore not particularly radical, or radical at all. This has been argued because the American Revolution was not a social revolution in the sense that the French Revolution was. Property relations in America were largely unaffected, and no distinctions among social classes were formally altered, in the way that they were in France of the 1790's, where a vast social transformation took place.

Nevertheless, recent historical thought has challenged this view and argued that the American Revolution was indeed radical, even if it differed from those in France, Russia, and China. Before 1760, America was a monarchical society peopled by subjects who thought of society as hierarchical and most of whom thought people were bound together by personal ties. Half a century later, however, this view had been transformed by the revolution's ideas. No longer subjects, all male citizens were now equal in civil rights. Theirs was the most liberal, democratic, and commercial society—in sum, the most modern society—in the world. America experienced a social transformation, not only a political "revolution." The change in thought that led to this transformation was indeed radical change, earning the American Revolution a distinct place in the history of radicalism.

In part, American radicalism was a rejection of the idea of monarchical man, who was subject to authority within a static hierarchical system that was based, according to its defenders, upon nature. In opposition to this vision of the human condition, Americans offered a liberal view of man, developed by Thomas Hobbes and John Locke. According to this view, by nature and in accordance with the laws of God, people are born to freedom, possessed of rights that cannot legitimately be stripped from them. In this view, espoused in the Declaration of Independence, people possess these rights as individuals, not as members of ascribed groups, that is, groups into which they are born and cannot change. Moreover, everyone's individual rights are equal. Here was an attempt to examine philosophically the roots of the human condition. It was, indeed, a radical theory.

Following by some thirteen years the outbreak of rebellion against constituted authority across the Atlantic, the French Revolution far exceeded its American counterpart in violence and in social turmoil and upheaval. The radicalism of the French Revolution consisted in part in its destruction of the class system of the *ancien régime*, with its "estates" of nobles and clergy and a third consisting of everyone else. The extremity of the change in France was dramatized by the Terror, with its busy guillotine and mobs raging for the blood of the aristocracy. Equally radical was the thought of Maximilien Robespierre, apologist of the Terror and proponent of virtue, or civic morality, and his protégé, Louis de Saint-Just, whose ideas exceeded Robespierre's radicalism in their adherence to rigorous Spartan ideals of the perfect republic.

The French Revolution ignited and inflamed the passions of Europe and led to the opening of numerous avenues of radical thought and action in the century that followed, avenues that led not only to the extreme left but also to the extreme right. Both communism and fascism have roots in the debacle that overtook Europe between 1789 and 1815, when France was finally pacified and a semblance of the old order restored. The spectacle of revolutionaries who lead the common people to the seizure of political power became a model for later revolutionaries.

Across the English Channel, another form of radicalism was developing. This radicalism was of the peculiarly English variety, combining the intellect with politics and having little to do with insurrectionary violence. For these reasons, it was sneered at by continental radicals. The British movement was philosophical radicalism, founded and led by English legal reformer and utilitarian philosopher Jeremy Bentham. Bentham's philosophy was radical in its insistence that all social, political, and legal institutions must either justify themselves as conforming to reason or they should be swept away by legal, deliberate, and, in some cases, gradual means. For Bentham, the roots of knowledge lie in studying the twin capacities of people for feeling and desiring pleasure and avoiding pain; pleasure and pain are the "sovereign masters." According to Bentham's principle of utilitarianism, maximizing the total sum of pleasure in society while minimizing pain is the proper goal of the state.

The state, however, is a poor vehicle for creating happiness, other than keeping order, regulating commerce, and the like. Attempts by the state to run commercial enterprises, provide for the poor, and much else are disastrous. Moreover, the British state of Bentham's day was, he argued, controlled by a parasitic aristocracy and royal family who taxed the productive to feed their wasteful pleasures, such as useless wars and inefficient administration. Those who ruled were unaccountable to a responsive electorate.

To unburden the entrenched upper classes of their power, the middle class and its values must be brought to power. Democratization was the radical solution advocated by Bentham and the philosophical radicals for the transfer of political power. If democracy was the instrument of enforcing accountability, a free press was its most important handmaiden to ensure that official misdeeds would be brought to public attention. "The more closely we are watched," Bentham wrote, "the better we behave."

On the continent of Europe, a host of schools of thought vied for influence early in the nineteenth century. Utopians such as the Frenchmen Claude Henri de Rouvroy and Charles Fourier attacked the evils of the emerging capitalist economic system that was fast industrializing Western Europe. Rouvroy (who served in the American Revolution on the side of the colonists) argued that society should be directed by scientists and industrialists to create a harmonious order. After his death, his followers advocated public control of the means of production and other socialist measures. Fourier, who is credited with creating the first nonrepressive utopia, also sought the key to a harmonious social system. He advocated the organization of society into communities of 1,620 people who would work according to their natural preferences.

The most influential nineteenth century radical theorist was Karl Marx, who worked with his intellectual partner, Friedrich Engels. Marx, like many other social analysts, was radical both in attempting to go to the root of human suffering and in proposing, or rather predicting, fundamental social change.

For Marx, the key to understanding society and social change is a knowledge of economic production and distribution. How work is allocated among various groups and occupations—the division of labor—is a key determinant of the economic system. Even more important is the ownership of the means of production, such as land and factories. A study of the past shows that conflict between "haves" and "have nots" is universal. These groups are social classes; all history is the history of class struggle.

The underlying reality of history is the scarcity of things. The Industrial Revolution of the capitalist economy appeared to create the means for the production of plenty for all. According to Marx, however, capitalism is beset by deep inner "contradictions" that it is unable to solve. Thus, the economy operates in a series of ever-worse boom-and-bust cycles. Depressions reveal the most ironic of capitalism's contradictions, the existence of enormous productive capacity that lies idle as workers starve.

Workers' suffering serves as a force to transcend the capitalist system. Suffering leads to organizations (labor unions and workers' parties) to improve the workers' situation. The most far-seeing leaders realize that the only solution to society's problems is a complete change in the social system and its underlying economic base. This change consists of abolishing the private ownership of the means of production and distribution and adopting collective or social ownership. In most cases, this change must come via violent revolution.

After the revolution, production will be increased considerably, so that scarcity will be a thing of the past. Society will be governed according to the principle, "from each according to his abilities; to each according to his needs." The coming of the new society is inevitable because it is part of history's inexorable logic, but its "birth pangs" can be lessened by those who organize on the basis of a correct understanding of the historical process. Thus, the role of the Communist Party is to hasten the historical process by making revolution.

Applications

The study of the phenomenon of political radicalism in all of its forms is required for an understanding of the twentieth century. It is scarcely too much to say that the twentieth century has been a century of radicalism. Originating in the nineteenth century, radicals such as anarchists, who rejected the existence of the state, and syndicalists, who advocated government by workers' groups, had some influence in Europe and elsewhere in the early twentieth century. More important were the offshoots of Marxian communism, especially those influenced by Russian revolutionary V. I. Lenin.

Lenin taught that the socialist revolution is not inevitable but contingent. Left to themselves, workers will go no further than improvements in their pay and conditions. Revolutionaries must make the revolution. The most effective way of making revolution is by a small, tightly disciplined group. Such a tiny group, the Bolsheviks ("majority"), seized power in Russia in 1917 and ruled a vast empire until 1992.

Much of the importance of Lenin's theory was its application to making revolution in Third World countries, where capitalism was not well developed and a ready supply of dissatisfied workers was thus unavailable as combustible revolutionary material. In China, Marxist-Leninism was combined with new elements to extend the applicability of communism farther in the Third World. Mao Tse-tung discovered an oppressed rural working class or proletariat among the peasantry, making socialist revolution a practical aim in agrarian societies. This view informed many communists from the 1950's onward in Asia, Africa, and Latin America.

Radicalism also visited the twentieth century in the form of fascism. Fascism was influenced by communism. Some fascist leaders, such as Benito Mussolini, were deeply influenced by Marxism. On the other hand, Joseph Stalin greatly admired Adolf Hitler, whose methods of governing closely paralleled his own in the use of secret police, terrorism, and concentration camps to cow or defeat real or imagined opposition. Hitler himself must be regarded as one of the most radical revolutionaries of all time.

World War II led to the demise of the most toxic European fascist regimes, and European communism grew progressively more arthritic, but radical politics of one sort or another spread throughout the world. In Western Europe, leftist groups, some of them youthful revolutionary terrorists, were active. In Africa, revolutionaries of both the left and the right spawned wars and uprisings, and in many cases they took power. Maoists fought wars of national liberation in Asia and Latin America, with bloody, sometimes horrific results. Thus, Pol Pot's communist Khmer Rouge regime in Cambodia killed a million people in pursuit of a radical political vision. In North Korea, Cuba, and Nicaragua, radical regimes came to power on the promise of "liberating" their peoples, only to oppress them far worse than the regimes they replaced. Radical groups in South America fought terrorist campaigns from the 1960's to the 1990's, always unsuccessful but nevertheless tragically bloody. Radical politics in the Middle East led to a long series of terrorist acts, such as the killing of Israeli athletes at the Olympic Games in Munich in 1972. More blood was spilled by terrorist acts in Northern Ireland and England from 1969 to 1994.

In the United States, radical politics took different forms. Usually (though not always) averse to terrorism, middle-class radicals of the 1960's and 1970's attacked the suburban status quo in the name of the poor, of the victims of the war in Vietnam, and of group oppression of various kinds, including those of race, ethnicity, gender, and sexual orientation.

Context

In sum, radical politics of one sort or another have deeply influenced the course of the twentieth century. With the end of the Soviet empire, leftist radicalism has diminished, though not disappeared. Radicalism in other parts of the world, such as the militant Islamic regime in Iran and communist insurgents in the Philippines and Peru, serve as reminders that the radical impulse, especially when allied with utopianism, is a potent, ever-present human possibility.

The study of political phenomena includes the examination of types of political ideology, action, and regimes. These may be divided into traditional, conservative, liberal, and radical types. Traditional refers to the political regimes and ideas of premodern societies. Conservative has two main subvarieties, one a corporatist type as found in continental Europe and the pre-Thatcherite Conservative Party in Britain, and the other market-individualist in orientation as in Thatcherite Britain and the United States. Liberal ideology is typified by the Democratic Party in the United States and the Christian Democrats in Italy; the social democratic type is exemplified by the social democratic parties in Germany and Sweden.

It is in this context that radical ideas, parties, styles of political action, and regimes gain their meaning. Radicalism may be of the Right or of the Left, but in the context of political action it advocates fundamental change in the social order and, typically, seeks to identify the roots of social problems or malaise.

Bibliography

Berlin, Isaiah. *Karl Marx, His Life and Environment.* 4th ed. New York: Oxford University Press, 1982. A classical account of Marx's thought written by one of the twentieth century's most distinguished intellectuals.

Gottschalk, Louis R. *The Era of the French Revolution, 1715-1815.* Boston: Houghton Mifflin, 1929. Classic general account of the French Revolution.

Halevy, Elie. *The Growth of Philosophical Radicalism.* 3 vols. Translated by Mary Morris. London: Faber, 1972. The classic account of the philosophical radicals, including their political, social, and economic thought.

Manuel, Frank Edward. *The Prophets of Paris.* Cambridge, Mass.: Harvard University Press, 1962. A lively and learned account of the utopian thought of Rouvroy, Fourier, and their followers.

Singer, Peter. *Marx.* New York: Oxford University Press, 1980. Brief but informative introduction to Marx's life and major ideas.

Charles F. Bahmueller

Cross-References

Capitalism, p. 197; Dialecticism, p. 540; Fascism and Nazism, p. 656; Irrationalism in Politics, p. 987; The Left and the Right, p. 1079; Marxism-Leninism, p. 1155; The New Right, p. 1293; Political Correctness, p. 1441; Scientific Humanism, p. 1784.

REALPOLITIK

Field of study: Political philosophy

The theory of realpolitik asserts that any means are acceptable for a state to use in pursuing its interests. The concept has influenced the foreign and domestic policy decisions of many major states during the nineteenth and twentieth centuries.

Principal terms
> GEOGRAPHIC REALITIES: parameters within which the leaders of a state must work, based on the availability of raw materials in areas under their control
> MUTUALLY EXCLUSIVE GOALS: frequently, two or more states find their strategic interests require the attainment of mutually exclusive goals, which may result in war
> POWER: ability of a state to pursue its strategic interests based on factors such the size of its armed forces, or its industrial capacity
> STRATEGIC INTERESTS: necessities for a state to survive and prosper, such as abundant supplies of food, raw materials, and energy sources

Overview

Realpolitik is a starkly materialistic theory of international and domestic politics. Adherents to this philosophy deny that considerations such as human rights and safeguarding the environment, or even honesty and justice, should enter into political decision making or international affairs. To a practitioner of realpolitik, the end always justifies the means. Lying, cheating, stealing, murder, and war are perfectly acceptable means to achieve the desired results. Historians and political scientists often associate the term realpolitik and its underlying tenets with Otto von Bismarck, chancellor of Germany from 1870 to 1890.

The theory of realpolitik rests on several premises, including strategic interests, geographic realities, mutually exclusive goals, and competition and conflict over these goals. According to this theory, states have strategic interests upon which their relative securities depend. The most basic of these interests is the security to continue to exist as independent states, which requires that they achieve power. Leaders must pursue policies that will ultimately increase the power of their state or decrease the power of real or potential enemies. Without power, there can be no true security, because the state's continued existence would rest on other states' lack of interest in destroying it, rather on its ability to defend itself. Therefore, states must constantly attempt to increase their power relative to the power of competitors. Increasing power may take the form of expanding their armed forces, developing revolutionary new weapons, or expanding their industrial production capacity.

Political leaders also have attempted to increase the power of their nations through imperialistic expansion in order to gain access to markets and raw materials, and to acquire areas into which the excess population of their nations may expand. Power also may be increased through alliances and international agreements. Attempts by political leaders to increase the power of their states and to limit the power of other states resulted in the explosion of imperialistic expansion during the late nineteenth and early twentieth centuries. Most of the European states, the United States, and Japan became involved in a race for colonies. Imperialistic competition became a primary factor in the massive world wars of the twentieth century, as did the complex web of entangling alliances that virtually guaranteed that any minor conflict between nations would escalate into a global war.

According to the precepts of realpolitik, leaders of states must attempt to increase the power of their state based on strategic interests and geographic realities. For example, if the state's industrial growth depends on a commodity not present within the area it controls, its leaders must attempt to secure access to areas where that commodity is present. Any means necessary to achieve that strategic interest, including war, must be pursued. Geographic realities determine most strategic interests. For example, a completely landlocked nation cannot compete in global trade, and thus increase its power, unless it secures access to a deep-water port. Its leaders may secure such access through negotiation, treaty, or international agreement. If attempts at negotiation fail, the leaders of such a nation may resort to war. Human lives mean nothing to the practitioners of realpolitik, as long as the desired end is achieved.

Realpolitik also has a domestic political dimension. Since security is the primary goal of all state policies, politicians must suppress what they conceive to be internal threats to the state, which they often interpret as any threat to their continued exercise of power. Political leaders in many different countries frequently have disregarded the constitutional rights of their citizens in suppressing political, religious, and social movements they consider subversive. Political leaders have also eliminated or neutralized individuals whom they considered dangerous to the state, often violating the laws of their nation in the process. Political leaders in all countries, including the United States, often have resorted to the use of realpolitik in domestic affairs.

Applications

Bismarck argued that in international relations, political leaders should base their policies on precisely defined goals. Those goals, when realized, should maximize gains in power while minimizing risk and cost. Paths to the desired goals might include the passage of favorable international laws, disarmament or arms limitations agreements, coalitions and alliances, collective security agreements, or aggressive war.

Many social scientists view Bismarck's foreign policy during the period 1862-1870 as a classic example of realpolitik in action. When Bismarck became minister-president of Prussia, Germany consisted of thirty-eight small states, each with its own currency, army, and tariff system. Prussia was the largest of the German states, but Austria was the most powerful. In only eight years, Bismarck managed to unify the small German States under Prussian leadership and form the German Empire that so profoundly influenced the course of twentieth century history.

Bismarck first increased the power of Prussia by expanding and modernizing its armed forces. To accomplish this task, he ignored the Prussian constitution and collected taxes illegally. Using the tax monies to turn the Prussian army into the most efficient fighting force in Europe, Bismarck proceeded to aggrandize his state territorially. He first attempted to maximize the power of Prussia through negotiation and international agreements whenever possible. When negotiation failed Bismarck did not hesitate to resort to war—three during the eight-year period of German unification. With each territorial acquisition, the power of Prussia increased. On several occasions, Bismarck deliberately misled the leaders of other states as to his intentions and future actions. Bismarck practiced his most notorious chicanery on France's Emperor Napoleon III, tricking him first into neutrality during the Austro-Prussian War (1866), then into fighting the Franco-Prussian War (1870-1871) that resulted in the unification of Germany under Prussian domination.

Bismarck negotiated many international agreements and settlements. When he deemed war necessary to achieve his ends, he always minimized the risks involved by signing alliances with other states against his potential enemies or securing the agreement of other nations to remain neutral. All Bismarck's policies were designed to maximize the security and power of the Prussian state, a power that he exercised. Once the unification of Germany was complete, he negotiated a series of alliances, such as the Triple Alliance with Italy and Austria and the Reinsurance Treaty with Russia, that greatly increased the power and security of Germany.

Bismarck also based his domestic policies on realpolitik. Under his leadership, the German Empire that he created adopted a democratic constitution that guaranteed all German citizens what are considered today basic human rights: freedom of speech, religion, press, and association; equality before the law; and trial by jury. Bismarck routinely violated those constitutional guarantees any time he believed the security of the state, or his own control thereof, was endangered. He instigated a three-year struggle called the Kulturkampf against the Roman Catholic church, because he thought the pope had too much power over German Catholics. He outlawed the Social Democratic Party because it was part of the international Marxist movement. Its newspaper was suppressed and several of its leaders imprisoned without trial, or exiled. Bismarck justified his actions by arguing that what he did was in the best interests of the state.

Bismarck's defenders point out that he was not the only politician practicing realpolitik in the late nineteenth century. They argue that all Bismarck's competitors used the same ruthless methods he did. Bismarck was simply the most able practitioner of realpolitik of his time. Ultimately, the principles perfected by Bismarck contributed heavily to the outbreak of World War I and to the inhumanity of that massive struggle.

Context

Political leaders have been practicing realpolitik since the beginning of recorded history. The principles of this essentially amoral political philosophy have contributed to, if not caused, every war in human history and all the suffering associated with those wars. Political leaders have used those principles to justify murder, tyranny, slavery, and injustice.

Cynics argue that the basic premises of realpolitik continue to dominate the international and domestic policies of most late twentieth century world leaders. They maintain that politicians care nothing for issues such as human rights or protection of the global environment; instead, they use those issues as tools to gain advantage over real or potential enemies. Constitutional guarantees, the cynics say, are ignored by politicians in their pursuit of security and power. Certainly, many events in the 1990's have suggested that the cynics are not entirely wrong.

If the cynics are correct, humanity would seem to be doomed to the recurrent cycle of war and tyranny that has marked history from its beginning. Unless informed citizens insist that their political leaders base foreign and domestic policies on principles such as justice and human rights, those leaders will continue to follow consciously or unconsciously the amoral philosophy of realpolitik.

Bibliography

Beres, Louis. *Reason and Realpolitik: U.S. Foreign Policy and World Order.* Lexington, Mass.: Lexington Books, 1984. Thoughtful examination of U.S. foreign policy through the lens of realpolitik. Argues persuasively that realpolitik has guided most U.S. foreign policy decisions throughout its history.

Burmeister, Larry. *Research, Realpolitik, and Development in Korea: The State and the Green Revolution.* Boulder, Colo.: Westview, 1988. Shows the often counterproductive effects of realpolitik on national development, using the model of South Korea.

Cusack, Thomas R. *Exploring Realpolitik: Probing International Relations Theory with Computer Simulation.* Boulder, Colo.: Lynne Rienner, 1990. Attempts to determine the extent to which realpolitik influences international relations using computer simulation.

Jensen, Kenneth, and Elizabeth Faulkner, eds. *Morality and Foreign Policy: Realpolitik Revisited.* Washington D.C.: U.S. Institute of Peace, 1991. Articles that seem to show that abstract principles and conventional morality have little influence on international relations.

Paul Madden

Cross-References

REGIONAL GOVERNMENTS

Field of study: Local and regional government

Regional governments—such as those of the individual states within the United States—are used in many countries to allow for local diversity within the framework of the national government. These governments vary greatly in their structures, in their functions, and in the amount of local autonomy that they exercise.

Principal terms

CONFEDERATION: form of government in which regional or subunit governments control the central authority and usually have the right to secede

FEDERALISM: system in which the central and regional governments have separate bases of authority

SUBUNIT GOVERNMENT: level of government that administers one of multiple regions into which a country is divided; called "states" within the United States, subunits are also known as provinces, cantons, departments, lander, and other names elsewhere

TOTALITARIAN GOVERNMENT: system of government in which the central authority puts no limits on the aspects of citizens' lives in which it may interfere

UNITARY GOVERNMENT: system of government in which a central government has ultimate authority; within such systems, subunit governments are controlled by the national government, which may alter or abolish them at will

Overview

Regional governments are those subunit governments found in many nations that have the same basic roles as the fifty states of the U.S. political system. Forms of regional government differ in the degrees to which their subunits have autonomy from central control. In a unitary system of national government, crucial power is in the hands of the central government. Such power is in the hands of the subunit or regional governments in confederal systems, and it is divided between the two levels within federal systems. To put this another way, the regional or subunit governments are dependent "creatures" of the state in a unitary system, while the equivalent regional governments have the right to secede or even to abolish the central government in confederal systems. There may also be subunits of the subunits, as is the case for counties or municipalities within the U.S. states.

Perhaps the most widely used example of a unitary system of national government is that of the United Kingdom of Great Britain and Northern Ireland. In that system, all power resides in the British Parliament, which may alter or abolish any subunit governments at will. Although historic regions known as counties or shires have some governmental functions, such functions are so limited and so closely controlled by

Parliament it may be said that regional governments do not truly exist in Britain. In saying that there are no regional governments in Britain, one must recognize that centuries-old treaties do govern the relationships between England and Scotland, for example, guaranteeing the Scots the right to their own parliament and legal system for local affairs. Scotland was joined to England to create Great Britain early in the eighteenth century by a treaty that continues to govern their relationship. Since this treaty is honored as an act of Parliament, the unitary system technically is still maintained in Britain. Similar arrangements govern the relationships among England, Wales, and Ulster (Northern Ireland). Although Parliament can change these relationships, the tradition-minded British are reluctant to do so.

France also has a unitary government which may appear to be federal because of the existence of ninety-five regional subdivisions known as "departments." French departments are not, however, autonomous governments, but merely subdivisions within an overarching national bureaucratic system. The authority of department officials is severely limited, and most basic rules are established by the central government in Paris. France also has local governments that have somewhat more autonomy than do the departments, but which are only given their autonomy by the central government, which can reclaim it. Again, tradition plays a role, as the ninety-five departments have existed since the Revolution of 1789, even though the central French government has gone through more than a dozen constitutions or regimes since then.

Within Europe, the only truly federal government is the Federal Republic of Germany, which now includes all of the four sectors into which Germany was divided at the end of World War II. The most significant recombination of these sectors was the addition of all of East Germany (the old communist regime known formally as the German Democratic Republic) at the end of the 1980's with the collapse of the communist regime. Germany is made up of several important regions, each of which is called a Land, and collectively are known as Lander. Each Land has substantial local governmental powers and is represented in the national Bundesrat, or upper house of the German legislature. Bundesrat members are selected by the legislatures in each Land, which make sure their members represent the interests of the regional governments. Technically, the Bundesrat is not as powerful as the Bundestag, or lower house of the legislature, but it has sufficient residual power to block some legislation and it controls how laws and policies are implemented. As is true of the fifty states in the United States, each Land is entitled to keep a wide variety of residual powers, and, in fact, the Lander probably have more power over their central government than states do in the United States.

The German federal system has its rules spelled out in a written constitution the terms of which are authoritatively interpreted by the German Constitutional Court. The highest in the land, it is in a position comparable to that of the U.S. Supreme Court, in that it can use "judicial review" to declare national and regional laws unconstitutional. Germany has not only the sole federal regime in Europe, but also has the only constitutional court with such wide-ranging powers.

Applications

Italy represents yet another variation in these patterns, principally because of the instability of its national regime. Italy has a multi-party, parliamentary government with such a large number of small political parties that no one party can win a majority in the legislature. As a result, coalitions of parties must be formed to elect a premier and form a cabinet. The inherent instability of such coalitions is demonstrated by the fact that the country had had forty-eight changes of government between 1945 and 1988—a new government on average once every eleven months. This instability is also reflected in the relations between the central and subunit governments.

The three main levels of Italian subunit governments are cities and towns (*comuni*); provinces; and regions. Politically, the comuni were the most important units throughout the 1970's, but, in administrative terms, the province was historically the major subdivision in the country. Provinces were controlled by prefects who were members of the national bureaucracy and members of the interior ministry in Rome. The relationship between a province and the central government was a unitary one, but the relationship between the province and its own comuni was somewhat looser and more "federal."

In the 1970's, a regional reform was passed to replace provincial with regional governments, but governmental instability and weak implementation meant that provinces lingered as administrative units and regional governments were instituted only slowly. Politics influenced this outcome since a center-right coalition feared potential communist control of regional governments if they were empowered as called for in the reform. The Communist Party then had considerable strength in the local governments in certain regions, and it did increase its strength in the regional governments that were finally empowered after a series of center-left coalitions were formed in the 1980's. The confusion of these practices and the instability of the national governments made it difficult to predict how the reforms would ultimately work. Generally, an unstable national government finds it difficult to assert authority over local units, and one possibility was that regional and local governments would continue to gain informal power even if the formal relationships appeared otherwise.

In principle, Italy is a unitary state with some ineffective trappings of federalism. On the other hand, the weakness of the national government means that the local patronage networks used to gather votes for electoral purposes become locally powerful at the subunit level. Another factor is the national division of the country between north and south—a division which is not only economic but also cultural. The industrialized north is divided internally between the industrial owners and the laboring groups, with religious groups playing a role. The less urbanized, agricultural south provides a large measure of support for the social and religious policies of the Catholic church. Each of these regions has its own cultural heritage which affects the degree of conservatism or radicalism of the area.

At the opposite extreme from unitary states, such as Britain and France, is the confederation of Switzerland, whose constitution defines the relationships between the national government and the twenty-two regions called "cantons." Of all the governments in Europe, Switzerland most closely fits the description of a confederation; however, the Swiss constitution assigns responsibility for national security, defense, and diplomacy only to the central authorities—the most limited range of powers given to any central government in Europe. Despite the formal weakness of the confederation government, it has faced no secession for several hundred years. Each canton has a broad range of local autonomous powers, which have been as jealously guarded as the well-known Swiss neutrality. Perhaps national authorities could hope for no more unity from such a small but diverse group as the Swiss, who speak four different languages within a small geographical area.

Regional governments assume a variety of forms on other continents. Africa offers the example of Nigeria, which has had nineteen separate states and a federal capital since 1978. The original colonial division was into two largely arbitrary political regions which Britain ineffectively used to try to represent the three biggest tribal groupings before abandoning it in favor of three divisions following tribal lines. Tribal rivalries and open warfare greatly disrupted Nigeria after it became an independent state in 1960, eroding the effectiveness of the national federal system.

Other former British colonies, such as Australia and Canada, which become strong and democratic nations in their own right, show a strong tendency to adopt federal systems. Australia has six full "states" and two smaller units called "territories." It has an elected national Senate based on the states and territories as subunits and a House based on proportional representation, as does the United States, but it uses a parliamentary system as in Canada and Britain.

Canada has ten full provinces and two sparsely populated territories. Its national parliamentary government consists of an appointed Senate and an elected House of Commons in which each province has a number of representatives based roughly on population. The key issue in the Canadian federal system is the uncertain and changing status of the French-speaking province of Quebec. This situation exemplifies both the need for, and the problems of, a federal system. French-speaking Quebec has always felt some danger of being overwhelmed by the larger number of English-speaking provinces (and citizens). The Canadian federal system allows Quebec a measure of special autonomy, but it also helps perpetuate controversy over how much uniformity is needed and how much diversity is possible.

At the extreme unitary end of the national government spectrum is the People's Republic of China. China, whether imperial, nationalist, or communist, has always shunned any official recognition of individual regional differences or federalism, even during periods when colonial powers, warlords, or powerful revolutionary groups were raging through the land. The traditional model has always been the notion of one united harmonious people led by a single "omnipotent" ruler. Such historic provinces, counties, and villages as exist in China have for centuries been officially controlled by the national government as a part of a gigantic bureaucracy no matter how weak the reality of that bureaucratic control may have been.

To the Western mind, it is confusing to learn the well-known Chinese adage: "Heaven is high and the emperor is far away." This means that anyone can ignore national directives, so long as the central authorities are too distant or too weak to compel obedience. To be sure, there have been emperors and communist leaders, such as Mao Tse-tung, who actually were in complete control of the country—at least briefly. There has always been a tension between the official centralized Chinese model and the reality of local autonomy.

Despite paper differences, this same basic observation could be made of the area now known as the Commonwealth of Independent States, the successor regime to the Union of Soviet Socialist Republics. Formally, the Soviet Union was a federal state so loosely constructed that each of its sixteen component "soviet socialist republics" had the right to secede in its constitution. In reality, Joseph Stalin exercised tight control through domination of the presumably "independent" federal and local officials through the hierarchically controlled Communist Party. Still, even in Stalin's time, and certainly in growing proportions after Stalin, quiet, unofficial local disobedience and passive resistance did occur.

Context

In the United States, Canada, Germany and Switzerland, much political activity occurs in the subunit governments because this level of government is meant to empower local or regional groups. Most Americans feel empowered to organize or change government since they can appeal to whichever local, state, or federal level they feel will be most responsive to their needs. The availability of different arenas for action empowers citizens to act on their own. In a unitary system, the citizen typically can only hope to influence policy through submerging themselves in collectivities large enough to contest for power on the national level. Perhaps the most striking contrast comes in the disempowerment of citizens in unitary totalitarian countries such as China. In 1989, many people around the globe were saddened to see Chinese students, a relatively tiny percentage of the urban population, try to muster the strength to overthrow a massive national government simply because they had no other level on which to contest national policies. The all-or-nothing contrast between the students' weakness and their hope that they could provoke the collapse of the government through national anarchy reflected the few options that they had. Citizens in a federal system might have attempted to act on other levels, but the Chinese had only one level on which to fight. This is true not only of dictatorial, totalitarian states, but also in democratic unitary states such as Britain and France. In a unitary state, it is said that subunit governments are creatures of the state and may be abolished at will. This is not an idle power; Britain's Prime Minister Margaret Thatcher did abolish some subunit governments, including the council for the City of London, thereby tightening her political control by threatening subunits that did not go along with her program. Despite the power of central government, however, the British Parliament rarely abolishes any of its subunits, as it depends heavily on tradition.

In France, the unitary system seems quite rigid. One widely read anecdote is about the French minister of education who supposedly knows what subject any class in any French public school is discussing at any given moment, simply by consulting his or her watch, as all classes are required to follow a rigid national curriculum. Such tight national control of education would be unheard of in America, where no such rigid uniformity exists.

Regional governments are not as widespread as local governments among the various nations of the world, but most nations in the world have some regional governments unless they are very small. As with local governments, the most important question is how much autonomy can the regional government have within a national structure which hopes to defend the entire nation. With so many different governments, individual variations are wide. The structures of these governments, however, typically fall into the broad categories of unitary, federal, and confederal forms of government along a continuum in which strong national governments are at the unitary end and strong regional governments are at the confederal end.

Bibliography

Curtis, Michael, et al., eds. *Introduction to Comparative Government.* 2d ed. New York: HarperCollins, 1990. Essays on the governments of Britain, France, Germany, Japan, the Soviet Union, China, India, Mexico, and Nigeria.

Dragnich, Alex N., Jorgen S. Rasmussen, and Joel C. Moses. *Major European Governments.* 8th ed. Pacific Grove, Calif.: Brooks/Cole, 1991. An excellent examination of the major European governments of Britain, France, Germany, and Russia from a very traditional institutional perspective.

Glendon, Mary Ann, Michael Wallace Gordon, and Christopher Osakwe. *Comparative Legal Traditions in a Nutshell.* St. Paul, Minn.: West, 1982. Succinct survey of the major legal traditions in the world from a comparative legal perspective.

Hunter, Brian, ed. *The Statesman's Year-Book.* 130th ed. New York: St. Martin's Press, 1993. Detailed information on every nation of the world, with extended descriptions of the subunit governments of the larger countries.

Kesselman, Mark, et al. *European Politics in Transition.* 2d ed. Lexington, Mass.: D.C. Heath, 1992. Examination of the governments of Britain, France, Germany, Italy, Sweden, Russia, and some of the smaller European governments.

Mahler, Gregory S. *Comparative Politics: An Institutional and Cross-National Approach.* 2d ed. Englewood Cliffs, N.J.: Prentice Hall, 1995. Relatively newer approach to comparative government which is distinguished by its separate discussion of the relationships between the central and subunit governments in Britain, France, Germany, Japan, Canada, Russia, Mexico, and Nigeria.

Richard L. Wilson

Cross-References

City Government in the United States, p. 266; Confederations, p. 391; County Government, p. 458; Federal Mandates, p. 662; Federalism in the United States, p. 668; Federations, p. 675; Indigenous Peoples' Governments, p. 903; Rural Community Government, p. 1763; State and Local Government, p. 1885; State Government, p. 1891.

REGULATORY AGENCIES IN THE UNITED STATES

Field of study: Functions of government

Regulatory agencies of the U.S. federal government set and enforce standards of behavior for other governmental units, businesses, and citizens. Few areas of human interaction are untouched; regulation itself is a fundamental and pervasive source of government control over social order.

Principal terms
CAPTURE: theory that regulatory agencies serve the very industries that they regulate for political reasons; the theory is largely discredited by empirical evidence
COMMAND AND CONTROL REGULATION: pejorative term used to describe traditional top-down or directive-based regulation, usually by those preferring deregulation or a system incorporating market incentives
COST-BENEFIT ANALYSIS: technique by which the costs and benefits of proposed actions are identified, assigned dollar values, and compared to calculate net results
REGULATORY NEGOTIATION: process in which regulations are devised through bargaining among interested groups and the regulatory agency in order to decrease conflict and enhance compliance
RISK ANALYSIS: technique by which risks are identified and evaluated, leading to decisions about how they might be managed

Overview

Of the various regulatory agencies that operate within the executive branch of the United States government, most are housed within the major departments. The Bureau of Alcohol, Tobacco, and Firearms, for example, belongs to Treasury. Others are so-called independent establishments, such as the Nuclear Regulatory Commission; a few are governmental corporations, such as the Pension Benefit Guaranty Corporation.

Internally, regulatory agencies follow one of two structural formats. Some, such as the Federal Election Commission, are headed by multimember boards selected by the president. Others are led by appointed administrators (for example, the Food and Drug Administration)—a system intended to enhance accountability and responsiveness to the executive department.

Regulation has developed into a significant federal activity. Regulatory agencies together employ more than 100,000 permanent full-time staff members and their administrative costs total billions of dollars. Compliance costs are billions more, though difficult to pin down; estimates by regulators are usually much less than those offered by the regulated.

During the first century of U.S. federal government, basic regulatory bodies such as the Army Corps of Engineers (1824), the Patent and Trademark Office (1836), and the Comptroller of the Currency (1863) were established within the executive departments. The birth of the Interstate Commerce Commission in 1887 marked the advent of the independent commission form and began a shift from state to federal authority. The New Deal era of the 1930's solidified economic regulation by the national government. Many new agencies were created in response to the Great Depression, such as the Federal Deposit Insurance Corporation and the Securities and Exchange Commission. Similar expansion occurred during the 1960's and 1970's, this time focusing more on social regulation. Government became involved in new areas such as consumer affairs, environmental protection, and workplace safety. A variety of industries, such as banking and telecommunications, were deregulated in the decade that followed. Mixed results led to debates about or movement toward re-regulation as happened in the case of cable television.

Federal agency intervention into the so-called free market has been justified on both economic and political grounds. The economic rationales stem from market imperfections of various sorts, such as lack of competition. The extreme case is a natural monopoly; for example, constructing more than one city water or sewer system would make less sense than regulating a single provider. Another economic rationale for federal regulation is destructive competition. This was the justification for airline regulation, which began in the 1930's. The existence of too many competitors in a market results in profit margins so thin that both service and safety can be jeopardized. Another economic rationale is lack of information. Since inadequately informed consumers cannot make rational decisions about purchasing goods and services—such as automobiles and doctors—without information, government oversight is needed. So-called externalities or spillovers are another economic rationale. These occur where third parties are affected by others' transactions. For example, everyone living within a watershed or airshed is hurt by harmful emissions from local producers who do not pay the costs of cleanup. A final economic rationale for government is the notion of public goods—the idea that some commodities are shared in common by definition. Without coordinated allocation, for example, the airwaves would suffer the combined chaos of having all those wishing to broadcast doing so across what is a physically finite spectrum.

Regulation is also justified for noneconomic, or political, reasons. One of the most important traditional reasons is the need to equalize power among interested parties. One rationale for the National Labor Relations Act, for example, was to balance the bargaining powers of workers and their employers. A similar rationale was advanced as an argument for regulating railroads in order to help farmers in the late 1800's. Another politic rationale is the need to compensate for income inequities. When gaps are deemed unacceptable, policies of redistribution result. Aesthetics is also a rationale. For example, preserving visibility at the Grand Canyon and in the Great Smoky Mountains is a significant force behind emissions standards in both areas.

Regulation in the United States is two tiered. State agencies add a second layer of regulation to that of federal agencies, and they often play more than one role. In areas such as environmental protection, individual states are typically responsible for implementing federal policies. Some industries, such as banking, face concurrent sets of rules at each level. In other cases states are the dominant or only government regulators of such matters as food pricing, insurance, occupational licensure, and public utilities.

Government regulation occurs through multiple mechanisms. As with all government agencies, those charged with regulatory authority engage in rule making to set standards. Adjudication is used to settle subsequent disputes. Various types of analysis are used to inform the process. One such tool is risk analysis, which involves three components. These are assessment, in which risks, their severity of harm, and their frequency of occurrence are identified; evaluation, wherein acceptable and unreasonable risks are distinguished; and management, in which decisions are made about how risks are to be controlled or eliminated.

Cost-benefit analysis is another common technique. As its name suggests, analysts attempt to assign explicit dollar values to all costs and benefits associated with proposed regulations. The intent is that only those regulations yielding net benefits should be adopted.

It should be noted that both risk analysis and cost-benefit analysis are controversial. For example, deciding how much, if any, risk may be tolerated in certain matters became more difficult as the science of detecting harmful substances improved from being able to detect parts per million to parts per billion, and then parts per quadrillion. Assigning dollar values to benefits such as an unobstructed view or saving a human life are considered by some to be impossible or even immoral.

Regulatory agencies must also enforce the regulations they adopt. Monitoring and inspection of those they regulate is an important part of their operations, consuming significant staff resources. Borders must be patrolled, smokestack emissions tested, meat examined, and so forth. Likewise, sanctions must be applied when violations occur for policies to be effective.

The result in the United States is an elaborate regulatory apparatus from which few social behaviors or interactions are totally excluded. There are limitations, however. Politicians can limit the scope of regulations by restricting an agency's legal authority or funding, for example. Regulation also lags behind constantly changing developments in business practice (such as the rise of "junk bonds" in financial markets), science (such as genetic engineering), and technology (for example, computer "hacking"). Nevertheless, the total breadth and depth of the enterprise make regulation a core feature of American government.

Applications

The U.S. Department of Agriculture (USDA) estimated that Americans spent more than $500 billion on food in 1989. Although federal law places basic responsibilities for quality and safety on manufacturers, the public relies on the regulatory system to ensure the quality and safety standards of the products that it eats. Food regulation is a fragmented and complex effort that has inspired more than thirty-five laws and twelve different agencies. The principal agencies involved devoted more than $800 million and almost seventeen thousand staff years to it in 1989 alone. The result was a food supply recognized as one of the safest in the world. Even so, the Centers for Disease Control reported that some six million illnesses and nine thousand deaths result from foodborne diseases each year.

The Food and Drug Administration (FDA) was created to be a significant part of this regulation effort. Located within the Public Health Service in the Department of Health and Human Services, it regulates the food, drug, and cosmetic industries. Its broad charge in the food domain was to ensure that domestic and imported food products (except meat and poultry) are safe, sanitary, nutritious, wholesome, and honestly labeled. The FDA also oversees animal drugs and food additives in animal feeds, and it shares responsibility for egg products.

The MacGregor Flavr Savr tomato was just one of the $1 trillion worth of products that the FDA was designed to regulate. This tomato was the first genetically engineered whole food to reach retail grocery stores. After scientists identified the gene that promotes softening in tomatoes, they reinsert a copy backward to retard the softening effect, thereby producing a tomato that can remain on the vine longer, become riper and more flavorful, and yet be not too mushy to ship. Its creator, a California biotechnology company named Calgene, spent ten years and $25 million on its development. The FDA approved Flavr Savr in 1994, after evaluating Calgene's data for four years and following final approval of its safety-review process by an advisory committee of twenty-eight scientists, academics, and other food experts.

The FDA's approval of the tomato had a number of applications. Most obvious was its impact on Calgene, whose investment and future profit—perhaps even its corporate viability—were at stake. Also at stake was consumer confidence in not only this product, but also others like it, as well as the food supply generally, should some harm result. In addition, the FDA's approval signaled its sanction of the science involved, setting an important precedent for consumers and the industry. Specifically, the agency was convinced that new antibiotic-resistant bacteria would not proliferate from the genetic engineering. Critics' calls for broader assessment of the benefits and risks of biotechnology are typical of the regulatory process as well.

Both the quality of the air that they breathe and the water that they drink are vital to Americans. The scope, rigor, and impact of government efforts to keep these basic natural resources in the United States clean also illustrate the power of government regulation. The Clean Air Act Amendments of 1970 required automakers to reduce engine emissions. The laws also required that the Environmental Protection Agency (EPA) establish national ambient air quality standards, that the individual states produce air pollution control plans to meet federal standards, and that citizens sue EPA to enforce the laws, if necessary. Congress also included specific goals and timetables for each activity. Automobile emissions, for example, were to be reduced 90 percent by 1975.

The immediate effect was EPA authority over all major sources of air pollution: mobile (vehicles) and stationary (especially coal-burning plants), existing and new.

Six pollutants were targeted by initial standards: suspended particulates, the soot and dust in the air; sulfur dioxide from coal combustion; the nitrogen oxides in smog; hydrocarbons, including gas and chemical vapors; carbon monoxide from automobile exhaust; and photochemical oxidants (later changed to ozone), which also cause smog. Limits were also imposed on other hazardous air pollutants such as vinyl chloride, and some, such as asbestos, were prohibited altogether.

The results of these regulations were generally positive. Automobile engine emissions fell substantially as a result of the introduction of unleaded gasoline and catalytic converters—the latter a technology invented after the act was passed. In fact, total lead emissions declined 97 percent between 1970 and 1991. Particulates fell more than 60 percent during the same period, carbon monoxide by half. Sulfur oxides and volatile organic compounds were also reduced substantially, although nitrogen oxides were not. In general, the air became cleaner.

The Federal Water Pollution Control Act Amendments of 1972 established goals of creating fishable and swimmable waters by the year 1983 and zero discharges by 1985. This legislation was based on equipment: Pollution sources were required to install the best practicable technology within five years and the best available technology within eleven years. As a result, the EPA drew up standards for 642 industrial processes and issued 67,000 effluent permits. Although the zero-discharge goal proved too optimistic and was eventually abandoned, the nation's waters became cleaner. Within a decade, the Council on Environmental Quality could report that most pollutants were either declining or holding steady. Violations of water quality standards for fecal coliform bacteria, dissolved oxygen, phosphorous, and lead all declined as well.

Context

Regulation falls squarely within the broader debate about the appropriate role of government in American society. On one side are laissez-faire capitalists, who argue that agency intervention merely substitutes government inefficiencies for those of the marketplace. On the other side are those who view regulation as the inescapable price of industrial and technological progress. U.S. presidents since Richard Nixon have attempted various strategies to manage or cut back on the growth of regulatory agencies. Nixon's Quality of Life review empowered the Office of Management and Budget (OMB) to examine agency proposals so that industry needs could be balanced with environmental and safety interests. Gerald Ford's administration used its Council on Wage and Price Stability to make anti-inflation analysis a routine part of formal rule making. President Jimmy Carter established the Regulatory Analysis and Review Group to bring economic analysis to the process and a semiannual calendar of forthcoming regulations to develop priorities.

Ronald Reagan's administration appointed antiregulation advocates to key positions, such as Secretary of the Interior James Watt. Its budget cuts, OMB review, and mandatory cost-benefit analysis were designed to dismantle or delay agency activity. As a consequence, significant deregulation occurred during this period. The list of industries affected includes airlines, buses, railroads, trucking, cable television, telecommunications, financial institutions, securities, oil, and natural gas. The net results were mixed. Airfares decreased dramatically for consumers, for example, but the number of airlines dwindled as fare competition intensified. By contrast, competitors proliferated following the antitrust breakup of American Telephone and Telegraph. In other cases, new problems led to the issuing of new regulations. Numerous savings and loan failures in the 1980's, for example, caused the demise of the Federal Savings and Loan Insurance Corporation; this led to the creation of the Resolution Trust Corporation to clean up the mess, costing taxpayers hundreds of billions of dollars. In 1994, Congress pressured the FCC to regulate the rate structure of local cable providers.

Naturally, proponents of regulation were quite alarmed by these trends. Regulatory agencies, they feared, were now captured by probusiness presidents. Critics perceived this dismantling of social regulation in particular as removing the safety net guarding Americans from such hazards as unsafe workplaces, faulty nuclear reactors, and environmental degradation—all of which resembled a leap backward to the nineteenth century.

If there is middle ground between the two camps, it is that both are interested in finding ways that regulation can be improved through reforms. Two areas of innovation in particular command attention: regulation through market incentives and regulatory negotiation. Market incentives are a response to the so-called command and control system. The goal is to replace or modify top-down directives with profit-oriented measures. Examples include permits that could be traded, such as routes and landing slots for airlines, broadcast bands, and rights to pollute. Another idea is setting emissions fees that simply charge companies money according to the amounts that they pollute. A third example is what are called bubbles, offsets, and banks. This system would set standards for an entire region, such as an entire airshed, making emissions "zero-sum," that is, each new form of pollution would have to be accompanied by an equivalent reduction elsewhere in the system. In regulatory negotiation, stakeholders draft rules with the assigned agency in a collective, consensual fashion. Although largely untried, the theory is that implementation, enforcement, and compliance will become easier as the regulatory processes become less adversarial.

Bibliography

Carson, Rachel. *Silent Spring*. Boston: Houghton Mifflin, 1962. Classic treatise, often described as the call-to-arms for the environmental movement. Carson raised public awareness by documenting the concentration of pesticides in the food chain and their harmful effects on fish and wildlife.

Congressional Quarterly. *Federal Regulatory Directory*. Washington, D.C.: Author. This biennial is the best descriptive source on regulation in the United States. Each issue contains a survey of recent developments, profiles of all national regulatory bodies, guidance on how to use the *Federal Register* and *Code of Federal Regulations*, and the text of many relevant statutes.

Downing, Paul B. *Environmental Economics and Policy*. Boston: Little, Brown, 1984.

Survey of the economics of environmental regulation. Though aimed at advanced readers, it does a particularly good job describing how market-based models of regulatory reform might work.

Nader, Ralph. *Unsafe at Any Speed: The Designed-In Dangers of the American Automobile*. New York: Grossman, 1965. Nader argues that automobiles have built-in safety defects, most notably Chevrolet's Corvair. Sales of the book soared after it was revealed that General Motors hired private detectives to investigate Nader. The book helped inspire both strong auto safety regulation and greater public interest in consumer protection.

Sinclair, Upton. *The Jungle*. New York: New American Library, 1960. First published in 1906, this novel exposing the terrible conditions in the meatpacking industry had a powerful impact on public opinion. President Theodore Roosevelt promoted passage of the Pure Food and Drugs Act the year after the book's publication.

Tarbell, Ida. *The History of the Standard Oil Company*. New York: Macmillan, 1904. A classic in muckraking journalism, this account of petroleum industry practices and arrogance materially contributed to fostering public support for economic regulation in the United States.

Tolchin, Susan J., and Martin Tolchin. *Dismantling America: The Rush to Deregulate*. New York: Oxford University Press, 1983. Polemic on the dangers of abandoning economic and social regulation that presented a lucid case for government intervention.

John Patrick Piskulich

Cross-References

The Arts and Government, p. 101; Business and Government, p. 177; Capitalism, p. 197; Commerce Regulation, p. 357; Consumer Politics, p. 445; Energy Management, p. 604; Environmental Protection, p. 617; Federal Mandates, p. 662; Government Agencies, p. 765; Government Powers, p. 772; Government Roles, p. 778; Political Economy, p. 1455; Public Utilities, p. 1640; Research, Development, and Planning, p. 1711.

RELIGION AND POLITICS

Field of study: Religion and government

A universal feature of human societies, religion encompasses sacred beliefs, observations, and obligations that define the relationships between individuals and groups and transcendental values and spiritual beings. In many societies the demands of religious beliefs and practices conflict with the political demands of governing institutions.

Principal terms

AMERICAN FUNDAMENTALISM: most conservative and countercultural wing of evangelical Christianity

EVANGELICALISM: conservative movement within Christianity distinguished by its emphasis on salvation through faith alone and the inerrancy of the Bible

POLITICS: institutions and processes by which laws are made and people are governed

RELIGION: people's understanding and practice regarding God, the gods, or a transcendent reality

RELIGIOUS RIGHT: political movement of late twentieth century United States, led by religious conservatives

Overview

Although human societies have differed radically, there are two things they all have in common: religion and politics. Throughout the ages most people have accepted the idea that the supernatural exists. As people attempt to understand and have a proper relationship with the supernatural, usually personified in one or more deities, they develop religious ideas and sacred practices, such as prayer, meditation, and sacrifice. Religious leaders often have great power since followers assume that, to one degree or another, the leaders speak for the gods.

At the same time, societies have always found it necessary to have some form of government to regulate human behavior. The institutions and processes by which people are governed may be referred to as politics. The role of government includes restraining human actions (such as preventing crimes), regulating society (such as inspecting food), and promoting the public welfare (such as requiring education). Political leaders are often powerful because they have the weight of law and the power of the state behind them.

Since both religions and political societies demand the allegiance of their members, and since religious and political leaders each have varying amounts of power, conflicts between religion and politics are common. For instance, the state may declare a war and require citizens to fight in it, but the religion of some citizens may teach them that all wars are wrong. Or, as has often been the case, a government may require people to worship a deity that they do not believe in.

Yet religion and politics often affect each other in a less direct, nonconfrontational manner. For example, in the Bible, the thirteenth chapter of Romans seems to require Christians to obey their governments. Similarly, Muslims are led by the Koran to pay their taxes and live moral lives. Citizens who take these commands seriously will be easier to rule than individuals who do not believe their religion requires them to do these things.

At a more theoretical level, religious ideas may indirectly influence political ones. For example, some scholars believe that Western ideas of equality arose because of the Christian conception that all individuals are equal before the eyes of God. Similarly, the authors of the Declaration of Independence seem to have based their theory of rights upon religious ideas when they wrote that "all men are created equal; that they are endowed by their Creator with certain unalienable rights; that among these, are life, liberty, and the pursuit of happiness."

Political ideas have also influenced religion, especially religious institutions. It has often been argued, for example, that the Roman Catholic church adopted many of the secular, hierarchical structures of the empire it supplanted. Another famous example is Henry VIII of England's break with the Roman Catholic church. In the late twentieth century, some advocates of gender and sexual equality attempted to use political means to force religious organizations to change their policies regarding the ordination of women and the condemnation of homosexuality.

It is more often difficult to measure the influence of religious and political ideas upon each other because so many different factors are involved. One may, for example, make a strong case for congregational church government on the basis of the Bible alone, without relying on political arguments. One might also make theological arguments for the ordination of women without relying on political ideas. The origin and influence of a given idea may be hard to pin down, but that does not mean that ideas of government and religion do not influence each other. To ignore the impact of religious and political ideas upon each other is a serious mistake.

The relationship between religion and politics may be described in three general ways. First, followers of a religion may completely withdraw from politics and society. Second, a religion may come to dominate a society's politics. Third, a relatively peaceful coexistence between religion and politics may arise.

The first of these models is not uncommon since most religions are primarily concerned with the supernatural. If a religion's leaders and followers were to focus on the supernatural, they might decide that participation in politics and society is either useless or of no great importance. In fact, involvement in politics and society, with their emphasis on acquisition and accomplishment, may even be viewed as a danger to one's spiritual existence.

A good example of a religion's retreat from culture is the early Christian church. In the Church's early years, believers were often persecuted by social and political leaders. Believers thought that Jesus Christ was going to return soon, so the early church fathers taught that individuals should focus on their relationships with God and avoid participation in politics and society. Similarly, some modern Buddhist and Hindu monks withdraw from society to seek spiritual perfection.

The second model, that of politics dominated by religion, may be seen in the West after 381 C.E., the year Christianity became the state religion of the Roman Empire. Throughout the Middle Ages, Christian ideas and leaders had a strong influence on European politics. In a like manner, beginning in the early seventh century, a number of Islamic countries were founded and dominated by religious leaders.

In the twentieth century neither of the above-mentioned models has been prevalent. It is possible, however, to find traces of each approach. In America, the Amish people continue to attempt to withdraw from society at large and from politics. Many people continue to retreat from society into convents, monasteries, and other places of spiritual refuge. In countries like Saudi Arabia, Iran, and Israel one may find modern adherents to the idea that government should be religious.

The third relationship between religion and politics is that of a peaceful and separate coexistence. The general reasoning behind this model is that religion and politics are concerned with different matters and should be kept in their own spheres. Advocates of this approach argue that religious institutions should primarily focus on the individuals' relationships with God and the state should worry solely about problems men and women have on earth. This view differs from the first model insofar as believers do not withdraw from the world; they may participate in society and politics without risking their spiritual salvation.

The idea that religion and politics can exist side by side, and that individuals can participate in both, has been advanced by a number of thinkers. Perhaps the most prominent supporter of this concept was Martin Luther, the leader of the sixteenth century Protestant Reformation. He proposed that religion and politics could be separated into completely different spheres. His ideas have had wide influence in the West.

The separation model has arguably become dominant in the West since Luther, but putting the principle into practice is difficult. In the United States, the First Amendment to the Constitution separates religion and politics. The relevant section of the Amendment reads: "Congress shall make no law respecting an establishment of religion, or prohibiting the free exercise thereof." At a minimum, this amendment prevents congress from creating a state religion or from interfering with the practice of its citizens' faith. Yet, while this principle seems simple, a number of difficult issues have come before the U.S. Supreme Court to show that it is not.

The First Amendment does not allow congress to form a state religion. It is not clear, however, if the First Amendment allows the national government to give support to religion in general. For example, one may question whether it should lend textbooks to religious schools, give grants to religious social programs, or exempt churches from taxes. One may question whether the government should be empowered to regulate the free exercise of religion if a religious practice is illegal (such as using drugs) or dangerous (handling venomous snakes, for example). At a more theoretical level, one may question whether the First Amendment prohibits religious citizens who feel their first allegiance is to God from holding public offices or supporting legislation on the basis of their religious beliefs.

Regardless of how the Supreme Court resolves these dilemmas, the questions themselves point to the tensions between religion and politics. Politics and religion come into contact in a number of areas. One will always affect the other in ways that some people do not like. This does not mean that religion and politics cannot coexist peacefully in a society. It does mean, however, that their relationship is likely to be tense. Hence the struggle to define their appropriate relationship is a never-ending one.

Applications

A development that illustrates the complex relationship between religion and politics is the rise of the religious right in late twentieth century U.S. politics. The religious right, which is also referred to as the new Christian right, the religious New Right, or the Christian right, is a political movement motivated by conservative religious principles and led by a variety of religious leaders.

In exploring this movement, it is first necessary to understand the specific religious groups that compose it. The bulk of the religious right is made up of evangelical Christians. Evangelicals differ from other Christians in their insistence that the Bible contains God's inerrant word, that salvation is found through faith in Jesus Christ alone, and that Christians should share their faith. Fundamentalist Christians are a subset of evangelicals, differing from their brethren primarily in their more complete rejection of modern culture.

Evangelicals are not a recent phenomenon in American religious history, nor is their participation in politics. For example, they were heavily involved in the abolitionist and temperance movements. After enjoying victories in these areas, Evangelicals began to feel increasingly isolated from the modern world. In the 1920's and 1930's they came to believe that America was moving away from its moral and religious base. As evidence they cited the repeal of Prohibition, the teaching of evolution in public schools, and the attacks made on the literal truth of the Bible by liberal theologians. In reaction to these events, many evangelicals withdrew from politics and secular society.

Evangelicals began to emerge from their isolation and participate in politics again the early 1970's as politicians began to court their vote. Most notably, Jimmy Carter ran for president as an evangelical Christian in 1976. The importance of his faith and the participation of this religious group was so evident that Time magazine labeled 1976 "The year of the Evangelical."

The return of evangelicals to politics in 1976 did not mark the beginning of the religious right, primarily because Carter was a liberal. As president he supported policies such as legalized abortion and the Equal Rights Amendment that alienated evangelicals. A date for the beginning of the religious right is 1979, the year Jerry Falwell, a Baptist minister who had a wide following through his television program, "The Old Time Gospel Hour," formed the Moral Majority. The primary purpose of this organization was to lobby elected officials on Christian issues and to elect supporters of the religious right's agenda to public office. Its creation coincided with the formation or expansion of several other Christian groups, including the Christian Voice, the Religious Roundtable, and the National Christian Action Coalition. In 1980 these groups and a variety of evangelical leaders successfully supported Ronald Reagan in his race for the presidency. Although Reagan was not noted for his church-going—as Carter was—he endorsed the religious right's agenda, for which he was substantially rewarded by the religious right at the voting booth. The fact that Carter did not receive the support of the religious right, and that Reagan did, is demonstration of the complex and strange turns that the relationship between government and religion can take. The religious right had two main objectives in the early 1980's. First, they wanted to encourage more evangelical Christians to participate in politics, either by voting or by actually running for office. The more important goal, for which the first was a means to the end, was to enact Christian legislation that they felt was necessary to make America moral again. The top legislative priorities of the religious right included making abortion illegal, returning prayer to the public schools, preventing sex education in the classroom, restricting homosexual rights, and generally shrinking the size of the federal government.

Initially the religious right assumed that the majority of the country agreed with them and that they could achieve their goals simply by encouraging people to vote. By the mid-1980's, however, it became clear that this was not the case. Although the religious right had a few successes, it was not able to elect many new supporters to office or pass its most desired legislation. In 1988, Pat Robertson, a pastor and religious broadcaster, ran for the Republican nomination for president, and lost by a large margin. It was becoming evident that the religious right was not, indeed, a majority.

This realization led to a second, more sophisticated, stage in the development of the religious right. Many of its initial groups, such as Falwell's Moral Majority, were disbanded or superseded by organizations such as Pat Robertson's Christian Coalition, the Eagle Forum, and Concerned Women for America. These groups retained most of the religious rights's goals, but they became much more politically realistic, recognizing the need to work within existing political structures, to compromise, and, in general, to care about results.

Using this new approach, evangelicals remained active and effective in politics. Working within the Republican Party, they were able to keep many of their goals in the presidential platforms of 1988 and 1992, even though some Republicans wanted to back away from issues such as abortion and school prayer. In addition, evangelicals took over several state-level party organizations in the late 1980's and in the 1990's, hence gaining the ability to nominate some of their own candidates and to make sure their issues remained before the public eye. Thus, while the religious right did not take over American politics, it became firmly enough entrenched to remain a political force into the twenty-first century.

Context

The rise of the religious right in the United States illustrates the complex relationship that religion and politics can have. The religious right's opposition to abortion, homosexuality, and sex education, for example, is largely informed by their understanding of the Bible. To have an impact on public policy, however, evangelicals must involve themselves in the secular realm of politics, from the mundane tasks of rounding up voters to the more exciting attempt to elect one of their own to the presidency.

Important questions can be raised about the means and ends of the religious right, or any religious political movement, such as whether it is proper for a group to legislate its religious beliefs, so that nonbelievers are bound by them. One might also ask if the church is an appropriate place to pursue political ends, and whether the merger of religion and politics might ultimately tear down religion instead of redeeming politics.

Different societies have come to different conclusions about these questions. Some cultures separate religion from politics, others have politics dominated by religion, and, in some societies, the two peacefully coexist. While the most common, the third model is quite often the most complex. The government will always regulate some aspects of religious life, and religious people will always participate in politics. To separate the two completely is not possible. All societies must deal with the vexing problems posed by the relationship between religion and politics. Though the ideal arrangement may never be found, it is clear that each institution has an important effect upon the other.

Bibliography

Johnson, Paul. *A History of Christianity*. New York: Atheneum, 1976. General history of Christianity with thorough discussions of the relationship between politics and the church.

Leege, David C., Lyman A. Kellstedt, et al. *Rediscovering the Religious Factor in American Politics*. Armonk, N.Y.: M. E. Sharpe, 1993. Attempts to define and measure the variables necessary to understand religion and politics in America.

Neuhaus, Richard John. *The Naked Public Square*. Grand Rapids, Mich.: Wm. B. Eerdmans, 1984. Important argument against excluding religion from public discourse in a democratic society.

Niebuhr, H. Richard. *Christ and Culture*. New York: Harper & Row, 1951. One of the finest analytical works on the relationship between Christianity and culture.

Niebuhr, Reinhold. *Moral Man and Immoral Society*. New York: Charles Scribner's Sons, 1960. Timeless examination of the use of religion and ethics in making public policy.

Wald, Kenneth D. *Religion and Politics in the United States*. 2d ed. Washington, D.C.: Congressional Quarterly Press, 1992. A social scientist's look at religion and politics in America, especially on the rise of the religious right.

Mark David Hall

Cross-References

Augustine's Political Philosophy, p. 121; The Bill of Rights, p. 134; Buddhism and Government, p. 152; Church and Government in History, p. 230; Church and State Relations in the United States, p. 236; Civil Liberties Protection, p. 291; Confucianism and Government, p. 405; Deism, p. 495; Hinduism and Government, p. 823; Islam and Government, p. 994; John of Salisbury's Political Philosophy, p. 1006; Liberation Theology, p. 1124; Theocracy, p. 1968; Vico's Political Philosophy, p. 2103.

REPRODUCTIVE POLITICS

Field of study: Civil rights and liberties

Reproductive politics concerns the conflicts arising over public policies relating to abortion, contraception, and population control. It encompasses the laws that governments enact in these areas, the ways in which these laws are enforced, and the efforts of special-interest groups to influence public policies.

Principal terms
ABORTION: medical procedure that terminates pregnancy, usually before the fetus is viable
FEMINISM: political ideology espousing equal legal rights for women and their liberation from oppressive social and economic institutions
"PRO-CHOICE" MOVEMENTS: umbrella term for organized groups whose aim is to preserve and broaden women's right to choose to terminate a pregnancy
"RIGHT TO LIFE" MOVEMENTS: umbrella term for organized groups who advocate restricting or eliminating the right to abortion in order to protect fetal life
ROE v. WADE: controversial 1973 decision by the U.S. Supreme Court that effectively legalized abortion
THERAPEUTIC ABORTION: abortion that is deemed medically necessary in order to preserve the life or health of the mother
VIABILITY: condition in which a fetus may—with reasonable medical intervention—sustain life outside its mother's womb (usually around twenty-four weeks)

Overview

Reproductive politics is a concept that encompasses a wide variety of conflicts over public policies having to do with the legal regulation of human reproduction. The causes of political conflict over issues such as abortion, contraception, and population growth policies are various and complex. These conflicts often reflect fundamental philosophical and religious disagreements about the nature of human reproduction and the rights and responsibilities of women in society. In developing countries, the primary reproductive issues involve conflicts over government attempts to reduce high population growth rates. In developed countries, where population growth rates are more stable, the primary reproductive issues tend to center on the rights of women to control their own bodies and their lives, against the sometimes conflicting interests of the state in protecting the life of the fetus, the health and well-being of the mother, and society in general. In all societies, reproductive politics is entwined with cultural, religious, and psychological attitudes and practices, and has often served as a surrogate for deep-seated conflicts about sexuality and morality.

In the nineteenth century, contraception and population control were the primary reproductive issues. In England, and other industrialized countries, it became a fashionable view among many intellectuals and government officials that overpopulation threatened economic growth and caused poverty. Despite the opposition of religious leaders, who feared that birth control would lead to widespread sexual immorality, organized groups formed to promote birth control in many European countries in the 1880's and 1890's. The gradual industrialization of Western societies in the nineteenth century reduced the need for agricultural manual labor and spurred calls for effective birth control methods, especially from people in the middle class. In the United States, birth control advocates ran into the obstacle of obscenity laws, which made it difficult in many states to publish and distribute birth control devices and descriptive literature. In 1873, the U.S. Congress passed the Comstock Act (named after Anthony Comstock, a famous moral zealot), which defined contraceptives as "articles of immoral use" and made it a federal crime to mail or transport them for sale across state lines. Many states enacted similar laws prohibiting the sale and distribution of contraceptives within their own state lines.

In the early twentieth century, birth control advocates, led by the heroic efforts of feminists such as Margaret Sanger in the United States and Marie Stopes in England, established birth control clinics and directly challenged laws banning contraceptives. By 1930, some three hundred clinics were opened in England, the United States, Germany, and Austria. Birth control came to be favored not only by feminists, who saw it as essential for women's liberty, but also by eugenics groups who saw contraception as a way to reduce what they regarded as excessive breeding of "inferior" people. By the late 1930's, feminists succeeded in encouraging the medical establishment to endorse contraception as a therapeutic health measure. In the 1940's and 1950's, many people in the United States and Western Europe came to accept the view of birth control as a legitimate means of family planning, despite continued opposition from the Roman Catholic church. The Planned Parenthood Federation of America, founded by Sanger, became the leading advocate of "responsible parenthood."

Although many U.S. states retained laws prohibiting birth control, such laws were seldom enforced. In 1965, the U.S. Supreme Court declared unconstitutional a Connecticut law that banned the manufacture, distribution, and use of birth control devices, even by married couples. Seven years later, the Court struck down a Massachusetts law that prohibited distribution of contraceptives to unmarried persons. In 1971, the U.S. Congress repealed the Comstock Act and six years later the Supreme Court nullified state laws prohibiting advertisement of contraceptives and their distribution to minors.

In the latter half of the twentieth century, abortion became the most contentious issue in the arena of reproductive politics, particularly in the United States. Conflict over abortion was fueled by the apparently irreconcilable antagonism between those fiercely dedicated to the protection of fetal life and those equally dedicated to advance the rights of women to make decisions about their sexual and reproductive lives without government interference. Yet, from colonial times until the early 1800's, abortions were generally legal and readily available in America. Opposition to abortion initially came mainly from the medical establishment, which aimed to put amateur abortionists out of business. By 1880, most states made abortion a criminal act, unless, in the opinion of a licensed physician, it was deemed medically necessary. Until the 1950's, this exception for "therapeutic" abortions, in practice, allowed middle- and upper-class women, who were likely to have regular physicians, to obtain abortions for almost any reason. Other women, especially the poor, were forced to seek abortions from unlicensed and unskilled practitioners, often with tragic results.

Progressive-minded members of the legal and medical communities in the United States led reform efforts in the 1950's and 1960's to change existing abortion laws. They sought to make physicians free to practice abortion if the physical or mental health of the woman was at risk, if a child was likely to be born with a grave physical or mental defect, or if the pregnancy was the result of rape or incest. Feminist groups called for repeal of abortion laws and to have the decision over abortion be a woman's alone, without interference from the state or the medical profession. Also in this period, reform efforts were aided by a growing number of scientists who popularized the view that world population was growing at a rate faster than the earth's resources could sustain. In response to these pressures, and over the strenuous objections of conservatives and the Catholic church, twelve state legislatures reformed their abortion laws between 1967 and 1973. At this point, the "right to life" movement organized itself to counter the trend toward liberal abortion laws.

Applications

The landmark Supreme Court decision in *Roe v. Wade* exemplifies the contentious nature of reproductive political issues. It also illustrates the difficulty of finding a democratic solution to the abortion question.

In 1973, the politics of abortion greatly intensified with the Supreme Court's decision in the case of *Roe v. Wade*. The case arose as a challenge by a pregnant woman to a Texas law which prohibited abortion except to save the life of the mother. "Roe" was a pseudonym for Norma McCorvey, an unmarried woman who was too poor to travel out of state to obtain a legal abortion, and unable to afford an illegal abortion in Texas. In court, the state of Texas argued that its law was justified to protect women from the medical risks of abortion and to protect fetal life. But, in an elaborate seven-to-two decision, the Supreme Court announced that the U.S. Constitution protected women and their doctors from unwarranted government intrusion into decisions to terminate pregnancies. Asserting that no consensus existed on the point at which life begins, and that the Constitution does not confer rights upon unborn persons, the Court said that states could not therefore intervene to protect fetal life until the point of viability. The state could intervene to protect maternal health, but only at the end of the third month of pregnancy. This decision, one of the most controversial in American political history, effectively legalized abortion throughout the United States.

The principal author of the decision in *Roe v. Wade*, Justice Harry Blackmun, viewed it as a reasonable compromise between the competing interests of women wishing to control their reproductive lives and the legitimate interests of the state in protecting the fetus and the mother's health. Indeed, three relatively conservative justices, all appointed by President Richard Nixon, joined in the majority opinion. Nevertheless, *Roe v. Wade* set off a firestorm of political activity. Abortion became a prominent and inescapable issue in state and national elections. Neither side in the raging debate was entirely satisfied with the Court's pronouncement. Opponents of abortion vilified the decision as legalizing the murder of innocent unborn children. Some Catholic church leaders advocated the excommunication of anyone professing support for the decision. Many feminist and other "pro-choice" groups saw the decision as a major step forward, but criticized it for falling short of establishing a positive constitutional right of a woman to choose abortion. In their view, this failing allowed Congress to deny funding that would ensure equal access to abortion services for poor women.

Right to life groups, growing in number and strength after *Roe*, directed unsuccessful efforts to amend the Constitution to protect fetal life explicitly. They proved more successful in helping to elect many "pro-life" candidates, including President Ronald Reagan. They prevailed in the fight to deny the use of federal funds to finance abortions for poor women, and in pressuring presidents Reagan and Bush to appoint judges to the federal courts who were unsympathetic to abortion rights. In the twenty years after *Roe*, right to life groups succeeded in getting state legislatures to pass numerous laws restricting women's access to abortion, including imposing a twenty-four-hour waiting period on women seeking abortion services, spousal consent and fetal-viability test requirements, and parental consent requirements in the cases of minors. The Supreme Court validated some of these restrictions, but announced in *Planned Parenthood of Southeastern Pennsylvania v. Casey* (1992) that restrictions placing an "undue burden" upon women seeking abortion were unconstitutional. To the dismay of right to life advocates, the Court reaffirmed in this important decision the right of women to choose abortion without unreasonable governmental interference.

The divisive nature of reproductive politics is illustrated by the attempts of some antiabortion groups to interfere with operation of abortion clinics. Though employing traditional civil disobedience tactics such as sit-ins and blockades, the activities of these groups occasionally erupted into violence. More than one thousand incidents of violence were recorded at abortion clinics between 1977 and 1994, including firebombs, assaults and, in several instances, the murders of physicians who practiced abortion and abortion clinic receptionists. After sometimes bitter debate, and much lobbying by pro- and antiabortion groups, the U.S. Congress in 1994 passed a bill, which became law, making it a federal crime to blockade or attack abortion clinics. Nevertheless, relentless efforts by some right to life groups succeeded in discouraging many physicians and doctors from providing abortion services. Pro-choice groups responded by making expanded access to abortion services a prime political objective. Pro- and antiabortion groups also regularly clashed over the use of foreign aid in support of family planning, over the role of abortion and contraception in the fight to stem teenage pregnancy, and over federal funding of sex-education in the schools and of fetal tissue research.

Context

The frequency and intensity of conflicts such as those described above reflect both the emotional and intractable nature of reproductive political issues. Democratic political systems, at their best, moderate social conflicts by channeling them through legitimate political institutions which create workable compromises. By contrast, reproductive issues such as abortion are often brought into the political arena by ardent activists who assume all-or-nothing stances. Feminists often regard any attempt to restrict access to abortion as demeaning to women, who they argue, ought to have absolute freedom of choice regarding their pregnancies. Those against abortion often assert, in equally absolute terms ("Abortion is murder!") the fetus' right to be born.

In the United States, the political conflict over abortion and contraception is further fueled by the fact that the U.S. Constitution is unclear on the critical questions central to these controversies. The Constitution speaks only in general terms of protecting rights to "life" and "liberty" of "persons," but it provides no decisive, unequivocal answers to the question of the rights of unborn children. Nor does the Constitution speak directly to the claims of women to have the freedom to terminate their pregnancies. These ambiguities cause the federal courts, which are charged with interpreting the Constitution, to become actively involved in making reproductive policy. But because federal judges are not elected, and because they commonly overrule democratically fashioned abortion-related laws, the role of the courts itself is a continuing source of controversy.

The politics of reproduction affects party politics as well, particularly in the United States. The strongest right to life groups, mainly Protestant fundamentalists, have been a potent force within the Republican Party. Some political observers see the potential for the creation in the future of a new political party that will be centered on moral issues such as abortion.

Though in the United States the abortion and contraception issues are cast in terms of a conflict between individual rights and the interests of the state, in most other countries reproductive politics is played out on a different field of political and philosophical assumptions. In European countries with traditions of social democracy—such as Sweden—concern for the quality of citizens' lives, especially that of newborns, encourages government-sponsored birth control education, maternity leaves, child care, and financial support for mothers and fathers of dependent children. By making childbirth less onerous, and also by actively promoting birth control to discourage teenage pregnancies, many European countries have relatively low abortion rates, and in turn, relatively little political conflict over the issue.

In nondemocratic countries, reproductive policies tend to be a direct function of government population policy. In the late 1970's, the People's Republic of China instituted a one-child-per-family policy in order to stem rapid population growth. This highly controversial policy sometimes led to state-imposed abortions and infanticide of female newborns, as families tried to ensure a male heir. Nazi Germany was notorious for employing abortion and forced sterilization as government tools for furthering misguided theories of "Aryan" racial supremacy. In the Soviet Union, government-directed efforts to accelerate industrialization led to the legalization of abortion, as women were needed to work outside the home. These "statist" reproductive policies reflect the assumption that the needs and interests of the nation take precedence over concern for the rights and interests of the individual woman.

Some nations face conflicts between the need to control the growth of their populations, often by use of liberal abortion and contraception policies, and the need to accommodate the conservative religious beliefs of major segments of their populations. India, for example, confronts a difficult reconciliation of the antiabortion beliefs of traditional Hindus and Muslims with the imperatives of family planning and economic development.

The future of reproductive politics worldwide will undoubtedly be shaped by the rise of novel medical technologies. Advances in birth control, such as the self-administered abortion pill RU-486, as well as advances in artificial womb and embryo transfer technology, will test the political abilities of all groups involved in the struggles to shape reproductive policies. These and future technological developments hold promise, especially to those political groups wishing to increase women's control over reproduction. Nevertheless these same technologies raise new and very troubling legal and moral questions for most right to life advocates and religious conservatives. The new technological frontier promises to be the battlefield for reproductive politics in the twenty-first century.

Bibliography

Bonavoglia, Angela, ed. *The Choices We Made.* New York: Random House, 1991. Collection of twenty-five oral histories, mostly of women, some well known, recounting their personal experience of having abortions. Told from a pro-choice perspective, the stories exhibit the emotional complexities involved in choosing abortion.

Craig, Barbara Hinkson, and David M. O'Brien. *Abortion and American Politics.* Chatham, N.J.: Chatham House, 1993. Data-intensive analysis of how the abortion issue affected American politics by two social scientists. Useful tables summarizing state and federal laws and public opinion on abortion.

Dixon-Mueller, Ruth. *Population Policy and Women's Rights.* Westport, Conn.: Praeger, 1993. Scholarly but accessible introduction to the complex problem of balancing efforts at world population control with concern for the human rights and dignity of women.

Garrow, David J. *Liberty and Sexuality.* New York: Macmillan, 1994. Exhaustively researched account of the events surrounding the landmark Supreme Court decisions in *Griswold v. Connecticut* and *Roe v. Wade* by a Pulitzer prize-winning historian. The best and most detailed history of the development of the constitutional right to privacy.

Luker, Kristin. *Abortion and the Politics of Motherhood*. Berkeley, Calif.: University of California Press, 1984. Based largely on interviews with activists on both sides of the abortion debate, the author examines the nature of their strongly-held beliefs. She argues persuasively that one's position on abortion is directly related to one's social position and one's view of women's proper role in society, sexuality, and technology.

Tribe, Laurence H. *Abortion: The Clash of Absolutes*. New York: W. W. Norton, 1990. Masterful, dispassionate examination of the abortion issue in America by a leading constitutional law scholar. Tribe covers abortion history, politics, and law in a brilliant yet readable treatise.

Philip R. Zampini

Cross-References

Activist Politics, p. 7; Citizen Movements, p. 248; Civil Rights and Liberties, p. 298; Feminist Politics, p. 682; Gay and Lesbian Politics, p. 732; Gender Politics, p. 738; Human Rights and International Politics, p. 848; The New Right, p. 1293; The Supreme Court: Role in Government and Law, p. 1935; Women in Politics, p. 2147.

THE REPUBLICAN PARTY

Field of study: Politics

The Republican Party, one of the two major political organizations in the United States after the Civil War, carries a tradition of limited government action in human and social service programs; a conservative approach to civil rights; and a close alliance with big business.

Principal terms

ABOLITIONIST: person who, during the debate over slavery, took the position that the institution should be abolished

"GILDED AGE": period from the end of the Civil War to the early 1880's marked by extensive strength of big business and deep corruption in the political process

GOP: Grand Old Party, the popular nickname for the Republican Party

NEW DEAL: series of sweeping reforms initiated in 1932 under President Franklin Delano Roosevelt to deal with the effects of the Great Depression

POLITICAL BOSS: local or state leader of the party machinery who delivers votes on election day in return for favors

POPULISM, POPULIST: political philosophy that prefers direct appeal to the people, especially regarding their economic interests

"RADICAL REPUBLICANS": members of the Republican Party during and after the Civil War who believed in immediate freedom and equality for African Americans and punishment of the South for its rebellion

Overview

By the middle of the twentieth century, the Democratic Party, established by Thomas Jefferson, was the oldest continuous political organization in the world. By contrast, the Democrats' major opponent, the Republican Party, had barely reached its one-hundredth birthday. The sudden birth, rapid rise, and long-standing power of the Republican Party is an important feature of United States politics.

For the first half of the nineteenth century, the Democratic Party dominated U.S. politics. Its opponents, first the Federalists and later the Whigs, were occasionally able to wrest control of the White House, but could never consolidate a lasting hold on both the executive and legislative branches of the federal government. Internal struggles during the 1840's and 1850's, including those over slavery, seriously weakened the party. The time was ripe for a serious opposition party.

The immediate situation that allowed the Republican Party to emerge came in 1854 when Congress debated the Kansas-Nebraska Bill. This bill would allow the settlers of each territory seeking to become a state to decide for themselves if the state would be "free" or "slave," that is, whether slavery would be forbidden or permitted within its borders. The issue was vital, because a series of compromises had kept slave and free states evenly balanced in Congress. The Missouri Compromise had set a geographical division, to the north of which no slave would be permitted. The Kansas-Nebraska Bill would wreck that delicate balance.

While the Democratic Party temporized, persons who wished merely to restrict the growth of the institution, joined by outright abolitionists, realized a new party was necessary, and on March 20, 1854, a group came together in a small school house in Ripon, Wisconsin. "We went into the little meeting held in a schoolhouse Whigs, Free Soilers, and Democrats," wrote one participant. "We came out of it Republicans." A new party had been born.

The party grew rapidly throughout the North and West. In addition to the party's antislavery appeal, the sharp decline of the Whigs had left a pool of experienced, ambitious politicians such as New York boss Thurlow Weed, New York governor William Seward, and Abraham Lincoln of Illinois, who soon filled the ranks of the Republicans. Within two years, the new party mounted a serious drive for the White House by nominating John Charles Frémont, hero of the Mexican War. Frémont swept New England and New York and took every state of the old Northwest except Illinois and Indiana. He lost the election to Democrat James Buchanan, but it was clear that the Republicans had an excellent chance in 1860.

The Democrats split in 1860, producing three different presidential candidates. Republican Abraham Lincoln, who had gained national prominence in a series of debates with Democrat Stephen Douglas during the 1858 Illinois senatorial election, won only a plurality of the popular vote (approximately 40 percent), but took firm control of the electoral college. The Republicans had already won or were winning the governorship of every northern state and strong majorities in both houses of Congress. In six years, the Republican Party had secured control of the federal government and half of the state governments. At the moment of the Republicans' initial triumph, however, the United States was poised on the brink of civil war.

The war, which forever changed the nature of the United States, inevitably changed the Republican Party as well, primarily through the rise of the "radical Republicans," the increase in party unity and discipline, an ever-closer alliance with big business, and the Republican identification with patriotism. Led by men such as Senator Ben Wade and Representative Thaddeus Stevens, the radical Republicans were avid for emancipation, equal rights for African Americans, punishment for the South, and destruction of the Democratic Party. Using the increased party discipline inspired by war, well-funded by munitions makers and others, and appealing to patriotism to stir popular enthusiasm, the radicals achieved many of their aims, at least in the short run. By 1868, the Republican Party, with the election of war hero Ulysses S. Grant to the presidency, had assumed control of American political life.

What followed, tagged by some as the "Gilded Age" and known by other historians as the lowest point of national disgrace, was a period in which the Republican Party presided over unprecedented political corruption and ruthless business misconduct. Republican bosses, such as Simon Cameron of Pennsylvania—dismissed from Lincoln's cabinet because of blatant misconduct—and Roscoe Conkling of New York, drew the Republicans closer to big business.

Popular disgust with political corruption and economic hard times helped revive the Democratic Party, and it drew its strength from urban immigrants, rural areas, and small business. In contrast, the Republicans strengthened their base among midwestern farmers, northern communities, and big business. Economic issues increasingly dominated political discussions, with the Democrats taking a more populist, middle- and lower-class stance, while the Republicans held to a conservative, big business position. This was most clearly articulated in the presidential election of 1896.

That year William McKinley, a Civil War veteran and solid if nondescript Republican party regular, was pitted against William Jennings Bryan, a spellbinding orator who had won the Democratic nomination after his sensational "Cross of Gold" speech advocating free silver—a populist economic plan anathema to big business and their Republican allies. During the election, the Republican propaganda machine flooded the country with pamphlets and other campaign literature emphasizing the dangers of Bryan, free silver, and the Democrats. Workers were warned that if Bryan won on Tuesday, there would be no jobs for them on Wednesday. So effective were the scare techniques that the Republicans were firmly established as the dominant national party, with big business as its key constituent.

The aberration during this period was the presidency of Theodore Roosevelt, one of the most energetic chief executives in American history. Roosevelt, who became president in 1901 following the assassination of McKinley, pushed through a series of reforms that limited the power of big business; established conservation through the national park system as a duty of the federal government; and increased U.S. influence and power internationally. After Roosevelt, however, the GOP reverted to form and it was left to Woodrow Wilson, the second Democratic president after the Civil War, to change the national direction.

During his first term, Wilson and the Democrats pushed through a badly needed, sweeping series of reforms, known as the New Freedom, that were deeply resented by many Republicans. During his second term, Wilson led U.S. participation in World War I and attempted to bring the United States into the League of Nations. He was thwarted by Republican opposition in the Senate; when the Republicans returned to the White House in 1920 under Warren Harding, they embarked upon what they called "a return to normalcy," a large part of which was designed to undo Democratic reforms.

"Normalcy" ended with the Great Depression, and the Democrats returned to the White House under Franklin Delano Roosevelt in 1932; they held the executive mansion and controlled federal government until 1952. During that time, the Republican Party had to define itself against the "New Deal coalition" of immigrants and their descendants, blue-collar workers, labor unions, white voters in the South, African American voters in the North, and the middle and lower classes nationwide.

The Republican response went through several phases. At first, they opposed Roosevelt's New Deal; then, as programs such as Social Security became indispensable elements in the U.S. social structure, Republicans accepted them but tried to limit their growth. Roosevelt's international activism, aimed at countering Adolf Hitler's rise in Germany and Japanese imperialism in the Far East, was first denounced by the GOP, then accepted as leaders such as Wendell Wilkie recognized the danger that faced the world. After the election of President Dwight D. Eisenhower in 1952, Republicans accepted the permanency of the New Deal and abandoned efforts to dismantle it.

With Eisenhower, the first of their party elected in almost a generation, the Republicans had a popular war hero whose own inclinations matched theirs: conservative minimal government at home, forceful anticommunism abroad. Indeed, the fear of communism dominated both political parties during most of the 1950's and 1960's, often skewing debate into a discussion over who was "soft on communism" rather than on who could best deal with American issues and interests.

This began to change in the watershed year of 1960 when Richard Nixon, Eisenhower's vice president, faced Democratic nominee John F. Kennedy in the presidential election. Domestic affairs, especially economic development and civil rights, had become more important, with the central issue being whether government intervention was desirable and effective. Even more notable, the modern mass media, especially the electronic media, played a decisive role in the 1960 campaign. The famous Kennedy-Nixon debates have been credited with tipping the balance in the thin margin of difference between the candidates, and ushering in a period when television took central stage in the electoral process.

The Republican Party responded to these changes by becoming increasingly more conservative in its philosophy, while skillfully exploiting the use of the media. In 1964, Barry Goldwater and the hard-line conservative wing took control of the party; although later Richard Nixon would somewhat restore the GOP's more centrist position, the party thereafter remained on the right wing of the political spectrum. Through this period, talented publicists and strategists used carefully crafted negative campaigns to impugn their Democratic opponent's competence and even patriotism. In a sense, genuine conservative political thought had been reduced to a series of sound bites.

The Republican Party had expanded rapidly from a protest group to a truly national party that embraced a set of generally accepted tenets based on a conservative approach to social action and civil rights; strong support of private enterprise, especially big business; and a strong foreign policy.

Applications

The 1884 presidential election matched Republican James G. Blaine and Democrat Grover Cleveland and marked the first time a major political party systematically and comprehensively used smear techniques, innuendoes, and negative campaigning. The election was one of the dirtiest in American history and set an unfortunate precedent for future contests.

In nominating Blaine, the Republicans created a dilemma for their party: A veteran of two decades of Congressional service, former Speaker of the House, and secretary of state, Blaine had accepted bribes thinly disguised as contributions or gifts. Although it is likely that Blaine sincerely believed he was innocent, public perception was less generous, and the Republicans knew they were vulnerable, especially since the Democrat nominee, Grover Cleveland, was widely known for his honesty.

The Republican tactic was to attack Cleveland. Party operatives discovered that as a young man, Cleveland might have fathered an illegitimate son. While the issue was unclear, Cleveland had accepted responsibility at the time, and did not deny it during the campaign. "Tell the truth," Cleveland commanded, while at rallies Republican supporters chanted: "Ma, Ma, where's my pa?"

Whether the assault on Cleveland's private character would have been successful is uncertain, for two events rocked the Republican efforts. First, incriminating correspondence from Blaine to a businessman with the warning, "Burn this letter," was published. Next, at a meeting in New York City, Blaine listened without comment as a leading supporter denounced the Democrats as the party of "Rum, Romanism and Rebellion." The bigoted remark lost the GOP massive votes in the urban North and Midwest, and Cleveland became the first Democratic president since the Civil War.

The presidential election of 1948 was the first to match a "mainstream" Republican against Roosevelt's New Deal coalition. Harry S Truman, who had assumed the presidency after Roosevelt's death in 1945, was seeking his own full presidential term against Thomas E. Dewey of New York, who had run against Roosevelt in 1944 and seemed assured of victory in 1948. Dewey's branch of the Republican Party was moderate on domestic issues, and actively interventionist in foreign affairs. It dominated Republican politics until the mid-1960's, when the much more conservative, and increasingly less tolerant, right wing wrested control.

Leading in public opinion polls, Dewey refused to address the issues that deeply affected average voters, while his obvious connection with big business reinforced public perception of an overly close relationship between monied interests and the Republican Party. By contrast, Truman's nationwide whistle-stop campaign, blasting Dewey and the "do-nothing" Republicans in Congress and emphasizing the benefits from Democratic government, appealed to the average voter. While Dewey and his staff thought it was undignified for a presidential candidate—much less a president—to seek votes as Truman did, voters gave Truman a smashing upset victory in 1948.

Although the Republican Party was largely created out of opposition to slavery, by the middle of the twentieth century it was identified with a conservative approach to civil rights and opposition to federal action to ensure equal opportunities for all Americans. This was by no means true of all Republicans and was generally an expression of the party's conservative nature, rather than an expression of intolerance. The historic Civil Rights Act of 1964 provides an example of Republican ambivalence on the issue.

Under the leadership of Lyndon B. Johnson, who became president after the assassination of John F. Kennedy, Congress took up the first comprehensive civil rights legislation since 1875. As passed by Congress in June, 1964, the act prohibited racial discrimination in public accommodations and employment, among other important provisions. Senator Everett Dirksen of Illinois, Republican Senate leader, was a principal backer, yet Senator Barry Goldwater and five other Republicans voted against the measure. Goldwater's vote was significant, because later that summer he was nominated by the Republican Party as its presidential candidate.

Although Goldwater lost in a landslide, four years later Richard Nixon unveiled the infamous "Southern strategy," which used covert racial appeals to drive a wedge between white Democratic voters and their party. Subsequently, the Republican Party, which had come into existence as an opponent of slavery and which had advocated equality during the Civil War and Reconstruction, all but excluded African Americans and other minorities from its ranks.

Context

Two basic tendencies have traditionally exerted themselves in the nation's political life. One has been activist, progressive, and liberal, urging government intervention to undertake efforts that private enterprise or groups cannot or will not undertake for themselves. This role has largely been filled by the Democratic Party, which, especially since Franklin Delano Roosevelt, has supported government involvement in issues as far-ranging as health care, old-age pensions, public works, and education. The second tendency has been passivist, restrictive, and conservative, preferring government to refrain from interfering with the free market. The Republican Party has been the chief exponent of this view, except in certain areas such as crime, morality, and communism.

In part because of the inherently economic divisions of the U.S. political system, the Democratic Party traditionally has retained control of the House of Representatives and often of the Senate. By contrast, the Republicans have extended their tenure on the White House. It is generally during periods of real or potential economic distress that a Democratic presidential candidate, such as Franklin Roosevelt, John F. Kennedy, or Bill Clinton, can assemble the electoral coalition needed for victory.

The Republican Party traditionally has believed in individual liberty in economic matters and restraint by the powers of government. This tradition has sometimes allowed attacks on labor, distrust of civil rights, and a disinclination to positive social action; however, it has also led the party to expose the preservation of the American union, the abolition of slavery, and the protection of individual liberties and traditional freedoms.

Bibliography

Boller, Paul F. *Presidential Campaigns*. New York: Oxford University Press, 1984. Witty and incisive look at the race for the White House since the early nineteenth century. Anecdotal material illuminates the nature of GOP candidates for the presidency.

Gienapp, William. *The Origins of the Republican Party, 1852-1856*. New York: Oxford University Press, 1987. Scholarly study of the all-important initial years of the Republican Party, showing how a protest movement was transformed into an enduring American political force.

Mayer, George H. *The Republican Party, 1854-1966.* 2d ed. New York: Oxford University Press, 1967. Essential study of the party, especially during its formative years and immediately following the Civil War.

Rapoport, Ronald, Alan I. Abramowitz, and John McGlennon. *The Life of the Parties: Activists in Presidential Politics.* Lexington: University Press of Kentucky, 1986. Lively, wide-ranging examination of various aspects of party operations and activities in the United States. Places the Republican Party within the context of wider political life.

Reichley, A. James. *The Life of the Parties: A History of American Political Parties.* New York: Free Press, 1992. Well-researched, well-written study, accessible to the general reader as well as to the serious student of American political life. Charts the course of events and provides excellent, thought-provoking analysis of developments.

Michael Witkoski

Cross-References

Business and Government, p. 177; The Democratic Party, p. 520; The New Right, p. 1293; Political Campaigning, Planning, and Financing, p. 1427; Political Campaigns in U.S. History, p. 1434; Political Machines and Bosses, p. 1468; Political Platforms, p. 1512; The Presidency in the United States, p. 1590; Presidential Elections in the United States, p. 1596; Two-Party Systems, p. 2033.

REPUBLICANISM

Field of study: Political philosophy

Modern republicanism emerged in the seventeenth century. It described regimes in which the people—as opposed to a monarch or nobility—exercise political rule through elected representatives.

Principal terms
ANARCHY: absence of rule, lawlessness; associated in classical thought with direct democracy
ARISTOCRACY: rule of the best or of the virtuous in classical thought; in contemporary life often misleadingly associated with rule of the rich or the upper class
CHECKS AND BALANCES: systems in government that keep complete authority from being placed entirely in one part of government; it requires that the various interests cooperate in order for government to act
FACTION: in James Madison's famous formulation, "a number of citizens, whether amounting to a majority or minority of the whole, who are united and actuated by some common impulse of passion, or of interest, adverse to the rights of other citizens, or to the permanent and aggregate interests of the community"
FEDERALISM: political system in which a national government and state or regional governments coexist
POLIS: Greek term referring to the city as an organic whole; sometimes misleadingly translated as "city-state"
REPRESENTATIVE GOVERNMENT: any regime in which the people elect officials to represent the people's interests
REPUBLIC: regime based on promotion of the public interest
TYRANNY: regime that violates basic human rights and oppresses citizens

Overview

If one asks a group of people what a republic is, they are likely to mention the following characteristics: the supreme power rests in the people; they elect representatives; they are not governed by a king or similar ruler. This modern understanding largely ignores an important philosophical debate that occurred in the seventeenth and eighteenth centuries. This debate encompassed philosophy, politics, art, and religion, and included a reevaluation of classical republicanism.

The English word "republic" derives from the Latin words *res* and *publica*, meaning the "public things" or "property of the public." The Roman philosopher Cicero's (106-43 B.C.E.) treatise *De Republica* defines a republic as the property of the people.

The people, it must be understood, are not just any assemblage of humans, but a community having a basic agreement with respect to justice and a partnership for the common good. Implicit in Cicero's treatise are three ideas taken from the earlier philosophy of Plato and Aristotle. First, humans are naturally social or political beings—they naturally seek out community with others, starting with the family and culminating in the polis; second, since only in the polis can humans fully realize their individual nature, the goal of the polis, then, is promotion of the excellence of its members; and third, the polis as a whole is more fundamental than its individual members, just as the proper working of the human body is more important than that of individual organs. This is an organic theory of politics; the requirements of the "organism" (the political community) take precedence over the requirements of its parts. From this it follows that rulers must always place the general, public interest over their own private interests. Such is Cicero's definition and some of the ideas on which it is built. This is classical republicanism; note how it differs from the definition given at the beginning of this section.

It is critical to emphasize that classical republicanism is not based on notions of natural or inherent rights, of consent of the governed, or even of limited government. These are distinctly modern concepts that are alien to classical thought. In contrast, classical republicanism justifies what, today, would be condemned as violations of natural or inherent rights. Slavery, for example, was consistent with this notion of government, as was the exclusion of sizable numbers of people from citizenship. The key concept of classical republicanism is that the good of the whole must take precedence, and this requires that each member performs the function best suited to his or her nature. If one is born a "slave by nature," to use Aristotle's term, it is best for the individual and city if one is enslaved to a "natural master." The task of ruling, then, is to properly order the polis, which requires involvement of the public.

The fundamental differences between ancient and modern political thought result from conflicting ideas about human nature. Classical republicanism is based on the presumption that each human has a certain purpose that is endowed by nature, and that it is the proper function of the polis to order itself accordingly. Underlying this idea is a division between what is and what ought to be—the actual and the ideal. The polis must look to the ideal, continually striving to approximate the best city. Hence the classical emphasis on the best regime and the reform of existing regimes. Niccolò Machiavelli broke radically with the classical tradition's concern with ideals. He rejects the notion that politics ought to be concerned with virtue. For Machiavelli, human nature is unchanging, and humans are acquisitive, grasping, and self-interested. As such, rulers should not ignore what is in favor of what ought to be; it is folly to think humans can be educated to virtue. Concern with creating an ideal state will lead to a neglect of political necessities. Machiavelli is concerned with actual human life—and human depravity—instead of virtue and the ideal regime.

Machiavelli divides regimes into principates and republics, the former ruled by princes, the latter by the people. The key to a successful republic lies in its founding: Those that are well-founded have long lives, while others decline and die after a relatively short time. For Machiavelli, the paradigm of the well-founded regime was the Roman Republic (510-31 B.C.E.). Within Machiavelli's discussion of this period lies a key precursor of modern republicanism. The ancients generally classified regimes into three categories: monarchy, aristocracy, and democracy, based on whether the one, the few, or the many rule. Machiavelli argues that a successful republic must combine each of these elements into one regime. In this way the vices of each part of the community are checked by the vices of the others. This is the root of modern concepts like checks and balances. American statesman James Madison, who eventually became president, showed a deep understanding of this in arguing that government must be designed so that ambition counters ambition. This emphasis on humans as naturally vicious indicates that government should be concerned primarily with restraining vice and not with promoting virtue.

Building on Machiavelli's grimly realistic views on politics, Thomas Hobbes and John Locke built their political theories on the need to create political society in order to provide safety and security. The desire to live in safety is, after all, a fundamental passion. Hobbes and Locke each speak of a prepolitical condition, the state of nature that preceded the creation of government. The uncertainty of life in the state of nature drives humans to agree to a social contract. The contract's legitimacy is based on individual rights rather than community good, and may therefore be viewed as a reversal of the classical priority of the whole over its parts. Modern republicanism assumes that the best way to promote the common good is through the protection of people's right to life, liberty, and property. Moreover, not only is government responsible, under modern republican precepts, for preventing vice instead of promoting virtue, it is also subject to the will of its members in its creation and dissolution. The idea of limited government based on consent implies that, if government violates the trust placed in it by the people, the people have a right to revolt and create a new government. This is the most radical political implication of modern thought. In this light, the problem of modern republicanism becomes the problem of carefully designing government that minimizes the likelihood that the public trust is violated. The idea that humans are fundamentally self-interested applies, of course, to officeholders. Just as vice must be restrained amongst the people by government, the potential for vice must be minimized within government.

Applications

The political experiment of the American Constitution is a direct application of these principles. For the Founders, republican government represented a mean between the tyranny of absolute monarchy and the anarchy of direct democracy; it allows for the prevention of the "disease of faction" (the sacrificing of the general interest to partial interests), which is the greatest threat to popular government.

The idea of virtue is not, however, completely lost to modern republicanism. Effective representative government relies on the faith that the collective wisdom, prudence, and judgment of officeholders will exceed that of the masses, since public life appeals, one hopes, to the sort of people who place the public above their own interests. As Thomas Jefferson argued, that government is best which provides for a "natural aristoi" in the offices of government. Aristoi is a Greek word meaning "the virtuous or best." The modern republic, combining this concept of public service with that of the priority of individual rights, radically alters classical republicanism while partially preserving its spirit. Modern republicanism provides a standard for free governments. Closely associated with its emergence is the idea of constitutionalism— the idea that legitimate government is based on a written constitution. The U.S. Constitution of 1787 is an excellent example. It is a legal document that attempts to codify the philosophical principles of the Declaration of Independence of 1776, which states that "all men are created equal" and are "endowed by their Creator with certain unalienable rights" including the "right to life, liberty, and the pursuit of happiness"; that just governments derive their powers from the "consent of the governed"; that when government deprives the people of these rights it is "their right, their duty to throw off such government, and to provide new guards for their future security." The Declaration sets the standard for the American republic. As Abraham Lincoln once said, its principles are a continual stumbling block to tyranny and oppression. This is not to suggest that they are—or ever have been—fully attained in practice. Slavery and its legacy of racial inequality represent the greatest challenge to the republic, because they are a direct challenge to the self-evident truth that all humans are created equal. Nor is race the only challenge. Whenever and wherever excessive government interference, unequal treatment of individuals under the laws, or official oppression of any sort appears, modern republicanism is a standard and a basis for turning back illegitimate authority and protecting inherent human rights. In other words, it is indeed a persistent obstacle and stumbling block to tyranny.

Context

Modern republicanism questions the capacity of any segment of society to properly order the entirety. Instead, modern republicanism assumes that governments are best trusted with the less ambitious goal of restraining vice. That is, they are best trusted with protecting citizens from each others' tendency to promote their own interests to the detriment of others. Much has been written of this radical shift away from the community and toward the individual as the starting point of political life. Many see Machiavelli's thought as the critical turning point in a process that ultimately produced a minimalist modern politics based on individual rights and with little regard to the promotion of community and citizen virtue. This is not to say that critics of modern republican thought would advocate a return to classical society. They would, however, support a thoughtful integration of the best of classical political thought with the best of modern political thought. During the founding of the U.S. republic, much debate centered on the excellence and the deficiencies of the classical republics. A sober deliberation suggested that certain aspects of classical republicanism ought to inform all political discourse. The Founders saw a place for the recognition that the community is an important entity, that happiness requires some degree of virtue, and that an excessive emphasis on individual rights might undermine the common interest. To this they added modern theories of natural rights, limited government, and the right of revolution.

Bibliography

Aristotle. *The Politics of Aristotle*. London: Oxford University Press, 1958. Book one offers a treatment of the nature of the political community, and book four offers a treatment of regimes in general.

Hamilton, Alexander, James Madison, and John Jay. *The Federalist Papers*, edited by Clinton Rossiter. New York: New American Library, 1961. Contains Madison's most forceful discussion in Federalist No. 10 of the dangers of faction under republican government, and how the proposed Constitution remedies this problem.

Kurland, Philip B. and Ralph Lerner, eds. *Major Themes*. Vol. 1 in *The Founders' Constitution*. Chicago: University of Chicago Press, 1987. Definitive collection of discourses and documents pertaining to the American founding.

Locke, John. *Two Treatises on Government*. Cambridge, England: Cambridge University Press, 1960. The source for much of modern liberal political thought.

Machiavelli, Niccolò. *The Prince*. Prospect Heights, Ill.: Waveland Press, 1982. Shows Machiavelli's radical break with classical and Christian thought.

——————. *The Prince and the Discourses*. New York: Modern Library, 1950. Machiavelli's major work on republican government, in the form of a commentary on the writings of the great Roman historian Titus Livy.

Matthew Westcott Smith

Cross-References

Aristotle's Political Philosophy, p. 83; The City-State, p. 272; Despotism and Tyranny, p. 527; Equality and Egalitarianism, p. 630; Government Powers, p. 772; Government Types, p. 785; History of Government, p. 829; Kant's Political Philosophy, p. 1025; Legitimacy, p. 1105; Liberal Nationalism, p. 1111; Liberalism, p. 1118; Montesquieu's Political Philosophy, p. 1228; Plato's Political Philosophy, p. 1396; Political Philosophy, p. 1505; Right of Revolution, p. 1744; Separation of Powers: Political Philosophy, p. 1809; The Social Contract, p. 1827; Spinoza's Political Philosophy, p. 1872; Tocqueville's Political Philosophy, p. 1981.

RESEARCH, DEVELOPMENT, AND PLANNING

Field of study: Functions of government

Encouraging scientific research and technological development has become an increasingly important governmental activity. Through the use of grants, contracts, or direct purchase, almost all governments find ways to support the work of scientists and engineers. These arrangements have produced a number of significant scientific and technological advances.

Principal terms

BASIC SCIENCE: research into fundamental scientific questions, undertaken without regard to practical application or commercial value. Also sometimes referred to as "pure" science

PEER REVIEW: process for determining the scientific merit of a project under consideration for government funding, usually carried out by other specialists from the applicant's field

R&D: popular abbreviation for research and development

SPIN-OFF: new product, process, or other application of a technology developed earlier for some other purpose

STRUCTURAL POLICY: set of governmental investments in infrastructure (roads and transportation systems, water projects, communication networks, etc.), science and technology, education, and other basic economic activities

Overview

Most modern countries maintain programs that subsidize, guide, and sometimes even directly manage the work of scientists and engineers. These programs are often part of a larger system of economic and industrial planning.

One of the major reasons that a government supports scientific research and technological development (commonly referred to as R & D) is to create products for its own use. Programs of this type are largely devoted to developing defense-related items such as weapons systems or surveillance satellites. Sometimes these technologies are later adapted for use in the civilian economy. These adaptations are known as spin-offs. Many commonly used computing, communication, and transportation technologies, for example, were originally developed for the military.

In addition, a number of countries provide funding for projects that, although potentially valuable, do not attract private investment because of their large start-up costs or lengthy development times. A case in point is the creation of communication satellite technology in the 1950's and 1960's. Learning how to build, launch, and operate these systems required several years of trial and error, with the expectation of numerous costly failures along the way, a task which was beyond the means of any single private company.

Finally, governments (principally those of the advanced industrial countries) often subsidize research in basic sciences like physics and astronomy. These are activities whose practical benefits, if they exist at all, will not be realized for many decades. This support has become increasingly important for scientists in fields that require large-scale, sophisticated (and extremely expensive) equipment such as experimental reactors or space probes.

The United States maintains a number of science and technology programs that are spread throughout the federal government. Agencies within the departments of defense, energy, and agriculture, along with the National Aeronautics and Space Administration (NASA), the National Science Foundation, and the National Institutes for Health account for nearly 90 percent of all federal R &D expenditures.

The funding for science and technology programs is administered through the regular budget-writing process, so other political agencies, like the Office of Management and Budget (which oversees federal spending), as well as the president and the Congress, can also play a crucial role in determining R & D priorities. The influence of nonscientific institutions in the funding of scientific research has been the focus of criticism, particularly from scientists.

A frequent complaint is that government officials (most of whom are trained as lawyers) do not fully understand the programs over which they are passing judgment. Lawmakers have made attempts to deal with this issue. In the early 1970's, Congress established the Office of Technology Assessment to provide scientific advice, and the president's Office of Science and Technology Policy (whose director advises the president) was created in 1976. Despite these reforms, some researchers feel that decisions regarding R & D initiatives are too much made on the basis of political considerations.

Critics also charge that the conventional budget process, which subjects all programs to an annual review, makes it difficult, if not impossible, for project managers to plan for more than a year or two into the future. Since some R & D programs may run for a decade or more, uncertainty over long-term funding can be a serious problem. Moreover, some observers feel that the bargaining and trade-offs that are a normal part of the budget process further politicizes science and technology.

Finally, some argue that the divided nature of federal R & D policy is inefficient. The United States has no central organization responsible for coordinating all of its various science and technology programs. The Office of Science and Technology Policy is general and nondepartmental, but, as already noted, it serves only an advisory role. There have been cases of government agencies openly competing over funding for duplicate projects.

In contrast to the United States, some countries seek to incorporate their science and technology programs into an overall strategy aimed at promoting economic growth and development. These nations see R & D as one fundamental part of a larger structural policy. The most prominent example of such a highly coordinated structural policy is that undertaken by Japan beginning in the 1950's. The Japanese government decided to concentrate its economic development efforts on a few key industries, most notably in the field of electronics. Toward that end, a strong set of linkages was established between its science and engineering community and its major industries, financial institutions, and universities. Many observers believe that this approach was largely responsible for the country's tremendous industrial growth in the latter half of the twentieth century.

Other nations have taken this strategy even further, attempting to manage their entire economies directly by establishing production targets and taking responsibility for allocating resources. This large-scale economic planning was a major feature in the so-called command economies of the former Soviet Union and communist Eastern Europe, and was still being practiced (to varying degrees) in the 1990's by North Korea, Cuba, and the People's Republic of China. The enormous complexities involved in such planning, as well as the uncertainties that are an inherent part of the R & D process, have led to results for these countries that generally have been viewed as unfavorable.

Public support of research and development can take a variety of forms. A common approach is for an organization, such as the National Science Foundation in the United States, to provide grants for individual researchers or laboratories to pursue individual projects. In order to ensure that these awards are based strictly on scientific merit, most granting agencies bring together a panel of specialists from the grant applicant's field (that is, the applicant's peers) to review applications for funding. Grants are made to applicants based on the recommendations of their peers. This process is called peer review. Not everyone, however, believes that peer review is completely fair. Some have claimed that the process tends to discriminate against researchers from smaller or less well-known institutions, as well as against women and minorities. In addition, it has been charged that because peer review is so heavily based upon current scientific beliefs and practices, it discourages innovation and new approaches.

Another approach to supporting R & D is for a government agency to enter into a contract with a private company to develop specific technological products. This is a common procedure in military-related fields. The United States Department of Defense, for example, may contract with an aerospace company for a new, high-performance aircraft. The approach is also used by the National Aeronautics and Space Administration to procure spacecraft systems and related hardware.

Finally, some public agencies maintain and operate their own R & D facilities. The United States, for example, has a large number of national laboratories scattered throughout the country. These were originally established for the purpose of creating military technologies. One of the original facilities, the Los Alamos National Laboratory in New Mexico, was instrumental in developing the first atomic bomb. All national laboratories, however, carry out a wide range of basic scientific work as well. In fact, the major challenge that has confronted these institutions since the end of the Cold War (and the resulting decrease in demand for defense-related hardware) is the conversion from military- to civilian-based R & D.

Another trend in government-sponsored research and development is toward international programs. In the face of rising research costs, many nations have found it advantageous to combine their efforts into a single joint venture. This has long been practiced in Western Europe, where a variety of scientific and technological projects are administered through cooperative efforts that often involve more than a dozen countries. Every advanced industrialized nation now carries out a significant portion of its R & D work through these collaborative programs.

Applications

Rocket technology has made possible a wide range of extremely valuable services, and it is responsible for the creation of whole new industries. Hundreds of satellites relay television and telephone signals, provide weather forecasting, aid in the navigation of planes and ships, and conduct remote sensing (oil, gas, and mineral exploration, environmental monitoring, and related activities) in orbit around the earth. In 1992, the revenues from commercial space activity in the United States alone totaled more than $5 billion.

The launching of satellites, scientific probes, and people into space has become such a matter of routine that it is easy to forget the immense technical difficulties that were involved in the development of modern rocketry. The history of this development, and its status today, demonstrates many aspects of government R & D policy.

Although the American scientist Robert Goddard had been experimenting with liquid-fueled rockets as early as 1926, the first modern launch vehicles of the United States military were built in the years following World War II. By the late 1950's, each branch of the service was working on its own set of projects: The Naval Research Laboratory had the Viking rocket and the Polaris missile, the Army Ballistic Missile Agency was building the Redstone and Jupiter rockets, and the Air Force had the Thor, Atlas, and the Titan programs.

As military projects, many of these rockets were designed primarily as weapons (specifically for use as medium-range and intercontinental ballistic missiles). They were, in some cases, patterned after German V-2 rockets captured during the war. Beginning in the mid-1950's, however, the Army and the Navy attempted to convert some of their missiles into vehicles for launching satellites into space. These efforts took on greater urgency after the U.S.S.R. became the first nation to orbit an artificial satellite (Sputnik 1) in October, 1957.

The first American attempt to reach Earth orbit was a conspicuous failure. On December 6, 1957, with millions of people watching on live television, an upgraded Navy Viking rocket that was to carry a three-pound satellite called Vanguard 1 developed a fuel leak just before launch and exploded.

Vanguard was was the first well-publicized disaster in American space history, but it was by no means an isolated incident. The Army successfully launched Explorer 1 on a Jupiter rocket one month after the Navy's attempt (and a Vanguard satellite did make it into space in March, 1958), but American rocket technology continued to have its share of setbacks.

In 1959, virtually all the military rocket programs were transferred to NASA, a civilian agency that had been established the previous year, partly as a response to the Soviet space program. Development continued, and U.S. rocket technology slowly improved. By 1960, NASA's successful launches began to outnumber its failures, although the failure rate was still over 40 percent. Three years later, the failure rate had been reduced to nearly 10 percent. From 1969 to 1992, NASA never experienced more than four launch failures a year. In eight of those years, its success rate was 100 percent. A little more than a decade after America's first ill-fated attempted rocket launch, a government-sponsored program had developed a proven, useable technology.

After many years (too many, according to some critics) of development, testing, and operation as a government program, a commercial rocket launching industry began to emerge in the late 1980's. In March, 1989, Space Services Incorporated became the first private company to launch its own rocket, which went on a suborbital flight carrying a scientific experiment. In August, McDonnell Douglas corporation successfully placed a British communications satellite into Earth orbit. Following these successes, and with help from the U.S. government, the commercial launch industry began to expand. Between 1989 and 1993, more than thirty private launches were conducted in the United States. Another forty were scheduled through 1997. The number of companies providing launch services grew from two to six. Approximately thirty years after the opening of the space age, rocket launching became a legitimate industry.

In addition to the fact that these companies make use of technologies originally developed under a government program (McDonnell-Douglas, for example, is a major NASA contractor), the commercial launchers are heavily reliant upon various forms of federal support. As much as 90 percent of their business comes from government-funded space projects. In addition, the U.S. Department of Transportation, which regulates the industry, underwrites a portion of its insurance. Finally, through international negotiations, the federal government provides some measure of protection against the subsidized launch programs of other countries. In short, public policy still plays a central role in fostering the industry's growth and development.

Context

Scientific research and technological development have become an increasingly important part of most modern economies, and they are often an essential element in such areas of public concern as economic growth, health care, education, and national defense. Although governments have sponsored science and technology projects of one sort or another for centuries (usually to provide for military needs or as a means of expanding commerce), the number and size of support programs increased rapidly in the years following World War II.

The primary catalyst for this growth was the onset of the Cold War. A widespread feeling at the time that the United States was falling behind in science and technology (a view that most observers now believe was incorrect) was directly responsible for the United States' decision not only to accelerate its own space program, but to expand its investments in many other technical fields as well.

During the late 1960's, when Cold War fears were declining and U.S. policymakers had become more concerned with other problems (such as urban poverty, race relations, and the war in Vietnam, to name only a few), the rate of growth in federal spending on R & D began to slow. The tendency since the mid-1970's was for specific programs to receive large increases in funding (in some cases temporarily) based upon perceived, politicized public needs, or upon the priorities of elected officials. During the administration of President Jimmy Carter, for example, the Department of Energy's budget for research into new sources of energy rose rapidly, a trend which was reversed in 1981, when President Ronald Reagan entered office. One of Reagan's major priorities was to develop a space-based defense against ballistic missiles—a program downgraded by President Bill Clinton after he took office in 1993.

Bibliography

Bryner, Gary, ed. *Science, Technology, and Politics: Policy Analysis in Congress.* Boulder, Colo.: Westview Press, 1992. Articles describing how the U.S. Congress has dealt with a range of scientific and technical issues.

Chubin, Daryl E., and Edward J. Hackett. *Peerless Science: Peer Review and U.S. Science Policy.* Albany: State University of New York Press, 1990. Strongly criticizes the process of peer review as it is practiced at the National Science Foundation and the National Institutes of Health.

Cohen, Linda R., and Roger G. Noll, et al., eds. *The Technology Pork Barrel.* Washington, D.C.: Brookings Institution, 1991. Highly critical account of government-funded R & D programs, with separate studies examining the space shuttle, communications satellites, and a number of alternative energy projects.

Hamlett, Patrick W. *Understanding Technological Politics: A Decision-Making Approach.* Englewood Cliffs, N.J.: Prentice-Hall, 1992. Framework for understanding how different groups (private businesses, legislatures, scientists, and engineers) influence the political process behind research and development.

Kernell, Samuel. *Parallel Politics: Economic Policymaking in Japan and the United States.* Washington, D.C.: Brookings Institution, 1991. Compares American and Japanese approaches to structural policy and economic planning.

Lambright, W. Henry. *Governing Science and Technology.* New York: Oxford University Press, 1976. Insightful analysis of how political factors influence the development of scientific and technical programs.

Logsdon, John M. *The Decision to Go to the Moon: Project Apollo and the National Interest.* Cambridge, Mass.: MIT Press, 1970. One of the first books to look at space exploration as a policy issue. Describes the politics of the U.S. space program from the 1950's to 1961.

Morin, Alexander J. *Science Policy and Politics.* Englewood Cliffs, N.J.: Prentice-Hall, 1993. Brief but thorough overview of the various agencies and institutions that govern U.S. science and technology policy. Useful as a general introduction.

Nelson, Richard R., ed. *National Innovation Systems: A Comparative Analysis.* New York: Oxford University Press, 1993. Essays describing the R & D systems of fifteen countries.

Smith, Bruce L. R. *American Science Policy Since World War II*. Washington, D.C.: Brookings Institution, 1989. Historical account of the development of U.S. policy toward the basic sciences in the latter half of the twentieth century.

W. D. Kay

Cross-References

Agriculture Management, p. 41; Budgets of National Governments, p. 158; Business and Government, p. 177; Energy Management, p. 604; Funding of Government, p. 724; Government Agencies, p. 765; Grants-in-Aid, p. 791; Industrialization, p. 916; Regulatory Agencies in the United States, p. 1678; Transportation Management in the United States, p. 2006; The World Health Organization, p. 2180.

RESOURCE MANAGEMENT

Field of study: Functions of government

One of the oldest functions of government, resource management became crucial to maintaining the power of the modern state after the industrial revolution, and continues to be an imperative of government in the increasingly interdependent world.

Principal terms

ENERGY CRISIS: shortage in the resources necessary to power civilization; usually refers to the 1973 and 1979 energy crises, which threatened the ability of developed societies to obtain or pay for the energy on which they run

ENVIRONMENTAL CRISIS: theory that the lifestyle of humankind is threatening the global ecostructure on which life depends; can also refer to instances of great environmental damage

INDUSTRIAL REVOLUTION: process of converting agrarian economies to a manufacturing base; customarily involves urbanization and a reliance on mechanical power sources

INTERDEPENDENCY: mutual dependence between countries by which each can somewhat influence the other and each is potentially vulnerable to disruption by the other

POSTINDUSTRIAL SOCIETY: society in which the service economy replaces manufacturing as the central economic sector, characterized by high levels of education and a concern with quality-of-life issues

TRANSNATIONAL ISSUES: issues that cross national boundaries and concern governments and citizens in many countries; also, problems that originate outside a government's jurisdiction

Overview

Mobilizing and managing resources is essential for a government to provide for the well-being of its people. It has become a crucial task for all governments in the twentieth century, but especially in democracies, where the people have the opportunity to reflect upon their prosperity and select their governments at regular intervals. The task has continued to evolve and expand in importance with the growing complexity and interdependency of social, economic, and political processes around the world.

There is some evidence that the concept of resource management existed even in the early history of Western societies or in traditional civilizations. Hunting and gathering societies, living off the earth, have occasionally moved the boundaries of their political communities when fish and game became difficult to acquire in their immediate surroundings, but such occurrences have been rare. The tools of acquisition in primitive societies rarely pose a threat to the regenerative processes of nature.

Limiting access to them by political means has been as unnecessary as it would be inconsistent with the notions of communal property prevailing in many traditional societies.

As modern state systems began to evolve in medieval Europe, however, the state rapidly assumed control over its most obvious resources. First, the impersonal city-state gradually replaced the family and religious-dominated political structures of previous eras. Political boundaries became fixed; eventually the extended territorial state displaced the city-state systems, and centralized political machinery emerged to link the capital to the people and territory throughout the realm. As these modern states began to emerge, so did concern with their resources. Where political authority rested on the concept of divine right monarchy or the state expanded by conquest, the basic resources of the realm—fish, game, timberland—were the property of the state. More precisely, they were the property of the king, given the highly personalized nature of states in much of Western Europe until well beyond the age of feudalism. Louis XIV's observation, "I am the state," could have been uttered by monarchs as early as William the Conqueror, one of whose first acts was to protect the royal forests of Norman England for the crown.

The next major development in the public management of resources occurred after the French Revolution ingrained the notion of popular sovereignty—that governments derive their legitimacy from the consent of the people, not their occupation by divine right monarchs—into Western political processes. The implication of this argument for resource management was straightforward: the state exists to protect resources for the common good, not the king's enrichment; to open through conquest new land for settlement by the people; and to protect those settlers in that land.

By the time of the French Revolution, this argument was already widely accepted in North America, especially in the English colonies, which, although established under the flag of commercial ventures such as the British West Indies Company, offered colonists access to land and resources in the New World. As early as the Plymouth colony, legal compacts began to reflect the concern of civil authority with resources that were clearly being treated, even in their apparent abundance, as finite. At Plymouth, the Founders regulated the cutting of timber on colony lands in 1626, less than a decade after touching shore. Elsewhere, colonies limited deer hunting, prohibited the setting of unnecessary forest fires, and, as early as 1681, decreed the protection of virgin forests even as land was being cleared for settlements.

Since that time, North America has occupied the center stage in resource management, for at least three reasons. First, North America was an extensive continent rich in basic resources: land with rich soil, vast timber forests, natural vegetation, and terrain favorable for settlement, crop cultivation and livestock rearing; game; water, usually clean and stocked with fish; and nonfuel metals, including gold and silver. It also was plentifully stocked with fuel minerals, enabling it to forge ahead of Europe economically during the nineteenth century in the Industrial Revolution and the subsequent revolution in lifestyles and living standards in the Western world. Finally, given the richness of the resource base in the United States, its industrial revolution raised environmental issues and policy choices involving resource utilization and management that industrializing European states rarely had the luxury of facing.

Concern with such issues as the environmental destruction attendant to resource development was not limited to North America. The term "ecology," for example, was coined by the German scientist-philosopher Ernst Haeckel in 1866. Nevertheless, it was in the United States that the great national parks were created as forestry and wildlife preserves during the nineteenth century, and the first enduring, broadly based environmental organization emerged—the Sierra Club in 1892. During the nineteenth century, European-trained advocates of scientific resource management trekked to the United States to practice their craft—men such as Gifford Pinchot, who became chief of the U.S. Division of Forestry during the 1890's, and was later a close personal adviser to Theodore Roosevelt, the first president of the United States to focus on environmental concerns.

Applications

The effect of the Industrial Revolution on resource policy in the United States was extremely mixed. On the one hand, industrialization produced a host of highly visible, new problems resulting from the growth of industry and population in urban areas, and an increasingly profligate, pollution-generating lifestyle. It consequently stimulated the conservation-minded to organize, and led urban environmentalists to focus on such resource issues as the overtaxed and often toxic water systems of America's growing cities. At the same time, the highly inefficient use of resources that characterized the industrialization process generated relatively little concern on the part of government or the public. The industrial age in general, and the expanding technologies of mass production in particular, was seen as heralding a period of superabundance in all things as technology rapidly increased, or promised to increase, the standard of living of the masses.

The icon of materialism and the myth of superabundance combined to preclude across-the-board attacks on the resource wastefulness and destructiveness of late nineteenth century laissez faire capitalism in the United States, but the growing scarcity of some resources could not go unnoticed. The frontier was at last closing; land was becoming finite. Industrialization was despoiling streams and already evincing the potential for doing greater damage to the physical environment. Social reform movements were developing in response to the often notoriously poor living conditions of workers in the cities. Environmental concerns formed a major part of the Progressive movement in U.S. politics, the term conservation itself growing out of environmentalists' efforts to construct reservoirs to conserve spring flood waters for use in subsequent dry seasons.

Between 1900 and World War I, the United States government gradually responded to these developments by stepping up its efforts to protect wildlife, fish, and timberlands, and by expanding its resource management activities well beyond preservation work into policies focusing on the efficient use of resources. The accomplishments were initially modest, in part because the environmental movement was split between the preservationists, who were focused on preserving wilderness exclusively for recreational use, and the conservationists, concerned with the efficient, scientific management of forest preserves. Nevertheless, by World War I, Pinchot not only had succeeded in convincing Roosevelt to host a national conference on environmental issues (in 1908), but also had been instrumental in organizing a series of subsequent state conservation congresses as well. The latter were not only concerned with the traditional topics pertaining to soil, water, and forest protection, but also addressed speculation in foodstuffs, the future ownership of public, non-agricultural lands, and issues involving manmade (infrastructure) resources, for example, public ownership of the railroads.

Then came World War I and the subsequent, postwar rush to return to highly materialistic, generally resource-wasteful, largely laissez-faire capitalism throughout much of the developed world. The binge was ended only by the Great Depression in 1929, a great reminder to all of the finite nature of prosperity and resources. The superabundance philosophy of industrialized capitalism was hard to sustain with a third to a half or more of nations' workforces idled by a global depression. At the same time, the Great Depression resulted in the U.S. government's taking specific new resource management responsibilities as a result of its involvement in such programs as the hydroelectric projects of the Tennessee Valley Authority, the soil conservation service, and the Civilian Conservation Corps.

World War II and the postwar plunge back into material gratification once again deflected attention from resource management, to survival during the war and to the improvement of living standards immediately after the war. As the U.S. population increased in affluence, however, it also increased in mobility, descending by the tens of millions on the country's park system. Postwar recreational needs thus prompted a substantial increase in the importance attached to national parks and habitat policy even during the 1950's.

During the 1960's, attention began to focus on many issues involving the destruction of basic resources in the process of economic growth: the threat to air and timber caused by the cars carrying people to the protected national parks; pollution from the coal-fired electricity plants supplying energy to their all-electric suburban homes; the spoilage of water caused by industrial expansionism; and similar issues. Even the new medium of television played a role in the process, keeping the environment on the public's mind and government's agenda through its coverage of natural disasters. The blowout at an offshore oil drilling platform near Santa Barbara, California, in 1969, for example, brought images of despoiled beaches and pathetic birds dying in their oily shrouds into the living rooms of the United States.

In the following decade, clean air and water acts, environmental protection acts, and cabinet-level environmental departments became fixtures in developed political processes throughout the Western world. Meanwhile, the heavy-industry-dominated, growth-oriented economies of the Soviet Union and communist Eastern Europe gave scant attention to environmental issues, even when siting and constructing nuclear power plants after the crisis at the Three Mile Island nuclear power plant in the United

States in 1979. The events in the 1970's that had the greatest impact on resource management policy, however, were the energy crises of 1973 and 1979, which decisively focused the attention of the world on the limited nature of resource wealth in general, and on the connection between energy resources and the high living standards of developed societies. Western civilization had largely come to run on imported petroleum by the 1970's.

The issues of access to and the affordability of foreign oil raised by these energy crises assigned still more new and rather specific resource management roles to government. Energy resource management became an integral part of coping with the growing number of megaproblems facing modern governments. These problems covered a multiplicity of public concerns, such as economic growth, quality of life issues, and national security, and involved a variety of different resources, not only the basic resources of water, land, and air, but also mineral resources, especially the fossil fuels of coal, oil, and natural gas.

The energy crises also provided Western industry, which had been placed on the defensive by relentless attacks from environmentalists during the early seventies, with the opportunity to counterattack—to build the Alaskan pipeline and nuclear energy plants, even if they posed a potential threat to the permafrost of Alaska or air of North America; to continue to use unmodified coal-fired electric plants, even though they carried a greater risk of causing cancer than costlier, scrubber-equipped systems; to defer expensive emissions controls on automobiles in order to keep people employed in manufacturing them in periods of recession, even though their emissions might cause acid rain. During the 1970's, policy choices involving the economy, energy, and the environment became increasingly zero-sum, that is, gains in one arena inevitably caused losses in another. Thus government had to widen its involvement in the area of resource management, especially where resource use in product production might involve social costs not apt to show up in the marketplace price of commodities, for example, the cost in air and water quality of allowing factories to function without environmental protection laws.

Context

Just as the middle of the twentieth century saw a shift in priorities from preservationist policies to efficient use and damage-control policies, so the principal trends in resource management shifted in the late twentieth century in response to the changing nature of the contemporary world.

For developed and developing countries alike, the world has become more economically interdependent. Resources are not only important for use by a country's own populace, but as export commodities to balance payments, support currency exchange rates, and earn income to pay for the imports necessary to raise the living standards of a people. The world is also increasingly interdependent environmentally. Reckless resources depletion or damage in one portion of the earth can potentially affect the global ecostructure, destroying the ozone layer or unbalancing the oxygen-producing system for the planet. As a consequence, governments gradually have moved toward greater resource planning and utilization on a global basis. The European Union, born from efforts to manage transnationally the coal and steel resources of Western Europe in the early 1950's, represents the most integrated arrangement for such planning, but is by no means the only one. Bilateral agreements between neighboring countries on specific topics, such as the United States-Canada treaty on acid rain to protect northeastern North American forests, are increasingly common. Even domestic legislation often reflects a transnational awareness. Whereas the principal environmental laws passed in the United States during President Richard Nixon's administration (1969-1974) had names such as the National Environmental Protection Act and were based purely on an assessment of the U.S. environmental and political scene, environmental legislation enacted in the 1980's, during the presidency of Ronald Reagan, carried titles such as the Global Climate Protection Act (1987) and the Ocean Dumping Act (1988).

This growing concern with resource planning, use, and protection on a global scale has not been at the expense of a national emphasis on resource management. President George Bush, a self-described environmental president, continued to push domestic environmental legislation focused on the United States during his years in office, such as the Clean Air Act amendments of 1990 and the emphasis on employing nonfossil, renewable fuel resources in the 1992 Energy Act.

Still, it can be expected that countries in the twenty-first century will continue to plan their resource policies in a global context. In part, this is because so many issues involving resources, for example, geopolitics, energy, political economy, and eco-politics, have become globalized. In a larger context, by the late twentieth century the ability of a government to provide the good life, or at least a better life, to its citizens had come to depend as much upon its ability to access and utilize the resources of others, as to manage those to be found within its own borders.

Bibliography

Becht, J. Edwin, and L. D. Belzung. *World Resource Management: Key to Civilizations and Social Achievement*. Englewood Cliffs, N.J.: Prentice-Hall, 1975. Somewhat dated but excellent broad-based discussion of the national and international importance of resource management and the role of resources in world affairs.

Butlin, J. A., ed. *Economics of Environmental and Natural Resources Policy*. Boulder, Colo.: Westview Press, 1981. Brief, information-laden work. The section on intertemporal and intergenerational problems associated with resource management makes this work especially worth seeking for advanced research.

Klee, Gary A., ed. *World Systems of Traditional Resource Management*. New York: V. H. Winston & Sons, 1980. Excellent, if rather historical, region-by-region guide to resource management in the late twentieth century.

Neher, Philip A. *Natural Resource Economics: Conservation and Exploitation*. New York: Cambridge University Press, 1990. For advanced research, a detailed examination of the economics of resource management for physical and biological, renewable and exhaustible resources.

O'Riordan, Timothy. *Perspectives on Resource Management*. London: Pion Limited, 1971. Written at a moment of great environmental concern, this book still offers an excellent, nuts-and-bolts introduction to the history of resource management and to late twentieth century issues in the field.

Switzer, Jacqueline Vaughn. *Environmental Politics: Domestic and Global Dimensions*. New York: St. Martin's Press, 1994. Excellent representation of the recent works on resource management, which increasingly focus on the environmental implications of resource policy, and the need to pursue it both in national political processes and through international collaboration.

Joseph R. Rudolph, Jr.

Cross-References

Energy Management, p. 604; Environmental Protection, p. 617; Industrialization, p. 916; International Agreements, p. 949; Land Management in the United States, p. 1045; National Economies, p. 1248; Public Works, p. 1647; Research, Development, and Planning, p. 1711; Social Democratic Parties, p. 1846; Supranational Government Institutions, p. 1922; Urbanization, p. 2071.

REVOLUTIONARY GOVERNMENTS

Field of study: Military

Revolutionary governments result from the overthrow of political systems in efforts to establish others in their place. Several general patterns tend to characterize such governments.

Principal terms

COUNTERREVOLUTION: revolution led by past leaders attempting to regain control

COUP D'ETAT: sudden takeover of government control, usually violent

PLURALIST POLITICAL MODEL: analysis of politics emphasizing the dispersion of power among many competing interest groups

POWER ELITE POLITICAL MODEL: analysis of politics emphasizing the concentration of power among the rich

REFORM: process involving change within the political system consistent with established political rules

REVOLUTION: overthrow of one political system as a part of the effort to establish another in its place

STATE TERRORISM: form of political conflict in which a government uses violence against various groups

TERRORISM: use of violence or the threat of violence in pursuit of political goals

Overview

Every political system attempts to translate power into legitimate authority. In some cases, however, political systems become defined as illegitimate by such a significant number of their citizens that radical political change results. A political revolution is the overthrow of one political system as part of the effort to establish another one in its place.

Revolution is quite different from reform. Reform involves change within the system consistent with established political rules, while revolution is a change of the system itself. A coup d'etat is also not a revolution; when one group of leaders overthrows another, violence may occur, but it is generally rather limited. A revolution, in contrast, involves widespread popular opposition to an established political system, and widespread violence is the likely result. For example, the Sandinista revolution in Nicaragua against dictator Anastasio Somoza, which ended in 1979, involved years of widespread violence. On the other hand, some revolutions, such as the overthrow of the Marcos regime in the Philippines in 1986, have been relatively free of violence.

Revolutions can occur within any type of political system and have a wide range of outcomes. The American Revolution, for example, ended the political control of the American colonies by the British monarchy and resulted in a democratic government.

The French revolutionaries of 1789 also overthrew a monarch and summarily executed many members of the feudal aristocracy, but in a few years monarchy returned in the person of Napoleon. Early in the twentieth century, the Russian Revolution replaced a system of monarchy with a socialist government based on the ideas of Karl Marx. Following the death of the dictator Francisco Franco in 1975, Spain experienced a mostly peaceful political revolution that resulted in a democratic government. Whether peaceful or violent, revolutions tend to follow several general patterns.

Common sense might suggest that revolution is more likely under conditions of extreme deprivation and oppression, but history shows that revolutions are actually more likely when people's lives are improving. Social improvements stimulate the desire for an even better life, and such rising expectations may outpace reality. As Crane Brinton has pointed out, revolutions are typically not started by starving, miserable people, rather they are born of hope, and their philosophies are optimistic.

Prerevolutionary societies are typically highly stratified. Disadvantaged people perceive themselves as unjustly deprived, with little chance for improving their lot within the prevailing political system. Sometimes, advantaged segments of society lose faith in their claims to legitimacy and become vulnerable to attack from below.

Revolutions are likely when an existing political system is unable or unwilling to change, especially to meet the demands of powerful segments of society. For example, monarchies in largely agrarian societies may be unable to meet the demands of a rising middle class based on industry and trade. A new and increasingly powerful segment of society may find revolution an attractive path toward greater power.

Thomas Hobbes observed that the center of political rebellion in seventeenth century England was the universities, a pattern that was repeated during the American political unrest of the 1960's. A successful revolution is likely to be led by an opposition that is not only militarily strong, but also has a well-expressed justification. Intellectuals are important for formulating principles to support revolution. Intellectuals may function as a revolutionary special interest group that expresses popular grievances and unites diverse opposition to the existing political system into a single revolutionary movement.

The successful overthrow of an old political system does not ensure the long-term success of a revolution. Revolutionary movements may be unified primarily by the hatred of the past government. Once the initial objective of political overthrow is accomplished, divisions within the revolutionary movement may intensify. More important, a new political regime faces the task of legitimating its authority. In the short run, revolutionary regimes face the danger of counterrevolution led by past leaders attempting to regain control of the society, as happened following the over-throw of the communist system in the former Soviet Union. To counter this danger, a revolutionary regime often eliminates the past leadership through exile or execution.

In general, the consequences of revolution cannot be defined as either good or bad. Certainly, revolution involves a radical disruption of established social patterns. In at least some instances, widespread death and destruction occur, and new governments are certain to be subject to political criticism. Historically, however, revolutions have launched many nations, including the United States, France, the Soviet Union, and China, into positions of world prominence. Recent revolutions in Cuba, Vietnam, and Nicaragua remind observers that revolution always evokes disagreement and conflict.

Applications

Theory maintains that social movements leading to revolutions frequently arise when large numbers of people believe themselves deprived of things they consider necessary to their well-being. Those who believe that they lack the income, working conditions, political rights, or social dignity they deserve can be expected to engage in organized behavior to bring about a more just political system.

It was Karl Marx's expectation that deprived industrial workers would eventually organize in opposition to capitalism. Marx claimed that capitalism deprived workers economically and politically by giving them low wages and little social power and psychologically by alienating them from their own creative potential. While no socialist revolution has occurred in the United States, labor unions and various political organizations of workers have arisen in an effort to address the sense of deprivation experienced by working-class Americans.

Deprivation is a relative concept. Regardless of the level of deprivation in absolute terms of money and power, people tend to evaluate themselves relative to a class they are familiar with. Relative deprivation is a perceived disadvantage based on comparisons with what other people have, or by some other established standard. Relative deprivation obviously arises if people use others in a more favorable position as a reference group, thinking that "there's no reason that we shouldn't have what they have." People also feel relatively deprived to the extent that they imagine how their lives could be more satisfying than they actually are.

In the nineteenth century, Alexis de Tocqueville examined the social uprising that became the French Revolution. Why, he asked, did revolution occur in France rather than in neighboring Germany, where the peasants were, in absolute terms, far more deprived? Tocqueville's answer was that, as bad as their plight was, German peasants had known nothing but feudal servitude and thus had no basis of comparison that would make them feel deprived. French peasants, on the other hand, had experienced steady improvement in their lives and were aware that society did not have to be the way it was. Able to imagine still further improvements, they experienced a keen sense of relative deprivation. Tocqueville concluded that steadily increasing prosperity, far from tranquilizing the population, generally promoted a spirit of unrest.

Later, echoing Tocqueville's insight, James C. Davies stressed the link between the birth of social movements and rising expectations. As life gets better, people quickly take the improvements for granted and look to the future for more. If the standard of living stops improving, or suddenly drops, people are likely to experience a pronounced sense of relative deprivation. Thus, social movements aimed at changing society are most likely to occur when an extended period of improvement in the standard of living is followed by a shorter period of declining circumstances.

Structural strain theory, developed by Neil J. Smelser, has become one of the most helpful approaches to understanding social movements. His analysis identifies six factors that foster social movements. The more these factors are present, the greater the likelihood that a social movement will develop. Smelser's theory also offers hypotheses about why collective behavior sometimes takes the form of a relatively unorganized mob or riot, and at other times takes the highly organized form of a political revolution or a social movement. The prodemocracy movement and corollary political revolutions that transformed Eastern Europe and the former Soviet Union in the late 1980's and early 1990's illustrate Smelser's six factors.

The first is structural conduciveness. The roots of social movements lie in social patterns that set the stage for significant social problems. Thus, the generally low standard of living in Eastern Europe, as compared to Western Europe, coupled with the lack of political participation by the majority of people, created widespread dissatisfaction.

Second, structural strain appears. The emergence of social movements is encouraged by strains within society, including any patterns of social conflict or of failed expectations. The prodemocracy movement in Eastern Europe gained strength because people there could readily see that the quality of life was far lower than that of their counterparts in Western Europe and lower than years of propaganda about prosperous socialism had told them to expect.

The third factor is the growth and spread of an explanation. A needed step toward organized collective behavior is the development of a clear statement of the problem, its causes, likely consequences, and what can be done to make matters better. A well-formulated analysis of the situation, spread throughout the society, encourages a well-organized social movement. Intellectuals propounded the notion that the plight of Eastern Europe was caused by deep economic and political flaws in the system. At the same time, movement leaders proposed strategies to increase democracy.

The fourth element is precipitating factors. While social movements are often a long time in the making, at some point, an event may precipitate the onset of collective action. When Mikhail Gorbachev came to power in the Soviet Union in 1985 and implemented his program of perestroika, people in Eastern Europe seized an historic opportunity to reorganize their political and economic lives as Moscow relaxed its rigid control.

The fifth factor is mobilization for action. Once precipitating factors have focused widespread concern on a public issue, collective action is likely to take place in the form of rallies, leafleting, building of alliances with sympathetic organizations, and similar activities, including demonstrations and lobbying. The initial success of the Solidarity movement in Poland, aided by the Reagan Administration in the United States and the Vatican, mobilized people throughout Eastern Europe to press for change. The rate of change accelerated as reform movements gained strength. Progress that had taken a decade in Poland required only months in Hungary, and only weeks in other countries.

Finally Smelser's theory factors in a lack of social control. The direction and consequences of any social movement are partly determined by the responses of various established authorities, including political officials, the police, and the military. Powerful repression by the state can weaken or destroy a social movement or revolution, while a lack of social control can encourage its growth. The former state of affairs was seen in the crushing of prodemocracy forces in the People's Republic of China. By contrast, Gorbachev adopted a policy of nonintervention in Eastern Europe, which propelled the drive for change there. Ironically, the forces his program unleashed in these neighboring nations soon spread to the Soviet Union itself, ending the historic domination of the Communist Party and leading to a new political confederation in 1992. It also laid the groundwork for three Baltic states, Estonia, Latvia, and Lithuania, to break away from the former Soviet Union and establish themselves as fully independent nations.

Context

A structural-functional analysis of the communist revolutionary phenomenon provides a fascinating study in irony. According to the dialectical materialism of Karl Marx, the key aim of communism was the provision of a prosperous, egalitarian life for all citizens. The more successful that socialist regimes were in realizing these economic objectives, the more they were likely, in so doing, to sow the seeds of their own destruction. The basic material needs of the people in socialist countries were more or less effectively met through the industrialization of their formerly agrarian societies. Socialism, however, while moderately successful in building basic heavy industries, was not as well suited as a market economy to running an economically and culturally diverse society, nor was it able to meet the higher philosophical and aesthetic needs of its people. A centralized economy was incapable, particularly in a totalitarian society, of meeting the escalating needs of people who continually observed the higher economic productivity of their Western European neighbors. The Marxist dictum of "from each according to ability to each according to need" not only failed to account for selfish motives, with the inevitable, variable investment of individual abilities to accomplishing the common good, but also was unable to adjust to the natural escalation of former, luxurious "desires" or "wants" to the status of "needs" for people whose basic needs had already been met by the socialist state. These higher material and nonmaterial needs could only be met within a different political context.

Only a truly democratic society could provide wider opportunities of self-actualization, both on a material and nonmaterial level, by offering heightened freedom in all phases of one's personal, religious, political, and public life. Thus, by realizing its own stated objectives of dialectical materialism, the Communist state latently set the stage for its own destruction, by initiating a revolution of rising expectations.

Bibliography

Ash, Timothy G. *The Polish Revolution: Solidarity*. New York: Charles Scribner's Sons, 1983. Analysis of the rise of the Solidarity movement and the political revolution it generated in Poland. Clearly illustrates the accuracy of Neil Smelser's structural-strain theory.

Brinton, Crane. *The Anatomy of Revolution*. Rev. and expanded ed. New York: Vintage Books, 1965. Comprehensive overview of the conditions which are likely to inspire, or retard, revolutionary activities, depending on a variety of social conditions.

Davies, James C. "Toward a Theory of Revolution." *American Sociological Review* 27 (February, 1962): 5-19. Describes the widely accepted social theory of revolution, linking the birth of social movements and rising expectations.

Skocpol, Theda. *States and Social Revolutions: A Comparative Analysis of France, Russia, and China*. Cambridge, England: Cambridge University Press, 1979. Analysis of the common elements precipitating revolutions in three widely disparate societies.

Smelser, Neil J. *Theory of Collective Behavior*. New York: Free Press, 1962. Presents one of the most influential and widely applied approaches to understanding the emergence of revolutions and various social movements.

Tocqueville, Alexis de. *The Old Regime and the French Revolution*. Translated by Stuart Gilbert. Garden City, N.Y.: Doubleday, 1955. Describes the common social factors underlying the American and French revolutions, as well as an analysis of the French milieu leading to the French Revolution.

Yuan, Gao. *Born Red: A Chronicle of the Cultural Revolution*. Stanford, Calif.: Stanford University Press, 1987. Personal account of a teenager's experiences during the Cultural Revolution in China from 1966 to 1969.

Robert D. Bryant

Cross-References

Anarchism in Marxist Thought, p. 72; Chinese Communism, p. 223; Civil Wars, p. 325; Colonialism and Anticolonialism, p. 351; Communist Parties, p. 377; Dialecticism, p. 540; Empires and Empire Building, p. 597; Force, p. 712; Hobbes's Political Philosophy, p. 836; Invisible Government, p. 975; Irrationalism in Politics, p. 987; Islam and Government, p. 994; Legitimacy, p. 1105; Military Structure, p. 1198; Political Economy, p. 1455; Socialism, p. 1865; Tocqueville's Political Philosophy, p. 1981; War, p. 2129.

REVOLUTIONARY PARTIES

Field of study: Politics

Revolutionary parties intend to replace, instead of join, the existing political order. This new order is to come into being, usually, under their direct supervision. They may attempt this change in an overt or covert fashion, through peaceful means or through violence.

Principal terms

DICTATOR: person who exercises absolute power in a state

IDEOLOGY: beliefs that form the theoretical basis for a political party

NATIONALISM: excessive devotion to the independence and advancement of one's own country

PROPAGANDA: information spread to promote or harm a cause, group, or nation

REVOLUTION: overthrow of an established government, usually in a brief time and often by violence

TERRORISM: use of violence, often in a systematic fashion, to achieve political goals

TOTALITARIAN: highly centralized form of government that grants neither recognition nor tolerance to opponents

Overview

Political parties exist to advance the shared interests of their members, usually by obtaining and retaining, as much as possible, control of the government. This often involves placing members of the party in the government, either through election or by appointment. Revolutionary parties have as their aim the complete overthrow of the existing government and its replacement by a regime of their own design; such changes are known as revolutions.

Revolutionary parties are distinguished from other political parties by the extent to which they desire a change in the existing conditions. Mainstream, nonrevolutionary parties, such as the Democratic and Republican parties in the United States, or the Labour and Conservative parties in the United Kingdom, generally accept the political process as a given, with need for reforms only, to correct minor flaws or disturbances in the system. For such mainstream parties, the basic question is how to gain more power and influence under the existing situation.

Parties that advocate more aggressive and sweeping changes in the fundamental political system are often known as reformist or, in the United States, progressive. While they accept the basic fundamentals of the existing political system, they believe that serious structural flaws need to be addressed in a radical fashion—literally, by going to the root of the problem. In the United States during the late nineteenth and early twentieth centuries, such progressive parties advocated the use of silver coinage in place of the strict gold standard, increased power for the average voter by allowing for the popular election of United States senators, and for the rights of initiative, recall, and referendum. In many poorer countries, land reform, debt reduction or cancellation, and nationalization of foreign businesses have often been the goals of progressive or reform parties.

Revolutionary parties neither wish to work as part of the existing political system nor to reform it. Rather, they seek to replace the status quo with their own political framework. They may seek to do this through peaceful means, such as winning electoral approval. This was accomplished by the African National Congress of South Africa; its long struggle was instrumental in finally dismantling the system of apartheid. Revolutionary parties may resort to violence, either in the form of a short coup d'etat or of a long-running guerrilla war, as happened in Algeria during the 1950's and 1960's. Parties may instigate a full-scale revolution that results in unexpected and unintended consequences. This was the case in France in 1789, and to some extent for the English, American, and Russian revolutions as well. Finally, a revolutionary party may utilize all these approaches, as was the case with the Nazi Party in Germany during the 1920's and 1930's.

There is a popular conception that revolutionary parties come mainly from the Left, but in truth they fall throughout the political spectrum. Throughout history, the Right has had its share of revolutionary parties. One example from Roman history is that of the rather loosely organized group which formed around Lucius Cornelius Sulla about 83 B.C.E. Sulla took Rome by armed force; there followed a systematic, violent, and cold-blooded series of mass murders, which effectively eliminated Sulla's enemies, leaving him free to declare himself dictator and impose highly conservative changes in the Roman political system.

During the 1920's and 1930's in Japan, secret military organizations took on the nature of revolutionary parties in their determination to sweep away recently established parliamentary and democratic institutions and replace them with a militaristic and nationalistic public policy that emphasized obedience and conformity. Such a change, these groups believed, was necessary to allow Japan to achieve its national destiny as ruler of Asia and the Pacific. While the outward form of the Japanese state remained intact, these groups were successful in changing its operations and bringing on World War II.

Perhaps the most notable revolutionary parties on the Right are the Fascists in Italy and the Nazis in Germany. Benito Mussolini, at one time a socialist journalist from a working-class family, used his editorship of the newspaper *Il Popolo d'Italia* to gain leadership of the Fascist movement. Having organized the Fascists, Mussolini was able to take advantage of social and economic unrest, and of the fear of a communist revolution that might result, to have himself appointed to the position of prime minister. By 1928 he had eliminated all competing political parties and established the Fascist Grand Council as the actual government of Italy.

Under Adolf Hitler, the Nazi Party pursued a similar, but much more thorough pattern, in Germany. Employing its tightly organized structure and through its appeal to Germans fearful of a communist revolution, the Nazi Party steadily gained electoral power, finally reaching the point at which Hitler was taken into the government as part of a conservative coalition. Once in office, Hitler ruthlessly disposed of the other members of the coalition and established the Nazi Party as first the de facto, and then the de jure, government of Germany.

Revolutionary parties also come from the Left. In Europe around 1848, a series of revolutions swept from France to Hungary, from Italy to Prussia, all of them essentially liberal in character and guided by revolutionary organizations that sought progressive reforms in their nations' governments. Later, the *caribari* (Italian for "charcoal burners," after the laboring class that supplied much of their initial membership) were another expression of this liberal brand of revolutionary party; their efforts under leaders such as Giuseppe Garibaldi led to the unification of Italy in 1870.

Undoubtedly the best-known revolutionary party from the Left is the Communist Party, which, under the leadership of Vladimir Lenin and Leon Trotsky, staged a brilliantly executed coup in November, 1917. This coup overthrew the democratic provisional government formed following the abdication of Czar Nicholas II. Once in power, the Bolsheviks survived a ferocious civil war and intense international aggression to establish communism in Russia and later throughout much of eastern Europe. In alliance with nationalist movements, communism was later a potent factor in Latin America, Africa, and Asia.

There are also instances where revolutionary parties have been created from the moderate center of the political spectrum. Such were the cases in English and American revolutions, in which the parties, at first seeking relatively moderate reforms, were forced by the intransigence of the elites in power to adopt increasingly radical positions. During the English Revolution, for example, King Charles I fostered, by his stubbornness, the more extreme groups behind men such as Oliver Cromwell. The more extreme groups began to dominate events and achieve more extensive changes than had been originally intended. In a similar fashion, the American revolutionaries found themselves forced into declaring independence as the only resort to losing even the modest freedoms they enjoyed at the beginning of their dispute with Great Britain. In both cases, however, moderates successfully restrained the more aggressive revolutionaries, so that there were no social upheavals such as those that occurred with the French or Russian revolutions.

Revolutionary parties may also be based on nationalism or, in some cases, race. The Indian National Congress, established by Mohandas Gandhi in 1915, and which eventually brought independence to India, was a nonviolent example of a nationalist party that was, in its ultimate aim, revolutionary. The Mau Mau movement in Kenya is an example of a revolutionary party that combined nationalism and racial consciousness, since it was directed against British imperialism in Africa, an imperialism that the Mau Mau perceived in both nationalistic and racial terms.

Another way to categorize revolutionary parties is by their internal structure. Some, such as those in the English or American revolutions, have been fairly loosely organized. In a sense, these can be characterized as gradual revolutionary parties. Their characteristics include their rising in response to specific grievances, usually over a period of time, and their tendency to seek redress or rebalance, rather than outright revolution, at least during the initial phases of friction. During the first phase of the Russian Revolution, the Mensheviks, a relatively moderate revolutionary party, fit this description, and in fact controlled the provisional government established after the czar's abdication. After less than a year, however, they were toppled by the more ruthless and better-organized Bolsheviks.

The Bolsheviks are an example of a tightly organized revolutionary party; the Nazis and the Chinese Communist Party also fit into this category. Such parties are often ideologically oriented; they have very rigid doctrines that govern their worldview and their activities. Their characteristics include a very definite plan for change that admits of no compromise (although, for tactical purposes, they may pretend to be amenable to compromise), the determination to eliminate all opposition, the use of violence to accomplish this end, and a disregard for conventional morality.

Applications

On May 5, 1789, King Louis XVI of France officially opened the gathering of the States-General, a collection of representatives of the nobility, the clergy, and the third estate, or middle class, to address France's severe economic crisis. Initial plans called for the three estates to meet separately, which would allow the clergy and nobility, although smaller in number, to dominate the proceedings. The third estate refused. Its famous Tennis Court Oath not to compromise followed, and by the end of June the King and the other two estates had capitulated. All three groups were merged. As historians have noted, this was the first really revolutionary event of the French Revolution, and it completely changed the political landscape.

Political parties began to form as deputies in the new Assembly discovered common principles or shared interests. By far the most organized, and among the most revolutionary, of these were the Jacobins, who, from the start, were determined to establish a French republic.

Officially known as the Society of Friends of the Constitution, the group received its better-known name because it met in the library of a Jacobin monastery in Paris. The Jacobins rapidly made contact with local groups, many of which had existed before the revolution. Soon, the Friends of the Constitution were established through-out the nation. The central club, in Paris, kept in constant communication with, and exerted control over, the local clubs through letters, visits, and periodic meetings.

The Jacobins were masterful in their use of all available propaganda techniques: pamphlets, newspapers, meetings, speeches, parades, and symbolic attire such as liberty caps. Jacobin propaganda spread the notion of republicanism and antimonar-chism, first through Paris and then throughout France. Jean Paul Marat, closely allied with the Jacobins, established the newspaper *L'Ami du peuple*, which was violent in its attacks on anti-Jacobins and helped further the Jacobin cause.

The Jacobin organization was taken over by its more radical members, chief among them Maximilien Robespierre, who were determined to create a "republic of virtue."

Their opportunity arose when the revolution swept away the governmental institutions of the monarchy without replacing them with effective forms of authority. The radicals were in control of the Jacobin organization, and the Jacobin organization was, by default, in control of France.

Once in power, the Jacobins sought to accomplish their truly revolutionary goals: The Catholic church was removed from its position of power. The French were encouraged to leave the church for a new, civic religion. The calendar, despised as a product of unenlightened superstition, was entirely recast in a more scientific, rational fashion. All traces of the monarchy were expunged. There was even an attempt, perhaps facetious, to change the name of the "queen bee" to "laying bee."

Most important of all, the machinery of the state was used to eliminate the party's enemies. Establishing the Revolutionary Tribunal in March, 1793, the Jacobins soon brought about the Reign of Terror, which sought out and punished enemies and traitors to the revolution. The Committee on Public Safety, rather than the National Assembly, became the actual power of the nation, echoed throughout France by smaller, local committees. The guillotine remained busy, and from April to July, 1794, Robespierre ruled as a virtual dictator of France. Robespierre's colleagues, fearful they would be next to face the guillotine, turned on their leader. He and his closest followers were executed. The revolution pulled back from the excesses of the Jacobins. By the middle of 1795, the Jacobins had been effectively eliminated as a political party.

Context

A political revolution is a fundamental change that is complete, pervasive, and usually radical. It is generally accomplished in a relatively brief period of time. Ironically, revolutionary parties, the agents which seek to implement such a change, often must plan and work diligently and even secretly for years or decades before engaging in their attempt to overturn, rapidly and completely, the existing government. The Bolsheviks under Lenin and Trotsky, for example, had been seriously preparing for revolution in Russia since at least 1900, but were taken by surprise by the 1905 uprising and were not ready for their own coup d'etat until after the successful overthrow of the czarist regime in 1917. In a similar fashion, the revolutionary groups in North America that agitated against British control of the colonies had been active, in some cases, since the end of the French and Indian War in 1763, but events did not allow them to mobilize more fully until 1775.

Revolutionary parties have varying degrees of organization. Some are centered around a single individual, and their aims are sweeping but vague. The violent Roman conservative movement which had the general and dictator Sulla as its leader was such a loosely organized revolutionary party. It was sufficiently unified to overcome its opposition (largely because of troops personally loyal to Sulla) and impose its version of government on the Roman state, but it lacked the cohesion to remain in power after Sulla's retirement from public life. At best, the revolutionary party of Sulla delayed the final fall of the Roman Republic by a generation; at worst, it showed later adventurers such as Caesar how vulnerable that Republic was.

Other revolutionary parties are more tightly organized. The Bolsheviks are a prime example of this discipline, as is the much less successful Communist Party in the United States (CPUSA), which has a considerable amount of discipline and internal organization but negligible impact on external events. Traditionally, the more extreme revolutionary parties, such as the Communists, the Nazis, and the Fascists, have been disciplined and tightly organized. Totalitarian regimes, such as those in Nazi Germany and Communist Russia, result from such disciplined groups. More democratic governments, such as those in the United States or England following their revolutions, come from revolutionary parties that are more loosely organized.

Finally, revolutionary parties have differing fates. Failure is the most common. The Levelers and Diggers in England during the seventeenth century, or the Black Panthers in the United States during the twentieth century, are examples of this. It is easy to see why revolutionary parties usually fail. Most revolutionary parties pit themselves against governments that not only are established but also possess immensely superior resources that, in most cases, they do not hesitate to employ. Even revolutionary parties that succeed, such as the Nazis or the Fascists, sometimes fail during their initial attempts at overthrowing the state.

Success, and then quick failure, has attended a number of revolutionary groups. The party triumphs over its opponents, but is quickly or gradually undone either by internal contradictions or a combination of external forces. The Jacobins ruled France for a period of approximately two years, four months of which Robespierre assumed a virtual dictatorship. Then, more moderate elements within the party, who feared for their lives, assumed power. In a similar fashion the Mensheviks toppled the czar in Russia, only to be supplanted by the Bolsheviks, who ruled for seventy-five years before they too fell. The Fascists were defeated and destroyed by external forces after they initiated World War II.

Lasting revolutionary parties discover a pattern of success, then adaptation. The party overthrows the existing government, gains power, and then adjusts to changing conditions in order to retain power. This is most obviously seen in the American Revolution, but the pattern has also been repeated in other cases, where revolution has been tempered by a resolution to adapt to conditions and profit by them.

Bibliography

Brinton, Crane. *The Anatomy of Revolution*. New York: Vintage Books, 1965. American classic on revolutions by a distinguished and readable historian. Starting point for understanding of the topic.

_____. *A Decade of Revolution, 1789-1799*. New York: Harper & Row, 1934. Study of the French Revolution, with emphasis upon the ideas and philosophies of the participants.

Ellul, Jacques. *Autopsy of Revolution*. Translated by Patricia Wolf. New York: Alfred A. Knopf, 1971. An interesting counterpoint to Crane Brinton's more pragmatic views.

Hyams, Edward. *A Dictionary of Modern Revolution*. New York: Taplinger, 1973.

Handy compendium, good for basic facts and definitions.

Kaplan, Lawrence, ed., with the assistance of Carol Kaplan. *Revolutions: A Comparative Study*. New York: Random House, 1973. Sets the sorts of revolutions and revolutionary parties within a framework.

Postgate, Raymond William, ed. *Revolution from 1789 to 1906*. New York: Harper & Row, 1962. Primary materials by and about revolutionaries.

Michael Witkoski

Cross-References

Chinese Communism, p. 223; Civil Unrest and Rioting, p. 317; Civil Wars, p. 325; Communist Parties, p. 377; Dialecticism, p. 540; Fascism and Nazism, p. 656; Insurgencies and Coups d'État, p. 930; Irrationalism in Politics, p. 987; National Liberation Movements, p. 1255; One-Party Systems, p. 1350; Political Violence, p. 1539; Revolutions, p. 1738; Right of Revolution, p. 1744; Russian Political History, p. 1770; Terrorism, p. 1962.

REVOLUTIONS

Field of study: Politics

A revolution is a process of deep and widespread social change in society, which often includes violence and the overthrow of the central government by armed citizens of that society. Revolutions make abrupt, fundamental changes in the government, constitution, national identity, socioeconomic order, and basic values of society.

Principal terms
EVOLUTION: gradual and continuous change in society and its
    institutions, typically not sought intentionally
IDEOLOGY: system of action-beliefs that describes, explains, and
    justifies the existing institutions in society
LEGITIMACY: belief that the government and key institutions should be
    supported and that their rules and commands should be obeyed
REFORM: fundamental change in the government, constitution,
    socioeconomic order, or basic values of society, which does not
    involve the violent overthrow of the existing government
RELATIVE DEPRIVATION: gap between what people believe they ought to
    receive under fair conditions and what they actually receive
UTOPIA: hypothetical place of ideal perfection, especially in laws,
    government, and social conditions

Overview

The term "revolution" has been used to describe many forms of change, ranging from unintended social changes such as were caused by industrialization to intentionally created change through armed struggle. Despite the popular tendency to label almost any change as a revolution, most social scientists now restrict the term to a relatively rare type of violent social change that is associated with a significant shift in the course of history for a particular society or region. For example, nearly all authorities agree that the term applies to England's Puritan Revolution in 1640, the French Revolution in 1789, the American Revolution in 1776, the Russian Revolution in 1917, the Chinese Revolution in 1949, and the Cuban Revolution in 1959. All these examples involve the violent overthrow of a government by its own citizens, the establishment of a new revolutionary government with a fundamentally different ideology and constitution, and a lasting change in the basic values of the people living in these societies.

Because revolutions typically involve the violent overthrow of existing governments, they share some of the characteristics of civil wars, insurrections, and coups d'état, and are associated with political violence, terrorism, and war. Nevertheless, revolutions are not identical to those other processes. Most wars do not stimulate the forces of revolution, and most incidents of political violence and terrorism are neither accompanied nor followed by revolution. Similarly, most civil wars, insurrections, and coups d'état neither accompany nor pave the way for revolutions. These other forms of violence can be distinguished from revolution on the basis of the type of political and social change they produce.

In contrast to revolution, which is a multistage process of social change, the coup d'état is an event of short duration. The typical coup d'état changes the top governmental officials and some of the policies pursued by the deposed leadership, but usually does not fundamentally change the basic values of society, the type of constitution, or the distribution of values. The coup d'état is often described as a palace revolution.

Although coups d'état usually do not result in revolutionary changes, during the course of a revolution, one or more coups d'état that have a significant effect on the revolutionary process may occur. For example, shortly after the start of the Russian Revolution in 1917, the Bolshevik Party, led by Vladimir Ilich Lenin, seized power from a less radical set of revolutionary leaders. This change in revolutionary leadership dramatically accelerated the breadth and pace of political, economic, and social change in Russia.

Civil wars, because they do not necessarily lead to the overthrow of the government, are different from both coups d'état and revolutions. Civil wars and revolutions are linked, however, because all major revolutions are accompanied by large-scale internal wars with intense and prolonged violence between the forces of change and the forces of resistance. Large segments of the civilian population are displaced by political violence, and, unlike the typical coup d'état, many civilians suffer casualties from terrorism and the course of the civil war.

Although revolution is an important source of social change, there are other ways that social change can occur. Much social change is evolutionary. According to German sociologist Max Weber, much of the urbanization and industrialization that took place in western Europe can be traced to the gradual spread of Protestantism. Protestantism established a system of values and beliefs that unintentionally fostered the spirit of capitalism, which, in turn, established conditions conducive to economic growth and widespread social change. Although much of this evolutionary change was unintended, in some countries it was intentionally sought by a variety of reform movements, which, over time, produced change that, in the aggregate, may have been as significant as the more dramatic change associated with revolutions. Thus, a revolution is simply a special type of social change that is distinctive because it is more violent, more intentional, and more rapid than other forms of social change.

Virtually all theories about the causes of revolution assume that widespread social discontent is a necessary, but not sufficient, cause of revolution. Conversely, societies in which the government is widely viewed as effective and legitimate simply do not spawn revolutions. If a lack of legitimacy increases the risk of revolution, it is important to know why governments lose legitimacy, and what kind of discontent is most likely to spur a revolutionary movement.

While sharp inequalities of wealth are likely to make the poor discontent about their immediate material conditions, this in itself rarely produces revolution. If the existence of a wealthy few living side by side with great numbers of poor people were a sufficient cause of revolution, human history would be marked by almost continuous revolutions. One reason that the poor do not revolt is because they have no hope that they can change their situation. They may be discontented, but if they do not believe that they can do anything to change their predicament, they are not likely to take action.

Leaders of revolutionary movements often stimulate hope among the masses by promises of utopia after the revolution. The very idea of a utopia encourages hope by presenting an alternative and ideal way of arranging society. The fact that a utopia can be described and explained makes it seem that alternatives to existing institutions are possible and desirable. Moreover, the promise of a utopian society constitutes the goal for the revolution, therefore providing a meaningful rationale for taking action. By drawing attention to the sharp contrast between the ideal society of utopia and the less-than-ideal existing social arrangements, utopian beliefs simultaneously stimulate both hope and discontent.

Because the poorest people in society rarely have much hope, they seldom attempt revolutions. Most revolutions have been attempted by people in the middle of the social order. To explain why these people are more likely than the poor to revolt, social scientists have focused on the notion of relative deprivation. One theory of relative deprivation ties together hope and discontent. According to this theory, continuous and absolute deprivation leads to despair, but a period of progress interrupted by a sharp, partial loss of previous gains can lead to revolution. This theory is supported by historical evidence, which suggests that several major revolutions occurred shortly after a period of steady improvement in social conditions was interrupted by a sharp decline. The period of improvement apparently gave the people experiencing the change hope for the future. When they experienced an interruption in this path of improvement, they apparently felt more deprived than those who did not experience any improvement, because the contrast between the ideal situation they expected to achieve and the actual situation in which they found themselves widened dramatically. Paradoxically, widespread progress is more likely to lead to revolution than a prolonged period of deprivation.

Because revolutions are made by humans and are not simply the result of natural forces, they require both leaders and a set of beliefs. Because it is the business of intellectuals to construct systems of symbols, virtually all revolutionary movements are led, in part, by intellectuals. In some cases, such as the Puritan Revolution in seventeenth century Great Britain and the Iranian revolution in the 1970's, the intellectuals are religious leaders as well as revolutionaries. In other cases, such as the French Revolution at the end of the eighteenth century and the Russian Revolution at the beginning of the twentieth century, the revolutionary intellectuals are anticlerical critics of the religious institutions. In each of these cases, utopian beliefs played a role in the mobilization and politicization of the forces involved in the revolution.

Applications

On July 4, 1776, the Second Continental Congress adopted the Declaration of Independence, declaring the thirteen American colonies independent of Great Britain. Although no two revolutions follow exactly the same path, the American Revolution illustrates some common features of revolutions: widespread discontent, politicization of the population, the outbreak of violence, the establishment of a parallel government by the forces of change, a substantial redistribution of wealth and power, and the ineffective use of force to crush the revolution in its early stages.

The British government's imposition of the Stamp Act on the American colonists in 1765 set into motion a series of actions and reactions that increasingly divided the population into two groups, those who defended the British government and its policies as reasonable and those who saw the British government as tyrannical. The Stamp Act caused immediate and widespread discontent. Merchants, lawyers, and prosperous tradesmen formed the Sons of Liberty, a mass organization that sometimes met openly and at other times secretly to promote opposition to the Crown. Members of this group destroyed taxed items and forced the resignation of official tax stamp distributors.

As violence increased—from spontaneous, isolated beatings of colonists who remained loyal to the Crown (the Tories) to planned major destruction of property as in the Boston Tea Party in 1773—opinions for and against the Crown crystallized. In an attempt to reassert British control over the colonies, Parliament passed the Coercive Acts in 1774, which included both a blockade of Boston Harbor and an authorization to the royal governors to quarter British troops in private homes. Committees of correspondence were formed to organize opposition to these measures. Under the direction of Samuel Adams, these groups later were able to supplant the more conservative town hall meetings and push the political agenda in a more radical direction.

The assemblies in Virginia and Massachusetts instituted a call for a parallel government that could speak and act for the people of all colonies. The First Continental Congress met in Philadelphia in September, 1774, with representatives from all colonies except Georgia. The aim of the congress was moderate: to restore unity between Great Britain and the colonies.

By early 1775, however, leaders calling for more radical action began to dominate discussions and meetings. They talked openly about revolution. Skirmishes with British troops at Lexington and Concord in Massachusetts preceded the Second Continental Congress, which organized an army and named George Washington, an American military hero in the French and Indian War (1756-1763), its commander. What had started as an effort by the colonists to secure rights to which they believed themselves entitled as British citizens had escalated into civil war. In January, 1776, Thomas Paine's inflammatory pamphlet, "Common Sense," was published. His outright call for rebellion found a large, receptive audience. Belated British attempts at conciliation failed, and consensus in the colonies rapidly shifted from continued protest within the British empire to an abrupt break with the Crown.

The War of Independence lasted more than five years. A larger proportion of the population was killed and wounded in this war than in any other conflict in U.S. history, except the Civil War. When the war finally ended in Yorktown, Virginia, on October 19, 1781, with Lord Cornwallis, the British General, surrendering his six-thousand-man army, the thirteen colonies had been molded into a new nation with a different constitution and a new government. The revolution substantially reduced the wealth and influence of the colonial upper classes through the confiscation of estates of British Loyalists who fled to Canada. The redistribution of property, together with the removal of the Crown's restrictions on land colonization in the west, accelerated the rise in size and influence of a middle-class gentry in the United States.

Context

Political scientist Harold Lasswell has defined politics as the process that determines who gets what, when, and how. Revolution enters into this definition in several ways: revolutions can determine how people and groups get what they want out of politics, and revolutions can determine who gets what. Those who lead and support successful revolutionary movements are typically the major beneficiaries of the newly established political order. Revolutions also can determine how much people get and how quickly they get it. Revolutions involve rapid and drastic changes in the distribution of values. Yesterday's winners are today's losers, and vice versa.

Although major revolutions are relatively modern in origin and relatively rare in occurrence, their appearance in the last three centuries has colored the political process throughout the modern world. The fact that revolutions have occurred means that they can occur again. The fact that no two revolutions are exactly alike means that it is not possible to precisely determine when and where the next one will occur. Thus, all governments that become unpopular face the risk of being overthrown in a revolution. Since that is a threat that rational governments want to minimize, most governments condition their policies and actions in light of that threat.

Politicians who might like to reverse changes that have already occurred have to consider the possibility that turning the clock back may trigger a revolution that will leave them in a situation they like even less. On the other hand, people who four or five centuries ago might have accepted deteriorating conditions without complaint, may be emboldened to push for a more active political agenda.

To a large extent, the threat of revolution forces modern governments to pay heed to the advice of Niccolò Machiavelli, the sixteenth century Italian philosopher, who advised rulers to avoid being hated. So long as governments are not generally seen as illegitimate, they can survive and avoid revolution even though they enjoy little popular support. The critical issue for governments is to maintain legitimacy in the eyes of the armed forces, because the military can be used to instill fear in those who might want to challenge the existing government.

The paradox facing democratic governments is that some of the conditions that nurture the health of democracy are also associated with the threat of revolutions. Just as healthy democracies require an informed and active citizenry, revolutions flourish when the general population is highly politicized. Because of this connection between politicized citizens and revolution, some theorists have revised their thoughts about the basic needs of democracy and argue that widespread apathy is a necessary condition for stable democracies. Even though this revision is criticized by other theorists, its existence points out how the mere threat of revolution has affected the way we think and talk about politics in the modern world.

Bibliography

Boswell, Jerry, ed. *Revolution in the World System*. New York: Greenwood Press, 1989. Unique in that it looks at revolutions from the perspective of a world system rather than from the conventional societal perspective. Index; lists references at the end of each chapter.

Brinton, Crane. *The Anatomy of Revolution*. Rev. and exp. ed. New York: Vintage Books, 1965. Classic historical analysis of the English, American, French, and Russian revolutions, easy to read and cited by virtually all other books about revolution. Index; annotated bibliography that is dated but still useful.

Calvert, Peter. *Revolution and Counter-Revolution*. Minneapolis: University of Minnesota Press, 1990. Brief introduction into the concept and theory of revolution. Index and bibliography.

Dunn, John. *Modern Revolutions*. 2d ed. New York: Cambridge University Press, 1989. Emphasizes the distinctiveness of various revolutions, illustrated through case studies. Subject index; extensive, but somewhat dated, bibliography.

Rule, James B. *Theories of Civil Violence*. Berkeley: University of California Press, 1988. Sociological analysis of violence, riots, and revolutions as discussed by political and social theorists such as Thomas Hobbes, Karl Marx, Émile Durkheim, Max Weber, Georg Simmel, Talcott Parsons, and Charles Tilly. Index and extensive bibliography.

Edward S. Malecki

Cross-References

RIGHT OF REVOLUTION

Field of study: Political philosophy

The right of revolution is generally based on the acceptance of the principles that political leaders have a responsibility to their subjects and that political power ultimately derives from the people.

Principal terms
CIVIL DISOBEDIENCE: refusal to accept a law considered unjust or immoral, as a means to draw attention to the law and force its change
DIVINE RIGHT OF KINGS: principle that the authority of monarchs is derived from God and subject only to God's sovereignty
JUST WAR: war or revolution that is justified in terms of its political objectives
MORAL FORCE: use of nonviolent action to change policies or laws, relying on one's moral position, rather than violence, to win
REGICIDE: killing of a monarch
SOCIAL CONTRACT: principle that sovereignty resides in the people, individuals subordinate their interests to those of the community, and rulers have the authority that the people grant them
TYRANNICIDE: killing of an oppressive ruler

Overview

The right to revolt, to resist and overthrow unjust political leaders, is not universally recognized. Political philosophers have debated this issue for centuries. While the ancient Greeks and Romans often glorified those citizens willing to act for the common good by removing tyrants, other ancient peoples assumed that the authority of rulers was sacred and not subject to challenge by common people.

In societies in which rulers were presumed to have derived their authority from their god or gods, people viewed challenges to the ruler in much the same way as challenges to the gods. The divine right of kings—the belief that power was granted by God—was commonly accepted in Europe and provided justification for centuries of rule by absolute monarchies. In other cultures, political rulers often were viewed as gods themselves. The pharaohs of Egypt, for example, were so ordained.

Once rulers were accepted as human, rather than as gods or chosen by gods, and as fallible, the stage was set for challenges to political authority. In societies such as those in ancient Greece and Rome, in which leaders were chosen by the political elite, the right to govern was considered conditional and generally subject to opposition. In more primitive societies, in which leaders were chosen based upon physical prowess or other skills, challenge was similarly expected. The identification of rulers as secular, separate from the religious leadership, removed that barrier to revolt.

The right to revolt became a major topic of debate in the seventeenth and eighteenth centuries, as a growing number of middle-class Europeans and colonists chafed under the rule of extravagant and corrupt aristocracies. Political commentators and philosophers began justifying challenges to the divine right of kings, and their arguments met with increasing support as people found themselves ruled by monarchs, often foreign-born, whose representatives were corrupt or incompetent. The stage was being set for revolution.

The most influential political and social thinker of the Romantic era was Jean-Jacques Rousseau. In the late 1700's, an absolute monarchy reigned in France. The king, Louis XVI, had the power to issue *lettres de cachet* ordering the arrest and imprisonment of anyone who displeased him, without giving reason or staging a trial. The king's court, including his wife, Marie Antoinette, were extravagant in their spending and uninterested in the welfare of the people. Interestingly, however, the king was supportive of the American Revolution, providing money and supplies to the colonists and ultimately providing most of the fleet that surrounded Cornwallis's army at Yorktown and led to the British surrender.

Rousseau provided the philosophical justification for revolution in Europe in his 1762 book *Du Contrat social (The Social Contract)*. He argued that sovereignty ultimately lies with the community and that the authority of rulers is derived from a social contract, that is, an agreement by the people to subordinate their interests to those of the community. The rights of the people cannot be given away; they accept the contract when they join the community. Rulers, acting for the community, agree to govern justly, if not reasonably. When rulers violate the contract, going against the general will of the people, the people have the right to remove them. The principle of the sovereign community was not new, but Rousseau's formulation of the argument found a receptive audience in revolutionary Europe, and its publication signaled the beginning of the end of the absolute monarchies in Europe. Rousseau, strong in his belief in revolution against unjust rulers, still appeared uncomfortable about the execution of Louis XVI. Revolution was easier to justify than regicide.

The more limited argument for revolution against unjust rulers advanced by John Locke in *The Second Treatise of Civil Government* (1690) focused more on violations of property rights than on the broader morality of revolt. In some measure, that may be why the American Declaration of Independence more closely followed Locke's argument.

Rousseau's work, more so than Locke's, continues to be a frequently used argument for revolution. He expressed concern, however, that people freed from one oppressive ruler might simply replace one tyrant with another. Much the same concern was expressed by Frantz Fanon in the 1960's in the context of the national liberation movements in Africa. Fanon stated the justification to revolt against colonial domination in moral and medical terms. He also argued that violent revolution was necessary to provide a cathartic experience for the people, who needed to overcome the mental bonds of colonialism. The violence was intended to assure that they did not return to the patterns of behavior created by colonial domination.

Revolutionary justifications have not always included violence. The nonviolent philosophies of Mohandas Gandhi, applied in the Indian rights movement in South

Africa and the struggle for Indian independence from Great Britain, and of Martin Luther King, Jr., in the U.S. Civil Rights movement, based resistance and revolt on moral justifications. Nonviolent means, civil disobedience, and noncooperation were to be used to demonstrate the greater moral force. At least one Hindu revolutionary has argued that violence is an extension of the moral force that Gandhi described, but the moral right to revolt against immoral authorities had deep roots.

Similarly, ideological justification for revolutionary action can easily be found. Marxists argue that class struggle is inevitable, with a proletariat, however it is defined, ultimately winning. The justification for revolution can be expressed simply in terms of moving society toward that ultimate utopia, communism. Indeed, there is an obligation to help realize the revolution. The idea that revolution is not only a right, but also an obligation, is not unique to Marxists.

Michael Walzer, in *Obligations: Essays on Disobedience, War, and Citizenship* (1970), argues that there is an obligation to disobey unjust laws and rulers. He further argues that oppressed minorities have an obligation to disobey and revolt, and that intellectuals have an obligation to report their understanding of the plight of oppressed minorities. These obligations are derived from obligations to the group: One should disobey unjust laws to bring them to the attention of society; members of oppressed groups should revolt to bring attention to the plight of their group; and intellectuals should participate in the revolt because they are part of the same group as the oppressed minority.

Applications

The American colonial leaders who planned and directed the revolt against British rule were clearly uneasy about their purpose. The Declaration of Independence provided a set of arguments describing the violations of the social contract and, thereby, justifying the revolt. The rights of people as derived from God and the laws of nature were reaffirmed. The relationship between the people and the government under the social contract was reaffirmed. The fact that the decision to change the government was not taken lightly was pointed out.

The rest of the document outlined the specific violations of which the king was judged guilty and stated that other means of correcting the violations had been attempted, without success. The Declaration of Independence charged the king with a lengthy list of violations, including refusing to agree to laws proposed for the common good, refusing to permit representation of the colonists and others in Parliament, dissolving legislative bodies in the colonies, obstructing the creation of judicial authority and selecting the judges himself, raising military authority over civilian, forcing colonies to support standing armies, interfering with trade, imposing taxes without consent, and interfering with local governance. The list concluded with charges that the king had, in effect, waged war against the colonies by employing mercenaries, inciting Indian attacks, impressing colonists into the British military, and so on. The document is an indictment, eloquently affirming the right to revolt and the objective of independence.

The language of the Declaration of Independence is clearly closer to that of John Locke in terms of the references to property rights and to the king waging war against the people than it is to the arguments advanced by Rousseau. A criticism of Locke has been that individual decisions concerning revolution may be fickle, prompted by anger one day and forgotten the next. The collective or community focus of Rousseau's conceptualization of the social contract and decisions on revolution would seem to be more conservative and consistent. The Declaration of Independence pointedly states that the decision to revolt was not taken lightly, perhaps to answer the criticism of Locke. The influence of the political philosophers of the time is clearly discernible in the document.

It is also noteworthy that some historians have challenged the view that an actual revolution occurred in the colonies. The revolutionary war ended British domination of the colonies, but there were few changes in American society. The elite that dominated colonial economic and political affairs, by and large, was the same elite that dominated U.S. political and economic affairs after the revolution.

Context

The relationship between the people and their governments is of obvious importance. It determines allocations of goods and services, tax burdens, and myriad other positive and negative interactions. How to address the problem of an unresponsive, unjust, or arbitrary government is an ancient question. In large measure, sovereignty is judged, in the twentieth century, to rest with the people in a society. Governments are created to achieve generally agreed upon ends. When that agreement ends, change is necessary. Whether revolution is necessary to effect the change is at issue. Change may be revolutionary in terms of its scope, or revolutionary in terms of the methods used. The arguments for a right to revolt provided by John Locke and Jean-Jacques Rousseau are illustrative of the most important issue, that is, who decides when revolution is necessary.

John Locke's view was that property and other personal interests were paramount. As long as the government did not interfere with the rights of the individual, there were no problems. Once an individual determined that the social contract had been broken, revolt became an option. Locke tended to focus on government in the abstract, rather than on the head of state or ruler. By contrast, Rousseau defined the contract more in terms of the community. Individuals were party to the social contract when they accepted the protection and benefits of the community. The right to revolt and the decision to do so rested with the community as a whole.

The two positions offer some explanation for the seeming futility of political action by relatively small groups. The terrorist violence of the last decades of the twentieth century was often carried out by ideological groups with few followers. Their potential to effect major changes in government policy or personnel was slight, even if their ideological justifications suggested an obligation to engage in revolutionary activity. They were revolutionary only in name and intent.

Rousseau's notion of a community right to revolt suggests a broader decision-making process. When enough people feel that their social contract has been violated to represent a fundamental change in the community view, revolutionary change is in order. In some sense, Rousseau's decision to revolt may be based on a majority or near-majority decision to exercise that right. A totalitarian or authoritarian government may be vulnerable if a majority of the people believe that the contract has been broken. Democratic governments, by their nature, should change to accommodate the will of the community, assuming that the mechanisms are in place to effect revolutionary change peacefully.

A right to revolt is an accepted principle in most societies. Whether it is accepted as a reasonable choice for individual people or groups is another question altogether. For example, Americans generally would accept the proposition that citizens in an authoritarian state have a right to change their form of government, to depose their current leadership, and to change their economic system. Americans generally would express disbelief if another American suggested essentially the same thing for the United States, but they likely would accept that person's right to propose a change.

Bibliography

Arendt, Hannah. *On Revolution*. New York: Viking Press, 1963. Arendt's comparison of the American and French revolutions is a classic philosophical study, in which the right to revolt against tyrannical rulers is a central theme.

Davies, James C. *When Men Revolt and Why: A Reader in Political Violence and Revolution*. New York: Free Press, 1971. Reader on revolution and political violence, including arguments by revolutionary writers and analyses of the violence born of national liberation struggles, political instability, and racial conflict.

Fanon, Frantz. *The Wretched of the Earth*. Preface by Jean-Paul Sartre. Translated by Constance Farrington. New York: Grove Press, 1963. A classic of the postwar national liberation period. It argues for violent revolution as a catharsis for people subjugated by colonial governments.

Greene, Thomas H. *Comparative Revolutionary Movements: Search for Theory and Justice*. Englewood Cliffs, N.J.: Prentice Hall, 1990. Greene looks at the history of revolution, including the preconditions, and assesses the theories concerning its causes.

Johnson, Chalmers. *Revolutionary Change*. 2d ed. Stanford, Calif.: Stanford University Press, 1982. Broad view of revolution as social and political change.

Laqueur, Walter, ed. *The Terrorism Reader: A Historical Anthology*. Philadelphia, Pa.: Temple University Press, 1978. Selections from the writings of Aristotle, Cicero, Plutarch, Thomas Aquinas, and others address the issue of tyrannicide; other writers examine the goals of revolution.

Walzer, Michael. *Obligations; Essays on Disobedience, War, and Citizenship*. New York: Simon & Schuster, 1971. Examines the obligations of citizens to resist unjust rule, in ways ranging from civil disobedience to war.

_____, ed. *Regicide and Revolution: Speeches at the Trial of Louis XVI*. New York: Columbia University Press, 1992. Using the speeches delivered at the trial of

King Louis XVI of France in 1792-1793, Walzer discusses the responsibilities of rulers and the people's right to revolt.

William L. Waugh, Jr.

Cross-References

Burke's Political Philosophy, p. 171; Civil Disobedience, p. 285; Civil Unrest and Rioting, p. 317; Civil Wars, p. 325; Colonialism and Anticolonialism, p. 351; Dialecticism, p. 540; Individual Versus State Rights, p. 910; Insurgencies and Coups d'État, p. 930; Locke's Political Philosophy, p. 1142; Marxism-Leninism, p. 1155; National Liberation Movements, p. 1255; Nationalism, p. 1268; Political Violence, p. 1539; Protest Movements, p. 1621; Revolutionary Governments, p. 1725; Revolutions, p. 1738; Right to Bear Arms and the Second Amendment, p. 1750; Rousseau's Political Philosophy, p. 1756; The Social Contract, p. 1827; Terrorism, p. 1962.

RIGHT TO BEAR ARMS AND THE SECOND AMENDMENT

Field of study: Civil rights and liberties

The right to bear arms is among the most controversial issues confronting U.S. politicians, the public, and scholars. The Second Amendment, according to some scholars, gives the people the general right to own and bear firearms. Others disagree with this interpretation. There is also controversy in the details of gun regulation.

Principal terms

CULTURE WAR: view that a "war" exists between two diametrically opposed cultures, one the conservative bedrock culture of middle America (which supports gun ownership), and the other governmental and academic policymakers (who consider private gun ownership anachronistic and counterproductive)

GUN CONTROL: regulations or limits on the ownership, manufacture, use, and sale of firearms

GUN LOBBY: group made up of firearms manufacturers, conservative activists, and sports groups that usually challenges attempts to pass and implement gun control legislation

MILITIA: in the sense known to the Founders, the entire population of adult males who are physically fit and politically eligible for military service

MORAL CRUSADERS: group of people, usually highly motivated and organized, who deem the status quo or a behavior as immoral or dangerous and who work to change laws to right the perceived wrong. Gun-control supporters and opponents are moral crusaders

ORIGINAL INTENT: conservative interpretation of the Constitution considers what the Founders meant—their original intent—and a liberal interpretation considers the Constitution as a contemporary document

RIGHT TO BEAR ARMS: right of the people, singly or collectively, to own firearms

SECOND AMENDMENT: amendment to the Constitution that specifies the right to bear arms

Overview

Understanding of firearms ownership in the United States hinges on a grasp of Anglo-American history and constitutional law. The frontier that English settlers in North America and their Anglo-American descendants inhabited seemingly necessitated the carrying of arms and legitimated an ideology of the individual's right to bear arms. Over time this way of viewing firearms became deeply ingrained. For example, the image of the pioneer or cowboy without a sidearm is incongruous. Guns were a critical part of the settling of the ever-moving frontier, and, following the Civil and

Indian wars, came to be found in both urban and rural "frontiers." Modern mechanization made firearms much more efficient than the Founders could have envisioned and relatively inexpensive. Merchandizing made guns easily accessible to most Americans. The concrete details of firearms, however, are secondary to their symbolic significance.

Firearms are part of the American mythos. The minuteman, for example, is a national symbol. Other romantic imagery involving firearms comes from the 1920's when the gangsters and lawmen spoke with their guns. American history, like that of many nations, glorifies the military, the hero, and wars.

From cheap novels about gunfighters of the Old West to gangsta rap, the firearm, crime, punishment, and violence came to be inescapable parts of the American cultural landscape. The plots of novels, films, and television shows are replete with iconic portraits of heroes and villains with firearms. In some films, it is arguably the firearms that have the featured role. This preoccupation with firearms is not found in European culture; Europeans often find American gun-related violence peculiarly disquieting. All European countries, having no recent frontier experience and no equivalent to the Second Amendment, tightly regulate the private ownership of firearms. In all peaceful European nations, homicide rates are less than a third of those found in the United States. It would seem that the linkage of firearms and violence would be inescapable and would invite significant policy intervention in the United States as well. This has not actually been the case, however, and the reasons for this, hinging as they do on Constitutional scholarship and the popular imagination, are very complex.

The Second Amendment to the U.S. Constitution is short and seemingly to the point: "A well regulated militia, being necessary to the security of a free state, the right of the people to keep and bear arms shall not be infringed." These few words, however, have engendered an outpouring of popular and scholarly articles and books. The words have provoked much political debate in the media and legislatures among policymakers, moral crusaders, and the general public. Basically, it is safe to say that there are two schools of thought concerning the Second Amendment. A significant school of thought among legal and criminological thinkers is that the Second Amendment is a right of the people (as are all other Bill of Rights guarantees). The Second Amendment, by this argument, grants individuals the right to bear arms for state and personal defense. The leading school of thought among policymakers and most other academics is that the Second Amendment exists solely to protect the right of individual states to maintain militias. From this point of view, the Second Amendment qualifies and strengthens the right of the states to maintain militias, has a strictly military meaning, and has little or no applicability to a right of people to keep and maintain deadly weapons for the protection of their lives and property.

Some experts have pointed out that a culture war exists between the two groups holding these opposing views, and that the debate over the Second Amendment and gun control is only one arena in which this conflict is being played out. This view of the debate places most control advocates in the liberal ideological camp, and casts gun control opponents as cultural and political conservatives. This grouping is correct in most, but not all, cases. Although few liberals have strayed far from procontrol positions, there has been more diversity about gun policy among conservatives. As public concern about violent crime translated into political action, moderate conservatives have moved toward a more procontrol stance, alienating some of their anticontrol constituency.

In the late 1980's and early 1990's, a number of scholars, proceeding from a liberal point of view, read the original work of the Founders and studied English and early American documents and history as they pertained to the right to bear arms. This research led to a new perspective on the issue that closely resembled the traditional view that gun ownership was protected and encouraged by the Bill of Rights. An implication was clear: If strict gun controls were to be enacted, it would be necessary to repeal what one law professor called the embarrassing Second Amendment. This interpretation has not enjoyed much attention from policymakers and the media, however, who continue to support increasingly restrictive qualifications on the right to bear arms but who believe that such restrictions can be implemented without reference to the Second Amendment.

Applications

Due to frontier-related ideology and imagery and the fact that gun-related crime was not seen as a serious problem in the last century, it is only in the twentieth century that gun control efforts became significant. The first gun control laws in the United States were enacted in large cities and in the rural South. In the South, the goal was to disarm poor whites and freed slaves. Some minor gun legislation appeared in the 1920's and 1930's as a response to the lawlessness of that period. These laws restricted ownership of fully automatic weapons, sawed-off shotguns, and heavy military ordnance. Much later, as a result of the popular concern over crime, assassinations, and political crime in the 1960's, the Congress passed the Gun Control Act of 1968. This law required all firearms dealers to be licensed, prohibited dealers from selling handguns to out-of-state residents, banned the mail-order sale of guns, and expanded the list of those prohibited from buying handguns: illegal drug users, convicted felons (excluding certain white-collar offenders), and the mentally ill. The Gun Control Act also barred the importation of certain nonsporting weapons. Its passage and enforcement had little or no effect on curbing violent crime but did move organized groups of gun owners and manufacturers to action. Legislative efforts to effect gun control on the federal level continued, largely unsuccessfully, until the late 1980's. Legislative opponents to gun control and the gun control lobby, a group that comprises gun manufacturers, conservative activists, and the National Rifle Association (NRA), stymied further attempts at gun control. In fact, pressure from these anticontrol groups gained the passage of the Firearms Owners Protection Act in 1986, which allowed out-of-state residents to buy rifles in any state whose laws allowed it. The law also banned ownership, manufacture, or sale of fully automatic guns after May 19, 1986. In 1989, President Bush, under authority of the 1968 Gun Control Act, banned the importation of forty-three types of semiautomatic rifles. Since many rifles of this type are made in the United States, this measure was largely symbolic.

As a consequence of public attitude toward violent crime in the 1990's, public opinion polls indicated an increase in support for more stringent gun controls, particularly in the form of waiting periods. The Brady Handgun Violence Protection Act (the Brady Bill) was passed by Congress and signed by President Clinton in 1993. This legislation provoked strong debate after it was first proposed in 1987. It mandates new and significant requirements on those wanting to buy or own firearms. Such requirements include a five-day waiting period to allow local police to conduct background checks on those who would buy handguns. The act states that the five-day waiting period should be supplanted in five years with a national instant criminal background check that will apply to all firearms. Opposition from organized gun owners' groups and lobbies was understandably fierce but failed to carry the day in the Congress. Efforts to overturn the Brady Bill in court proceeded not on Second Amendment grounds, as that was viewed as a dead issue by litigants, but rather on Tenth Amendment grounds, that is, that the federal government, by forcing local law enforcement officials to conduct background checks, is exceeding its authority. Tenth Amendment challenges to the Brady Bill alleged that the federal government improperly assumed powers not delegated to it by the Constitution. Powers not delegated specifically to the federal government are "reserved to the States respectively, or to the people," the Tenth Amendment reads. Therefore, the argument goes, the states cannot be ordered to carry out federal functions without compensation. The litigants in these cases were local law enforcement agencies supported by various groups of firearms enthusiasts, such as the NRA.

Other federal initiatives, backed by alliances of mayors, public health officials, and the leadership of some police organizations, included a proposal for the Treasury Department to raise the fees firearms dealers pay the government in order to do business. This would have the effect of forcing small, independent dealers out of business, thus allowing fewer firearms in circulation.

In addition to federal initiatives toward gun control, numerous states and localities have qualified the right to bear arms by banning civilian carriage of firearms altogether (outside of hunting or target shooting contexts), banning guns from schools, courthouses, and airports, banning minors from any carriage of weaponry (outside of hunting or target shooting contexts), and banning types of weapons, for example Saturday night specials and so-called assault rifles. In the absence of a Supreme Court ruling overturning some of these actions, it appeared that more gun control efforts were in the offing. On the other hand, scholarship supporting the original intent view of the Second Amendment and a general reluctance to tamper with the Bill of Rights (despite efforts in Congress to repeal or circumvent that amendment), meant that further gun control efforts encounter continued resistance. In response to the fear of crime mentioned above, however, some states have enlarged the franchise to carry concealed firearms. The effects of this legislation will not be apparent for decades.

Criminologist Gary Kleck, in an award-winning work, *Point Blank* (1991), argues that most gun control efforts will fail. Moreover, in that and earlier works he points out that many of the fundamental assumptions of procontrol groups are illogical and are based on faulty interpretation and dissemination of data and wishful thinking. Some useful and important points Kleck makes that challenge the procontrol position are that guns are an extremely effective means for legitimate self-defense and are so used by citizens in approximately one million legal interventions per year. Firearms accidents, he also argues, are far less common than procontrol groups would have the public believe. Finally, he points out that various "successful" control efforts have proven to be failures and even counterproductive. He does suggest an "instant records check" that would seriously modify existing firearms sales practices. Kleck's ideas have been attacked as too control-oriented and as not control-oriented enough by partisans on both sides of the issue.

Context

The Second Amendment developed out of English historical and legal experience and directly out of American Revolutionary experience. Its inclusion in the Bill of Rights was no accident and was clearly intended to afford white, male freeholders the right to self-protection and to support a militia. As such, the Second Amendment was a response to prevailing political ideologies and realities of its day. The private ownership of firearms was critical to the successful settlement of the United States. Private ownership has also contributed to the history of political violence and the growth of violent crime in the United States.

The pressure for more restriction on firearms is a reflection of the fear of crime, especially inner-city crime, held by many Americans. Thus, gun control supporters and opponents have popular support. Opponents generally argue for an original intent view of the Second Amendment. Gun control supporters base their arguments on a commonsense view of the issue and find further support for their point of view in public opinion polls.

Neither gun control advocates nor opponents are satisfied with the status quo. Supporters of the existing controls advocate more controls. Opponents advocate rolling back gun control laws and challenge newly proposed controls. Despite the efforts of gun control opponents, it is likely that they will continue to fail in legislatures and the courts even if some scholarship supports the validity of their interpretation of the Second Amendment. The very real problem of violent crime, the media-engineered fear of crime, and the politicians responding to crime will continue to influence public opinion far more than scholarship.

Bibliography

Halbrook, Stephen P. *A Right to Bear Arms: State and Federal Bills of Rights and Constitutional Guarantees*. Westport, Conn.: Greenwood Press, 1989. Detailed examination of the actions of state legislatures and the Constitutional Convention. A good text for background on the Second Amendment and related state guarantees of the right to bear arms.
Kates, Don B. *Firearms and Violence: Issues of Public Policy*. San Francisco: Pacific

Institute for Public Policy Research, 1984. The best single source for scholarly articles supportive of gun ownership and an individual-rights interpretation of the Second Amendment.

_____. "Handgun Prohibition and the Original Meaning of the Second Amendment." *Michigan Law Review* 82, no. 2 (November, 1983): 204-273. A major scholarly work on the original intent of the authors of the Second Amendment.

Kleck, Gary. *Point Blank.* New York: Aldine de Gruyter, 1991. The most useful reference on gun control laws, practices, and suggested policies available. Argues objectively about which policies do, and which do not, work. Excellent bibliography.

Kopel, David. *The Samurai, the Mountie, and the Cowboy: Should America Adopt the Gun Controls of Other Democracies?* Buffalo, N.Y.: Prometheus Books, 1992. Contrasts gun controls in the United States with those of Japan and Canada. Puts the laws of other democracies in a useful cultural context.

Malcolm, Joyce. *To Keep and Bear Arms: The Origins of an Anglo-American Right.* Cambridge, Mass.: Harvard University Press, 1994. Exploration of the historical and intellectual background of the Second Amendment.

Nisbet, Lee, ed. *The Gun Control Debate: You Decide.* Buffalo, N.Y.: Prometheus Books, 1990. Evenhanded, large, and important collection of articles by noted scholars and policymakers.

Tonso, William R., ed. *The Gun Culture and Its Enemies.* Bellevue, Wash.: Merril Press. Collection on the sociocultural "war" over gun ownership issues in American society. The contributors believe that a culture of gun ownership and enemies of that culture are in conflict.

Wright, James D., Peter H. Rossie, and Kathleen Daly. *Under the Gun: Weapons, Crime, and Violence in America.* Hawthorne, N.J.: Aldine Publishing, 1983. A seminal and critical work that examines many assumptions of the progun and antigun positions.

Zimring, Franklin E., and Gordon Hawkins. *The Citizen's Guide to Gun Control.* New York: Macmillan, 1987. Useful, brief overview of the many aspects of gun control issues from a procontrol perspective.

F. Frederick Hawley

Cross-References

The Bill of Rights, p. 134; Civil Rights and Liberties, p. 298; The Constitution of the United States, p. 425; Lobbying and Lobbyists, p. 1130; The Media and the Conduct of Government, p. 1167; Policy Development and Implementation, p. 1414; Public Policy, p. 1633; Right of Revolution, p. 1744.

ROUSSEAU'S POLITICAL PHILOSOPHY

Field of study: Political philosophy

Jean-Jacques Rousseau attempted to reconcile the conflicting concepts of individualism and collectivism, creating a framework for a just government that could guarantee individual freedom in keeping with a humane and moral society.

Principal terms

COLLECTIVISM: system in which people as a group share in the ownership, control production, and distribute property

DISCOURSE: formal dialogue, lecture, sermon, treatise, or serious piece of writing

GENERAL WILL: unbiased and just will of the group, disassociated from the will of any individual

INDIVIDUALISM: concept that the individual is the starting point for political theory

SOVEREIGNTY: authority and power over a community, nation, or territory

Overview

The life of Swiss-born Jean-Jacques Rousseau (1712-1778), according to his biographers, abounded in contradictions, inconsistencies, and paradoxes. He loved humanity, especially the lost, yet he quarreled constantly and had few friends. He promoted the disciplined, productive life but he could not keep jobs himself in France or on the Continent, becoming an undisciplined drifter, a tramp, and later during his final years, an exile and fugitive. He proclaimed the good life to be the simple, solitary life in sylvan woods; yet he pursued the role of political activist and man of the world. He professed extreme piety and family virtues while frequenting with the low life in taverns and living with an unmarried woman who bore him five children.

His writings also take on the contradictions, inconsistencies, and paradoxes of the life he led. They reveal Rousseau's penchant for offering within the same work divergent, often opposing views that seemed incompatible. For example, did Rousseau champion the noble primitive life or the highly sophisticated political world? Did he advocate anarchic freedom or state control? Extreme individualism or social collectivism? Toleration of or persecution for nonconformity? Property rights for the individual or communal living? To his critics, Rousseau responded that he was indeed systematic. With careful and repeated readings of his works, he argued, they too would eventually comprehend how he reconciled the roles of the individualistic noble savage with those of the member of society. His critics would see how his political philosophy formed an organic, idealistic whole.

For over two hundred years, scholars have sought to find the unity of principles within Rousseau's works. They have read him in a variety of fashions, labeling him at times as a liberal, a conservative, a populist, an asocial individualist, and even as a totalitarian. From the mass of scholarly writings about Rousseau and his philosophical thoughts emerges one certainty: Everything Rousseau wrote about was related to politics. In search for the good and just life, Rousseau sought to reconcile two mutually antagonistic forces, individualism and collectivism.

In the first treatise which brought Rousseau fame, *Discourse on the Sciences and Arts* (1750), he passionately rejected the eighteenth century notion that progress in the sciences and arts of civilized nations had uplifted and purified their citizens' morals. On the contrary, Rousseau asserted, development of civilization had corrupted the natural goodness of the people who, in turn, fell prey to the artifices of sophisticated artists and scientists. The exception was the folk artist—untainted, intuitively engaged in the artistic search for truth and virtue, and not dependent on others to set false moral standards.

Although this first discourse established Rousseau's reputation as a political thinker, the fiery treatise lacked the systematic and well-reasoned approach of a comprehensive political philosophy. Three works published later, however, did provide key elements to Rousseau's political philosophy: *Discourse on the Origin and Foundation of Inequality Among Men* (1755); an article in *Encyclopédie*, "Political Economy" (1755); and *The Social Contract* (1762).

In his discourse *Inequality*, Rousseau returned to a familiar theme: that developing civilizations undercut the moral fabric of simple, rustic-hearted people, causing them to forfeit their freedom and free will. Rousseau mourned the passing of the primitives living peacefully and contentedly, engaged in hunting, fishing, and tilling the soil. These noble savages were by all accounts superior to civilized society. Rousseau reasoned that growing population pressures forced these primitives to settle in communities, and to develop cooperative, family-based lives.

Tracing the evolution of the human race, Rousseau argued in *Inequality* that when these displaced primitives began drawing boundary lines and claiming property, that signified the beginnings of civilization. Property, in Rousseau's eyes, became the major source of conflict and injustice in civilized society because the aim of property ownership is not to satisfy real needs but to accumulate more than what others have. Property and ownership of things begets social inequalities; some become wealthy, exploiting their poorer brethren. Some communities grow into powerful states, and their deceit, hypocrisy, jealousy, and greed increase, eventually leading to murder, mayhem, crime, and war.

In his discourse "Political Economy," Rousseau reluctantly accepts the reality of private property, politicized society, and the necessity of government; he realizes there is no hope of humankind returning to the golden age of primitive, simple living. In this article, Rousseau focuses on the administration of a moral and just state, visualizing citizen groups uniting voluntarily in a common cause. This would be a society of free people who made the laws they lived under, each having an independent will but each being part of a public will. By common consent of all citizens, they would share in administering the state, moving it toward meeting their common interests and goals.

These three discourses, according to Ramon Lemos in *Rousseau's Political Philosophy* (1977), revealed Rousseau's evolving political philosophy. His first discourse seems to view corrupt civilization as incompatible with the primitive. The second discourse, *Inequality*, however, hints that morality may be possible without entirely abandoning civilization and society. The third discourse, "Political Economy," extends Rousseau's position one step further: Moral deliverance is attainable within the social system. Lemos indicates that the final shift in Rousseau's philosophic thinking came in *The Social Contract* (1762), in which he advocates rebuilding the existing society so that the individual may attain genuine morality.

In *The Social Contract*, Rousseau demonstrates how a heightened sense of morality may be achieved when the proper and right relationships are established between a government and its people. He proposes the creation of a just state, one built upon the sovereignty of its citizens, who would be treated equally under the law, a state small enough so that each individual might vote on all laws. The opening sections of *The Social Contract* reflect Rousseau's concern with the loss of innocent individualism, but he realized it was impossible to return to this pristine stage. In the transformation of individuals from a natural state to a collective society, Rousseau calls for a social contract, a contract that binds these individuals to live together as a harmonious community. The last portions of *The Social Contract* develop Rousseau's plans for establishing and operating an ideal government. He advocates a collectivized system to ensure the necessary moral unity and discipline among its members. This was to be achieved through the social contract, with individuals relinquishing their desires and interests to support those shared in common. This common desire is the general will. Individuals had voted for the laws in the first place, Rousseau so reasoned; individual freedom was neither lost nor forfeited. Hence, individuals should obey willingly the laws based on popular consent.

For the good of its citizens, the state became supreme over the individual, including the threat of banishment or the death penalty for nonconformists or criminals. Rousseau concluded that a powerful state was the servant of its people because it was based on consensual governing by the people, offering higher types of freedom and happiness than found in individualistic freedom.

The most important political ideas of Rousseau, as drawn from the discourses described above, are these: that the innate goodness and naturalness of individuals have been corrupted by civilization's conventions, emphasis on rationality, covetous taste, and unjust political systems; that the people are sovereign in governing society; that the basis of legitimate political obligation is consent of the people; and that there is no antagonism between the individual and the state, freedom and authority, liberty and equality for those who subscribe to Rousseau's concept of general will, that is, the common good of all.

Applications

Rousseau's views were widely read and discussed, not only by the intelligentsia and aristocrats but by commoners. Rousseau's passion for his subject and his magnetic literary style brought political theory and social speculation into the shops and streets. He often articulated the longings of peasants, the lower-middle class, and artisans.

Yet for all of the discussions generated by his works, none of his models or blueprints for an ideal political state were actually tried out. Even Rousseau admitted that his ideals could not operate within the restrictions of the realities of the eighteenth century world. Rousseau, however, did dramatize some of his convictions in his novel, *Julie, ou la Nouvelle Héloïse* (1761). A series of letters revealed the forbidden love of aristocrat Julie d'Etange for her tutor Saint-Preux, a love thwarted by Julie's disapproving father. Rousseau's novel depicted the corrupting influence of city life, the defects of education and artificial social conventions of the times as contrasted with the satisfying benefits of rustic living in Alpine mountains and the idealized concept of friendship and trust. The basic principle found in *The Social Contract*—that a person is individually good when living in harmony with nature but turned bad by a corrupt society—was applied by Rousseau to his part novel, part educational tract *Émile* (1762). Rousseau charted the development of Émile, the son of a free and noble savage, from infancy to manhood, under the charge of an unorthodox tutor. Rousseau also prepared a similar agenda for Émile's future mate, Sophie, a simple peasant girl with no town artifices.

In *Émile*, Rousseau advocated that children be protected from corrupt society until the age of twelve, avoiding bookish learning by exposing them to the perfecting powers of nature, allowing them to unfold naturally from within with no overt force being exerted, experiencing life directly through their own built-in curiosity. After age twelve, Rousseau believed in introducing rational activities, permitting children to evaluate and form critical judgments. Only useful subjects, such as science, agriculture, and the manual arts, were to be learned. During late adolescence, youngsters should travel, studying the problems of government and being equipped for intelligent citizenship. Rousseau also thought that children should be encouraged to participate in benevolent projects; for by doing good, he reasoned, individuals become good. Older adolescents, Rousseau believed, should be introduced to religion where they may find God through nature, not theology.

Rousseau's reputation as a political philosopher throughout Europe during the 1760's led to his being asked to apply his insights to the new constitutions of Corsica in 1764 and of Poland in 1769. Rousseau responded by suggesting that the constitution of Corsica use these principles, drawn mainly from *The Social Contract*: that citizens take an oath to subordinate their individual desires to a government based on social equality, where none is rich, where state socialism prevails in lieu of private property, where individuals share common property according to what they produce; that government officials be chosen and changed frequently by voters in free elections; that there be no capital city because such cities corrupt government and its citizens. Rousseau's suggestions were never implemented.

When the Polish Convention in 1769 asked Rousseau to make suggestions for Poland's constitution, he proposed that their monarchy be an elective post. He further proposed that the government continue to be in the hands of the aristocratic senate, with the serfs having no voice because they might misuse freedoms given them. He suggested that taxes be levied on land and property, and that because Poland was a large country, it should become a confederation of smaller entities, each with its own legislature but subordinate to Poland at large. Again, Rousseau's ideas were not implemented.

Rousseau's political schemes saw little application during his lifetime. His ideas did have great influence, however, on general conceptions of governance. The movers and shakers of history since the eighteenth century were influenced by Rousseau's ideas.

Context

Rousseau ranks as one of the most influential figures of the French Enlightenment, a philosophical movement of the seventeenth and eighteenth centuries. The French Enlightenment rejected the authority of tradition as represented by the church and state of France. The movement instead looked to reason, especially in regard to attaining truths through scientific inquiry. For example, Montesquieu—like British scientific experimentalist Francis Bacon—made scientific studies of comparative governments. Others in the movement, such as Voltaire, focused on the necessity of freedom and liberty to counter political absolutism and injustice. Voltaire supported political and religious tolerance, deism, pacifism, and the belief in the individual's ability to make moral progress. The objective of the French Enlightenment was to reform French society and its decaying institutions.

Although Rousseau was active in the Enlightenment, he also stood apart from it. For example, he recognized the importance of reason, but he criticized those who overstated reason's importance at the neglect of emotions and intuition. He firmly believed that virtue resulted from spontaneous feelings welling up from the heart as well as the head. Moreover, Rousseau was particularly incensed with English philosopher Thomas Hobbes's views that people are self-seeking, brutish, continually warring with one another, and must be ruthlessly subjugated by absolute rulers. Rousseau could not accept Hobbes' materialistic assumptions because Rousseau idealized the common individual and believed that human perfection could be achieved.

Critics have pointed out that Rousseau, who accused others of overemphasizing rationalism, sometimes tended to go to the other extreme, exaggerating sentiment and emotion. His concern with the noble savage, peasants, and children, and his glorification of nature and the individual personality, have led to Rousseau's being considered a founder of the Romantic movement, a revolt against eighteenth century rationalism characterized by an outpouring of emotions and the senses. Rousseau's works published after his death in 1778, the *Confessions* and *Reveries*, are prime examples of romanticism.

Rousseau's influenced on his contemporaries' political views was considerable. He was lionized because of his unconventional behavior and pronouncements, his strange dress and boorish manners, and his general deportment. When he got into trouble with the church and state authorities of France over the publication of both *Émile* and *The*

Social Contract and had to flee France in 1762, Rousseau's influence on political thought waned. Although his *Julie* and *Émile* remained popular, Rousseau's political ideas were neglected until 1789.

The French Revolution of 1789 rekindled great interest in Rousseau's political ideas. Revolutionaries took up Rousseau's cry of popular sovereignty, and the grand slogan of "liberty, equality, fraternity" became a potent propaganda weapon. Beleaguered aristocrats of the day confirmed their own positions as well by citing Rousseau's thoughts. Revolutionary leaders used Rousseau's arguments to justify their own totalitarian edicts suppressing individual liberties and political parties for the good of unity within the state. Rousseau's idea of the general will was thus distorted.

Rousseau's political writings also influenced the American Revolution, especially inspiring Jeffersonian democracy, the idea that legitimate political authority rests in the consent of the people. Moreover, Rousseau deeply influenced German political philosophers Immanuel Kant, Georg Hegel, Friedrich Engel, and Karl Marx.

Rousseau's political thoughts continue to be relevant. Much serious study, debate, and scholarship continues on the perennial issues Rousseau raised: material progress, politics, governments, and moral freedom. Studying Rousseau's political views in the context of contemporary societies is very likely to continue.

Bibliography

Cullen, Daniel. *Freedom in Rousseau's Political Philosophy*. DeKalb: Northern Illinois University Press, 1993. Examines Rousseau's concepts of natural, civil, and moral freedom, attempting to clarify current debates on morality and politics.

Lemos, Ramon. *Rousseau's Political Philosophy: An Exposition and Interpretation*. Athens: University of Georgia Press, 1977. Rousseau is often a cryptic and enigmatic writer; Lemos tries to present in accurate paraphrase what Rousseau wrote.

Levine, Andrew. *The General Will: Rousseau, Marx, Communism*. New York: Cambridge University Press, 1993. Applies Rousseau's concept of the general will to Marxist, socialistic, and democratic theories.

Masters, Roger. *The Political Philosophy of Rousseau*. Princeton, N.J.: Princeton University Press, 1968. Helpful textual analyses of Rousseau's major works of political philosophy.

Masters, Roger, and Christopher Kelly, eds. *The Collected Writings of Rousseau*. 3 vols. Hanover, N.H.: University Press of New England, 1990. Rousseau's dialogues, discourses, observations, and letters. Useful commentary.

Miller, James. *Rousseau: Dreamer of Democracy*. New Haven, Conn.: Yale University Press, 1984. Assesses Rousseau's political convictions, chronicles Rousseau's rise and fall, and applies Rousseau's views to modern democracies.

Roosevelt, Grace. *Reading Rousseau in the Nuclear Age*. Philadelphia: Temple University Press, 1990. Applies Rousseau's educational and political views to contemporary issues of war, peace and education.

Richard Whitworth

Cross-References

Burke's Political Philosophy, p. 171; Dialecticism, p. 540; General Will, p. 745; Hobbes's Political Philosophy, p. 836; Idealism, p. 855; Individual Versus State Rights, p. 910; Kant's Political Philosophy, p. 1025; Legitimacy, p. 1105; Locke's Political Philosophy, p. 1142; Marxism-Leninism, p. 1155; Montesquieu's Political Philosophy, p. 1228; Neo-Idealism, p. 1287; Political Philosophy, p. 1505; The Social Contract, p. 1827.

RURAL COMMUNITY GOVERNMENT

Field of study: Local and regional government

Rural community government is one variety of local government. Typically, it includes towns and townships, villages, and rural county government of communities with less than 10,000 in population that are outside of a central city and its suburbs.

Principal terms

COMMUNITY: people living in a specific area and having similar interests or characteristics

COUNTY: large territorial division of local government

INCORPORATED AREA: city or town whose charter or constitution is granted by the state

METROPOLITAN AREA: region that encompasses at least one big city and outlying suburban communities

RURAL: less densely populated, often agrarian

SUBURBAN: outside of a central city, but usually within commuting distance of its core

TOWN: small localized population; also a unique form of government in New England

TOWNSHIP: type of local government in some Mid-Atlantic and North Central states

UNINCORPORATED AREA: territory that does not have a state charter, and that usually relies on county government for its services

VILLAGE: incorporated minor municipality, or formal unit of local government, or compact settlement usually smaller than a town

Overview

Rural community government is found outside of the central cities and their suburbs. In the past, rural communities were synonymous with farming and agrarian areas. By the latter part of the twentieth century, however, some rural areas had become communities for retirees, experimental sites for new businesses and industries, or work-at-home stations for computer information systems.

Compared to cities, small towns are usually less complex, both socially and economically. Cities usually have more diversity of lifestyles and racial, ethnic, and age groups. As a consequence, rural local governments usually provide fewer services to more homogeneous populations than do city governments. There is more evidence of personality in small communities, because of the close and constant interrelationships among their residents. Unlike their counterparts in more impersonal cities, citizens of small towns cannot avoid interacting with each other. Small towns tend to have minimal service needs and prefer not to regulate or limit individual behavior. Thus, public responsibility is somewhat narrowly defined, in an attempt to maintain the lowest possible taxes. In the small town, the scope of government is often limited to the roles assigned to it by shared values of the electorate. Moreover, distinctions between citizens' public and private roles is easily blurred. Rural politics are thereby more personal politics, involving friends and neighbors.

There are more than 16,000 township governments in twenty states, as classified by the U.S. Bureau of the Census. Townships serve inhabitants of these defined areas without regard to population concentration. Two groups will be discussed separately because of their rural local government significance: New England towns and North Central townships.

Most of New England is divided into small towns under 10,000 in population and averaging twenty-five to thirty square miles in area. Many were established before the revolutionary war after evolving from early settlements centered around religious congregations, protective stockades, and village centers. With population growth, some communities grew into cities or suburban municipalities—mostly in southern New England. Some remote rural sections of Maine, Vermont, and New Hampshire remained as unorganized territories. Functions that may be performed elsewhere by active county governments are done by town governments in New England. This makes the town government the most dominant type of local government in this region.

New England town government originated as an experiment in direct democracy, in which the people at large are the legislative body. Originally, eligible male residents were empowered to vote on almost all significant issues. A citizen assembly, the town meeting, allowed direct participation in local lawmaking, establishing the tax rate, electing officials, and approving the budget. The board of selectmen was charged with running the town, and elected for one-year terms. This administrative board could appoint other officials (such as tree wardens), plan meeting agendas, propose budget items, review bills for payment, and carry out the town's official business. Other prominent elected officials included the town clerk, treasurer, assessor, tax collector, and constable.

In more than three hundred years of operation, town meetings have evolved in a number of ways. Voting electorates have been expanded to include women, minorities, and nonmembers of the church. State governments have assumed more responsibilities in education, highways, law enforcement, health, and welfare. Urban growth often has ended the luxury of many town meetings, which become unwieldy as populations reach 5,000. In southern New England, more dramatic growth forced change to a representative town meeting, for which voters elect 100 to 150 representatives, who actually conduct the town meeting. All eligible residents may attend meetings and discuss issues, but only the elected representatives may vote. Attendance at town meetings has declined to less than 25 percent, which parallels local voting patterns in other municipal forms of government.

Townships outside of New England are found mainly in fifteen mid-Atlantic and midwestern states, where a wide range of structure, capacity, and service delivery is found. Few services are available in rural areas, compared with numerous services given in more populated, urban townships. Pennsylvania, for example, divides its townships into different classes, while in Michigan townships provide a wide array of services. New Jersey's urban townships resemble other common forms of city government, such as city councils with mayors.

Rural townships provide few services within their territory. For example, most maintain only those roads not under federal, state, or county jurisdiction, some perform functions in assessment and equalization of property for taxation, and others serve as election precincts. Other functions vary, but may include fire protection and cemetery maintenance. Other important service areas are handled by counties and special districts, which enjoy a larger tax base.

The governing boards of most townships outside of New England comprise three to five persons each and are called "supervisor," "trustee," or "township" boards. Townships tend to elect other local officials such as clerks and treasurers and sometimes constables, road commissioners, and justices of the peace. Approximately half of the townships operate without paid employees, however, because volunteer government is common in rural areas. One hundred townships in the United States, however, have at least twenty-five or more paid employees. Various reform studies have recommended dissolving townships, especially the smaller ones under 2,000 population, and turning their responsibilities over to other local governments. Most of these small units, however, continue to survive.

Another prime provider of services to rural areas is county government. These services may be in addition to those of other providers (such as small municipalities, towns, or villages). They may be the only services provided to unincorporated areas that have no other local government. Unincorporated areas do not possess charters from their states that establish their political identities. Although they may look like towns, they are not governments.

While counties are the most nearly universal type of local government in the United States, they are not modeled in one standard form. In New England they are either weak governments or nonexistent. From a historical and legal perspective, counties are closely tied to state governments and only possess those powers granted to them by their states. It is important to note that many counties are severely limited in their ability to assume broader responsibility. In the South, counties are significant as general purpose local governments and the county seats and courthouses represent major centers of power. Nationwide, counties are the prime local governments in rural areas, while city governments dominate the urban landscape. Over 70 percent of the nation's 3,041 counties are mostly rural and four-fifths have fewer than 50,000 residents. A number of rural counties have had to evolve into partial or total urban service providers as the nation's population became more suburban after World War II. Rural county governments usually have significant roles in property tax assessment and collection, law enforcement and judicial administration, road maintenance, record keeping, public health and human services, planning and land use, parks and recreation, and libraries. California, for example, permits its counties to become very active in providing numerous services for its smaller cities and towns.

Counties typically have a major governing body of elected officials. While their titles may vary, boards of "commissioners" and boards of "supervisors" are most prevalent. There are numerous variations in size and responsibility of these governing boards, which often involve the merger of executive, legislative and even judicial authority. An elected executive group is quite common.

Rural counties often provide the only safety nets for public services at the grassroots level. While some boards may meet only once a month, other elected administrators, such as county clerks, sheriffs, treasurers, registers of deeds, coroners, and prosecuting attorneys carry on the county's daily business. That many of these officials are elected reveals a public preference for participation and control.

Partisan politics play a major role in many county governments. In the South, the Democratic Party has dominated, often with little competition, while in the West, Republicans have often dominated. The election of specialized administrators who lack professional credentials creates many problems. County officials must devote much time to getting elected or holding on to their positions. Often, their profession-alism is compromised to suit key elements of the community.

Applications

The plight of the small northern Maine border town of Grand Isle, population 558, illustrates some of the extreme challenges that face rural local governments. During the early 1990's, there were allegations of secret unposted meetings of selectmen, misuse of town funds, nepotism, conflicts of interest, lack of quorums, and disagree-ment over the wording of minutes of previous meetings. These issues were first revealed in an article by a *Bangor Daily News* reporter. Even before the above problems had surfaced, this tiny town experienced financial stress in attempting to support its own school system and new water and sewer treatment plants. The majority of Grand Isle's voting population are senior citizens on fixed incomes, and the townfolk believe that they cannot afford a full-time town manager. Town decisions were made by three elected board members, who were not well versed in municipal law and who lacked ethical perspective. Protracted conflict occurred among the board members, which led to delays in town employees' being paid, signing of blank treasurer's warrants by local officials, and an investigation on possible violations of Maine's right-to-know law by the district attorney's office. One selectman resigned after winning a seat with only eight write-in votes during the previous election year. He was rendered powerless because he could rarely attend meetings, which were scheduled by the other selectmen, who could make decisions in his absence.

A conflict of interest question arose when two selectmen voted to pay the third selectman $337 for 225 bales of hay for a road repair project. The difficulty of separating personal business from the public business proved difficult for these elected officials. Extensive disagreements and general embarrassment to the town continued to escalate as part of a personal feud among present and former board members. Even in the best of times, small-town governments have to pull together to survive the poor economic conditions that frequently challenge their existence. The romantic view of the delights of citizen government by laypersons and the suspicion of experts culminated in a crisis in town government. The result was an investigation by the state and collective rethinking of the issue by people of the town.

Another example is found in Champaign County, Ohio, that illustrates the variety of government units and players in rural local politics. This rural county of 30,000 people is forty-five miles west of Columbus, Ohio, and traditionally dependent on agriculture. In the late 1980's, concern of business and government leaders arose about the need for more proactive economic development strategies. A major effort was undertaken by an ad hoc citizens group and a variety of established groups (Urbana Chamber of Commerce, Urbana City Council, Champaign County Board of Supervisors, County Extension agents, and the Ohio Department of Development) to address the problem and create a database for an economic development plan. A survey of citizens and businesses revealed a very strong support for businesses in the county, but also the need for additional management training seminars for area companies.

This collaborative approach produced a partnership between key government agencies and support for strategies that would help retain businesses and encourage their expansion. It also led to the hiring of a planner who would guide the implementation of goals approved by a task force. This coalition of rural government officials and businesspersons also succeeded in obtaining financial support from the state government. What on the surface appeared to be a classic problem of governmental fragmentation, with duplication and competing interests at the local level, was nurtured as a positive leadership base. Moreover, the strong grassroots coalition strongly advocated the county's planning and developmental interests and future needs. This bottom-up approach proved that the various, often competing, interests could work together to improve the climate for business, the local economy, and the tax base.

Context

Rural community government is one of the major variations of local government found in the United States. It provides essential services to the population outside of the central metropolitan areas. Less densely populated areas need a general-purpose government to provide basic services such as public safety, public works, and health and human services. They are supplemented in many cases by special purpose districts (water, sewer, solid waste districts, and school districts).

Traditionally, rural local government has been characterized as amateur, using part-time citizen volunteers. This characterization may be contrasted with the more specialized, professional bureaucracy of the city or county governments. This smaller, more personal local government is also known for defending the community against perceived encroachments, such as environmental standards imposed by the state or national governments. The ability of these little rural governments to survive conflicts with the larger cities, state, and federal governments is often in doubt. These smaller units of government may seek to continue their existence, but often find that they need to enter into cooperative arrangements.

Many small communities, however, have found themselves becoming more professional, especially in the area of executive reform. Communities have appointed administrators who bring knowledge and experience to government administration. This may occur in any rural, local government or small municipality, which may hire an expert for advice. Some rural county commissioners have hired outside, professional county managers as well, not only advisers.

In the typical New England town, an administrator, with management responsibilities in budgeting and personnel, may report to the board of selectmen or town council. Small municipalities, governed by other forms of local government, such as the mayor-and-council arrangement, have also begun to seek and appoint professional leaders. These leaders are likely to bring more proactive styles of leadership that seek to enhance the community's quality of life and economic growth. While it is not uncommon for communities to remain amateur, with total layperson leadership, the future price for this may be quite high. American traditions of limited government and citizen participation are being challenged by the changing demography of rural America, as they once were challenged by the progressive reform period of the early twentieth century in urban areas.

Bibliography

Duncombe, Herbert S. *Modern County Government.* Washington, D.C.: National Association of Counties, 1977. Excellent analysis of urban and rural American county government.

Flora, Cornelia B., and James A. Christensen, eds. *Rural Policies for the 1990's.* Boulder, Colo.: Westview Press, 1991. Specialized collection of essays on major public policies, especially social and economic, affecting rural America.

Lancaster, Lane W. *Government in Rural America.* 2d ed. New York: D. Van Nostrand, 1952. Most comprehensive treatment of rural community governments. Though in many ways dated, the book offers excellent historical documentation.

Martin, Roscoe C. *Grass Roots.* 2d ed. Tuscaloosa: University of Alabama Press, 1964. Classic study based on four university lectures on the unique features of rural governance.

Swanson, Bert E., Richard A. Cohen, and Edith P. Swanson. *Small Towns and Small Towners: A Framework for Survival and Growth.* Beverly Hills, Calif.: Sage Publications, 1979. Provides a guide for studying towns, including their culture, norms, values, social structure, economy, and politics.

Vidich, Arthur J., and Joseph Bensman. *Small Town in Mass Society: Class, Power and Religion in a Rural Community.* Princeton, N.J.: Princeton University Press, 1968. Detailed case study that explores the foundations of social life, institutions, and power structures in a small New York village dominated by a ruling economic elite.

Wikstrom, Nelson. *The Political World of a Small Town: A Mirror Image of American Politics.* Westport, Conn.: Greenwood Press, 1993. Colorful academic case study of West Point, Virginia, which includes twenty-eight tables. Focuses on anatomy of town government and the political process.

Zuckerman, Michael. *Peaceable Kingdoms: New England Towns in the Eighteenth Century*. New York: Alfred A. Knopf, 1970. Historical account of New England towns in the eighteenth century. Includes detailed appendices, notes and index, and a splendid chapter on town meetings.

G. Thomas Taylor

Cross-References

City Government in the United States, p. 266; County Government, p. 458; Disaster Relief in the United States, p. 558; Federalism in the United States, p. 668; Fire Protection, p. 700; Grassroots Politics, p. 797; Local Governments, p. 1136; Political Machines and Bosses, p. 1468; Regional Governments, p. 1672; State and Local Government, p. 1885; Town Meetings, p. 1993; Urbanization, p. 2071.

RUSSIAN POLITICAL HISTORY

Field of study: Comparative government

Russian political history has been determined by a search for order and stability. Possessing few natural borders, the Russian people have been subject to repeated invasions from Europe and Asia. The threat of attack has encouraged the development of a strong, centralized government that does not tolerate dissent.

Principal terms
BOYAR: member of the hereditary Russian nobility
CZAR (TSAR): Russian emperor
DUMA: representative assembly
GENERAL SECRETARY: functional leader of the Communist Party during the Soviet period
PERESTROIKA: attempt by Mikhail Gorbachev to restructure the Soviet economy to be more responsive to the needs of ordinary people
POLITBURO: body chosen by the Central Committee of the Soviet Communist Party to conduct party business when the Central Committee was not in session
SERFDOM: servile labor system under which Russian peasants were bound to the land
TABLE OF RANKS: formal bureaucratic structure created by Peter I, establishing fourteen grades of state service
WARSAW PACT: military alliance formed in 1955 between the Soviet Union and her client states in Eastern Europe

Overview

The vast open geography of the Eurasian plain has made the region a natural avenue of invasion for centuries. Neither the grassy steppes of southern Russia nor the forest of the north have prevented Asiatic conquerors or European armies from sweeping into the very heart of Russia and wreaking havoc upon her inhabitants. Each new invasion has brought with it new ideas, but also has reinforced the desire of Russians to secure their frontiers against future threats.

Slavic tribes who moved eastward into modern Russia during the sixth century mixed with Finns and Turks. Although these peoples sometimes allied with or were subjugated by Asiatic hordes, a centralized state did not emerge to unify the region for several centuries. During the ninth century, Scandinavian Vikings, known as Varangians, began to establish fortified trading centers in the river valleys of Russia and the Ukraine. The Varangians gradually mixed with the Slavic peoples of the region and a powerful confederation of city-states, centered at Kiev, emerged. The prosperity of the Kievan-Rus Empire was based on its domination of the trade routes from the Baltic to the Black Sea.

Important trade links with Constantinople led to Byzantine cultural influence throughout the empire. The people of the Kievan state accepted Orthodox Christianity in 988, and the prince of Kiev claimed supremacy over the Church in the Byzantine tradition. Kievan scholars adopted the Cyrillic alphabet devised by Byzantine missionaries, and Russian craftsmen imitated the art and architecture of the Greek world.

The rulers in Kiev wanted to model their government on the absolute power of the emperor in Constantinople, but they were forced to concede a significant amount of authority to the princes who governed the other major cities of the empire. All of the princes consulted councils of boyars, hereditary nobles. The boyars helped to write laws and performed a variety of diplomatic and judicial functions. During the twelfth century, rivalries within the royal family weakened the Kievan state and greatly enhanced the power of the boyars. This decentralization of power made the Kievan-Rus Empire vulnerable to invasion.

During the thirteenth century, Russia was attacked from both east and west. Swedes, Lithuanians, and the Teutonic Knights pushed eastward from the Baltic coast. At the same time, Mongolian armies conquered the land east of the Dnieper River and their Tatar allies formed the Golden Horde, which extracted taxes and military recruits from their Slavic subjects. For nearly two centuries, the princes of Russia were forced to humble themselves before the Tatar khan, as western states such as Poland and Sweden absorbed land occupied by Orthodox Slavs into their kingdoms.

The grand dukes of Muscovy submitted to Tatar overlordship while consolidating their lands and power. In 1380, Dimitri Donskoii raised Moscow's prestige by defeating a Tatar army on the Don River. Donskoii did not break the power of the Golden Horde, but he did achieve a reduction in tribute. Although the rulers of Muscovy hated the Tatars, they adopted their military tactics and their concept of conscription.

The disruption of trade resulting from Tatar domination transformed Russia into a rural society in which peasants were increasingly reduced to serfdom under the control of boyars. Those who wished to preserve their freedom fled to the southern frontier to form cossack bands.

During the late fifteenth century, Ivan III transformed his position from grand duke to czar by ending tribute to the Golden Horde and by marrying the niece of the last Byzantine emperor. Moscow then emerged as the spiritual center of Orthodoxy and the political center of a new Russian state. During the next two centuries, Russia was forced to compete with Sweden and Poland for supremacy in eastern Europe. Despite many setbacks, the region controlled by the czar in Moscow continued to expand in all directions. The Russian state defined itself as the defender of the Orthodox tradition and the autocracy of the czar.

The trend toward autocratic centralization and expansion culminated with the reign of Peter I (1696-1725). Russia's victory over Sweden and the Ukrainian cossacks made Russia the dominant power in eastern Europe. Impressed by Western technology, Peter forced European fashion on the Russian nobility and utilized foreign advisers to modernize his nation. He reformed Russian government by replacing the boyar duma with an appointed senate that drafted laws at the request of the czar. In order to ensure competent leaders for the military and the bureaucracy, state service was made compulsory for the nobles and the gentry. The Table of Ranks was created, with fourteen grades. Only the top eight carried the privileges of nobility, and only members of the top rank could pass their title to an heir. The nobility was freed from compulsory state service by the end of the eighteenth century, but it continued to dominate the officer corps and the bureaucracy until the Revolution of 1917.

The liberal notions of equality that sprang from the French Revolution posed a direct threat to the autocratic traditions of Russia. Throughout the nineteenth century, the Russian government remained staunchly conservative. Czar Nicholas I (1825-1855) created a comprehensive system of censorship and a well-developed internal spy network to guarantee that his people were not infected with liberal ideas. Although the Russian government freed the serfs in 1861, communal land ownership prevented the development of an independent yeoman class. Manufacturing was generally state-sponsored and directed toward the benefit of the military.

In response to social unrest in 1905, Czar Nicholas II (1894-1917) established an elected duma. Unfortunately the new duma had little power and the suffrage was manipulated by the czar's ministers.

The defeat of Russian military forces during World War I sparked a democratic revolution in March, 1917. A provisional government controlled by the duma granted civil liberties to the Russian people, but it refused to withdraw from the war. A second revolution led by Vladimir Lenin in November, 1917, brought a Marxist-oriented government to power and sparked a four-year civil war that devastated the Russian economy.

The new Union of Soviet Socialist Republics was dedicated to the dictatorship of the working class. Class enemies were hunted down by the secret police and killed or imprisoned in work camps. Banking and industry were nationalized. The Communist Party set policy for the government.

During most of its seventy-four year history, the Soviet Union was a federation of fifteen republics, each with its own national soviet. The central government consisted of a Supreme Soviet, the legislative body of the federation; a presidium that exercised policy-making authority; and a council of ministers, consisting of the heads of executive agencies. Members were elected by universal suffrage, but the candidates for office were chosen by the Communist Party and were unopposed on the ballot. Real power rested in the hands of the party.

Members of the Soviet Communist Party elected representatives to party congresses. A congress chose a central committee that ran the affairs of the party when a congress was not in session. Within the central committee were the Politburo and the secretariat. The members of the Politburo initiated all policies for the party, and the secretariat controlled personnel. The general secretary of the central committee was the head of the party, the leader of the secretariat, a member of the Politburo, and the most powerful person in the Soviet Union.

Communist ideology replaced the Russian Orthodox church as the theology of the state. Russians made up only 52 percent of the population, but dominated the upper ranks of the party. Party leaders used a combination of propaganda, terror, and Russian nationalism to retain the loyalty of their people. World War II and the Cold War that followed played upon traditional fears of invasion and reinforced Russian xenophobia.

During the 1980's, General Secretary Mikhail Gorbachev attempted a dramatic reformation of the Soviet government. He attacked the rampant corruption within the bureaucracy, eased censorship, and initiated a decentralization of the Soviet economy. Resistance to change by party functionaries led to a deterioration of the economy and forced Gorbachev to liberalize the political system. He introduced multicandidate elections and attempted to shift power from the party to the legally constituted institutions of government. In an attempt to retain their power, high-ranking Communist officials organized a coup d'etat in August, 1991. When the coup attempt failed, the Soviet Union disintegrated and each of the constituent republics gained independence.

After December, 1991, the Russian Republic functioned under the leadership of President Boris Yeltsin. When disagreements between Yeltsin and the Russian parliament over economic policy led to streetfighting in 1993, Yeltsin used the military to dissolve the parliament and arrest its leaders. The Russian people approved a new democratic constitution in December, 1993, which increased the power of the president.

Applications

In the twentieth century, Russia continued its search for stability and secure borders. Soviet leader Joseph Stalin utilized the chaos caused by World War II to expand Russian power and influence in an effort to guarantee that the Soviet Union would never again be invaded. As many as twenty million Soviet citizens were killed during World War II. Hundreds of towns were completely destroyed by the German army, and thousands of Soviets were forced to labor for the benefit of the Nazi war machine.

Suspicious of the capitalist West, Stalin demanded the creation of friendly governments in Eastern Europe to act as buffers against future incursions. Along the Baltic coast, the Soviet Union simply annexed Lithuania, Latvia, and Estonia during the course of the conflict. Large portions of Finland, Poland, Czechoslovakia, and Romania were also seized. In countries liberated by Soviet troops, local Communist parties were given prominent roles in the formation of new governments.

Although the United States and Great Britain gave reluctant approval to the Soviet demand for a sphere of influence in Eastern Europe, both nations became concerned about the growth in Soviet power after World War II. By 1948, Communist governments loyal to the Soviet Union controlled Poland, Czechoslovakia, Hungary, Bulgaria, and Romania. The Soviet sector in Germany was also taking on a distinctly Communist character. A Communist rebellion in Greece and an attempt by the Soviets to stop Western access to Berlin were viewed as signs of Soviet aggression.

Efforts by the United States and its Western European allies to contain the spread of Soviet influence led to a Cold War between the two power blocs. The Soviets responded to this challenge by forming a military alliance with its client states in Eastern Europe, ostensibly to protect socialism from the threat of Western capitalism.

Known as the Warsaw Pact (1955), the alliance was used as a pretext for military intervention in Hungary in 1956 and Czechoslovakia in 1968 to preserve Russian domination of the region. The Soviet government also used the Cold War to stifle dissent. Internal criticism of the Communist leadership was viewed as a threat to national security. Just as in the days of the czars, dissidents were either killed, exiled, or sent to work camps in Siberia.

Ironically, the lifting of censorship during the Gorbachev era drowned the Soviet leadership in a flood of criticism. Nationalist groups within the republics demanded separation from the federation, while democratic reformers within Russia pushed for an end to the totalitarian system of Communist, one-party rule. In the chaos that followed, the Soviet Union not only lost its East European empire, it also suffered internal collapse and economic decline.

The post-Soviet Russian republic lacked the cohesion of the Soviet Union or the czarist empire. While President Yeltsin's economic reforms opened new opportunities for entrepreneurs to acquire wealth, millions of Russians were disenchanted by their loss in status. Foreign capitalists harvested Russia's natural resources, while Russian nationals were often taunted and harassed in the states of the former Soviet Union. Pressure by minority groups within the Russian republic for greater autonomy added to fears of instability, and organized crime replaced the state police as the most dreaded oppressor of the common people.

The results of the parliamentary elections held on December 12, 1993, illustrated the desire of many Russians to return to a civil society that stresses order and stability. Fifty-eight percent of the Russian electorate voted for a new constitution giving the president the power to form his own cabinet and rule by decree if necessary. Yet nationalist and communist candidates opposed to President Yeltsin were able to win a large bloc of seats in the new parliament. The fascist-oriented Liberal Democratic Party won 23 percent of the vote, placing second behind Yeltsin's Russia's Choice Party. Liberal Democrat Vladimir Zhirinovsky promised to reestablish the old Russian empire and ties with the West. In their search for stability, the Russian people in the early 1990's were again looking for a strong leader who would set their nation on a clearly defined course.

Context

More than eleven centuries of Russian history reveal that the Russian people have tolerated strong, centralized governments in order to guarantee their security. Subjected to repeated invasions, the Russians began a policy of expansion during the fifteenth century in order to secure their territory from attack. During the czarist period, Russians were unified by the Byzantine traditions of the Russian Orthodox church and an autocratic ruler. For much of the twentieth century, Russia controlled a vast, multicultural empire unified by Marxist ideology and a totalitarian government.

The Russian political system established after the fall of communism in 1991 was based on the Western European model of parliamentary democracy, with power shared by an executive president, a popularly elected legislature, and an independent judiciary. Elections were to be by universal suffrage, and a wide variety of political parties emerged in Russia, making it difficult for any single party to dominate the legislature.

Democracy did not have deep roots in Russia. While Russians exercised new civil liberties, they also were subjected to the confusion of a multiparty system. Disputes between the executive and legislative branches of government stalled economic reform and created a vacuum in leadership. The loss of a common purpose fragmented Russian society, as the loss of subject nations weakened Russia militarily. While few Russians desired to reconstruct a totalitarian government, many soon yearned for a return to order and stability.

The collapse of the Soviet regime also had a major impact on the world community. In a global context, it meant an end to the Cold War. Emerging from decades of Russian domination, the nations of Eastern Europe were forced to confront ethnic and religious conflicts within their borders. Czechoslovakia and Yugoslavia splintered; Georgia was plunged into civil war. All suffered from economic dislocation without a strong Russia available to impose order on the region.

Bibliography

Barbour, William, and Carol Wekesser, eds. *The Breakup of the Soviet Union: Opposing Viewpoints*. San Diego, Calif.: Greenhaven Press, 1994. Short essays dealing with diverse theories about the collapse of the Soviet Union and the impact of that collapse.

Crowley, Joan Frances, and Dan Vaillancourt. *Lenin to Gorbachev: Three Generations of Soviet Communists*. Arlington Heights, Ill.: Harlan Davidson, 1989. Short, readable political history of the Soviet Union, divided by ruling generations.

Florinsky, Michael T., ed. *McGraw-Hill Encyclopedia of Russia and the Soviet Union*. New York: McGraw-Hill, 1961. Excellent, though dated, reference work containing entries by noted scholars in the field.

Lincoln, W. Bruce. *The Romanovs: Autocrats of All the Russias*. New York: Dial Press, 1981. Brilliantly written work detailing the strengths and weaknesses of the autocrats who ruled Russia for four hundred years.

MacKenzie, David, and Michael W. Curran. *A History of the Soviet Union*. 2d ed. Belmont, Calif.: Wadsworth, 1991. The best one-volume text on the Soviet Union in print. Readable and scholarly. Selective bibliography of both secondary and reference works.

Vernadsky, George. *A History of Russia*. 6th ed. New Haven, Conn.: Yale University Press, 1969. Interpretive volume tracing Russian history from its beginnings through the fall of Khrushchev. Particularly significant for its analysis of the Kievan and Mongol periods.

Yeltsin, Boris. *The Struggle for Russia*. Translated by Catherine A. Fitzpatrick. New York: Times Books, 1994. Personal account of the collapse of the Soviet Union and the struggle for democracy in Russia by that nation's leading political figure at the time.

Thomas D. Matijasic

Cross-References

Autocracy and Absolutism, p. 127; Chinese Communism, p. 223; Communist Parties, p. 377; Empires and Empire Building, p. 597; General Will, p. 745; Geopolitics, p. 759; Marxism-Leninism, p. 1155; One-Party Systems, p. 1350; Police States, p. 1408; Revolutionary Governments, p. 1725; Revolutions, p. 1738; Superpowers and World Politics, p. 1916; Totalitarianism, p. 1987.

SANCTIONS

Field of study: International government and politics

A means of coercing a country to stop or reverse behavior deemed illegal, immoral, or dangerous, sanctions are prohibitions on international economic and social exchange with the offending country. Sanctions have been frequently used, especially since World War I, as an alternative to using military force to punish aggression or lawlessness.

Principal terms

BOYCOTT: refusal to have dealings with another, especially refusal to buy products

COLLECTIVE SECURITY: countries cooperating to secure their respective territories by assenting to international laws and to sanctions for countries that violate the laws

DIPLOMATIC RECOGNITION: formal acknowledgment by one country of the legitimate sovereignty of another

EMBARGO: a prohibition on commerce or trade

FREEZING FOREIGN ASSETS: prohibiting foreigners from withdrawing their assets (bank accounts, bills payable, stocks, bonds, and other forms of investment) from one's country

MOST-FAVORED NATION (MFN) STATUS: the granting of equal treatment in such matters as tariff rates to the commerce of each country to which MFN status is given, usually reciprocally

Overview

Sanctions are various means used to put pressure on a foreign country. In general, sanctions are nonviolent alternatives to war. Among the most important sanctions are economic measures. These may include trade embargoes or restrictions on investment in the target country, freezing or even confiscating the target's foreign assets, or milder steps such as denying most-favored-nation status, reducing foreign aid, or curbing tourism. Countries may also resort to a range of diplomatic sanctions, including expelling foreign diplomatic personnel, recalling their ambassadors from the target country, breaking off diplomatic relations, or refusing to grant diplomatic recognition to a new nation or regime. Such sanctions, which are not economic, may nevertheless have powerful economic effects as investors and traders cut back their business activity to reduce their risks in the event of any further deterioration of relations.

Generally, sanctions are a weapon of stronger powers against weaker ones. If a weaker country tried to use sanctions against a stronger one, the stronger power might threaten to use force to induce the weaker to relax the sanctions. On the other hand, a weaker country has little recourse if a stronger country or coalition of countries chooses to use sanctions against it. The major problem with using sanctions is that they are usually a two-edged sword: not only the target country, but also the sanctioning country may suffer economic losses from the interruption of their commerce. Sanctions have become more common during the twentieth century as economic interdependence has increased. Interdependence makes sanctions more effective, since the target country will have more to lose from any reduction in its commerce, but interdependence also increases the cost of using sanctions. This is another reason why larger countries are more likely to use sanctions than smaller ones, because if a larger country sanctions a smaller one, the resulting loss of commerce is likely to be proportionately less for the larger country than for the smaller one. For example, United States economic sanctions against Haiti or Cuba inflict far greater injury on those countries than on the United States itself, since U.S. trade with those small countries is a small fraction of total U.S. trade, whereas before sanctions most of the trade of those small countries was with the United States.

Sanctions are especially useful in situations in which employing military force may be more difficult, more costly, more unpopular, or counterproductive. For example, it would generally be counterproductive to threaten military action against an ally, yet sanctions or threats of sanctions have often been used to influence allies, most commonly in trade disputes.

Sanctions are more effective and less costly to impose if a coalition of countries invokes them. If only one country applies sanctions against another, other countries might simply take the economic place of the country applying the sanctions. The sanctioning country would simply lose business without imposing much of a cost on the target of the sanctions. This is an important reason why sanctions are especially popular as weapons of collective security. Broad cooperation makes them more likely to succeed.

Both the League of Nations (1920-1945) and its successor, the United Nations (U.N.), which was founded in 1945, provided explicit rules spelling out the circumstances under which the world community would be justified in using sanctions against errant governments. Article 16 of the Covenant of the League of Nations stipulates that all member states should implement a complete economic embargo against any member deemed to have committed an act of war against any other member. Other articles of the U.N. Charter authorize the use of economic and diplomatic sanctions against states that, according to the U.N. Security Council, are a threat to peace. Other international organizations, such as the World Trade Organization (WTO), have also defined the circumstances under which members may legitimately employ trade sanctions against other member countries violating WTO rules. As the twentieth century progressed, sanctions became more widely recognized as a legitimate instrument for enforcing international law.

Sanctions are used either for general or specific purposes. The most common general purpose is to undermine a foreign government considered illegitimate or dangerous. Such sanctions are not directed against any particular act of the target government, but against its very existence. Sanctions used for specific purposes aim to stop or reverse some particular action by a foreign government, without necessarily challenging the government's right to exist. Common specific purposes include opposing an act of military aggression or opposing economic policies contrary to either international law or the sanctioning country's interests.

Increasing concern about enforcing universal standards of human rights has prompted the use of economic sanctions to pressure countries to curb human rights abuses. This is a considerable extension of the use of sanctions. Traditionally, international law upheld the sovereign authority of states to do as they pleased within their own boundaries, as long as they respected foreign lives and property. The U.N. Charter in 1945 first defined comprehensive and universal human rights. Much of the impetus for this new development came from the worldwide horror at Nazi Germany's genocide against Jews and Eastern European peoples and Japan's atrocities in the course of its Asian conquests. Since then, private international organizations dedicated to exposing human rights violations and mobilizing public opinion against them have expanded enormously. The pressure of public opinion has occasionally induced countries to impose sanctions against other nations for extreme human rights violations.

There has been considerable controversy over the extent to which sanctions can be effective as an alternative to military force. Many liberals and proponents of international law consider sanctions to be morally superior to the use of force as a means of maintaining international order and enforcing international law. Those who call themselves realists often argue that sanctions are difficult to enforce in the absence of any effective world government. Realists contend that military force remains the ultimate arbiter of international disputes. They believe that sanctions can at best supplement rather than replace military power. There can be little doubt, however, that since 1945 recourse to war has become less common and the use of sanctions more common.

Applications

Sanctions have been used dozens of times since the end of World War I. Three cases serve as examples. In one case, Allied economic sanctions during 1940-1941 forced Japan to choose between giving up its conquests in China and Indochina and initiating war against a combination of powers almost certain to defeat it. Japan responded by initiating war in December, 1941.

In a second example, Arab oil-producing countries began to restrict oil sales to the United States and its allies for their support of Israel during the October, 1973, war between Israel and Arab countries led by Egypt and Syria. The boycott failed to disrupt support for Israel, but did quadruple world crude oil prices. In another example, many nations, international organizations, and even local communities imposed sanctions on South Africa during the 1970's and 1980's to protest against the oppression of the black majority of the country by a white minority regime. The regime had imposed a system of controls, known as apartheid, on the non-white population. These sanctions probably contributed to the dismantling of the apartheid system during the early 1990's and to democratic reforms culminating in free elections held in 1994.

The Allied economic sanctions against Japan are among the most important of many cases of sanctions imposed against a country to oppose an act of aggression. Japan had been gradually expanding its control of northern China since its 1931 conquest of Manchuria, the northeastern region of China. Japan launched a full-scale invasion of most of the rest of China in 1937. Other countries protested, but little effective action was taken to punish Japan. Both Japan and China continued to trade and buy war materials abroad.

The U.S. Neutrality Acts, which were passed by Congress beginning in 1935, prohibited Americans from making loans or selling war materials to any countries at war. Over the objection of President Franklin D. Roosevelt, isolationists in Congress had refused to limit the embargoes to only the aggressor. The president's supporters did manage to add a major loophole to the laws: It was up to the president to declare when a conflict constituted a war. Despite millions of troops engaged in combat, Roosevelt did not declare the Japan-China conflict a war, so the Neutrality Acts never applied. He wished that China not be impeded from buying arms from the United States, but thus neither could he prevent private arms sales to Japan. After repeated Japanese bombings of Chinese cities, however, he successfully urged U.S. aircraft manufacturers to place a "moral embargo" on sales to Japan of bombing aircraft and related equipment.

An official U.S. embargo began in earnest only after the Japanese occupation of the northern part of French Indochina (now Vietnam) in September 1940, following the conquest of France by Nazi Germany. Japan aimed at closing off one of the few remaining avenues for China's foreign trade, having already conquered most of China's seaports. At first the U.S. embargo applied only to scrap iron and steel needed by the inadequate Japanese steel industry. This embargo did not, however, deter Japan from further aggressive moves.

The decisive tightening of the embargo occurred in July, 1941. In response to Japan's occupation of the remainder of French Indochina, the United States, Great Britain, and Britain's allies froze all Japanese assets and placed such restrictions on trade with Japan as to practically constitute a complete embargo. Japan could no longer import essential supplies. Japan was especially vulnerable to the cessation of oil imports. Once the embargo was in place, U.S. diplomatic demands on Japan began to harden until Japan was left with the choice of abandoning all its conquests of the past ten years, of slow economic strangulation, or of further expansion to try to conquer areas that produced what Japan needed most. Some argue that the sanctions failed because they did not deter Japan from launching a war, but that was not necessarily the sanctions' purpose. Sanctions succeeded in forcing Japan into a corner so that either by war or diplomacy Japanese aggression could be checked.

The Arab oil embargo against Western powers in 1973-1974 has often been cited as proof that in the modern, interdependent world, economic power can best military power. Militarily weak Arab oil-exporting countries successfully withheld a vital resource from the West and its vastly greater military power. The embargo did fail, however, to have much impact on support for Israel. What it achieved was a quadrupling of world oil prices. This, understandably, benefited the Arab exporters, but it also increased their incentive to end the embargo and resume selling rather than lose lucrative Western markets to non-Arab producers. The oil price increase plunged many countries into a deep recession, combined for the first time with inflation as well. Despite these heavy economic costs, not everyone in the Western world was hurt; British and U.S. oil interests certainly prospered. The advantages accruing to Western oil interests probably worked against a united Western response toward breaking the embargo, since any economic pressure against the Arab world would have probably required cooperation from the oil companies. Since the Arab oil-exporting countries were mostly led by conservative, anti-Soviet regimes, the United States also had to consider whether undermining those governments or taking military action might increase Soviet influence in the Middle East. Thus both domestic business interests and global security issues presumably tempered the U.S. response.

South Africa's has been the most prominent of a growing number of cases of sanctions applied in order to force domestic policy changes. Like most such cases, the issue was human rights. The South African apartheid regime denied political rights to the nonwhite majority, so the sanctions were aimed not only at reforming government policy, but also at a political revolution that would grant nonwhites full citizenship. The case of Rhodesia (now Zimbabwe) during the 1970's was similar. In both cases, sanctions were voted by the United Nations, the British Commonwealth, and many individual countries, but few countries fully implemented the sanctions recommended by international organizations, and even those sanctions that were imposed were widely violated. Worldwide popular pressure resulted in the gradual tightening of the sanctions. Though the sanctions were never severe, they contributed to the international isolation of the minority regimes and probably helped force them eventually to concede power to the black majority.

Context

The growing prevalence of sanctions in international relations reflects several trends: increasing economic interdependence, the decreasing legitimacy of militarism, the growing global importance of public opinion, and the increasing popular concern for human rights.

Economic interdependence continues to increase as industrialization proceeds globally. When agriculture was the economic base of human existence, countries could be more self-sufficient. Trade was a matter more of luxury than necessity. As industrialization proceeds, however, countries become increasingly dependent on resources and markets far beyond their own borders. Most modern nations would be devastated by cessation of foreign commerce. Thus the power to withhold trade will remain a potent weapon in the modern world, particularly whenever nations are able to cooperate to sanction renegade regimes.

War is certainly not extinct, but it has become so costly and destructive, even for the victor, that nations are increasingly reluctant to solve disputes by violence. In the twentieth century, wars of conquest have seldom succeeded. The most common form of war is now civil war, rather than outright wars of conquest, although admittedly many civil wars are veiled wars of conquest. The threat of sanctions in an interdependent world certainly contributes to the growing popular belief in futility of militarism.

Gradual democratization and a revolution in communications technology have magnified the importance of public opinion throughout the world. Regimes that offend global sensibilities, whether by military aggression, human rights violations or whatever else, are increasingly likely to be held to account by world public opinion. Sanctions are often more widely supported than military action against an errant nation.

Increasing popular concern for human rights throughout the world has given a new impetus to popular pressure to impose sanctions against repressive regimes. Many people no longer wish to be implicated, through trade or other forms of intercourse, with repression.

Bibliography

Alerassool, Mahvash. *Freezing Assets: The USA and the Most Effective Economic Sanction*. New York: St. Martin's Press, 1993. Examines one important case: the U.S. freezing of Iranian assets after U.S. Embassy personnel there were taken hostage in 1979.

Daoudi, M. S., and M. S. Dajani. *Economic Sanctions: Ideals and Experience*. London: Routledge & Kegan Paul, 1983. Argues that since the 1960's the conventional wisdom has held that sanctions are largely ineffective, whereas previously they were held in high esteem, but that study of dozens of cases indicates that neither of the two extreme views is accurate.

Doxey, Margaret P. *International Sanctions in Contemporary Perspective*. New York: Macmillan, 1987. Readable, short general introduction to the modern use of sanctions, with many individual cases discussed and an entire chapter on South Africa.

Hufbauer, Gary Clyde, Jeffrey J. Schott, and Kimberly Ann Elliott. *Economic Sanctions Reconsidered*. 2d ed. Washington, D.C.: Institute for International Economics, 1990. This survey of 108 cases of economic sanctions from 1914 to 1989 is probably the most comprehensive study of the uses and effectiveness of economic sanctions.

Leyton-Brown, David, ed. *The Utility of International Economic Sanctions*. New York: St. Martin's Press, 1987. Useful collection of articles dealing with several important themes and cases.

Licklider, Roy E. *Political Power and the Arab Oil Weapon: The Experience of Five Industrial Nations*. Berkeley: University of California Press, 1988. Arab efforts to reduce Western support for Israel during and after the 1973 Arab-Israeli war represent one of the few important attempts of militarily weak countries to influence strong ones. Licklider concludes that this effort largely failed.

Martin, Lisa L. *Coercive Cooperation: Explaining Multilateral Economic Sanctions*. Princeton, N.J.: Princeton University Press, 1992. Examines sanctions as a problem of international cooperation. Using statistical analysis, Martin finds that the involvement of international organizations facilitated cooperation, and that the decline of U.S. power has not made cooperation more difficult.

Renwick, Robin. *Economic Sanctions*. Cambridge, Mass.: Center for International Affairs, Harvard University, 1981. Evaluates sanctions primarily as an alternative either to using military force or doing nothing.

James H. Nolt

Cross-References

Diplomacy and International Negotiation, p. 552; Food Politics, p. 706; Foreign Relations, p. 718; Genocide, p. 752; Human Rights and International Politics, p. 848; International Agreements, p. 949; International Law, p. 956; International Relations, p. 969; Peace, p. 1390; Supranational Government Institutions, p. 1922; Terrorism, p. 1962; Trade with Foreign Nations, p. 2000; Treaties, p. 2020; United Nations, p. 2045; War, p. 2129.

SCIENTIFIC HUMANISM

Field of study: Political philosophy

As the belief that science can and should be used to enhance human dignity, scientific humanism was a basic tenet of the "brain trust" behind the socialist party's rise to power in Great Britain after World War II. The foremost spokesman for this creed was the political scientist Graham Wallas.

Principal terms
CAPITALISM: system of free market (laissez faire) economics
FABIAN SOCIETY: group of British intellectuals who advocated democratic socialism
HABIT PHILOSOPHERS: authority figures who perpetuate habitual modes of thought
HUMANISM: doctrine that exalts human dignity, particularly that of the individual, and rejects the supernatural
INTELLECTUALISM: view of human nature that exaggerates the importance of reason, as opposed to anti-intellectualism, which exaggerates the nonrational
SOCIALISM: belief in state ownership of industry

Overview

The historical relationship between modern humanist thought and democratic theory can be traced back to classical Greece. The fifth century B.C.E. philosopher Protagoras claimed that the value of all things should be measured in terms of their effect upon human beings. Moreover, Protagoras left no room for doubt about the unequivocal relationship that existed between his humanism and his politics. From this doctrine, which took mankind as the measure of all things, he derived a remarkable corollary for his times: a doctrine of equal rights that included women and slaves. He then backed up his beliefs with a call for sweeping social reforms to be instituted by democratic means.

From Protagoras to the present, humanism has been an ally to freedom's cause. The first step toward adding science to this alliance was taken in the sixteenth century, when the Polish astronomer Nicolaus Copernicus used a simple and elegant mathematical formula to overthrow the ancient, Earth-centered view of the solar system, replacing it with his heliocentric or sun-centered theory. The scientific revolution had begun. The crowning event took place a little more than a century later when Sir Isaac Newton drew upon the scientific heritage of the previous century to formulate the law of universal gravitation—a single law whereby all motion in the heavens and Earth became intelligible and predictable. Science was now the authoritative definer of the universe.

By the eighteenth century, Europe was struck by a virtual mania for applying the new scientific method to all areas of human inquiry. While the idea that science would produce useful knowledge for the betterment of humankind was as old as science itself, it was during this century that scientific humanism, the belief that science and human progress are inextricably connected, took hold. It now seemed that humankind could use the scientific method to establish a rational world in which the dream of human fulfillment could be realized. For some, there now seemed to be no limits to human progress. In the late eighteenth century, the Marquis de Condorcet summed up the optimism of the times in the language of political freedom. Looking back upon the victories of the scientific revolution, Condorcet predicted a future in which further scientific progress would render both tyrants and slaves obsolete.

But if the eighteenth century Enlightenment was the great age of optimism, it was during the second half of the nineteenth and early part of the twentieth centuries that scientific humanism met with its greatest success in the work-a-day world of practical politics—the election of the socialists to power in Great Britain in the aftermath of World War I. This movement was the brainchild of the Fabian Society, a small group of intellectuals who met for the first time in 1854. The Fabian socialists—a name they took to signify that they intended to imitate the delaying tactics of Fabius, a famous Roman general—preached gradualism, not revolution. Like Fabius, they opted for a war of attrition, but theirs was an intellectual war waged in the pages of newspapers, journals and books. They were confident that once the freedom-loving British people realized that socialism was the only economic system compatible with democratic freedom, victory would be theirs. The economic and social forces of the capitalist citadel would fall, defeated at the polls by freedom-loving citizens. This conviction—the belief that if people were shown what was right they would do right—accounts for the patient collection of facts that became such a marked feature of Fabian activity.

Nowhere is the penchant for rigorous factual analysis that characterized the Fabian movement better exemplified than in the scientific humanism of Graham Wallas (1858-1932). In his youth Wallas enjoyed all the material benefits common to the lifestyle of England's middle class. Unfortunately, he did not get on well with his father, the Reverend Mr. Wallas, which might account for his later distaste for organized religion and his suspicion of those in authority. After graduating from Oxford in 1881, Wallas began a career as a preparatory teacher, preparing young men for college. This career came to an abrupt halt, however, when religious scruples prevented Wallas from taking communion as required by the school authorities. Dismissed from his teaching post in 1884, he spent a year studying in Germany, where he became interested in that country's burgeoning socialist movement. Upon his return to England in 1886, he joined the Fabian Society. He was a leading member of the society until he resigned in 1904 over his disagreement with the organization's position on the question of tariffs. This disagreement was over a matter of principle, not personalities, and he remained on good terms with the Fabians for the remainder of his life. Wallas entertained two brief forays into politics, one as an elected member of the London County Council (1904-1907), the other as a member of the Royal Commission of the Civil Service (1914-1915). However, it was as a public lecturer and teacher of political science at the London School of Economics (1895-1923) and at the University of London (1914-1923) that he earned his fame. Wallas was not only the first person to apply the theory of the mind developed by the American psychologist and philosopher William James to the study of political behavior, he was also a pioneer of an empirically based social science. He is probably best remembered, however, for his lifelong commitment to and struggle on behalf of the freedom, equality, and economic security of the British people.

Applications

Although Wallas was the author of numerous essays and five books, he never presented a carefully worked out political philosophy. Nevertheless, when what he says about human nature in his many essays and five books is pieced together, an embryonic but coherent theory of politics does emerge. Much of what he had to say about politics centers around his objections to both "intellectualism"—the tendency on the part of some to exaggerate the importance of reason in politics—and "anti-intellectualism"—the tendency of others to ignore reason's importance in human affairs. Wallas considered both perspectives, derived as they were from a lopsided view of human nature, as hazardous to the moral health of a nation. He was convinced that a people unaware of their own natures were doomed to become the victims of their own ignorance.

For Wallas, the capitalist doctrine of laissez faire, or free market, economics provided a prime example of the perils inherent in "intellectualism." The capitalists believed that the competitive forces that resulted from rational individuals pursuing their own selfish ends were directed by an "invisible hand" toward an equitable distribution of wealth. In Wallas' view, the harsh facts of reality shattered any hope that capitalism would advance the interests of the poor. The same "invisible hand" that provided friendly ideological support to capitalist entrepreneurs had proved to be a hostile fist that squeezed the bulk of the working poor into the misery of poverty. Yet capitalism provided no compassion for its victims. For in capitalist theory, reason was all important. Feelings, emotions, and desires—with the crucial exception of inordinate desire for wealth—could only interfere with the mechanical precision of the free market. Pity for the plight of the working class and the destitute had no theoretical validity.

But Wallas did not single out the "intellectualism" inherent in capitalist theory as the sole source of blame. If the exaggeration of reason lent the illusion of intellectual legitimacy to the "philistine" doctrine of laissez faire, it was the proclivity toward "anti-intellectualism" on the part of those whom he (with tongue in cheek) called "Habit Philosophers" that presented the major obstacle to reform. The philosophers of habit were all those unaware of the new science of psychology who held positions of authority in society. All too often, they unwittingly exploited the ignorance and fear of the masses by perpetuating and reinforcing habitual modes of thinking that supported the evils of capitalism and denigrated human dignity. When Wallas spoke of the "philosophers of habit," he meant almost all authority figures—mothers, fathers, teachers, preachers, military generals, captains of industry, and so on. He did not intend to imply that they conveyed a monolithic set of ideas—like a traditional school of philosophic thought. To the contrary, the philosophers of habit bombarded their fellow citizens with a virtual cornucopia of truths, half-truths, and downright falsehoods, some which through constant repetition became part of the habitual assumptions, ideas, and "commonsense" notions that formed the national character of the English people.

Wallas recognized that certain habitual thoughts that produce quasi-automatic behavior, such as obedience to the law and civility to others, are the glue that holds modern nation-states together. But he was also aware that other habitual thoughts slowly eat away the moral fabric of a democratic society. For example, most philosophers of habit who were themselves victimized into thinking of women in terms of home and hearth perpetuated the myth that women are by nature unsuited for any kind of political participation, including the right to vote. Such thinkers were responsible for promoting the notion that members of certain racial and ethnic groups are by nature ill equipped to participate in the democratic process. But perhaps the most destructive ideas to the social welfare were those that added to the inequalities inherent within the capitalist system. Wallas found two pervasive habits of thought held by citizens to be particularly pernicious and damaging to the socialist cause. The first was the idea that individuals are greedy by nature; the second, the notion that a life of poverty indicates an indolent nature. By transmitting and reinforcing such ideas, the philosophers of habit became the handmaidens of capitalist theory. Before the goal of socialism could be realized, such ideas had to be changed. It was to this task that Wallas dedicated his professional life.

What kept Wallas' hope in the possibility of change alive was his own view of human nature, according to which human beings inherit their impulses, but not their responses to them. He also believed, however, that when a person forms the habit of responding to the same impulse in the same way time after time, what is really a learned response gives the appearance of being part of one's nature. Most important, because habits are learned they do not represent eternal forms of human behavior, and because they include not only ways of reacting but also ways of thinking, they are the key to overcoming social evil. They can be singled out, analyzed, and changed.

In order to accomplish the herculean task of changing the habits of a nation, Wallas turned to science. But it was not the deductive methods of physical science that he embraced. Rather, Wallas was a pioneer of the inductive approach common to the empirically oriented social sciences of today. Firm in the conviction that the more unaware a people are of their own nature, the more likely they are to be dominated by it, he advocated amassing statistical data to bring the errors of their habitual half-unconscious assumptions to light. He never wavered in his faith. Faced with a mountain of uncontestable statistical data, the myths of racial, ethnic, and sexual superiority would be crushed. Moreover, the English people would conclude that the only economic system logically compatible with democracy was socialism. Wallas' perseverance paid off. He lived to see the formation of Great Britain's first socialist government when the Labour Party assumed the reins of power in the aftermath of World War I.

Context

Great Britain's first socialist government did not command an absolute majority in Parliament. It was therefore unable to effect a legislative agenda that restructured British society along egalitarian lines and it quickly lost control of the reins of power. Reinstated in 1929, again without a parliamentary majority, the party split over economic issues arising out of the Great Depression, and it was succeeded by a coalition government in 1931. It was not until 1945 that the socialists again formed a government. This time they commanded an absolute majority; however, they quickly learned the problems of governing. The most pressing ideological problem the Fabians faced was a consequence of the fact that the socialism of the Labour Party was very catholic in nature, ranging as it did from a small Marxist strain to a trade unionism of the bread-and-butter variety. This factionalism within the socialist ranks forced compromise. In the hurly-burly world of real politics, compromise for the Fabians meant surrendering noneconomic ideals to the more politically pressing concerns of economic policy. But even within the economic sphere, the responsibility of governing forced negotiations and concessions until many socialists were complaining that it was often hard to distinguish the pragmatic positions of the Labour Party from those of the Conservative Party. Fabian radicalism had given way to political pragmatism.

How successful were the early Fabians in achieving their humanistic ends? Because they believed economic security to be essential to human dignity, they had set out to eradicate poverty. Under socialist direction the state did use its legislative and administrative power to humanize capitalism. If nothing else, a social net was established that lessened the suffering of those who fell through the cracks of the economic system. Thus, six years later, when the Conservatives came to power, a substantial segment of British industry had been nationalized. The Fabians cannot, however, take sole credit for any major piece of legislation; they were part of a socialist coalition. Nor were they responsible for a worldwide ideological movement. But they can take credit for recognizing that as long as socialism clung to a rigid, undemocratic Marxist doctrine it would be doomed to remain a tiny, insignificant force in a country that had passed through the economic and social turbulence of the Industrial Revolution and emerged as the most prosperous nation in the world. The Fabians never deviated from their democratic path. So while their ideological radicalism may have given way to political pragmatism, they always remained sensitive to changes in public sentiment, ready to cast aside extraneous beliefs, clinging only to their essential commitment, which was the gradual enhancement of human dignity within a framework of democratic freedom.

Bibliography

Burtt, E. A. *The Metaphysical Foundations of Modern Science*. Garden City, N.Y.: Doubleday, 1954. History of the scientific revolution. A modern classic, this is philosophical criticism at its best, written for the general reader.

Cole, Margaret. *The Story of Fabian Socialism*. Stanford, Calif.: Stanford University Press, 1961. For years one of the leading commentaries on the subject, this is a detailed but readable history. It covers the origin of the Fabian Society to the years immediately following World War II.

Matson, Floyd W. *The Broken Image: Man, Science, and Society*. Garden City, N.Y.: Doubleday, 1966. Exceptionally well-written account of how modern science can serve the quest to understand what it means to be truly human.

Shaw, G. Bernard, ed. *Fabian Essays in Socialism*. Gloucester, Mass.: Peter Smith, 1967. A collection of public lectures delivered by prominent members of the Fabian Society in 1888, this is the most comprehensive statement of Fabian socialism yet published. Includes "Property Under Socialism" by Graham Wallas.

Wallas, Graham. *The Art of Thought*. New York: Harcourt, Brace, 1926. Observations derived from Wallas' many years as a teacher on human thought processes.

_____. *The Great Society: A Psychological Analysis*. New York: Macmillan, 1914. Analysis of life in a large nation-state, expanding Wallas' case against "anti-intellectualism."

_____. *Human Nature in Politics*. 3d ed. London: Constable, 1938. Although this analysis of representative government (originally published in 1908) is now mostly out of date, it remains important as a statement of Wallas' argument against "intellectualism."

_____. *The Life of Francis Place, 1771-1854*. 4th ed. London: George Allen & Unwin, 1925. Biography of a political activist whom Wallas regarded as a great influence on his own life. First published in 1898, the book traces the life of Place from his beginnings in poverty to his rise to the centers of political power in Great Britain.

_____. *Our Social Heritage*. New Haven, Conn.: Yale University Press, 1921. Surveys various ways that human beings relate to their social, economic, and political environments.

Wolfe, Willard. *From Radicalism to Socialism: Men and Ideas in the Formation of Fabian Socialist Doctrines, 1881-1889*. New Haven, Conn.: Yale University Press, 1975. Written with grace and style, this is easily the best book for general readers on Fabian socialism. It places the Fabian socialist philosophy in historical context and contains an excellent biographical sketch of Wallas that focuses on his intellectual development.

Thomas J. Mortillaro

Cross-References

The British Parliamentary System, p. 146; Capitalism, p. 197; Democracy, p. 513; The Left and the Right, p. 1079; Liberalism, p. 1118; Marxism-Leninism, p. 1155; Political Economy, p. 1455; Radicalism, p. 1661; Socialism, p. 1865; The Welfare State, p. 2135.

SECESSIONISM

Field of study: Politics

Secessionism is the political withdrawal of a region from a country's governmental system. Usually the region in question claims sovereignty, although sometimes a region might seek to join a different country. Often the secession is challenged by the parent country, which has an obvious interest in maintaining its own territorial integrity.

Principal terms

AUTONOMY: degree of freedom for a regional government to make its own laws and policies within a larger governmental system

FEDERATION: governmental system in which some powers are allocated to the central government and others are allocated to the various constituent parts (states, provinces, regions) of the country

NATION: group of people bound together by a common language, culture, history, ethnicity, religion, or other factors

NATION-STATE: country whose population constitutes a single nation

SELF-DETERMINATION: the principle that a nation has a right to govern itself

SOVEREIGNTY: principle that an entity (usually a national government) wields supreme authority over its designated territory

Overview

Secessionism is a region's formal withdrawing of its participation in an existing country's political system. When a part of a country successfully secedes, it severs its political ties to the central government. In so doing, the seceding region may attempt to join a different country; usually, however, a seceding region declares sovereignty and attempts to be recognized as a country in its own right. Yet the mere declaration of sovereignty does not confer statehood, as a state must formally be recognized as such by other states in the world community. Further, the secession may be opposed, politically and militarily, by the parent country.

Secessionism, as opposed to other methods for securing political independence, implies that the seceding region had in some way joined the parent country in the past. Often a seceding region has existed as part of a federation of semiautonomous governments. Typically the various parts of the federation have their own histories that distinguish them from one another, and these differences serve as the justification for having formed a federation (rather than a unitary state) in the first place. In a federation, the various parts are accorded a measure of autonomy, or the authority to make and execute policies in certain areas, such as education and land use. Although this framework is designed to accommodate differing attitudes, needs, and interests among the parts of a federation, it also creates conflicts that might be exploited by secessionists. Indeed, in rare cases, a federation even will accord to its component parts a specific right of secession. Such was the case with the Soviet Union, although this constitutional "right" did not translate into practice for most of the country's history.

If a region joins a union voluntarily (which is not always the case), it presumably anticipates a net benefit from membership. Regions later can be motivated to secede when the costs of membership are perceived to outweigh the benefits. Of course, a formal cost-benefit calculus is seldom performed; instead, public opinion within the region begins to settle on the belief, correct or otherwise, that the region is being exploited by the central government. Sometimes the perceived exploitation is economic in nature. If a part of a country believes that it is contributing a disproportionately high share of taxes to a central government that in turn redistributes wealth to the poorer and perhaps less productive parts of the country, the wealthy region might question the value of remaining in the union. Similarly, if a poor region believes that its economic plight is caused by exploitative industrial and employment policies in the country, it might seek to control its own economic system. It should be noted, however, that economic issues by themselves are rarely potent enough to precipitate secession. More often they are addressed through legislation, strikes, boycotts, and other means.

Nationalism represents a much more potent driving force for secessionism. Many countries can be considered multinational, that is, comprising more than one nation. This can pose problems when one predominant nation holds the reins of power. To the extent that any group considers itself to be unique (in culture or religion, for example), that group might chafe at being governed by others. When this happens, members of the predominant nationality are perceived, perhaps correctly, to be indifferent or hostile to the interests of the minority nationalities. Governmental policies and laws are perceived to promote the interests of the dominant nationality over those of other national groups. Even when the central government includes representatives of many different groups (or nations), the policies which result can be seen by nationalists as homogenizing, and therefore destructive to national groups. Nationalists therefore tend to see secession and independent statehood as a valid and logical solution to such perceived injustices.

Predictably, secessionism does not usually sit well with the remainder of the country. If the seceding region's claims of exploitation are true, the rest of the country could lose the advantages it had been receiving. Even if the seceding region had not in fact been exploited, its absence still could hurt the country as a whole; most federal systems are founded with a belief that the whole is greater than the sum of its parts. The withdrawal of a region destroys the wholeness of the federation, and sets a precedent which might precipitate a complete disintegration of the country. For these reasons, central governments often respond to acts of secession with military force, and the country descends into civil war. Such wars pit the principles of self-determination against those of political cohesiveness and territorial integrity.

On what does a sovereign government base its claim of ultimate authority in a territory? In modern republics that claim is based, at least in part, upon consent of the governed and upon a hypothetical social contract between the rulers and the ruled. These principles disallow meddling and intervention by foreign forces outside the polity. Yet can a segment of the polity itself legitimately negate the social contract? The Founders of the United States believed so when they declared independence from England, although they emphasized that the people can only resort to revolution after exhausting the various other options available to them. A century later the justifying principles of the American Revolution were seized by the Southern states in their attempt to secede from the Union.

Perhaps a state or province belonging to a federation has a better claim to a right of secession than a part of a unitary state. Perhaps a historic nation in a multinational country has a better claim than a group without such status. Nevertheless, nonnational groups do press claims of autonomy and sovereignty, and nonfederal states are subject to secessionism. One of the most difficult issues of secessionism is adjudicating these claims. Not only must groups decide whether to press such a claim, but also countries experiencing secessionist movements must choose how to respond, and third parties must decide whether to intervene and, later, whether to recognize a newly declared state. These choices have implic ations far beyond issues of justice: If self-determination is held as a paramount principle, then one might expect (or even desire) a proliferation of small, highly homogeneous states. Taken to its extreme, though logical, conclusion, self-determination would terminate in anarchy, with sovereignty accorded to each individual. Although one might never expect that extreme outcome, certainly the character of the international system, and the human condition itself, hinges in large part upon how secessionism is addressed as a tool of national and economic self-determination.

Applications

A classic example of secessionism is, of course, that of the American South. The admission of California to the Union in 1850 gave the antislavery North a majority in the Senate and the House of Representatives. The South felt the North was using its superior political and economic power at the South's expense. Differing attitudes about slavery involved not only issues of morality, but also of property rights, economics, and states' rights. After increasingly bitter confrontations in the Congress and scattered violence throughout the country, South Carolina seceded from the Union on December 20, 1860. In February, 1861, it and six other Southern states formed the Confederate States of America, which eventually grew to include eleven states. The remaining states of the Union fought the Confederacy in the Civil War, which four years later terminated in the defeat of the South and the reestablishment of the Union.

The South's secession was motivated by ideological principles and economic interests, rather than nationalism. Although the Confederacy sought recognition as a legitimate entity, it would be difficult to call its struggle one of "nationalism." The language, religion, culture, ethnicity, and history of the Northern and Southern populations were not appreciably different. The South's secession instead was a test of the right to exit a voluntary federation—an exercise of states' rights rather than national self-determination.

Some have drawn parallels between the South's attempt to secede from the United States and the successful acts of secessionism from the Union of Soviet Socialist Republics at the end of the 1980's. Unlike the states of the United States, however, each of the Soviet Union's fifteen republics was based on a different predominant nationality (such as Russian, Ukrainian, or Estonian). Also in contrast to the United States, the various republics of the Soviet Union had been forcibly incorporated, either as parts of the old Russian empire or as a result of conquests during the World War II. Third, the Soviet Constitution guaranteed each of its union republics the right to secession—a right not accorded to the states of the United States. It should be noted, however, that the Communist Party seldom considered itself bound by constitutional limitations, and in fact used threats and force on various occasions to maintain the territorial integrity of the Soviet Union. Yet with the reforms of Soviet president Mikhail Gorbachev in the mid- and late 1980's, leaders of various republics began to push for greater autonomy and, eventually, outright independence. With a few exceptions, Gorbachev's government permitted the secession of each of the republics. By the end of 1991, all fifteen republics of the Soviet Union had become independent states. The Soviet Union was no more.

The independence movements of the former soviet republics in many ways can be considered nationalistic. Nationalist pride and lingering hatred of Russian domination explain much of the popular support for secessionism in many of the republics. Yet a perceived Russian domination was not the only factor motivating the secessionist drives. Indeed, the Russian republic itself seceded from the Soviet Union. The republics' desire for independence was in part a reaction to the authoritarian excesses of the Communist central government, as well as the economic privations of the citizenry. Perhaps if the Soviet Union had been a unitary state at the end of the 1980's it would have experienced a revolution. Instead, the fault lines of the federal structure and the feelings of national, economic, and political oppression worked together to disintegrate the union.

Tellingly, the drive for independence did not end with the separation of the Soviet Union into fifteen independent states. Many of those new states were themselves multinational, and many of the minority nationalities began pushing for greater autonomy and even independence. Crimea's desire to secede from Ukraine is illustrative. Crimea, a peninsula on the Black Sea, was part of Russia since 1783, until premier Nikita Khrushchev transferred it to Ukraine in 1954. The transfer was largely symbolic, since all territories—Russia, Ukraine, and Crimea—remained under the jurisdiction of the Soviet Communist Party. Yet with Ukraine gaining independence in 1991, the largely Russian population of the Crimea expressed a desire to reunite with Russia. Both nationalist sentiments and economic desires (Ukraine's economy was even worse than Russia's) drove the Crimea's desire to secede, and threatened to fracture Ukraine.

Russia itself faced still greater threats of secessionism. Even as part of the Soviet

Union, Russia was constituted as a federation of eighty-nine regions, with twenty-one of the regions designated as autonomous by virtue of their predominantly non-Russian populations. When Russia gained its independence from the Soviet Union in 1991, the desire for self-determination and the impulse toward secessionism spread to many of those component parts of Russia. Some of the border regions sought to reunify with what they perceived as their national brethren—the North Ossetians in Russia with the South Ossetians in Georgia, for example. Other ethnic groups, such as the Tatars, sought independent statehood. In many cases, the conflicts between the central government in Moscow and the non-Russian regions became increasingly violent.

Secession can provoke conflict and even civil war, but it also can fulfill the principle of self-determination as a peaceful solution to political differences. Two examples from the early 1990's represent both outcomes: a peaceful separation of the Czech-dominated and Slovak-dominated regions of Czechoslovakia into separate states, and the bloody war between Serbs and Bosnians after Bosnia seceded from the Serb-dominated federation of Yugoslavia. It is difficult, therefore, to classify secessionism as legal or illegal, stabilizing or destabilizing, just or unjust. It is a political action whose merits may be judged on a case-by-case basis.

Context

Although it has been hailed as the antidote to oppressive empires, secessionism can threaten any state that has a measure of diversity. Particularly with the collapse of the bipolar political order that characterized the Cold War, secessionism became more widely practiced as a practical solution to perceived exploitation and as a tool for fulfilling nationalist goals. It continues to threaten not only multinational federations, but even unitary states with national minorities. Secessionism, the preferred tool of nationalists, counters its opposite trend in the post-Cold War world: integration. That is, while the states of Western Europe surrender a measure of sovereignty to a European Union, and while many advocate an expanded role for institutions like the United Nations, and while myriad technological advances in communications, transportation, and trade "shrink" the world, there is at the same time a trend toward breaking countries into smaller, more homogeneous states.

The interplay of these two opposite trends—integration and nationalism—will in large part determine the future of the international state system. The outcome depends on how the actions of national groups, regional groups, governmental leaders, and foreign policymakers address secessionism.

Bibliography

Buchanan, Allen. *Secession: The Morality of Political Divorce from Fort Sumter to Lithuania and Quebec*. Boulder, Colo.: Westview Press, 1991. Concerned with developing a theory about the morality of secessionism, it concludes that there is in fact a moral right to secession.

Buchheit, Lee C. *Secession: The Legitimacy of Self-Determination*. New Haven, Conn.: Yale University Press, 1978. Analysis of the moral basis for secessionism as a means for achieving self-determination.

Carrére d'Encausse, Hélène, and Franklin Philip, trans. *The End of the Soviet Empire: The Triumph of the Nations*. New York: Basic Books, 1993. Focuses more on the secession of Eastern European states from the Soviet Union than on the secession of the various republics.

Cohen, Lenard J. *Broken Bonds: The Disintegration of Yugoslavia*. Boulder, Colo.: Westview Press, 1993. Describes the creation of Yugoslavia as a multinational and multiethnic federation, and its dismantling in the early 1990's. Has a high level of historical and statistical detail, with numerous tables, notes, and charts.

Dunlop, John B. *The Rise of Russia and the Fall of the Soviet Empire*. Princeton, N.J.: Princeton University Press, 1993. Analyzes the disintegration of the Soviet Union, placing special emphasis on Russia's efforts to achieve political autonomy.

Moynihan, Daniel Patrick. *Pandaemonium: Ethnicity in International Politics*. New York: Oxford University Press, 1993. Analysis of how ethnicity is used as a basis for self-determination. Argues that ethnicity will remain a major force in the international sphere.

Steve D. Boilard

Cross-References

Civil Wars, p. 325; Colonialism and Anticolonialism, p. 351; Federations, p. 675; Independence Movements and Transitions, p. 896; Nationalism, p. 1268; Race and Ethnicity, p. 1654; Self-Determination, p. 1796.

SELF-DETERMINATION

Field of study: Political philosophy

In international law the principle of self-determination recognizes the right of peoples to direct their own political destinies. This includes their rights to follow their own political philosophies, determine their own forms of government, and establish systems of government free from external pressures of interference.

Principal terms

AUTONOMY: self-government of a region or minority group within a larger state

EXTERNAL SELF-DETERMINATION: political separation of nations from alien national bodies in order to form their own nation-states

FOURTEEN POINTS: issues enumerated in a 1918 foreign policy address in which U.S. president Woodrow Wilson articulated the goal of self-determination for the component nations of the former Austro-Hungarian and Ottoman empires

INTERNAL SELF-DETERMINATION: political separation (or secession) of a minority within a national population to form a separate nation-state

MINORITY: national group that differs from the rest of the community in ethnic origin, religion, language, or culture

NATION: body of people who share a common culture and feel bound to one another as a group; they usually occupy a single geographical region and may or may not form a nation-state; the term is also used for a modern sovereign country

NATION-STATE: complex political entity governing a clearly distinct geographical area and people who share a common culture, history, or ethnicity

NATIONALISM: social and emotional force that binds a people together through their shared culture or history in support of a nation-state

PEOPLE: in a political context, synonymous with nation

SECESSION: voluntary separation of a region or a people from a larger polity

Overview

Self-determination is the right of a group with a distinctive identity to determine its own destiny. Essentially, the principle stipulates that each nation—a group defined by its common history, traditions, language, and ethnic background—has a right to a sovereign state of its own and freedom to choose its own leadership. This is an ancient principle that has generated particular attention in the twentieth century. It has its origin in the eighteenth century proposition that governments must rest upon the consent of the governed. Following the French Revolution of 1789, the postmedieval form of the theory of the divine right of kings, which had been the dominant political system of the early modern period, received a mortal blow. It was replaced by the divine right of the people. The principle has come to be closely associated with President Woodrow Wilson, and is generally considered to be one of the "Fourteen Points" of a foreign policy address he gave to the U.S. Congress on January 8, 1918. It was immediately hailed by world opinion as the moral foundation of peace and has since become one of the fundamental principles of international society.

Since its inception, subsequent developments within the League of Nations and especially the United Nations have imbued the principle with legitimacy and currency. Even though it was not included in the Covenant of the League of Nations, it served as a guideline for much of the reshaping of states following the end of World War I. Winston Churchill and Franklin Roosevelt later included self-determination in the 1941 Atlantic Charter, which was to culminate in the foundation of the United Nations. Since then, it has become the major driving force in legitimizing scores of nationalist ambitions and in some cases has been used to justify claims of outright secession. Indeed, in its most extreme use, self-determination had been known to be interpreted as the right of disaffected groups to break away from the state to which they formally belong in order to establish one of their own.

A serious problem with which the international community has not been able to come into grips, is how to reconcile the principle of self-determination with that of the territorial integrity of a state. On one hand, self-determination seeks to grant minority groups the right to break away from a state; on the other hand, international law seeks to guarantee the territorial integrity of all states. The synthesis of state and nation brings with it a problem which is full of difficulties and dangers: the problem of national minorities. Nearly all states in the world have minorities. In many, the various minorities taken together constitute more than half of the total population of the state. Although allowing complete liberty of self-determination to all minorities who seek it could lead to anarchy, there have been cases in which widespread sympathy has been given to nations that have dared to undertake precisely such an endeavor. The complexity of this problem became acutely apparent soon after most of the African and Asian nations attained independence. Although the Bandung Conference of Non-Aligned Nations in 1955 gave its full support to the principle of self-determination as basic to all fundamental human rights, many African and Asian signatories still systematically denied that right to minority groups wishing to break away within their own nations. Similarly, in the Organization of African Unity, minority groups have challenged the principle of territorial integrity, seeking to override it with what they considered a higher principle: self-determination. This was the case in Biafra (Nigeria), Katanga (Zaïre), and Eritrea (Ethiopia). Nigeria had to fight one of the bloodiest civil wars in the history of independent Africa in its bid to deny the right to self-determination to the Ibo-speaking people of its Eastern Province.

Nevertheless, the sacred rights of self-determination have been known to be subordinated and in some cases sacrificed outright to the rights of state sovereignty. This meant simply that the territorial integrity of the state took priority over the political aspirations of the nation. In 1920, a Committee of Jurists appointed by the Council of the League of Nations rejected national self-determination as being recognizable by positive international law and ruled that in the absence of express provisions in international treaties, the right of disposing of national territory is essentially an attribute of the sovereignty of every state.

Applications

The difficulties of applying self-determination became more apparent when it was time to bring the principle down from abstraction to working reality. Translating it from ethical and political precepts to binding legal norms would eventually prove to be one of the most trying tests the big powers would face, especially within the United Nations. The existence of the Cold War would further complicate the situation as self-determination would lend itself to some of the most arbitrary and sometimes absurd interpretations. In Germany, Korea, and Vietnam, lines were literally drawn to demarcate the spheres of the two great opposing blocs, which in each case were two bitterly opposed regimes, each claiming to represent the national will of its citizens.

Indeed, it is clear from the way this principle has been applied that it represents conflicting interests. This is because, in most cases, governments endorse the notions of internal and external self-determination only when they suit their own national interests. The Soviet Union found it an excellent principle to use in debates against the West and its colonies; the West held it eminently applicable to the peoples of the Soviet Union, as well as the latter's satellites in Eastern Europe. Although the Soviet Union interpreted the principle as a blank check for absorption and domination in Eastern Europe, the Western colonial powers saw it as a tool of self-destruction of their empires in the Middle East, Asia, and Africa.

A typical example of the difficulties internal self-determination ran into was presented by the former Soviet Union. Vladimir Lenin defined national self-determination as the political separation of nations from alien national bodies to form their own national states. Initially, he supported unequivocally a people's right to national self-determination, but apparently neither expected nor desired that right should include secession. Nevertheless, the Declaration of November 15, 1917, of the Rights of the Peoples of Russia included the proclamation of equality and sovereignty of all national groups, and the right of each to self-determination, including the right to secede. Following that declaration, many borderland groups such as Azerbaijan, Belorussia, Estonia, Georgia, Lithuania, Latvia, and Ukraine applied these rights by proclaiming their own independence. Later, of course, they were all reintegrated into the Soviet state—some by armed force. The necessity of having to use armed force, coupled with unfavorable international public opinion, impelled the Soviet Union to redefine its understanding of the concept of self-determination. Thus, in 1923, Joseph Stalin would make a complete turnaround by announcing that the right of the working class to consolidate its power would always take precedence over the right of a people to self-determination. Stalin made it absolutely clear that the Soviets would embrace self-determination only when it involved a breach in the imperialist structure and that it would not tolerate it where it involved a separation from the communist fatherland.

External self-determination had its most ardent expression in the United Nations. It was directed mainly against the colonial empires. In the late nineteenth century, many non-Western peoples were subjected to colonial rule, often within newly defined territories. The anticolonial powers later insisted that self-determination had relevance only in the colonial realm and made it a weapon aimed primarily at the victorious imperial powers. The actions of the colonized peoples were given the force of law by the United Nations, as self-determination was applied and achieved in most cases through the famous Resolution 1514. As a result of the efforts of the anticolonial movement within the United Nations, self-determination became a powerful force resulting in the creation of more than eighty new states in a little more than two decades. The West eventually became suspicious and distrustful of the application of the principles, and of the intentions of the African and Asian states and of the Soviet bloc, which championed the anticolonial cause in the United Nations. At that time, the principle of self-determination became more of an instrument of division than cohesion among the member nations.

Although the international organization has been effective in the field of external self-determination, it has been more reluctant to support claims of internal self-determination. Despite the fact that international lawyers have been divided on the question of whether self-determination is a right, the speedy application of the concept to most former colonial territories has been remarkable. Nevertheless, the same United Nations that gave a substantial boost to the colonized territories in their quest to achieve self-determination also denies the same right to minorities within national territories. Indeed, international law supports the preeminence of the population within the total national territory over parts of the population or territory within it. Under international law, a minority cannot seek self-determination whether on its own initiative or with the help of any outside power because such an action would dismember or damage an existing state. Any departure from this rule must be ratified by the majority of a country's total population.

Context

Following World War I, the focus of self-determination was in Europe. The experience of World War II and its aftermath is in many respects the reverse of the first war, and by the end of that war, the focus had shifted from Europe to Asia, the Middle East, and Africa. Despite its usefulness in international law, the concept has been criticized for the various ambiguities that exist in its practice and interpretation. For example, it recognizes the right of all peoples to self-determination, whereas the definition of "peoples" and the territories to which it applies remains largely ambiguous. Part of the confusion arose from the fact that the United Nations could not come up with a practical working definition of the term self-determination. Even though the U.N. Charter endorses the principle, many questions were left unanswered. How are the people to whom the principle applies to be defined? Does it apply only to people constituting a majority within a certain territory, or does a minority people have the same right? Who speaks for the people in order to set the process in motion?

This confusion has been complicated further by virtue of the fact that there has never been any substantial consensus on where the rights of the state stop or where those of the nation begin. International jurists as well as other guardians of international law could not come up with a satisfactory distinction between the territorial integrity of a state and the right to self-determination, which sometimes may mean the right to secede. While the state has an indisputable prerogative and duty to defend its own existence (the right to sovereignty), a minority group within that state is equally endowed with the right to overthrow the state (right to internal self-determination). In the first case, the state perceives the act as one of secession, and its perpetrators as revolutionaries, while in the latter case, members of the minority group perceive themselves as nationalists and freedom fighters. The right to self-determination has as yet found no stable place in the international legal structure, and the likelihood that one day it will be accepted by states as a policy to be applied consistently and across the board is slim. In the meantime, it is a right to be defended in lofty terms when it is politically expedient and to be rejected when it is not.

Bibliography

Cobban, Alfred. *The Nation-State and National Self-Determination*. Rev. ed. New York: Thomas Crowell, 1970. Notes that self-determination was expected to end imperialism and the oppression of colonies. Observes instead the proliferation of tiny states. Cobban explores the underlying bases for this development. He concludes that if every nation were to become sovereign as a state, international chaos might result, causing wars and preventing the development of world government.

Cristescu, Aureliu. *The Right to Self-Determination: Historical and Current Development on the Basis of United Nations Instruments*. New York: United Nations, 1981. Complains that although the right to self-determination had become a universal rule and a fundamental human right according to conventional and customary international law, it was being denied in various parts of the world. Considers territorial integrity still to be the paramount principle governing states.

Emerson, Rupert. *Self-Determination Revisited in the Era of Decolonization*. Cambridge, Mass.: Center for International Affairs, Harvard University, 1964. Reviews several cases illustrating key problems involving self-determination in the postcolonial era. Suggests that in its interpretation, it means that all overseas colonial peoples have the right to be liberated from alien rule.

Knight, David B., and Maureen Davies. *Self-Determination: An Interdisciplinary Annotated Bibliography*. New York: Garland Publishing, 1987. Has over five hundred entries on self-determination and related issues. It is indispensable for scholars who are interested in carrying out research on this subject.

Olusoji A. Akomolafe

Cross-References

Africa: Politics and Governments, p. 21; Asia: Politics and Governments, p. 108; Geopolitics, p. 759; Independence Movements and Transitions, p. 896; Indigenous Peoples' Governments, p. 903; Initiatives and Referendums, p. 923; Leagues, p. 1072; Liberal Nationalism, p. 1111; Mill's Political Philosophy, p. 1204; Nationalism, p. 1268; Nonaligned Movements, p. 1319; Pacific Islander Governments, p. 1362; Pan-Africanism, p. 1369; Realpolitik, p. 1668; Secessionism, p. 1790; Treaties, p. 2020; Underdeveloped Nations, p. 2039; World Government Movements, p. 2174; World Political Organization, p. 2186.

SELF-INTEREST IN POLITICS

Field of study: Politics

Rational-choice theory is an approach to the study of politics that seeks to identify and explain the self-interests which lie behind the political behavior of individual citizens, elected and appointed public officials, political parties, and the courts.

Principal terms
CORPORATISM: political system in which principal economic functions (such as banking, industry, labor, and government) are organized as corporate entities
LINE RESPONSIBILITIES: duties of government personnel who perform services directly for citizens
NORMATIVE POLITICAL THEORY: any political theory that recommends values, standards, and norms for political thought and action that are based on intellectual explorations
RATIONAL BEHAVIOR: behavior based on reason and logic, rather than emotion
SELF-INTEREST: regard for one's own advantage or interests

Overview

Self-interest as the primary explanation for politics is based on what is called rational-actor or rational-choice theory. This theory is based on the premise that the behavior of individual units of political action—including persons, institutions, or economic firms—should be viewed as furthering self-interest, which is limited only by the quality of information and perceived costs of carrying out actions.

At the core of a view of politics as flowing from self-interest are many assumptions about politics and political actors, including citizens, elected officials, and those appointed to government positions. These include the idea that individuals are basically egoistic, self-regarding, and instrumental in their behavior, acting on the basis of the consequences for their personal (and family) welfare. Other assumptions include the ideas that individuals have well-formed preferences, or interests that they perceive, rank, and compare easily; that the rankings of interests and preferences are logically consistent; that individuals always seek the greatest possible benefits at the lowest cost when acting on decisions; and that individuals act rationally when they pursue their preferences in consistent and efficient manners, seeking net maximization of benefits over costs, and paying little mind to how others may judge the effects of their rational self-interested choices.

Scholars who seek to explain politics through a self-interest model assume that individuals possess considerable prior knowledge when they make political choices, at times even perfect knowledge. Such scholars view an individual's preferences as fixed by factors not affected by their participation in the political system. When they discuss political institutions, they make gross assumptions about the extent to which collective entities, such as cities, political parties, and bureaucracies, can be treated as unitary actors with fixed interests—such as the view that a city's primary interest is economic growth and keeping taxpayers from leaving. They also assume that political actors only have a single maximizing course of action open to them if they wish to act in a self-interested way—such as an elected official's maximization of votes.

Scholars who consider the centrality of rational self-interested actions by citizens and leaders as explanations for politics and the operations of political institutions ask a variety of questions. Are market metaphors from economics upon which rational self-interested actor studies are based appropriate for the study of politics? Can the welfare of a collective political body (such as a city or bureaucracy) best be understood by the study of the pursuit of self-interest by individuals? Do citizens make actual decisions by their conscious consideration of self-interest? Can individual self-interest and political institutions be understood by using theories, premises, and techniques from economics such as cost/benefit analysis (which is used to determine the costs and benefits of specific actions to individuals), and the idea that citizens usually act only after a consideration of how to maximize their comparative advantages over others? Does politics as private self-interested behavior negate the emotional bases of politics? Do most, or all, citizens, simply pursue goals or objectives out of self-interest when they act politically, and pursue goals for other reasons, such as ambivalence caused by unreconciled conflict, frustration, or meeting requirements of their structured roles in bureaucracies? Can rational-choice theory and the notion of all political actors as self-interested fully explain politics in complex political institutions, such as bureaucracies, courts, and legislatures, which may be viewed as bodies which create incentives for actors to behave in accordance with rules set out by the institution to limit the impact of individual wants or interests on agency operations? Are there some political actions, such as voting in Congress or in elections, that are better explained by theories of individual, rational self-interest? What role does cultural context play in determining whether leaders and citizens act as self-interested individuals and whether rational choice theory is a valid conceptualization of politics? What roles does altruism, one's relationship to others, have on the validity of politics viewed as individual self-interested actions? Can individuals adequately perceive the objective conditions in which they are acting and thus be disciplined by their perception of the political marketplace?

Political theorists have been concerned about the implications of viewing politics in a democracy as simply the outgrowth of individual self-interest. They ask what effect the study of politics as self-interest has on our understanding of the role of values, political philosophies, and institutions on political action. They also ask what effects assumptions about citizens and leaders acting only on self-interest have on the consideration of the possibilities of a good society in traditional democratic theory and on the objective of the rule of law in legal theory. Can concern for the social values that underlie democracy be included in a theory of politics that highlights individual self-interested preferences as the central cause of individual political behavior? Is the assumption that self-interest is an empirically established component of human nature antithetical to normative political theory and to the consideration of the effect of power inequalities on citizens and groups in society? Is rational-choice theory—which views democracy as a procedure to harness the uncurbed individual self-interests of leaders and citizens and accepts uncritically the results of self-interested actions—destructive of democracy? Does it undermine the importance of the fears of the Founders as to the problems of faction and the politics of self-interested individuals?

Applications

The U.S. Congress is typically viewed as a political institution in which the self-interest of its members for reelection is the primary basis for both their individual actions and the decisions made by Congress as a whole. David Mayhew asks whether the members' self-interested need for reelection fully explains what Congress does as an institution. He views the major activities of Congress members to be advertising their names among voters, claiming personal credit for positive government actions, and position-taking through their votes or speeches. Mayhew finds that the organization of Congress meets well the electoral needs of its members and, most important, that achieving electoral needs does not necessitate much conflict among members, who can usually get what they need without denying other members the opportunity to protect their own interests in reelection. Mayhew argues that the maintenance of Congress as an institution is not hurt by individuals operating to secure their reelection, in part, because needed internal leaders of Congress are repaid with prestige, perquisites, committee chairmanships, and memberships on committees that help sustain voter support.

Mayhew emphasizes, however, that self-interest alone does not explain the constancy in lawmaking over the years in Congress. Norms, external events, opinion cleavages among members of Congress that cross party lines, problem-solving propensities, and the ease and difficulty of putting together winning coalitions, not simply electoral incentives as the self-interest model would predict, explain the actions of members of Congress.

Self-interest alone does not predict congressional action because collective outcomes in Congress are more than a summation of individual voting decisions in the districts. Gary Jacobson argues that the path that leads from aggregate political conditions to individual voting decisions to aggregate congressional election outcomes is quite complicated. Even so, a congressional candidate's electoral strategies provide a critical connecting link between individual interest and voting. For Jacobson, the decline of party politics in the United States has fostered a system of individual responsiveness with collective irresponsibility that has led to the inability of the nation to deal effectively with problems and a consequent loss of public faith in political institutions.

Self-interest as a basis for congressional decision making is limited by the quality of information that members of Congress have on the electoral effects of a vote which they are about to make in Congress. Legislators simply cannot identify the wants of all the attentive and inattentive (unknown) publics who are interested in a particular vote. They can easily estimate neither the direction and intensity of the preferences of attentive publics or the potential preferences of inattentive publics nor the probability that citizens and groups will transform potential preferences into real preferences and political action.

Members of Congress, especially those new to Congress whose concerns about operating in their self-interest are most acute, demonstrate great difficulty in weighing preferences according to the needs and possible needs of attentive and inattentive publics. They simply do not know when to give special weight to consistent supporters. Information may be nil as to inattentive publics and less than precise for attentive publics. Therefore, even if a member of Congress were to try to act simply on the basis of self-interest, it is not clear that it is possible to vote on such terms.

Most important, there is evidence that members of Congress do not simply act on self-interest and out of a concern for reelection. Policy choices and the need for party or presidential support in the future also influence their voting. Moreover, each time members are reelected, they can draw more upon the advantages of incumbency, as well as their improved skills as a politician, and their improved staffs to deflect voter criticisms of their voting records and to persuade voters to support positions which they may at first oppose. There also is a lack of clarity of long-term costs and benefits to members of Congress if they vote certain ways on particular pieces of legislation. The practical difficulty of holding a member of Congress accountable for votes made in the past suggests another reason why self-interest alone may not explain voting in Congress as well. Only where a proposed law has a clear impact on a member's own district must a member of Congress act based on self-interest by simply responding to constituent preferences out of concern for being reelected.

Glenn Parker argues that there has been a change in the style of members of Congress since the mid-1960's. Congressional styles in the 1990's are far more attentive to the needs of individual constituents. This is realized through more frequent (government-paid) travel back to the home district and more thorough casework by congressional staffs to meet the specific needs of constituents as they seek benefits from federal bureaucracies. As a result, reelection has increased for incumbents, especially for the congressmen and senators who seem least representative politically of their districts and states. This change, in turn, has given members of Congress increased freedom from their fears of non-reelection. Parker argues that they are now free to pursue personal legislative goals, such as policies which are of less interest to constituents, to accept leadership positions in Congress, and to follow the directives of party leaders. Thus, the reduction of electoral competition reduces the degree to which self-interest and the need to be reelected dominate the thinking of members of Congress.

In addition to the study of Congress, self-interest as a basis for political action has had a major impact on our thinking about the possibilities of collective action by citizens with regard to the theoretical positions of pluralism, corporatism, and Mancur Olson's pathbreaking public choice analysis of the organization of interest groups and leadership strategies. Complex rational-choice models of individual behavior that incorporate individual self-interest models are used to explain behavior in political institutions such as bureaucracies, courts, and the presidency. They have become a fixture in the modern study of politics. For example, with regard to bureaucracies, William Niskanen's *Bureaucracy and Representative Government* (1971) includes an influential model of how all rational public officials seek to maximize their agencies' budgets. Patrick Dunleavy offers a radically different model which argues that rationally self-interested top officials have few incentives to maximize budgets. Instead they pursue strategies to reshape or remodel their agencies as small, elite, staff organizations that have few line responsibilities.

Moreover, recent public-choice theories and studies argue against following many of the primary assumptions about politics which are found in the first wave of work by public-choice scholars: that voters' preferences are exogenously fixed; that political parties simply compete to win elections; that politicians simply accommodate voters' and citizens' preferences while governing; that politics occurs in situations of perfect information; and that decision makers act on single maximizing courses of action.

Context

Approaches to politics that emphasize self-interest and rational actions by individuals got their theoretical impetus from classical microeconomics, or the theory of the firm, developed by Adam Smith in the eighteenth century. For Smith the pursuit of individual self-interest should lead to collective welfare. While Smith did not mean for his economic theories to explain political action, concepts of marginality in economics in the late nineteenth century transformed his insights into meanings that led to the basic view of rational self-interested action in economics. Later welfare economists developed formal theories of social decision making in which rules are developed for aggregating individual preferences, drawing upon the formal models of Kenneth Arrow and Amartya Sen. By the 1970's rational-actor theory, and the view that self-interest in the source of individual action, whether that of a citizen or leader, led to the study of a diverse set of political phenomena: voting, coalition formation, peasant revolts, discrimination and marriage, group formation and strength. By the 1980's, rational-choice scholars argued that individual preferences could be aggregated to express a common good and rational, self-interest models could be applied to the study of political institutions, norms, and political culture both in the American context and in the comparative study of national, mostly postindustrial nations.

In the future, political science can be expected to develop more complex theories and empirical studies that emphasize the rational pursuit of self-interest by individuals to explain citizen and political institution behavior in the United States and in other nations. Many distinguished political science departments now have rational-choice scholars working within the major subfields of the discipline: American politics, international relations, comparative politics, and political theory. Given that major questions continue to be raised about the reliance on rational-choice and self-interest models as the sole approach through which to study politics and political institutions, most major political science departments continue to be made up of theorists and empirical scholars who do not employ rational-choice models as their primary approach to the study of politics.

Bibliography

Arnold, R. Douglas. *The Logic of Congressional Action.* New Haven, Conn.: Yale University Press, 1990. Important attempt to explain congressional policy preferences, decisions, and strategies of coalition leaders.

Downs, Anthony. *An Economic Theory of Democracy.* New York: Harper and Row, 1957. Pioneering study that views American democracy as a product of actions by citizens who rationally pursue their self-interests.

Dunleavy, Patrick. *Democracy, Bureaucracy, and Public Choice: Economic Explanations in Political Science.* New York: Harvester Wheatsheaf, 1991. Major study of how contemporary rational-choice or self-interest approaches to politics explain the place of bureaucracies in American democracy.

Jacobson, Gary. *The Politics of Congressional Elections.* 2d ed. Boston: Little, Brown, 1987. Leading work on congressional elections and the incumbency advantage.

Mayhew, David R. *Congress: The Electoral Connection.* New Haven, Conn.: Yale University Press, 1974. Seminal study of the U.S. Congress which views the need of members for reelection as primary to congressional action.

_____. *Divided We Govern: Party Control, Lawmaking, and Investigations, 1946-1990.* New Haven, Conn.: Yale University Press, 1991. General study of Congress that suggests limits on the ability of members of Congress to act simply on the basis of self-interest and the need for reelection.

Monroe, Kristen Renwick, ed. *The Economic Approach to Politics: A Critical Reassessment of the Theory of Rational Action.* New York: HarperCollins, 1991. Distinguished collection of original essays on the application of self-interest, rational-choice theory to contemporary politics and political institutions.

Olson, Mancur. *The Logic of Collective Action: Public Goods and the Theory of Groups.* Cambridge, Mass.: Harvard University Press, 1965. Pathbreaking study of interest groups and collective action which considers the self-interests of group members and leaders as primary bases for the political strength of groups.

Parker, Glenn R. *Homeward Bound: Explaining Changes in Congressional Behavior.* Pittsburgh: University of Pittsburgh Press, 1986. Argues that in the 1970's and 1980's members of Congress developed ways to be more attentive to the needs of constituents, opening the way for them to be less concerned about self-interest and reelection when voting and accepting leadership positions.

Ronald C. Kahn

Cross-References

Clientelism, p. 337; Congress, p. 412; Corporatism, p. 452; Democracy, p. 513; Hobbes's Political Philosophy, p. 836; Iron Triangles, p. 981; Legislative Functions

SURVEY
OF
SOCIAL
SCIENCE

ALPHABETICAL LIST

CATEGORY LIST

POLITICS